PENGUIN BOOKS

LOCAL GOVERNMENT IN BRITAIN

Tony Byrne was born in 1937 and went to school in Liverpool. He took
a degree in economics at the University of Bristol, and in government
at the University of London. He has taught in schools in Liverpool and
Somerset, was an adult education officer and an examiner for the
Yorkshire and Humberside Council for Further and Higher Education, and is now lecturer in government and social administration at
the Somerset College of Arts and Technology in Taunton and at
the University of Plymouth. For some years he was chairman of the
Taunton Marriage Guidance Council and has been secretary of the
Taunton Workers' Education Association. His other books are *Social
Services Made Simple* and *British Constitution Made Simple*, both
written with the late Colin Padfield. He is a semi-professional musician
and plays the saxophone with a local dance band.

Local Government in Britain

Everyone's Guide to How It All Works

SIXTH EDITION

TONY BYRNE

PENGUIN BOOKS

PENGUIN BOOKS

Published by the Penguin Group
Penguin Books Ltd, 27 Wrights Lane, London w8 5TZ, England
Penguin Books USA Inc., 375 Hudson Street, New York, New York 10014, USA
Penguin Books Australia Ltd, Ringwood, Victoria, Australia
Penguin Books Canada Ltd, 10 Alcorn Avenue, Toronto, Ontario, Canada M4V 3B2
Penguin Books (NZ) Ltd, 182–190 Wairau Road, Auckland 10, New Zealand

Penguin Books Ltd, Registered Offices: Harmondsworth, Middlesex, England

First published 1981
Second edition 1983
Third edition 1985
Fourth edition 1986
Fifth edition 1990
Reprinted with revisions 1992
Sixth edition 1994
10 9 8 7 6 5 4 3 2 1

The artwork for all the figures throughout this book
was prepared by Nigel Andrews at Capricorn Design

Set in 10.5/13 pt Monotype Ehrhardt
Typeset by Datix International Limited, Bungay, Suffolk
Printed in England by Clays Ltd, St Ives plc

In memory of C. F. P.

Contents

List of Text Figures

List of Tables

Glossary
See also Index

Abatement the withholding of central grant to a local authority: see Holdback, below

Accountability the condition of being held responsible and answerable for decisions and actions (or inactions) which affect others and which are usually undertaken on their behalf: typically officers are accountable to councillors (members) and the latter are accountable to the local populace and electors (p. 65)

ACC The Association of County Councils: one of several societies of particular types of local authority (p. 401)

AEF Aggregate External Finance (replaces Aggregate Exchequer Grant; see p. 308)

AMA The Association of Metropolitan Authorities: another local authority association, for those in metropolitan areas (p. 401)

APSAS the Association of Public Service Administrative Staff

Audit the checking of local councils' income and expenditure to detect errors, abuse, waste or illegality (p. 348)

Balances the reserves held by local authorities as a result of savings of income over expenditure; may be used to balance any subsequent deficits arising from an excess of expenditure over income (e.g. to keep down council tax)

Block grant central government's financial aid to local authorities; it is 'unhypothecated', i.e. it is not directly allocated to particular services; it forms the major part of the Revenue Support Grant (p. 315)

Borough (or in Scotland, **Burgh**) an old term still used to denote certain (mainly urban) local authorities entitled to have a mayor (or provost) instead of a chairman of the council, and other minor privileges. In England, such Borough (or district) councils may be metropolitan (of which London Boroughs are a particular case) or non-metropolitan (p. 50)

By-laws legally enforceable regulations created by the council and which help to control social life in the local community (p. 367)

Capital expenditure spending on 'real' and costly items (highways, land, housebuilding, machinery etc.), cf. current or revenue expenditure (on wages, heating, etc.) (p. 341)

Capping the placing, by central government, of an upper limit on the proposed budget and council tax levied by local authorities; formerly rate-capping (p. 324)

Cash limits the maximum allowance made (usually by the government) for increases in the cost of expenditure due to inflation (prices and wages increases) (p. 329)

CCT compulsory competitive tendering, the requirement that local authorities invite firms to bid for contracts to supply services otherwise provided directly by the authority itself (pp. 272, 306)

Chief Executive Officer (CEO) a chief local official who acts as head of his local authority's team of chief officers, often heads his own department and may sometimes be entitled Chief Administrative Officer, General Manager or Director of Administration (p. 263)

CIPFA the Chartered Institute of Public Finance and Accountancy, comprising accountants and financial managers from local government and the public services; publish data and journals and help in the development of SSAPs (see below)

Circular a government document sent to local authorities for the purpose of explanation or guidance, on legislation etc. (p. 368). (But note there are also 'circulars' sent out to local authorities by the local authorities' associations, and others sent to local parties by party central offices.)

Clawback the mechanism whereby excess spending of some

councils is recouped from all. The government apportions money to councils according to a formula based on what they are deemed to need; if the total of councils' claims exceeds the total grant available, money is 'clawed back' from every council (p. 474)

COG Chief Officers' Group or management team (p. 266)

Collection funds local authority financial pools comprising receipts built up from government grants, community charges and business rates (p. 328)

Commissioner for Local Administration (CLA) popularly known as the 'ombudsman', he or she is responsible for investigating complaints against local councils (p. 422)

Community charge a flat rate tax or levy; otherwise known as resident's charge or poll tax (p. 325)

Community council a very local and small-scale form of local government, found in Wales and Scotland (p. 449)

Community politics concern and action involving very local issues at street or neighbourhood level (p. 442)

Corporate management a system whereby senior administrators (especially chief officers) and/or councillors regularly meet to determine, and co-ordinate, the execution of policy through a unified or collective approach (p. 230)

COSLA the Convention of Scottish Local Authorities (p. 402)

Council tax a tax for local authorities; levied on each household according to value of property but allowing a 25 per cent discount for single adult households (p. 333)

Creative accounting the use of financial devices and procedures (such as adjusting allocations and nomenclatures) to present expenditure accounts in such a way as to maximize grant entitlement and to minimize or escape government spending (capital or revenue) limits or penalties

Credit approval the government's allocation of permission for local authorities to borrow and spend on capital items (p. 341)

Derogation a special relaxation or redertimination of the government's council tax cap (p. 476)

DFE the central government's Department for Education (p. 367)

Direct labour (DLO) use of a council's own workforce, instead of an outside contractor (p. 470)

Director a local authority chief officer such as Director of Social Services (p. 269)

DoE the central government's Department of the Environment (p. 375)

Financial year the period from 1 April in one year to 31 March in the following year

GLC the Greater London Council; the former top tier of London's government, abolished 1986 (p. 113)

GREA Grant Related Expenditure Assessment: a central estimate of what each local authority needs to spend; it helps determine (block) grants to councils (p. 313); but see SSA below

HIPS Housing Investment Programmes: what the government agrees councils should spend on housing (building, repairs, renovation grants) (p. 340)

Holdback the withholding of some of the (block) grant to those councils which exceed the spending targets set by the government (p. 474)

Hung (or balanced) council where no party has an overall majority (p. 149)

ICSA the Institute of Chartered Secretaries and Administrators

ILEA the Inner London Education Authority: a special body, abolished in 1990, which was responsible for education in part of the Greater London area (p. 121)

INLOGOV the Institute of Local Government Studies, part of Birmingham University (p. 257)

LASS local authority (personal) social services department(s) (p. 97)

LBA the London Boroughs Association (p. 401)

LGMB Local Government Management Board (p. 276)

Local authority associations groupings of councils of the same type (p. 401)

Local income tax (LIT) a proposed council tax on income-receivers (p. 324)

LRT London Regional Transport (p. 119)

Metropolitan a conurbation area containing metropolitan districts (or boroughs) and, until 1986, metropolitan counties (p. 50)

NALGO a trade union: the National and Local Government Officers' Association (now UNISON) (p. 257)

Neighbourhood councils very local, non-executive, semi-official bodies (p. 452)

Non-domestic rates a tax on business properties; known as the Unified Business Rate, it is determined by the government and distributed to local authorities (p. 328)

Ombudsman see Commissioner above

OMT Officers' Management Team (p. 270)

Penalties loss of grant where a council exceeds GREA and/or target (p. 474)

Planning gain the benefit or asset that a local authority may derive from negotiations with developers who seek planning permission, e.g. a leisure facility

Policy and Resources Committee (P and R) the main committee of the council; here councillors are responsible for overall policy, management and finance (p. 234)

Poll tax a local tax or levy, collected from those listed on the register of residents or electors, see community charge above (p. 325)

Precept the council tax collected by charging authorities (district councils) for county councils, parish/community councils or for joint authorities/boards (p. 316)

Prescribed expenditure allocation (PEA) the blocks of capital expenditure allocated to local authorities by the government (p. 340)

Privatization contracting out councils' work to private firms (p. 376)

PSS social services department of the local authority (p. 97)

PTAs Passenger Transport Authorities (p. 510)

PWLB the Public Works Loan Board: a government body which lends to local authorities (p. 338)

Qualgo quasi-local government organization; a form of 'quango' or semi-independent board in the field of local (as opposed to central) administration such as the ILEA, Police and Fire Authorities and Passenger Transport Authorities (p. 105)

Rate-capping the placing of an upper limit on councils' or joint boards' rates/precepts; now budget-capping or council tax-capping (pp. 337, 475)

Rates a tax on property levied by councils for their own or (as a precept) others' revenue; based on property's (rateable) value (p. 316)

Resident's charge a local tax collected from those living in the area of a local authority; similar to community charge/poll tax (p. 325)

Residuary bodies panels or groups of government appointees who handle and wind up the remaining affairs and commitments of the abolished metropolitan county councils and the GLC (p. 121)

Revenue budget the main financial statement of a local authority containing details of planned revenue income and expenditure for the forthcoming year, often supported by information relating to previous years and projections for the future

RSG Revenue Support Grant (sometimes known as Standard Spending Grant) (p. 315)

Safety net the transfer of funds from gaining authorities to losing authorities in the early years of introducing the system of the unified business rate and community charge

SAUS the School of Advanced Urban Studies, part of Bristol University

Shire the non-metropolitan county (p. 50)

SOLACE the Society of Local Authority Chief Executives (p. 269)

Special responsibility allowances payments to councillors with additional duties (p. 194)

SSA Standard Spending Assessment – the government's estimate of what local authorities should spend to achieve a common level of service provision (p. 315)

SSAP Statement of Standard Accountancy Practice describes methods of accounting (approved by the accountancy bodies), a number of which are being developed for particular application to local authority accounting practice

SSD local authority social services department (p. 97)

SSG Standard Spending Grant (also known as Revenue Support Grant) (p. 315)

Surcharge a financial penalty on those responsible for illegal spending (p. 348)

Supplementary rate (or precept) an extra levy, in addition to the regular, annual local tax (p. 346)

SWD local authority social work department (Scotland) (p. 77)

Taper the diminishing proportion of grant attracted by a council's spending when it exceeds a threshold level (p. 313)

Target a guideline level of council expenditure set by the government (p. 474)

Transitional relief (or community charge reduction) government subsidy to reduce the community charge/poll tax for those who would otherwise experience excessive increases

Unified business rate (UBR) see non-domestic rates (p. 326)

Unitary single tier and all- or most-purpose authorities (pp. 47, 60)

Ultra vires beyond the powers; illegal (p. 57)

VFM value for money (p. 356)

ZBB Zero Base Budgeting; theoretically it implies analysing or justifying any expenditure at all on a service/function and starting from scratch, cf. Programme Budgeting – or PPB – which may be used in times of economic growth and incrementalism (p. 277)

Preface to the First Edition

There is much public ignorance of and misunderstanding about local government: according to one survey, some 20 per cent of the British public cannot accurately name a single local government service. But local government is not unique in this respect, judging by the similar results produced by surveys of public understanding of the national government, the EEC and the legal system.

Such widespread ignorance, sometimes referred to as 'political illiteracy', may be understandable if not excusable. It takes energy, persistence and patience to master the intricacies of any large organization, be it the Ford motor company, the National Health Service or a government department such as the Ministry of Agriculture.

This book seeks to provide a reasonably clear and up-to-date account of what local government is, what it does and how it does it. I have aimed to achieve a balance between description and analysis, between law and practice and between institutions and issues. Being based essentially on secondary sources, the book makes no claim to originality, nor does it attempt to contribute to theory.

In writing this book, I have had in mind a number of overlapping groups of reader:

(1) the *consumer* who needs to know how local political decisions affect him;
(2) the *activist* who, as a citizen, wants a part in the decision-making process;

(3) the *student* who seeks an understanding of local government as part of his academic studies;

(4) the potential or *new entrant* to local government who wishes to know something about the world of the local authority.

It is ambitious to try to satisfy all these groups, and in a book of this size one can hope to do little more than provide an outline and an introduction to certain themes. I have treated the subject in a fairly conventional way, and I make no apology for this, since the book is intended as an introductory text. Detailed references, and a bibliography of more specialized works, are provided for the benefit of those who wish to pursue the various themes and issues in greater depth. Some of the works mentioned, such as Stanyer's *Understanding Local Government*, are highly original and commendable.

Comments or questions from readers will be welcome so that the text can be suitably amended at a later date.

Local government is a branch of public administration, and its study helps to form one of the 'social sciences': that is, studies which seek to apply to social affairs the scientific methods of observation, comparison and conjecture. But social science is not an exact science and there are many areas where ideas about relationships and the causes and consequences of events remain inconclusive. There are many 'ifs and buts' because we are dealing with a world (human society) which lacks certainty or uniformity; it is dangerous therefore to generalize. This is perhaps especially true of local government in Britain, which includes 500 principal local authorities and covers such different territories as England, Scotland and Wales, highlands, lowlands, conurbations, market towns and seaports. Each area and local authority is unique: it has its own traditions, history, problems and social structure . . . in short its own political culture.

However, as the late Professor J. Mackintosh said, the study of political institutions and theories connected with it depends on the patient accumulation of instances. Furthermore, local authorities do have many common features and are subject to a number of common influences and constraints, not the least important of which is the law. Consequently we can say that a local government 'system' does exist and we are able (with caution) to suggest some general tendencies which operate within it.

One thing which can be said with certainty is that local authorities live in exciting times! Nationally, our economic performance has faltered and we have sought salvation (at least in part) by joining the Common Market. At the same time, a diminished faith in our political system has been manifested both in a review and reform of a number of our institutions (the civil service, the House of Commons, the National Health Service) and in our adoption or contemplation of certain exotic devices (ombudsmen, referendums, proportional representation, a written constitution).

Local government has not escaped scrutiny: indeed it can claim to have had more than its fair share of searching inquiry over the past twenty years; and since the 1960s local authorities have undergone substantial changes in their structure, in the allocation of responsibilities and in their internal organization. Confidence and optimism, sustained and reflected in their expanding budgets, have given way to retrenchment of spending plans and reductions in services. Local authorities have (perhaps only for the moment) been spared the challenge posed by devolution, but they are experiencing a longer-term and less conspicuous threat. This has been described as 'de-localization' and it is caused by the loss of certain services, the greater quest for equal (national) standards and the insinuation into local politics of national parties and pressure groups. In these ways local authorities are being homogenized – just as our town centres are losing their local character by the spread of national chain stores and building societies. However, there may be some gains from these developments, and in any case they are still far from complete.

Students, councillors and officers have had to cope with these developments, and it has not always been easy. This book deals with a number of them. Its preparation has been stimulating for the author, but it would have been an impossible task without the generous assistance of a number of friends, colleagues, specialist practitioners and students (past and present). My debt to published work will be obvious to the reader. I have also received helpful information and documents from central and local officials in England, Wales and Scotland. In particular, however, I wish to acknowledge the help I have received from the Rt Hon. Edward du Cann, MP; from Brian Bailey, John Blackmore, John Chant, Mike Dearden, Mr S. E. Harwood, John Pentney, David Perrin, Brian Tanner, Barry Taylor, Phil Trevelyan and Colin Vile (all of Somerset County Council); from Don Alder, Michael Clark, John Davis, Mr I. Locke, Mr S. Price, Mike Porter and Derek Rumsey (all of Taunton Deane Borough Council); and from Rosemary Morris (Kent County Council). I am confident of the accuracy of their answers: I only hope I have asked the right questions. Any errors of omission or commission are entirely mine and while I have tried to make it entirely up to date, the book has come to fruition at a time of considerable change in local government.

I am also grateful to David Hencke of the *Guardian* and David Peschek of Local Government Information Services for advising me on certain sources, and to David Smith of the Conservative Central Office for allowing me access to local government records.

I should also like to thank my teaching colleagues Barrie Foster and Russell Pearce; the library staffs of the Somerset College of Arts and Technology, Bristol and Exeter Universities and Taunton library (in particular Bryan McEnroe); the NJC for allowing me to quote extracts from their scheme; and the Controller of HM Stationery Office for his permission to reproduce material from official sources.

Neil Middleton of Penguin Books has been most considerate in regard to unavoidable delays over deadlines. And his encouragement and help have been most welcome.

Finally, I must thank my wife Sari and my children Celie and

Dan for their support and for enduring my more than usual preoccupation and periods of silence.

Taunton, February 1981   Tony Byrne

Preface to the Second Edition

An American wit, parodying Lord Acton, has opined that 'Government is boring; Local Government bores absolutely'. Many people in local government would it were true! They seek more settled times – a return to normalcy, where they can get on with administration and the delivery of services, instead of adapting to the latest change and awaiting the next one. Professor Stewart's description of local government as 'the government of difference' is perhaps more apt, though for unfortunate reasons.

The exciting times referred to in the First Edition of this book have continued and this new edition takes account of the related causal and consequential changes (up to January 1983). The book was originally scheduled as a reprint with corrections. Fortunately I was able to take advantage of the opportunity to thoroughly revise the text and bring it up to date; I am grateful to the publishers for agreeing to this.

I must also express my gratitude to a number of people who have contacted me or otherwise communicated their generous and encouraging remarks about the first edition, or have provided me with additional information or perspectives. In particular I wish to thank Professor George Jones of the London School of Economics, William Thornhill of Sheffield University, Professor Ken Newton of Dundee University, Professor D. E. Regan of Nottingham University, John Gyford of University College London, Alan Parker of Teesside Polytechnic, Mr K. J. Bridge, Chief Executive, Humberside County Council, and Arthur Godfrey of the *Local Government Review*. I am also grateful to Peter

Stuart of Somerset County Council Law Library, Bryan McEnroe of Taunton Library, Stuart Macwilliam of Exeter University Library and Phil Lawton of Somerset Health Authority.

For local government watchers there has been a lot to see in the past two years – legislation, legal battles, resource restrictions and service reductions. Unfortunately our sights are being narrowed here by government economy measures. Thus as part of the 'Rayner exercise' in cutting 'waste' in public expenditure, the OPCS has now ceased to collect and collate the local government election returns; consequently, after forty years, it is now impossible to follow trends and patterns in local government voting turnout. This, in itself, is not a vitally important matter; but it is another indication of the unfortunate recent tendency to downgrade Local Government in Britain.

Taunton, January 1983   Tony Byrne

Preface to the Third Edition

It is tempting to suggest that for local government in Britain George Orwell's choice of the year 1984 was remarkably prescient, for 1984 saw the passage into law of the Rates Act. This permits, for the first time, the limitation of local councils' rates by (Big Brother) central government; and eighteen local authorities have been selected to have their rates thus capped in the year 1985–6.

As this legislation proceeded through Parliament there was massive protest and lobbying, and considerable opposition among MPs, including many prominent members and former leaders of the Government's own party; indeed one former (Conservative) Secretary of State for the Environment described the legislation as 'a deplorable Bill which raises major constitutional issues. It is a classic example of elective dictatorship' (Geoffrey Rippon, House of Commons, 22 December 1983).

With the Government's overwhelming majority (of 144 seats) in the House of Commons, parliamentary opposition is weak and frustrated, and as a result many detect that the task of opposition has, at least to some extent, shifted out to local government. In so far as this is (or is perceived to be) true, it helps to explain the acrimony which has characterized local–central relations in recent years – and is likely to continue, with arguments over rate-capping and derogation, and over targets and grants: already a number of councils are threatening to 'do a Liverpool' and deliberately to refuse or delay the declaration of a rate/budget. And 1985–6 will witness the débâcle over the abolition of the metropolitan authorities and the redistribution of their responsibilities; members (especially Labour members) in metropolitan counties are resigning or threatening to resign their seats in order to force by-elections and thus test public opinion on the issue in the hope of embarrassing the Government and discrediting its plans.

Such is the continuing pace of change in the world of local government that I have found it necessary to undertake a further revision of the text, for which opportunity I am grateful to Penguin Books. However, I have left some of the figures unaltered either because the recent changes are not significant, or (as with the election turnout figures) because the data is unfortunately not available.

Taunton, September 1984   Tony Byrne

Preface to the Fourth Edition

So much continues to happen in the world of local government that to blink is to miss something – legal judgments, elections, nominations for rate-capping, financial brinkmanship, changes in party control, fluxing conventions – and, of course, the annual (at least) Local Government Act (there have actually been twelve such Acts since 1979).

Ideally, therefore, to observe local government in Britain, one needs a compound eye, for local government is not a single entity. Local authorities may exhibit a number of common features, and there is an underlying legal framework. But the essence of local government – and ultimately its *raison d'être* – is its diversity, as local authorities serve differing communities. Local government might be described as 'bespoke' government in respect of local policy choices and decisions, and local procedures and practice – at least in theory, if not practice.

In practice, there are strong forces at work which are seriously undermining this potential for local choice and diversity. John Banham, the Controller of the Audit Commission, has described Britain as 'a highly centralized society with a central government machine that lacks – and inevitably will always lack – the information, skills and attitudes to manage the services for which ministers are nominally accountable to Parliament . . . The public expenditure process and Parliamentary procedures perpetuate the myth of central control. The mythology is dangerous since it simultaneously encourages delusions of competence at the centre and a dangerous, dependent attitude at the local level . . . Indeed public administration in Britain appears to combine the worst of all worlds: most of the costs associated with centrally managed economies but few of the potential benefits. The choice is clear: replicate in Great Britain the present administrative arrangements in Northern Ireland, or devolve much more power, responsibility and accountability to the local level. From a management point of view, least (central) government is best government' (*Public Administration*, Winter 1985).

He might have added that it is also best from a democratic point of view. Indeed, recently, Patrick Jenkin, the former Secretary of State substantially responsible for the abolition of the metropolitan counties and the GLC and for the introduction of rate-capping, has himself spoken of '. . . a greater and greater degree of centralization . . . that measure of central control is really hostile, inimical to what local authorities stand for. They ought to be substantially independent bodies. The more that central government tries to influence them the less efficient the system has become.'

Things might change. Particularly important here is the system of local government finance. To quote John Banham again, he describes it as 'a most ghastly shambles . . . one of the biggest administrative bog-ups it's been my misfortune ever to see . . . part of a system that's generating waste and inefficiency at local level on a scale that I find deeply depressing.' The opposition parties are highly critical of the grant system, and the Government itself has announced proposals for changing it.

Meanwhile, in this new edition, I have tried to incorporate a number of the recent events and changes. I would like to thank my wife Sari for her painstaking revision of the index, and for her vital support throughout.

Taunton, May 1986   Tony Byrne

Preface to the Fifth Edition

Since the first edition of this book there have been over fifty pieces of legislation dealing with local government. Despite recent reassurances from local government Ministers that there is to be a period of stability and consolidation, there are already signs of further Government-inspired change for local authorities – in finance (in response to problems with the poll tax), in functions (planning, pollution, waste disposal) and perhaps in structure. This is very unsettling for those who just want to get on with the job of providing public services.

Yet government is about change and how to manage it. It is said that good management copes with change, better management anticipates change, and the best management creates changes (though presumably not just for its own sake). Certainly, local authorities experience their own organic or self-induced change – in party politics, in local problems, in their own management arrangements, for example.

This new edition seeks to take account of such changes, and also those arising from the Local Government Finance Act 1988 and the Widdicombe Report (1986), with its consequential Local Government and Housing Act 1989.

I wish to thank Peter Stuart, Somerset's Law Librarian, for his help. And my debt to those who write and concern themselves with the place of local government in Britain today is at least partially acknowledged in the References and Further Reading section.

Taunton, May 1990   Tony Byrne

Note on 1992 revised reprint In this reprint, I have made a number of amendments and additions – such is the volatile state of local government. A fuller treatment will be given in the next edition: the General Election should by then have resolved some uncertainties.

Taunton, February 1992   Tony Byrne

Preface to the Sixth Edition

It would be trite to remark that much has happened in and to local government since the previous edition of this book. With 150 pieces of legislation affecting local authorities since 1979, change has become endemic. Some of the changes are continuations of existing developments – contracting out, tight budgets, opting out, etc., whilst others are new, or rather repeats of earlier policies, such as the introduction of a new system of local tax, the redistribution of responsibilities and, above all, the reorganization of the structure of local government.

Before the last General Election (1992) a prominent government minister, Chris Patten, declared that local government needed a reorganization 'like a hole in the head'. By the time this new edition is published the legislation will have determined the details of the new structure for Scotland and Wales, and the fate of the English authorities will be settled soon after.

Once the reorganization has taken place (no simple or quick matter) local government may be able to look forward to a period of relative calm. The Prime Minister said he wishes to see an improvement in general–local relations and a renaissance in local government. The introduction of the Secondment Initiative Programme and the government's newly established (1993) regional offices should facilitate better understanding and coordination with local authorities – all perhaps made easier with a (long-heralded) revival in the economy.

This is not to suggest that problems will not remain – inadequate sources of local tax, capping, loss of functions to non-elected bodies, etc. This makes it all the more regrettable that the reorganization has not been accompanied by a fundamental examination of the essential role of local government and its financing. If there is a calm, it may be short-lived.

April 1994   Tony Byrne

Recent Landmarks

1966–9 Royal Commissions on Local Government – in England, Redcliffe-Maud Report, in Scotland, Wheatley Report

1967 Maud Report on Management in Local Government

1970 Local Authorities Social Services Act – social services departments created

1972 Local Government Act (1973 in Scotland) – reorganized structure

1972 Bains and Paterson Reports on management in the new authorities

1973 National Health Service Act – from 'tripartite' to 'unified' structure; local authorities lost health function to Area Health Authorities.

1974 Local Government Act – Local Commissioners (ombudsmen) created (1975 in Scotland)

1976 Layfield Committee Report on Local Government Finance

1976 Education Act – compulsory comprehensive schools

1976 'The party's over' (Anthony Crosland, Secretary of State)

1978 'Organic Change' White Paper – proposed increasing the role of city councils

1979 Education Act – rescinds 1976 Act

1980 Local Government Planning and Land Act – introduced block grants; competitive tendering; compulsory sale of council housing

1980 Education Act – parent governors; parents' right to choose school

1981 Spending targets and penalties introduced

1982 Local Government Finance Act – supplementary rates abolished; Audit Commission established

1982 Housing Benefit introduced

1984 Rates Act – introduced rate-capping

1985 Local Government Act – abolished GLC and Metropolitan County Councils

1985 Local Government (Access to Information) Act

1986 Widdicombe Report on the Conduct of Local Authority Business

1987 Abolition of Domestic Rates etc. (Scotland) Act – introduced community charge or poll tax

1988 Local Government Act – further compulsory tendering of council services

1988 Local Government Finance Act – community charge/poll tax for England and Wales; and national business rates

1988 Education Reform Act – local financial management in schools; power to opt out of LEA control; national curriculum; polytechnics independent of LEAs

1988 Housing Act – opting out; 'pick a landlord/tenant'

1989 Local Government and Housing Act – Government's response to Widdicombe Report: restricts officers' political activities; requires parties to share committee seats; bans councils' rent subsidies (see Appendix 16)

1989 Children Act – introduces a new statutory framework for local authorities' work with children and families

1990 National Health Service and Community Care Act – removes local authority representation on health authorities; local authorities given the lead role in arranging the provision of social care in the community

1990 Environmental Protection Act – increased responsibilities for local authorities

1991 Criminal Justice Act – implications for local authorities' costs

1992 Local Government Act – Commission to review structure and electoral arrangements in England's non-metropolitan areas

1992 White Paper on structure of local government in Wales

1992 Local Government Finance Act – abolishes community charge/poll tax, introduces council tax

1992 Education (Schools) Act – sets up independent inspection system (OFSTED); schools to be inspected every four years; school performance indicators to be published

1992 Further and Higher Education Act establishes further education and sixth-form colleges as corporations independent of LEAs (in 1993)

1993 White Papers (two) on police – to be more autonomous; local authority representation to be reduced to one half

1993 White Paper on structure in Scotland and (a second) in Wales

1993 Trade Union Reform and Employment Rights Act – provides for Careers service to be privatized

1993 Leasehold Reform, Housing and Urban Development Act – extends sale of council houses through rents-to-mortgage scheme; council tenants' rights to repairs made statutory; sets up Urban Regeneration Agency

1993 Education Act – promotes school opt-outs to grant-maintained (GM) status; sets up Funding Agency for GM schools; sets up Schools Curriculum and Assessment Authority (SCAA); inefficient LEA schools to be subject to take-over by specifically appointed bodies ('commissions')

1993 Working party report on internal management

1993–4 Reports by Local Government Commission on the structure of local authorities in parts of England

1993–4 Local Government (Wales) Bill

1993–4 Local Government etc. (Scotland) Bill

1. What Local Government Is

The governance of a modern society is an enormous task. In Great Britain, for example, half of the nation's annual income flows through the hands of the government, and some 30 per cent of the labour force are employed in the state sector. Government is, therefore, 'big business'.

For this reason most countries find it necessary to decentralize their administration, in other words to arrange for services to be provided and decisions to be made away from the centre or capital and 'in the field' or locally. Such decentralization can take a number of forms. The simplest is known as *deconcentration*, whereby the officers of the central government (the civil servants) are dispersed into local and regional offices such as the local tax or benefits office. Another simple form is *functional decentralization*, in which a particular service or function is hived off from the central government to a semi-independent organization commonly referred to as a 'quango' (quasi-autonomous non-governmental organization). Among their estimated 2,000, examples include the Post Office, the Arts Council, the British Council, the Gaming Board, the Housing Corporation, the Rural Development Commission, the National Council for Vocational Qualifications and the Scottish Development Agency. *Regional devolution* (or regionalism) is more complex and involves the limited transfer by the central government of political and administrative authority to a regional body, such as a Scottish or Welsh Assembly. Local government is an example of such devolution, but on a more local basis. Local government is self-government involving the administration of public affairs in each locality by a body of representatives of the local community known as the local authority (or council). Although subject to the central government in many ways, local authorities possess a considerable amount of responsibility and discretionary power.

Local government, then, is one of a number of forms of decentralization. This fact helps to explain why it can be so confusing: it resembles so many other administrative structures to be found in the modern state – ministries, departments, authorities, boards, corporations, bureaux, councils and so on. Consequently it is not surprising that many people mistakenly believe, for example, that local authorities run the hospitals (which are actually the responsibility of appointed Health Authorities or self-governing trusts) or think that social workers are paid by the Minister responsible for social services (in fact they are employed by the local authorities, who pay their salaries out of the rates and council tax).

There are, however, a number of characteristics which mark out local government as a distinctive form of public administration. Thus local government is *elected*. Although some areas (parishes and communities) are small enough to need only a simple meeting of all the local people, most local authorities consist of representatives chosen by the members of the community at properly constituted elections. These elected members form the local 'council', which then recruits the full-time paid staff of the authority, including engineers, accountants, teachers, clerks and bin-men. These employees are not civil servants, though they are organized at the town hall or county hall into departments such as the Education Department, the Housing Department or the Social Services Department.

It follows that local government is *multi-purpose*: every local authority has many jobs to do and a variety of services to provide. An individual local authority may be responsible for the provision of schools, homes for the elderly and training centres for the handicapped; fire services; road building and maintenance, and traffic management; and the control of the environment through

County/Regional councils

Metropolitan boroughs
and London borough councils

Non-metropolitan district councils

Figure 1 *The structure of British local government (since 1986)*

the regulation of building and land development. By contrast, the 'quangos' and public corporations tend to be concerned with just one particular service or field of activity, such as health (the Health Authorities), water (the National Rivers Authorities) or racial discrimination (the Commission for Racial Equality).

The third feature of local government is the *local scale* of its operations: each authority has responsibility in its own area only. As we have seen, some of these areas (the parishes and communities) are very local in scale. But most of the more important authorities operate over the area of a county or region, or over a district (part of a county or region).

Fourthly, local government has a quite clearly *defined structure*. This consists of either two tiers made up of fifty-nine large county or regional councils plus 455 smaller district councils, or (in the conurbations of England) sixty-eight single-tier London boroughs and metropolitan district/borough councils. (In some parts of Britain, the parish or community makes a third tier.) This is illustrated in Figure 1. (The diagram is not intended to suggest a hierarchical or power relationship between the two tiers.)

The next feature of local government is that it is *subordinated* to the national authority, which is Parliament. Local authorities come into existence as a result of legislation passed by Parliament, and all such authorities are subject to the law. If a local authority steps outside the law (for example by failing to do something which the law requires it to do, such as not providing schools) it will be liable to the rigours and sanctions of the law in the same way as private people are. Parliament alone has sovereignty: local authorities exercise power to the extent that Acts of Parliament allow. (Membership of the European Union qualifies this.)

Although local authorities carry out those responsibilities handed on to them by Parliament, it is misleading to see them simply as agents acting for the central government in the administration of certain services. While subject to certain controls operated by the central government, the local authorities work in partnership with it, and they possess a freedom and initiative which justifies their being described as bodies exercising local *self*-government.

Enabling them to do this, and the last important feature of local government, is the *local tax system*, comprising (from 1993) a local council tax on residents and a rate (or property tax) on businesses. Locally determined taxes (in the form of 'rates') have been collected by local authorities for centuries. Although local taxation has not been the chief source of local government incomes in recent years, it is still important (see Chapter 11) and provides local authorities with some degree of independence and flexibility.

Local government forms part of the administrative structure of the country, and it may be useful, before going further, to summarize the work of the two other main components of this administrative structure, namely central government and the quangos.

Central government and the quangos

Central government is composed of about a hundred Ministers of the Crown, responsible to Parliament. Most of them are elected MPs (from the majority party in the House of Commons), though some will be peers (members of the non-elected House of Lords). The central government forms the executive branch of the nation's political system, and it is headed by a Cabinet of senior Ministers, under the leadership of the Prime Minister.

Central government is national, not local, and has to take the whole country into its consideration, administering services uniformly across the nation. Thus the services carried on are national, not local, in scale. The necessary finance is derived by the Treasury from national taxation.

Civil servants are recruited to carry out government policies and administer the statutes passed by Parliament. They are both advisers to the government and administrators of government policy. Although the main government departments (or Ministries) are in London (for the most part in Whitehall), there are regional and local offices in the main towns and cities of Britain. So we have Ministers, each heading a government department, and civil servants, who are directly responsible to the Ministers through a hierarchical structure ranging from the permanent secretaries (civil servants) at the top advising Ministers personally, down to the assistant clerical and administrative officers, who help to put the laws and regulations into effect at the community level (for example, by assessing and collecting income taxes, keeping records, etc.).

Quasi-governmental organizations or 'quangos' are independent agencies set up to perform some service or to administer an industry free from direct government control (though subject to some restraints exercised by Ministers, who are responsible to Parliament). There are about[1] 2,000 such bodies, and in addition to those previously mentioned (p. 1) examples include British Rail, the Welsh and Scottish Development Agencies, the Grant Maintained Schools Trust, the British Library Board, the Royal Fine Arts Commission, the National Mobility Office, the Further Education Funding Council, the Museum Commission, British Coal, the Atomic Energy Authority, the Independent Broadcasting Authority, the National Enterprise Board, the Countryside Commission and Remploy. Collectively, quangos are responsible for one fifth of public sector spending,[2] which is nearly as much as local authorities (see Chapter 11).

The role of these organizations varies. They may be *advisory* (for example the School Curriculum and Assessment Authority

(SCAA) or the British Safety Council); *executive* (the Business and Technical Education Council or the Public Works Loan Board); *industrial–commercial* (British Rail or British Nuclear Fuel); *promotional* (the Training Boards, the Millennium Commission, the Research Councils or the General Practice Finance Corporation); *regulatory* (the Monopolies Commission, OFWAT or OFSTED); *coordinating* (the National Blood Authority or the Urban Regeneration Agency); *semi-judicial* (the Commission for Racial Equality or the Health and Safety Commission); or they may be *conciliatory* in function (the Advisory Conciliation and Arbitration Service or the Central Arbitration Council). Many in fact combine several roles and are therefore difficult to classify.

The number and variety of these organizations and bodies reflect the range of activities which fall within the sphere of 'government' in its widest sense. At the beginning of the last century, the main task of government was internal peace and defence against external enemies. Gradually government has widened its view and extended the scope of its activities, particularly with the development of the Welfare State and the 'managed' economy.

The degree of control over these bodies exercised by government Ministries varies. Most of the boards or managing committees, however, are appointed either by the Prime Minister or a Minister, and they are given a general responsibility defined in either a charter (like the BBC and the Arts Council) or a statute (like the Countryside Commission, the Commission for New Towns and most of the others). The staff of these bodies are not civil servants; they are employees of the particular corporation, commission, authority, council or board. Nevertheless, the political responsibility rests with the government Minister.

Quangos are given considerable freedom from direct government control so as to keep politics, which may be irrelevant or prejudicial to their various ostensible functions, out of their day-to-day operations, whether commercial (as with the nationalized industries such as British Coal or British Rail) or cultural (such as the BBC) or semi-judicial (such as the Charity Commission).

The administrative structure in Britain is summarized on p. 8 in Figure 2.

The justification for local government

Local government exists and it is difficult to imagine its disappearance. However, it is worth considering some of the reasons which are advanced to justify its existence.

(1) Local government is seen as an *efficient* method of administering certain services. This efficiency is explained on one or more of the following grounds: (a) local authorities consist of members who are drawn from the local populace and who therefore have local knowledge and a commitment to the local area and its people; (b) local authorities are multi-purpose bodies and can therefore, theoretically, secure a greater degree of coordination and policy integration: for example, since the same council is responsible for planning, roads and housing, the liaison between these different services and departments is easier and closer; (c) public administration generally benefits from the existence of local authorities because they off-load responsibilities from central government departments and the civil service, who would otherwise be overburdened with work.

(2) Having a fair degree of independence, the local authorities can take initiatives and *experiment*: they can seek a variety of solutions to society's problems. In this way they may innovate and pioneer new services or methods of administration, and successful ideas may be spread to other authorities. For example, in 1847 Liverpool Council made the first appointment of a Medical Officer of Health; other authorities followed suit later. Similarly, certain cities in the late nineteenth century (notably London and Birmingham) developed the first council housing. More recently, individual local authorities have originated such schemes as devolved budgets to schools, free birth control, comprehensive education, mobile libraries, bottle banks, advice centres

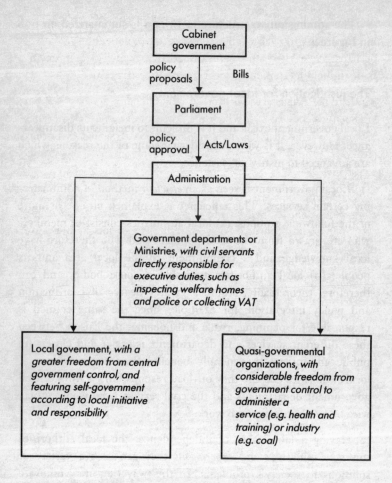

Figure 2 *British administrative structure*

for housing or consumer affairs, rents-to-mortgages and free bus travel and special housing for pensioners; many local authorities, or even government, have since adopted these ideas.

(3) Local government can be said to encourage citizenship or *democracy* and to promote 'political education' in its widest sense. It does this by involving large numbers of people in the political

decision-making process. While people may find the affairs of a modern state too large and complex to understand, they will perhaps more easily and naturally participate with their neighbours in helping to manage local community affairs:

Nowhere has democracy ever worked well without a great measure of local self-government ... Where the scope of the political measures becomes so large that the necessary knowledge is almost exclusively possessed by the bureaucracy, the creative impulses of the private person must flag.[3]

In Britain, there are currently some 25,000 local government councillors, that is, members of the public who are elected to the principal local authorities. A significant proportion of these are members of social groups which are distinctly under-represented in national politics, for example women and manual workers. Furthermore, experience in local government has frequently proved to be a stepping-stone to national politics: as many as one third of M Ps are or have been local councillors.

Councillors of course are elected, and the frequent elections which occur in local government give the general public an opportunity to exercise and practise the right to vote. In some ways this relationship between elector and elected is closer at the local than at the national level, and helps to create an awareness among local voters of their ability to influence decisions. Local government is more accessible and thus accountable. It is therefore likely to be more responsive to local wishes.

(4) Local government is seen by some as a barrier or *defence* against an all-powerful central government and the abuse of power. Certainly in the nineteenth century it was held that the existence of a strong local government system helped to disperse political power and diminish the danger of an over-centralized state.[4] Today we tend to see local government more as a means to influence central government; for example, through the various local authority associations (see p. 401), which may seek to influence government policy in such matters as transport subsi-

dies, conservation, rural postal services or economic development. Furthermore, the diffusion of decision-making power is justified on the grounds that numerous errant policies among a variety of local authorities cause less harm than one big policy failure by the central government.

(5) Local government may be justified simply on the grounds of *tradition* – that it has from time immemorial been a part of the British way of life, part of our heritage and of our culture. A more sophisticated view is that of Edmund Burke (1729–97): 'That which *is* must be good because it has stood the test of time.'

(6) Finally there is support for local government from those who, like the American Founding Fathers of the eighteenth century, believe that there should be no taxation without *representation* – that since local authorities have the power to impose taxes (the council tax), the tax-payers should be represented on the body which determines how that money should be spent. This is a fundamental precept of parliamentary government (and has been since the signing of Magna Carta in 1215). Many feel it is equally applicable at the local level of government.

The Widdicombe Committee on *The Conduct of Local Authority Business* summarizes the case thus:

The value of local government stems from its three attributes of:
  (a) pluralism, through which it contributes to the national political system;
  (b) participation, through which it contributes to local democracy;
  (c) responsiveness, through which it contributes to the provision of local needs through the delivery of services.[5]

It goes on to add the comment that 'Local government has no independent right to exist. Its continued existence is based on the contribution it can make to good government. It needs to be able to demonstrate that it is a more effective means of government than local administration'.

The critics of local government

However, the case for local government is not overwhelming or unanimous: there exists a contrary view, that of the 'centralists', who are critical of its existence on a number of grounds:[6]

(1) Local government allows a variation in the standard of provision of local services which may be regarded as inequitable or unfair in an age of equality, or at least equality of opportunity. For example, in operating the '11-plus' examination and selective secondary education, some authorities allowed half of their secondary pupils to go to grammar schools, while in other areas the figure was only 20 per cent. Similar variation may be found in other areas of education (such as in the extent of the provision of nursery or adult/community education) and in other services, such as the provision of special housing for the elderly, hostel accommodation for the mentally disordered, youth services, or the levels of provision of home helps, occupational therapists and social workers.

(2) Doubt is cast on the efficiency of local government administration. Many authorities are felt to be too small to be effective in the provision of some or all of their services (see p. 55). In addition, there is scepticism about the amount of coordination and integration of services which is achieved in practice within local authorities. Moreover, the speed of modern communications means that central government can be as effective in dealing with local problems even though local government is nearer.

In addition local government is seen as either too bureaucratic or too party political to be efficient or sufficiently responsive to public opinion. An alternative to central government intervention here is seen in the privatization of local services.[7]

(3) Though local authorities may be progressive and pioneer new services, equally they may drag their feet and be closed to new

ideas and change. Thus local government is criticized as encouraging narrow or 'parish pump' attitudes and policies.

(4) Finally there is the danger of exaggeration and over-idealization. The notion that local government acts as a bastion against excessive state power and as a catalyst to the release of simmering community participation may be far too ambitious a claim. In practice, as we shall see later (Chapter 12), the central government exercises considerable control over the policies of local government, and the general public shows a considerable lack of enthusiasm for local government matters.

Arguments or views such as these may convince some people that local government should be abolished altogether.[8] The main consequence, in practice, has been a tendency to closer control and supervision of local authorities by the central government, which could ultimately threaten the existence of local government in view of the comment above by the Widdicombe Committee.

2. An Evolving System

The British are renowned for their respect for tradition. The British system of government is equally famous for its reliance on conventions and unwritten codes of behaviour, in preference to formal written codes which often purport to be immutable. Change, however, is inherent in laws and constitutions, as it is inherent in life. The way in which local government has adapted to changing circumstances is the subject of this chapter.

History has imprinted itself with particular clarity on our system of local government. Understand our history and you go a long way towards an understanding of the present local government system, for we still have the same essential forms (for example, committees), the same basic geographical divisions (such as counties and parishes), the same sort of local leaders (the councillors) and the same sort of offices (such as mayors and provosts) as we have had for centuries. All the main elements have evolved to meet the new challenges of a complex society and to ensure sensible democratic government.

Before 1800: the early system

The feudal system in England lasted until the sixteenth century. It was based on land tenure or holding, with the king, as lord paramount, granting tracts of land to barons, nobles or bishops, who in turn granted portions to freemen. It was a social order or hierarchy, each person having duties towards or rights over those above and below. Central government was carried out by the king with his *curia regis* (or council). Justice was administered by judges, holding the king's commission, who visited the localities to supervise local administration and ensure justice, order and peace.

Local government grew out of the local communities of parishes, townships (some of which were boroughs) and counties, the boundaries of which were found even in Anglo-Saxon times. The local communities formed naturally, and leaders (such as the hundredman, the shire reeve or sheriff, and the Justice or Conservator of the Peace) emerged or were appointed by the king to help to carry out the basic tasks of the local communities – the prevention of crime, punishment of offenders, the provision of poor relief and welfare, the control of nuisance, the management of common lands and property, etc.

These essential local government activities were in fact dealt with by various bodies: self-help groups, voluntary associations and sometimes commercial undertakings. Formal legal authorities, what today we would call 'local authorities', provided a fourth agency, but they were not necessarily the most important, and in many areas the units of civil government merely filled in the gaps left by the other bodies.

In the course of time, many of the non-statutory bodies (charities, guilds, the Church and the manor) declined, and many of their functions were taken over by the nascent local authorities. From the late Middle Ages, around the fifteenth century, three types of civil authority became firmly established: the parish (based on the church parish), the shire (county) and the corporate town (borough or burgh).

The parish became responsible for local law and order (appointing a local constable), for providing common amenities (through a surveyor of highways) and for dealing with social distress (through overseers of the poor). These officers were elected or served on a rota basis. Some general supervision was exercised by the 'vestry', a local committee which in some places was elected and in others was appointed or self-selected. Further oversight was provided by Justices of the Peace (appointed by the Crown), who exercised authority on a county-wide basis. They were responsible for checking local affairs and administration, inspecting accounts and making appointments, but they had direct responsibility for such matters as highways and bridges, weights and measures, as well as the traditional duties of maintaining the peace and punishing petty crimes.

The corporate towns (called 'boroughs' in England and Wales, 'burghs' in Scotland) were those urban areas which had at some time obtained a charter from the Crown entitling them to certain privileges. These included the right to establish their own administration (in the form of a 'corporation'), to own corporate property (guild halls and town halls) and to have a separate 'bench' of magistrates or JPs; they may also have been entitled to call themselves 'cities'.

This was the picture, much simplified, of local government at the end of the eighteenth century. The real picture was very complex, however, and there were many variations among the regions and areas. In some areas charities were strong and active; in others responsibilities had been taken over by special statutory bodies, such as Turnpike Trusts (to build and maintain roads) or Improvement Commissioners (to provide water, lighting or sanitation). And there was considerable variation in the method of election or selection of officers, vestries and corporations. A generalization that can safely be made, however, is that the 'system' was rudimentary, and by today's standards many local authorities were inefficient and corrupt.

Over the course of the next two centuries local government appears to have undergone three distinct phases of development, which we now consider.

1800–1880: stress and improvisation

By the beginning of the nineteenth century the impact of industrialization and urbanization was becoming clear. Problems of poverty, disease, crime and squalor were demanding attention.

The response was substantial, though piecemeal and sometimes reluctant,[1] so that by the mid nineteenth century there was more active concern about the problems of society than there had been at any time before. However, it was a community response rather than an official response: private enterprise developed estates and provided water and gas; voluntary groups and charities provided schools, housing and hospitals; self-help and pressure groups urged the provision of parks and other cultural and social amenities.

From the official side it was soon apparent that the existing authorities could not cope with the problems they were now facing. The parishes were too small or inept, and they began to lose some of their traditional functions to higher authorities. For example, in England and Wales the inadequacy of the parish constables led to the setting-up of police forces in the boroughs in 1835 and in the counties in 1839 and 1856 (all modelled on the Metropolitan Police, created in 1829). Similarly, being unable to cope with the mounting social distress, the parishes lost their individual responsibilities for poor relief in 1834, when the Poor Law Act placed this responsibility on to groups (or 'unions') of parishes, which then operated under *ad hoc* elected Boards of Guardians.

Such *ad hoc* (or special-purpose) authorities were not new: a number of Turnpike Trusts and Improvement Commissioners had been created by Local (or Private – see p. 78) Acts of Parliament in the eighteenth century. These bodies proliferated in the nineteenth century (often by-passing the existing public authorities), so that we find local commissions or 'boards' for cleaning, paving or lighting the streets, for road building, for slum clearance, sewers, burial and for water supply.

Furthermore, general Acts of Parliament led to the creation of more *ad hoc* bodies, just as the Poor Law Amendment Act 1834 had created Boards of Guardians. Local health boards were set up under the Public Health Act 1848, highways boards under the Highways Acts 1835 and 1862, and elementary school boards under the Education Act 1870. Each of these local boards had its own elected body (the board itself), its own officials and its own rates.

Some existing local authorities showed initiative and foresight: they promoted local Acts and obtained the powers to take action themselves.[2] There was thus some administrative tidying-up, as corporations, and especially Boards of Health, took over some of the functions of the Improvement Commissioners.

In addition, there were some attempts to reform local government in the towns, since it was the towns which were most affected by economic and social changes (including an astonishing growth in population[3]). In 1835 the Municipal Corporations Act, affecting 178 corporate boroughs in England and Wales, was passed. In an attempt to remove corruption and inefficiency, the Act required the corporations to be elected by ratepayers, to hold council meetings open to the public and to have their accounts regularly audited. In this way, a uniform constitution for most (about two thirds) of the boroughs was established.

The Municipal Corporations Act 1882 added another twenty-five old boroughs to this scheme, and in the meantime all new boroughs (some sixty-two were created between 1835 and 1876) adopted this form of local government. Uniformity was enhanced by the Public Health Act 1872, which *required* the establishment of health authorities throughout England and Wales – whether they took the form of borough councils (for the towns and cities), Boards of Health (for urban areas) or Boards of Guardians (for rural areas) – and the obligatory performance of health functions and responsibilities.

But a number of the old corporations had gone unreformed and had dwindled into insignificance as the *ad hoc* bodies assumed real power. In other towns and villages there was no common pattern either: the vestry, manorial officers, guardians, Improvement Commissioners, charity trustees, Justices of the Peace, all jostled each other for authority. Consequently local government was fittingly described in the 1870s as 'a chaos of areas, a chaos of authorities and a chaos of rates'. The structure was the product of a continuous patching-up exercise: it was not purpose-built.

1888–1930: the period of ascendancy

Such chaos as existed in England and Wales before 1888 was described and condemned by the Royal Sanitary Commission (1868–71), and there was some attempt at improving and tidying up the situation by the Public Health Act 1872, which divided the country into *rural* and *urban* areas for the purpose of public health services such as sanitation. But the demand for a more thorough-going reform had been growing since the 1830s. In particular there was a call to set up in the counties a form of representative government similar to that established for the boroughs. The call was resisted by the country gentry, largely because of fear of an increased rate burden which they thought would result from a more open and more active county government.

The Reform Act 1832 had revised the allocation of parliamentary representatives to reflect the changed distribution of the population. In removing the parliamentary franchise from many ancient boroughs ('rotten' or 'pocket' boroughs), the effect was to leave the disfranchised boroughs somewhat powerless and exposed. Hence the reforms of the Municipal Corporation Act 1835 (see p. 17). In a similar way, the Reform Act 1884, by extending the parliamentary vote to agricultural workers, threw into sharp relief the anomaly of the non-elected character of the county authorities composed of Justices of the Peace. Consequently the Local Government Act 1888 created elected *county councils*, based largely on the existing counties.[4] Initially their responsibilities were limited to highways, asylums, weights and measures and police, but these were increased substantially over the next forty years.

The Local Government Act 1888 also created *county borough councils*. These were to be all-purpose authorities, independent of the county councils and based on existing boroughs. The criterion for their creation was population: a town with a population of 50,000 or more could claim county borough status. Some eighty-two towns[5] did so, much to the dismay of the county MPs, who had originally sought a qualifying figure of 150,000 population. Those boroughs which failed to gain county borough status remained as non-county boroughs and became *district councils*, for local government purposes, within the counties.

The rationalization of the local government structure was largely completed by the Local Government Act 1894. This created elected *urban district councils* (UDCs) and *rural district councils* (RDCs), which were based on consolidated sanitary districts. Like those of the *non-county borough councils*, the main functions of the district councils were public health and highways.[6] Under the same Act, *parishes* were revived by the creation of parish councils, which, except in parishes of under 300 electors (where they might simply have meetings of all parishioners), were elected.

The system of local government was completed in 1899 when twenty-eight *metropolitan borough councils* were established for the London area, which had at that time the largest city population in the world. In 1888 a separate London county area had been created by removing parts of Middlesex, Kent and Surrey, and the *London County Council* was established on a similar basis to other county councils. In 1899 the 'district' authorities were being added, with the City of London (the square mile in the heart of London) being left as a separate authority in deference to its unique character and tradition.

Local government now had an established structure which was based on rational principles and provided a large measure of uniformity. In addition, all local authorities (councils) had a constitutional basis and operated on openly democratic lines. The stage was set for the local government system to enjoy some fifty years of ascendancy. It enjoyed increased status in the eyes of the general public, it became a pathway to a desirable career, and, above all, the central government was increasingly willing to entrust it with important responsibilities.

Some of these responsibilities were simply transferred from existing local government bodies when the new authorities were

Figure 3 *Local government in England and Wales at the end of the nineteenth century*

set up: in 1888 the county councils and county borough councils acquired the administrative functions of the Justices of the Peace, which covered rating, licensing, asylums, highways, weights and measures and police. Similarly, some of the JP's functions were passed on to the new district councils in 1894, though the districts' most important functions came in the same year from the transfer of the functions of the public health and highways boards. Further important transfers were soon to follow. In 1902 the School Boards (see p. 16) were abolished, and in their place local authorities set up committees (known as 'local education authorities') to provide schools and other educational services such as meals (introduced in 1906) and medical inspection (introduced in 1907). Under the Local Government Act 1929 the Boards of Guardians (see p. 12) were abolished and their functions transferred to local authorities, who created Public Assistance

Committees to continue the Guardians' former financial and welfare services.

Meanwhile new responsibilities were being assumed by the state, and many of these were placed in the hands of local government. In 1890 local authorities were permitted to build low-cost houses, and in 1919 they were given central government subsidies to encourage them to do so (as a result of which 1 million council houses were built in the years 1919–39). Under the Town Planning Act 1909, local authorities acquired the power to control the use and development of land, and while the legislation was modest in its provisions, it was greatly strengthened in 1919 and was extended to rural areas under the Town and Country Planning Act 1932.

Following the Unemployed Workmen's Act 1905, local authorities were permitted to anticipate the creation of a national network of Labour Exchanges by setting up local labour bureaux to help the unemployed to find work. (They could also finance the voluntary emigration of those out of work.) The same legislation strengthened their powers to spend money on public works for the purpose of creating jobs, a scheme originated in 1886 by Joseph Chamberlain. For school-leavers, the Education (Choice of Employment) Act 1910 allowed local education authorities to make special provision for advising and placing young people in employment (later to become known as the Youth Employment Scheme or the Careers Service).

During this period, local authorities were also providing employment opportunities directly, as a result of their expanded trading activities. There was considerable development by local government, by means of the Private Bill procedure (see p. 76), of what are usually called 'public utilities' – public transport, water, electricity and gas supply – although some of this apparent expansion was due to 'municipalization', that is, the takeover of private enterprise provision by local authorities. Apart from these activities there was considerable variety in the nature of municipal enterprises, which included the provision of a racecourse (Doncaster), a municipal bank (Birmingham), river ferries (Birkenhead), a telephone system (Hull), a civic theatre (Manchester) and numerous crematoria, slaughter-houses and dock undertakings.

In the meantime, local authorities' powers in respect of health – already well established in the environmental field (see p. 16) – were being extended to personal services. These included the provision of sanatoria for tuberculosis (1921) and community care services for the mentally subnormal (1913) and the mentally ill (1930). Concern at the welfare of children and young people found expression in the Midwives' Act (1902), the Children's Act (1908) and the Maternity and Child Welfare Act (1919), all of which had an immediate effect on the role and scope of local authorities.

Thus, over a period of some fifty years local government enjoyed something of a 'golden age', the symbol of which was the Local Government Act 1933. This was a consolidating measure, designed to clarify, confirm and in effect set the seal on the constitution, structure, powers and functions of local government in England and Wales.

1930–74: the period of 'decline'

For the next forty years, local government was in retreat: it no longer assumed such pride of place in the career orientation of bright school-leavers; it was losing status in the eyes of the public and became the subject of a number of unlikely sounding television serials; its management processes came in for criticism when the aldermanic system, the proliferation of committees and the ethos of 'Buggins' turn next' were contrasted with foreign systems and in particular with modern business management.[7] But the more tangible evidence of a decline lay in four other directions:

(1) *Loss of functions.* As the result of a policy of nationalization, local authorities lost their responsibilities for electricity and gas supply when these were taken over by electricity and gas boards

in 1947/8. Local government had never been the sole provider of these services, but its role was a substantial one, supplying about one third and two thirds respectively of the nation's gas and electricity consumption in 1945. Similarly, under post-war legislation (notably the Water Act 1945) many local authorities lost their responsibilities for water supply, as smaller water authorities were absorbed by the larger local authorities or joint water boards. Between 1945 and 1970 the number of water undertakings shrank from 1,250 to about 300. Under the Water Act 1973, English and Welsh local authorities lost all responsibility for water and sewerage to regional water authorities (private water companies from 1989).

These developments have been described as a return to the *ad hoc* system of the nineteenth century. But this resurgence is not confined to the field of public utilities. Under the National Health Service Act 1946, all local authority hospitals (about 1,700) together with voluntary hospitals (about 1,300) were transferred to Regional Hospital Boards. Under the National Health Service Act 1973 local government lost the remainder of their personal health services (including vaccination, health visiting, district nursing, ambulances and health centres) when these were transferred to the newly created *ad hoc* Regional and Area Health Authorities in order to create a more unified (and uniform) health service.

Similar developments occurred in the field of social security, for while local government inherited the function of public assistance (or poor relief) from the Boards of Guardians (see p. 16) when they were abolished in 1929, the local authority Public Assistance Committees which administered the system within the local government soon found themselves deprived of clients (whom they could barely afford to support) when, in 1934, the central government set up its own *ad hoc* Unemployment Assistance Board. In 1948 this became the National Assistance Board (then, in 1966, the Supplementary Benefits Commission, and subsequently Income Support in 1986–8), and it removed from local government completely the function of public assistance.

Further instances of the transference of local government functions to *ad hoc* bodies may be cited: under the River Boards Act 1948 (extended by the Water Resources Act 1963) the control of river pollution became the responsibility of River Boards. Under the Road Traffic Act 1930, the responsibility for licensing passenger road services passed from local authorities to regional traffic commissioners. The Transport Act 1947 transferred many canals and harbours to the British Transport Commission, and under the Transport Act 1968 special Passenger Transport Authorities have been established to manage the provision of local buses and trains in the larger urban areas (see p. 510).

However, the re-emergence of semi-independent public boards was not the only way in which local authorities lost functions. The central government itself has taken over direct responsibility for a number of services, for example the building and maintenance of trunk roads (under the Trunk Roads Acts 1936 and 1946) and rating valuation (under the Local Government Act 1948). For a short time, 1972–4, local authorities in effect found that central government had become responsible for the determination of council housing rents (under the Housing Finance Act 1972).

It is felt by some that another element in this aspect of local government 'decline' is the upward transfer of functions from the lower-tier authorities to the upper-tier ones. This has occurred most clearly in the case of the district councils. Although there were some exceptions, in 1944 district councils lost to the county councils their responsibility for providing elementary schools; in 1946 they lost their health and police functions, and in 1947 their fire services and planning functions.

This transfer between tiers has occurred in another sense. Under the direction of the Home Secretary, the number of police forces in Britain has been reduced from over two hundred in 1946 to fifty today. This is partly a consequence of the transfer from district to county councils under the 1946 Police Act. But it is also due to the fact that many police forces are now administered by joint committees of neighbouring county councils (for example the Avon and Somerset Constabulary).

(2) *Failure to attract new functions.* It has been suggested that local authorities have failed to acquire certain new responsibilities to which they would seem to have a claim. Under the New Towns Act 1946, the development of New Towns (such as Cumbernauld, Milton Keynes and Cwmbran) was placed in the hands of appointed boards instead of the proximate local authorities, and for nearly twenty years (1959–77) it was intended that the New Towns when completed should be transferred from the Development Corporations to the New Towns Commission rather than to local authorities. (This was changed in the 1977 Act and local authorities will now acquire the New Towns' assets and management, though some authorities are apprehensive about the costs involved.)

In 1949, under the Special Roads Act, the government announced plans to build motorways. It was not, however, the major local authorities who were to be responsible but the Ministry of Transport (operating through Road Construction Units). In 1967, in pursuance of a policy to preserve and enhance the environment, the Countryside Commissions were set up. Yet their functions (of encouraging the provision and development of facilities for open-air recreation) could perhaps have been undertaken by local authorities, if necessary through joint committees.[8] In 1965, under the government's National Plan, regional economic development machinery was established, in the form of Regional Planning Boards and Councils.[9] Although local authorities had representatives on these Planning Councils, at the time of their creation it was felt that local government was again being overlooked and by-passed. Indeed, in a leading article entitled 'Exit the Town Hall', *The Times* said, 'It is beginning to look as if confidence in it [local government] and practice of it may prove to be a passing phase in British political evolution.'

(3) *Loss of financial independence.* One of the characteristics of local authorities is that they have the power of taxation (see p. 4) and are thus able to finance their activities. Rates have never been the sole source of income, however, as local authorities have

also received income by way of rents, sales, service charges, fines and legacies. Since the nineteenth century, beginning with police grants, local authorities have also received grants from the central government. Between the 1930s and the 1970s the proportion of this grant revenue in local authority budgets grew substantially, as the figures in Table 1 indicate. As a result, it is argued, local authorities have lost much of their independence – 'he who pays the piper calls the tune'. (See Chapters 11 and 12.)

(4) *Increased central control.* In the course of the twentieth century, the central government has sought to control the activities of local authorities in a number of other ways. Legislation in the 1940s, setting up the post-war health, education and welfare services, required local authorities to submit their proposed schemes (for the administration and development of these services) to the Minister, or else gave him or her wide discretionary powers over local authorities undertaking those services. The central government has also developed substantial powers to intervene in local authorities' appointment of senior officers, to inspect certain local government services and to determine the charges which local authorities make for certain services. In addition, the volume of informational and advisory documents from the central government (called 'circulars') has grown in such a way as to give the central government considerable additional powers of persuasion and influence over the affairs of local government. The situation is well illustrated by the career of Aneurin Bevan. He is said to have been elected to Tredegar Urban District Council (in 1922) only to find that power resided in the county council. Having got himself elected to Monmouth County Council (1928), he found that power had gone to the central government. Subsequently he went there (1929) becoming Minister of Health (1945) and thus responsible for local government!

A number of explanations have been put forward to account for the apparent decline of local government. Firstly, it is suggested

Table 1 *Local government income (revenue account)*

Year	Grants £m	%	Rates £m	%	Other £m	%
1933	122	27	149	33	176	40
1953	469	36	443	33	413	31
1963	1,158	37	1,031	33	901	29
1973	4,422	45	2,682	28	2,660	27

Source: Local Government Finance (the Layfield Report), HMSO, 1976, Table 25; W. A. Robson, *Local Government in Crisis*, Allen & Unwin, 1966, Table 1.

that rates as a source of income are inadequate: they lack 'buoy-ancy', that is to say that they do not automatically produce a higher yield in revenue as incomes rise generally (see p. 320). As a consequence local authorities have of necessity come to rely more and more on central government grants.

Secondly, local authorities lost another source of income when gas and electricity were nationalized. The notions of nationaliza-tion and centralization are normally associated with the rise of socialism. The Labour Party was swept to power in 1945 (remain-ing in office until 1951) and while Labour is usually seen as an ally of local government (having historically developed many of its roots there) this time its commitment to central state ownership outweighed its predisposition to municipal enterprise.

Thirdly, the notion of equality had been gaining general ap-proval throughout the century. The privations and camaraderie of the Second World War gave it a substantial boost. Thus, following the Beveridge Report (1942),[10] the Welfare State was established. Social security and health services were unified and centralized to secure more uniform and equal treatment through-out the nation. And to the same end the activities of local government in the fields of education, welfare and housing became subject to greater central government oversight.

Fourthly, the radical doctrine of state intervention in the

economy, usually associated with the economist J. M. Keynes (1883–1946) and often referred to as 'Keynesian economics', became official government policy during and after the war. In 1944 the government pledged itself to a policy of full employment (in contrast to the heavy unemployment of the 1930s) and this required 'budget management' by the government, that is to say that in times of threatened depression the government would spend money to boost the economy, even if it meant that its budget was in deficit and not balanced with income from taxation. Conversely, where demand in the economy was excessive and inflation threatened, the government would seek to reduce state expenditure and perhaps private spending too, for example through higher taxes, tighter credit facilities and higher interest charges. This is generally known as fiscal and monetary policy. Local authorities have inevitably been caught up in this new 'demand management' role of government as they are big spenders, and in this way they have lost some of their freedom and autonomy.

Fifthly, local government may be said to have 'declined' because of its outmoded structure, which was mainly established in the nineteenth century, when the population was much smaller and population settlement quite different. At that time there were few if any suburbs, nor was there a 'drift' of population such as we have experienced in this century towards the South and East. Increased mobility, especially with the spread of motoring, and modern transport and communications, has made the nineteenth-century local government boundaries meaningless. In many ways, therefore, the structure was out of date from its inception: boundaries were wrongly drawn (for instance, county boroughs were made too small) and with the possible exception of London (see p. 113) insufficient account was taken of the nascent conurbations (the large urban areas, which stretch around the cities of Birmingham, Manchester and Glasgow, for example).

Coupled with this was the notion that local government units were too small to be efficient. Business enterprise had shown that 'bigger is better' in the sense that economies could be achieved in large-scale units – increasing the size of production unit can lower the unit costs (just as a double-decker bus can carry twice as many people as a single-decker but still only needs one driver and four wheels). Thus 'the process of technical change, by making such economies possible, encourages a shifting of responsibility for particular functions from lower to higher levels of government'.[11]

Assessing the fortunes of a private company or the business sector in general can be a fairly objective and precise exercise: one can refer to profits records, balance sheets, etc. It is much more difficult to make a similar evaluation of local government, which is very subjective and open to varying interpretations.

In the previous pages we have indicated some ways in which local government generally has declined since the 1930s, in contrast with its expansionary and optimistic phase from the later nineteenth century. However, we must beware of the danger of exaggeration. It could be argued that a number of the functions lost by local government were not very significant. For example the central government, in building motorways and taking over trunk roads, became responsible for less than 5 per cent of the nation's public highways; local authorities have retained responsibility for the remainder. Overall, it is not unreasonable to suggest that local authorities have retained their most important functions, and indeed they have markedly expanded their provision of these, as for example in the fields of education, leisure and the welfare services.

In addition, local government has acquired some new or enlarged responsibilities: for instance in the environmental field (including planning, town development, National Parks, pollution control and civic amenities) and in the field of welfare (such as children's services, consumer protection and community care for the mentally disordered). As a result of these developments, local government expenditure in the 1950s and 1960s increased not only in real terms but also as a proportion of total national expenditure (see Chapter 11).

Moreover, we must distinguish the substance from the shadow.

Extensive central government control exists in law, but how much is exercised in practice? For example, although he has the power to do so, only rarely does a Minister issue general directions to local authorities (and not always successfully even then – see pp. 372, 388, 586).

In so far as local government has experienced a decline in the ways described in this chapter, this *in itself* is not to be decried, for society changes and the machinery of public administration must change accordingly. What appears as a loss to local government may represent a net gain to society: thus the removal from local government of public assistance or gas supply may provide the greater benefits of lower costs and less uneven standards of service.

Finally, it may be added that local government has to some extent suffered at its own hands – by failing to take advantage of existing permissive powers and by failing to adapt itself and its structures to changing circumstances. It has also been suggested that too many authorities have developed a culture of 'submissive dependence' on central government.[12]

Scotland

The development of local government in Scotland quite closely parallels that of England and Wales. However, the relatively large number of burghs and their tradition of local self-rule provided Scotland with a more pervasive framework on which to build the structure of modern local government.

Burghs, like the English boroughs, were established in the Middle Ages as trading communities. Their primary function was to make profits and so supplement the king's revenues, but they were also set up to extend royal influence within the kingdom. In time many of these burghs flourished and grew into towns, and councils of burgesses were entrusted to collect the revenues and regulate trading practices. Subsequently they began to assume responsibility for the management of local affairs generally. Alongside these 'royal' burghs there developed a considerable number of 'barony' and 'regality' burghs, established by landowning Scottish nobles and bishops and having similar trading privileges. By the end of the sixteenth century, there were some 350 burghs of one kind or another in Scotland.

The Church, in the form of the 'kirk session' (similar to the English parish vestry – see p. 14), had long taken upon itself the responsibility for caring for the helpless poor and for providing some school education. In practice the cost of these services was met largely from church collections. But they were also partly financed from rates levied on the property owners (or 'heritors') of the parish. Assessment for rating was undertaken by committees of local landowners in each county, known as 'commissioners of supply'. Gradually the functions of these magnates widened to include such matters as the establishment of police forces, registration of electors and the management of roads, though in some cases the responsibility was shared with the Justices of the Peace.

So in the eighteenth century there was a rudimentary form of local government in both the urban and rural (or landward) parts of Scotland. But, as in England and Wales, Scottish local affairs in the late eighteenth and early nineteenth centuries suffered from the twin defects of corruption, due to the closed, self-appointing system of selecting councillors, and of impotence in the face of the problems arising from rapid industrialization, population growth and urbanization.[13] One consequence was that the larger, mainly royal, burghs were reformed: under the Burgh Reform Acts 1833 these councils were made subject to open election.[14] Many burghs, however, remained unreformed until 1900 (see below).

A second consequence was the creation of numerous *ad hoc* bodies. In the smaller burghs, alongside the old councils, popularly elected commissions were set up to provide police and basic improvement services, such as sanitation, lighting and water. Following the Police Acts of 1850 and 1862 new (non-burghal) towns were allowed to establish similar multi-purpose police commissioners, and by the end of the nineteenth century there were about one hundred such 'police' burghs.

In 1845, following a Royal Commission report, elected parochial boards were established to take over responsibility for the relief of the non-ablebodied poor. Subsequently, these boards became responsible for certain aspects of public health. In 1857 local boards were set up to take care of the mentally disordered. And under the Education Act 1872, locally elected school boards were formed to administer the new system of popular education.

In 1889 elected county councils were established in Scotland which took over most of the functions of the commissioners of supply and the JPs (both of which remained in being, partly to administer the police through joint committees), together with some of those of the *ad hoc* bodies. Similarly, under the Burgh Police Act 1892 the functions and relationships between the police commissioners and the burgh councils were clarified and rationalized. The reform momentum continued under the Town Councils (Scotland) Act 1900, when *all* burghs were required to have regularly elected councils, each headed by a 'provost' (or mayor) and 'bailies' (aldermen). At a lower level, elected parish councils were created in 1894 and given responsibility for poor relief.

For administrative purposes county councils were obliged to delegate a part of their responsibilities to county road boards (appointed by the county council) and to district committees, comprising representatives from the county council, town councils and parish councils and responsible for roads and public health. Consequently, despite some measure of rationalization, Scotland's local government in the early twentieth century was a complex network consisting of 200 town councils (the burghs), 33 county councils, 869 parish councils, nearly 1,000 school boards and a host of police commissions, county road boards, district committees and joint standing committees.

However, this complex structure was somewhat simplified by the Education (Scotland) Act 1918, which replaced the school boards with thirty-eight education authorities based on the coun-

Figure 4 *Local government in Scotland 1929–74*

ties and large burghs. And finally, the whole local government structure was re-cast by the Local Government (Scotland) Act 1929, under which:

(1) The various types of burghs were reduced to two, 'large' or 'small', depending on whether their population exceeded or fell below 20,000. (Towns with under 700 inhabitants lost their burghal status. In 1947 this figure was raised to 2,000.)

(2) The four largest burghs (Glasgow, Edinburgh, Dundee and Aberdeen) became 'counties of cities' (all-purpose authorities like county boroughs in England) and they, together with the county councils, became responsible for the provision of school education.

(3) Parishes, district committees and standing joint committees (with their commissioners of supply) were abolished and their functions transferred to the county councils.

(4) District councils were set up in the landward (rural) areas.

(5) The rates of the various authorities were combined into a consolidated county and burgh rate.

(6) Functions were divided between the county councils and the more local authorities: (a) the large burghs were responsible for all *except* education and valuation; (b) small burghs were responsible for housing, public health and amenities; (c) district councils

had statutory responsibilities for amenities (parks, allotments, entertainments, footpaths) but might also receive delegated authority from the county council for such services as lighting, sewerage and refuse.

(7) As a consequence of the division of functions, the councils of the counties were to contain representatives from the town councils of the burghs.

Like local government in England and Wales, the Scottish system had its critics. The need for structural revision was officially recognized in 1963, when the government published a White Paper, *The Modernisation of Local Government in Scotland* (Cmd 2067). This was not acted upon because, following a change of government, a Royal Commission was appointed in 1966 (under the chairmanship of Lord Wheatley) to undertake a thorough-going review of local government in Scotland. This Commission thus ran parallel to the Royal Commission, under Lord Redcliffe-Maud, which was considering local government in England (see pp. 44, 56).

3. The Structure of Local Government

Local government today has a dual structure, comprising single-tier metropolitan and London boroughs, and the two tiers of counties and districts (in England and Wales) or regions and districts (in Scotland). This is a relatively new arrangement, being the combined result of the Local Government Act 1972 (which applied to England and Wales), the Local Government (Scotland) Act 1973 and the London Government Act 1963, together with the Local Government Act 1985. The new structure is also the product of a great deal of criticism, inquiry, debate and argument.

As we saw in the previous chapter, the old structure, established mainly at the end of the nineteenth century, had become out of date and inappropriate to twentieth-century circumstances. It was increasingly seen as an incubus and has been blamed for local government's loss of functions and general decline.[1] The words of the Royal Commission on Local Government in Scotland could have referred to the whole country: 'Something is seriously wrong with local government . . . the system is not working properly . . . At the root of the trouble is the present structure of local government.'[2]

The old structure: 1888–1975

Until the reforms of the 1960s and 1970s, local government in Britain comprised three different structures:

(1) The single-tier all-purpose authorities called 'county boroughs' in England and Wales, and 'counties of cities' in Scotland. About 15 million people, or about 25 per cent of the population, lived under this system in 1965.

(2) The two-tier system that existed in the administrative county of London, the London County Council (LCC) having responsibility over the whole area for such functions as education, planning, health and welfare, and the twenty-eight boroughs having responsibility for public health and housing. About 3 million people, or about 5 per cent of the population, lived in the LCC area in 1965. (About 8 million, or 15 per cent, lived in the area of Greater London. See Chapter 5.)

(3) The three-tier system of the counties, districts (including urban district councils, rural district councils and non-county borough councils – see p. 19), and parishes which operated in the remainder of Britain[3] and thus covered about 40 million, or about 70 per cent of the population. Under this system, the county councils had responsibility for the broader functions of education, planning, welfare and police, and the district councils for public health, housing and amenities. Within the RDCs, parishes held meetings of all parishioners or, where the population was large enough (200 or over), formed councils with responsibility for such things as allotments, footpaths and recreation grounds, some of these being exercised concurrently by the RDC.

The faults which have been detected in this structure over the course of the century are numerous. They may be summarized as follows:

(a) Many local authorities had become too small, with the consequence that they were unable to provide some of the services expected of them,[4] or they provided inferior services.

(b) There were great disparities in the sizes of local authorities of the same type. In 1966, out of a total of 140 top-tier local authorities in England and Wales (outside London), twenty-two had populations of over 500,000 and forty-one had populations of less than 100,000. Similarly, at district level, out of a total of 1,298 local authorities ninety-five had populations of over 50,000 while 184 had populations of less than 5,000. As a result, many top-tier local authorities were actually smaller than some second-tier authorities, so that population size was no longer an accurate guide to the status or functions of a local authority. (In Scotland, this was less of a problem because in 1929 the Scottish burghs were revised to take some account of population variations. See p. 33.)

(c) The structure no longer reflected the social geography of the nation: what may have been appropriate for the later nineteenth century no longer suited Britain in the second half of the twentieth. Movements in the population and developments in transport and communications, electricity, housing and medicine made many local government boundaries seem irrelevant and redundant. For example the distinction between town and country (as exemplified in the county council–county borough and the rural district–urban district bifurcations) no longer seemed appropriate, as people were regularly moving between the two environments for employment, leisure or education: they were no longer distinctive communities. A similar situation existed in the conurbations, where there were collections of separate local authorities and no authority with an overall responsibility or perspective.

(d) The division of functions among local authorities inhibited their effective performance. This occurred in two ways. Firstly, some services were complementary to one another, but their close liaison and coordination was obstructed because responsibility for them lay in the hands of different local authorities. For example, housing was the responsibility of the district councils while welfare functions – accommodation for the homeless, care of the elderly, community services for the mentally and physically handicapped – were carried out by the county councils. Secondly, the *same* function could be divided among different local authorities, and this fragmentation could reduce its effective performance, as, for example, in the area of the comprehensive planning and control of land development and transport.

Generally, therefore, it was felt that there were too many local authorities (about 1,500, excluding parishes) and that larger units would be more effective and more economic. Furthermore the existing system was regarded as confusing for the public, especially since it was compounded by complexities such as delegation, joint schemes and *ad hoc* provision.[5]

Some of these anomalies were inherent in the sense that they were allowed into the original structure. For example in 1888 four county boroughs came into existence with populations well below the statutory requirement of 50,000 (see pp. 18-19). But most of them have arisen as a result of social and economic developments. It is perhaps surprising that the system did not respond to such changes and adapt itself to them. We consider this in the following section.

Attempts at reform 1900–1966: England and Wales

The local government structure created at the end of the nineteenth century did not remain completely unaltered until the reorganization of the 1970s. The founding legislation did allow for boundaries to be changed and for councils to be merged or altered in status. The process was quite cumbersome, involving the relevant local authorities, the central government and, for major changes, Parliament. But the system was used, and it led, for example, to the creation of twenty-one new county boroughs and over a hundred county borough boundary changes in the years 1889–1925. These changes cost the county councils an estimated 3 million loss of population and some £14·5 million loss of rateable value (revenue). It thus caused them considerable anxiety and heightened the enmity which existed between town and country authorities.

The consequence was a full-scale inquiry in the form of the

Royal Commission on Local Government 1923–9. Essentially, this had two consequences: (1) it stemmed the growth of county boroughs by recommending that the minimum population be raised from 50,000 to 75,000 (enacted in 1926); (2) it led to a massive reduction in the number of district authorities (UDCs and RDCs) from 1,606 to 1,048 during the years 1931–7.[6] This followed from the Royal Commission's recommendation (enacted 1930) that county councils should be *required* to conduct a review of the district authority areas. Nevertheless, the central government was moved to comment that 'the changes have not in every case been as comprehensive as would have been wished'.

The 1939–45 war prevented the issue of reform being taken any further, but in 1945 the government appointed a five-man Local Government Boundary Commission to 'consider the boundaries of local government areas in England and Wales (except London) and related questions such as the establishment of new county boroughs'; their objective was to secure 'individually and collectively effective and convenient units of local government administration'. They were also advised to take account of such factors as community of interest in the localities, their physical, economic and social characteristics, financial resources and local opinion.

The Commissioners felt that they had been given plenty of instructions but not enough powers. In their report for 1947 they made some very trenchant criticisms of the local government structure, and on the ground that a major disorder demanded drastic treatment they went beyond their terms of reference and recommended a substantial reorganization. Their proposals included: (1) two-tier county systems (like that of London – see p. 19) for the conurbations; (2) most-purpose authorities for the medium-sized towns (like the Scottish large burghs – see p. 33); (3) a uniform system of district councils formed from the UDCs, RDCs and boroughs. But the government, in the form of the Minister of Health, Aneurin Bevan, in effect rejected the report and the Commission was later dissolved.

In taking this action, the government declared that it was not the right time to introduce far-reaching changes in local government structure. It also acknowledged the fact that the various types and tiers of local government were at odds with one another over the direction which reform should take, since inevitably one authority's gain was another's loss. This divergence of opinion was revealed most clearly in 1953, when the local government associations (the organizations representing the different types of local authority – see p. 400) held a number of joint conferences and issued reports. These reports were largely concerned with defending and espousing the virtues of their own particular types of local authority, and generally supporting the existing system with some modifications. However, the Association of Municipal Corporations, representing the county boroughs and non-county boroughs, was alarmed at the others' suggestion that county boroughs with populations of under 75,000 (nineteen of them) should be demoted, while no new county boroughs should be created without a population of at least 100,000. In reply, the AMC advanced the figure of 50,000 as the population minimum for county borough status.

The government sought to cool tempers among the local authorities by announcing that it had faith in the existing system and did not propose to embark on any extensive reform. 'The present system has, over many years, stood up to the severest tests. It responded well ... There is no convincing case for radically reshaping the existing form of local government in England and Wales.'[7]

The Local Government Commissions 1958–65

Nevertheless some changes were needed and to this end the government set up two Local Government Commissions (for England and for Wales) under the Local Government Act 1958. They were to be advisory, not executive; that is, they could propose changes but the government and Parliament would make the decisions. They were also given some general guidelines, based substantially on an amalgam of the local authority associations' earlier proposals. Thus, in what were called 'General Review Areas', the Commissioners could propose changes in the area and status of county councils (which would then review district council areas) and county boroughs (taking 100,000 as a loose population criterion for the latter). In the five 'Special Review Areas', based on the conurbations apart from London, the English Commission could be more assertive and (1) deal with *all* the local authorities, (2) re-distribute functions, and, in particular, (3) propose 'continuous counties' (counties in which there would be no 'islands' of independent county boroughs) where they thought it appropriate.

For a number of reasons, the work and achievements of these Commissions were limited. In the first place, their terms of reference were inadequate: in one sense they were too vague and in another too restricted (for example, by excluding the consideration of functions in the General Review Areas). Secondly, the procedure was cumbrous, providing as it did for innumerable consultations and opportunities to raise objections, so that delay was inevitable and inordinate (some reports took up to four years to produce[8]). Furthermore, a number of the recommendations were rejected outright (those of the Welsh Commission for example – see p. 42). Finally, the English Commission was prematurely dissolved in 1965 when the government announced its intention to set up a Royal Commission, under Lord Redcliffe-Maud, to undertake a more fundamental review of local government. (The Welsh Commission had already completed its work – see below.)

Nevertheless, a number of reports were issued[9] and some changes took place. For the General Review Areas, proposals were made to revise a number of county boundaries and to amalgamate some of the smaller counties. Similarly, boundary changes were proposed for county boroughs, with some demotions and new creations. For the Special Review Areas, apart from some adjustments to the boundaries and status of counties and county boroughs, the 'continuous county' system (an urban two-tier system like that in London) was recommended for Tyneside and South East Lancashire, while a joint board of neighbouring county councils was recommended for Merseyside.

Some of these recommendations were accepted by the government and became operative. For example, the Isle of Ely was merged with Cambridgeshire and a number of county boroughs were created, including Torbay, Luton, Solihull and Teesside. Other proposals were rejected, either outright (such as those for Wales) or after sustained protest and inquiry (such as the proposed abolition of Rutland County). The remainder languished and lapsed when, in February 1966, the setting-up of the Royal Commission was formally announced.

It has been suggested that 'the significance of the period from the Second World War to the passage of the Local Government Act 1958 is that it was a period of great changes in local government, *except* in the structure of local government'.[10] As we have seen, the structure has not changed fundamentally throughout the century (until the 1970s). We now consider why this is so.

Why reform was delayed

Despite the fundamental changes in society and the mounting pressure for structural reform, local government remained substantially unchanged until the 1970s (except for London – see p. 113). This may be partly explained by exigencies, such as the costs involved in reorganization, the pressures on governments' legislative timetables and the problems caused by war and reconstruction. Nor was there any real fervour from the general public.

Secondly, there was no agreed alternative: a number of schemes were proposed of more or less equal appeal (or repugnance). Differences of opinion were bound to arise as some groups sought to promote *efficiency* (which frequently meant larger or single-tier units), while others sought to emphasize and enhance the cause of *democracy* (which often amounted to the retention of small local authorities, usually in a two-tier structure) and yet others pursued the goal of *simplicity* (which implied a uniform pattern of authorities). In other words, the whole basis of reform was in dispute and implied deadlock or compromise (as exemplified in the numerous boundary changes outlined above).

Finally, there were political reasons for delay. Any reform was bound to threaten some interests, and every local authority or group of authorities sought to justify its own continued existence. The government at Westminster could not afford to ignore or alienate large blocks of local government opinion. (A more cynical view was that the central government preferred to keep local authorities small, numerous and divided in order to sustain a dominant position.) Moreover, party politics were involved, since changing local government authorities and boundaries could affect the composition of constituencies and so large numbers of local government votes and party majorities.[11] In fact, it appears that when reform did appear it was to a large extent the result of pure chance.[12] Before examining this reform, it is appropriate to consider developments in Wales's local government structure.

Wales

The Local Government Commission for Wales (see p. 40) produced a draft report in 1961. It recommended the reduction of counties from thirteen to five. Following considerable protest, it deliberated further and revised its recommendations to seven new counties. Again there was strong reaction from the local authorities, and indeed the Commission itself was not entirely happy with its own conclusions, as it felt that its terms of reference were somewhat inadequate: '. . . we cannot help wondering whether, had we been allowed to consider at least the redistribution of functions, we might not have done a better job.'[13]

In response, the government thanked the Commission for its report, but rejected its proposals. It then acknowledged the limitations of the terms of reference by setting up a departmental inquiry (under the Welsh Office) in 1965 to consider the functions and finance, as well as the boundaries, of local authorities in Wales. Despite the inauguration of a Royal Commission in England in 1966, it was decided to persist with the Welsh inquiry, and in 1967 a White Paper was published.[14] This proposed that the county boroughs should be reduced from four to three, the counties from thirteen to five, and the districts from 164 to thirty-six. The scheme also proposed the introduction of an appointed Welsh Council with advisory functions.[15]

Inevitably, with various ideas for reform going before the English Royal Commission, it was felt that the proposals for Wales were premature. Subsequently, the proposals were changed, partly as a result of the Royal Commission's report (see below) and partly as a result of a change of government in 1970.

The Redcliffe-Maud Report

Local government is the only representative political institution in the country outside Parliament; and being, by its nature, in closer touch . . . with local conditions, local needs, local opinions, it is an essential part of the fabric of democratic government. Central government tends, by its nature, to be bureaucratic. It is only by the combination of local representative institutions with the central institutions of Parliament, that a genuine national democracy can be sustained.[16]

Thus did the Royal Commission on Local Government in England 1966–9 (led by Lord Redcliffe-Maud) defend the concept of local government. It went on to say that a local government system should possess four qualities: the ability to perform efficiently a wide range of important tasks concerned with the well-being of people in different localities; the ability to attract and hold the interest of its citizens; the ability to develop enough inherent strength to deal with national authorities in a valid partnership; and the ability to adapt itself to the process of change in the way people work and live. These qualities were missing from English local government, which was found to be suffering from four structural defects, namely:

(1) The local government areas did not fit the pattern of life and work of modern England, and the gap was likely to widen with social, economic and technological changes.

(2) The fragmentation of England into seventy-nine county boroughs and forty-five counties, exercising independent jurisdictions and dividing town from country, had made the proper planning of development and transportation impossible. The result had often been an atmosphere of hostility between county boroughs and counties and this had made it harder to decide difficult questions on their merits.

(3) The division of responsibility within each county between county council and a number of county districts, together with the position of county boroughs as islands in the counties, meant that services which should have been in the hands of one authority were fragmented among several, making it more difficult to meet needs comprehensively.

(4) Many local authorities were too small in size and revenue and consequently lacked qualified manpower and technical equipment to be able to do their work well.

Furthermore, and partly as a consequence of these failings, there were deficiencies in local government's relationships with the general public, who saw local government as too complex and irrelevant to their daily lives, and with the national government, who doubted the ability of local governors to run local affairs and consequently restricted their activities.

As a result of this analysis, the Royal Commission members were unanimous in their view that the structure needed changing, and there was near unanimity on the principles which should underlie the reformed structure. These stated that local authority areas must be so defined that they enable citizens and their elected representatives to have a sense of common purpose. Consequently,

(1) The areas must be based upon the interdependence of town and country.

(2) In each area, all environmental services (planning, transportation and major development) must be in the hands of one authority. These areas must be large enough to enable these authorities to meet pressing land needs, and their inhabitants must share a common interest in their environment.

(3) All personal services (education, personal social services, health and housing) must also be in the hands of one authority.

(4) If possible both the environmental and the personal groups of services should be in the hands of the same authority: through the allocation of priorities and coordinated use of resources, this single authority can relate its programmes for all services to objectives for its area considered as a whole.

(5) Authorities must be made large enough to be able to command the resources needed for the efficient provision of services.

(6) The size of authorities must vary if areas are to match the pattern of population, but a minimum of around 250,000 is essential.

(7) On the other hand, authorities must not be so large that serious managerial problems arise or elected representatives cannot keep in touch with constituents. Consequently a maximum of around 1 million is appropriate as a general rule.

(8) Where the area required for environmental services contains a very large population, a single authority for all services would not be appropriate; here, responsibilities must be divided between environmental and personal services and allocated to two operational tiers of authority.

(9) The new local government pattern should as far as practicable stem from the existing one.

In trying to determine the appropriate units for the new local government structure, the Royal Commission was thus laying down four criteria: efficiency, democracy, the pattern of living and the existing structure of local government. These were not all necessarily compatible. For example, research for the Royal Commission had shown that there existed some 130–140 areas which could be described as coherent socio-geographic units (that is, having patterns of living which combined town and country). But these areas were of varying sizes and were generally too small for the effective performance of the main services. The Royal Commission therefore had to strike a balance between the claims of efficiency, democracy, community and continuity.

In striking this balance, the Royal Commission concluded that most of England should be divided into fifty-eight areas, each having a population in the range of 250,000 to 1 million with a *single-tier* or 'unitary' authority to carry out all the local government responsibilities (that is, it would resemble the county borough system). In three other areas of England, all densely populated conurbations, the environmental group of services would have to deal with such large populations that a single authority would be too unwieldy, too difficult to control democratically and, for the purposes of the personal services, too remote. In these 'metropolitan' areas therefore, a *two-tier* structure was recommended (somewhat like the London system of local government – see p. 115). The top-tier metropolitan authority would be responsible for the mainly environmental services, while the smaller metropolitan district authorities were to provide the more personal services.

In addition, the Royal Commission recommended two partial or non-operational tiers of local government. At very local level, 'local councils' were to be elected with the duty of representing local opinion and perhaps with some powers to provide some local services. At the regional level, eight 'provincial councils' were to be set up to represent the main local authorities in those regions and be responsible for drawing up the provincial strategy and planning framework within which the main authorities would operate.

Reactions to these radical proposals were mixed. The Association of Municipal Corporations (representing the boroughs and county boroughs) accepted the report to some extent. The Labour Party endorsed most of the proposals, although the Labour government's projected legislation[17] included plans to increase the number of metropolitan areas to five and to defer its decision on provincial councils until the Royal Commission on the Constitution had reported.[18]

Hostile comment came from those, notably the Rural District Councils Association and the County Councils Association, who argued that the large unitary authorities would be remote, bureaucratic and unresponsive to local needs, and that the proposed local councils were inadequate, a mere sop to satisfy the demands for local democracy. In effect, these critics were saying that unitary authorities were government but not local, that local councils were local but not government, while the provincial councils were neither local nor government. Instead they favoured a two-tier system of local government throughout England.

They were not alone in this. Many other critics thought that the Royal Commission had sacrificed democracy in the pursuit of consistency and of efficiency (even though, as others pointed out and the Royal Commission acknowledged, there was no conclusive evidence that larger units of administration were more efficient). Indeed the Royal Commission did not produce a unanimous report, for one member wrote a powerful memorandum of dissent[19] because he believed that the main report had given too much weight to the principle of concentrating responsibilities into single-tier authorities, but that in making these areas the appropriate size for effectiveness (between 250,000 and 1 million) it had undervalued the important principle of population settlement. He felt that his colleagues on the Commission had compromised in the wrong direction and had gained the worst of both worlds, as many of the proposed areas would be too small for environmental services and too remote for personal services. His own proposals for a two-tier structure (plus local and provincial councils) sought to give greater recognition to the 'facts of social geography' (rather like the Royal Commission on Scotland's local government – see p. 64) by creating small regional authorities, to exercise mainly strategic functions, and district authorities, for the more personal services.

In June 1970 the Conservative Party won the general election and local government reform was back in the melting pot. The Conservatives were anxious to avoid unitary authorities for a number of reasons. In the first place there was no great enthusiasm from any quarter – for many of the public the whole exercise was somewhat remote, and most people were at least used to the two-tier system (only 25 per cent lived in county boroughs). For members and officers, the unitary system threatened possible redundancy. For a number of Conservative MPs, the parliamentary constituency changes which may have resulted from the proposed local government reforms appeared unwelcome (especially where a rural constituency might be merged into an adjacent city). Fear of amalgamation and perhaps loss of political control also caused a number of county councillors to press the new government to retain the two-tier structure.[20]

Then in 1971 the government published its own proposals,[21] which accepted the two-tier system for the metropolitan areas, but rejected completely the unitary authorities which had been proposed for the rest of England. Instead, the whole of England (and Wales[22]) was to have a two-tier system. The first tier was to be based largely on existing counties; the main change was to occur at district level, in the second tier.

The Local Government Act 1972

Under this Act (operative from April 1974) the eighty-two county boroughs were abolished outright. The fifty-eight *county councils* in England and Wales were reduced to forty-seven (thirty-nine in England and eight in Wales), with populations ranging from 100,000 (Powys) to almost 1·5 million (Hants), and responsible for most of the planning, protective and personal services. Within

Figure 5 *Local government in England and Wales* (*outside London*)
1974–86 (*Metropolitan county councils ceased to exist in April 1986*)

these counties, 1,249 borough, urban and rural district councils
were replaced by 333 *district councils* or *boroughs*[23] (of which
thirty-seven are in Wales). Their populations ranged from 422,000
(Bristol) to 18,670 (Radnor), and these councils are responsible
for such services as housing, environmental health and amenities.
However, a number of responsibilities, such as planning and
amenities (parks and museums etc.), are shared between the two
sets of authorities.

The Act also created six *metropolitan counties* (Greater Manchester, Merseyside, West Midlands, Tyne and Wear, South Yorkshire and West Yorkshire), ranging in population from just over 1
million (Tyne and Wear) to 2·7 million (West Midlands) and
having responsibility for the broad environmental services (planning, transport, highways). Within these metropolitan counties
were created thirty-six *metropolitan districts* (or *metropolitan boroughs*) ranging from 173,000 (South Tyneside) to over 1 million
(Birmingham) and having responsibility for such services as
housing, education, welfare and environmental health. A number
of other services, such as planning and the provision of amenities,
were a shared responsibility.

In England, the parish was retained as a third tier of local
government. In those districts where they existed before 1974,

parish councils have been re-established. Elsewhere they have been created either automatically (if the population is large enough) or at the discretion of the district council (see p. 447). There are currently some 7,200 *parish councils* in England. In the other parts of the non-metropolitan counties local government electors may hold parish meetings to discuss parish affairs and perhaps to take some decisions (see p. 448ff). In Wales the situation is similar except that parishes have been replaced by 'communities', which are entitled to have community meetings and/or community councils with a role similar to that of parishes in England, acting as a forum and a voice for the locality. In particular they can claim to be consulted on planning applications, and they may opt to exercise control over the provision of allotments, burial grounds, footpaths, bus shelters, recreation grounds and street lighting. Altogether, throughout England and Wales (though not in every district – see pp. 447, 450) there are about 11,000 parishes and communities, of which about 8,000 have elected councils. Collectively, they are known as 'local councils' to distinguish them from the larger 'principal' authorities (see p. 447).

The Local Government Boundary Commissions

The Local Government Boundary Commissions (not to be confused with the Local Government Boundary Commission 1945–9) are permanent bodies set up under the Local Government Acts of 1972 (England and Wales) and 1973 (Scotland). There are three such Commissions, one each for England, Wales and Scotland, and each comprises about half a dozen people (usually from an academic or public service background – Sir Edmund Compton, an ex-civil servant and the first 'ombudsman' in Britain, was the chairman of the English Commission until 1978).

It is the Commissions' function to keep under review the local government areas (including their names) and their electoral arrangements (including the number of councillors and the

Counties and regions

Metropolitan areas
(districts/boroughs)

Figure 6 *The local government areas of Britain*

Key to Figure 6	Population	(1991)	Population
1. Avon	959,000	29. Highland	204,300
2. Bedfordshire	547,000	30. Humberside	866,000
3. Berkshire	774,000	31. Isle of Wight	132,000
4. Borders	103,500	32. Kent	1,547,000
5. Buckinghamshire	665,000	33. Lancashire	1,408,000
6. Cambridgeshire	690,000	34. Leicestershire	914,000
7. Central	272,100	35. Lincolnshire	605,000
8. Cheshire	975,000	36. Lothian	749,600
9. Cleveland	547,000	37. Mid Glamorgan	539,600
10. Clwyd	411,800	38. Norfolk	767,000
11. Cornwall	481,000	39. Northamptonshire	599,000
12. Cumbria	499,000	40. North Yorkshire	742,000
13. Derbyshire	944,000	41. Northumberland	308,000
14. Devon	1,057,000	42. Nottinghamshire	1,026,000
15. Dorset	680,000	43. Oxfordshire	598,000
16. Dumfries and Galloway	148,400	44. Powys	117,400
17. Durham	596,000	45. Shropshire (Salop)	417,000
18. Dyfed	354,000	46. Somerset	478,000
19. East Sussex	728,000	47. South Glamorgan	406,800
20. Essex	1,553,000	48. Staffordshire	1,053,000
21. Fife	354,000	49. Strathclyde	2,306,000
22. Gloucestershire	541,000	50. Suffolk	657,000
23. Grampian	506,100	51. Surrey	1,002,000
24. Gwent	447,500	52. Tayside	394,000
25. Gwynedd	241,100	53. Warwickshire	487,000
26. Hampshire	1,573,000	54. West Glamorgan	363,200
27. Hereford and Worcester	693,000	55. West Sussex	721,000
28. Hertfordshire	994,000	56. Wiltshire	580,000

Not shown are the 3 Scottish Island Councils of Orkney (19,570), Shetland (22,270) and Western Isles (31,660).

The shaded areas (of the recently abolished Metropolitan County Councils) contain the following Metropolitan Districts/Boroughs:

A   Greater London – comprises 32 London Boroughs: see p. 116.

B   West Midlands – comprises Birmingham City (1,006,000), Coventry City (305,000), Dudley MB (309,000), Sandwell MB (294,000), Solihull MB (201,000), Walsall MB (263,000), Wolverhampton MB (248,000).

C   South Yorkshire – comprises Barnsley MB (224,000), Doncaster MB (293,000), Rotherham MB (255,000), Sheffield City (529,000).

D   West Yorkshire – comprises Bradford City (475,000), Calderdale MB (194,000), Kirklees MB (381,000), Leeds City (717,000), Wakefield City (317,000).

E   Greater Manchester – comprises Bolton MB (263,000), Bury MB (179,000), Manchester City (439,000), Oldham MB (220,000), Rochdale MB (205,000), Salford City (231,000), Stockport MB (288,000), Tameside MB (221,000), Trafford MB (216,000), Wigan MB (312,000).

F   Merseyside – comprises (a) Knowsley MB (157,000), (b) Liverpool City (481,000), (c) St. Helens MB (181,000), (d) Sefton MB (295,000), (e) Wirral MB (336,000).

G   Tyne and Wear – comprises Gateshead MB (204,000), Newcastle-on-Tyne City (278,000), North Tyneside MB (195,000), South Tyneside MB (157,000), Sunderland MB (297,000).

The Merseyside area (F) is highlighted to illustrate the district/borough pattern in the metropolitan areas.

patterns of wards and county divisions – see p. 123). They would normally be expected to undertake reviews of principal areas at intervals of ten to fifteen years, unless otherwise directed by the Minister.

Following their reviews, they are required to make proposals to the appropriate Secretary of State for changes which they consider desirable 'in the interests of effective and convenient local government'. Such proposals may include the alteration of boundaries, the abolition or creation of local government areas, the conversion of a metropolitan area into a non-metropolitan and vice versa. As regards areas, most of their work so far has been to consider the districts' reports on parishes and communities in England and Wales, and certain anomalous boundaries in other local authorities generally. Alterations are effected, with or without alteration, by the Secretary of State by means of an order (or statutory instrument) which is passed through Parliament, some of the objections, if any, having been already heard at a local inquiry if necessary. Meanwhile, the Commissions have also been engaged in reviewing electoral arrangements (such as warding) in most local government areas (see p. 123).

Reorganized but not reformed?

The Local Government Act 1972 substantially altered the face of local government in England and Wales. Apart from the creation of the six metropolitan areas (with their county and district councils) and the reduction in the number of county districts by 75 per cent, the county borough 'islands' were abolished; some of the smaller counties disappeared through amalgamation (especially in Wales); some new counties were created; and there have been innumerable boundary changes (only five counties retained their territories completely intact). It was widely anticipated that these changes would promote efficiency and improve services while at the same time retaining an ample measure of democratic control and involvement:

There is considerable advantage in having units of population sufficiently large to provide a base for ... effective organization and a high quality of service ... The Government obviously must seek efficiency, but where the arguments are evenly balanced their judgement will be given in favour of responsibility being exercised at the more local level.[24]

However, the critics of the reorganized system were legion. The substitution of the two-tier system for the proposed unitary authorities did not assuage the feelings of those who felt the new system to be remote and insensitive. In some ways the prescribed antidote has become poisonous, as the parish and town councils have acted as a focus and rallying point for old loyalties so that the hoped-for melding of new communities has been slow to develop.

A different kind of criticism has come from those on the left of British politics. They see the reorganization as a stratagem for the greater centralization of power. This has occurred in two directions: firstly from local to central government, and secondly from significant levels of working-class participation and influence to the more exclusive, elitist influence of the business and professional sectors of society.[25] In effect, the capitalist state is seen as mopping up pockets of resistance which local councils represent (see p. 587, note 53).

Most of the criticisms, however, tend to point in the other direction – that, broadly speaking, the scale of reorganization was inadequate and far too many small authorities remain and exercise vital responsibilities (such as education and social services). Even the metropolitan counties were felt to be too small in that their boundaries have been drawn rather tightly around the urban areas, thus incorporating too little of the rural hinterland.[26] This arrangement to some extent reinstated the town–country dichotomy (see Chapter 10) and hindered successful planning and housing programmes, which often require inter-authority co-operation. Relations between local authorities have been soured in other ways, in particular by the division of responsibilities under the 1972 Act. The most contentious area here is that of

'concurrent' powers, where both tiers were given responsibilities
for the same service (notably planning, but generally too in the provision of amenities). In many parts of the country this has not
worked smoothly and there have been some notable cases of outright hostility (see p. 396). Recent legislation should improve
matters here (see p. 458). A further criticism concerns the effectiveness of the county or regional tiers. They are supposed to
exercise a broadly strategic role, but this is made difficult by the
fact that they do not control the administration of so many
services – those which lie in the hands of the districts and of *ad hoc*
bodies. This was particularly the case in the metropolitan areas.

Apart from any other consideration, this system of sharing
responsibilities (compounded by 'agency' arrangements – see p. 82)
adds to the public confusion about local government. The reorganization was intended to 'de-mystify' the system for the person in the
street by making the structure simpler and clearer, but the creation
of a double two-tier system, the complicated division of services
(not just as between the metropolitan and the non-metropolitan
areas, but between England and Wales) and the proliferation of
names (including boroughs, cities and town councils) makes the
system apparently as complex and perhaps irrelevant as ever. This
criticism would appear to be reflected in the fact that election
turnout has not improved since the reorganization (see p. 142).

Finally, there is the government's removal from local government of personal health services and responsibilities for water
provision.[27] This has not only added to public confusion, but
also suggests a continued lack of confidence in local government
by the central government – in contrast to the aspirations of the
Royal Commission, which declared:

The whole Commission is unanimous in its conviction that if the
present local government system is drastically reformed, its scope extended to include functions now in the hands of nominated bodies and
the grip of central government relaxed, England can become a more
efficient, democratic and humane society.[28]

The reorganized system of local government is essentially an evolution from the system established in the late nineteenth century, and in this respect it carries with it the virtues of that system. But it also has many of its defects. The reorganized system does work, but there are many who believe that it does not meet the major problems that local government has to face as effectively as a more radically reformed system would have done.

Abolition of the metropolitan counties

Based on the White Paper *Streamlining the Cities* (1983), and following lengthy and controversial debate, the Local Government Act 1985 abolished the metropolitan counties and the GLC in April 1986. In eliminating these upper tier authorities, the Government sought to 'remove a source of conflict . . . save money . . . [and] provide a system which is simpler for the public to understand' (Para. 1. 19).

Underlying the proposals is the Government's view that these authorities were created (in 1972 and 1963 respectively) at a time when resources seemed plentiful and that there was a need for strategic planning to cater for continuing growth. But since the 1970s growth has faltered and 'incrementalism' (spending) has been replaced by 'decrementalism' (cuts). Thus the Government aimed (1) to reduce public sector spending, (2) to improve efficiency (or value for money) and (3) to attack the 'national overhead' through cuts in the civil service, the removal of one tier of the NHS (see p. 98) and higher revenue targets for nationalized industries. Abolition of the upper tier of metropolitan local government is seen as local government's contribution to this general objective and to the Government's prime objective to 'tackle inflation and to improve efficiency in all sectors of national life'.

The Government saw metropolitan counties as secondary and superficial; they had 'too few functions' which resulted in their finding it 'difficult to establish a role for themselves' – indeed they had sought to encroach on that of the district councils, thus producing 'conflict and uncertainty'. Worse had been their inclination to 'promote policies which conflict with national policies which are the responsibility of central government'. Thus the capital offence of the metropolitan counties has been to 'consistently exceed [the] targets' of expenditure set by the Government. In abolishing these large top tier authorities, the Government also claimed to be bringing local government closer to the people by distributing their functions to smaller, more local authorities, i.e. the borough councils. In the event, the responsibilities of the metropolitan county councils (and the GLC) have been transferred not only to the boroughs but also to a number of ad hoc joint boards, including joint police authorities, joint passenger transport authorities and joint fire and civil defence authorities (for most of which one of the constituent councils has assumed the role of the 'lead' council), and to 'residuary bodies' (authorities appointed to handle and wind up those responsibilities which could not otherwise be allocated: see p. 121). In the case of London, the arrangements are particularly complex and confusing (see p. 121). Thus, it may be doubted whether the reorganization really has made local government less remote in these areas, with only about 20 per cent of the metropolitan counties' expenditure having been transferred wholly to the boroughs as such.

Furthermore, a recent study of the relationships between the tiers in the metropolitan areas shows that reports of inter-tier/authority conflict have been exaggerated.[29] It shows that conflict has occurred, but that it was limited to certain functions and areas only. There is already evidence to suggest that the new arrangements will experience similar problems.[30] Moreover, private management consultants have suggested that the Government's assertions about the metropolitan authorities' excessive spending were overstated and misleading, and that abolition will produce no significant savings.[31] Another study[32] concludes, 'Notwithstanding the criticisms directed against them, the extent to which their activities are constrained by non-local factors and their apparent lack of legitimacy, the Metropolitan Counties cannot be regarded as redundant . . . due consideration must be given to the difficult circumstances in which they have had to operate, to the fact that historically they have been operating for an extremely short period of time, and to the fact that people's selective memories of the system they replaced are strong ... Our conclusion then must be that the case for Metropolitan Counties remains a powerful one.' As *The Times* (1 August 1985) has commented, 'A convincing case for abolition has yet to be made with intellectual vigour and sufficient fact ... ministers will seem to believe that in this matter assertion can substitute for argument.'

Others have interpreted the reorganization as pure political opportunism, with a Conservative Government removing seven strongholds of Labour power and opposition. Indeed Edward Heath, a former Conservative Prime Minister, has declared the reform to be 'the greatest act of gerrymandering* in the last 100 years of British history.' (See also pp. 105, 119.)

Further proposals and prospects

Clearly the issue of local government structure is not settled. The Labour Party, for obvious reasons, was totally opposed to the abolition of the metropolitan county councils and the GLC, and at the 1987 General Election both the Labour and Alliance opposition parties' manifestos contained commitments to further reorganization (see p. 458), including the restoration of the GLC. Earlier, Labour had produced two sets of proposals: one, known as 'organic change',[33] involved a limited redistribution of respon-siblities in favour of the larger, urban, non-metropolitan county districts (such as Bristol, Hull or Nottingham). The other had a longer-term perspective and envisaged a regional structure throughout England. It was based on the criticism that reorganiza-

---

*i.e. the manipulation of boundaries for party political advantage. An alterna-tive is to manipulate the social – and voting – composition of wards, e.g. through housing policies. See the *Independent*, 20 July 1989, and p. 468 below.

tion was a 'botched job' and that for planning purposes in particular the 'two-tier county–district structure . . . [was] irrelevant'.[34] Consequently, in 1978 and more recently the Labour Party came out with the proposal for twelve regional councils, with 200 most-purpose authorities forming the second tier (like Scotland's Island Councils). (See p. 458–9.) The Liberal Democrats (formerly the Liberal/SDP Alliance) also propose the conversion of the county–district system into a single tier of unitary authorities, though overlaid by a new system of regional councils.

The Conservatives have a distaste for regional councils. But they now appear to be looking more favourably on the idea of unitary authorities across the country. In 1991, triggered by the violent reactions to the poll tax/community charge (see p. 333), there was a flurry of government proposals for local government reform covering finance, management and structure. Consultative papers were issued on the structure of local government in Scotland (see pp. 70–71), England and Wales. The paper on Welsh local government was the most prescriptive. It proposed the replacement of the existing eight county and thirty-seven district councils with twenty unitary authorities deriving from existing boundaries (though the paper provided alternative plans for thirteen to twenty-four). Subsequently in March 1992 and 1993 White Papers outlined a revised scheme of twenty-three unitary local authorities, involving the restoration of many traditional county names and a number of main cities (Cardiff, Swansea) regaining control of their own affairs as pre-1974 (see p. 36). They are to come into existence in 1996 following the legislation of 1994. The proposals have received some support. But there is hostility from the Labour Party and trade unions, who have pledged a policy of non-cooperation and amendment.

For England, the proposal was to set up a Local Government Commission in 1992 (thus replacing the Boundary Commission). Under the chairmanship of John Banham, a former head of the CBI and of the Audit Commission (see p. 352), it was to review the structure, boundaries and electoral arrangements of all the main councils (except those in London and the metropolitan

Figure 7 *Proposed unitary authorities for Wales*
Source: Welsh Office

areas). Under the Local Government Act 1992, the Commission (an independent body of thirteen people drawn from a cross-section of councillors, administrators, academics and private business) was duly appointed by the Secretary of State for the Environment, and given guidance on procedure – publicity, consultation, timings and drafting, together with policy guidance – to heed local loyalties and preferences, costs and benefits, history and traditions, accessibility, responsiveness and democracy. Above all, the changes, if any, should 'better reflect the identities and interests of local communities and secure effective and convenient local government'. In general, therefore, the criteria are those of efficiency, simplicity, community and democracy.

Thus taking account of local opinion and loyalties and of submissions from local authorities and other interested parties, the Commission was to outline proposals (including, perhaps, the status quo) for each area and then put these out for wider consultation before a final report and recommendations are submitted to the Minister.

The paper stated a clear preference for a structure based on unitary (i.e. single-tier) authorities as this, by replacing the two-tier system, would reduce bureaucracy and operating costs, improve coordination of services and improve people's understanding and thus increase accountability. It suggested that in some areas the 1974 reorganization had not settled down or been accepted. Thus it is proposed that some existing or merged districts will become all-purpose authorities; in others it will be the county council assuming sole responsibility. However, there is to be no wholesale abolition of districts or counties, so that in some areas the two-tier system will continue if this is thought best. Within this, the roles of parish and town councils are to be enhanced. Originally, the reformed structure was to be in place in 1994, but now the review process is to be completed by 1994 and the new authorities in place by 1996.

So far, the Commission has produced a number of reports, in the form of viable alternative structures together with their main recommendations. The emerging pattern is modelled on the unitary format, though there are considerable variations in size of unit and the two-tier structure has found favour and been recommended for Gloucester and Lincolnshire, for example. Some of the authorities created in 1974, those which have apparently not found acceptance or legitimacy (Avon, Humberside), have been recommended for abolition.

Unlike the Royal Commission of 1966–9, there is less attempt to identify a 'right size' for local authorities. This is largely a product of compulsory competitive tendering and the move to enabling rather than providing ('steering not rowing'). Thus in recent years we have seen a greater readiness among local authorities to work together in partnership with the private and voluntary sectors to deliver services. It is also a shifting scene as services are not only contracted out (and in; see pp. 272, 306) but as they opt out (in the form of grant-maintained schools or housing associations).

In the end much will depend on the view taken by the Minister (and Parliament), who will promulgate the changes in the form of Parliamentary Orders. Ministers have already declared that they will not necessarily accept the Commission's proposals.

The Local Government Commission's review has been criticized on a number of counts – that the review is taking place in a vacuum,[35] that the procedure has lacked rigour,[36] that its proposals have been inconsistent[37] or, conversely, that it is working to a preconceived national blueprint. It has been accused of lacking sufficient awareness or sensitivity to public views, and its estimates of savings have been condemned as inaccurate. And there are those who are concerned that the recommendations are pointing to a reduction in the number of councillors – by about half – thus reducing the degree of democratic representation provided by local government (especially in comparison with other European countries). Others have accused it of political intrigue – pandering to vested interests[38] or seeking to pick off councils which are unpopular with the Government and protecting party seats.[39] As a result, at one point the chairman threatened to resign, and the Government lost some of its enthusiasm for the whole exercise and the likely costs of upheaval. And the Chairman of the Commission, at the outset, declared that 'if it aint broke, don't mend it'.

There has been considerable in-fighting among the councils under review. And the parties have been divided (especially locally) over the issue, though in general Labour and the Liberals have criticized the Government's failure to consider the regional dimension and have accused it of gerrymandering in its reform of Scotland and Wales (see p. 71).

Thus has local government become a party political football, albeit one of third-division impact as a result of its limited public appeal: a public attitudes survey in 1970 showed that 77 per cent favoured no change in local government or didn't know or care about it,[40] though the anti-abolition campaigns of the metropolitan counties and the GLC, as well as the introduction of the community charge (poll tax), may have raised public consciousness.

Scotland: The Wheatley Report

The Royal Commission on Local Government in Scotland 1966–9 (under Lord Wheatley) praised the work of the local authorities in Scotland, but found the structure of local government to be gravely defective:

Something is seriously wrong with local government in Scotland . . . the local government system is not working properly – it is not doing the job that it ought to be doing. At the root of the trouble is the present structure of local government. It has remained basically the same for forty years, when everything around it has changed. (paras. 1 and 2)

More specifically it pointed to the following defects:

. . . local authorities on the whole are too small. The boundaries pay little heed to present social and economic realities. Services are often being provided by the wrong sorts of authorities and over the wrong areas. The financial resources of authorities do not match their responsibilities. (para. 3)

And as a result:

. . . the services that local government provides do not operate as well as they should. Staff are not always deployed to the best advantage. Plans . . . are often not fully realized. Friction tends to build up between neighbouring authorities because of an artificial conflict of interest, created by the structure of local government and nothing else. The ratepayer's – and the taxpayer's – money is frequently wasted on maintaining two or more separate organizations where one would do perfectly well. Some important services have outgrown the structure, and have had to be taken away from local authorities altogether. (para. 4)

Thus the faults are similar to those diagnosed for England's local government (see p. 45). Not unexpectedly, the overall consequences are also similar:

Looked at as part of the machinery for running the country, local government is less significant than it ought to be. It lacks the ability to speak with a strong and united voice. Local authorities have come to accept, and even rely on, a large measure of direction and control from the central Government. The electorate is aware of this . . . The question is being asked . . . whether . . . local government is worthwhile maintaining at all. (para. 5)

The Royal Commission answered this last question with a firm 'yes' – 'local government of some kind is absolutely indispensable' – but only if it is fundamentally reformed.

The Royal Commission believed that the structural defects 'were so deep seated that surface patching would not do'. Consequently, the reforms were to be thorough-going and were to rest on a foundation of solid principle which would allow the new structure to (a) function as a whole and (b) be capable of coping with future social changes and demands on local government.

In order to provide the groundwork for such a system, the Royal Commission then set down four basic objectives of reform:

(i) Power: Local government should be enabled to play a more important, responsible and positive part in the running of the country – to bring the reality of government nearer to the people [and in particular away from central government].

(ii) Effectiveness: Local government should be equipped to provide services in the most satisfactory manner, particularly from the point of view of the people receiving the services. [This implies a reallocation of functions for discharge at appropriate levels.]

(iii) Local democracy: Local government should constitute a system in which power is exercised through the elected representatives of the people, and in which those representatives are locally accountable for its exercise. That is, local councils should be genuinely in charge of the local situation and elected local councillors really answerable for its actions.

(iv) Local involvement: Local government should bring the people into the process of reaching decisions as much as possible, and enable those decisions to be made intelligible to the people. (paras. 126–160)

These were to be the ideals of the new structure as a whole. But in the quest for appropriate *units* of local government, the Royal Commission emphasized three criteria:

(1) Functional viability. The Royal Commission examined the main functions (actual or potential) of local government and, after considering the scale on which they should be discharged and the extent to which they could be combined in the same hands, drew conclusions about the size of area, population and resources requisite for each. On this basis it said there was a *prima facie* case for three levels of local government (regional, intermediate and local).

(2) Correspondence with communities. It was felt important to match authorities with communities as closely as possible. After examining the social geography of Scotland, the Royal Commission concluded that a pattern existed, made up of four types of community – the region, the shire, the locality and the parish.

(3) Democratic viability. Local authorities must have a sufficient range of functions to create local interest and provide opportunities for councillors to exercise real choice while at the same time keeping the councillors' duties within the compass of ordinary members of the public serving in a part-time capacity.

Clearly these criteria were not entirely compatible. Some sort of compromise was inevitable. In order to avoid fragmentation and to ensure that all local authorities had a sufficient range of functions, the Royal Commission rejected the idea of a four-fold structure to match the four-level community. Instead it sought to concentrate responsibility on just two sets of local authorities. This would have the added virtue of consistency – of as uniform a structure of authorities as could be achieved without undue violence to the pattern of communities.

The final result of the analysis[41] was the recommendation of a two-tier structure consisting of:

(1) Seven regional authorities, based on an amalgamation of existing counties and ranging in population from 2·5 million in the West Region to 145,000 in the South West Region;

(2) Thirty-seven district authorities, based on counties and counties of cities which had been enlarged and/or partitioned;

(3) At a very local level community councils could be set up throughout the new districts where there was sufficient local/popular support. They would have no statutory powers and would not be local authorities as such. Essentially their role would be a representative one: to give expression to the views of the community. They would also be entitled to do anything to improve the amenity of the area, and indeed might act as agents for the local authorities in the day-to-day running of certain services.

(4) Responsibilities would be divided between the two sets of authorities. The regional authorities would be responsible for transportation, water, sewerage, drainage, education, social work, housing and police; the districts for environmental health, libraries, building control and licensing. Functions such as planning, parks and recreation would be shared between them.

The Conservative Government at Westminster made no radical changes to these recommendations – as it had to the Royal Commission report on English local government – partly because the proposed scheme fitted in with that party's preference for a two-tier system of local government, and partly because they had less at risk politically in Scotland than in England.

Nevertheless the government did respond to the criticism that the district authorities would be too few, too remote and too restricted in function. Consequently the number of districts was increased and they were given more responsibilities (notably housing). In addition, the island authorities were given a separate, virtually all-purpose (region *and* district) status, and another two regions were added to the seven proposed. (Some of these changes were forced on the government during the Bill's passage through Parliament.)

The Local Government (Scotland) Act 1973

The resulting Act created, with effect from May 1975:

(1) Nine regions, each with a Regional Council, and ranging in population from under 100,000 in the Borders to nearly 2·5 million in the Strathclyde region, and in area from 500 square miles in Fife to 10,000 square miles in the Highlands.

(2) Three island councils, two with populations of about 20,000, one with 30,000.

(3) Fifty-three districts, each with a district council and ranging in population from 856,000 in Glasgow to just over 9,000 in Badenoch and Strathspey in the Highland region.

Functions were divided between the two sets of authorities largely as recommended by the Royal Commission, except that housing became a function of the district authorities and the island authorities were each given responsibility for most functions (except fire and police services, for which purposes they combine with the Highland Regional Council).

Provision was made for the creation of community councils along the lines recommended by the Commission. (By 1979 some 1,343 such councils had been approved by the government.)

Figure 8 *Local government in Scotland since 1975*

Predictably, the regional tier has been criticized as too big and remote; as over-bureaucratized, cumbersome and inefficient; as varying too greatly in area, population and resources.[42] In particular, the huge Strathclyde region (containing half of Scotland's population) has come in for criticism.

The Royal Commission had anticipated some of the criticisms, saying for example that while the Strathclyde region was big, it nevertheless did comprise a meaningful and identifiable community.[43] Furthermore, it stressed that democracy could be enhanced rather than diminished by increasing the size of the local government unit:

It is when local government operates at the scale which its services demand that true local democracy emerges; because that is the point where power and responsibility can be properly entrusted and where the administration of services can be responsive in the right way, that is through pressures from within [the local authority] rather than from without [from central government]. (para. 162)

However, the expectation that the bigger and more powerful local authorities would stimulate a greater public participation has been disappointed: voting turnout and the contesting of seats has not noticeably increased since the reform, apart from an initial improvement in the first elections in 1974[44] (see p. 145).

The other main criticisms have been directed at the distribution of functions, and in particular at the transference of housing and refuse disposal from the regions to the district councils[45] and the souring of relations between the two tiers of authorities over the vexed question of shared responsibilities for certain services (as has happened in England and Wales).

On the other hand, one potential problem – devolution – has disappeared (at least for the present). At one time, there was speculation that Scottish local authorities (whatever form they were to take) might have had their functions gradually usurped by the prospective Scottish Assembly.[46] Following the referendum in March 1979 (where only 34 per cent voted in favour of the devolution proposals) the scheduled devolution of power to Scotland (and Wales) was formally dropped by the Government.

In 1979, the Secretary of State for Scotland set up a committee of inquiry into local government in Scotland (under the chairmanship of Anthony – now Lord – Stodart). Its terms of reference limited its scope to a tidying-up exercise, though many of the district councils were hoping for something more radical. The Report (February 1981) formed the basis of the Local Government and Planning Act 1982 which (among other things) rationalized the division of concurrent responsibilities among the two tiers of local authorities by some modest adjustments (mainly in favour of the districts) in the fields of tourism, planning and leisure provision, and (in favour of the regions) in the field of industrial promotion and development. In April 1984 another committee (Montgomery) reported on its inquiries into the workings of the Island councils. The Report applauded the operation of these most-purpose authorities and recommended that their powers be consolidated and perhaps extended (e.g. into airport management).

The 1993 review

A consultation paper on local government in Scotland was issued in 1991 (alongside those for England and Wales, see p. 60

above). It contained some very general proposals, the only firm commitment being to the retention of the three Island councils. The paper suggested a preference for the unitary model, but left the details of number, size and powers for public consultation. It also suggested that police and fire services should be organized on a larger scale than other local services, and that water and sewerage may be best dealt with by independent authorities. Many people in Scotland feared that the latter implied water privatization (as had occurred in England and Wales in 1989) and there was protest at the prospect.

The Government did indeed consider privatization of water as part of its reform. However, in the end it announced (in July 1993) that water and sewerage were to be transferred to three separate appointed bodies and thus away from direct provision by local authorities. On local government structure, the nine regional and fifty-three district councils, together with the three Island councils, are to be replaced by twenty-five new unitary councils. The legislation began its passage thorough Parliament in 1994 and the reorganized system is to be in place by 1996, with an estimated saving of £110–£330 million over the first five years. (See p. 72 for proposed structure.)

The proposals for Scotland have received considerable criticism – from those who see no point in the reorganization and from those who want an independent commission (as in England) and see the Minister's plans as a political ploy to manipulate party advantage. The local authorities' association COSLA has described the plans as 'tendentious and insulting'. The former Liberal Party leader, Sir David Steel, has called the proposals 'corrupt', and the Labour Party and the trade union UNISON have threatened a policy of non-cooperation.

A Note on local government in Northern Ireland

Following the Report of the Review Body 1970 (Macrory), local government in Ulster was reorganized into twenty-six District

Numbered Areas
1. Dumbarton and Clydebank
2. East Dunbartonshire
3. North Lanarkshire
4. City of Glasgow
5. East Renfrewshire
6. West Renfrewshire
7. Clackmannan and Falkirk
8. The Lothians

Figure 9 *Proposed unitary authorities for Scotland*
Source: Scottish Office

Councils and nine Area Boards. The district councils are responsible for local environmental services (noise and smoke control, food hygiene, abattoirs, pests, refuse, street cleaning, cemeteries), for entertainments and recreation (museums, sports facilities), licensing and consumer protection, and for markets and gas undertakings. Councillors are elected for four years at a time, by way of proportional representation (using the Single Transferable Vote method, with electoral wards grouped into district electoral areas).

Of the area boards, four are responsible for health and social services and five for education and libraries. They are made up of 30–40 per cent district councillors and the remainder appointees of the Minister. For housing there is an appointed Housing Executive, and there is a single Fire Authority. The other services are run directly by the Department of the Environment for Northern Ireland.

4. The Functions of Local Government

Local government has a number of functions – providing a voice for the local community, acting as a buffer to the central government, supplying local services, recruiting people into the political process and off-loading the central administration. More briefly we can say that local government has a *political* (or representative) role and an *administrative* (or executive) role. In this chapter we are concerned with the latter.

The principle of 'ultra vires'

An essential element of any democratic system of government is the rule of law: that government is not arbitrary or unrestrained but operates according to the law of the land, and members of the government are subject to the law in just the same way as ordinary members of the public.

As public authorities, local authorities in Britain are subject to the rule of law. Before they can act (impose charges, build schools, make by-laws, acquire property, etc.) they must be able to point to the statutory authority (normally an Act of Parliament) which authorizes such actions. If a local council were to take action which was not sanctioned by the law (say by opening a chain of fish shops) or if they exceeded their lawful powers (providing a laundry service where they were only permitted to provide public wash-houses[1]), they would be acting illegally, or *ultra vires.* When a court finds a local authority thus acting beyond its powers, it will declare these actions illegal and may punish members or officers of the authority (see p. 350). In contrast, private organizations or individuals can act in any way whatsoever as long as it is not forbidden by law. We can do what is not prohibited; local authorities can do only what the law explicitly allows them to do: what is permitted.

However, local authorities do have some freedom to act. In the first place, besides those powers explicitly conferred on them, there are those which are derived by reasonable implication or inference – powers which facilitate the discharge of their explicit powers, such as acquiring special equipment or appointing and training staff. Secondly, while Acts of Parliament mostly require local authorities to undertake certain 'mandatory' duties (such as building schools or providing gipsy caravan sites), some statutes merely allow local authorities to exercise optional or permissive powers as they see fit (such as taxing unoccupied properties or providing museums, nurseries or general caravan sites). Thus local authorities have a certain discretion as to which services to provide and to what standard, and indeed in what form they will be provided[2] (for example, in the provision of meals on wheels, an authority can decide whether to provide them seven days a week or just one or two, whether and what to charge and whether they should be provided in-house, through voluntary organization or by private contractors (subject to CCT – see pp. 272, 306)).

In addition to providing services, local authorities have a regulatory role (indeed, this is the essence of all government). Thus local councils are responsible for granting (or refusing) licences for taxis, market trading, etc., and for registering (and approving) private welfare homes and child-minding. Furthermore, they can exercise a general regulatory power over the community through by-laws. These are as much the law of the land as Acts passed by Parliament, but are of local application only (e.g. prohibiting cycling on footpaths, banning dogs from beaches or parks, determining the opening times of public parks or banning the consumption of liquor in public places). Such laws have to be approved by the Minister (who may indeed provide models or examples for councils to adopt where appropriate).

Thirdly, local authorities have the freedom to spend a certain sum of money for any purpose which in its opinion would be to the benefit of the area (except where this runs counter to other statutory provisions). Such spending is restricted by law: initially, when the scheme started in 1963, such expenditure was limited in amount in any one year to the product of a 1d rate (see pp. 316, 380), raised to 2p under the 1972 Act (Sec. 137) (Sec. 83 of Scotland's 1973 Act)[3] and known as the 'free tuppence'. In recent years, councils have been spending 32 per cent of what is permitted (compared with only 7 and 17 per cent in 1982 and 1983 respectively, though some councils – 25 per cent – spend nothing). In all, spending here amounts to only 0·5 per cent of total expenditure by local authorities.[4]

With the abolition of domestic rates (see p. 326) a new (for many, less generous) scheme was introduced under the Local Government Act 1989 (Sec. 36) – known as the 'free resource' – which limits such spending to a per capita figure of £5 in single-tier authorities, £3.50 in parishes/communities and £2.50 elsewhere. Also, whilst in the past councils often used this resource to promote local economic development, the 1989 Act (under Sec. 33) limits this activity to only certain councils (e.g. 166 of the 296 English districts and to fourteen of the London boroughs).

The justification of the *ultra vires* principle is that it protects the community against possible tyranny, extravagance and hare-brained or politically motivated adventures by its local council. However, it could be argued that the ballot box is a sufficient safeguard and that the operation of the *ultra vires* rule is too restrictive. Professor Keith-Lucas has written, '. . . our local councils are narrowly limited in their powers and duties. There is a lack of enterprise among them, and a feeling in many people's minds that they are unimportant and rather dull'.[5] Apart from thus inhibiting enterprise, voting turnout and council membership, it was argued strongly by the Maud Committee[6] that the principle of *ultra vires* 'robs the community of services which the local authority might render . . . encourages too rigorous oversight by the central government . . . contributes to the excessive concern over legalities'. (And it was pointed out that foreign systems of local government do not have such restrictions.)

The private business sector can also be adversely affected by this rule, as in 1991 when the House of Lords declared local authorities' interest-rate swaps (or 'swaptions'; see p. 359) to be illegal, with the result that a number of banks lost large sums of money. Following a subsequent investigation, the Legal Risk Review Committee (Alexandra) recommended the abolition of *ultra vires* in its 1992 report *Reducing Uncertainty – The Way Forward*. (The Audit Commission, however, is opposed to this.)

The Maud Committee recommended that local authorities should be given a 'general competence' to do whatever in their opinion is in the interests of their areas, in addition to what is already specified in legislation and subject to their not encroaching on the duties of other governmental bodies and to safeguards for the protection of public and private interests. A similar recommendation was made by the Royal Commissions on local government in England (Redcliffe-Maud) and Scotland (Wheatley) in 1969. Others take a similar view,[7] including the Labour and Liberal Democrat parties. The Widdicombe Committee (see p. 130), however, took the opposite view.

Official response to this suggestion has taken the form of a marginal increase in the power of local authorities to spend money for the benefit of their inhabitants (the 'free resource', see above). However, the Local Government Acts of 1972 (England and Wales) and 1973 (Scotland) do make provision for local authorities to acquire statutory powers somewhat more easily (through the rationalization and consolidation of many private Acts and making them of general application to local authorities, as happened through the Local Government Miscellaneous Provisions Acts of 1976 and 1982). We now therefore consider the acquisition of powers by local authorities.

The source of powers

As we have seen above, local authorities are required to operate according to the law. Parliament is the source of law, but there are different kinds of law which can apply to local government. The most important derives from *Public Acts* (the most usual kind of legislation). Some of these Acts, such as the Local Government Acts of 1972 and 1973 or the Local Government Social Services Act 1970, apply specifically to local government. Others deal with a general service or function and confer powers on local authorities along with other official bodies, as did for example the Education Act 1944, the National Health Service Act 1946 and the Housing Finance Act 1972. Most of these Acts are introduced (as Bills) by the Government. But some legislation affecting local authorities may be originated by backbench MPs, as *Private Members' Bills*. Recent examples include the Traffic Calming Act 1992 and the Local Government (Overseas Assistance) Act 1993, both of which enhanced local authority powers.

There are some Acts which permit local authorities to exercise certain powers if the authorities themselves formally 'adopt' them and thus choose to exercise them. These are usually called 'adoptive' or 'enabling' Acts. An example is to be found in connection with the licensing of private hire vehicles in the Local Government (Miscellaneous Provisions) Act 1976. However, they are of relatively little importance these days.

An individual local authority (except a parish or community council) wishing to extend the range of its powers beyond those conferred by public legislation can promote a *Private Bill* in Parliament. The procedure involves special meetings of the council, compulsory advertisement and public announcement, and the engagement of legal counsel for part of the parliamentary proceedings; it is thus complex, lengthy and costly,[8] and only about ten local authorities a year promote such Private (or 'Local') Acts. For example, the Southampton Corporation Act 1960 empowered that local authority to construct a bridge across the River Itchen;

the Abingdon Market Place Act 1978 allows that authority to ban vehicles from the market place in order to help conserve the historic town centre; the Kensington and Chelsea Corporation Act 1977 enables that borough to ban the leaving of refuse outside commercial premises, and also empowers it to carry out the work necessary for the maintenance of the external decoration of any listed building or any building in a conservation area; the Cornwall County Council Act 1984 provides the power to ban dogs from beaches; and the Birmingham City Council Act 1985 allows city-centre motor racing.

Finally, local authorities can seek to extend their powers by applying to the Secretary of State (the Minister), who has the authority, delegated to him by Parliament, to confer certain powers or duties. In some cases he alone has discretion (for example, if a local authority is seeking power to acquire property by compulsion, the 'compulsory purchase order' needs to be confirmed only by the Minister). In most cases, however, the Minister will have to submit his 'orders' for parliamentary approval. Parliament seldom rejects such Ministerial Orders, though they are often challenged (for example by other local authorities) and may be amended.[9] One of these powers is the power to confirm local authorities' by-laws (such as to control cycling on footpaths, the opening times of public parks, the behaviour of people in libraries, unauthorized tipping of waste or sticking posters, etc.).

Who does what

In examining the reorganization of local government in Chapter 3 we had an indication of the division of responsibilities among the various tiers and types of local authority. It may be useful at this point to draw the threads together before analysing the various functions in further detail. Table 2 attempts to do this.

There is some logic underlying this distribution, in that the 'bigger' services are administered by the 'bigger' authorities.

Broadly, the functions are allocated between the two main tiers on the basis of operational efficiency and cost-effectiveness. Thus it is both cheaper and more effective to have responsibilities such as major planning, police and fire services operated over fairly large areas. Similarly it was strongly argued by the Redcliffe-Maud Report[10] and the Wheatley Report[11] that the education service should be administered over an area containing at least 200,000–250,000 people in order that such authorities should have at their disposal 'the range and calibre of staff, and the technical and financial resources necessary for effective provision' of the service. On the other hand services such as allotments, public health and amenities can be effectively administered over smaller areas, and are thus the responsibility of district (and even parish/community) authorities.

There is, however, no universal agreement about this general distribution of functions. There is even less agreement about such services as housing and social services (social work): on operational grounds a good case could be made out for their being administered by either tier; services administration varies among the different parts of Britain (see Table 2).

However, the scale of operations is only one criterion. In the allocation of responsibilities, regard has rightly been given to the need for democratic control and responsiveness to local needs. Furthermore, in practice, the rationality of the system has been undermined by the respect which has been paid to history and tradition: for example, the district authorities in England and Wales not only have long experience (and expertise) in housing but also have substantial political influence which they could use to defend themselves against any threatened loss of the housing (or other) function.

Another complication is that the allocation of responsibilities among the local government tiers is not clear-cut: many responsibilities are *shared*. Shared responsibilities can take a number of forms, including (1) *concurrent provision*: whereby several types of local authority all provide the same service, such as car parking, amenities or caravan sites; (2) *joint provision*: whereby several

Table 2 *The responsibilities of local authorities*

	Metropolitan		England and Wales Non-Metropolitan		Greater London	Scotland		
	Joint Authority	District Councils	County Councils	District Councils	Borough Councils	Regional Councils	District Councils	Island Councils
Social Services		●	●		●	●		●
Education		●	●		●	●		●[2]
Libraries		●	●		●	●		●
Museums and Art Galleries		●	●	●	●		●	●
Housing		●		●	●		●[2]	●
Planning – Strategic		●[4]	●		●[4]	●		●
– Local		●		●	●		●	●
Highways		●	●		●	●		●
Traffic Management		●	●		●	●		●
Passenger Transport[6]	●		●			●		●
Playing Fields and Swimming Baths		●		●	●[1]		●	●
Parks and Open Spaces		●		●	●		●	●
Refuse Collection		●		●	●		●	●
Refuse Disposal	●[5]	●[5]	●[8]		●		●	●
Consumer Protection		●	●		●	●		●
Environmental Health[7]		●		●	●		●	●
Police[3]	●		●			●		
Fire[3]	●		●			●		

1 Shared by groups of London boroughs.

2 Except in Highlands, Dumfries and Galloway and Border regions, where the function is regional.

3 Some areas have Joint Police Forces and Joint Fire Brigades. In London the police authority is the Home Secretary; the Fire and Civil Defence Authority runs the Fire Brigades.

4 Strategic planning in metropolitan districts is coordinated by a joint committee of the districts in each former metropolitan county area. A joint planning committee also handles strategic planning for London.

5 In metropolitan areas, refuse disposal may be either a joint authority or a district council function.

6 Passenger transport in London is carried out by a separate body, London Regional Transport.

7 Regional and Island councils in Scotland control water and sewerage, in addition to the usual environmental health duties.

8 In Wales, the Waste Disposal Authority and Waste Collection Authority are the same, being the district council in both cases.

9 In Wales some districts operate a library service.

For a more detailed analysis, see Appendix 2 and Appendix 10.

local authorities join together by forming a joint committee or board for the provision of a common service, such as crematoria or communications (for instance, the Forth Road Bridge Joint Board, a combined provision by the Lothian and Fife Regional Councils); (3) *shared but divided provision*: whereby several tiers are responsible for a service, but each is responsible for a separate part or aspect of that service, as with refuse collection and disposal (in England) and planning development and control;[12] (4) *reserve powers*: as in the case of housing (and, until recently, planning control), whereby the English county councils may assume responsibility under certain circumstances (for such undertakings as providing houses for certain employees, such as police or teachers); (5) *claimed powers*: whereby certain responsibilities are initially allocated to one set of authorities, but may be claimed by individual local authorities from another tier, such as the district councils in England and Wales, which can claim to maintain unclassified roads in urban areas;[13] (6) *agency powers*: whereby a local authority can arrange (by mutual agreement) for another local authority to carry out functions on its behalf and be suitably reimbursed. This power to delegate or transfer responsibility is widely available, except that it is specifically prohibited in the case of education, police, social services, national parks, finance (other than rate collection and valuation) and diseased animal control. It is quite widely used, but it varies considerably among both local authorities and services. For example, many district councils have agency agreements to maintain highways and street lighting for county councils and for the provision or maintenance of sewerage for water companies. Services may also be transferred when an authority defaults (see p. 366).

Furthermore, local authorities have a number of joint arrangements for the provision of services. These take a variety of forms and include statutory joint authorities or boards, joint committees, joint forums, lead authorities and arm's-length suppliers.[14]

Further complications arise from the fact that in some cases non-providing local authorities must be advised and consulted about matters relating to certain services. For example, parishes and community councils must be consulted about planning matters by the appropriate planning authority. Similarly, district authorities are normally given representation on bodies that are the responsibility of the counties (as in the case of school governing bodies in the English and Welsh non-metropolitan areas).

Enough has been said to illustrate the main point: that while it may be possible to indicate in a broad way the allocation of responsibilities among local authorities, for any particular local authority its range of responsibilities will depend on its status, the use it makes of agency and claiming powers, and the use it makes of its permissive powers – all of which will depend in turn on its size, local needs, finance, party politics and the vitality of local voluntary organizations and pressure groups.

The range of services

The range of local government responsibilities is extensive (especially compared to local government in European countries).[15] It is no exaggeration to say that it provides services 'from the cradle to the grave'. Table 2 gives a stark indication of this, and Table 16 (p. 299) shows the relative importance of each function in terms of expenditure. The wide range of activities is well illustrated by the fact that some public information booklets produced by local authorities to outline their functions contain up to 1,000 separate headings. Here we shall try to put some flesh on the bare bones by describing some of these responsibilities in more detail. We can conveniently group them into five categories (Table 3); though it is not always easy to decide the allocation of some services.

(1) Protective services

Protective services seek to protect the citizen from various dangers.

Table 3 *Categories of local government services*

Protective	Environmental	Personal	Recreational	Commercial
Police, Fire	Highways	Education	Sports	Markets
Consumer	Environmental	Careers	facilities	Transport
protection	health	Housing	Museums,	Smallholdings
Diseases of	Transport	Social work	galleries	
animals	Planning	Homes	Theatres	
Licensing	Parking	Aids	Camp sites	
Emergency		Meals		

(a) *Police.* The organized provision of local police services has been a local government responsibility since the mid nineteenth century, but since the Police Act 1946 small local forces have disappeared and some of the county-based forces have been amalgamated (or 'combined'). It might well be that in the not too distant future Britain's police forces will be organized on a regional basis, and indeed some people argue strongly in favour of a national system.[16]

Police forces are superintended by the police committee of the local authority. This committee is special in that it comprises two thirds councillors and one third magistrates. In London the boroughs have no police committees, as the Metropolitan Police Force is under the direct control of the Home Office.* In fact the Home Secretary has considerable powers of inspection and regulation of all local police forces and he must approve the appointment of chief constables. However, of greater public concern is the effectiveness of the control exercised by local police committees. It is widely felt to be inadequate, partly as a result of the

---

* Government White Papers and a Police Bill in 1993 proposed to reduce local councillor representation to half, though in London it is proposed to create a local authority police committee to manage the Metropolitan Police instead of the Home Office. The latter will continue to play a key role, however, since the police are both servants of the Crown and employees of the local authority.

amalgamations producing bigger and remoter forces. (Since 1946 the number of forces has fallen from 200 to 50.) But this unease is also due to the fact that under the Police Act 1964 the duties of the police committee are limited to maintaining the police force and appointing the chief constable. The latter is responsible for the general operational management of the force and consequently many committee members' questions and probings are allegedly blocked and deflected by the chief constable on the grounds that members are trespassing into his operational territory or that revealing certain information would be contrary to the public interest.

(b) *Fire.* The provision by local authorities of fire-fighting services was not generally obligatory until 1938. Under the Local Government Acts of 1972 and 1973, fire authorities are required to cooperate and assist one another and, like police services, fire brigades may be amalgamated under a single chief fire officer. Apart from fire-fighting, fire authorities are also concerned with fire prevention, and under a number of statutes (notably the Fire Precautions Act 1971 and the Health and Safety at Work Act 1974) a wide variety of premises (residential, educational, leisure and employment) are required to obtain fire certificates. These are issued by the fire authority (county councils, the boroughs' joint boards, regional and island councils) if they are satisfied that adequate fire precautions and safety facilities (such as fire escapes, alarms, fire doors) exist. Local authorities may provide loans to enable such adaptations as are necessary. In the first instance, it is normally the district authorities who (in the pursuance of building regulations) inspect and require the occupier of premises to obtain fire certificates.

(c) *Consumer protection.* Local authorities appoint inspectors (often known as trading standards officers) whose task it is to test the weights and measures of local trading concerns and to take legal proceedings against fraudulent traders and similar offenders – those giving short measure, for example. In recent years their work has extended into other areas of trading practice, such as charges and credit facilities and false or misleading descriptions of goods and services. Consequently, local authorities are empowered to make purchases locally for test purposes, and inspectors have the right of entry to premises.

Local authorities have similar powers in relation to their food and drug responsibilities, which include the enforcement of regulations regarding the production and sale of food and drugs – their purity, safe storage, labelling and fitness for consumption. For this purpose local authorities appoint inspectors and many will also appoint a qualified public analyst. Inspectors have the right of entry to premises and the right to take food samples for testing. Under the Food Act 1992 and the Environmental Protection Act 1990 local authorities took over much of the responsibility of the Health and Safety Executive (for example in the control of pesticide use in commercial premises).

Local authorities are empowered to set up consumer advice centres. These provide general pre-shopping and post-shopping advice to consumers, assessing product claims and facilitating the investigation of complaints. There is considerable variation across the country in what is provided here, and some local authorities rely on local voluntary provision (by Citizens' Advice Bureaux, for instance). This variation is due partly to financial stringency but also to differences of principles and politics: councillors have varying opinions about how far local authorities should go in advising consumers on appropriate purchases and how far it is the proper role of local authorities to take a pro-consumer stance and campaign against questionable trading practices.

(d) *Diseases of animals*, such as tuberculosis, swine fever, foot and mouth or rabies, can be directly or indirectly injurious to humans. Consequently, legislation seeks, through local authorities, to control such disease by regulating the movement of livestock and by promoting certain preventive measures (such as sheep dipping). Local authorities issue licences for the movement of animals, and farmers must keep records of such movements.

(e) *Licensing* has already been mentioned. Broadly it takes two forms: (i) Licensing which seeks merely to regulate certain trades or activities, such as pawnbroking, money-lending, taxis, massage treatment, gun-ownership, street-collecting, cinemas, theatres, employment agencies, child-minding or private nursing homes. Such licensing or registration normally involves inspection or compliance with particular regulations (such as safety facilities or refraining from exhibiting certain films). (ii) Licensing which involves regulation, but also provides a source of revenue or local taxation, such as dog licences (until 1988), waste-disposal licences or licences required for killing or dealing in game. The amounts of money raised here are very small.

(2) Environmental services

Environmental services control and improve the physical environment.

(a) *Environmental health* is perhaps the best known and most firmly established local government function (see Chapter 2). Although in 1974 local authorities in England and Wales lost their responsibilities for the supply of water and main sewerage to *ad hoc* water authorities, they have for instance in recent years become responsible for smoke and noise abatement, the regulation of caravan sites, the control of poisonous waste disposal and the enforcement of health and safety at work regulations. Their more traditional responsibilities, undertaken by environmental health officers (often on the basis of by-laws), include: the control of nuisances (such as waste tips, insanitary or overcrowded premises, unfenced mines and quarries) and offensive trades (such as glue-making, fat-extraction and tanning); the enforcement of building regulations (which lay down criteria for the construction and design of buildings, including such matters as the adequacy of drains, insulation and accessibility); refuse collection, street cleaning and the instituting of proceedings against litter offenders; the provision of public toilets; the provision of cemeteries and cremat-oria (and the disposal of dead bodies where no one else can be found to be responsible); and the control of vermin (by requiring or perhaps undertaking the destruction of vermin – most commonly rats, mice and lice – affecting persons or premises).

Many of these activities aim at preventing the outbreak of disease. When an outbreak of a 'notifiable' infectious disease (smallpox, diphtheria, typhoid, cholera, dysentery or anthrax) does occur, local authorities have the duty to inform the local health authority. Local authorities also have powers to prevent the spread of diseases through disinfection of premises and people and the compulsory removal to hospital of infected persons.

(b) *Highways, traffic and transport.* Roads take a number of forms and local authorities are involved in all of them. Motorways are the responsibility of the central government,[17] which organized their construction through Regional Construction Units (which then broke down into sub-units run by local authorities and acting as agents for the central government). RCUs were disbanded in the early 1980s (with much of their remaining work being contracted out to private contractors). Trunk roads are also the responsibility of the central government, but it is normal practice for local authorities to act as agents and undertake their building, maintenance, lighting and speed restriction. When such roads become 'de-trunked' (as when a parallel motorway is built) they become the full responsibility of the local authorities. The county councils have recently been pressing for the outright responsibility for trunk roads to be transferred to local authorities.

All other public roads and bridges are the responsibility of local authorities, mainly the county and regional and island councils. District councils have the right to claim responsibility for the maintenance of urban non-classified (i.e. less busy) roads; in practice they often undertake maintenance of these and other roads as agents of the (county) highways authorities. Responsibility for lighting may be similarly delegated, as may the provision of pedestrian crossings, footpaths, seats, shelters, speed limits, etc. Such agency agreements are often preferable to the claiming arrangement, as the latter can give rise to discontinuous or patchy coverage of responsibility.

Traffic management involves responsibility for such devices as signals and roundabouts and for regulations such as those covering one-way streets, speed limits and the prohibition of certain vehicles. They are the responsibility of the highway authorities, but may be delegated along with highway maintenance. Decisions concerning street parking restrictions rest with the highway authority, but district authorities may provide off-street parking in their own right. Local authorities have a statutory duty to promote road safety and the prevention of accidents. For this purpose they usually appoint a road safety officer who organizes publicity to encourage road consciousness and the formation of local voluntary groups (for cycling, motorcycling proficiency, etc.), often in conjunction with the police and the schools.

Local authorities may provide passenger transport services, though it has only occurred in metropolitan counties, the GLC, Strathclyde regional council and about forty district councils.[18] Metropolitan boroughs are (since 1986) responsible (via joint boards) in their areas, while in London the GLC's role has been transferred to London Regional Transport (LRT) (see p. 119). Otherwise, county and regional councils are responsible for coordinating and rationalizing such provision (though less so following the Transport Act 1985), for which purpose they must draw up and submit to the central government five-year transport programmes which must be revised annually (in the form of Transport Policies and Programmes, or TPPs). Local authorities may assist in the provision of public transport through grants (including subsidies for the running of mini-buses in rural areas).

(c) *Planning.* Britain is a small and densely populated country. Land space is limited and its use needs to be carefully monitored, guided and, if necessary, controlled in the interests of the community as a whole. This is the realm of town and country planning, an essentially twentieth-century function of local government.

Planning is important, therefore, because it affects the way individuals dispose of their property (land) and because it affects their living environment. Broadly, local authorities are charged with responsibility for the preparation of plans, the control of development and the conservation of the environment.

'Structure plans' set out for a ten-year period the broad policy or strategy of the local authority for the use of land in the area of the county or region/island. They cover such concerns as the lines of proposed roads, the sites of public buildings and open spaces, and the allocation of areas for such uses as housing, schools, agriculture and commercial premises, and they thus imply an element of economic planning. These plans are based on a survey of various factors, including population, economic activity, communications and traffic, each of which is likely to affect the scale and nature of land use and development. In drawing up its structure plan, the local authority must consult other appropriate bodies (including constituent district councils and neighbouring councils) and must submit the plan to the Secretary of State for approval.

'Local plans' cover smaller areas, filling in the details, and are also submitted to the Secretary of State, but do not necessarily require his confirmation. Local plans have to be certified by the county council as conforming to the structure plan. Metropolitan and London boroughs have 'unitary development plans' which combine local and structure plans. The Government has proposed the abolition of the counties' structure plans, thus creating a single-tier system of development planning at district level, though counties would be responsible for drawing up 'Statements of County Planning Policy' on those matters that need to be dealt with at county level (such as major highway schemes, major commercial development, minerals, waste disposal). The new district plans would not require ministerial approval (though they could be 'called in').[19] This plan has since been dropped.

All of these plans must be well publicized and there must be ample opportunity for objections from the public.[20] The consequence of objections is a public inquiry or a local hearing, and the final decision rests with the Secretary of State, in the case of structure plans, and with the local planning authority in the case of the local plan.

Having settled their plans, local authorities are then responsible for the implementation of those plans through the process of the control of development. All development – from the big housing estate or shopping centre to the individual house extension or conversion, and the location and size of advertisements – must obtain prior planning permission[21] from the local authority (the district council). Where such permission is refused or involves unacceptable conditions, appeal may be made to the Secretary of State, who may hold an inquiry before making a decision. There are some 650,000 such appeals a year in England and 40,000 in Scotland, and most are dealt with by correspondence. Where there is an inquiry the Minister rarely overturns the decision of the local authority. (In some cases, involving matters of national, regional or technical importance, the Secretary of State may appoint a Planning Inquiry Commission.)

Planning often appears to be a rather negative exercise, and planners are sometimes characterized as 'inverted Micawbers', waiting for something to turn down. However, town and country planning has many overtly positive aspects. Local authorities may acquire land (perhaps through compulsory purchase orders) with a view to its development either directly or by attracting industry (through the provision of loans or factory space). They also have powers to reclaim and improve derelict land. In both these respects the powers of councils in the inner urban area are especially great; one of these is the possibility of 'planning gain' or betterment, where private developers provide amenities for the authority in recognition or as a condition of planning approval.

Councils also have certain powers related to conservation. They can require special planning applications for the demolition or alteration of 'listed buildings' (those listed as of special architectural or historic interest or importance). Trees and woodlands may be protected by local authority 'preservation orders'. Local planning authorities may make grants or loans available for the maintenance of listed buildings. Finally, councils are empowered to preserve and enhance the natural beauty of the countryside by creating country parks and setting up nature reserves. They are also responsible for the recording and protection of rights of way. A number of their conservation functions are exercised in conjunction with the Countryside Commission.

(d) *Emergencies.* Local authorities have made some sort of provision for the possibility of Britain being involved in a war, such provision normally including the formulation of an emergency plan, though a number of councils have dragged their feet after declaring themselves 'nuclear free zones'. They also have contingency plans for natural disasters or hazardous conditions, such as abnormally heavy snowfalls, floods or extensive oil pollution. Under such circumstances, the emergency planning officer would be responsible for the coordination and execution of the appropriate services (perhaps in conjunction with outside bodies, such as the armed forces or health services).

Environmental services often seem dull in the sense of their being devoid of conflict and controversy. There are good reasons for this – we can normally expect the bins to be emptied, the dead to be buried or the public lavatory to function without a fuss. On the other hand there are many areas of dispute in this field. In the area of planning, apart from issues such as compulsory purchase or refused planning applications, there are the larger-scale issues of planning blight, the damage caused to communities by large-scale redevelopment and the running down of town centres (e.g. as a result of too many out-of-town superstores), etc., which give rise to neighbourhood action groups and civic societies. In the field of transport, there are the problems of routing, parking and pedestrianization, and the broader questions of social need and loss of amenity. Questions of highway design, road crossings (at school/peak traffic times), car parking and lighting are being raised in relation to the incidence of crime, especially against women and children.

(3) Personal services

Personal services seek to enhance personal welfare.

(a) *Education*, taken as a whole, is the local authorities' most costly service (see p. 299). Their basic responsibility laid down in the Education Act 1944 (England and Wales) and 1945 (Scotland) and the Education Reform Act 1988, is to provide, without charge, adequate primary (including nursery) and secondary education for the 9·2 million schoolchildren in Britain (in some 35,000 schools, of which 5,000 are secondary). This implies the provision and staffing of schools, the enforcement of regular school attendance and the provision of transport and maintenance and clothing grants for the children. Other welfare services include the supply of milk, meals and child guidance services, as well as special arrangements for the education of handicapped or special needs children at home, in hospital or in schools.

State schools are 'maintained' by local education authorities (LEAs). Many of these in England and Wales – about one third – are known as 'voluntary aided' or 'voluntary controlled', implying their foundation by a voluntary organization (usually the Church) which continues to exercise a management role in spite of dependence on LEA financial support. The management committees or boards of governors of schools and colleges are currently being reformed (following the Taylor Committee Report 1977 and the Education Acts 1980 and 1986) to include (alongside the LEA appointees) a stronger representation of members of the public, both (elected) parents and (co-opted) business people (see p. 198). Under the Education Reform Act 1988, the governors have important new powers. In particular, they now have the responsibility for managing their school/college budget, under the system of LME or LMS – the local management of schools. Some governors have gone further, under the Act, and, following a vote among parents, they have opted out of LEA control and become grant-maintained (GM) by the central government through a funding agency. In 1993, there were 1,500 such schools, though, as a result of the Education Act 1993, the Government anticipates a figure of over 4,000 by 1995. This option was introduced in Scotland under the Self-Governing Schools (Scotland) Act 1990.

Beyond the secondary school stage, LEAs were until 1993 responsible for the provision of courses in tertiary or technical colleges, sometimes known as colleges of further education, and in sixth-form colleges. In 1993, all these (500) colleges became independent of local authorities and set up as state corporations (quangos, in effect). Local authorities (on a joint or 'pooled' basis) up to 1990 were also responsible for part of the higher education system in the form of polytechnics and monotechnics. Under the Education Reform Act 1988, most of these have now become self-governing and have been re-titled universities, and are thus funded through the Higher Education Funding Council. They also provide grants for students entering higher education courses.

Despite the trauma of public expenditure cuts in recent years, there is still much talk of 'continuing education' – the opportunity for those who wish to go on learning after leaving school, or who fared badly in school and need a second chance, or who need to keep up with and adapt to economic and technological change in society. Apart from further education, what is known as 'adult education' plays an important role here, especially for those whose schooling finished early (and about one third of Britain's population left school before the age of fifteen). Except for some formal and examination-orientated studies, adult education is largely associated with so-called leisure-time classes – needlecraft, cookery, woodwork and art, for example. In recent years a fusion has occurred between adult education and youth services (but often also including schools, voluntary groups and volunteer tutors and parents), giving rise to 'community education'.

The main educational issue of the 1960s, however, was the comprehensive school. The post-war system of segregating secondary school children according to the results of tests given between the ages of ten and eleven (the '11-plus') was increasingly condemned as unfair and elitist. By the mid 1970s most LEAs had 'gone comprehensive', and the Education Act 1976 sought to compel the remaining LEAs to do likewise. However, the Conservative government's Education Act 1979 restores to local authorities their freedom to determine their own system of secondary education. In doing so the government is also attempting to enhance parental choice (of their children's schools) and parental participation (in the management of those schools, as governors). However, over the past twenty years it is in the field of nursery and primary education especially that parents have been encouraged to participate, as helpers and quasi-'teachers'. At the same time, the policy of designating certain parts of towns as 'educational priority areas' (EPAs) was an attempt to equalize educational opportunities by diverting extra resources to areas of deprivation.

Freedom is a strong feature of the British education system, for although the Secretary of State is required 'to promote the education of the people . . . and secure the effective execution by local authorities, under his control and direction, of the national policy' of education, in practice LEAs are given a substantial degree of autonomy. The British system of education is perhaps the most decentralized in Europe. However, this can have its disadvantages in that it may create too great a variety (of teaching methods, of subjects, of exam standards). The periodic discoveries of low levels of literacy and numeracy have given rise to the 'great debate' on education and the greater monitoring of standards, with demands for closer links with the world of industry. These developments have moved government policy in the direction of greater curriculum uniformity. Under the Education Reform Act 1988, a national curriculum (consisting of three core subjects – English, Maths and Science – and seven foundation subjects) has been introduced, together with plans for universal assessment and testing at the ages of 7, 11, 14 and 16.

(b) *Careers.* Most councils have had long experience in providing employment services for young people. Since the Employment and Training Act 1973 all local (education) authorities are required to provide vocational advice and guidance for pupils and students attending educational institutions (except universities) and an employment service for those leaving or having recently left such schools and colleges. If the local authority so decides, this service may be extended to young people in employment, thus providing a parallel and alternative service to that provided by the employment division of the Department of Employment (formerly the Manpower Services Commission, or MSC).

The 2,000 or so careers officers may be visited at their local careers office or they may hold interviews with individual school and college students on school and college premises. Some may specialize in work with the disabled or the long-term unemployed. More generally they visit educational establishments regularly to talk to groups of students about local and perhaps national employment opportunities and prospects, explaining the requirements and facilities for further education and training, including that provided through the Training and Enterprise Councils (TECs, or LECs in Scotland).

In the 1970s the careers service tried to cast off the rather unfavourable image of the old youth employment service. It has also had to face the problems of serious juvenile unemployment. However, together with the Department of Employment it is playing a large part in a wide range of schemes to try to deal with the situation, such as work experience, job creation, community work and youth training.

(c) *Personal social services* are concerned with the social welfare of people of all ages and conditions, but their main attention is focused on the more vulnerable groups in society – the elderly, children and the handicapped. Broadly speaking, local authorities are required to promote social welfare by making available advice, guidance and assistance, and by providing a range of facilities. These facilities include residential homes or hostels and foster care; day-time care, training and occupation centres; help in the home, including laundry, meals and practical aids; and the support and advisory work provided by social workers, be it on an individual (casework) or group basis, or in a community setting (working with voluntary and tenants' groups).

Traditionally the emphasis has been placed on residential care and even today over 50 per cent of welfare expenditure takes this form. However, since the 1950s, increasing emphasis has been given to the concept of 'community care'. Thus, in order to avoid or postpone the need for residential care of the elderly, community support has been broadened by way of home helps, aids and adaptations, special equipment, recreational facilities and help with travelling. Special 'sheltered' housing schemes have also been developed (in conjunction with housing authorities and voluntary associations). Consequently, only about 3 per cent of persons of retirement age are in residential or hospital care.

Similar forms of provision, including facilities for occupational therapy and sheltered employment, have been developed for the physically and mentally handicapped (i.e. those with learning difficulties), often in cooperation with local voluntary groups. The intention here is to provide rehabilitation and reduce the numbers in long-stay hospitals and homes, partly to avoid the danger of institutional neurosis (or over-dependence) and partly to lower costs.

There has been a significant increase in expenditure on these community services over the past twenty years, following the Social Work (Scotland) Act 1968, the Local Authority Social Services Act 1970, the Chronically Sick and Disabled Persons Act 1970 and the Disabled Persons Act 1986, and partly as a result of central pressure on councils to provide for the mentally disordered, with the inducement of 'joint funds' from the NHS. This has been greatly reinforced by the NHS and Community Care Act 1990 (operative, mainly, from 1993), which seeks to shift the emphasis of welfare from hospitals and residential care to domiciliary and community care. (There is also a change in the form of provision, with local authorities themselves being less responsible for actual provision and more for arranging (through contracts) for others (private and voluntary bodies) to provide; a clear manifestation of the 'purchaser–provider' split, so evident

in the NHS; see below). However, there are many wide variations
between the different local authorities' provision, due in part to
differences in resources, but also to differences in councillors'
values, priorities and political wills. The mixed result is sometimes
described as 'territorial injustice'.

Similar difficulties exist in the provision of services for children. Recent legislation (e.g. the Children Act 1989) is placing
extra demands on the local authority social services departments.
Apart from their traditional role as provider of care for children
deprived of normal family life (through fostering and residential
care in community homes), they have now to devise comprehensive adoption facilities, provide a thoroughgoing monitoring
system to prevent child-abuse, and supervise young offenders in
the community on a caring rather than a punitive basis. Some of
these services will only be adequately developed as more resources
become available to the personal social services.

(d) *The National Health Service.* The NHS, until its reorganization in 1974, was a tri-partite organization: one arm (the hospitals)
was administered by appointed hospital boards; another arm (the
family practitioner services) was administered by appointed local
executive councils; and the third arm was administered by local
authorities, who were responsible for a number of health services
including health centres, home nursing, health visiting, maternity
and child clinics, school medical services, family planning, vaccination and ambulances. Local government lost responsibility for
these services when they transferred (in 1974) to Scottish Health
Boards (15) and English and Welsh Regional (14) and Area (98)
Health Authorities. The 98 Areas became 201 District Health
Authorities (DHAs) in 1982 (though 40 have merged since then).

These health authorities are responsible for most health services.[22] They are appointed bodies and have always included
members drawn from local authorities though this has now
ceased under the NHS and Community Care Act 1990. This Act
also initiated the separation of responsibility for arranging provision from actual supply of service (as with community care,

above). Consequently, health authorities purchase or commission services from the providing units (e.g. hospitals) on the basis of contracts, and so most hospitals have become NHS trusts. This is another example of the internal market or purchaser–provider split. Half of the DHAs have geographical boundaries that broadly match those of the main local authorities. This co-terminosity – greater before 1982 – was deliberate and aimed to facilitate liaison between local government and the health services. Furthermore, in order to promote the coordination of health and welfare services (especially for groups such as the elderly, the mentally disordered and discharged hospital patients) joint consultative committees, joint planning teams and jointly financed projects have been established. Another aspect of the NHS is of particular interest to local government: the Community Health Council or, in Scotland, Local Health Council. There is such a local health council for every health district. Their purpose is to monitor the health services and represent to the health authorities the views of the consumer. By law at least half of the members of health councils must be drawn from neighbouring local authorities.

Thus local government has a continuing interest in the nation's health services. This is perhaps inevitable, since the boundary between health and welfare service is not clear-cut, and many people felt that a reorganized and strengthened local government system could be strong enough to take over responsibility for the NHS.[23] While this now seems out of the question in the immediate future, the idea is by no means dead and buried (and it has been partially revived by the Griffiths Report on *Community Care* (1988)).[24]

(e) *Housing* covers a wide range of services, some of which could be said to fall within the environmental and protective fields. Thus, as an adjunct to public health, local authorities have long been empowered and (through subsidies) encouraged to clear slums and re-develop or rehabilitate whole areas (now known as 'general improvement areas' and 'housing action areas'). Similarly they have developed powers to control overcrowding. In general, their principal statutory duty is to undertake periodic reviews of housing conditions in their areas.

It was in response to the need to rehouse persons displaced by slum clearance that council housing was introduced in the nineteenth century. However, it was not until general subsidies began after 1919 that the building of council houses began on a large scale. Local authorities currently provide about a quarter of housing accommodation in Britain (i.e. they supply about 5 million dwellings).

Central government grants have been paid to encourage local authorities to provide housing. They are also intended to reduce rent charges to tenants. However, when it was felt that such subsidized rents were too indiscriminate and wasteful, the Conservative government passed the Housing (Finance) Act 1972 which required local authorities to charge 'fair' (generally higher) rents, but with reductions for those on low incomes. This policy was welcomed in many quarters as fair, rational and long overdue, as well as contributing to a reduction in state expenditure. Elsewhere (generally on the Left) it was condemned as inflationary, exploitative and profiteering, and also autocratic, since local authorities were no longer free to decide their own rents. Councillors at Clay Cross (Derbyshire) actually refused to implement the law and were displaced by housing commissioners, appointed by the Secretary of State. These councillors were saved from threatened imprisonment by the Labour government, which restored local authorities' housing powers in 1975. However, the other main part of the 1972 Act was left intact. This is the scheme whereby tenants in *privately* rented accommodation receive rent allowances according to their income. Rents are settled (if necessary with the assistance of rent officers and rent panels) and the role of local housing authorities is to process tenants' claims and disburse the appropriate allowances (for which they are largely re-imbursed by the government). Since 1982–3, rent rebates and allowances are called 'housing benefits'.

In recent years governments have tended to give added emphasis to the policy of housing conservation and improvement. Local authorities are responsible for the distribution of housing renovation grants and for ensuring that any conditions attaching to them are complied with. Generally speaking the grants are payable for housing conversions (into flats, for instance) and for improvements (like the installation of amenities such as running water or a WC or thermal insulation). Local authorities have the power to compel owners to improve their properties. The most important grant condition concerns future occupation: in order to prevent abuse, restrictions are placed on the immediate future use or occupation of the improved properties. In addition certain grants are not payable if the property exceeds a certain rateable value. Overall the number of such grants increased substantially in recent years, from 128,000 in 1968 to 200,000 in 1980, but have since declined and there is now a waiting list.

The most controversial aspect of housing is the sale of council houses (see Norwich case, p. 584). Since 1980 it has become incumbent on local housing authorities to sell some of their housing stock. The broad objective is to extend the property-owning element of our democracy. However, critics point out that there should always be a sizeable proportion of rented accommodation (which the private sector is failing to provide) and that the private sector can be left to supply adequately for owner-occupation. Also, in recent years, local authorities have been restricted to using only a limited proportion (25 per cent) of the proceeds of house sales for new building (which has fallen significantly), the remainder being used for debt repayment. In addition, local authorities already promote owner-occupation through the provision of mortgage advances (up to 100 per cent in some cases), by guaranteeing the repayment of loans from building societies and, most recently, through rents-to-mortgages schemes.

Under the Housing Act 1988, council tenants now have the right to opt out of their local authority tenancy and transfer to another landlord, where the latter is prepared to take over the housing stock and manage the property in a 'social' (rather than purely commercial) manner. The transfer can only take place if a

majority of tenants on individual housing estates vote in favour –
but, unusually, those who fail to vote are counted as voting in
favour of the transfer!

Local authorities have other important housing responsibilities.
These include the provision and control of caravan sites in
general, and of gypsy sites in particular (though the latter is
currently under review). Local government retains its ancient
responsibility of providing accommodation for the homeless (but
this is under serious review). Since the Housing (Homeless
Persons) Act 1977 the responsibility (currently affecting some
120,000 households) has been transferred to local housing authorities from social service departments. Another more recently developed 'welfare' service is the local authority provision (either
direct or indirect) of housing advice and aid centres.

(4) Amenity services

Amenity services provide for citizens' leisure time and, more than
any other, tend to be taken for granted, mainly because they have
long been provided by local government and have become very
closely identified with it – museums, art galleries, parks and
gardens (now including country parks), libraries and playgrounds
are typical examples. Many were established in the nineteenth
century, the formative years of local government, and their
foundation stones and commemorative plaques bear the names of
many civic leaders of earlier generations.

The past thirty years have witnessed a significant growth in
leisure time, and local authorities have made an equally significant
contribution to the provision of facilities for active forms of
recreation, either indirectly through grants and assistance to
sports clubs, or through the direct provision of facilities such as
sports centres, swimming baths, squash courts, ski slopes and
skating rinks as well as the longer-established bowls, golf, tennis
and other recreational grounds.

On the cultural and entertainments side, local authorities have
continued to subsidize art galleries, museums and exhibitions in

addition to making their own direct provision, and their library services have diversified into such areas as information provision, audio-visual materials, sound archives and special services for the disadvantaged groups.

There has been a noticeable expansion too in the number of municipal theatres, and in local authorities' promotion of groups and festivals of drama, music, crafts and dancing as well as such events as regattas, flower and agricultural shows, particularly in areas where local authorities are promoting tourism and holiday-making. For this purpose they may also provide long-distance footpaths, camp sites and perhaps hotels and restaurants. Since the Local Government Acts of 1972 (England and Wales) and 1973 (Scotland), the financial limits on local government expenditure on such entertainments have been removed. But public expenditure cuts are jeopardizing existing provision.

(5) Trading services

Trading services are services for which local authorities make commercial charges. They charge fees for a large number of services, including further education, day nurseries, school meals, residential care, home helps, car parks and sports facilities. These charges are generally below the full economic cost and are often scaled to take account of users' ability to pay. Apart from housing, such charges bring in only about 15 per cent of the costs. Consequently they are substantially financed by local taxes and central government grants (see Chapter 11) and are not classified as *trading* services. What distinguishes the trading services is, firstly, that their charges aim substantially to cover costs (in aggregate they cover about 90 per cent of costs) and, secondly, these charges do not normally allow for differences in the incomes of users. (In addition it may be added that it is only the profits and losses of the trading services – and unlike other services, not their gross income and expenditure – which are brought into account in the general rate fund.)

This distinction is not always clear, as certain services

traditionally classified as trading (such as markets) may regularly make losses and have to be subsidized from the rates. Some are perhaps run at a loss because they bring wider benefits – such as making the area more lively and attractive, which enhances local property values and job opportunities (and so rate revenues). The best illustration of this is local authorities' attempts to attract commercial enterprises to their areas through offering low-rented land and premises (using their 'free resource' power under Sec. 137 of the Local Government Act 1972, amended 1989; see p. 76). For example, the GLC set up a technology centre where newly formed companies could develop their ideas for new products.

As we have seen, there are some rather unusual municipal trading services, including Birmingham's bank, Hull's telephone system and Doncaster's racecourse, but more generally they include allotments and smallholdings, markets, civic airports, conference and exhibition centres, estate development and beach undertakings.

The importance of trading services has declined, especially since the nationalization of gas, electricity and water. And there is a general reluctance to involve local government further in competition with private enterprise, partly for political reasons (to avoid 'creeping socialism') and partly for economic reasons (to avoid the waste of inefficient management). Such arguments are not conclusive and are examined further in Chapter 11.

(6) Legal Services

Legal services do not fall within the mainstream of local authority responsibilities, but there is a connection. While in Scotland the probation service is part of the social-work department's role, in England and Wales the only link is through local authorities having to help finance, and perhaps help compose, the county and metropolitan/London borough probation committees which organize the service locally. Similarly, local authorities contribute to the running costs, and perhaps the membership, of the magistrates' committees which manage the magistrates' (JPs) courts and juvenile courts, and the coroner service. Elected councillors also help to constitute various local tribunals and appellate bodies, such as those that deal with appeals on school placements and property valuation and council taxes.

Reorganization 1986

The Local Government Act 1985 abolished the metropolitan counties (see p. 57) and the GLC (see p. 119) in 1986, and redistributed their responsibilities among the local authorities in these areas. Most of the functions of the metropolitan counties were transferred to the metropolitan borough councils (which have thus become the sole principal local authorities in these areas). A number of the functions (planning, highways and traffic management, waste disposal) require that there is considerable coordination, cooperation and sharing of specialist staff resources by the boroughs. However, certain functions – those of a 'county-wide' nature (i.e. police, fire, civil defence, public transport) – were transferred to statutory joint authorities or boards* (or what are becoming known as 'qualgos': quasi-autonomous local government organizations). There is also an appointed 'residuary' body for each metropolitan county area, responsible (temporarily) for such matters as the management of remaining debts, superannuation schemes, etc.

The Government's stated aims in reallocating the functions were to: (i) reduce costs; (ii) simplify the administration; (iii) bring the services closer to the public; (iv) remove the inter-tier conflicts; and (v) remove or reduce local government's spending over and above Government guidelines by getting rid of some of the main culprits.

* Joint *boards*, unlike joint committees, are corporate bodies created under law by Ministers and/or Parliament, not by councils themselves. Unlike joint *committees*, boards have a 'life' of their own (i.e. they continue in being regardless of changing membership); they can hold property, levy charges or precepts and raise loans.

However, the changes have been criticized as 'piecemeal tinkering' and as being motivated by party political considerations rather than administrative rationality (see p. 59). It is widely felt that the reform was too hastily devised and lacking in adequate planning and research (though the Government did ultimately produce a figure for estimated savings of £100 million per annum). Abolition is also seen as unnecessary, since local authorities' ('excessive') expenditure is now significantly controlled through local (council) tax limitation or 'capping' (see p. 324). Above all, the joint boards have been criticized for creating public confusion, for fragmenting what should be a coherent approach to urban problems, and for diminishing accountability and democracy by further manifesting the 'corporate state' (or corporatism – not to be confused with corporate management: see p. 240) where governmental decisions are made by organized bodies on behalf of the public, who may have little or no say, or control. It is also widely believed that bodies such as these tend to be wasteful of expenditure; clearly the Government believes this since, for the first three years, the Minister has had control over the board's manning levels and finances (precepts), i.e. they are rate/tax-capped.

There is already evidence both of increased costs and of public confusion in these areas,[25] as well as considerable anxiety by many voluntary, charitable and cultural organizations about their role and status – and there are murmurs of 'me too' by some districts in the shire counties. There are also some in the Government who wish to pinpoint accountability by creating single-tier local government throughout Britain and removing the confusion caused by county precepts on the districts' council tax; see pp. 316, 317.

5. London's Local Government

London's system of local government has a number of distinctive features – a consequence of its importance as the nation's capital and of its preponderant size. With a population of nearly 7·5 million, London contains one in seven of the nation's population.

Local government in London has always posed difficulties owing to the rapid and continuous growth of its urban population. An immediate problem is to determine what and where exactly London is. Up to the nineteenth century, for local government purposes, it consisted essentially of the ancient City of London: the square mile of heartland which was governed by a Corporation consisting of aldermen, sheriffs, liverymen, freemen and justices – all functionaries of medieval origin. Around this nucleus lay the ancient counties of Middlesex, Kent, Surrey and Essex, which were governed by JPs and parish vestries. The increasing urban development of London led to the creation of numerous *ad hoc* authorities – turnpikes trusts, Commissioners of Police, Boards of Guardians, and Boards of Commissioners with powers of sewerage, paving and water supply – all operating over limited areas. Thus by the mid nineteenth century there were some 300 such bodies (with about 10,000 members) all functioning in the area which became known as the 'metropolis' owing to its substantial population growth and urbanization. (In the period 1801–61 the population increased from 865,000 to 2·8 million in the area subsequently covered by the LCC.)

The Municipal Corporations Act 1835 (see p. 17) had not applied to London. Instead, because of its special problems,

London was the subject of a separate report by the Royal Commission on Municipal Corporations in 1837. This considered the feasibility of placing London directly under the jurisdiction of the central government. On balance the report recommended a system of local self-government for London by extending outwards the authority of the City Corporation. This was not acted upon, but in 1854 another Royal Commission reported and emphasized the problems created by a multiplicity of uncoordinated authorities and communities within the vast urban sprawl of the metropolis and its surroundings, promoted by the railway development of the mid nineteenth century. However, this Commission rejected the notion of a single elected council for the whole of the London area on the grounds of size: that local government should be based on local knowledge and a community of interest, neither of which, it felt, would be possible with a single authority. London was more a collection of communities. The result was a compromise. Under the Metropolis Local Management Act 1855 a two-tier system was to replace the haphazard arrangements then existing. An area of 75,000 acres (containing 2·8 million people) was clearly defined. It contained ninety-nine parishes, but most of these were grouped into districts, each under a district board. These vestries (fifteen) and district boards (twenty-three), together with the City, which remained unchanged, were to continue as the primary units of local government in London, with responsibility for local sewerage and drainage, paving, lighting and street cleaning. Superimposed on this pattern of authorities was a new central body, the Metropolitan Board of Works. It had forty-five members, indirectly elected from the constituent parish vestries and district boards, with a term of office of three years, and it was given responsibility for main sewers throughout the metropolis. However, it was to become more than just a sanitary authority, for subsequently it acquired responsibility for (and achieved some notable successes in) flood prevention, fire services, housing provision, building controls and street improvements. It also had a supervisory role in relation to the public health activities of the primary authorities.

However, such control was weak and did not prevent some dereliction of responsibility by the vestries and boards. The Board of Works lacked authority (being indirectly elected) and failed to inspire civic pride. Furthermore its position was undermined by the continued existence of a number of *ad hoc* authorities within its territory. These included the Metropolitan Asylums Board (established 1867), which arranged for the grouping of Boards of Guardians and their provision of accommodation and hospitals; the London School Board (established 1870), with responsibility for the provision of state elementary schools in London; and the Port of London Sanitary Authority (established 1872), providing for public health in the dockland areas. Meanwhile, water supply was in the hands of nine private companies and gas in the hands of three more.

Subsequently there developed a movement for the reform of local government in London. Various pressure groups were involved – the Municipal Reform Association (founded 1866), the London Municipal Reform League (1881) and perhaps above all the Fabian socialists, who saw London as pioneering a 'brave new England' of municipal enterprise (otherwise known as 'gas and water socialism'). Such notions aroused the hostility of the City and the fears of those who foresaw the ignorant masses holding sway over the richest and most prestigious city in the world. Consequently, the argument became not whether to rationalize the government of London, but how to do so, and in particular which tier or level of authority was to predominate – the county or the district authorities.

The reform of local government in London took place as a result of the insistent pressure of those who argued that, like every other town, London should have a directly elected body to represent ratepayers. But the more immediate reasons were (1) the alleged corruption and investigation of the Metropolitan Board of Works (in 1888) and (2) the fact that the rest of English local government was being reorganized (see pp. 18-19). However, the reform was controversial and modest in scope, partly because of the widespread fears and opposition of those who foresaw a socialist London re-creating something approaching the Commune, the left-wing revolutionary government which ran Paris in 1871, after the Franco-Prussian war. Thus under the Local Government Act 1888 an elected London County Council (of 124 councillors and twenty aldermen) replaced the Metropolitan Board of Works and became responsible for its functions. But the new LCC was given few additional powers, and its area of administration, to be known as the Administrative County of London, covered only the Metropolitan Board of Works' former territory, despite the growth of population. Furthermore, the forty-one vestries and district boards plus the City remained untouched, thus detracting from the authority of the LCC to speak for London – a situation which was exacerbated by the continued existence of numerous *ad hoc* bodies including the Metropolitan Asylums Board, the Boards of Guardians, the Metropolitan Police, Burial Boards, School Boards and the Thames Conservancy Board.

Despite its inauspicious beginnings, the LCC soon grew in stature, partly because of its endeavours and achievements, and partly because of the eminence of its members, such as Lord Rosebery, who became Liberal Prime Minister in 1894–5, and Sidney Webb, a leading member of the Fabian Society. Socialist members[1] and non-members called for greater powers for the LCC. They wanted a municipal takeover of water, gas, transport and the docks. They also envisaged a programme of action to deal with housing, unemployment and land speculation. In the process, they sought the abolition of the numerous vestries and boards in their midst.

These proposals were offensive to Conservative opinion and, following the recommendations of a Royal Commission Report of 1894, but partly also under pressure from the larger vestries themselves, the Government passed the Local Government Act 1899. This Act reorganized the lower tier of London's local government by replacing the mass of vestries and boards with twenty-eight municipal boroughs, each with an elected council. (The City remained unaffected.) They were given significant responsibilities for public health, housing, libraries, recreation and rating, and the whole arrangement seemed clearly aimed at reducing the power of the LCC by enhancing that of the boroughs: a counterweight to the actual or threatened excessive power of the top tier. Consequently, the Act was criticized as having, in effect, broken up London into a collection of twenty-eight power centres (or 'Birminghams'), and further that, being artificial creations, these centres lacked any civic identity of the sort that Birmingham and other county boroughs could reasonably claim.

However, it would be inaccurate to see the London boroughs as county boroughs (see pp. 18-19). They were really a new genre of local authority: something more than town councils but less than county borough councils. Equally the LCC was unique as a county council, for it lacked some of the powers and authority which other counties possessed. Nevertheless, in the course of time, its prestige mounted, and in parallel with other local authorities in Britain the LCC became responsible for a whole range of functions, some of which were new, such as planning (1909) and education welfare (1907), and some of which were transferred from *ad hoc* bodies, such as school education (1902) and health and welfare services (1930).

Meanwhile, the population pattern was changing (see Table 4). The population of inner London (the 117 square miles of the LCC area) stopped growing in the twentieth century and indeed began to fall. The surrounding area of nearly 600 square miles (outer London – the area which covered that originally designated to the Metropolitan Police in 1829) continued to grow rapidly.

Developments in electricity, slum clearance, transport and communications were increasing the mobility of the population and thus reducing the validity of the administrative boundaries and the division of responsibilities. Under the impetus of the LCC, the concept of 'metropolitanism' began to emerge: the idea of a government for Greater London as a whole (both the inner and the outer areas) and having responsibility for services such as public health, planning, housing and transport, on the grounds

Table 4 *The population of London*

	City of London	Inner London*	Outer London†	Greater London conurbation
1801	128,269	959,310	157,980	1,117,290
1851	127,869	2,363,341	321,707	2,685,048
1901	26,923	4,546,267	2,050,002	6,596,269
1951	5,324	3,347,956	5,000,041	8,347,997
1961	4,767	3,492,879	4,499,564	7,992,443
1971	4,245	3,031,935	4,420,411	7,452,346
1981	5,893	2,496,756	4,199,252	6,696,008
1991	4,100	2,530,500	4,359,400	6,889,900

*Comprising the County of London after 1888 and the inner boroughs after 1965.

†After 1965 the outer London boroughs.

NOTE: this Table is based on the official (Census) definition of Inner London, comprising 14 boroughs; it thus differs slightly from the area of ILEA (see p. 116).

that these could be effectively handled only by a single authority operating over the wider area.[2] As if to demonstrate the point, in 1933 the LCC's transport functions were transferred to the London Passenger Transport Board, a new *ad hoc* body with responsibility for services in and beyond the Greater London area.

In 1940, the Royal Commission on the Distribution of the Industrial Population (Barlow) drew attention to the growth of London, which was being accelerated by the 'drift' of the population to the South and East. Also, the problems of reconstruction after the war, coupled with the increase in commuting[3] between inner and outer London, were threatening the integrity of the Green Belt (the zone of protected countryside surrounding London) and led to the urgent consideration of a strategy for planning in the London region.

The immediate result was the Abercrombie Plan of 1944, which recommended the creation of a ring of small new towns around London and the setting-up of a regional planning board. But planning was not the only problem, and clearly something more comprehensive was needed.

In 1945, while the Boundary Commission looked at the rest of England and Wales (see pp. 38-9), a special committee under Lord Reading was appointed to inquire into and advise on the local government problem within the County of London. But this committee was soon disbanded when it was realized that the scope of the inquiry was too narrow and the problem of London government needed to be considered within a regional context. This wider inquiry took the form of a Royal Commission.

The Herbert Commission

London had outgrown its nineteenth-century local government structure. In recognition of this fact, the Royal Commission on Local Government in Greater London (1957–60) was to examine the Greater London area, within and beyond the LCC area, and it therefore included those built-up areas which identified with London but technically formed part of the separate counties surrounding London (the 'Home Counties'[4]). Thus the social unit of Greater London was not reflected in its local government structure: services were administered by seven county councils, three county boroughs, twenty-eight London boroughs, the City Corporation and seventy-one UDCs, RDCs, and non-county boroughs, apart from half a dozen *ad hoc* authorities. As the Royal Commission commented,

The machinery is untidy and full of anomalies. There is overlapping, duplication, and in some cases gaps ... The fact that local government in London does manage to hang together and avoid breakdown says much for the British knack of making the most cumbrous machinery work ... judged by the twin tests of administrative efficiency and the health of representative government the present structure ... is inadequate and needs overhaul. (paras. 286, 696) ... none of these major functions [except environmental health] can be discharged best by the local authorities which exist under the present structure of local government, and ... some of them cannot be adequately discharged at all. (para. 672)

The report of the Royal Commission, published in 1960 (Cmnd 1164), was unanimous in its recommendations for change. Its detailed proposals for a two-tier structure were based on the principle of having as many services as possible concentrated in the hands of the borough councils, except where these could be better performed over the wider area and thus by an 'umbrella' or supra-borough authority. This body was to be the Greater London Council. The Commission recommended that:

(1) The London County Council and the Middlesex County Council be abolished and replaced by a Greater London Council (GLC) whose jurisdiction would also include the metropolitan areas of Essex, Kent, Surrey and Hertfordshire together with the county boroughs of Croydon, East Ham and West Ham. The area thus created would cover about 600 to 800 square miles and contain some 8 million people.

(2) Within that area covered by the GLC, the existing local authorities were to be reduced from ninety-five to fifty-two, to be called Greater London boroughs (except the City, which was to retain its ancient identity).

(3) Greater London boroughs were to have responsibility for the local services of housing, health, welfare, libraries and non-major roads. The GLC would exercise the wider, strategic, functions of fire, ambulances, main roads and refuse disposal. In education and planning the GLC would be the main authority, but the boroughs would have executive powers, that is the GLC would draw up the development plan for Greater London, but the boroughs would deal with local planning applications; in education, the GLC would be the local education authority, owning

the schools and appointing teachers, but the day-to-day running and maintenance of the schools would rest with the boroughs. The GLC would also have some concurrent and supplementary (shared) powers in the fields of housing, open spaces, sewerage and drainage where these functions cut across or involved several boroughs, such as large housing and redevelopment schemes or the very large London parks.

The Government responded favourably to the report, though it did propose some amendments. Reactions elsewhere were more hostile: some, such as Middlesex, sought to preserve their own existence; others, such as the LCC, were afraid of the upheaval to services which the reorganization would cause; and inevitably there were fears, especially in the Labour Party, about the threat to party fortunes. An independent panel considered the local authorities' comments and there was further acrimony and review as the Bill went through Parliament. The result was the London Government Act 1963 (which came into operation in 1965). Under the Act:

(1) An area of local government, somewhat smaller than that suggested by the Royal Commission, was designated as Greater London. It was to have an elected council of a hundred councillors (reduced to ninety-nine in 1973) and sixteen aldermen. (Aldermen were abolished in the GLC in 1977 and in the London boroughs in 1978.)

(2) The area was divided into thirty-two London boroughs (plus the City), each with an elected council comprising councillors and aldermen.

(3) Functions were allocated largely as recommended in the Royal Commission report,[5] with the notable exception of education. Since the boroughs were now to be fewer and larger than originally envisaged, it was felt appropriate to give them responsibility for education. However, in order to preserve the unity of the education services built up by the LCC, it was decided that the inner London boroughs would not individually control educa-

☐ Outer London
■ Inner London Education Authority area

	Population in thousands			Population in thousands	
	1991	(1983)		1991	(1983)
Barking and Dagenham	146	(150)	Hounslow	209	(200)
Barnet	300	(294)	Islington	174	(162)
Bexley	219	(218)	Kensington and Chelsea	145	(134)
Brent	249	(254)	Kingston upon Thames	138	(133)
Bromley	295	(299)	Lambeth	257	(245)
Camden	182	(175)	Lewisham	241	(231)
City	4·1	(5.5)	Merton	172	(165)
Croydon	319	(320)	Newham	221	(210)
Ealing	282	(284)	Redbridge	231	(227)
Enfield	263	(263)	Richmond upon Thames	164	(160)
Greenwich	214	(216)	Southwark	227	(215)
Hackney	188	(186)	Sutton	171	(169)
Hammersmith and Fulham	156	(150)	Tower Hamlets	168	(144)
Haringey	212	(204)	Waltham Forest	218	(215)
Harrow	204	(199)	Wandsworth	265	(258)
Havering	233	(240)	Westminster, City of	188	(184)
Hillingdon	237	(234)			

Figure 10 *Greater London and the London boroughs*

tion. Instead, in that area (the original LCC area) education would be administered by a special committee of the GLC, called the Inner London Education Authority (ILEA), consisting of members of the GLC from inner London, together with a representative from each of the twelve inner London borough councils (who were responsible for rate-funding the service).

Various criticisms have been levelled at the reform outlined above. There were those who thought that the reorganization did not go far enough, and that the boundaries of the GLC area had been too tightly drawn, and others who argued for a regional structure for the local government of London and the South-East. At the other extreme were those who genuinely believed that no major reorganization was necessary.[6] In between were those who felt that the allocation of functions was unsatisfactory and that inadequate attention had been paid to the functions of the *ad hoc* bodies.

Nevertheless, the new London system was, to some extent, used as a model for the reorganization of local government in the other conurbations of England (see pp. 46–50). And a subsequent study of the London system of local government concluded that 'neither the best hopes nor the worst fears of the protagonists in the discussion which preceded the reforms appear to have been justified . . .' and on balance 'the new system represents a distinct advance in the evolution of London's government'.[7] Clearly, the study envisaged further change and drew particular attention to the problems caused by the sharing of responsibilities between the two coordinate tiers of authority (the GLC and the boroughs). This problem was reiterated in the Marshall Report in 1978.

The Marshall Report (1978)

The original aim of the 1963 Act was to create a mainly strategic authority (the GLC) for the Greater London area, while leaving the delivery of services in the hands of others (the boroughs). In practice it had been felt, especially by the Conservative members of the GLC, that the GLC's strategic role had gone by the board and it was involving itself in too many other activities. Consequently, when the Conservatives gained power in the GLC elections of 1977, they appointed Sir Frank Marshall, a lawyer, ex-chairman of the Association of Municipal Corporations and a former Conservative leader of Leeds City Council, to undertake an inquiry.

The Marshall report rejected the idea either of the abolition of the GLC or of expanding it to a wider-ranging regional authority (as some had suggested). Instead its recommendations sought to clarify and enhance the GLC's strategic role while leaving the boroughs with local executive functions. For example, to deal with the areas of greatest dispute, the GLC would drop out of the ILEA and from housing provision. It would thus concentrate on the setting of broad objectives for all London; it would oversee local policies; and it would assume overall control of resources (authorizing capital expenditures and distributing the central government grant among the boroughs). The scheme envisaged other transfers, including the transfer of some functions from the central government to the GLC (such as London's trunk roads and public transport – especially British Rail – pricing and investment). The plan thus involved some devolution of power: from the central government to the GLC and from the GLC to the London boroughs. As *The Times* concluded, the report was 'a constructive attempt to find a useful and clearly defined role for the GLC in the middle of the sandwich of power'.[8]

Abolition of the GLC: the Local Government Act 1985

In 1979 the Conservatives won the General Election and replaced the Labour Government; conversely (but being in mid-term, quite typically) in 1981 Labour won control of the GLC from the Conservatives. The Government in effect ignored the Marshall Report, and instead stumbled into a much more radical and controversial policy: the abolition of the GLC. First, in 1980 the Government set up an inquiry into the future of the ILEA – much to the chagrin of most of the (Labour) inner London boroughs. The inquiry followed an earlier report by a group of London Conservatives, which referred to ILEA's poor educational standards and lack of democratic and financial responsibility and urged its dismantlement. In 1981 the Government announced that the ILEA was to be retained, but this did not stop the argument or the uncertainty.

Second, in December 1981, the House of Lords declared the GLC's transport subsidy – known as 'Fares Fair' – to be excessive and illegal, thus confirming Lord Denning's earlier judgement in the Court of Appeal. Apart from the immediate financial turmoil, this decision brought allegations that the Lords and the judiciary were being political and helping the Government to implement its public expenditure (local government cuts) policy. The case had been brought by Bromley Borough Council and also illustrated an element of the conflict which could arise between the boroughs and the GLC when their party complexions differed – and when ratepayers baulk at the GLC's precept (see p. 316). But the issue also increased calls for the removal of GLC responsibility for transport.[9] This took place in 1984 when London Transport was replaced by London Regional Transport (a 'quango' appointed by the Transport Secretary)[10] because under the GLC 'transport services were not integrated, not economic and . . . not efficient' (Secretary of State for Transport in the debate on the London Regional Transport Bill 1983). However, there are now (1993) plans for privatization.

Finally, there was mounting pressure for the total abolition of the GLC – partly from those who wished to see its functions transferred to the boroughs (as housing virtually has been); partly from those who saw it as merely duplicating the functions of other authorities; and from those who argued that it was redundant since it had so few responsibilities, having lost planning responsibility for the docklands area to a development corporation in 1980 and losing transport to London Regional Transport (LRT) in 1984.

In the White Paper *Streamlining the Cities* (1983), the Government declared that the GLC (and the metropolitan counties) represented 'a wasteful and unnecessary tier of government'; it lacked functions and *raison d'être*, especially since its policing (by 'the Met') is the direct responsibility of the Home Secretary and responsibility for London Transport (run by the GLC since 1969) had been transferred to London Regional Transport. In addition, the GLC was deemed the nation's principal 'overspender' (i.e. above the government's target guideline) to the extent that it had lost entitlement to any government block grant (see p. 313). Within this context, the villain of the piece was the radical and outspoken leader of the (Labour) GLC Mr ('Red Ken') Livingstone. So the rationale behind the abolition of the GLC was an unfortunate mixture of politics, personality, economics and administration.

In April 1986, under the Local Government Act 1985, the London boroughs (plus the City of London) took over responsibility from the GLC for most of its functions, but special arrangements are laid down for many of these. Thus strategic planning is undertaken by the boroughs through a joint Planning Advisory Commission and, where appropriate, under guidance of the Minister. For many of the transferred functions, the Minister requires adequate cooperative arrangements among the boroughs and exercises reserve powers where such cooperation is lacking (thus five Waste Regulation Authorities have been formed for refuse disposal). Thirdly, for certain services (e.g. fire and civil defence) statutory joint boards (comprising borough councillors) have been established. The ILEA was to be abolished but was instead replaced by a directly elected body in 1986; however, under the Education Reform Act 1988, the ILEA was abolished after all (in 1990) and its responsibilities transferred to the constituent inner London boroughs (which receive specific grants to facilitate their new role).

The GLC's responsibility for land drainage and flood protection has gone to the Thames Water Authority; the Arts Council is now responsible for the South Bank complex and the GLC's responsibility for listed buildings and conservation has transferred to the Historic Buildings and Monuments Commission. Further allocations involve the Sports Council, the Theatre Trust, the Lee Valley Regional Park Authority and central government itself. Finally, an appointed London Residuary Body (LRB) was made responsible for those items that could not easily be transferred elsewhere (GLC debts, superannuation, properties, etc.).

In all, London is administered by seventy to eighty (according to definition) different bodies. (For example there are sixteen waste disposal bodies: four statutory, twelve in the hands of the boroughs, but with eleven of them formed into three voluntary groups, together with a London-wide waste regulatory body.) Apart from the diminished accountability and public confusion this has caused, it is doubted by many whether any savings will result (especially since many of the GLC staff have been taken on by the successor authorities). Initially, many of these bodies have precept limits (i.e. local tax capping), and London (1986–7) was treated relatively well in the distribution of Rate Support Grant (sceptics have suggested that this was to make reorganization an apparent cost-cutting success and/or to boost the Conservative Party's chances in the London borough elections). Today only 40 per cent of London's public services are controlled by elected or indirectly elected ('quelgo') bodies. The other 60 per cent of services are run by central government, quangos or 'privatized' companies (see *The London Government Handbook*).

Thus, London has become unusual among capital cities in lacking a metropolitan governing body, which already creates problems. Many believe that the new arrangements cannot last. Certainly the Labour and former Alliance parties have promised a restoration of a GLC-type authority, and even the Conservatives have now signalled plans for an (appointed) London-wide strategic body and (in a White Paper, 1993) for a police authority. Others have called for a Minister for London, as with Wales, Scotland and N. Ireland.[11]

6. Local Government Elections

We have seen that one of the main features of local government is that it is elected. The members of local authorities – the councillors – are chosen by popular ballot, in keeping with the democratic nature of Britain's system of government. Both in theory and in practice, the electoral system in Britain's local government displays a number of democratic features – the right to vote is widespread, as is the right to stand as a candidate; the administration of elections is impartial and uncorrupt; there is plenty of advance notice about elections; the ballot is secret, and it is simple. Finally, the result of the election is direct and immediate: the composition of the council is changed to reflect the voters' preferences, the candidates who gain the majority of votes being deemed elected and becoming councillors for a fixed period of 'office'.

On the other hand, there are a number of aspects of local government elections which diminish its democratic impact. They include the low turnout at the polls; the numerous uncontested seats; the ignorance and confusion about such things as 'warding' or 'election by thirds'; and the possible injustice of the simple majority system of choosing winners. We examine these aspects in more detail below.

The administration of elections is the responsibility of the Returning Officer, usually a senior officer who often doubles as Registration Officer (see below). He is responsible for advising voters of the pending election and the location of the polling stations or (in Scotland) polling places. He also appoints polling officers, who distribute the ballot papers and supervise the polling stations (schools, village halls, public buildings, etc.). The Returning Officer oversees the counting of the votes and declares the winners. He must also receive the nominations of the candidates and check their qualifications and their election expenditures (see p. 127).

The boundaries of local authorities are not determined by those authorities: this is the responsibility of the Local Government Boundary Commissions (see above, p. 51), appointed but impartial bodies who are also responsible for reviewing the electoral districts within local authorities (called 'divisions' and 'wards') in response to population changes.

The right to vote

There is a widespread franchise in local elections; indeed the right to vote is almost universal. Anyone who is at least eighteen years of age and a British subject (or a citizen of the Irish Republic or of the Commonwealth) is entitled to vote. But certain people may be disqualified: those detained in psychiatric institutions; convicted prisoners; and persons convicted of corrupt and illegal practices in elections.[1] In order to vote, however, an elector's name must appear on the local authority's Register of Electors. This Register (which is used for national as well as local elections) is compiled each year by the Electoral Registration Officer (usually a senior official of the district council). He lists the names of residents in the electoral area who are of voting age on the qualifying date (10 October), together with 'attainers' – those who will reach voting age during the following twelve months. (In the City of London, non-residents may register to vote on condition that they occupy property there with a rateable value of at least £10 p.a. Known as the 'business vote', this additional qualification had applied to all local authorities prior to the 1969 Representation of the People Act.) The Register is published in draft form (in about December) and, following appeals over omissions and exclusions or other errors, the final Register is published and is ready for use on the following 16 February.

Voting

Voting is simple enough – a matter of marking an 'X' against the name of one of the candidates listed on the ballot paper (unless there are several seats to be filled, in which case a number of Xs will be required – see p. 131). The Representation of the People Act 1969 allowed candidates to add to their names a short description (in no more than six words) of themselves and what they stand for. In practice that often means simply stating the candidate's party or putting the word 'Independent'. This has helped to remove some confusion and erroneous voting, especially in those constituencies, such as Wales, where several candidates might have the same surname (such as Jones or Thomas).

Voters who cannot attend the poll (at the local polling station, which is open 7 a.m. to 9 p.m.) are allowed to vote by post if they have moved house after the qualifying date, if they are ill or disabled and housebound or if they are engaged in religious observance for the day of the election. Electors who are working outside Britain, such as fishermen or military service personnel, are allowed to vote by proxy, that is they can nominate a person to vote on their behalf. The Representation of the People Act 1985 extended absent voter rights to holidaymakers, and to parish/community council elections. On average about 2 per cent of electors vote by post or proxy, and an estimated 7 per cent of adults (i.e. 2·5 million)[2] do not register for voting and are therefore not entitled to vote – a figure which may have increased with the introduction of the poll tax/community charge, and could affect marginal seats (see p. 333); indeed in 1993, the Office of Population, Censuses and Surveys (OPCS) estimated that one-fifth of the electorate was missing in inner London. There is some dissatisfaction with the present registration system as so many people move house and fail to vote (by post or by making the journey to their former home polling area). It has been suggested that a 'rolling' register system be adopted, and in 1993 a Private Member's Bill to that effect was (unsuccessfully) introduced into Parliament.

The winner

The winner of an election is determined on the basis of 'the first past the post' – a simple majority is all that is required. Thus if there are three candidates and they receive votes as follows – Ellington 4,000, Basie 3,000, Herman 2,000 – Ellington is declared the winner. The same system is used in the General Election for Members of Parliament and it has come in for severe criticism in recent years on the grounds that:

(1) It exaggerates victories and distorts the true results. Thus in our example, while Ellington had 4,000 votes and was declared the winner, he actually had more electors against him (the 5,000 who voted for the other two candidates). The distortion is magnified if we introduce political parties: for example suppose that Taunton is divided into five electoral divisions for the purpose of electing five councillors to Somerset County Council. Suppose also that Ellington is a nominee of the Conservative Party, and that in the other four divisions his party colleagues were equally successful (that is, they each had simple but not overall majorities). That would result in a 'clean sweep' for the Conservative Party in representing the Taunton area, and the other parties would be completely unrepresented even though they attracted sizeable voting support. Islington borough provides a recent case (where, in 1982, the Labour Party won 51 of the 52 seats with only 51·9 per cent of the vote).[3] In practice, parties gaining the most votes may even fail to gain power (a majority) in the council.

(2) It creates upheavals whenever power changes hands. Thus,

when a council changes hands from say Conservative to Labour, there is a lurch in policy in such matters as secondary school organization, council house rents or concessionary bus fares.

(3) Somewhat contradicting the previous point, it is argued that the simple majority system creates permanent majorities on local authorities – areas come to contain 'safe' Labour or Conservative councils. Consequently it may be that complacency or even corruption develops because there is no effective opposition.

The remedy for such defects in the voting system is often held to be some kind of *proportional representation*, in which parties would be allocated seats in proportion to the volume of votes they attracted. This would be fairer and it might well produce coalition councils which could avoid lurches in policy. On the other hand, it might add to public confusion and obscure accountability and a clear choice for voters, since there may be no clear party majority (though this is already the case in nearly one-third of councils; see Chapter 7). Problems would also arise under the proportional system at by-elections.[4]

The right to stand

A candidate must be at least twenty-one years old and be a British (or Irish) citizen. In addition, he or she must possess one of the following qualifications:

(1) be registered as an elector for the area;

(2) have occupied land or property in the area for at least twelve months prior to nomination;

(3) have his main or only place of work in that area for at least twelve months prior to nomination;

(4) have been resident in the area for the previous twelve months, or within three miles in the case of the parish/community council

in England or Wales (requirements for Scottish communities vary).

On the other hand, a candidate (or elected councillor) may be *disqualified* if he or she:

(1) is (or has within five years of the election been) a declared bankrupt;

(2) as a member of the council has been found to have incurred or authorized expenditure which is unlawful and exceeds £2,000;[5]

(3) has been found guilty of an offence which leads to a prison sentence (without option of a fine) of at least three months;

(4) has been found guilty (in his local authority area) of the criminal offence of corrupt and illegal practice at an election (this would include such actions as bribing or using undue influence on an elector, impersonation, hiring vehicles to convey electors to the polls, indiscriminate sticking of posters or exceeding permissible election expenses – see p. 130);

(5) is a paid employee of the local authority (though there are certain exceptions here; for example, state school teachers can be co-opted on to committees (see pp. 197–8) and as an employee of the county he or she can be a member of a district council even though that authority appoints members to the County Education Committee). The government is currently (1993) considering a relaxation of the rules here, starting most obviously with staff in GM (opted-out) schools and colleges/universities.

All these disqualifications except (5) last for varying lengths of time, but most typically for five years. It is perhaps surprising that members found guilty of corruption (receiving bribes, non-disclosure of a financial interest etc. – see p. 205) are not subsequently disqualified unless they come into category

(3). (Councillors can be dismissed if they fail to attend for council business for a continuous period of six months or used council property/resources for personal or party political purposes.)

Perhaps the most controversial of these disqualifications is (5), and many people (especially trade unionists) have argued for a relaxation of this part of the law. It is said, for example, that it is unreasonable to exclude council employees while allowing local businessmen such as estate agents, architects, building contractors etc. to qualify, since the latter may have just as much to gain from influencing council policy. The issue was considered by the Committee on Conduct in Local Government 1974 (see p. 209), which concluded that on balance it should remain unchanged. The rule reflects a more general principle, the 'separation of powers',[6] in that it attempts to avoid the situation in which a councillor who is in the employment of his own local authority might be tempted to manipulate policy to his own advantage (for example in the grading of posts). To make doubly sure, a councillor may not become an employee of his authority within twelve months of his ceasing to be a member.

In 1986, the Widdicombe Committee Report *The Conduct of Local Authority Business* found some 16 per cent of employed councillors working for (other) local authorities or 'twin-tracking' (especially teachers). The Committee was concerned here about such political activity by senior officers and its compromising effects on their ability to serve and advise their employing authority with impartiality. It smacked of self-advancement, nepotism and 'jobs for the boys'. Consequently, it recommended that such officers should be disqualified from being councillors. Thus, under the Local Government and Housing Act 1989, senior employees of local authorities (some 50,000)[7] may not be elected members of any council (nor may they engage in political activities of any kind; see pp. 261-2), though exceptions may be permitted.

Election expenditure

Candidates in parliamentary elections are required under the Representation of People Act 1985 to put down a 'deposit' of £500 (£600 for the European Assembly election) as an indication that they are contesting the election seriously; the money is returned if they achieve not less than 5 per cent of the total poll. This requirement does not apply to local government elections, but candidates are required to produce the written support of a proposer and seconder and (except in parishes and communities) eight other electors for that area. Candidates are also required to nominate an election agent (they can if they wish act as their own agent) whose function is to assist in the election campaign, but who is specifically charged with keeping an accurate record of the candidate's election expenditure. These accounts must be submitted to the returning officer, who will check to see that the statutory limits have not been exceeded. The object of these restrictions is to equalize election chances between rich and poor candidates. Currently, the limits are £192 per ward or electoral division plus 3·8p per elector.[8]

The electoral sequence

Normally we do not know more than a few weeks in advance the date of a forthcoming General Election for members of Parliament: the decision rests with the Prime Minister (the only limitation being that a Parliament must not go beyond five years before it is dissolved and faces re-election). Local councils, however, have a fixed term of office, so that their election arrangements follow a regular sequence (apart from by-elections – see note 4 – and exceptions which occur as a result of boundary changes), and local government elections normally occur on the first Thursday in May.

All councillors are elected for a fixed term of office of four years. In most local authorities (counties, parishes and communities in England and Wales; all London authorities; all Scottish authorities) councillors are elected *all together* every fourth year: this is known as the 'whole council' system (or the 'county system'). For the purpose of these elections, the local authorities are divided into electoral 'divisions' or 'wards'[9] some returning one member, others two or three. In the metropolitan districts, *one third* of the councillors are elected in each of the three years when there is no county election. This is known as 'election by thirds' (or the system of 'partial renewal' or of 'rolling elections') and the local authority is divided into wards with each ward returning (usually) three councillors (or a multiple of three according to the size of the council). Non-metropolitan district councils may themselves choose which of the two systems to adopt. If they opt for the whole council system (and 205 out of 333 have) they normally hold these elections in the mid-term year of the counties. Thus the election sequence runs as Table 5.

It is argued by its supporters that the system of elections 'by thirds' has the merit of keeping in closer touch with public opinion, as there are elections in three years out of four. Also there is greater continuity in council policy and administration as new members of the council will form only a minority and can be 'shown the ropes' by existing councillors who form the majority. Some would claim that this system of gradually changing the composition of councils prevents the full-time officials from 'getting on top' by browbeating new and inexperienced councillors. But it has been argued more cynically that the system of election by thirds is favoured only because the frequency of elections is a device to keep local party machines in motion. In practice it is the large town district councils (apart from metropolitan districts) which have opted for the 'thirds' system: these areas have a longer tradition of local party politics.

Against this system, and in favour of 'whole council' elections, is the argument that elections can be frustrating where they provide only for partial change: that it takes three or four years for a complete change to occur. Apart from frustration and

Table 5 *The local elections cycle in Britain*

	1987	'88	'89	'90	'91	'92	'93	'94	'95	'96	'97
County councils	·	·	✓	·	·	·	✓	·	·	·	✓
Metropolitan and some non-metropolitan districts	⅓	⅓	·	⅓	⅓	⅓	·	⅓	⅓	⅓	·
Most non-metropolitan districts,* all parishes and communities (England and Wales)†	✓	·	·	·	✓	·	·	·	✓	·	·
Scottish regions and islands, and London boroughs	·	·	·	✓	·	·	·	✓	·	·	·
Scottish districts	·	✓	·	·	·	✓	·	·	·	✓	·

* Some may not conform as the election year of any particular non-metropolitan district council will depend on the year it opted for the 'whole council' system. A local authority can apply to change its electoral system at any time, but not more than once every ten years, and it must have a 60 per cent majority vote at the council meeting in support of the proposal. Boundary changes can also interrupt the normal sequence.

† In Scottish communities, the election arrangements vary considerably.

disillusionment, it may be that the public get confused by these partial elections, and perhaps their frequency reduces public interest. Certainly elections cost the councils time and money, not just in terms of the formal electoral arrangements, but also time spent electioneering (does it encourage permanent electioneering?), and, perhaps above all, the need to recast the membership and chairmanship of committees and representation on outside bodies.

Just as the arguments are well balanced, so too is public opinion. A survey for the Widdicombe Committee showed that 47 per cent of the public favour the whole council system, while 44 per cent prefer to vote for part of the council each year.[10] And the Widdicombe Committee itself recommended the county system,[11] as does the Local Government Commission in its current reports on structure. Whilst this is also the Conservatives' preferred system, the Labour Party are in favour of having annual elections in local government.

Voting behaviour

Since elections in Britain are conducted on the basis of secret ballot, we cannot know who votes, how they vote or why they vote as they do (or do not). We must rely substantially on social survey evidence, which is inevitably somewhat limited and patchy. It is also often inconsistent.

A survey for the Maud Report[12] suggested that those with the most favourable attitudes to voting are 'likely to be men, to come from the middle age group (35–64), to come from socio-economic groups 1 and 2 and to have had more than a primary type education'. Those with less favourable attitudes are 'likely to be women; to be under 35 and over 64; to be semi- or unskilled manual workers; and to have had only an elementary or secondary education'. When the same survey investigated those who said they had voted at the last local elections, it found a close relationship to the attitude findings, except that there was no difference in (claimed) voting between men and women (although a MORI poll in 1993 indicated that young women were least interested in politics and least likely to vote). Other surveys[13] confirm some of these findings, particularly the research for the Widdicombe Committee.[14] Thus, in general:

(1) *Age* seems to make a difference in preparedness to vote: people under thirty-five appear to be less likely to vote than their elders. (It may be, of course, that older people exaggerate their declared readiness to vote in response to survey questioning.)

(2) *Sex* seems to make no difference (there is no 'gender gap'), as men and women appear equally likely (or unlikely) to vote, though young married women appear to be the group least likely to vote.

(3) *Class* appears to make little difference in influencing the propensity to vote (somewhat in contrast to America, where studies suggest that the middle class are more ready to vote than the working class).

(4) *Activists*, that is party members and those who identify with and are strongly committed to a party, show a greater than average inclination to vote.

(5) *Owner-occupiers* are more likely to vote than are tenants who rent their accommodation (especially private tenants).

(6) *Mobile* people, especially recent newcomers to an area, are less disposed to vote in local elections.

(7) *Race*. Black Britons seem to vote less often than whites, while Asian turnout is average or over.

It may be noted that 'voting behaviour' can involve more than merely voting. There is the activity of registering to vote, and evidence suggests that, overall, some 7–10 per cent of adults may not be so registered (with perhaps up to 20 per cent in Inner

London). Non-registration is particularly high (30–50 per cent) among young people, the unemployed and the black and Asian community. Reluctance to pay the community charge/poll tax may have exacerbated this problem – indeed it is estimated to have deterred 350,000 potential (and largely non-Conservative) voters.[15]

It is important to bear in mind that these are no more than tendencies drawn from a few local surveys. Any individual local election can reveal considerable variations in behaviour patterns. One particularly interesting development in recent years is the apparent emergence (or restoration) of local factors in voting for councillors. Much has been said and criticized about the overbearing influence of national attitudes and trends on local elections (e.g. how people feel about John Major or Margaret Thatcher's Conservative Government will be manifested in how they vote for local authority councillors). And there is much evidence of such local impact by national politics (see pp. 165–6). But there is evidence too that *local* issues are often influential, as in the success of low poll tax councils in 1990, and these are perhaps becoming increasingly significant (see p. 166), hence the (not unwelcome) difficulty of discerning national or general swings and trends in local election results.

Voting turnout

One well-documented area of electoral behaviour is that of turnout. An examination of the electoral statistics shows considerable variations in the pattern of voting between different parts of Britain (for example Wales compared with England); different types of local authority (for example metropolitan county councils compared with non-metropolitan county councils in England); different (individual) local authorities of the same type; and the same local authority at different times.

One of the factors which affects turnout is the existence of political parties. Generally, it is believed that parties boost popular participation in elections (through canvassing, greater publicity, etc. – see Chapter 7). However, this can be offset where parties dominate or virtually monopolize particular authorities (tradition-ally the Tory shires or certain Labour boroughs).* Here elections can be seen as foregone conclusions and of relatively little impor-tance, though in recent years voters have become more volatile in their voting allegiances, so that even 'safe' seats are changing (party) hands (as with the collapse of Conservative control of so many counties in the 1993 elections). In contrast, it is evident that polling tends to be higher where seats are marginal and the result is uncertain.[16]

The data in Table 6 (pp. 144–5) indicate some regional and national differences in relative turnout/polls and the contesting of seats. Table 8 displays similar differences in party orientation. More detailed information shows other interesting differences in the (local) political cultures of England, Wales and Scotland and their sub-areas. For example, in Scotland the three Island councils consist entirely of Independents, and in Welsh and Scottish districts between 20 and 25 per cent of councils are non-party. (Non-partisan politics is a notable feature of parish and commu-nity councils.)

It was suggested earlier (p. 131) that too-frequent elections may cause a decline in local political interest. If this were so, we would expect to see a lower turnout of electors in those local authorities, notably metropolitan districts, that hold annual elec-tions (using the thirds system) as compared to those authorities, such as counties, that hold elections every fourth year. The figures in Table 6 give some support to this view, since up to 1990† the metropolitan districts consistently polled below

---

* For example in 1992 Labour held 63 of the 66 council seats in Barnsley MB and 17 of the 20 seats in Monklands CD (Scotland), whilst in Castle Point DC the Conservatives held 37 of the 39 seats.

† After 1988, the metropolitan districts became single-tier authorities with the abolition of the metropolitan county councils (and the GLC).

40 per cent while the counties mainly polled over 40 per cent. On the other hand, those non-metropolitan districts which elect their council by thirds experience turnouts which exceed those of the metropolitan districts – for example in 1978 the average was 42·3 per cent (compared to 36 per cent for the metropolitan districts) and in 1979 the figure was 77 per cent (compared to 74·4), perhaps because they are smaller and constituents identify more closely with them. Nevertheless, within the non-metropolitan districts, the turnout is higher (up to 7 per cent higher) in those districts polling every four years.[17]

Clearly, there are other factors influencing events. One such general factor is the size of the ward/division; the smaller the ward, the higher the turnout. Another factor is almost certainly the incidence of non-contested seats. In general, turnout tends to be higher in those authorities where a larger proportion of wards/divisions are left uncontested: in other words, where there is a fight it will tend to be a good one.[18] Two other important influences seem to be population size and stability of population. The larger the local population, the lower the turnout tends to be. And a mobile and changing population will also lower the turnout.[19]

The most striking and apparently consistent feature of the statistics in Table 6 is the low level of turnout by voters.[20] At around 40 per cent, the poll is low in comparison to that in parliamentary elections (which have ranged from 72 per cent to 84 per cent since 1945). The exception was 1979, when the local and parliamentary elections were held simultaneously: electors simply put their 'X' on two ballot papers instead of the usual one. The uniqueness of this event was shown in 1980 and subsequent years, when the average poll in local elections was back to 40 per cent. In 1985 it was 41·1 per cent in (England and Wales).* Clearly, the reorganized (post-1974) local government system has

* Figures supplied by the Conservative Central Office; official figures ceased to be published in 1979.

not succeeded in attracting voters as had been hoped by some advocates of reorganization in the early 1970s[21] (see Appendix 3). The introduction of the community charge/poll tax was intended to raise public interest in local government and boost turnout, and there was some increase in polling, for example in the metropolitan districts where there was an increase from 38·8 per cent (in 1988) to 46·3 per cent (in 1990). But there was no significant change in the Scottish regions/islands and even the metropolitan districts' turnout fell back (see Table 6).

The low polls in local government elections are widely held to reflect a lack of interest, and local electorates are derided as apathetic. There may be some truth in this: an inquiry for the Maud Committee (1967) showed that among those who did not vote in local elections were substantial proportions of electors – over 20 per cent in some places – who said they were not interested in local elections or they did not know, or did not know enough, about the election taking place.[22] A survey for the Widdicombe Committee (1986) revealed 34 per cent who did not know who to vote for because local elections are so complicated.[23] It also concluded that Britain's local election turnout 'is almost bottom of the international league table'. And a survey in 1991 made a similar point but also suggested that the number of people who think their vote is effective in deciding how their locality is governed has fallen since 1965.[24]

However, instead of blaming the public for their ignorance or apathy, perhaps we should look elsewhere for an explanation. It may well be, for example, that people see local authorities as essentially administrative rather than decision-making bodies, so that it little matters to electors who sits on the council: even if the election totally changes the composition of the council, the administrative end-product will be the same. Rightly or wrongly, council decisions may be seen as not very important, since it is felt that the central government and Parliament make the strategic decisions (hence the impact of national politics on local elections – see pp. 165–7). At local level, much policy-making is often no more than an adjustment here and there – whether to raise the fees for adult education classes by 50p rather than £1; which particular schools to close down; what kind of comprehensive school system or sheltered housing design to adopt. These are administrative details which may be of interest to councillors and officers, but are hardly issues of principle to excite the general public. In the nineteenth century the 'improvers' battled with the 'economizers' to persuade the public of the need for municipal provision of water, public health or building controls, but perhaps all the battles of principle have been won, so that now local authorities can be run on a simple care and maintenance basis.

Yet there *are* issues in local government, and policy decisions *can* give rise to considerable argument – and high polls (see p. 554, note 20). Current and widespread examples include the sale of council property, concessionary bus fares, direct labour versus contracting out ('privatization') and rate/council tax levels.[25] While there may be no specifically Conservative or Labour way of paving the streets, awkward political questions remain to be dealt with: whose street is to be repaved first? Who will get the contract? Why not spend the money on a sports hall instead? As Professor George Jones has said,

Political parties are not artificially imposed on local government. They grow out of a local environment, and competition between them reflects clashes of local interests and views on public policies. They differ in their attitudes as to what is prudent spending, over priorities, the pace of development of services, and over who should receive what benefits. Such differences involve differing concepts of equality and liberty, different attitudes about who is deserving or the under-dog and about the scope of public collective activity and enterprise.[26]

To a considerable extent, the current centrally imposed expenditure cuts have reintroduced the nineteenth-century argument, only these days it is more a matter of the 'cutters' versus the 'preservers' of services.

Why, then, does the low turnout persist? Some people blame the councillors – 'they're all the same, so what's the point?' The

Widdicombe survey (Vol. 3) found 66 per cent who believed that 'the people you vote for say they'll do things for you but once they're in they forget what they've said'. Others blame the complexity of the local government system. There is the confusion caused by the voting system(s), which is compounded where elections occur out of sequence (as when boundaries are changed) or where the districts' partial elections coincide with the whole council elections of the parish/community (often involving many of the same candidates).

Another possibility is that the low poll is a deliberate and adverse comment on local government – that people are voting with their feet. Yet the converse may just as well be true: that people are basically satisfied with the services provided and do not therefore wish to promote any significant changes. Indeed the Widdicombe survey (Vol. 3) found a high level (70 per cent) of satisfaction and support for local authorities. Thus, the low poll may be seen as an accolade for local government.

Rather than take too rosy or pessimistic a view of election turnout, maybe we need to adjust our perspective. It may be argued, for example, that the 70 per cent turnout in the General Election is an unreasonable paradigm – after all, General Elections occur infrequently and are accompanied by a lot more publicity and 'bally-hoo'; there is far more personalizing in national politics, with the media concentrating on the party leaders in particular (there are often no such obvious leaders in local authorities). Many people may thus be turning out to vote for rather superficial or synthetic reasons. Besides, voting in a General Election may be held to be a civic duty (like filling in one's tax return) and this attitude has not yet penetrated to local elections. Is it fair, then, to compare local with national elections? Perhaps the 40 per cent figure is a good indication of a genuine interest in politics in Britain – after all, in both the 1979 and 1984 EEC Assembly elections the poll was only 32 per cent rising to 37 per cent in the 1989 election (local election turnout in the USA and Canada is, on average, 25 and 33 per cent respectively). It might even be argued that the local government figure is a *desirable* level of participation, since too avid and active an interest in politics can be politically destabilizing and dangerous.[27]

Furthermore, it may be argued that elections should not be seen as the sole or even the principal criterion of political interest. The vigour of the local press and other media, the growth of 'consumerism' in the form of welfare rights groups or direct action events (rent strikes, marches, sit-ins), the formation of local pressure groups such as civic societies or education campaigns – all of these indicate a vitality of local political awareness and commitment, but using methods which supplement or substitute for the electoral system: after all, polling is only one means of gathering opinions.

Lack of candidates

Less defensible is the large number of uncontested seats in local government elections. The figures in Table 6 show that the proportion of uncontested seats in recent years has amounted to over 20 per cent in many areas (especially in the Welsh and Scottish districts – indeed in the Scottish Island elections, the figure is over 50 per cent, and in the Highland Region it is 40 per cent[28]), though the emergence of the SDP in 1981 has led to more electoral contests, and in 1982 the overall figure was only 1 per cent.[29] (And by contrast it is worth noting that some 13 per cent of councillors are members of more than one council, with as many as 28 per cent in some types of authority.[30]) Before the reorganization of 1974–5 the figures were often much worse: in 1967 the Maud Report commented that 'Recruitment of candidates . . . was a problem in almost all the authorities we visited. In some areas it was difficult if not impossible to find sufficient people of even the minimum calibre considered adequate willing to accept nomination.'[31] The Committee found that over 40 per cent of members of principal authorities had been returned without having to contest elections. 'It seems likely that about one in three of county councillors and about one in two of rural district councillors have never had to fight an election.'[32] (See Appendix 3.)

By contrast, in General Elections, despite higher costs and more demanding campaigns, there is no shortage of contestants: no constituency has fewer than three candidates. In the elections of 1974 (Oct.) and 1979 there were 2,252 and 2,576 candidates respectively for the 635 seats, in 1983 there were 2,579 candidates for the 650 seats, and in the 1992 election there were 2,948 candidates for 651 seats.[33]

Why is there a shortage of public-spirited citizens willing to run for election locally? Many explanations have been put forward, and these are dealt with in some detail in the next chapter. Here it will be sufficient to say that there are two main reasons:

(1) Many of those who have *been* members give up for reasons of time; loss of income; frustration with the methods and controls or with party politics; mobility, especially in pursuit of a career.

(2) Many members of the public do not seek to *become* councillors because they think it might interfere with their business interests or their voluntary activities elsewhere; they are insufficiently informed about local government; or they are just not interested.[34]

In response to such attitudes a number of proposals have been made to try to improve the situation. These were elaborated in the Maud Report (Vol. 1) and include:

(a) the internal reorganization of local authorities by streamlining committees and departments, concentrating responsibility and making greater use of management services – all with a view to making council membership less time-consuming and less frustrating (see Chapter 10);

(b) reducing the degree of Whitehall interference in local government, and giving local authorities a greater general competence (see Chapter 12);

(c) providing more publicity about the activities of local govern-ment through open meetings, improved facilities for the press and publication of discussion papers, and a greater encouragement to schools to include local government studies in their curricula (see Chapter 13);

(d) improving the image of local government, partly through (c) above, and partly through such changes as the abolition of the aldermanic system (see pp. 196-7) and compulsory retirement from membership at the age of seventy;

(e) increasing the opportunities for membership by increasing the scope for release from employment to undertake council duties; reducing election costs by allowing a free postal delivery of election material; and by allowing candidates to stand in the local authority area of their principal place of employment;

(f) the payment of part-time salaries to the leading councillors who give most time to their council duties;

(g) the building of closer relations between local authorities and voluntary organizations;

(h) more training courses for members.

Some of these suggestions – the abolition of aldermen, pay-ments to councillors, the expansion of public relations and the reform of internal structures – have been acted on over the past ten years. Most occurred at the time of reorganization in 1974-5. It is difficult to compare the incidence of non-contested elections in the pre- and post-reorganization periods, but there appears to be some evidence of improvement: for example, in the non-metropolitan county councils, the proportion of non-contested seats fell from a figure of about 50 per cent in the 1950s and 1960s (see Appendix 3) to a figure of 12 per cent in the 1970s. However, bearing in mind that the number of local authorities has been reduced (from 1,500 to 500) and the number of members similarly reduced (from 42,000 to 26,000) it would be surprising if the recruitment picture had not improved.

Table 6 *Local government elections: principal authorities in Britain (selected years)*

Area/Type of authority	Year (1)	Total of electors (2)	Total of councillors (3)	Councillors returned unopposed (4)	% returned unopposed (5)	Councillors elected (6)	Electors in contested areas (7)	Total poll (8)	% poll (9)
COUNTIES – ENGLISH	1973	19,354,642	3,129	396	12	2,731	17,386,510	7,399,655	42·6
	1977	20,195,908	3,129	376	12	2,753	18,397,510	7,795,341	42·3
	1985	22,211,838	2,005	33	1·6	1,969	22,032,571	9,020,828	41·0
	1989	—	—	—	2·1	—	—	—	39·2
	1993	—	—	—	—	—	—	—	37·2
COUNTIES – WELSH	1973	1,982,126	578	109	19	468	1,647,836	906,830	55·0
	1977	2,055,199	578	122	21	456	1,714,085	874,323	51·0
	1985	1,966,449	494	129	26	364	1,460,874	752,723	45·8
	1989	—	—	—	—	—	—	—	44·0
	1993	—	—	—	—	—	—	—	38·2
REGIONS – SCOTTISH AND ISLANDS	1974	3,704,758	507	77	15	430	3,445,472	1,708,792	50·1
	1978	3,809,212	508	134	26	374	3,356,403	1,509,476	45·0
	1982	3,881,552	520	110	21	410	3,586,549	1,540,773	42·9
	1986	3,948,194	524	8	15	435	3,754,717	1,711,040	45·6
	1990	—	—	—	8·5	—	—	—	45·9
DISTRICTS – ENGLISH Metropolitan	1973	8,327,570	2,514	66	3	2,445	8,204,197	2,744,195	33·4
	1976	8,466,953	2,517	13	0·5	838	8,116,271	3,151,964	38·8
	1978	8,482,364	2,517	7	0·3	930	8,327,862	3,099,025	36·1
	1979	8,652,318	2,508	9	0·4	978	8,291,576	6,174,319	74·4
	1986	—	—	—	2·9	—	—	—	39·3
	1988	—	—	—	2·1	—	—	—	40·1
	1990	—	—	—	6·4	—	—	—	46·3
	1991	—	—	—	4·5	—	—	—	40·8
	1992	—	—	—	1·5	—	—	—	32·5
London boroughs	1974	5,300,915	1,867	22	1	1,845	5,182,440	1,893,009	36·0
	1978	5,195,451	1,908	0	0	1,908	5,111,143	2,213,507	43·3
	1982	5,005,832	1,014	2	0·3	1,012	5,000,625	2,213,386	43·8

Year									
1986	5,113,730	1,914	3	0·1	1,911	5,107,386	2,5210,2	45·4	
1990				0·5				48·1	
DISTRICTS – ENGLISH									
Non-metropolitan (or shire)									
1973	19,354,642	13,560	1,665	12	11,879	17,416,523	6,730,485	38·6	
1976	20,228,191	13,614	2,207	16	11,388	17,082,398	7,560,057	44·3	
1978	3,000,429	1,989	47	7	628	2,487,184	1,053,301	42·3	
1979	20,807,223	13,510	2,269	19	9,840	17,186,806	13,216,753	76·0	
1987	—	—	—	11·3	—	—	—	44·0	
1988	—	—	—	4·3	—	—	—	41·6	
1990	—	—	—	3·7	—	—	—	48·6	
1991	—	—	—	12·4	—	—	—	48·1	
1992	—	—	—	3·4	—	—	—	38·3	
DISTRICTS – WELSH									
1973	1,982,126	1,521	281	18	1,240	1,690,233	847,131	50·0	
1976	2,046,375	1,513	316	21	1,194	1,709,809	909,300	53·0	
1979	2,084,700	1,521	396	27	1,119	1,675,048	1,288,467	77·0	
1987	—	—	—	—	—	—	—	40·7	
1988	—	—	—	—	—	—	—	42·1	
1990	—	—	—	—	—	—	—	45·8	
1992	—	—	—	—	—	—	—	33·8	
DISTRICTS – SCOTTISH									
1974	3,655,775	1,110	223	20	887	3,173,701	1,636,859	52·1	
1977	3,735,784	1,114	247	22	867	3,230,280	1,540,280	48·2	
1980	3,808,438	1,123	289	25	834	3,184,075	1,469,496	46·2	
1984	3,887,914	1,152	250	22	902	3,387,754	1,493,280	44·1	
1988	—	—	—	13	—	—	—	45·5	
1992	—	—	—	—	—	—	—	41·4	

Source: Office of Population Censuses and Surveys Electoral Statistics; Registrar General (Scotland) Annual Reports (adapted); J. M. Bochel and D. T. Denver, *The Scottish Regional/District Elections,* Dundee Univ. (various years); *Scottish Government Yearbooks,* Edinburgh Univ.; C. Rallings and M. Thrasher, *Local Elections Handbook(s),* LGC; London Boroughs Association and London Research Centre; individual local authorities.

NOTES. In 1979, local government elections coincided with the General Election. Apart from any other consideration, this meant that the polling stations were open for an hour longer than normal.

The figures in columns (4) and (6) do not always add up to those of column (3) because some elections are held only for part of the council, and also because some seats may be left vacant, as when an election is cancelled (countermanded) due to death of a candidate.

For data on elections in the (now defunct) Greater London Council and the metropolitan county councils, see Table 6 of earlier editions of this book (up to and including the fourth edition, 1986).

However, the proportion of seats which remain uncontested is still significant. It may be that service on the newer, larger authorities is more demanding of councillors. But it may also be that the local government changes were too much for some of the older or longer-standing members, as they were for many London councillors in the early 1960s: in 1973 there were murmurs from some of them about the authorities becoming too big, too remote, too managerial or too bureaucratic. In terms of the 'brave new world' of efficient local government and in terms of attracting members of the 'right calibre', this shedding effect may have been no bad thing. But many felt that, in the process of change, local government was losing its 'soul': it was being seen purely as a mechanism for effective administration and the delivery of services (the 'instrumental' view). What was being over-looked or devalued was its 'organic' aspect: that local government should be seen as an extension or a natural expression of the community. The Maud Report showed an awareness of this problem:

The proposals . . . would encourage more men and women to offer themselves for service in local government . . . But organizational changes . . . will not of themselves achieve our purpose fully. A general change of attitude is needed most of all. The characteristic *result* of local government action is seen in such material things as schools, homes, traffic signs and refuse-bins. But the *purpose* of such action is invariably *human happiness.* And the action itself is taken by *people*, for *people* . . . (Vol. 1, p. xii)

It has also been argued that current participation levels at least provide a fair reflection of society; that there is perhaps a danger in trying to increase overall participation rates, as this may result in a disproportionate increase in influence by one class or interest.[35] How far local government is attracting the right people and fairly reflecting the community is examined in Chapter 8.

So far we have considered the formal organization of local government – that which is based on law or long established precedent. We now turn to examine part of local government's 'unwritten constitution'[36] – an informal, but increasingly crucial, element in local authorities: political parties.

7. The Political Parties

It is very difficult to assess the real extent of party politics in local government, partly because it is changing (especially in the 1970s as a result of reorganization), but mainly because of the problem of definition – when does a group of like-minded councillors become a 'party'? Is a group of active campaigners who seek but lack representation on the council a political party? Do labels always mean what they say – for example how many 'Independent' members are really disguised party men, and how many of those councillors bearing party labels really participate on a party basis?[1]

The vast majority of local government decisions involve no party politics.[2] Yet in some authorities they obtrude into virtually every issue, no matter how minor or routine,[3] and will vary so considerably among the different types of local authority and the different areas of the country that generalization is difficult. Much will depend on:

(1) whether the local parties are branches of national parties (Labour, Conservative, Liberal Democrat, Scottish Nationalist, etc.) or

(2) are purely local organizations, not connected with a national party (ratepayers' associations, tenants' groups, etc.);

(3) the personalities, experience and motives of the councillors, especially the local party leaders;[4]

(4) the political culture,[5] traditions and conventions of the local area.

Consequently, the local party system may be:

(a) *one-party monopolistic:* where a party holds an overall majority of seats (80 per cent or more) and maintains that position over a long period;

(b) *one-party dominant:* where one party persistently has a majority of seats of about 60 per cent and over;

(c) *two-party:* where the leading party has no more than 60 per cent of seats and there is genuine competition from another party, with the reasonable possibility of power changing hands between the two rival parties (as is basically the situation in British central government);

(d) *multi-party:* where third and other parties have at least 10 per cent of seats and power is shifting among the parties following elections or is held jointly in coalitions (several parties combining to form an alliance and thus together enjoying a majority position). Where there is mutual hostility and a failure to cooperate, the parties exercise only a negative form of 'power'; these may be known as 'hung' (or balanced) councils;

(e) *non-existent:* where the majority of the council, say 60 per cent or more, are non-partisan (that is, independents); party members of the council are in a minority and perhaps divided into several small parties.

Within these categories may be found a host of others – for example where parties fight elections under their own labels but drop their separate identity within the council chamber. Parties will vary enormously in the extent to which they exercise discipline over their members, appoint party 'whips' (who resemble school 'prefects') or hold party meetings to predigest council business. Some parties are no more than loose groupings, perhaps bound together by a vague philosophy or by a dominant personality. Like national parties, local parties are outwardly monolithic but inwardly fragmented and often fall out among themselves over policy issues in order to protect a sectional interest, a locality or a particular service. This is often the case where there is a dominant party: in practice that party may divide into several rival semi-parties or factions.

The variety of party systems is rich in local government. The pattern is illustrated, though not completely, in Table 7 (which accepts at face value the labels supplied by the local authorities).

Local party politics in the past

It is often suggested, usually by critics of party politics, that parties are something new to local government: a twentieth-century phenomenon. This is not an unreasonable belief, for to some extent it was the Labour Party, seeking to create a power base, which penetrated local (urban) politics and established at large the devices of party organization, discipline and local policy programmes; these devices were new to local government,[6] and the other parties were slow to copy them. But the concept and experience of political parties were not new. Acknowledged historians of local government have stated: 'By 1890, it would indeed be difficult to find any great English town ... with a municipal council elected on other than party lines.'[7] Numerous studies attest to the vitality of party politics in nineteenth-century local government – in Leeds, Sheffield, Exeter, Liverpool, Manchester and Oldham for example, where the parties were in conflict over such issues as public health expenditure,[8] municipal transport, education and its relationship to religion. The broadest division was between the 'improvers', who wanted to spend along the lines of the 'gas and water socialists', and the 'economizers', who did not. Such a division was well illustrated by the London County Council virtually from its inception in 1889, when the 'Radicals' (or 'Progressives') clashed with the Conservatives (or 'Moderates') over just this issue.[9] What is mainly new to twentieth-century local government is the form rather than the fact of party politics.

However, it is apparent that in the course of the last eighty years party politics have become much more widespread in local

Table 7 *Party systems in local government, 1992 (1988 and 1979)*

	Number of LAs		%		Definition
Non-party	36	(41) (81)	7	(8) (16)	60 per cent or more seats held by Independents
One-party monopolistic	51	(64) (52)	10	(13) (10)	80 per cent or more seats held by one party
One-party dominant	134	(173) (187)	26	(34) (36)	60–80 per cent seats held by one party
Two-party	100	(87) (109)	19	(17) (20)	Two parties, with the leading party having not more than 60 per cent of seats
Multi-party	193	(146) (92)	38	(28) (18)	Third party or parties having 10 per cent or more of seats
	514	(514) (521)	100	(100) (100)	

Based on information from *Municipal Year Books 1980, 1989, 1993* and press reports.
NOTE. The number of councils fell with the abolition of the GLC and Metropolitan County Councils in 1986.

Table 8 *Political control of local authorities in Britain, 1992 (1988 and 1979) respectively*

Overall majority of seats on each council held by:	England County councils	District councils	Metropolitan District councils	London councils	Total
Labour	9 (5) (3)	82 (61) (53)	26 (29) (20)	13 (16) (14)	130 (111) (90)
Conservative	19 (11) (39)	88 (139) (164)	2 (1) (11)	12 (10) (18)	121 (161) (232)
Other	0 (1) (0)	27 (3) (9)	0 (0) (0)	3 (2) (0)	30 (6) (9)
Independent	0 (0) (1)	14 (24) (27)	0 (0) (0)	1 (1) (1)	15 (25) (29)
NOC	11 (22) (2)	85 (69) (43)	8 (6) (5)	4 (4) (1)	108 (101) (51)
Total	39 (39) (45)	296	36	33 (33) (34)	404 (404) (411)

Overall majority of seats on each council held by:	Wales			Scotland			Gt Britain
	County councils	District councils	Total	Regions and Islands	District councils	Total	Total
Labour	5 (4) (3)	17 (16) (16)	22 (20) (19)	4 (4) (4)	22 (24) (6)	26 (28) (10)	178 (159) (119)
Conservative	0 (0) (1)	1 (3) (2)	1 (3) (3)	0 (0) (2)	5 (3) (9)	5 (3) (11)	127 (167) (246)
Other	0 (0) (0)	1 (3) (5)	1 (3) (5)	0 (0) (0)	4 (5) (9)	4 (5) (9)	35 (14) (23)
Independent	1 (2) (3)	10 (9) (8)	11 (11) (11)	5 (5) (4)	13 (11) (16)	18 (16) (20)	44 (52) (60)
NOC	2 (2) (1)	8 (6) (6)	10 (8) (7)	3 (3) (2)	9 (10) (13)	12 (13) (15)	130 (122) (73)
Total	8	37	45	12	53	65	514 (514) (521)

Based on information from *Municipal Year Books* 1980, 1989, and press reports.

NOTES. The discrepancy between the NOC (no overall control) or mixed system of Table 8 and the multi-party of Table 7 arises from different definitions – a multi-party system can have a majority party.

Variation in number of councils arises from the abolition of the GLC and Metropolitan County Councils in 1986.

Table 9 *Local authorities run on party lines* (as a percentage of all local authorities of that type)*

	1992	1988	1983	1979		1972
County councils	98	96	92	92	County councils (England and Wales)	59
London councils	97	97	97	97	London councils	97
District councils (England and Wales)	93	90	90	88	County borough councils	99
District councils (Scotland)	77	79	72	70	Scottish county councils	68
Regions/islands	58	58	50	67	Scottish burghs	43
					Non-county boroughs/ rural boroughs	63
					Urban district councils	70
					Rural district councils	27

* i.e. at least half of the councillors on the council openly belong to a party (see Table 7).

Source: Municipal Year Books 1993, 1989, 1984, 1980, 1973 and press election reports.

government. On the evidence of the last few years, this trend is continuing, especially as a result of reorganization in the mid 1970s. This is illustrated in Table 9.

Prior to reorganization, the smaller and more rural authorities were the ones least likely to operate on party lines. It was anticipated that this situation would change as the rural authorities were merged with the urban and as the smaller authorities were thus enlarged. The figures indicate the extent to which this has occurred, though they cannot tell us how active these parties are or whether they are no more than old wine in newly labelled bottles – perhaps no more than electoral ploys. (It may also be that erstwhile Independent members have taken off their masks of neutrality and openly adopted the party label to reveal their true affiliation.) We must therefore examine the consequences of party politics in local government.

The operation and effects of local party politics

As so often elsewhere in local government, it is difficult to make safe general statements about the role of party politics – so much will depend on the local party system, the local political culture and the influence of personalities. All that can be done here is to indicate some of the effects. The existence and the form of political parties is likely to affect local authorities in the following areas:

(1) *Elections.* There are a number of likely effects here. In the first place, the existence of party competition is likely to reduce the number of uncontested seats.[10] Even where the seat is 'safe' and the likely result is well known (a fact which will probably deter the independent), a rival party is likely to field a candidate if only to 'wave the flag' or give new candidates their first experience of elections.

Secondly, the existence of parties will influence the number and composition of the candidates who stand for election. As we shall see (p. 180), a large proportion of councillors have said that they entered local government at the suggestion of a party. And it is far easier to fight an election on a party 'ticket' than organize and finance your own campaign. Thus parties are responsible for the entry of many members to local government office: they are important agencies for recruitment.[11] In many, especially urban, areas, party competition is keen and so too is competition to stand for election. For this purpose, the candidate has to be selected and nominated by his party (usually by a relatively small committee of the local party). Who we as electors can vote for is therefore often determined for us by the party machines. And while there may be some guidance from the national party on policy, on campaign procedure or in respect of choice of candidates, local parties are usually free to follow their own judgement (or prejudices). Some choose intellectuals or those from a professional background; some choose the party loyalist regardless of background; and others may prefer the ideological 'hardliner' or those who are union-sponsored.

Thirdly, election turnout is likely to be higher where there is a party contest. This is partly because voters can easily recognize or identify (national) party labels, whereas it requires considerably more effort to discern individual non-party candidates and their election 'platforms'. The better turnout[12] is also a consequence of the better election organization and greater publicity which the parties are likely to foster – for example in informing the public about the issues, the candidates and even simple things such as the location of the polling stations. (Not that this increased turnout is necessarily a good thing, for example if people have simply turned out to vote like zombies, without considering the issues or seeking to exercise any real sanction over the elected representatives.)

(2) *Public interest.* We have already seen how parties are likely to encourage members of the public to participate as candidates or as electors. In addition it is likely that the parties will help to stimulate interest in local government affairs by spreading knowledge about issues and personalities, and indeed even by performing an 'educative' role by providing information about such basic aspects as the structure and functions of the local authority. (Such a consequence would be mainly as a by-product of the campaign.) Much of this information will get little further than its own party members, though even this is not insignificant as a step to public participation. But in the process of campaigning, canvassing, sloganizing and conducting arguments through the local press and other media, the parties will have some impact on the stimulation of public awareness and interest.

(3) *The authority's operation and policy decisions.* This is the most difficult area in which to make general statements, since so much will depend on the number of parties; their 'style' (struc-

ture, discipline, outside links etc.); the local traditions and experiences; the size of the council and the size of the authority's area; whether there is a majority party etc. Here we must deal in general tendencies, and many of these are based on the operation of local parties in the more 'political' urban areas. This narrowing of focus is partly due to the fact that most academic research has tended to concentrate on the bigger urban authorities (see note 12, p. 557), so that we know rather more about their party systems. They have developed a broadly 'Westminster' pattern of party politics which can provide a useful model for the study of local party politics generally. One finding is that Labour councils are most likely to provide services to members (Thomas Report: see note 49, p. 563 below).

It is common practice for Labour, Conservative, Liberal, SNP, etc., councillors to form themselves into party 'groups' within their local authorities. Such groups, depending on their size, will often appoint officers – chairman, whip, secretary, leader (if not the chairman) – from among their own members, and perhaps a policy committee (sometimes called the leader's coordinating committee). Inevitably, there is a more or less close relationship between the group and the local constituency party (especially in the Labour Party) and members of the latter may actually attend and speak (though not vote) at group meetings. (These 'outsiders', together with the group's officers, form what is called the 'caucus'.[13]) However, this relationship varies among local authorities. It also varies among parties in that Labour, compared to the Conservatives, has a much more systematic and structured relationship set down in the model standing orders originally drafted by the national party organization in 1930. These purport to give the local party some potentially significant influence over the local groups' policy-making powers. In practice, that influence appears to be limited or variable, and is complicated by the cross-membership of councillors who are also active members and office-holders in their local party. Most party groups meet less than once per month (though Labour groups tend to meet more often; see Widdicombe Report, Research Vol. 1).

What is the *role* of the party group? It is here that we observe the significant impact of parties on the operation of local authorities. The functions of the party group are numerous[14] and may include:

(a) Choosing members to serve on various committees, to act as chairmen of those committees, to choose the leader of the party group and to nominate the mayor/chairman or provost/convenor of the council, where this is separate from leader. In about 5 per cent of councils the majority party does not take all the committee chairmanships and in 13 per cent they do not take a majority of seats on all committees; 20 per cent have committees comprising only majority party members, though these committees are usually deliberative rather than executive; see Widdicombe Report, Research Vol. 1. (In the case of Regina v. Greenwich London Borough Council, ex-parte Lovelace, June 1989, it was held that it was lawful for a council – in effect the majority party – to remove from its committees councillors who were opposed to the policy of the council and replace them with others.) Under the Local Government and Housing Act 1989, committees are now required to have a membership reflecting, *pro rata*, the party composition of the council (though informal one-party committees may continue);

(b) formulating policies for the various council services;

(c) determining the group's attitude to policy proposals which emerge from other sources – especially from chief officers of the authority and from committee reports and recommendations. In this task, individual differences can be thrashed out in the privacy of the group meeting, so that in council or committee meetings all members of the group will speak and vote according to the party 'line';

(d) determining tactics regarding debates, votes and other procedures at council and committee meetings;

(e) enforcing discipline and helping to present a united front in the public activities of the council;

(f) keeping members informed and primed, especially on the

work of committees (since most members will sit on only a few such committees);

(g) scrutinizing existing policy and administration, and perhaps dealing with constituents' complaints;

(h) as a consequence of several of the above points, helping to promote the coordination of the authority's policy and administration.

Many of these activities resemble those of Parliament, and in some respects the local party groups go further than the parliamentary parties, for example in the holding of 'epitome' or dress-rehearsal meetings (prior to council and perhaps committee meetings) at which they vet committee minutes and reports, determine their party 'line' on policy and devise their tactics – who is to speak, in what order, whether they will move for a referral back etc. The result is that the subsequent council or committee meeting will have been pre-empted: the proceedings will be cut and dried and the result a foregone conclusion.

However, not all party groups will attempt to pursue all those objectives. This is obviously the case where no party has a clear majority (e.g. as was the situation in Liverpool during 1974–83 or in the many 'hung' county councils since 1985; see p. 149.[15] Here there is a greater tendency to compromise or cooperation (though it is important to distinguish between the effectively hung and those – about half – where it is nominal, such as where Conservatives get regular support from Independents). But even where a majority does exist, there may be strong differences within the party which disciplinary threats or patronage blandishments cannot overcome. Thus, where party cohesion is weak, there can be frequent conflict between members from different districts of the authority or among different age groups (the young Turks $v.$ the old guard) and perhaps, above all, between members of different committees – especially over such issues as economies and where cuts should fall.[16] Further, while it may be frequent practice for the majority party, by virtue of its superior numbers, to assume a majority on the key committees and to monopolize the key posts (the chairmanship of committees and perhaps of the council),[17] not all such parties take full advantage of their opportunity.[18]

Generally the Conservatives claim to have little truck with many of what they see as inflexible and restrictive party devices[19] such as 'whipping' (e.g. only 23 per cent of Conservative party groups in power always vote together at council meetings, compared with 59 per cent for Labour; see Widdicombe Report, Research Vol. 1, 1986) and while there may be more need for a formal structure and discipline in the Labour Party (for ideological and other reasons),[20] even here there are considerable variations among local Labour groups. By analogy, just as the Labour Party at national level is constantly trying to settle the issue of the proper relationship between the Parliamentary Labour Party and the mass party outside (especially as manifested in the party conference), so there are numerous local disputes over the same theme – how autonomous is the local group, and how independent-minded can individual councillors be allowed to be?

Similarly there are variations in the extent to which local party groups initiate policies. Some groups have policy or advisory committees which act as a source of policy ideas, and it has been claimed that 'in many authorities operating on party lines the party group makes a more significant contribution than any single "constitutional" committee towards general policy initiation'.[21]

That was written in 1967 and even then it was probably unusual for such policy initiation to occur. More often party groups appear to be so overwhelmed with the size and complexity of their existing programmes that they are unable to disentangle themselves and think in broad and longer terms. Consequently, much policy emerges instead from individual committees or the senior officers of the authority. (The introduction of policy committees throughout local government since the reorganization of the 1970s is intended to change this situation – see p. 232ff.)

To sum up, we may conclude with Gyford[22] that

party Groups provide a useful means of exchanging information between members, of pleading cases before a sympathetic audience, and, if effectively organized, of securing the passage through committee and full council of approved recommendations, whatever their source. They also serve to encourage debate and criticism and to ensure, through the existence of Minority Groups, that local Government enjoys the equivalent of a Parliamentary Opposition ... They find it more difficult to operate as co-ordinating devices and as policy initiators.

These limitations are even more apparent in those local authorities where the party system is little developed. And in local government generally it is worth repeating that a great deal of business is not transacted on party lines. 'In committees and sub-committees free discussion and even "cross-voting" is quite common and on many issues there is little evidence of party discipline.'[23]

Political parties: curse or blessing?

There is some evidence to suggest that Labour control of a local authority will tend to increase the levels of that authority's expenditure on education, housing and welfare services, in contrast to expenditure when the Conservatives are in control.[24] Thus in terms of the size and the composition of a local authority's provision, which party is in control is clearly important. However, as we have seen, the mere existence of parties can have very significant effects on the working of local government. The question is whether these effects are desirable or not. The arguments are extensive and quite evenly balanced. Here we must content ourselves with a résumé of the main points.

The arguments *in favour* of parties in local government can be grouped as follows:

(1) *Participation.* As we saw earlier (p. 156), parties help to mobilize voters. Turnout tends to be higher where parties contest local elections, partly because of the better organization and

publicity which they bring. But it is largely due to the fact that parties simplify and crystallize the main issues for the general public. Parties present a publicly known set of principles and policies, as local party manifestos are becoming much more common. At the very least party labels will provide instant indicators of the candidates' policy orientations – what they stand for (or against). In contrast, for electors to sift through a collection of independents' election addresses is to expect too much from the real world.

We also saw (p. 155; see also p. 180) how parties help to recruit council members and reduce the number of non-contested seats. It is also worth pointing out that membership of local government tends to be more representative of the community than is the House of Commons[25] (or the British component of the European Assembly). It is unlikely that local authorities would draw on such a cross-section of the community if it were not for the recruiting activities of the parties. In general then, a smaller proportion of uncontested seats and higher turnouts are the by-products of party competition.[26]

(2) *Public interest.* We have pointed out that parties can help to stimulate and sustain a general interest in local government (p. 156), though it is difficult to gauge the extent of this. Again, at the very least, the party 'ding-dong' at council and committee meetings provides plenty of copy for the local press, and to a lesser extent local radio and television.

(3) *The working of the council.* The main advantage claimed for political parties here is the coherence they can bring to the work of the authority. Parties are 'organized opinion' and where they hold a majority position within the council they can provide a programme of internally and mutually consistent policies. This is much more difficult to achieve in an authority comprising independent members. And there is the added gain of responsibility: with a single party holding a majority and in office, the electors can pin responsibility for the authority's achievements and failures fairly and squarely on the shoulders of that party: it alone may be

held accountable in debates, public meetings and above all at election time when people can vote for or against the incumbent 'team' of party councillors.

It is also claimed that having parties in the council chamber helps to diminish the possibility of domination by officials: parties will have their own views on policy and perhaps some research facilities with which to challenge official reports.[27] Issues like council house sales, education priorities, transport policy etc. can receive deeper and more structured analysis than would be the case in the non-party authority (an argument which resembles the one that favours the entry of 'political advisers' or 'departmental cabinets' into central government). Party groups keep members better informed and may also enhance regularity of attendance at council meetings (members' absences often have to be explained to the party whips). In a number of councils, the leader (i.e. head of the majority party) and committee chairmen form a policy group (or 'cabinet').

(4) *Central government relations.* It is frequently asserted that central government is stifling local government (see p. 370). Supporters of party politics point out, however, that in terms of local government's relations with the central government the existence of local parties can facilitate some influence in an upward direction. Members of local party groups – many of them respected and influential figures within the national parties – can have the case for local government raised in Parliament either directly (where the councillor has become an MP) or through sympathetic MPs of their own party, and this may be particularly effective for the party whose national leaders constitute the central government (see p. 584, note 31).

The advocates of parties claim too much. To a large extent this is because they take the 'ideal-type' two-party system as their model. In practice it cannot be assumed that parties will produce majorities, and thus the pursuance of consistent policies and constructive opposition cannot be assured. The benefits of local party government will depend on the nature of the local party system. Besides, as we have seen (p. 160), parties often take little initiative in the development of policy, and some of the claimed advantages of parties have been obviated by internal reforms of local authorities (see p. 232). Furthermore, in terms of elections, it is not necessarily the case that parties increase the poll, and even where they do so, it is not necessarily a good thing since many can be induced to cast their vote through blind loyalty or prejudice and in complete ignorance of the points at issue.

The arguments *against* parties can be considered under the following headings:

(1) *Participation.* Parties distort the composition of councils by squeezing out the independents: the bearing of a party label has become the necessary if not sufficient condition for election success. Apart from voters' actions, there is a certain amount of self-selection (or denial) here as independent-minded people will be deterred from local politics by the party regimentation and the 'rail-roading' of decisions in the council chamber. Others are discouraged from standing, not because they are non-partisan but because they do not wish to reveal (e.g. in election campaigns) their affiliation for social or business reasons. This latter group may be small (the Maud Committee believed it to be only 1 per cent), but they are significant because they represent sections of the community (such as business or professional people) which arguably should be adequately represented.[28]

Another aspect of this issue arises from the fact that, in the process of selecting candidates, parties may use the wrong criteria – rewarding loyalties and services to the party and perhaps thereby overlooking those with the desirable qualities of a councillor (see p. 155). The whole process may also create cynicism if it appears to degenerate into a self-perpetuating clique arrangement – especially likely where one party dominates the council.

(2) *Elections.* Where one party does so dominate, electors may be discouraged from voting because they see the result as a foregone conclusion. However, perhaps the greatest indictment of parties in this field is the impact of national issues. Rightly or wrongly

electors identify local party groups with the national parties and either vote for their party election after election through blind loyalty and without regard to local issues, or they switch their voting support among the local parties in response to the actions (or inactions) of the central government party: in effect it is national rather than local politicians who are being held accountable on local election day. Thus a general dissatisfaction with the Thatcher government, or say its foreign policy (e.g. supporting the USA over its bombing of Libya in 1986), will be reflected in a uniform swing against Conservative councillors throughout the country regardless of their individual worth and irrespective of local issues. Professor Miller found that over four-fifths of the electorate vote in accordance with their national political preferences when they voted in local elections:

Local effects seem to move about one tenth of local voters away from their national preferences and toward 'less political' candidates (Alliance and others . . .). And local influences may determine the local choice of another tenth of local voters who have no national preference.[29]

Local elections thus become miniature general elections, and the good councillor is penalized along with the bad if his party is out of favour nationally: the councillor becomes 'protest fodder' and the quality of local government is jeopardized. 'Those who treat local polls as surrogate general elections are merely playing the centralist game.'[30]

This is well displayed in Figure 11. It shows a remarkably close relationship between voters' attitudes to the national parties and the local parties in one local authority.[31] Further illustration occurs in Table 10, which shows a congruence between the local voting in twenty large cities and in proximate General Elections.[32]

The close relationship between national trends and local voting patterns appears to be further confirmed by recent events. In 1981 a series of spectacular Parliamentary by-election successes by the Social Democrat/Liberal Alliance was accompanied (though somewhat less spectacularly) by Alliance gains in local

Figure 11 *Birmingham and the national swing*
(NOTE: *Swing = [% gain by major party + % loss by other] ÷ 2*)

Table 10 *Local (city) elections and General Elections, 1965–79*

Date	Labour control	Conservative control	Other or no overall control
1965	17	2	1
1966	General Election – Labour wins		
1970	1	16	3
1970	General Election – Conservatives win		
1973	16	3	1
1974	(Feb) General Election – Labour wins		
1974	14	3	3
1974	(Oct) General Election – Labour wins		
1978	6	11	3
1979	General Election – Conservatives win		

elections. Then in 1982 we witnessed the 'Falklands factor' – when the widespread national support for the Government's policy of armed retrieval of the Falklands carried unusually large numbers of Conservatives to victory in the local elections. Similarly in 1992–3 there were sensational Liberal Democrat victories in Parliamentary by-elections followed by outstanding gains in the county council elections.

It should be noted, however, that even in these elections there were many aberrations and unexplained local variations, when Conservative candidates lost heavily. Such variations can occur as a result of candidate personality or local performance, and so on.[33] There is a danger in generalizing about local results, turnouts and trends; not only are there considerable variations among individual council results (in turnout, party allegiance, etc.) but there are significant (and fascinating) variations *within* local authorities, i.e. differential patterns or trends in party support or 'swing' and in turnout as between wards or divisions of the same local authorities. It does appear that local issues are actually becoming a more significant factor in local elections: that with the limitations on resources since the mid 1970s, difficult *local choices* are having to be made about priorities, what services to cut, which staff to shed, which client groups to disappoint.[34] And in one recent survey, 56 per cent of respondents claimed to vote in local elections on the basis of local rather than national issues.[35] Intense involvement with parochial issues – known as 'community' or 'pavement politics' – has long characterized the Liberal approach (see p. 456), and as multi-party politics and 'hung' councils become more commonplace, so does the importance of local factors, including the level of rates or council tax.[36] In the 1990 elections there was the 'London effect', in which low poll tax Conservative boroughs bucked the trend to Labour.[37]

(3) *The working of the council.* The main criticisms in this area are five-fold. Firstly, party-based councils are prone to treat too many items of business as party issues (see p. 156).[38] This may not only prevent the issues being dealt with on their own merits, as national policies are adopted in doctrinaire fashion by local party groups, but it may slow down the whole process of decision-making and implementation, as parties seek to obstruct and score points off one another. There is the danger of too much

party bickering and not enough civil engineering! This is especially likely in a multi-party system where no party has a majority (some officers regard the hung council situation as 'sheer hell'[39]). Some such criticisms were directed at Liverpool City Council following the Toxteth riots in July 1981 and the school disturbances in 1982. In 1991 Avon CC's hung council had to choose between three different (party) budgets. (It is said in favour of the hung council that at least the parties have to confer together to reach decisions, even if it takes longer.) There is the added danger that deadlock in the council chamber can result in power slipping into the hands of the officials.

Secondly, and conversely, wise decision-making can be jeopardized because chief officers (to preserve their impartiality) are normally absent from the meetings of party groups and cannot therefore provide the sort of guidance and advice which they would be called on to give at council and committee meetings in non-partisan authorities. Where there is a party system, the party group decisions are often final, the council/committee meeting becomes a formality and officials are too late to make a contribution (for example it is suggested that the GLC's legal conflict over its fare subsidies could have been avoided if it had been more fully advised by its officers[40]). Furthermore, where the official does make a contribution to the council/committee discussion he will often feel frustrated by seeing his advice ignored and decisions being made 'on the nod' (for a graphic illustration, see p. 291; see too notes pp. 599–600).

Thirdly, where control of the council is subject to frequent, see-sawing change of party control (every four years at 'whole-council' elections), policy lurches can be time-consuming and wasteful, and again may be very frustrating to the officers and staff, as well as the local population (as in Tameside's switchback on comprehensive schools – see p. 373).

Fourthly, the party system is condemned as undemocratic. As in Parliament, the elected members are expected to 'leave their minds outside the chamber' and slavishly obey the dictates of the party caucus. They cannot exercise their independent powers of judgement: once the party decision is made – even where only one vote had decided the issue – party solidarity requires members to toe the party line. Free speech is stifled and individual initiative is dampened; council debates become sterile, set pieces; minds are closed and decisions are pre-determined. This criticism has even greater poignancy in so far as there is an input to the decision-making from outside, either in the form of the 'outsiders' sitting in the caucus meetings (see p. 157) or in the form of the manufacture of policies by the parties' national headquarters. But what has been of greatest concern recently is the abuse of power by majority parties, such as the use of council funds for apparently party political purposes and 'advertising' (e.g. the GLC's anti-abolition campaign, and the campaign against rate-capping; in 1985 Bristol Council (Labour) was criticized for holding a free – on the rates – public seminar on social security reform as it was seen merely as a vehicle for publicizing the Labour Party's views on that subject), or the virtual cornering or hijacking of decision-making procedures to exclude, perhaps completely, minority party groups (see p. 286) or even some of its own members, as allegedly happened in Liverpool's (Militant) Labour Party (and prompted an inquiry by Labour's head office in 1986).

More generally it is alleged that a number of councils have become 'poisoned' by ideological politics, with the result that councillors and/or staff are being harassed and intimidated, party supporters or sympathizers are given sinecure jobs (some as 'advisors'), other council posts (senior officers, head teachers, even gardeners) are determined by party affiliation or support, and it may even reach down to the determination of school syllabuses, or the purchase of books. Some councils have banned what they regard as obstructive or conspiratorial chief officer group meetings (see p. 270). A further development is the appointment to chief officer posts of partisan members of neighbouring councils (known as 'twin-track politicians': see pp. 173–5, 261). More obvious is the impact on policy decisions, with councils veering into areas which some commentators regard as inappropriate or irrelevant to local politics and which bring local government into disrepute (see note 17, p. 599), an example of which was the ban on the purchase of, or advertising in, certain newspapers by councils which sympathized with the printers in dispute in 1986 with News International. Such action by Derbyshire was declared illegal in 1990. (Other councils ban publications from their libraries for political reasons.) Concern has also been expressed about management (or technical) decisions being overlaid or influenced by political or ideological considerations in such areas as competitive tendering contracts or the local administration of services (decentralization or 'going local'; see pp. 445–6), and school governors.[41]

Finally, political parties are often condemned for engendering artificial and unnecessary conflict, that 'the regular stirring up of political feeling in small communities is harmful'.[42] The implication here is that small communities are naturally consensual and in harmony.

Clearly a number of these points are based on exaggerations. For example, party discipline and 'rubber-stamping' is by no means universal even in those authorities with a developed party system (see p. 156), for not only are there different party systems but local parties operate in more or less their own unique way (e.g., in some authorities majority parties do not take majorities on all committees (see p. 158); or in some, party groups are formally constituted as council committees; and Widdicombe provides evidence of an actual decline in the partisan appointment of officers. But later research suggests an increase in party activity[43]).

As regards the absence of chief officers from crucial group meetings, there is evidence of ways having been found round this problem[44] and besides, as we have seen (p. 161), most business is transacted without regard to party considerations. Under the 1989 Act (following Widdicombe; see p. 176) officers' terms and conditions of service have been amended (through LACSAB, see p. 252) to allow them to attend and provide advice to councillor party groups (including minor parties). Requests for such advice will have to pass through the chief officer who will be responsible for nominating the officers involved.

The assumption that the small community is more in harmony without political parties is even more questionable. Even if there were no parties, there would be conflicts of personality (among councillors or between officials and councillors); or clashes over sectional interests (such as tenant groups or shopkeepers); or rivalry among territorial blocks (councillors from a formerly autonomous area forming a separate identifiable group within the council and protesting their area's relative neglect within the larger amalgamated unit of local government); or there may be functional competition between different committees and services. When 'independent' councillors thus form cliques or unspoken agreements we have an emergent or concealed party system. The 'open' political parties cannot create conflict from nothing: their aim in this respect (if indeed they are aware of having an aim) is to heighten people's awareness of issues and their relationship to those issues. Indeed local parties can help to overlay some of the local divisions and reduce petty squabbles and parish-pump attitudes. Further, it may be argued that parties make a positive contribution to the well-being of the community, in that many councillors are initially recruited by the parties and subsequently move on to give service to voluntary organizations.[45]

The assertion that there ought to be 'no politics in local government' and that the council should 'pull together in the best interests of the community' leaves two vital questions unanswered. First, what *is* the community? Is it the adult population? people who live in families? sport fanatics or culture vultures? motorists or pedestrians? Sunday shoppers or worshippers? And, second, what is *best*, and who decides what this is? Politics is about choice – 'who gets what' – and it is not at all obvious whether the town would benefit, say, more from the provision of a new sports centre or from the installation of central heating on a council housing estate. Parties may distort some of the issues, but they do not create them, and to a large extent they help to articulate and clarify them for the public at large. Above all, parties do not exist by command of the law: they exist because they attract popular support. If they were as dreadful as their critics suggest, independ-

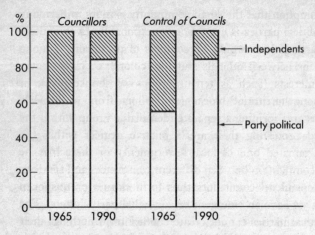

Source: based on figures in *Municipal Yearbooks*

Figure 12 *The decline of the Independent councillor*

ent candidates would do far better in elections than is currently the case. In England and Wales in 1975 there were thirty-one councils wholly non-party or entirely composed of independents; in total there were some 4,000 independent or non-party members (17 per cent of all councillors). In 1989 there was only one such council (the City of London Corporation), and the number of independents or non-party councillors had fallen to just 10 per cent of the total[46] (see Figure 12).

However, such was the concern of the Government about the developments in local party politics, that in 1985 it appointed the Widdicombe Committee to inquire into 'the practices and procedures governing the conduct of local authority business'.

The Committee confirmed that there had been an increase in party politics in local government and that local party politics had 'taken on a new intensity'. This took a number of forms, including an increased ideological orientation (e.g. with some 63 per cent of councillors now believing that their first duty is to implement the party's election manifesto); a greater polarization of the parties and an increased propensity to organize themselves within their authorities; a tendency to control officers more and to challenge established frontiers between members and officers;[47] and a greater penetration of national issues into council business.

Nevertheless, it found that there was still a considerable bi-partisan approach to local administration, and that a number of important local inter-party agreements or conventions had developed to moderate the erstwhile conflict or potentially harmful consequences.[48]

In many authorities the Committee found a number of benefits in the party system, such as increased democratic choice, enhanced coordination, greater consistency, better accountability. But it also found cases of abuse and corruption, such as showing favour or allowing party considerations to influence staff appointments, planning permission, the allocation of services or the allocation of funds (e.g. to outside groups). It was also critical of councils wasting time scoring party points during council business and engaging themselves on national rather than local issues. Consequently, while the Committee expected to see a continuing trend towards political organization in local authorites, it did 'not regard this in itself as either desirable or undesirable'. But the growth of party politics has caused 'definite strains and stresses', and as a result the Committee concluded that there was a need to take account of this growth: to provide some formal recognition of local party politics and introduce some clarifying and regulatory measures.

Some of the Committee's proposals (which it hoped to see implemented partly in legislation, but also in codes of conduct and explicit, publicly available local arrangements) dealt specifically with party politics; others were more general in nature but did bear indirectly on party matters. Among its recommendations were:

(a) all decision-making committees should reflect the composition of the full council, and should comprise only elected members (or where non-elected members, such as co-opted members or advisers, attend, they should not vote);

(b) council meetings should provide opportunities for business chosen by minority parties and providing a period for question time;

(c) national parties should seek to ensure that local party groups: (i) keep a publicly available list of those attending their meetings; (ii) limit the number of non-councillors so attending and preclude their voting at such meetings; (iii) debar from attendance anyone disqualified from council membership following surcharge (see p. 348); and (iv) apply the principle of conflict of interests and disclosure at group meetings (as well as in normal council and committee meetings; see pp. 205–6);

(d) officials at the rank of principal officer and above should be barred from political activity (including holding office in a party, holding or standing for public elected office, canvassing or speaking/writing in party political debate);

(e) staff appointments should be based on merit and fair and open competition (with provision for an independent assessor in the selection of chief executives, for whom dismissal should only be permitted where at least two-thirds of council members concur);

(f) chief executive officers (see p. 265) should be legally responsible for all appointments, discipline and dismissal of staff below principal officer level, and also for initiating discipline and dismissal of staff above that level;

(g) local authorities should be allowed to attach staff to party groups (so long as they are clearly identified and are limited in numbers and seniority);

(h) officers should be allowed to attend party group meetings (provided requests from the groups are directed through the chief executive officer).

In an interim report (July 1985) the Widdicombe Committee recommended that local authority publicity of a party political nature should be made illegal, and that council's powers to issue publicity generally should be clearly confined, i.e. in effect to sections 142 and 111 of the Local Government Act 1972 (sections 83 and 69 of the 1973 Act in Scotland). The committee commented that 'tone and presentation is important and it should be controlled . . . on matters of political dispute and sensitivity, it is wrong for public funds to be spent on material that is strident, sloganized or partisan in style'. But many (including some of the committee) disagree and feel that persuasion is a legitimate objective for councils when providing information; that central government itself uses persuasive information; or that the position of local government has changed so dramatically in recent years that constitutional principles and the law courts are no longer sufficient for its protection. Nevertheless, the Government quickly pushed through the Local Government Act 1986 to prevent 'propaganda on the rates'. The Act prohibits the financing or the publication by local authorities of material 'designed to affect public support for a political party'. The Government is empowered to issue codes of recommended practice regarding content, style and distribution of local authority publicity, but it may well introduce more legislation to restore the wider powers it sought but lost when the legislation was amended in the House of Lords. These powers were strengthened in the Local Government Act 1988.

In response to the main report of the Widdicombe Committee, the Government has endorsed many, though by no means all, of the recommendations; it has already implemented some of them, and proposes to implement others, largely through the Local Government and Housing Act 1989. Thus (a, above) is agreed, with the proviso that advisers be suitably experienced or expert and (with the exception of teachers) should not be disqualified from council membership; (b) is agreed except for the question-time suggestion; (c) is accepted; (d) is accepted in principle, but officers will be identified as those who are chief officers or hold 'sensitive' posts that may involve giving advice to councillors, having contact with the public and media or exercising delegated discretionary powers, or more generally, those officers with salaries of between £19,650 (Scotland), £19,632 (England and Wales) and £21,354 (London) per annum (1991) or more. (The figure is subject to the Minister's determination, and is currently linked to officers' pay scale, at 'spinal point' 44 (a salary grade).) Collectively these form the 'politically restricted' group of officers; (e) is agreed except for the special provision for the chief executive officer; (f) is accepted in so far as an officer (rather than necessarily the chief executive) is identified and he or she is responsible for staff appointments up to the level of the politically restricted group – in matters of discipline and dismissal, councillors will continue to be involved (subject to certain safeguards); (g) was originally rejected on the grounds that 'it is inappropriate for local authorities to employ at public expense staff whose purpose is to undertake political support duties for a particular party group or councillor rather than serve the council as a whole'[49] (especially as they would have to be available to all party groups), but these have now been approved, though limited to a maximum of three per authority and with a salary maximum (in 1993) of £24,842 (from the original figure of £13,500); (h) is accepted (see p. 261).

Items (a) and (d–g) are being given effect in the Local Government and Housing Act 1989. The others will be legislated for at a later date or simply commended for action by the appropriate bodies, be they the national parties, local authority organizations and associations and local councils themselves.

Some critics of political parties in local government find solace in the thought that, as the standards of services become more uniform throughout the nation and as control by the central government is extended, so the scope for local party politics diminishes. Whether this optimism is justified is doubtful, but they also like to comfort themselves with the thought that the extensive nature of party politics in Britain reduces the scope for what many people see as a far more sinister phenomenon – the pressure group (see p. 403).

8. The Councillors

There is something of a shortage of people willing to stand for election as councillors. As we have seen, in some areas there are as many as 50 per cent uncontested seats for major local authorities, and overall the figure is something like 20 per cent. In addition, there are a small number of vacancies on the local authorities of Britain – council seats which remain unfilled because no one is willing to serve (although some of these vacancies are temporary – the result of death or resignation and awaiting a local by-election). In 1991, Secretary of State Michael Heseltine, speaking at the Conservative Party Conference, publicly proclaimed that 'it is getting harder to attract people to serve on councils. Not just people of the necessary calibre – it's often difficult to attract anyone at all. And it's affecting all parties.'

Who'd be a councillor?

Such deficiencies are not altogether surprising considering the disadvantages of being a councillor. Chief among these is the time it consumes – the average councillor spends 74 hours per month on his or her public duties (see pp. 188–91). This is a large amount, and it can cut severely into his or her social life. It can also interfere with business and earnings. Others find it a physical and mental strain, and many councillors find their duties frustrating. This may be the result of experience with the administrative machinery – the limited powers of local authorities, restrictions by the central government, delays in reaching or implementing decisions or difficulties in obtaining finance.

Alternatively, the reluctance to serve may be the result of bad relationships with other councillors, either on a personal level or via party politics – the Minister (above) blamed 'the local politicking that Labour has introduced into the culture of local authorities over the last two decades'. Others may be put off by what they see as hostility or ignorant attitudes of the public. We get some idea of the scale of these difficultries from Table 11, which is based on a survey of councillors.[1]

There are other reasons why people are unwilling to enter or remain in local government service. For some, the times of meeting[2] are inconvenient – for example, evening meetings may not suit those who dislike night driving, while afternoon meetings may be awkward for housewives and mothers. Meetings at any time may be difficult for those in full-time employment and attendance may involve some loss of income. Although the Employment Protection (Consolidation) Act 1978 requires employers to allow their employees to take reasonable time off to attend public duties, it may be done grudgingly, jeopardize promotion prospects and create friction with colleagues.[3] A more recent report suggests that in so far as employers are reluctant to allow councillors time off to perform their council duties (which is a particular deterrent to those at the beginning of their careers) it may be feasible to consider making payments of councillors' allowances (see below) directly to employers.[4] The Widdicombe Committee found private employers compared well with the public (State) sector, though it found wide differences in practice among the former and urged a more positive and flexible approach; they also found manual workers in particular had problems with lost earnings and getting time off. (In view of the apparent abuse by some local authorities in granting virtually full-time paid leave of absence, the Committee recommended that there be a statutory upper limit on paid leave which public sector employers may grant employees for council duties, and the Government has imposed a maximum of 208 hours p.a. (1989

Table 11 *Councillors' probable reasons for eventually giving up council work, and ex-councillors' reasons for leaving*

	Councillors'* probable reasons for giving up %	All ex-councillors' reasons for leaving %	Ex-councillors' (under 65) reasons for leaving %
Personal reasons:			
Ill-health/tired/found it a strain	22	23	⎱ 21
Old age	21	7	⎰
Interference with business or family life	17	14	15
Amount of time given	5	18	25
Moving from area	5	13	16
Became MP	1	—	—
Council reasons:			
Frustrations of party system	5	8	⎱
Frustrated by other aspects of local government organiza- tion	12	13	⎰ 22
Other answers/not answered	12	4	1
Total	100	100	100
(Numbers)	(1,044)	(401)	(289)

*Excluding those who said: 'Can't think of anything.'
Source: *The Management of Local Government* (Maud Report), HMSO, 1967, Vol. 2.

Act).) Some potential councillors are put off by the increasing complexity of council business, the central controls and financial constraints and having to cut budgets and reduce services, or the perceived vilification of local government by the central government,[5] and others may be put off by their image of local government (parochial, bureaucratic, corrupt, etc.). Further (as we have seen in Chapter 6 above), some local seats are so safe, either in personal or in party terms, that it is regarded as a hopeless task to fight an election there.

Although professional and business/managerial occupations appear to be well represented in local government,[6] there is a feeling in some quarters that many potential councillors from such a background are lost to local government on account of their mobility, especially in the pursuit of their careers. However, while there is clearly something in this, a study in Bristol[7] suggested that many such people are lost to local government because they prefer to give their services to voluntary organizations (partly because it affords greater status).

The problem may be eased in so far as a reorganized system of unitary authorities is likely to result in far fewer councillors – a reduction of 50 per cent seems likely. However, this would not be good for democracy, especially since (excluding local councils) Britain already has fewer councillors than many countries abroad. For example, whereas in Britain there is one councillor per 2,200 of the population, in most European countries the figure is below 500. (A number of these issues were considered by the working party on councillors in 1993; see p. 245 below.)

In spite of these obstacles, why are so many people willing to become councillors? For example, in 1978 for the 3,466 seats in England and Wales which were contested (about 200 were not) there were some 9,000 candidates. According to one survey[8] only a minority of councillors themselves had the idea of standing: these were often driven to seek election in order to promote or campaign against a specific issue. Over three quarters said they were asked to stand, and most of these said they had thought little or not at all about becoming councillors beforehand. About one third had been asked to stand by political parties and another third by personal friends or acquaintances. Others were asked by organizations such as trade unions (which may 'sponsor' them, as they do MPs),[9] or religious, welfare, business or civic groups.

Once on the council, there are a number of satisfactions to be gained from being a councillor:

(1) One of the most important seems to be that of giving service to the community. (Some may treat it as a form of apprenticeship before standing for Parliament. In the 1992 General Election a record number of parliamentary candidates – 880, or almost 50 per cent – came from a local government background, either as current or ex-councillors. This may be an indication of local government's importance as a national political issue; see Chapter 14.)

(2) There is a certain prestige attached to being a councillor (although the Maud Report doubts the importance of this these days[10]).

(3) Many find satisfaction in council work (decision-making, leadership, involvement) as a contrast and compensation for their paid employment (which may be more routine and undemanding or lacking authority). Retired members may find it a substitute for their former employment. And the hen-pecked husbands or intimidated wives may find it a compensation for their lack of status at home.

(4) The town hall has been described as 'the best club in town' and many councillors do find that membership of the council can enhance their private and social life.

Portrait of the councillor

There are about 25,000 councillors in Britain's principal local authorities – about 1 per 2,200 of the population (plus some 70,000 parish and community councillors). Like MPs they are elected as local representatives. But just how *representative* of their community are they? How typical are they of the person in the street?

The pattern varies somewhat among communities and types of

local authority – for example, London borough councillors tend to be younger than the national average councillor; there are fewer women councillors in Welsh and Scottish councils. Overall, the picture[11] reveals that councillors are not a cross-section of the community: they are *un*typical. Compared to Britain's population as a whole, councillors tend to be:

(1) older – 50 per cent of councillors are over the age of fifty-four, and less than 10 per cent are under thirty-five years of age; this contrasts with the national population figures of 37 per cent aged fifty-five and over, and nearly 30 per cent aged between twenty-one and thirty-four; 25 per cent are retired (compared to 16 per cent in 1976);

(2) male – less than one councillor in five (19 per cent) is female (compared to 12 per cent in 1964 and 17 per cent in 1976);

(3) owner-occupiers – 85 per cent of councillors own their home, compared to 60 per cent for the population as a whole;

(4) white-collar in occupation – only 5 per cent of councillors have an occupational background in semi-skilled or unskilled manual work, compared to the national figure of 24 per cent; on the other hand, they contrast with the national figure of 23 per cent by having (especially among the Conservative members) 59 per cent in professional, managerial and intermediate white-collar jobs. Despite much press speculation, only 36 per cent have jobs in the State sector (i.e. about the same as the national figure);

(5) better educated – while 20 per cent of the population experience education at A-level or above (1983 figure), the proportion of councillors is 40 per cent;

(6) better paid – earnings of occupied councillors (in 1976) were approximately one third higher than the national average: no doubt a reflection of their educational and occupational background, and age; in 1985, some 40 per cent of councillors had incomes of £10,000 or over, compared to the national average earnings figure of £9,000 p.a.

Table 12 *Councillors by age, 1985*

Age-range	% of whole adult population		% of councillors	
21–24	9·3 ⎫	28·7	— ⎫	7
25–34	19·4 ⎭		7 ⎭	
35–44	18·8 ⎫	34·1	19 ⎫	44
45–54	15·3 ⎭		25 ⎭	
55–64	15·5 ⎫	27·8	27 ⎫	46
65–74	12·3 ⎭		19 ⎭	
75 and over	9·1	9·1	3	3
	100	100	100	100

Source: 'The Local Government Councillor', *The Conduct of Local Authority Business* (Widdicombe) Research Vol. 2, HMSO, 1986, Table 2.3; OPCS Monitor *Mid-1985 Population Estimates.*.

NOTE. Figures refer to England and Wales.

These are national average figures: the social composition of any particular council will vary with local circumstances. For example, in rural areas farmers will tend to be well represented; in Labour-dominated areas there will tend to be more members from a working-class background; there are more women councillors in metropolitan and London Boroughs, the metropolitan districts and Scottish districts.[12] Much too will depend on the turnover of councillors in the area, and on the method of recruitment (whether members are recruited through political parties, for instance, see p. 180).

It may be argued that our local councils should be more of a cross-section of the community: that only in this way can councillors really understand the issues and problems which are felt by the ordinary man in the street. For example, does the lack of women councillors explain the apparent inadequacy of nursery provision, while there is an arguably ample supply of municipal golfing facilities? In other words, better balanced councils would

Table 13 *Councillors by political party membership and age, gender, activity status, socio-economic group and income (1985)*

	Conservative %	Labour %	Liberal %	Independent %	Other* %	All Councillors %
Age: 60+	37	32	22	52	30	36
45–59	42	33	30	36	33	37
18–44	19	33	49	11	33	26
Gender: Male	78	83	79	81	81	81
Female	21	17	21	19	19	19
Activity status:						
Employed full- or part-time	64	59	74	47	67	60
Unemployed	2	8	3	1	2	4
Retired	24	22	13	40	30	25
Permanently sick/ disabled	—	2	—	1	—	1
Looking after a home	9	6	9	9	7	8
Other	—	1	—	—	—	1
Socio-economic group:						
Professional	11	6	15		5	9
Employers/managers	42	20	28	37	26	32
Intermediate non-manual	14	22	23	11	30	18
Junior non-manual	8	11	15	6	2	10
Skilled manual/own account non- professional	10	25	8	14	14	16
Semi-skilled manual	1	8	4	5	—	4
Unskilled manual	—	2	—	1	—	1
Armed Forces/NA	12	8	8	16	5	11
Income:						
£15,000+	25	7	18	14	33	16
£10,000–£14,999	22	23	29	17	2	22
£6,000–£9,999	23	28	23	27	25	26
Up to £5,999	22	38	23	29	23	28
None	1	1	2	2	—	1
Refused/NA	8	4	3	10	12	7
Base	(595)	(496)	(133)	(224)	(43)	(1,557)

* Includes Scottish Nationalist, Social Democrat, Plaid Cymru (Welsh Nationalist) and other parties.

Source: 'The Local Government Councillor', *The Conduct of Local Authority Business* (Widdicombe), Research Vol. 2, HMSO, 1986, Table 4.5.

make for a better balance of services, of priorities and of justice. A current illustration is the campaign for better design and planning and street lighting to make the urban environment less hazardous or threatening to women and mothers of young children.

On the other hand, it may be felt that the atypical (some would say elitist) composition of our local authorities has certain advantages – that age brings experience and wisdom; that certain occupations (especially business and managerial) bring useful contacts; and that, above all, managerial and administrative ability is necessary for the work councillors have to do.

The Maud Committee[13] concluded that

It is neither possible, nor in our opinion is it desirable, that councils should in some way be representative of all the varying interests, economic groups, income or education levels in the community ... The qualities of the member should be related to what he is expected to do ... The qualities required ... are:

(a) The capacity to understand sympathetically the problems and points of view of constituents and to convey them to the authority and, at the same time, to interpret and explain the authority's policies and actions to those whom they represent.

(b) The capacity to understand technical, economic and sociological problems which are likely to increase in complexity.

(c) The ability to innovate, to manage and direct; the personality to lead and guide public opinion and other members; and a capacity to accept responsibility for the policies of the authority.

The councillor's role

The duties of councillors are little stated in law, and to a large extent therefore they must turn for guidance to the conventions and practice[14] of their local authority. (Many of these will have been set out in the authority's standing orders – see p. 219.) Legislation – the Local Government Acts 1972 (England and

Wales) and 1973 (Scotland) – does require their attendance at council meetings (see p. 129) and disclosure of financial interest (see p. 205). They have the right of access to the local authority's official documents in so far as this will enable them to carry out their responsibilities as a councillor (but see p. 213) and they can by law claim an attendance allowance (see pp. 191–2). Councillors' discussions enjoy 'qualified privilege'. Normally it is understood that individual councillors have no lawful authority: that executive power is exercisable only by the council as a whole, as a corporate body (and operating within the powers given to them by law – see p. 352). Consequently all questions are decided by the vote of the members of the council, each voice and each vote counting equally.

However, local authorities have the power to delegate responsibility, and they frequently use it, especially in relation to committees (see p. 220). As a consequence of this and of other practices and conventions[15] in individual local authorities, the theoretical parity (of authority) among members is very different in practice.

Councillors will find that they have a variety of overlapping and perhaps conflicting roles and responsibilities, and they must try to achieve a satisfactory balance among them. Thus, they are:

(1) *Representatives*. They are elected to represent a ward or division, but they are also expected to have regard for the interests of the whole of the local authority area. This dual role can be difficult, especially justifying it to local constituents[16] – a problem compounded in the case of the councillor who also sits on a lower-tier council (see p. 397).

(2) '*Ombudsmen*' or citizens' referees. As such they have to deal with, or 'trouble-shoot', problems and issues raised by individual constituents' grievances (such as school closures or allocations, adult education fees, road or council house maintenance, and planning permission).

(3) *Community leaders.* This is a wider aspect of the above, where councillors become 'democratic advocates' on behalf of their

constituents, i.e. consumer watchdogs of all local services, public or private. Here, councillors can play an important role in monitoring the quality of services provided to their constituents by other agencies (such as the NHS). Agency representatives may be invited to address special council or committee meetings. Or, more usually, councillors are appointed to represent the authority on various outside bodies. This can provide important opportunities for councillors to exercise leadership and influence as well as being consumer champions and advocates and 'charter-seekers'. This would involve a combination of some of the above roles.[17]

(4) *Managers*. Here they must oversee the administrative machinery of officers and staff, to see that it is fair (as above) and efficient.

(5) *Policy-makers*, helping to shape policies and plans in the council and committees. In this and the previous role, they are expected to identify needs, set objectives and establish plans to meet those needs, and subsequently to review achievements (sometimes known as monitoring or 'progress chasing').

(6) Above all, councillors are *politicians*, seeking to resolve conflicts. In pursuit of this aim, they will exercise some of their other roles, but they must also be motivators and persuaders, trying to influence, sway, convince – be it their committee members, constituents or party fellows. Inevitably, many councillors will also adopt a narrower political role in having a commitment to a political party.

Analysing the role of the councillor in this way suggests a degree of fragmentation. Yet many aspects are congruent and reinforcing. For example, as a recent report states, 'The representative role of the councillor is indivisible from his or her role in policy formulation or the scrutiny of performance. The roles are mutually interdependent and inform each other.'[18]

In Parliament, some MPs become Ministers and shape government policy. Other MPs play a supporting role or, in the case of the Opposition, a critical and probing role (asking questions, making critical speeches, attempting to influence policy, especially through committee investigations, etc.). Finally, there are those MPs who are content to play a more passive back-bench part (going along with the party directives, raising constituency matters from time to time, etc.).

Similarly, councillors vary in the roles they play. Some, variously known as 'delegates' or 'tribunes',[19] are mainly interested in playing the representative role – dealing with complaints and speaking for particular areas or groups. This seems especially true of newer, less experienced, 'lighter' members. Others, known as 'statesmen' or 'trustees', will seek to play a more active part in policy-making, whether in broad terms (setting general objectives, determining priorities, etc.) or in the area of particular services, such as housing or education. Thus, in local government, we have something equivalent to the parliamentary front- and back-benchers, and to government and opposition, since 'the growth of political party organization within local government has significantly altered the role of the councillor. The fact that in many authorities there is a majority party – which forms the administration – and a minority party or parties which form the opposition, challenges the pretence that all councillors have equal power and equal responsibilities. In practice they do not, and not only in majority councils.'[20]

The demands of council work

Being a councillor is a heavy commitment: the Robinson Committee[21] (1977) found that on average a councillor spent seventy-nine hours a month on his duties. This is a significant increase since the Maud survey (1967) which found the average to be fifty-two hours – a reflection among other things of the fact that in 1974–5 the number of principal local authorities (i.e. excluding parishes/communities) was reduced from 1,857 to 521, and the number of councillors from 46,000 to 26,000 (with a further loss of 700 in 1986). While some evidence suggests a further increase in hours,[22] the authoritative Widdicombe Report shows that the average councillor now spends seventy-four hours per month on council business. But there are considerable variations among types of local authority; for example, for County Councillors in England the figure rose from 90 to 101 hours per month in 1974–86.[23]

This average figure conceals substantial variations, however. There are variations among individual councillors, since obviously they are not all equally devoted to their duties. For example, councillors who are retired from employment appear to give more time than do councillors who have a self-employed occupation. There are also variations among local authorities, for example, according to the number of committees in the council (see p. 220). Furthermore, being a leading councillor, such as mayor,[24] Lord Provost, committee chairman or party leader, usually involves a far greater commitment – up to and even well over a hundred hours per month.

Table 14 gives a breakdown of the time spent by the average councillor on public duties. In more detail, they include:

(1) Council and committee meetings, including sub-committees. These involve attendance, preparatory work (reading relevant papers such as reports, etc.), attending party meetings, personal contacts, meeting council officers and travel.

(2) Dealing with electors' problems (especially housing matters) and holding 'surgeries' at which the councillor makes himself available for consultations by constituents, including pressure groups. Sometimes councillors will visit constituents and they may organize open forums on local issues of the day.

(3) Serving as a nominee of the council on other organizations, such as health authorities, school governors and water authorities.

(4) Miscellaneous duties, including conferences, training courses, meetings of local organizations (such as Age Concern, Round Table and Shelter), site visits, ceremonies, speech days, fetes and various other semi-social functions.

Table 14 *Time spent by councillors on their public duties*

	hours per month	
Attendance at council and committee meetings	21	
Preparation for meetings	18	
Travelling to meetings	7	
Party meetings	5	
Electors' problems	13	
Meeting organizations on behalf of the council	8	
Public consultation	2	
Total	74	

Electors (17%) · Attendance (28%) · Organizations (11%) · Consultation (3%) · Party (7%) · Travel (10%) · Preparation (23%)

Source: 'The Local Government Councillor', *The Conduct of Local Authority Business* (Widdicombe), Research Vol. 2, HMSO, 1986.

A 1991 survey showed the average time spent by councillors to be eighty-two hours per month,[25] and a later one puts the figure at ninety-seven hours.[26] But the average councillor is hard to find. The number of hours any one councillor will spend on public duties will depend on whether he is a member of the controlling group, his seniority and the amount of time he is prepared to give.

The number of years of service also varies. The 1986 Widdicombe Report drew attention to the development of the tendency for members to serve for only two terms. Indeed councillor turnover has become such that newly elected members can become chairs of meetings at the beginning of their term rather than having to serve a long apprenticeship as in the past. The 1991 survey (above) showed that 42 per cent of councillors did not seek a second term of office – due to the time commitment, the effect on job opportunities, the inadequacy of financial allowances and the lack of childcare facilities. There is evidence to suggest that the proportion standing down (at least in county council seats[27]) is not increasing. However, the 1992 survey suggests that the situation will worsen, especially for high-calibre people, if workloads increase as a result of reorganization into single-tier unitary councils. It also suggests that many will be deterred (through feelings of isolation or exclusion) if cabinet-style executive boards develop among local authorities (see Chapter 9).

A recent review of local authorities found that 'the most common complaints . . . from councillors were not about the costs of being a councillor but about the time-consuming nature of their duties and the often unfocused nature of the debate in which they had to engage.'[28] A solution to this problem is for councils to review the way they manage their business. In so far as the problem is timing rather than just length of time involved, this implies altering the times (and places) of meetings (see p. 219), such as differentiating the use of meetings in different parts of the committee cycle (see p. 223) and varying the nature and purpose of committee meetings, by emphasizing different aspects of their role at different times – such as budget and policy framework, policy development and review, general debate, etc. This would provide a clearer focus for councillors. Councils should also consider how they structure their agendas and the clarity and quality of the information they provide. More fundamentally, councils should seek to avoid the duplication of decision-making, though in part this may require action by the government (see p. 221).

Payment

In view of the considerable time which is involved in being a councillor it may seem reasonable to suggest that councillors should be paid for their endeavours. Up until the reorganization of local government in 1974–5, councillors received no payment as such, just expenses and loss of earnings allowance, which had been introduced on a systematic basis in 1948. This arrangement was superseded as a result of the Local Government Acts of 1972 and 1973 (since amended by the Local Government, Planning and Land Act 1980; see p. 195), when attendance allowances were introduced, and councillors in principal local authorities (that is, excepting parish and community councils) are now entitled to claim an *attendance allowance* for approved duties up to a maximum (£18·25 per day in 1989–90). Most local authorities do actually pay this maximum to their members (although not all councillors bother to claim). The allowances are taxable, after deducting certain expenses. Absence through illness also now qualifies for payment.

What constitutes 'approved duties' is determined by each local authority, and there are considerable variations (for example, some may recognize 'surgery' expenses or may provide secretarial help, while others may not), but all must recognize council and committee meetings for this purpose. In 1985, councillors reported receipt of financial allowances for an average of twenty-five hours per month of the seventy-four spent on council duties (compared to thirty-three of the seventy-nine spent in 1976). Almost one in ten councillors reported receiving no financial allowance, with 17 per cent receiving over £100 per month and 5 per cent over £200. However, the majority (almost a third) received between £25 and £50 per month. The overall average was £75 a month. Those councillors receiving the highest amounts were mainly 'council leaders' – those with responsibilities such as committee chairmen – and on average these councillors claim about double that of the 'back-bench' councillors. Nearly all local authorities pay special non-taxable allowances to the chairman of the council (the mayor, convenor or Lord Provost) of between £500 and £3,000 per annum, to cover the extra cost (civic expenses) of high office. In addition, all councillors can claim for travel and subsistence expenses necessarily incurred in the pursuit of council business (see below). In the early 1980s an estimated 100 councillors (mainly Labour) lived on these allowances (which may amount to £6,000–£7,000), i.e. they are professional local politicians. Now, 1 per cent of councillors claim to have no income other than their financial allowances,[29] and less than half of all councils claim to have any full-time members.[30]

The issue of payment is controversial. Members of the public are often quick to accuse councillors of self-seeking and not deserving of trust. Yet being a councillor can be costly: according to 1976 figures, about 40 per cent of working councillors lost pay if they stayed away from work, and about one in five of these lost as much as £50 or more a month, even taking attendance allowances into account. Overall, the cost of local authorities' expenditure on members' allowances and expenses amounted to £28 million in 1985 – or under 0·1 per cent of their total expenditure.

The Wheatley Report (p. 64 above) and the Robinson Committee (1977) recommended a more substantial and uniform payment to councillors. In the words of the former, 'There is a job to be done, and the labourer is worthy of his hire.' It argued that a better system of payment would attract more people to stand for election: that in the light of 'the demanding and responsible nature of local government service . . . service given [ought no longer] to be its own reward' and that a standard system of payments would be far simpler and less invidious than the current arrangements.

The payment of councillors may have other merits. It might help to bring in a broader cross-section of the community (assuming this is desirable) and possibly a more committed, professional approach to the task. It might also help to stimulate public interest in the work and workings of local government. Finally, it might be argued that the adequate payment of councillors would help to eliminate corruption by reducing the disparity between the financial position of so many councillors and that of their officials and of the businessmen they must regularly meet.[31]

However, the Robinson Committee rejected the notion of a full-time salary on the grounds that it

would irretrievably damage the voluntary principle . . . would endanger the relationship between elector and elected . . . would endanger the relationship between members and officers by tending to blur the well-established distinction between their respective roles ... Further, we do not believe that public opinion is ready to accept the idea of full-time salaried councillors.[32]

It was also concerned about the likely cost.

While many of these points are by no means self-evident, it may be added that on the one hand such payments might attract the wrong sort of person on to local authorities, while on the other hand there is little if any evidence that payment would attract candidates: according to the Maud Report some two thirds of the elected members questioned thought that councillors should not be paid, and it did not appear that finance was a dominant influence on ex-councillors in giving up council work (see p. 179). In the survey of electors, only just over 10 per cent mentioned finance as a means of attracting more people into local government.[33]

Consequently the Robinson Committee (1977) recommended the abolition of the current attendance allowance (both because it was unfair and because it was surrounded by public misunderstanding and suspicion) and its replacement by a multi-component system of payment. This would comprise: (1) a basic nominal payment for all councillors; (2) an element to take account of expenses incurred (a figure of £1,000 for members of main authorities was suggested for (1) and (2) together); (3) a financial loss allowance, to compensate for lost earnings as a result of engaging in approved council duties (as existed up to 1974–5, when the Local Government Acts were implemented); (4) special responsibility payments for those councillors, such as committee chairmen, who have to spend extra time on council affairs. The burden of office on such 'leaders' would vary with the size of the local authority and so a sliding scale was suggested for these extra payments (from £3,000 per annum in an authority with 400,000 population to £750 per annum in authorities below 50,000).

The overall cost of this scheme was estimated at some £30 million per annum, assuming full take-up of payments (all 1977 figures).

Under the Local Government, Planning and Land Act 1980, local authorities were empowered (though not required) to pay *special responsibility allowances* (SRAs) (of between £525 and £5,125 per annum in 1990, according to size) to certain (leading) councillors, such as committee chairmen. In addition, councillors had the option of claiming attendance allowances (as above) or alternatively of claiming a *financial loss allowance* (to compensate for loss of earnings caused by attendance at council meetings; up to £29.70 per day (1990)). Such payments may have assisted the emergence of the full-time councillor, though the Widdicombe inquiry found only 1 per cent of councillors claimed financial loss allowance, and only 43 per cent of councils paid special responsibility allowances, and under 1 per cent of councillors received more than £5,000 a year from all three types of payment (i.e. excluding travel and subsistence expenses).

The Widdicombe Committee was critical of this system on grounds of its complexity, uncertainty and its possibly encouraging unnecessary meetings. Consequently, it recommended instead that all councillors should in future be entitled to flat-rate annual payment (varying with type and size of council) plus, for 'key' councillors, special responsibility allowances (SRAs) – all amounting to a total of £75m (1991 prices). Subsequently in 1990, under the Local Government and Housing Act 1989, the Government introduced such a scheme, though limited to a global sum of £39m (increased to £45 million in 1993). Councils now have an allocation varying with size and type of council and population from which they must pay councillors a basic allowance and, where appropriate (for up to one third of the council), SRAs (though no member may receive over £8,120 (1993/4) in SRA). On top of this, councils may pay attendance allowances (up to a maximum of £21 per day). Meanwhile, the Labour Party has plans for some councillors to be salaried – and the Conservative Government has shown an interest; see p. 245.

A recent working party report, *Community Leadership and Representation: Unlocking the Potential*, believes this scheme to be too rigid. It wishes to see councils have more discretion to pay allowances, including payment for attendance at party group meetings. And while the Labour Party has plans for some councillors to become salaried, the working party report found little support for such a development. Indeed, while they accepted that payment does have a part to play, in general they 'question the extent to which improvements in the allowance system will of themselves or alone make people more likely to stand for election or stay on as councillors'.[34]

Non-elected council members

In addition to elected members (councillors) local authorities have often drawn in other members of the public by the appointments of (1) *aldermen* (though this office has now been abolished) and (2) *co-opted* members, neither of them directly or publicly elected.

(1) *Aldermen*, or in Scotland 'bailies', were elected to individual councils by existing councillors.[35] They had no special role as aldermen/bailies. They tended to be older and somewhat more prestigious than the average member. In some respects they were more 'powerful' in that they often chaired committees, and in England and Wales their term of office was twice that of ordinary councillors (six years instead of three years, before 1974). In Scotland, their term of office was the same as that of (burgh) councillors.

For the most part aldermen were actual or former councillors, though legally anyone who was qualified to stand for election as a councillor (see p. 127) could be appointed. However, their numbers were limited to a maximum of the equivalent of one third of the council (one sixth in the London boroughs): thus a council of twenty-one councillors could add seven aldermen to their number.

The aldermanic system was introduced mainly to secure a

measure of stability and continuity, especially where the whole council could be replaced in a 'clean-sweep' election. In addition, it was justified on the grounds that it could bring on to the council persons of ability and experience who might have been unable or unwilling to gain a place through open election. However, the system was clearly undemocratic and there were some notable instances of abuse – a marginally superior party might shore itself up by taking all the seats on the aldermanic bench. Consequently, under the Local Government Acts of 1972 and 1973, the office of alderman/bailie was abolished.[36]

(2) *Co-opted members* (or *additional members*) are similar to aldermen in that they are chosen by the council itself (on the recommendation of its committees). The system of co-opting members is often used in parishes to fill council vacancies, or the appropriate district council may have to resort to co-option if the parish council is too low in membership through lack of candidates. The procedure is used in other local authorities to augment the membership of committees, but these co-opted persons do not become members of the local authority (the council) as such, though they can claim expenses and allowances.

Legally, any local authority committee (except the finance committee) or sub-committee may co-opt persons from outside the council, and normally the council will set down in its standing orders (see pp. 219) its arrangements for co-option, such as the numbers and composition (for example a certain percentage of women on the social service committee). Some committees may be obliged to co-opt, because the law may require the representation of specific groups or interests, and without co-option the committees may be deficient in this respect. The 1944 Education Act requires education committees to include people who are experienced in education or acquainted with educational conditions in the area. Existing councillors (such as teachers in private schools) may themselves fulfil this requirement but otherwise they will need to be co-opted in order to comply with the law.[37] In Scotland, the law is more precise: Scottish education committees must appoint outsiders, including at least three persons interested in the promotion of religious education and two teachers from maintained schools (Local Government (Scotland) Act 1973).

In practice, apart from Scotland, education committees do tend to co-opt fairly regularly, while other committees are far less consistent (especially in district councils, where only 26 per cent have any co-option, compared with London Boroughs where the number is 83 per cent). But rarely do co-opted members form a substantial proportion of committee membership. Legally they can comprise up to one third of the membership of most committees, but they can constitute up to 49 per cent of education committees, and even 100 per cent of sub-committees, though they rarely ever do so. In 1965, there were about 16,000 co-opted members (i.e. one for every three elected members). In 1985, the number had fallen to 6,000 (or one for every four).

Where there is a statutory requirement to co-opt, co-optees become full members of their committees with powers to speak and, until the 1989 Act, vote (though while they may claim financial loss allowance, they may not claim attendance allowance). Where co-option is discretionary, it is left to each council to determine the status of such members.

Co-opted members usually become full committee members, with powers to speak and vote, and it is not unknown (though rare) for a committee chair to be a co-opted member. However, co-opted members do not become members of the local authority (the council) as such; they will usually be confined to the field of their committee.

There are two broad types of co-opted member: (a) a person chosen on an individual or personal basis as having expertise or local notability (perhaps as a long-serving ex-councillor) and (b) a person chosen as a representative of some outside interest – the Church, a teachers' union, a welfare society or the local chamber of commerce. In the case of 'representative co-option', the local authority will often leave it to the outside body itself to select the representative.

The sort of people who get co-opted to local authority committees are of a very similar mould to councillors themselves – which is not altogether surprising, since they must have the qualifications of a councillor[38] (see p. 127), and they are likely to be interested in council work and to know council members (perhaps as relatives). Some are chosen to provide them with a trial run at local authority committee work; others are chosen for party political reasons (and may as a consequence be subject to the party whip system). Allegations of party manipulation or of nepotism call in question the whole principle of co-option.

Briefly stated, the *advantages* claimed for co-option are as follows:

(i) It can provide expertise (cheaply) which may be lacking among the members and the officials or which may be sought as an alternative or counter-weight to that of the local government officers. (In a rather similar way, some Ministers bring in 'outsiders' to their departments in Whitehall.)

(ii) Outsiders can give a wider, perhaps fresher perspective and reduce the danger of parochialism; and, in so far as they are independent, they can help to diminish a preoccupation with party politics.

(iii) A larger number and a wider range of people can be brought into the political process, especially those who can give only a limited amount of time, or who would be otherwise deterred by having to go through the election process.

(iv) In the 'representative' form, co-option can promote the exchange of ideas with outside organizations and so enhance mutual understanding and cooperation between them.

The *disadvantages* may include the following:

(i) The involvement of co-opted members may be regarded as undemocratic, not simply because they are not elected and are therefore not accountable to anyone, but because they may be appointed for purely party motives and may even include candidates who stood unsuccessfully in the election.

(ii) They may upset committee relations with the local authorities' own 'experts' – the officers – and indeed, in so far as co-opted members are unfamiliar with local government procedures, they may upset councillors with their biased or 'starry-eyed and impracticable' ideas.

(iii) They may provide dangerous openings for pressure groups, with the consequent unreasonable distortion of priorities in individual local authorities' provision.

(iv) They can become the 'tail that wags the dog' in those councils (e.g. hung) where they hold the balance among the confronting parties.

The Widdicombe Committee was critical of co-option on the grounds that it blurred the accountability of elected members and detracted from the democratic basis of local government, besides which it could distort the political balance of committees. It therefore proposed that co-option should be banned from all decision-making committees, though non-voting members or 'advisers' should be permitted. This has been agreed by the Government (see p. 175 above).

Standards of conduct

Self-denigration is said to be a national pastime in Britain, especially in the 1970s, and local government is as likely to run the gauntlet as are trade unions, management, Parliament, moral standards, sporting achievements or education standards. So, from time to time it is alleged that the quality of local government is not what it used to be.

Such denunciations have become especially intense in the years since the Second World War. In 1948, a respected historian commented on 'candidates of illiterate speech and low social standing . . . tongue-tied [in council debates]'.[39] In 1960, a senior civil servant[40] averred that '. . . despite the first-class people there are on every sort . . . of local authority . . . by and large local government is not drawing as good a quality of councillor or as many outstanding leaders by way of councillors as it used to do'. In 1961, a professor of government wrote that '. . . our councils are filled with retired people, with women whose children have grown up, and with a few others who can afford the time, or see some particular advantage in being on the council'.[41] In July 1963 *The Times* headed an article 'Petticoat and Pensioner Rule in Council Chambers'.

Partly as a consequence of this onslaught, the Government appointed the Maud Committee on the Management of Local Government (1964–7). Its terms of reference were 'to consider in the light of modern conditions how local government might best continue to attract and retain people of the calibre necessary to ensure its maximum effectiveness'. This implied that the Government had confidence in the quality of current councillors (and officers), but that there were doubts about the immediate future.

These doubts were reinforced in the research work which was undertaken for the Maud Committee:

Many chief officers . . . thought that members were unable to grasp issues of any complexity . . . only a small minority . . . made any real contribution in committee . . . Instances were found of dismal standards of discussion . . . Evidence of a decline in calibre is insubstantial. It does seem clear, however, that the increasing complexity of proposals for innovations are tending to increase the gap in understanding between member and officer, and . . . frequently . . . members take decisions without an adequate understanding of the issues involved.[42]

To be fair, the blame clearly did not always lie with councillors themselves; it was at least partly due to the fact that 'in many spheres, local government had become so highly technical that its intricacies were in large measure incomprehensible to the layman'[43] – be it environmental planning, engineering and building techniques or finance and budgetary procedures. As the Salmon Commission put it, '. . . members [of local authorities] may enter public life with little preparation and may find themselves handling matters on a financial scale quite beyond their experience in private life'.[44] An ex-leader of the GLC has recently condemned the shortage of young, enthusiastic and discerning councillors (see p. 287).

The Maud Committee itself declared that it is difficult to both measure the quality of councillors and discover hard evidence for its alleged decline. Instead, it looked to the future, and suggested that councillors should possess the following qualities:

(a) The capacity to understand sympathetically the problems and points of view of constituents and to convey them to the authority and, at the same time, to interpret and explain the authority's policies and actions to those whom they represent.

(b) The capacity to understand technical, economic and sociological problems which are likely to increase in complexity.

(c) The ability to innovate, to manage and direct; the personality to lead and guide public opinion and other members; and the capacity to accept responsibility for the policies of the authority.[45]

To secure councillors with these qualities, it suggested a number of changes to the then existing practice, including compulsory retirement at seventy, training courses, greater opportunities for release from employment, review of the councils' meeting times, increased co-option, reduction in the number of committees and a reduction in central government controls over local government. Some of these points have been dealt with above; others will be covered in later chapters. Here it is appropriate to comment on two aspects: training and facilities.

Training and support

There is little systematic *training* for councillors. Although most local authorities provide some form of general induction procedure for new members and perhaps some briefing on areas of special interests, such as housing, social services or the financial aspects of the authority's work, a frequent complaint from councillors is that 'on election they had only a limited idea of what the role of councillors was and no one told them what to do, how to do it or how to use the council's resources. They were given the minimum assistance possible provided they turned up to the necessary meetings.' Consequently it is small wonder that some first-time councillors become quickly disenchanted. However, some councils see training and support for their members as an essential ingredient of their pursuit of quality public service.[46] And the political parties often make some such provision for their councillors (for example, in 1993 the Conservative Party set up 'Performance 2000', a service for their councillors which includes induction courses, media training and regular briefing on legislation).

Similarly, the facilities available to councillors to help them in their work vary considerably from one authority to another. In relation to secretarial assistance, the Bains Report said, 'Some authorities already provide some facilities for members, but in very few is there anything approaching a comprehensive service.'[47] As the publishers of a recent book on councillor support services have said, 'Local government is the biggest business in the country, but all too often those who control it, the elected members, have to take decisions and make policy without a proper level of professional support services.'[48]

One study suggests that the 'Councillor's role has been perceived as a part-time leisure activity rather than as a professional or career activity. As a result ... the facilities to support the representational role are limited.'[49] It is further suggested that while the task of local government is becoming more complex and demanding, such that the days of the dedicated amateur approach are no longer relevant, officers' needs have received attention to the neglect of members'. Consequently, it is recommended that there should be more systematic training for members (both induction and continuing) and more adequate support services (in the form of accommodation, transport, crèches, secretarial assistance and information services). The most recent working group on local government management suggests that the installation of such facilities as fax machines or word processors in councillors' homes or the costs of childcare should be clearly allowable expenses.

The growing politicization of local government led the Widdicombe Committee to state that

there is need for councillors and senior officers to develop a better understanding of each other's roles. Councillors need to understand and respect the delicate balance which officers must keep between serving the council as a whole and providing adequate advice to the majority party. Senior officers need to understand and respect the political aspirations of councillors ... The scope for misunderstanding will always be greatest when a new council is elected ... elections can result in 50% or more councillors being new ... there is a need for induction training for new councillors ... and current arrangements are patchy ...[50]

Consequently it recommended local authorities (in conjunction with the Local Government Training Board) to provide more training to secure better understanding by councillors and officers of each other's roles, responsibilities and aspirations. This has been endorsed by the Government.

Corruption

If the 1960s were concerned with the quality of councillors, the 1970s were concerned with their integrity – or rather apparent lack of it. Such concern, however, is by no means a modern phenomenon: in 1834 the Royal Commission on Municipal Corporations (see pp. 17, 107) criticized the way members enjoyed rent-free use of municipal property, held entertainments at public expense and misappropriated corporation income. Throughout the nineteenth century there were numerous scandals involving the Boards of Guardians (see p. 17) and rumours of 'jobbery' in the granting of contracts. In 1888 the allegations of corruption in property development by the Metropolitan Board of Works were such that they led to the appointment of a Royal Commission of Inquiry. Then, in the 1920s and 1930s there was another upsurge of rumour and suspicion about the activities of elected Guardians and councillors – partly due to the supposed vulnerability of the growth in incumbents from poorer backgrounds.

In an attempt to prevent such abuses, the central government used the system of inspection (originally developed to improve efficiency in certain services – see p. 364), and local authority finances became increasingly subject to the professional audit (of their accounts) by the district auditor (see p. 349). Parliament has increasingly required councils to open their meetings to the public and press, and it has established local commissioners to investigate complaints of maladministration. Local authorities themselves have laid down codes of conduct in standing orders (see pp. 218–19), and to promote greater openness they have established a number of public relations activities (see p. 437).

In addition a number of legal restraints have been placed upon councillors – notably (1) the disqualification of being an employee of the authority or for unauthorized expenditure exceeding £2,000 (see pp. 128, 551); (2) the duty to make a 'declaration of pecuniary interest'; and (3) the regulations against corrupt practices. As the other points are dealt with elsewhere, we shall briefly deal with the last two points here.

Pecuniary interest

Councillors are unique in public life in that their duties are of an executive nature and yet they are not responsible either to an employer or to an appointing authority: their responsibility to the electorate is tenuous to say the least. On the other hand, by the very nature of local government's functions, councillors are likely to encounter a conflict of interests between their own private interest or benefit and those of the community they represent (especially in such areas as planning decisions, awarding building contracts or allocating council house tenancies). To help to guard against the temptations of such situations, it has long been a requirement[51] that councillors who have a direct or indirect financial interest in any matter which is before the authority must at the meeting where the matter is under consideration disclose the fact that they have an interest (except in certain cases – see below) and thereafter refrain from speaking or voting on the matter. Members must declare an interest as soon as practicable after the start of the meeting. Alternatively, where the interest arises because they or their spouse is a member, partner or employee in a business which has dealings with the authority, or they are tenants of authority property, they may give a general written notice of his interest; they need then make no oral disclosure at the meeting. A record or register of such notices and of disclosures made at meetings is kept by the authority and is open to inspection by members of the council (in England and Wales) or by local electors (in Scotland) (somewhat parallel to MP's register of interests). Breach of this provision is a criminal offence, and between 1964 and 1974 some twenty members were prosecuted for failing to disclose a pecuniary interest in the business before their council.

However, the law is not totally rigid in this matter, and the Secretary of State has the discretionary power of dispensation. He can (and does) remove from individuals or groups of members the ban on speaking and/or voting in council or committee, usually where the pecuniary interest is somewhat remote or where the incidence of disabilities would be such as to decimate the council or committee concerned. Such general dispensation has been granted, for example, to councillors who are tenants of council houses or have children at state (LEA) schools.

Corrupt practices

The Prevention of Corruption Acts 1906 and 1916 (and their predecessor, the Public Bodies Corrupt Practices Act 1889) were the product of the report in 1888 of the Royal Commission on the Metropolitan Board of Works (see p. 109 above). This report had stated that

it might have a wholesome effect if it were distinctly made a criminal offence to offer to any member or official of a public body any kind of payment, fee, or reward having any relation to the affairs of the body of which he was such a member or official, and also to make the person accepting any such payment . . . amenable to the criminal law.

This legislation has no doubt had the desired salutary effect, but it has not of course eliminated corruption. In recent years, much publicity has been given to cases in which councillors have been convicted under that legislation for taking bribes in respect of the allocation of council houses or the granting of planning permission. The penalties include imprisonment, fine, surrender of the corrupt gift and disqualification from office. Between 1964 and 1974, sixteen members (and twenty-two officials) were convicted for such offences, or similar ones.

The most notorious prosecutions occurred in 1974, when a number of leading councillors in the North of England were imprisoned for corruptly securing lucrative contracts for a private architect, John Poulson. It was this 'Poulson affair' which jolted public opinion and gave rise to several official inquiries into standards of conduct in public life.

The first of these reported in May 1974,[52] the second in July 1976.[53] Neither was unduly concerned at the extent of corruption. 'Our own judgement . . . is that standards of conduct in local government are generally high.'[54] 'We have heard no evidence to give us concern about the integrity and sense of public duty of our bureaucracy as a whole . . .'[55] But they do admit that corruption is difficult to measure. 'There is no objective way of making a true assessment of the amount of public sector corruption that exists now or whether the amount has changed over recent decades.'[56]

However, this view was not entirely supported by at least one member of the Royal Commission, who suggests that certain recently changing factors 'may have enabled corruption to creep into bodies which have rightly enjoyed a long standing reputation for very high standards of honesty and unselfish service'.[57] These factors include:

(a) the growth in power of certain councillors and committees as a result of changes in the planning and building functions of local government;

(b) the emergence of one-party domination in many authorities;

(c) the uncertain tenure of chief executive officers (in contrast to the older-style clerks), which might inhibit their pursuit of a suspicion of corruption by councillors, his employers;[58]

(d) the diminution in the degree of central government control of local government;

(e) the emergence of a 'Robin Hood syndrome', whereby, with the aim of providing services 'in the public interest', more quickly or adequately, members lose their patience with the ordinary processes of government and start to cut corners;

(f) councillors' lack of training, and their inadequate remuneration.

Despite their belief that 'the picture is still of an essentially honest service', the reports themselves saw no room for complacency, and they recommended a number of changes to improve the situation and reduce that minority who 'do not measure up to acceptable standards of probity in public life'. Broadly they sought to do this by (i) further discouraging corruption, for example by suggesting stronger penalties and recommending that, in charges of corruption, the burden of proof should rest on the defence (thus implying the presumption of guilt rather than innocence[59]); (ii) making it easier to investigate suspected corruption, for example by increasing police powers of access to information, including information held by the Inland Revenue and other official agencies.

For local government, the more comprehensive recommendations are to be found in the report of the Committee on Conduct in Local Government (1974). This made the following proposals:

(a) Councillors (and officers) should be required to disclose a pecuniary interest orally whenever it arises (that is, exceptions would no longer be allowed).

(b) Such councillors should be required to withdraw completely from the meeting (except where they had a dispensation from the Secretary of State).

(c) Such disclosures, withdrawals and dispensations should be recorded and be open to inspection by local electors (by councillors in the case of officers' disclosure).

(d) There should be a compulsory register of certain pecuniary interests of councillors (paid employments, local land holdings, company interests and tenancies of council property), to be annually revised and open to inspection by electors.

(e) The use for private gain of information received through membership (or employment) in a local authority should be a criminal offence.

(f) Central government departments should consider giving further advice to local authorities on procedures for the award of contracts and the management of comprehensive development.

(g) Consideration should be given to extending the power of local commissioners ('ombudsmen' – see p. 422).

(h) Local authorities should have clear arrangements for the systematic review of their internal procedures from the point of view of probity.

(i) Local authorities should have clear and well publicized arrangements for receiving and investigating complaints.

(j) Local authorities should pursue vigorous policies of public communication, especially to publicize their policies and procedures.

(k) In conjunction with the central government, local government should establish a national code of conduct based upon those principles which already govern the best practice among individual authorities.

(l) Political parties should ensure that rules of conduct in local authority party group meetings are no less strict than in those of the authority itself.

(m) Councillors (and employees) should treat their non-pecuniary interests (such as family ties) on the same basis as the law requires them to treat their pecuniary interests.

(n) Councillors (and employees) should ensure that hospitality given or received in connection with their official duties can always be justified in the public interest; and that official facilities or allowances to which they are entitled are used strictly for the purposes of their official duties.

(o) Members of the public should take action if they have evidence of misconduct on the part of any member or employee of a local authority.

The most immediate result of all these inquiries and suggestions has been the joint publication by the local authority associations and the government of a National Code of good behaviour in local Government. This reiterates a number of the recommendations and seeks specifically to guide the conduct of councillors and more generally to provide an explicit public standard by which local government can be measured by those outside it.[60]

That such action was desirable was not doubted by Richard Crossman, who wrote, 'The truth is that the moral standards of local government have declined until the relationship between members of public bodies and outside business interests are freely tolerated.'[61]

It is difficult to judge its success. If corruption has diminished in scale, it may be the result of other factors. As Doig says, 'The fact that there have been no large corruption cases since the mid 1970s is less the consequences of locking up a handful of rotten apples than the steady decline in the big spending and the relationships of the previous decade . . . the modest amounts (of fraud) . . . may not justify increasing the present local government audit staff.'[62]

The Widdicombe Committee approved the current methods of overseeing members' interests (i.e. the 1972–3 legislation which dealt with pecuniary interests, and the Code of Conduct for non-pecuniary interests, such as friends, relatives or club member-ship). But it concluded that there should be more emphasis on openness, and proposed (like the Redcliffe-Maud Committee and the Salmon Commission) that there should be registers of mem-bers' interests placed on a statutory basis in order to enhance public confidence in the integrity of councillors. The Government has accepted this (see Local Government and Housing Act 1989, and p. 176), with the exception of non-pecuniary interests (which it feels would be too general and perhaps intrusive), though individual councils may set up such registers on a voluntary basis.

In addition, under the 1989 Act the Code of Conduct has been given statutory force and now requires all councillors taking office to affirm that they will be guided by the Code in carrying out their duties and all councils will monitor and report regularly on whether councillors are observing the Code.

It is possible that the increase in the contracting out of local authority functions may reduce corruption (at least within authori-ties). But local government reorganization may provide further opportunities as 'systems get stretched and valuable assets are easily lost track of . . . a new dash to sell assets could be good news for crooks'.[63]

In 1993 the Audit Commission uncovered over 100 local government frauds (of not less than £500 each) amounting to £2·5m, though about half of these were perpetrated by outsiders* against the councils. This is an increase from seventy-five cases in 1985 (worth £1·5m) – an increase which may be due to local authorities' difficulties (in competition with the private sector) of recruiting strong financial staff. In some cases it is also suggested that it is due to left-wing Labour councils deciding to cut spending on their finance departments in order to use hard-pressed finance for front-line public services. But although a number of Labour councils (such as Lambeth LB and Monklands DC) have been in the headlines for alleged fraud, nepotism or gross mismanagement, so too have some Conservative-run councils (such as West Wiltshire DC and Westminster LB). In the 1990s, there were a number of cases (and prosecutions) involving former council staff who had set up companies and been awarded contracts to provide council services. In 1993, the Welsh local government Commissioner ('ombudsman' – see p. 422) severely criticized Brecknock district council over councillors who allocated council houses to their relatives in advance of other people on the waiting list.

The complete elimination of corruption is impossible – after all, corrupt dealings are conducted in secret and are therefore difficult to assess or prove: in 1983–4 there was considerable disquiet at allegations about freemason membership influencing police promotion and inquiries, but there was no conclusive evidence.

Codes of conduct and declarations of interest will have little impact on the dishonest, though they may dissuade the pliant. And there is one fundamental dilemma: the introduction of greater scrutiny and regulations can seriously damage the morale and feeling of mutual trust within an organization. In particular, it may inhibit the leadership and initiative of management. Before we turn to management, in the next chapter, perhaps we should conclude by putting local government corruption into perspective: local authorities are local, their activities are watched by the

---

* The 'insider' offences were largely committed by employees (such as the obtaining of council goods by a purchasing officer, collaboration with a contractor to overcharge the council, or a housing benefits officer making payments to himself). In 1992 a city treasurer was imprisoned for making false expenses claims.

press, they are in many ways more open and exposed to public
scrutiny than are government departments, 'quangos', political
parties, charities and private enterprise. There may *appear* to be
more corruption in local government simply because there is
more light and more detection. And overall, local and central
government show a very high standard of probity relative to
other sectors as far as fraud is concerned.[64]

Access

A number of councils have set up closed one-party committees
(sometimes with special rules or powers) which have excluded
minority party members and denied them access to relevant
records and information. In 1984, in the so-called Hackney case,
the court declared that opposition councillors should not be
barred from attending sub-committee meetings (see note 26,
p. 584, see too R. *v.* Sheffield City Council 1985).

However, it has long been the practice of local authorities to
restrict access to council records exclusively to members of the
relevant committees for reasons other than party political. This
was highlighted in 1982 (in the so-called Birmingham case) when
a councillor sought to examine the case file of a social services
client. Lord Denning ruled that such files were only accessible to
committee members. However, on appeal to the House of Lords,
it was instead declared that 'a councillor is entitled by virtue of
his office to have access to all written material in the possession
of the local authority of which he is a member, provided he has
good reason for such access'.

The most recent development here is the Local Government
(Access to Information) Act 1985, which clarifies and extends the
right of councillors to council documents, subject to certain
limitations of confidential items. This Act* also increases the

* In practice this Act operates by adding clauses to the Local Government Acts
of 1972 and 1973. In consequence, the Public Bodies (Admission to Meetings)
Act 1960 – see p. 441 – is superseded.

opportunities for public access to sub-committees and to council papers such as agendas, reports, minutes, letters, memoranda and other background documents. Some councils are accused of evading the law by forming informal working parties and secret panels or by charging excessively (and deterrently) for copies of documents. The Widdicombe Committee suggested that the former would be a not unexpected consequence of councillors being (wrongly) unable to develop policy options in confidence before presenting their final choice for public decision. The Committee therefore suggested that purely deliberative committees and sub-committees could be reasonably excused from the requirements of the 1985 Act. The Government has not accepted this suggestion (though the 1991 consultative document *The Internal Management of Local Authorities in England* seems rather more persuaded; see pp. 245ff.). However, as a result of the decision of the Court of Appeal in R. *v.* Eden District Council ex-parte Moffat 1988, local authorities are reviewing their procedures to ensure that any of their bodies exercising executive power are designated as committees or sub-committees; further, they are admitting all councillors who wish to attend (member-level) working party and panel meetings, and requiring such bodies to consider closely their grounds for excluding the press and public when this occurs.

The Widdicombe Committee was also concerned that the law allows the council, and thus in effect the majority party, to determine whether a member needs to inspect a document or attend a meeting in order to carry out his or her duties, and further that the law enables councillors to have access to documents not available to the public and in which they may have a pecuniary interest. The Government is to amend the law in this latter respect, and in 1993 it began a review of the whole operation of the 1985 Act. In the meantime, in pursuit of the open government aspect of the Citizen's Charter, the Government has proposed statutory rights of access to personal records and health and safety information (including safety of food, transport, public places and consumer goods, and environmental health risks). It will extend individuals' rights under the Data Protection

Act 1984 to manually held files (though it only applies to information created after the new legislation is passed).

More generally, concern has been expressed that the 1985 legislation became too tightly drawn as it passed through Parliament. Originally it was intended to allow public access to any document relating to any matter discussed in public by the local authority, i.e. not just those relied upon in producing council reports. Some councils, however, have adopted the broader approach.[65] But others use exempted business (confidential items) as a device for disguising policy matters.

9. Internal Organization: The Council and its Committees

How local authorities organize themselves to carry out their responsibilities varies from one authority to another. But they all follow a broadly similar pattern, and certain forms or procedures are universally adopted where they are required by law. Briefly it can be stated that all local authorities will conduct their activities through a council of all members, aided by a number of committees (comprising small groups of members), which work in close collaboration with senior officers, who are employed by the council and head the various departments of the council. This is illustrated by Figure 13. In this chapter we shall be mainly

Figure 13 *Basic structure of a local authority*

concerned with the work of the council and its committees. The officers and staff of local authorities are more fully examined in Chapter 10.

The council

By 'local authority' we mean those groups of people who are elected to be councillors and form councils, the bodies which take authoritative decisions for their local areas. But all councils delegate much of their work to smaller groups (committees) or to individuals (officers). Such delegation occurs because councils are too large to be effective decision-making bodies (some have over a hundred members), and council members, meeting only as a whole group, would not develop sufficient expertise. Further, most councils do not meet frequently (many meet only five times a year) and their meetings (of perhaps three hours' duration) do not give them enough time to exercise close supervision of the work of the many departments and employees of the council.

Consequently, most of the activity at full council is concerned with (1) the ratification (through voting) of decisions and actions which committees have taken since the last full meeting of the council, and (2) the discussion of committee reports, analyses and recommendations which may then be approved, amended, rejected or 'referred back' for further consideration to the committee concerned.

The council itself will determine what or how much is delegated to committees and will often reserve to itself the more important policy matters. It thus remains the ultimate decision-making body. However, as the Bains Report (see below) pointed out, the way councils exercise that role differs widely from one authority to another. At one extreme the council receives and considers the reports and minutes of every committee: at the other extreme, members individually may receive the relevant papers but very little may go before the full council unless members specifically

Figure 14 *A council setting*

request it. In between these two types are those councils which receive and consider summary reports and may as a consequence debate major matters arising from them.

Council meetings are presided over by a chair, who may be variously entitled chair or mayor (in England and Wales), provost or convenor (in Scotland), according to the type of local authority. However, most of the council discussion is led by the chairs of the various committees. Officers also attend council meetings, but they do not normally speak: their role on these occasions is mainly a consultative one – to be 'on tap'. The other officials present are the clerks. They are responsible for distributing any relevant papers and for taking the minutes (a written summary) of the meeting. These minutes are subsequently open to inspection by the public.

One type of council setting is illustrated in Figure 14.

Council meetings

The frequency and timing of meetings are matters which are left largely to the local authorities themselves to decide. By law, all principal councils (that is, all except parishes and communities) must hold an annual meeting. Some authorities meet monthly or even more often; others meet only quarterly. The timing of meetings is an important consideration, as it can affect attendances. Urban authorities tend to meet in the evening; other authorities meet in the daytime for the convenience of councillors who have to travel long distances (e.g. the Western Islands council in Scotland meets for four days at a time), though this may present problems in getting release from employment.

Council meetings are formal affairs, and much ceremony may be attached to them – the civic mace may be carried and the chain of office worn. Meetings may start with prayers. Speech-making, the conduct of debate and other procedural matters are quite closely controlled, usually in what are called 'Standing Orders'.[1] (Under the Local Government and Housing Act 1989, the Minister is empowered to prescribe particular procedures and Standing Orders.) Members of the public may attend as observers. In all these respects, council meetings resemble those of Parliament.

The leader of the council

In Britain, the *chair* of the council is elected by councillors from among their number. He or she is not therefore elected directly by the people, as in the USA. Consequently (and partly because of the tendency to rotate the office) the office is ceremonial rather than effective: the chair is a figurehead rather than a political force, unlike the council *leader*, who is normally head of the majority party. However, in some local authorities, the chair acquires a pre-eminence by way of social standing, hard work, experience or sheer ability.[2] As a result, the chair may develop a permanence and so combine chairmanship with leadership of the council. In many local authorities, usually those where parties are strongly developed, council leadership is openly and formally acknowledged (perhaps in standing orders). However, in these circumstances it may be difficult to combine this role with that of chair, since the latter requires a non-partisan approach, so that the roles of leader and chair will be separated and come to resemble that of (political) Prime Minister and (non-political) monarch. (The Speaker of the House of Commons plays such a non-political role; so do a number of national presidents, as in West Germany or Italy.) It is also quite usual for there to be a council *leader of the opposition*, as in Parliament. However, unlike chairmanship, the office of leader is not statutory but is informal and based on convention and practice.

Committees

The Local Government Act 1993 standardized the power of local authorities to form committees. The number, size, composition and powers of committees in any local authority are determined by each individual council and laid down in the Standing Orders. Generally, the functions of local government committees are to: (1) take particular interest in one aspect or area of the local authority's work (education or highways, for instance); (2) closely supervise the administration of that area; (3) formulate policies or lines of action; (4) deal initially with any problems which arise in its field of special interest.

Committees are usually required to report their discussions back to the full council. This may be something of a formality, simply in order to keep the council informed, as in cases where the committee is delegated the power actually to decide issues of policy; such powers were significantly increased in the Local Government Act 1972. But more usually the purpose is to gain approval of the council for the actions which the committee may recommend (closing certain schools, selling council houses, undertaking a redevelopment scheme, etc.). And, by law, certain matters cannot be delegated to committees: the power to raise loans or to determine the community charge rests with the council alone. Obviously, where a committee has to await the approval of the council before it can act, there is delay involved, but this may be regarded as a reasonable price to pay for greater democratic control. In such cases, the committees are advisory rather than executive in nature. Nevertheless, they do a lot of the detailed groundwork and sifting on behalf of the council and have been aptly described as the 'workshops' of local government (though of course much of the work of local government occurs in the departments and among senior officers).

Types of committee

There are many different kinds of committee in local government. The most usual categories are as follows:

(a) *Horizontal* and *vertical.* Those committees which concentrate on the administration of a single service (such as education or housing) are usually called 'vertical' (or service) committees. Other committees may be concerned with a particular function that directly affects many or all other council activities (though often having little contact with the general public), and because they cut across other services these are known as 'horizontal' (or functional) committees – finance or staffing, for example.

(b) *Special* and *standing.* Special (or *ad hoc*) committees are formed to deal with a particular problem (for instance, flood) or event (for instance, Jubilee celebrations) and are disbanded when circumstances permit. Standing committees are more permanent, being re-appointed annually to fulfil the roles outlined in (a) above.

(c) *Joint.* These are formed by two or more local authorities when they share an interest in some activity or problem (a national park or other amenity). In many instances these committees are called 'boards' or 'authorities' – the Avon and Somerset Police Authority is an example.

(d) *Statutory.* While local authorities have considerable discretion as regards the committees they appoint, they are nevertheless required by law to appoint *certain* committees. The most important of these are police, education and social services. (Before the reorganization legislation of 1972–3, the list of such committees was considerably larger, though in all cases only the relevant type of local authority was affected. Under the Education Act 1993, education committees will cease to be compulsory.)

Size and membership of committees

For the most part, membership of committees in local government is confined to currently elected members of the council, the councillors. (Co-opted members are an exception to this rule – see p. 197.) These members are allocated to committees by the full council, though much of this work is often done in advance by a special 'selection' committee (which usually consists of more senior councillors). In this allocation process, arrangements vary among local authorities. Statutory committees may have certain constraints on their size or composition – police committees must comprise two thirds councillors and one third magistrates (this is to change), and education committees must contain members who have experience in education. It is normal for some account to be taken of councillors' own preferences, the balance of the parties, the representation of wards or districts and the balance of age and experience of members. Where a party dominates the council, it may well use its advantage to predominate in each of the important committees (but see p. 158).

The size of committees is a matter for the individual council to determine and there is wide variation. The desirability of having small and workmanlike committees needs to be balanced with the democratic desire to have a proper representation of areas and interests. The importance and even perhaps the popularity of a committee is likely to affect its size. As we have seen (p. 222.), some committees will find it necessary to co-opt members from outside the elected membership of the council.

The operation of committees

Usually, the first task of a committee is to appoint a chair, though often this may be done for it by the whole council, and where there is a majority party the allocation of such positions is often a foregone conclusion.

Naturally, committees are usually smaller in membership than the full council. Committee meetings are less formal occasions than full council meetings, and officers are expected to play an active role by answering questions and giving advice. Indeed, a lot of committee time is spent hearing and reacting to the reports by chief officers on such matters as the council's budget, a housing development scheme or the planned closures of certain schools. From such questions and discussions will emerge the committee's views, and these views, or 'resolutions', together with the 'minutes' (written summaries of the committee's proceedings) are usually submitted to the next meeting of the full council.

Just as the full council meets at regular intervals, so do committees – they go through a regular 'cycle' of meetings (though, like the council, they may have special or emergency meetings). By law, their meetings are open to the public, but for certain items a committee (and indeed the full council) can exclude the public and press by going into 'closed' session (meeting 'in camera'). These items are usually of a confidential nature, such as those where a council is negotiating for property or where a housing committee is discussing rent arrears or evictions. On occasion, a member of the public may be invited to address a committee. (Whilst local government has no Official Secrets Act such as that operating in central government, local authorities usually have a clause in their standing orders which prohibits the disclosure of council or committee matters until this is authorized by the council. For many matters this occurs in the normal course of events, e.g. in open council or committee meetings; and council minutes are made available for public inspection at the council offices or public libraries.) Under the Local Government (Access to Information) Act 1985, council sub-committees became open to the public, subject to certain limitations concerning confidential matters (see also p. 210).

As we have seen (p. 205), when items occur at committee or full council meetings in which any councillor has a pecuniary interest, such as owning a property which the council may wish to acquire or running a business which it may wish to employ, he or she must declare an interest and take no further part in the discussion or voting on that item.

The role of chair

Chairs of committees do not merely control the conduct of committee meetings and speak on behalf of their committees at council meetings (like Ministers speaking in Parliament). They will be in regular contact with the departmental chief officers, especially prior to committee meetings. Occasionally they may call emergency meetings of the committee. And they may also, as its chair, meet members of the public – to explain the council's policy on school closures or housing rents, for example. The precise role of chair will vary among local authorities and may or may not be set out in their standing orders.[3] However, the mayor or any person presiding at a council meeting does have the legal right to exercise a second, or 'casting' vote and may, rather than act impartially, thus vote in accordance with the policy of his or her party (see Regina *v.* Bradford City Council ex-parte Corris, May 1989).

Generally speaking, a committee chair's job is a responsible and onerous task. Between committee meetings a chair may have to deal with urgent issues – on lesser issues this power may be delegated to the relevant official – and take decisions on behalf of the committee (which he or she will subsequently have to get its approval for). This is known as 'chairman's action'. However, in a recent court case it was held that a chair is not legally entitled to take decisions alone (R. *v.* Secretary of State for the Environment ex-parte Hillingdon LBC, 1985). The Widdicombe Committee recommended that 'chairman's action' should be legalized, but the Government disagreed, on the grounds that it would breach the essential local government principle of corporate decision-making and would undermine the proposals for proportionate representation on decision-making committees (see p. 173); instead it believed that councils should be able to convene small urgency committees (of, say, three members).

The pros and cons of the committee system

Historically, committees exist in local government because the modern local government system was largely preceded by a collection of *ad hoc* authorities (Boards of Guardians, Boards of Health, School Boards) which were more or less simply amalgamated when local authorities were created, so that the latter became a system of ready-made committees and departments. Furthermore, it has been convenient (and sometimes mandatory) for local authorities, on the acquisition of an extra responsibility, to create a committee (and a department) to administer that function.

There are, however, some more positive reasons for setting up committees:

(a) They off-load the full council, which can consequently spend less time on details and devote greater attention to overall policy matters.

(b) They can save the time of councillors, since different matters can be considered at the same time in the different committees – they can be dealt with in parallel rather than in series.

(c) Their existence can simplify the tasks facing the council through the division of labour and the specialization of responsibilities.

(d) Such specialization should facilitate greater knowledge and expertise by councillors (aided where appropriate by co-opted outsiders).

(e) Further, such specialization should produce more effective supervision and control of the local authority's administrative areas.

(f) Committees are generally smaller in size and their procedures are more informal, which may encourage councillors to speak more freely.

(g) Finally, committees provide a useful point of contact with the officials and help to keep them in touch with public opinion (though see pp. 285–6).

It is difficult to envisage local government trying to operate without committees, and many councillors would feel that they are not sufficiently involved unless they personally are a member of at least one committee.[4] However, committee systems can be abused and thus create problems. Among the principal dangers are the following:

(a) Rather than save time, committees may actually waste it. They may do this in a number of ways – by going into excessive detail and talking endlessly, by creating unnecessary sub-commit- tees and working parties, by delaying decisions while waiting for another committee to make a decision which affects its work, and so on. Besides, there may be simply too many of them. In the past, they often grew without regular review, and as a result there was overlapping and duplication of function. Committees may also be accused of dispersing or clouding responsibility.

(b) While committee members may become experts in the field of administration covered by their committee, they may also become narrow-minded and fail to see the work of the council as a whole.

Indeed, there is the real danger of insularity (especially among vertical committees and their related departments), with members (and officers) identifying too closely with 'their' service: rivalry, jealousy and protectiveness may follow. Councils have usually tried to secure some coordination in the work of their committees and departments by various means, for instance through horizontal committees, such as finance, or by ensuring that there is cross-membership within the vertical committees (some members sitting on several committees). Some relied on the machinery of the political parties, and perhaps most assumed that the chief administrative officer – the clerk – would provide a sufficient overview of the local authority's affairs. But in the 1960s these arrangements were increasingly felt to be inadequate – hence the setting-up of the Maud Committee (see p. 201).

The Maud Report

Such criticisms were most stridently and tersely stated in the Maud Report (*Report of the Committee on the Management of Local Government*, 1967). That inquiry found that many of the principal local authorities had thirty or more committees and forty or more sub-committees.[5] The same report showed that one large local authority sent out 700–1,000 sheets of official paper (agenda, reports etc.) each month to committee members. Consequently, preparation for, travel to and from, and attendance at meetings were making considerable demands on the time of members and officers. The Committee also expressed its concern that 'the association of each service with a committee, and of a department and a principal officer with both, produces a loose confederation of disparate activities, disperses responsibilities and scatters the taking of decisions'. It concluded:

The virtues of committees are, at present, outweighed by the failures and inadequacies of the committee system ... It becomes increasingly difficult for committees to supervise the work of the departments because of the growth of business, lack of time and the technical complexity of many of the problems. The system wastes time, results in delays and causes frustration by involving committees in matters of administrative detail. The system does not encourage discrimination between major objectives and the means to attain them, and the chain of consequential decisions and action required. We see the growth of business adding to the agenda of committees and squeezing out major issues which need time for consideration, with the result that members are misled into a belief that they are controlling and directing the authority when often they are only deliberating on things which are unimportant and taking decisions on matters which do not merit their attention.

Some local authorities had become aware of the deficiencies of their committee structure and their internal arrangements generally, and some had undertaken interesting and sometimes controversial reorganizations (in Newcastle and Basildon, for example). Other local authorities had more conventional arrangements, but sought to achieve greater coordination through the creation of special 'policy' or 'management' committees or by enhancing the role of one of the horizontal committees.

The Maud Committee may have been influenced by some of these developments. It was not only outspoken in its criticisms, but radical in its recommendations. It proposed that:

(1) Each local authority should create a small 'management board' of councillors with considerable delegated powers. Its functions would be to develop policy, review progress and generally coordinate the work of the council (rather like the Cabinet at central government level).

(2) Committees and departments should be drastically reduced in number (a figure of six was suggested) and certain separate functions should be grouped.

(3) These committees would have deliberative rather than executive responsibilities.

(4) There should be a chief officer for each local authority who should have general management abilities which he should use to supervise and coordinate the work of other principal officers and their departments.

(5) More responsibilities should be delegated to officers, and members should generally become less involved in the day-to-day administration of services, decisions on case-work and routine inspection and control.

The Maud Report stimulated a great deal of interest and discussion. But it also provoked much hostility: in whole or in part it was regarded as too radical by many local authorities, who believed that their particular system was already adequate to the task. Some argued that the proposed management board would not only be undemocratic but would clash with the principle of the 'collective responsibility' of all councillors. Apart from this, many councillors were afraid of 'losing control' to the officials or of becoming second-class councillors in contrast to the 'elite' appointed to the management board.

However, the Maud Report did cause some local authorities to review their internal organization and procedures, and certain councils began to introduce a number of diluted Maud-type reforms.[6] They received added impetus from the publication of the two Royal Commission reports – the Redcliffe-Maud Report for England and Wales and the Wheatley Report for Scotland – in 1969. Thus there was a reduction in the number of committees and sub-committees;[7] central or 'policy' committees were established; chief executive officers were appointed or clerks had their positions enhanced to give them some formal authority over other chief officers in the authority, who were formed into management teams; departmental functions were amalgamated or grouped and the 'directorate' approach was adopted, chief officers becoming responsible for several areas of activity (such as planning and transportation, or leisure and amenities).

Such moves were encouraged in the 1970s as a result of the reorganization of the local government structures and in particular by the tide of support which accompanied the Bains Report and the Paterson Report. These were the product of two committees set up in 1971 to produce advice on management structures for the new local authorities which were to be established under the reorganization Acts of 1972 (England and Wales) and 1973 (Scotland). These reports were more favourably received than was the Maud Committee Report of 1967, for a number of reasons. In the first place they were not as radical as Maud: all councillors would continue to be substantially involved in the work of the council, as committees were to continue to play an important part, and the controversial idea of a high-powered (some called it 'oligarchical') management board was dropped. Secondly, their recommendations were less dogmatic and presented local authorities with a number of alternative schemes (for the grouping of services, the number and role of committees etc.) from which to choose. Thirdly, the Maud Report had educated (or 'softened up') local authorities to the idea of reform in their internal arrangements. Fourthly, local government was to be comprehensively reorganized and new internal structures would be required: experience of reforming Greater London (1963) had indicated that merely modifying existing structures would not be sufficient to meet the changed circumstances. This view was endorsed by both the Redcliffe-Maud and Wheatley Royal Commissions (1969). Finally, the Local Government Acts of 1972 and 1973 removed a number of the legal constraints on local government (concerning the compulsory appointment of officers and committees or the scope of delegation), which made it easier for the new authorities to adopt new management structures. However, it has been remarked that 'the extent to which the Bains Report has been accepted is in its own way both exciting and disturbing'.[8]

Bains, Paterson and the 'corporate approach'

The Bains and Paterson Reports of 1972 were very similar both in their general approach and philosophy, and in their detailed recommendations. Similarly they reflected many of the sentiments expressed in the Maud Report and in the Redcliffe-Maud and Wheatley Reports, though they provided more in the way of detail. Above all they emphasized the desirability of a 'corporate' (or integrated) approach to the management of local authority affairs, in contrast to the traditional, departmental approach (so strongly criticized by Maud – see p. 227), which lacked a sufficiently unified attitude towards the development of policies for the locality. Despite the coordinating role performed actually or potentially by senior officers (such as the clerk or the finance officer) or by committees (such as the finance committee), the Paterson Report concluded:

In general, the process of formulating policies and devising plans to implement these policies is carried out independently within the various service committees and their respective departments, each making separate recommendations to the full council. Although there is now widespread recognition that the activities of any one committee or department interact to a substantial degree with those of other parts of the organization, particularly in terms of their end-effect on the public, there is still very little in the way of formal coordination across the whole range of an authority's activities. (para. 3.5)

Furthermore, although the finance committee could exert some overall influence, its effectiveness was limited because

its members are in no position to assess whether the sum total of the various departmental spending proposals really represents a cohesive programme geared to achieve the authority's objectives; they lack guidelines to assist them in reconciling the competing claims for the services for finance; they are concerned only with the financial implications . . . and not with the deployment of other important elements of resource necessary for the implementation of the programmes. (para. 3.6)

The two reports, then, are concerned with coordination, not merely to provide better services and prevent errors (such as housing estates lacking community facilities, or education and housing provisions being out of phase), but also to promote efficiency, avoid wasteful duplication and ensure value for money.[9]

However, there is a third reason for seeking the corporate approach in local government management. The perception of local government should not be

limited to the narrow provision of a series of services to the community ... It has within its purview the overall economic, cultural and physical well-being of the community and for this reason its decisions impinge with increasing frequency upon the lives of its citizens ... Local government is about, and more important, for people. (Bains, paras. 2.10, 2.13)

Such overall responsibility and the interrelationship of problems in the community calls for the wider-ranging, less mutually exclusive, corporate approach. Such an approach is unfortunately limited by the fact that *other* public bodies are responsible for such matters as income maintenance, health services and (except in Scotland) social work with offenders and water supplies.

Corporate management

Both the Bains and Paterson Reports take as their basis a corporate approach to the management of local authorities. Management, generally, has been described as consisting of forecasting, planning, organizing, commanding, coordinating and controlling.[10] Corporate management aims at securing a unity to these processes, both individually and collectively. For local authorities this implies the development of comprehensive policies and cohesive programmes of action – a unified approach to the formulation and implementation of policies and plans to meet the needs of the community. As the Paterson Report puts it,

The ultimate objective of corporate management is to achieve a situation where the needs of a community are viewed comprehensively and the activities of the local authority are planned, directed and controlled in a unified manner ... (para. 5.3)

The Bains and Paterson Reports both outline management structures to support such an approach, and despite some differences of detail[11] the two sets of proposals are very similar (see Figure 15). Thus they recommend that at *councillor* level:

(1) The number of committees should be reduced by organizing them as far as possible on a 'programme area' basis, grouping together those activities which are closely related in terms of their purpose or end-result (such as education, libraries and amenities, or transport, highways and planning). These programme areas or spheres of activity arise from, and seek to match, the broad objectives of the local authority. Each of these spheres of activity thus would have its own objectives and programme for meeting them, and the committees would be responsible for each programme and the allocation of resources within it. Consequently, the committee structure would be directly geared to the needs and objectives of the authority, and a 'mini-corporate' approach would be developed at committee level rather than a single-service or departmental view.

(2) A central management committee, which the reports call a Policy & Resources (P&R) committee, should be established to provide coordination and guidance to the council on overall or strategic policy, priorities, resource allocation and major programmes, to coordinate advice to the council, especially from the specialist committees (and officers), to exercise overall control over major resources and to coordinate and control programme implementation. For these purposes, it would have a close working relationship with other committees, some of which might actually form sub-committees of this central policy committee. (In contrast to the Maud Report, here it is recommended that the pre-eminence of the policy committee – Maud's management board – shall be moderated or balanced by the service committees continuing with a policy-making and executive role: they would not be merely advisory.)

(3) Area joint committees should be set up to plan and coordinate

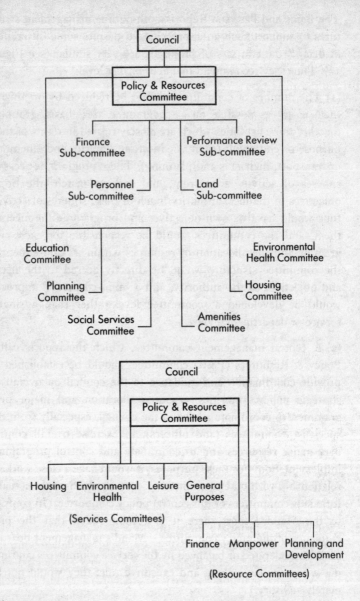

Figure 15 *Sample committee structures proposed by Bains (upper) and Paterson (lower)*

the provision of services which are closely related but separated (such as housing and social services in non-metropolitan areas) or provided concurrently (such as planning). These committees would consist of members from the county and district councils in the areas.

(4) At *officer* level, a chief executive officer (CEO) should be appointed to head the full-time officers' side of the local authority. He or she would become the council's principal official adviser on matters of general policy and would be responsible for securing coordination of advice on the forward planning of objectives and services, for the efficient implementation of policies and for ensuring that the authority's resources are most effectively employed (which implies keeping under review such matters as the organization and manpower policies of the council). He or she would also be responsible for the maintenance of good internal and external relations.[12] His or her key role would be to lead the officers' management team (chief officers' group). As a general rule, the CEOs should not head departments, as this may detract from their other responsibilities.

(5) A small group of about six chief officers, under the leadership of the chief executive officer, should form the officers' management team (OMT). It would act as the counterpart of the members' policy committee,[13] providing a forum in which chief officers would develop a corporate identity. This team would be responsible for the preparation of plans and programmes in connection with the council's long-term objectives, and for the general coordination of the implementation of those plans.

(6) Where appropriate, departments should be amalgamated or grouped into 'directorates'. This grouping should not normally go as far as the grouping of committees (recommended in (1) above), since that might jeopardize the highly prized professionalism or expertise which is one of the strengths of local government. Enforced amalgamations might also give rise to some illogical

groupings and to the problem of control. But, perhaps above all, drastic departmental groupings might lead to the re-creation of the one-committee/one-department link which so fostered the development of departmentalism in the past. Bains and Paterson indicated a number of alternative arrangements (see Figure 16). These were to be guidelines rather than blueprints for local authorities.

(7) More decision-taking should be delegated to officers, the general principle being asserted that 'issues are dealt with at the lowest possible level consistent with the nature of the problem'.[14] Thus, as a general rule, members would not normally be involved in detailed or routine low-level decision-making. Nevertheless, the 'constituency' role of members would require them to be aware of and sensitive to local needs and feelings, and consequently both reports recognized that members may genuinely have occasion to be involved in matters of detailed policy execution.

At the other extreme, both reports emphasize the important role of the full council. In spite of the delegation to officers, the enhanced role of the chief executive officer and the key role of the policy committee, the council is to remain the ultimate decision-making body in a real rather than a merely formal sense. It should provide 'a forum for public debate and for the open challenge and questioning of policy and its application' . . . it is 'the body in which the authority's broad objectives and the major commitment of resources should be fully discussed and decided'.[15] Councils should not degenerate into ritualistic talking shops or rubber stamps.

Much can be said about the concept of corporate management as exemplified in the Bains and Paterson Reports. Here, limitations of space forbid more than a brief comment.

The two reports have been described as accounts of what the minority of local authorities were doing for the enlightenment of the majority. Certainly their central theme – that the whole of a

* = Members of Officers' Management Team

Figure 16 *Alternative departmental structures (adapted from the Bains Report)* local authority's activities should be carried out by a group of people all working towards the same general end – seems convincing and desirable, and seemed especially so at that time, when local authorities were about to become bigger and cover more diversified geographical areas. Furthermore, in a period of scarce resources, there is an obvious need for their rational allocation, for determining objectives and ordering priorities, and subsequently monitoring results for effectiveness. Not that this necessarily implied restraint or retrenchment: financial management, planning, personnel management and policy in general were to become much more positive and forward-looking instead of simply reacting to events on a piecemeal basis. In short, the multifarious roles of the local authority were to be seen in the round, as a totality. 'Problems do not arise in neat compartments or individual packages, but rather as a tangled, interrelated mass needing a corporate approach to solve them.'[16]

However, some critics quickly denounced the proposals as a 'bureaucrat's charter' and feared that members might become overawed with the new language and procedures and would find it difficult to counter the collective advice coming to them from the officers' management team and the chief executive officer. And there was the fear that the new corporate structures and processes might lead to the general public's becoming further mystified and confused about local government. Thus the changes were seen as a further manifestation of managerialism and technocracy at the expense of democracy (in the same way that many people allege that the country is really run by the civil service). In so far as it is true, one solution has been to increase the training and competence of councillors. Another approach has been to strengthen member control through the party group as 'the caucus strikes back' (see p. 157 and p. 168). But others have interpreted the changes as a 'dual elite' takeover or dominance (see p. 292).

Others foresaw the danger of the new approach being implemented because it was fashionable, with local authorities setting up the machinery of corporate management without a proper understanding of how it should work. As Paterson says, 'We would stress that the corporate approach is not merely a question of structure – equally important are the processes needed to sustain it and the genuine willingness of all concerned to make it work . . .' (para. 4.35). Corporate management is 'a total style of management, not merely an isolated technique' (para. 5.1). In particular, there was a fear that old attitudes would persist among committee members and officers, who would identify too closely with *their* service, neighbourhood, political party or interest. In contrast to the Maud Report, the Bains and Paterson Reports had made this more likely by compromising on the matter of committees and giving them an executive rather than a merely advisory or consultative role.[17] In so far as the policy committee consists of service committee chairs, and the officers' management team of departmental chief officers, effective corporate management would be severely jeopardized, as it would be difficult for these individuals to act otherwise than in a representative or partial capacity.

Similarly, the position of the chief executive in relation to the other chief officers was stated in somewhat ambiguous terms, although all three reports sought to enhance the role of the chief executive beyond that of the traditional clerk (always a lawyer). Paterson says they were to be 'head of the authority's paid service . . . with direct authority over and responsibility for all other officers except . . . where they are exercising their professional judgement'. The Bains Report gives the chief executive the same initial description, but qualifies it by adding:

the range of issues and problems facing any local authority is too numerous and varied for the Chief Executive to grasp in detail, and Heads of Departments must therefore retain the responsibility for the effective and efficient running of the services for which their departments are responsible. (para. 5.13)

This leaves open the question of the relationship between the chief executive and the other chief officers. As head of the paid service, how authoritative is the chief executive to be? Equally uncertain is the relationship between the chief officers and the management team, and, in particular, just how binding upon the officers the decisions of the management team should be. One thing has become clear, however, chief executives no longer have a predominantly legal background, with only 43 per cent being lawyers (compared with 68 per cent in 1975).

Local authorities had many decisions to make about how far they would adopt the corporate approach and the ways in which they might adapt the Bains and Paterson models to their particular circumstances. Before we turn to see what has happened, it should be noted that in some respects the work of the two reports was pre-empted by government action. The Local Government Acts of 1972 (England and Wales) and 1973 (Scotland) *required* the appointment of certain chief officers and committees (for education, social work, police, etc.). The same legislation also allocated related functions (such as housing and social services or structure and local planning) among different tiers of local authorities (see p. 50). This introduced some constraints and precluded certain organizational possibilities which Bains and Paterson may have considered desirable.

The corporate approach since 1974–5

On a very wide scale, especially in Scotland, local authorities adopted the management recommendations of the Bains and Paterson Reports.[18] 'The concept of a corporate approach to management has been so thoroughly absorbed into the ethos of local government that it no longer provokes the discussion it did in the 1960s. There are nevertheless differences of emphasis.'[19] Some made adaptations, but others adopted corporate forms without a clear understanding of the requisite relationships and operations for it to work successfully. One study[20] of a sample of local authorities has discovered three broad types of management system in operation:

(1) The 'professional departmental approach' which, while per-

haps having the outward appearance of a reformed, corporate system, actually operates in the older, more traditional ways, with policy ideas emerging from the departments and the service committees, the policy committee and management team playing a relatively small coordinating role, and the chief executive liable to operate rather like his or her predecessor (the clerk) and being seen as no more than 'first among equals'. Within this arrangement, there is a tendency for the department and committee system to be in a one-to-one relationship, though some inter-departmental working parties may exist. Such arrangements are most likely to be found among the non-metropolitan authorities.

(2) Local authorities with the 'developed corporate approach', as the title suggests, have established corporate structures and operate them in an appropriately corporate fashion, with each part of the machinery fulfilling its proper role – the chief executive acting as policy adviser and director of the officers' management team, which resembles a corporate planning unit and acts in a directing relationship to the individual departments. Similarly, the policy and resources committee sees itself as 'custodian of the corporate plan' and will seek to assert itself over the service or programme committees. Such arrangements are mainly to be found among the urban or metropolitan authorities.

(3) The 'collaborative approach' is found among those local authorities that had developed some corporate processes and were working towards the 'developed' system. These authorities thus exhibit features of the other two systems. Being new authorities based, for the most part, on amalgamations of former councils, they are trying to evolve cautiously and incrementally. Their constituent elements (the policy committee, the chief executive, the management team, the service committees, the inter-departmental working groups) are composed in different ways and exercise varying roles and degrees of ascendancy.

The existence of such variations is in no way surprising. As the research report says, corporate management 'is a phrase to which people react in emotional rather than rational ways' and it is pointed out that many members exhibit a great deal of suspicion of corporate management. The same is true of many chief officers, particularly education officers, some of them believing that their particular service suffers as a result of the corporate approach. Consequently, the assumption of a corporate form of management may be a façade hiding regular inter-committee or departmental battles. Indeed, corporate management has been applied in so many different ways and with so many different levels of understanding that it has 'become a phrase to which it is increasingly difficult to give a real meaning'.[21]

There appears, in fact, to have been something of a retreat from corporate management. Some local authorities unthinkingly adopted the form or machinery of corporate management without the appropriate attitudes and processes. Subsequently, when it did not appear to be working, it was deemed a failure and partly or wholly abandoned. A number of chief executives have either been dropped or have assumed departmental responsibilities. In 1993, the working party report on internal management, *Community Leadership and Representation: Unlocking the Potential*, declared that while 'most authorities already have a policy committee which explicitly provides strategic direction to guide the running of the authority's affairs and sets out the authority's vision for local people . . . [others] need to use their policy committees specifically to identify what they want to achieve for their communities, and how it can be achieved' (para. 4.11(i)).

It is perhaps unfortunate that the 'corporate revolution' should have coincided with restraints on public expenditure and strong pressures on local authority resources. Political pressures have compounded this situation, as

the opposition parties (usually Conservative) took up the cry of inefficient structures and too much bureaucracy. Thus by the election swings of 1976 and 1977 a head of steam had been built up in many local authorities for change and change away from the existing (corporate) structure.[22]

Although party politicization and the emergence of party leaders may encourage a unified approach to management, it may be subject to short runs where there are electoral swings and party polarization. Paradoxically, with hung councils, the corporate approach may be more difficult to achieve initially, but may last longer in spite of changes in the composition of the council.

Other local authorities have weathered the storms of reduced resources and perhaps increased politicization, and have continued their development of corporate management and planning systems. This seems to be due to their having a strong initial commitment to a corporate approach and some early experience of working that system.[23] Thus we see once again the influence of local political and administrative cultures in shaping the operation of local government. These are considered further in Chapters 13 and 14.

In the meantime, the corporate approach is having to cope with a number of other developments, some deriving from government policies. The first is the problem created by uncertainties and fluctuations in revenues. Many local authorities developed corporate plans or strategy documents that set out targets and specified goals for the council. But such corporate planning relied upon a degree of certainty about future finances. This became increasingly problematical with changes in RSG/block grant and tax-capping (see pp. 472–4) and such planning began to wane.

Second, the trend towards greater accountability in local government has led to the development of decentralization, with patch systems, neighbourhood offices (even neighbourhood chief executive officers; see p. 446). Clearly such arrangements can weaken or jeopardize corporate management; indeed one view is that decentralization is 'the very antithesis of corporate management'.[24] The third involves opting out or the hiving off of various local authority services to government-appointed agencies (or quangos), such as Housing Action Trusts, Urban Development Corporations or the Grant Maintained Schools Trust – which further undermines the corporate concept.[25] Finally, there is competitive tendering and the contracting-out of services (see p. 272, 305–7), which in itself need not present a threat, but which in practice often appears to do so:

The name of the game for the service chief officer will be survival . . . Coordination and the subordination of interests to achieve a wider benefit to the local authority or local community will not win contracts . . . (the officer's) ambition will be more heavily focused on his own service, and he will not be prepared to accept those compromises demanded in the name of the community or the wider local authority interest, if he will lose the contract.[26]

One consequence of this is that service managers will demand different services, information, advice and skills from their central departments – finance, personnel, legal – which, if they are not forthcoming adequately enough, they may seek to develop themselves or buy in from outside.

However, a further consequence has been to move the Government to initiate a wide-ranging review of local authorities' internal management and decision-making arrangements.

Reforming internal management

In 1991, Michael Heseltine, as Secretary of State for the Environment, expressed concern at the shortage of people willing to become councillors. In large part he blamed 'the procedural wrangles, the proliferation of committees and the scheming that goes on in smoke-filled rooms . . . [which] . . . have all discredited the system. There are simply too many councillors spending too much time – achieving too little'.[27] The speech had been preceded by the Government's publication of a consultative document, *The Internal Management of Local Authorities in England.* This provided a wide range of options for organizing (and improving) the management of councils and implied that local authorities, where appropriate, may experiment and adopt a variety of committee and management arrangements. These could include a cabinet–

backbench system, elected mayors or appointed council managers. The paper raised questions as to the desirability of delegated powers for chairmen, salaries for councillors, referendums on local spending and the power to dissolve councils and hold elections as appropriate. The wisdom of having two different election systems (of 'thirds' and 'whole council') was also questioned. The objectives of any subsequent change in management arrangements should be to promote more effective, speedy and business-like decision-making; enhance scrutiny of decisions; increase interest in local government by the public; and provide councillors with greater scope for their constituency work.

Of those who responded to the consultation paper, nearly half were in favour of leaving the present arrangement unchanged. Subsequently a working party (comprising councillors, officers and representatives of the local authority associations, the Audit Commission, the LGMB, civil servants of the Department of the Environment and a professor of government) was set up to review and report on current management practice in local government, to consider suggestions for change received in response to the consultative paper and to suggest possible experimental models of internal (or 'political') management. In explaining its role, the working party report says:

In all areas of the public sector new management styles are being developed to deal with new roles and new circumstances. Local government is at the forefront of these changes . . . the increasing . . . diversity of provision . . . opens up opportunities for choice and improved services. The local authority has to look not only to its traditional role as provider of services but also to one where the emphasis is now more on specifying requirements, coordinating functions and monitoring performance. The existing committee structure and many features of common practice grew up as the best way of managing service provision; it may not be the best way of running an authority, with a new role, in the 21st century.[28]

The working party recommended that all local authorities should review their committee and internal management arrangements to assess the extent to which they are appropriate for achieving the review's main objectives of strengthening the role of all elected members and developing the framework for effective leadership within local authorities. The local authority associations are urged to promote such reviews and to disseminate good practice and encourage innovation and diversity.

After outlining a number of current management arrangements (formal and informal) currently operating in various local authorities, the report illustrates a number of management models which, given due government approval where necessary, local authorities may (voluntarily) experiment with, according to local circumstances. (The Bains Report was felt to have been somewhat overprescriptive.) These models may be executive or non-executive in orientation. Of the former, some – such as the directly elected single- (mayor) or multi-member executive – are not recommended, largely on the grounds that such systems could confuse accountability and create difficulties in the relationship between the executive and the separately elected council (i.e. a potential clash of supremacy or of mandates) as well as making it difficult to ensure political neutrality of officers with two masters. Other models include the single-party policy committee with a limited range of executive powers; the lead-member system where – like government Ministers – senior councillors have delegated control and executive powers over aspects of the council's services; the 'cabinet' system, the membership of which has individual and collective executive powers; and the 'strong political executive', drawn from the council but (like a collective presidential system) having a separate legal entity and taking many (even all) decisions on behalf of the council.

The advantages claimed for these executive models are that they would provide clear political direction for the authority, make clear where accountability lies, provide a more efficient, quicker and coordinated decision-making process, and provide a confidential forum for the ruling group to test the range of policy options with its official advisers. In their annual report for 1992, the local government Commissioners (ombudsmen) for England also endorsed the idea of separating councils' decision-making process from that of scrutiny (along the lines of Parliamentary select committees).

However, such proposals are unlikely to find universal support, and the most obvious objection will come from the councillors who find themselves excluded from the executive body, however constituted.[29] Whilst recognizing this problem, advocates of the 'cabinet' system suggest that backbench councillors could have enhanced area-advocacy and consumer-advocacy roles together with a degree of rotation or alternation with the frontbench roles[30] and greater investigatory powers (through Parliamentary select committee-type scrutinies).[31]

The working party also felt that there was a strong case for councils experimenting with a non-executive or advisory committee, which should be single party (where there is a majority) or multi-party (dominant party coalition). On the grounds that 'most major policy decisions in practice are taken not by the full council, its committees or sub-committees but elsewhere within the ruling group . . . or in consultation with the leadership of other groups . . . the majority party . . . through its leading members and especially its leader, is a de facto executive . . . Formal authority may rest with the full council, or with the committee . . . [but] the real authority rests with individuals.' The result is that, due to the law and other formalities, councillors often 'spend unnecessarily long hours in meetings which purport to take decisions which in reality have been taken elsewhere'. By aligning appearance with reality 'there should be clearer policy guidance and recommendations being issued to executive committees'. Clearer accountability will be achieved, since 'such a system would also clarify the source of recommendations being put to committees'. Hence it is recommended that councils should be allowed (notwithstanding the 1989 Act (see p. 158)) to establish such deliberative committees on a formal basis.

In view of the proposed reorganization of local government in Scotland, the Government, in 1993, issued a consultation document on *The Internal Management of Local Authorities in Scotland*. It provides a number of ideas (about committee structures and size of councils) for discussion, including that of directly elected provosts or council managers and the introduction of 'cabinet' government by small groups of senior councillors. It also proposes to require councils to appoint heads of the paid service (as is already the case in England and Wales; see p. 266).

Whatever the form of decision-making and coordination, it is obvious that most of the work of local government is conducted in the 'field'. Most of us encounter local government on the roads, in the car parks, playing fields, sports halls, etc. And most of the staff employed in local government do not work at the headquarters (the Town or County Hall) but in a host of institutions and depots, area offices, nurseries, schools and colleges; hostels, homes, day centres; workshops, training centres; libraries, fire stations and building/engineering sites and stores. We examine local government staffing in the next chapter.

10. Internal Organization: The Officers

The local government service is the local government equivalent of the civil service, consisting, that is, of paid employees whose job it is to carry out the policy decisions of the elected politicians. Local government officers are therefore 'bureaucrats' in the sense that, in the interests of efficiency and fairness, they are appointed and promoted on merit rather than fear or favour, and they do their work (such as allocating school places, grants or council houses) impartially and in accordance with the council's declared policy and rules of procedure. This is not to deny that they may become 'bureaucrats' in the pejorative sense of becoming slow, rigid, unsympathetic and, above all, exercising power without being held to public account. As we shall see, there are mechanisms and procedures which seek to minimize such undesirable tendencies.

The central government has a civil service of 565,000 employees (in 1979 it was over 700,000). Like the civil service, local government employment is large, with some 2·2 million employees (down from 2·3 million in 1979 – see Table 15). Unlike the civil service, however, it is not really one single service: each local authority recruits and employs its own staff. There is no single employing body, and local government officers cannot be posted from one part of the country to another, as a civil servant can. In practice, however, salaries and conditions of service have become substantially standardized throughout the country as a result of the emergence of national negotiating machinery, trade unions and the Local Government Training Board (now the Local

*Includes architects, accountants, engineers, public health
inspectors, social workers, technicians

Figure 17 *The structure of local government service*

Government Management Board; see p. 277). Recent developments (allowing local authorities more flexibility to introduce
performance-related pay and short-term contracts of employment,
together with contracting out and out-sourcing etc.) are altering
this situation.

Table 15 shows the large number of different kinds of employee
in local government. Traditionally, they are divided into officials
or 'officers' (professional, technical and clerical staff, or 'white-
collar workers') and 'servants' ('blue collar', or manual workers,
including refuse collectors, gardeners, cleaners or road workmen).
Each group has its own conditions of service, superannuation
provisions and negotiating machinery.

However, there is a third group of employees whose existence is
crucial to local government but who are classified neither as officers
nor as servants. These are teachers, social workers, firefighters
and the police. In this chapter we are primarily concerned with the
first group, the officers: it is they (about 0·5 million) who form what
is known as the 'local government service'.[1]

Table 15 *Local authority employees (full-time or equivalent), 1979–93*

	1979	1984	1988	1993
Education: teachers/lecturers	629,312	608,526	585,591	555,906[b]
others	467,058	424,740	439,635	410,356
Construction	155,336	132,897	131,738	94,356
Transport	31,688	27,694	3,813[a]	2,275
Libraries and museums	37,453	37,042	38,964	38,601
Recreation, parks, baths, tourism	97,767	87,026	99,415	85,093
Environmental health	25,200	23,397	24,248	23,681
Cleaning, refuse collection/disposal	60,852	51,035	47,372	32,093
Housing	54,256	62,073	70,858	76,068
Social services	234,653	251,562	273,186	282,972
Town and country planning	24,369	23,038	24,011	26,629
Fire service	45,892	46,204	47,315	47,576
Police (inc. clerks, cadets, wardens)	172,521	182,117	186,651	200,892
Local courts and probation staff	17,599	21,600	24,319	27,197
Miscellaneous	303,876	288,549	290,611	310,818
Total (= 8·5% of national workforce)	2,358,686	2,267,500	2,286,327	2,214,513

Source: Employment Gazette (monthly).

NOTE: Of the total, Scotland has some 300,000 local government staff.

Occupational groups	
Chief officers	0·3%
Administrative, professional, technical and clerical	20%
Teachers, police, firemen	30%
Manual	50%
	100

[a] Reduction reflects creation of public transport companies in October 1986.

[b] Education figures reflect transfer of polytechnics from local government 1989, but not teachers and lecturers who transferred in 1993.

The figures in Table 15 show a changing pattern in the distribution of these different occupations. This is in response to a number of factors including changing priorities (government or local authority), structural and functional changes (such as the decline in the school population, the transfer of polytechnics and colleges), competitive tendering and contracting out of services, the introduction of housing benefit, community charge and community care, etc.

Negotiating machinery

Since 1944, local government has developed a national negotiating machinery known as the National Joint Council for Local Authorities Services. This comprises a number of separate committees, about forty in all, covering such occupational groups as firefighters, youth leaders, manual workers, engineering craftsmen and teachers. Their function is to negotiate national salary scales and conditions of service. There are thus two 'sides' involved – the employers (or management side) and the employees (the staff side). In practice, the employers' side is drawn from representatives of the local authorities' associations (such as the Association of County Councils – see p. 401) and the staff side from the trade unions such as UNISON (formed in 1993 through the amalgamation of the NALGO, NUPE and COHSE unions).

The multiplicity of negotiating bodies makes the negotiating machinery very complex and liable to create inconsistencies and unfairness, as well as being difficult to operate. However, the problems were reduced by the creation in 1948 of an advisory and coordinating body, the Local Authorities Conditions of Service Advisory Board (LACSAB).* Apart from advising on pay and conditions and giving guidance on implementation, it also

---

* LACSAB, the Local Government Training Board (LGTB) and the Local Authorities Management Services and Computer Committee (LAMSAC; see p. 277) merged into the Local Government Management Board (LGMB) in 1991.

provides information and recommendations on general legislation, reports on how national decisions are working out in practice and responds to requests for advice on specific issues. In addition, at regional level, there are Provincial Councils which keep the national bodies in touch with local opinion on conditions of service matters. They also oversee and assist with the local implementation of national agreements and hear local disputes and staff appeals.

The terms and conditions of employment resulting from the negotiations – sometimes called 'Whitleyism' – are implemented by individual local authorities (except parishes and community councils, to which the agreements do not apply), although the agreements only provide guidelines for minimum rather than necessary conditions, and local authorities are free to improve conditions where they see fit. Where a local authority fails to meet the minimum agreed provisions, employees can appeal through the well-established machinery. It is perhaps ironic, though probably inevitable, that individual councils are advised on matters of implementation by their officers, that is their employees.

Officers and conditions of service

In this chapter we are primarily concerned with the administrative and professional staff of local government – the officers. These comprise various grades and statuses: the professional and special-ist officers; general (or 'lay') administrators; technicians; and clerical and other office staff. These are generally referred to as 'the APT & C' grades. Under the Local Government Acts of 1972 and 1973, local authorities are required to 'appoint such officers as they think necessary for the proper discharge by the authority of such of their . . . functions as fall to be discharged by them'. Certain officers are, however, required by law to be appointed: these include Chief Education Officers, Directors of Social Services, members of fire brigades, Chief Constables, public analysts, agricultural analysts and Inspectors of Weights and Measures. (Local authorities are also required by law to designate officers for the posts of head of the paid service, a monitoring (or propriety) officer and financial administration; in practice these roles may be combined except monitoring and finance offices.)

All such officers 'hold office on such reasonable terms and conditions ... as the local authority think fit' (Section 112). Some – the chief officers – have their own separate national negotiating machinery. But for the majority of local government officers their conditions of employment are determined by the National Joint Council for the Administrative, Professional, Technical and Clerical staffs, and these conditions are set out in a detailed scheme[2] sometimes called the 'charter' or 'purple book'. This originated in 1946 and represented a breakthrough in the establishment of the principle of equal pay for equal work throughout the country (except for the GLC, which had its own scheme).

The National Joint Council for the APT & C staffs is regularly negotiating and reviewing the scheme of conditions of employment. As a result there will be regular adjustments in hours, holidays, leave of absence, sickness payments and, above all, salaries.

Before 1946 the rates of pay varied haphazardly among local authorities, partly as a result of local trade-union pressure and partly as a consequence of local party politics. However, variations will still occur, partly because of local authorities' differing management structures and partly because of variations in the local employment situation. It is particularly likely where authorities abolish departments and replace them with trading agencies (as Berkshire CC did, for example, in 1992[3]). A number of councils (e.g. Harrow LBC) are breaking away from national agreements to develop their own local pay scales, in some cases to deal with the problem of excessive staff turnover (as in Kent CC, which has experienced a 20% turnover in recent years).

Salaries and grading

Apart from certain (designated) chief officers, the scheme divides the staff of the local government service into three groups (there were five up to 1983), each with a number of salary scales:

(1) *Administrative, professional, technical and clerical (APT & C)*. In 1993, the salary ranged over six scales from £5,229 to £15,063 for those doing *clerical* work (such as filing, typing, checking documents, processing claims for grants or other payments) or *technical* work (such as that of draughtsman, librarian, building inspector and engineering, laboratory, planning or accounting technician). The actual salary scale will vary according to degree of responsibility and level of work undertaken. Thus there is a salary range for *senior officers* of £15,629 to £18,231 and for *principal officers* of £17,721 to £22,032. These latter posts are available for the more experienced and qualified officers, and it is here that we find education officers, housing officers, planners, lawyers, accountants and engineers. Their work often involves controlling large or important sections of a department and the leadership of teams of officers. At the top are the *chief officers* and *senior managers*, whose work involves giving advice on policy and managing whole departments or groups of departments. Their salaries can range from £22,887 to £69,075, but the actual levels will depend on the size of the local authority and its population. In England and Wales, chief executive officers have a separate salary scale from other chief officers, currently £33,573 to £85,275.

These are the national scales (for 1992–3), which vary with size of population in the authority area. But the scales are only guidelines, and councils can agree to pay over the scale rates, some on the basis of performance-related pay. About half a dozen chief executives receive over £100,000 p.a. (but to put this into perspective, while the CEO of Birmingham MBC receives £92,000 p.a. (1993), the chairman of the East Midlands Electricity Board gets £250,000 p.a.).

(2) *Special classes*, which comprise a variety of occupational groups each with its own grade and salary scale, for example social workers £11,268–£19,656 or residential and affiliated staff £6,852–£23,169.

(3) *Miscellaneous*, which comprises another range of occupational groupings such as meals supervisors, telephone supervisors and traffic wardens whose duties are neither wholly clerical nor wholly manual. The range is £8,000 to £11,000.

Generally speaking, grading in all posts depends on such factors as experience and level of responsibility as well as qualifications. This gives each local authority some discretion in grading posts in relation to the national scheme.

Recruitment, appointment and promotion

Recruitment to local government traditionally relied on the grammar-school leaver. Before the Second World War local government provided an occupation opportunity with some status and security. Entrants were expected to study and gain professional qualifications (in law, engineering, housing administration, etc.). Since the war (at least until recently), local government has faced competition from other employers and as a consequence has either had to lower its entrance requirements or has moved 'up market' to recruit A-level students and graduates.[4] The situation eased during the high (especially youth) unemployment of the 1980s, but demographic change has led to a falling off in the number of school-leavers and thus a return of the recruitment problem. There are already shortages in a number of areas, ranging from lawyers and accountants to social workers and trading standards officers. Extra pay, 'golden hellos' and attractive employment packages are being offered in many authorities to combat the problem. This problem has eased somewhat in the current recession, but will intensify as the economy returns to growth and fuller employment.

Appointment is based on (desirable) bureaucratic principles: the aim is to appoint on the basis of merit and eliminate the possibility of nepotism or favouritism. Any relationship between a candidate and a councillor or officer of the authority must be disclosed, and canvassing for an appointment is prohibited (though it still occurs[5]).

Promotion too is based on merit or performance as well as qualifications. Officers, especially young clerical entrants, are encouraged to move among departments in order to obtain a wider administrative experience. Officers are also generally encouraged to undertake approved courses of education and training to obtain qualifications, especially those in the administrative and professional grades: the aim is to develop certain skills and promote in officers a broader and more positive interest in their daily duties.

The education and training of local government officers has long been exhorted by NALGO,[6] now UNISON. And, although well developed (e.g. the Local Government Examinations Board was established in 1945), it was given a substantial impetus with the setting-up of the Local Government Training Board (now the Local Government Management Board) in 1967. By helping to spread the costs of training among local authorities, the aim was to deal with the problem of the small authorities which had difficulties in financing the training of their staff; it also aimed at stopping the less training-conscious authorities 'poaching' trained staff from other authorities.

The underlying purpose of this training is to increase the effectiveness of local government manpower. Training courses include induction, training in clerical skills, training for supervision, preparation for administrative and professional qualifications, and instruction in the principles of management. Some training is carried out at work itself or at home (through distance learning courses), but a great deal is given in colleges on a day-release or block-release basis. A number of higher management courses are provided by the University of Birmingham's Institute of Local Government Studies (INLOGOV). However, while education and training have much expanded over the past fifteen years, its cost is now being more carefully counted, and there is a growing insistence that training and post-entry education should be job-related and effective, i.e. less purely academic and more geared to problem-solving and practical application, increasingly in the direction of business-related skills and the Investing in People programme. BTEC and National Vocational Qualifications (NVQs) focus on the development and testing of skills and competences, and professional bodies such as the ICSA and the IRRV place increased emphasis on financial and management information, systems management and marketing as well as developing strategies for greater business awareness, continuous professional development (CPD) and credit accumulation and transfer (CAT); CIPFA's new training scheme 'recognizes the realities of the new world in which we find ourselves'.[7] The highly regarded MBA has now been adapted to the public sector. In their recent revision of the qualifying scheme the ICSA perceive the needs of local government to be similar to those of the private sector, because of the more commercially oriented approach to local authority activities as manifested in CCT and contracting out, cost-centre management, service level agreements, business plans and internal trading accounts.

Security of tenure

The substantial security enjoyed by local government officers is well known, and in the past has proved an attractive feature of local government employment. However, local government officers can be relegated, suspended or dismissed on grounds related to discipline or efficiency – for example, unauthorized disclosure, persistent lateness or absenteeism. And an officer's employment can be terminated where a 'closed shop' (trade-union monopoly) exists, as it does in a number of local authorities (though much depends on the political composition of the council, and government legislation is now making the closed shop illegal).

Local government employees can also be made redundant – no longer an empty threat in these days of expenditure cuts, and an increasing number of staff are being employed on fixed-term contracts.

Local government officers must not only behave properly, but they must be seen so to behave. The APT & C scheme (p. 253) states:

The public is entitled to demand of a local government officer conduct of the highest standard and public confidence in his integrity would be shaken were the least suspicion ... that he could in any way be influenced by improper motives.

As a consequence and to reinforce this general goal a number of precepts are laid down:

An officer's off-duty hours are his personal concern, but he should not subordinate his duty to his private interests or put himself in a position where his duty and his private interests conflict.

(An example might be taking on an inappropriate part-time job such as a local authority planner or architect undertaking technical or presentational work for an applicant for planning permission.)

No officer shall communicate to the public the proceedings of any committee meeting etc., nor the contents of any document relating to the authority unless required to do so by law or expressly authorized to do so.

If it comes to the knowledge of an officer that a contract in which he has any pecuniary interest ... has been, or is proposed to be, entered into by the authority, he shall ... give notice ...

It is difficult to know how far employees live up to these standards. Statistics for the period 1965–75 show that ninety local government employees (including forty dustmen and seventeen policemen) were convicted of offences under the Prevention of Corruption Act (see note 5), and for the period 1967–79 about 1,000 cases of fraud were reported, though this 'does not indicate extensive dishonesty having regard to the scale of local government operations, and many of the sums [frauds] include very small sums'.[8] (Most of the offenders here were those who generally handled small amounts of money. The (illegal) offering of gift vouchers as inducements to local officers who order products for councils appears to be quite widespread among major firms.) Furthermore, officers can be placed in awkward situations when they suspect or allege corruption among their colleagues or councillors: they risk possible victimization and pressure to resign.[9]

Politics

Another potentially hazardous area for local government officers is party politics. The APT & C scheme declares that the officer

... should not be called upon to advise any political group of the employing authority either as to the work of the group or as to the work of the authority, neither shall he be required to attend any meeting of any political group.

A similar provision exists in the conditions of service of chief officers. The aim is to reinforce the political impartiality of the local government service, which, like the civil service, is expected to show disinterested loyalty to whichever political party group controls the council. The situation can be more difficult in local government because parties are a new phenomenon for many authorities, and because local government officers are responsible to the council as a whole rather than to the council chair or committee chairs. (Civil servants are responsible to individual Ministers, not to Parliament as such. However, the question is sometimes raised there whether the Opposition, or indeed MPs generally, should be briefed by officials.) Meanwhile, for local government the questions remain to be decided among the local authorities: should (chief) officers develop special relationships with the majority party and its leaders? Should they appear at party caucus meetings, as a growing number appear to be doing,[10] and if so on what conditions? How should they balance this relationship with the minority parties and the council as a whole? The Government has recommended that officers' terms and conditions of service be amended to allow officers to attend party meetings (on request via the Chief Executive).

There is a strong convention that local government officers, especially more senior staff, should refrain from open support of political parties. Otherwise members might lose confidence in the impartiality and objectivity of professional advice and may doubt the speed, enthusiasm or even the direction with which their decisions were being implemented by the officials. Similarly, members of the public might come to suspect that they were not receiving fair treatment from their local administrators. Nevertheless, local officers play a quite public role (in committees, etc.).

However, while we as a society restrict the political rights of local government officers, we compensate them with security of tenure: we do not (as in the so-called 'spoils system') change our officials when we change (by election) our council. Nor do we elect our officials (as in some parts of America, where they may elect their 'strong' or executive mayor). Like civil service employees, British local government officers are 'permanent' (subject to what has been said on pp. 257 and 467). And by law (under the Local Government and Housing Act 1989) all appointments to paid office must be made on merit. The issue has arisen because of the increasing tendency for councillors to become involved in the appointment of staff.[11] Consequently it is proposed that members will be involved in the appointment of those officers in the politically restricted group (see below); and 'the proper officer' (i.e. the head of the paid service; see p. 266) will be responsible for appointments outside that group. Members may continue to be involved in matters of discipline and dismissal, but must take into account the accompanying report of the proper officer.

The law also intervenes to keep officials away from party

politics by making membership of a local authority legally incompatible with paid employment by that authority.[12] This does not altogether prevent an officer from becoming a councillor, since he or she may be free to stand for election and serve as an elected member for *another* local authority. Clearly this may jeopardize the principle of official impartiality, especially where the candidates fight the election under party banners. However, a concerned local authority can insist that an officer does not 'put himself in a position where his duty and his private interests conflict'. Indeed, under the scheme senior officers must obtain the consent of the council before 'engaging in any other business or take up any other additional appointment'. But a number of recent cases caused concern[13] and invited the attention of the Widdicombe Committee. As outlined above (p. 174) the Committee recommended that senior officials should be barred from political office (the so-called 'twin-trackers') and the Government has made provision for this in the Local Government and Housing Act 1989. Under this Act, officers are deemed to fall into the *politically restricted* category if they hold senior posts and/or their work is of a sensitive nature (see p. 175). A criterion salary level of between £19,600 and £21,300 has been given (see p. 176), though the Minister has the power to alter this, and also to declare exemptions. Not only may such officers not stand for political office (with the exception of parish/community membership) but (under their contracts of employment) they must desist from such political activities as canvassing at elections, holding office in a political party, or speaking or writing publicly on matters of party political controversy. Officers may, however, by request and through the chief officer, attend party group meetings to give professional advice. And others may be appointed (with a salary of up to £22,842 (1993)) in order specifically to assist and advise party groups. Such party *political advisers* will be appointed on political criteria and will be limited to a maximum of three per authority. (They are currently employed in some forty local authorities.[14])

It has, however, been argued that this disqualification for

council membership is no longer valid, particularly for the majority of the two million employees in local government who play no part in policy advice or formulation. Apart from depriving employees of their rights as citizens to take part in the civic life of their community, it denies both to local government and to the public the benefits of the pool of skill, experience and enthusiasm which such employees may possess. In addition it is argued that local government should follow the tendency of other forms of employment towards greater participation by employees in decision-making. (In practice, some local authorities such as Basildon, Slough and Hampshire have allowed manual and staff workers speaking rights at council and committee meetings.) The Committee on Conduct in Local Government (see p. 209) considered these arguments but concluded that it was in the public interest that the law should remain unchanged. However, the issue is being kept alive by the trade unions and by the publication of the Bullock Report on industrial democracy.[15] However, following the Widdicombe Report, the Local Government and Housing Act 1989 is even more restrictive by excluding an estimated 50,000 officials from holding political office.

The role of local government officers

Local authorities have wide discretion in appointing officers (see p. 75), and officers are appointed on such reasonable terms as the authority thinks fit (p. 251), with conditions being agreed collectively through the National Joint Council under the guidance of the Local Authorities' Conditions of Service Advisory Board (now merged into the LGMB), though these are not binding on individual authorities. The relationship between officers and councillors is not defined in legislation, but the National Code of Local Government Conduct recognizes that whereas councillors are responsible to the electorate, officers are responsible to the council, to give advice and carry out the council's work. Thus the primary task of local government officers is to implement the policy decisions of the council. In the Middle Ages everyone was expected to spend a few days in the year making up the local roads, whereas highway engineering today requires skill and training, as do all modern local government services – social work, housing maintenance, planning, architecture. The trend to specialization continues. Elected councillors themselves lack both the experience and the time: hence they employ full-time paid officers and other staff.

Not all officers are directly concerned with the delivery of services. Many are providing back-up or support services. Just as local authorities have 'vertical' (or service) and 'horizontal' (or functional) committees (see p. 221), so they have vertical departments (such as the education department and the social services department) and horizontal departments (such as finance). Officials in the latter departments help only indirectly to implement policy. Their immediate function is to provide support services for the other, 'delivering', departments.

A third and perhaps less obvious role of officials is to advise on policy. It is no longer possible these days (if it ever was) to say that members make policy and officers merely carry it out. Officers, especially senior officers, not only have experience and professional training: they also have a commitment to their service – whether in education, social work or engineering. As a result they will have ideas, pet schemes and ambitions which will inevitably be communicated to councillors, especially committee chairs. In some ways it is true to say that the members' task is to keep a rein on officials' enthusiasm and tell them what the public will not stand! Apart from the fact that ideas will emerge from the administrative process itself, administrative experience provides other lessons. Officers too will exercise a negative influence, checking members' exuberance and advising them what is not feasible (for legal, financial or other reasons) or warning them of possible snags and suggesting alternatives. This officer–member relationship is explored further below (p. 283).

The chief officers

Chief officers head the departments, or, in some cases, as 'directors', groups of departments. (The exception is the chief executive officer – CEO – who, following the Bains recommendation, in most local authorities does not have a department. See Chapter 9 and p. 269.)

The Chief Executive Officer

While not mandatory, 90 per cent of authorities have a chief executive. However, the role varies: in some authorities the CEO is no more than first among equals; elsewhere he (there are only four women CEOs) is genuinely in managerial control of the council's operations. The Widdicombe Committee considered that the post of CEO needed to be formalized and enhanced in order to improve corporate management, to secure a clearer relationship between officers and members, and to promote the interests of accountability and better management within the officer hierarchy. They recommend that (a) the post be made mandatory, (b) he should be designated as head of the authority's paid service, with overall managerial responsibility for the discharge of functions of officers, and (c) he be given additional responsibilities, such as securing proper party balance on committees, determining councillors' need to inspect documents or attend meetings, to advise on the legality of any proposed action by the council or to be involved in discipline of senior (as well as junior) staff.

In response, the Government has rejected (a), but under the Local Government and Housing Act 1989 (sec. 5), now requires all principal authorities to designate an officer as *monitoring officer*. It is his or her duty to alert the council to any situation where the council or a committee/sub-committee or an officer may be about to do or may have done something unlawful, improper or which would constitute maladministration. (This post can be assigned to the CEO or, more usually, the solicitor but not the chief finance officer; see below.) Such advice takes the form of a report, which must be considered by the full council within three months. In addition, the Act requires local authorities to designate an officer (usually the CEO) as *head of the paid service*, whose duty would be to advise the council on the coordination of its functions and the organization (including discipline) of its staffing.

A chief executive's duties may include the following:

(i) to act as head of the council's paid service, with authority over all other officers so far as this is necessary for the efficient management and execution of the council's functions;

(ii) to act as leader of the chief officers' group (COG) and (through the policy and resources committee) as the council's principal adviser on matters of general policy. It is his responsibility as such to secure the coordination of advice on the planning of objectives and services, and to lead the management team in securing a corporate approach to the affairs of the authority generally;

(iii) to be responsible, through his leadership of the COG, for the efficient and effective implementation of the council's programmes and policies, and for ensuring that the resources of the authority are most effectively deployed towards these ends;

(iv) to review the organization and administration of the authority and make recommendations to the council (through the P & R committee) if he considers that major changes are required in the interests of effective management;

(v) to be responsible, as head of the paid service, for ensuring that effective and equitable staffing policies are developed and implemented throughout all departments in the interests both of the authority and the staff;

(vi) to be responsible for the maintenance of good internal and external relations.

Other Chief Officers

The chief officer is primarily a manager and he or she must recognize that any major decision cannot be made without an impact on other services. In general, the role of the chief officer includes:

(i) membership of the chief officers' group (COG), which secures a corporate approach to the affairs of the authority (see p. 237);

(ii) responsibility for the efficient and effective implementation of the council's and committee's policies and programmes within his or her department and within the corporate plan;

(iii) acting as principal adviser to his or her committee;

(iv) responsibility for the maintenance of good relations with the community with regard to the service provided.

Under the Local Government Finance Act 1988, each authority's *chief finance officer* has the responsibility of advising the authority about any of its decisions which might involve unlawful action and/or expenditure (including that which exceeds the authority's resources). Thus, in order to provide a system of checks and balances, this role cannot be combined with that of the monitoring officer above (though government recognizes that this may lead to a difference of opinion between the two officers on occasion). In effect this will restore the position which existed before 1974, when there was a ban on the posts of clerk and treasurer being held together.

Although in any one day most of the work of chief officers is totally unpredictable, their work generally falls into four general areas or directions, each of which involves a combination of administration and politics, in the non-party sense of the word.

(1) Working within their own department. Here they exercise an administrative or managerial role – overseeing the execution of policy, being responsible for the allocation of work and the general standards and efficiency of working methods, staff appoint-

Figure 18 *A chief officer's domain*

ments, discipline and general morale and leadership. Apart from managing the current work of the department, chief officers also see their role as a policy-formulating one (see p. 284). When the chief officer is heavily involved in working outside his department, some of this work, especially the management aspect, is likely to be shared with or devolved upon their deputies, who are most frequently appointed in the county authorities.[16]

(2) Working with other departments. This is likely to involve a lot of the chief officer's time in councils where the corporate approach has been developed and inter-departmental mechanisms have been instituted (such as officers' management teams and inter-departmental working parties – see pp. 235, 270). This is particularly likely in the case of the larger authorities, but there are differences among the departments, especially between the service (vertical) departments and the function (horizontal) departments such as the chief executive's or treasurer's. A particular problem for chief officers is balancing the claims of their individual departments with those of the authority as a whole as represented by the chief executive officer and the treasurer (or chief finance officer) as well as the authority's secretary/solicitor (or director of central/corporate services).

(3) Working outside the department with other authorities. This

would involve relations with other local authorities (such as district councils) and liaison with government departments (such as the local Department of Social Security or Department of Employment) and semi-government bodies (such as the Health Authority, the Further Education Funding Council or the Forestry Commission). Some chief officers have direct links with Whitehall departments or their regional outposts in, for example, discussions over educational matters, building programmes or local government finance. In addition many chief officers act as advisers to the local authority associations (see p. 401), they are frequently engaged in the activities of their own professional associations such as the Association of Directors of Social Services (ADSS) or the Society of Local Authority Chief Executives (SOLACE) and all of them are expected to play some part in the public relations side of their department, including relations with the media and pressure groups. The actual amount of time involved here will vary, especially among departments and different types of local authority (the incidence being heaviest among the metropolitan authorities). (See note 15.)

(4) Working with councillors. This occurs mainly in the formal setting of committees, but involves a considerable amount of time in preparations for committees, including the briefing of committee chairs before meetings. Again certain officers are more heavily involved than others: the treasurer or secretary are called on to attend many committees. The Maud Committee (1967) was critical of the extent to which members were involved in the detailed aspects of administration (for instance, choosing furniture or colour schemes for homes or constituting selection committees for minor posts such as junior library assistant). The Committee urged greater delegation of authority to officers, with members concentrating on broader policy matters (especially in the management board – see p. 228) and on their representative or constituency roles (especially in their non-executive committees). As we have seen (p. 230), the general tenor of the Maud Committee was endorsed by the Bains and Paterson Reports, but they were less

radical (and arguably more persuasive) in their detailed recommendations. Consequently, it is interesting to observe that there is a feeling among some officers that members are becoming increasingly involved in departmental administration (with more regular visits to the departments, etc.) to the extent that some of them, especially committee chairs, are becoming virtually full-time.[17]

Departmental reform

Despite the strictures of the Maud Report and the recommendations of the Bains and Paterson Reports, the number and form of local authority departments have not changed greatly, especially in England and Wales. Few local authorities have adopted a thoroughgoing directorate approach (of grouping departments). Most have retained the traditional departmental/professional structure, but with some inter-departmental links such as programme teams (sometimes known as the matrix system).[18] Where the directorate form has been adopted in substance (not merely in change of title), it has been mostly in the areas of technical or recreational services.

Change has been much more dramatic in the formal designation of a head of the officer structure. By 1975 only one major local authority in England and Wales had not appointed a chief executive officer.[19] Most of them had been given, at least formally, the responsibilities recommended by Bains and Paterson, with the important exception that a large minority had given their chief executive a department. These local authorities argued that a non-departmental chief executive officer would become too detached and isolated. For the most part, their departmental responsibilities involve such central support services functions as personnel, management services, public relations, corporate planning and research. This is in contrast to the functions of the traditional and largely superseded clerk's department, which was responsible for legal services, committee administration and electoral registration. The latter responsibilities are now usually in the hands of the local authorities' secretary or chief administrative officer.

In the appointment of chief executives, local authorities were urged[20] to have regard to managerial ability above all. Professional and technical expertise and background should no longer be the main criterion (as in the appointment of other chief officers and as traditionally in the appointment of lawyers as clerks). The top local government post therefore was to be an open field to officers from any background. The Mallaby Committee in particular envisaged a place for 'lay' administrative officers (that is, officers whose work in local government is of a general administrative nature, like that of the top civil servants, rather than those who specialize in education, finance or engineering). In practice, local authorities have tended to appoint their former Clerk (or Town Clerk) to the post of chief executive, although some have appointed treasurers, and of 101 chief executives appointed 1989–91, only thirty were lawyers. Only a few have gone outside local government (for instance to the civil service, the water industry or the district audit service) for their appointments.[21]

A third area of change in the administrative arrangements at officer level is in the universal creation in the 1970s of officers' management teams (OMTs) or chief officers' groups (COGs). In the early 1960s these were rare; by 1970 more than half the local authorities had them; by 1975 all local authorities had them. There are, however, variations in the size of these teams, in the proportion of chief officers included and in the frequency of their meetings.[22] A few councils have developed joint councillor–officer management committees.

However, as John Stewart has pointed out, much of the so-called corporate management has only reconstituted the old departmental or functional approach,[23] though in other cases it has complemented it, and this has been useful since no single principle is perhaps appropriate or adequate for organizing the affairs of a community. The Widdicombe Report has given a higher organizational profile to the political dimension. Individual councils are developing additional approaches, such as those based on area and neighbourhood (see p. 446–7).[24]

The new public management

Over the past fifteen years there has been an increasing re-orientation (or 'marketization') of the public sector, towards a greater private business style of operation (encouraged or initiated by the government via compulsory competitive tendering (CCT), the Citizen's Charter, VFM audits, etc., as well as the constraints imposed by such things as capping and cash limits). This has created what has been termed a 'private style of public management'.

CCT and other (often government) initiatives have generated the purchaser/provider (or client/contractor) split and the 'contract culture', with authorities becoming 'clients' buying (under agreed contracts) services or products from outside suppliers or from their own arm's-length organizations or companies (typically, direct service or direct labour organizations – DSOs or DLOs). The most recent development here has been in social services, with many councils setting up not-for-profit companies to take over the running of their residential care homes. In education, LEAs, in competition with others, have become the providers of services (legal, payroll, psychological testing, etc.) for 'client' schools.

With service (or 'vertical') departments having to demonstrate their real costs (i.e. without the often hidden subsidies of the central servicing departments), systems of interdepartmental charging have developed, 'cost centres' are being identified and time costing has been developed for the services of council solicitors, architects, etc. This will become more apparent with the imminent application of CCT to the bulk of professional white-collar jobs in local authorities. Some authorities have devolved central service functions to service delivery ('vertical') departments (who thus manage their own finances, personnel, etc.). And throughout local authority departments private business concepts and practices are being applied (such as value-added analyses, formulation of business plans, etc.).

Departments have shrunk or begun to merge (e.g. education and social services) as work has been contracted out or services devolved/transferred – to schools (via LMS or through opting out), to housing associations, or perhaps to local community self-management (e.g. tenants). In some authorities, whole or large parts of departments have been transferred ('externalized') to the private sector (through 'outsourcing' contracts,[25] perhaps with the transfer of staff). Hierarchies have become shorter as ranks of middle managers disappeared or as managers have been given greater autonomy and responsibility (for managing budgets, utilizing staff, as well as giving value for money and sustaining a clientele).

The trend to devolve responsibility to middle and first-line managers seeks partly to concentrate power in the hands of those who are closer to the consumer and partly to increase efficiency and effectiveness through greater flexibility of decision-making and the innovation and enthusiasm which can flow from the 'ownership' of decisions. As one chief executive officer has said, 'Good management will more and more be seen as removing barriers to colleagues' and subordinates' performance by enhancing their contribution and releasing their potential'.[26]

As a consequence, the role of officers (and members) is changing. Chief officers are developing a different relationship to their middle, more autonomous, managers. Chief executives are becoming managing directors,[27] and the management function is tending to divide – into those who specify and buy in or contract for services; those who provide services; those who monitor, inspect and regulate or audit services obtained; and those who are responsible for the overall strategy of the authority.

As a result of these changes and in so far as the contract culture and management 'revolution' continues, managers will need to acquire a range of skills. These include especially for the purchaser/client manager, those of policy development, negotiation, networking, communication and political awareness. Services/contractor managers need the skills of leadership and people management, business and marketing and operational management.[28]

Modern management, as developed in the private business sector, seeks to lead by example and the generation of a sense of purpose or 'mission', rather than, as in the past, control and constraint. Staff are to be motivated by sharing the goals or 'vision' of the organization. This sense of commitment allows the management system to become 'loose-tight', i.e. the structure can be loose (e.g. through devolution and decentralization) but there is still tight integration because of the common cause. In his book *Thriving on Chaos*, Tom Peters says, 'The boss with a vision is political in the very best and purest sense of that word. He or she . . . is constantly out "campaigning" – campaigning for the support, energy and wholehearted participation of everyone in the organization.'

Quality

In local government, the 'mission' is increasingly centred on the consumer and the quality of services provided to him or her. Competitive tendering and the threats of services opting out (schools, housing estates) has made councils more service conscious. So have the reports of the Audit Commission and the 'ombudsman'. Some local authorities had already been influenced and stimulated by private sector management practices and by the writings of such management 'gurus' as Tom Peters. They had begun to produce customer charters and service commitments before the government's Citizen's Charter of 1991. (For example, in 1990, the Audit Commission reported that two thirds of councils employed staff to monitor service delivery.[29]) Nevertheless this has now generated considerable activity among local authorities in pursuit of the Charter's six principles of standards and performance, openness and clear information about services, choice and consultation of users, courtesy and helpfulness, straightforward avenues for complaint and putting things right, and value for money. Thus by 1992, over 90 per cent of local authorities had become or were becoming involved in quality initiatives.[30] A number of local authorities have been awarded the prestigious 'Charter Mark' as a result of their efforts (in 1992 there were eight, including Braintree DC, Bromley LB and Kent CC).

Instead of measuring just costs or 'inputs', more attention is being paid to the 'outputs' or outcomes of local authority activity, especially those identified by performance indicators (see p. 282). And councils are committing themselves to the achievement of stated levels of service (aided by the specification involved in tendering and contracts), with redress or compensation to the public where standards fail. They have also set up complaints systems, but many seek to avoid complaints and prevent faults in service delivery by regular monitoring of results, developing systems audit and by creating quality circles and adopting quality standards such as BS 5750 and TQM.[31]

There are inevitably differing judgements and opinions on these developments. There are those who take a very positive, inspirational attitude, that change is inevitable if not good and local authorities should see problems as an opportunity and 'run with it',[32] and indeed there are calls to go further.[33] Others give cautious approval and see the public–private distinction as too stark or exaggerated.[34] Some see the Citizen's Charter as creating too narrow a focus.[35] There are sceptics who see the new 'private style of public management' as superficial and amounting to no more than 'Have a nice day!', whilst others are very concerned at the effects of the importation of private sector business methods and attitudes on the concept and practice of public service.[36] Much more critical are those who detect a further manifestation of capitalist over other values, and see the management changes as 'managerialism' and disguised forms of discrimination or worker exploitation (i.e. through performance measurement, flexible arrangements for pay and conditions, etc.).[37]

Management services

(1) *Personnel management*

The Bains Report argued that local government tended to lag behind industry and other areas of the public service in its recognition and development of the personnel management function:

There must be a greater awareness of the importance of personnel management in local government. Manpower is a leading resource of any authority and must be properly deployed. The appointment of the senior officer responsible for personnel management is crucial . . . (p. xv)

Personnel and establishment officers had traditionally confined themselves to the oversight and administration of salaries and conditions of service. Bains and Paterson emphasized that they should take a wider and more positive approach to promote the effectiveness of (costly) human resources and to create opportunities for flexibility and change when it becomes necessary. Thus personnel management, or human resources management (HRM), should encompass manpower planning, recruitment techniques, training, career development and industrial relations.

In practice, while the personnel function has received greater recognition by local government, it has not achieved the important role envisaged by Bains.[38] This is partly because it is new to many councils and is having to establish itself at a time of economic restraint and expenditure cuts. But it is also due to the distrust shown by many chief officers who

. . . see it as negative rather than positive . . . as being there to stop them doing what they want to do, and what they are there to do. They feel that personnel does not understand the professional needs and difficulties of the departments.[39]

Furthermore, the personnel function tends to react to events rather than initiate activities:

Frequently it has to wait to be consulted by other officers on questions of staffing, or possibly even industrial questions. Frequently also O & M and work study are dependent on requests from chief officers, committees or the unions. These problems are heightened where employees are seen as being employed by the department rather than the authority.[40]

(2) *Management techniques*

The Maud Report recommended that local authorities should adopt 'a systematic approach to the processes of management'. Subsequently local authorities have taken an increasing interest in management processes, techniques and services. Impetus was added by the creation of the Local Authorities Management Services and Computer Committee (LAMSAC) in 1967. This body's function is to coordinate research, development and training, to establish a central information library and to act as a clearing house for local authorities. It cooperates with the government and other bodies and advises local authorities on latest management services.

In 1989 it was decided to set up the Local Government Management Board (LGMB) by merging LAMSAC with LACSAB (the employers' coordinating body; see p. 252) and the Local Government Training Board. This took effect in 1991.

Management services help management to plan, control and improve the activities of the organization. Broadly their role is either to assist the planning and decision-making process or to promote the efficiency of execution and value-for-money (VFM) expenditure. Some of the services will be grouped and centralized in a Management Services Unit; others may be dispersed and utilized in individual departments. The following is a brief description of the main management techniques.[41]

Planning, Programming and Budgeting Systems (PPBS) have been defined as methods of establishing what an organization is aiming to achieve – what its *objectives* are; which *activities* contribute to these objectives; and what is actually being achieved, or what the *outputs* are (such as the number of old people rehoused or the miles of road re-surfaced) in relation to expenditure.[42] A similar technique is *management by objectives* (MbO), which generally seeks to pinpoint key tasks and set work targets for officers.

More measurable or quantifiable forms of work may be set targets as a result of *work study*. As the name implies this involves the investigation of work processes and the various factors which affect their operation (such as the layout of the office) with a view to improving their efficiency. It is often used as the basis for incentive bonus schemes, in refuse collection for example. It may also be used for job evaluation and the grading of posts.

Organization and methods (O & M) is concerned with the structure of an organizational unit and the way in which that unit operates to achieve its objectives. It is often applied to administrative arrangements to secure more efficient methods, for example by simplifying procedures and delegating more routine clerical operations so as to enable the professional staff to devote more time to their professional work.

Operational research (OR) is used to establish a more rational or scientific basis for management decision-making. It uses complex mathematical techniques, and local authorities receive information and guidance from the Local Government Operational Research Unit (established in 1965). The technique has been applied to operations such as refuse disposal, purchasing methods and urban planning.[43]

Another decision-making technique is *cost-benefit analysis* (CBA). This attempts to go beyond the immediate direct (or primary) costs and benefits of a service or project by taking into account the indirect or 'external' costs and benefits. Many of the latter are intangible and difficult to measure, since they involve social considerations. For example, the relative financial cheapness of high-rise dwellings may be offset by the social costs of the possible family distress they cause. But this analysis does have the merit of extending perspectives, of reducing to statistical terms matters which would otherwise be the subject of unscientific value judgements and of facilitating detailed consideration of alternative courses of action.

Network analysis may be used once a new project has been approved. It aims at providing a plan of action by analysing the project into component parts and recording them on an arrow network diagram. The implementation stages and the inter-relationships of the various activities then become clear and the work – such as school building or engineering projects – can be programmed. This procedure can give rise to a number of ancillary techniques such as *critical path analysis* (CPA), *programme evaluation and review* (PERT) and *resources allocation and multi-project scheduling* (RAMPS).

Many of these procedures will involve substantial use of the computer. Its advantages stem from its ability to store masses of information and solve very complex problems with speed and accuracy. The creation and accessing of databases and the general process of information systems management is now commonplace. *Performance indicators*, and various financial information and management techniques, such as *policy reviews* and *zero-base budgeting* (ZBB),[44] are becoming more prominent.

How efficient is local government?

It is not easy to measure local government efficiency, since there are no indices of success as there are in the business world (such as profits or market penetration figures). Local government has to satisfy three criteria:

(1) *Relevance:* Is the local authority doing the right thing, pursuing the right policies, providing the appropriate service? A local authority's operations may be highly efficient but they may be irrelevant to the problems to be solved. Should local authorities engage in such activities as housing, refuse collection or transport services or should these be left to private enterprise or other public bodies? The answer to this will depend on one's moral and political values as well as economic considerations. There is no simple test of what is 'right' for local government[45] (see Chapter 14).

(2) *Effectiveness:* If it is accepted that local authorities should provide certain services, such as welfare for children or the elderly, they may still be wasteful of resources even if they are efficient in making such provision. This may be due to their pursuing the wrong policies which limit the effectiveness of the operations. For example, a local authority may be building residential homes more cheaply than ever before or more cheaply than other local authorities, but the institutional form of care may not be contributing much to the welfare needs of deprived children or the elderly.

(3) *Efficiency:* Having identified a correct course of action, the local authority must seek to operate efficiently so that its actions are in themselves not wasteful, extravagant or incompetent. There is certainly a danger of inefficiency in this sense, since local authorities do not have the financial discipline of the market: they cannot make losses since they have the power of taxation. Furthermore, how does one measure inefficiency or extravagance? How much time should a social worker spend with a client? How many hours per week should a GCSE student receive in tuition? Some guidance can be obtained by making comparisons with other authorities, but such comparisons are difficult because local authorities vary considerably in their physical, social and economic characteristics. Local authorities' internal audit (see p. 349) and the government's external audit[46] may provide a check, as they detect unreasonable expenditure. But traditionally their function is to investigate the legality of financial transactions (for example that the correct fees have been charged and collected).

The various management techniques outlined above seek to improve the efficiency of local government operations. But many people are sceptical of the progress in this field,[47] pointing to the growth in local government manpower and rising local government costs (reflected in the local tax levels). Much of this is, of course, due to inflation (labour costs absorb some 70 per cent of local government expenditure) and part is due to increased responsibilities which the government has placed on councils. Some is also due to improved conditions of service (itself enhanced by the growth in trade-union activity in local government). Reorganization in the 1970s, with its widespread upgradings and golden handshakes, also added to costs, at least in the short run.

Perhaps the most significant change which is taking place is in the area of programme or output budgeting. Traditional indicators of performance in local government have been in terms of inputs: in the size and funding of the authority and its services (and so to a large extent local authorities have been more interested in improving – that is, expanding – services than merely reducing rates/taxes). Much more attention is now being given to performance and output measurement. This involves the clarification of objectives and the devising of techniques to measure the achievement of those objectives. Expenditure is thus considered in terms of its purpose or the activity it finances, for example the tons of rubbish collected per dustman, or in housing, the number of dwellings improved to a planned standard, or in education, the number of children acquiring basic skills by a given age.[48] A very public and nationwide example is the publication of schools' test and examination results.

However, useful as such steps are, there are problems, especially in defining suitable output measures for many services and in particular those of administrative personnel. Bains suggested that performance should be subject to annual review, and 60 per cent of authorities have established performance review systems; a lot more is being done in this area. Consequently, many more indicators are being devised, such as staff–student ratios, student retention (or drop-out) rates, area cleaned per hour, library-book stock or issues per head, numbers of visits, inspections or cases dealt with per week, speed of response to letters or complaints, etc. The pursuit of the '3 Es' (economy, efficiency and effectiveness) is not easy, and satisfactory performance indicators are difficult to devise in services where quality as well as quantity is important. But the Audit Commission regularly provides data to enable local authorities to compare their own performance with that of a group (or 'family') of authorities with similar features (e.g. see Appendix 15).

Following the Citizen's Charter and the Local Government Act 1992, the Audit Commission (see p. 352) has a duty to specify a list of indicators of performance which every local authority in England and Wales is obliged to report annually. In 1993 the Commission produced a list of 152* such measures of performance (many of which are not new) and local authorities are due to publish the specified information in local newspapers by the end of 1994 and regularly thereafter (with the Commission itself publishing summaries).

Although local government is often denigrated for its inefficiency, in 1985 the Audit Commission (and see p. 350) concluded that 'the best of Local Government is better than the private sector and much better than the NHS or Whitehall at delivering services'. (This was reiterated by Graham Mather of the IEA in 1990). And on the evidence of recent surveys, the general public seem well satisfied with the services provided by local authorities. Thus, the Consumers Association[49] found nearly two thirds of those interviewed thought local authority services were good value for money and four out of five were satisfied overall with the quality of their services. A survey for the Audit Commission[50] revealed 54 per cent were satisfied with council services. The Widdicombe Committee[51] found more than 70 per cent of respondents very or fairly satisfied with the performance of their councils, and a survey for Professor W. Miller[52] found a figure of 75 per cent. Furthermore, as Miller discovered, although there may be a general preference to cut services rather than raise rates, when voters 'are confronted with specific cuts in the big-spending services then they tend to favour the maintenance of those services'. Nevertheless, council management has been criticized following the child-abuse revelations in Staffordshire ('pindown'), Orkney and Leicestershire, the interest-rate 'swaps' in Hammersmith and Fulham, and the financial losses or waste in the

---

* Not all of which applied to each authority. The list has since been reduced.

Western Isles and Brent councils. And there have been numerous reports by the Audit Commission that detailed failings in local authorities in a variety of areas, including rent arrears, special needs education, police, property management, support for the arts and surplus school places.

Local authorities face other problems in trying to give value for money. Councillors, as elected politicians, may wish to see reductions in overall expenditure and rates, but will urge particular expenditures, especially for their own localities.[53] And unlike their opposite numbers in the business world, the top managers (chief officers) are not autonomous: the chief executive officer does not have the authority of a managing director of a company or an American 'city manager' to 'hire and fire', and the chair of the council or of a major committee has nothing like the authority of the chair of a public company. Besides, broadly speaking local authorities are anxious to avoid redundancies; as good employers, they are normally conscious of their responsibilities as regards the employment situation in their areas. But perhaps the biggest contrast to the business world is local government's system of dual management. We consider this below.

Member–officer relationships

Like Whitehall, local government is characterized by the system of 'dual management', i.e. the political management of the elected members and the executive management of the appointed officers. The traditional view of the relationship between members and officers is that of master and servant: the council issues orders and the officers carry them out. Such a view is based on the rational, democratic principle that councillors are elected to make policy decisions and the expert is engaged to execute those decisions. Furthermore, the law appears to support such a view: in the Bognor Regis case (1965) the QC conducting the inquiry concluded that

... if a Clerk is not answerable to his council he is answerable to no one. In my view he is the employee of his council and it is to them that his primary loyalty and duty lie and it is to them that he is answerable for his actions.[54]

In practice, the notion that the council formulates policy is substantially qualified by the fact that many responsibilities are delegated to officers (especially since the Local Government Acts of 1972 and 1973).* But a more important modification lies in the long-standing fact that local government officers advise the council and its committees. This is both inevitable and desirable: after all, the officers are full-time and permanent, and with training and experience acquire considerable expertise. Members can therefore scarcely avoid placing considerable reliance on their judgement: the range of policy and individual matters of administration is too great to be managed by part-time members. According to the Maud Report:

In nearly two thirds of the authorities we consulted officers were said to make a significant contribution to the initiation of policy and in nearly a quarter they were said to play the major part.[55]

It is this advisory role which was clearly articulated in the Maud Report, which consequently, in the words of the Bains Report, 'exploded the myth of policy being a matter for the elected members and administration for officers'.

We do not believe that it is possible to lay down what is policy and what is administrative detail; some issues stand out patently as important and can be regarded as 'policy'; other matters, seemingly trivial, may involve political or social reaction of such significance that deciding them becomes a matter of policy and members feel that they must reserve to themselves consideration and decision on them. A succession of detailed decisions may contribute, eventually, to the formulation of a policy . . . policy making can arise out of particular problems when consideration of a new case leads to the determination of general guides to action which have a general application.[56]

* For illustration, see Appendix 13.

Thus administrative details shade imperceptibly into policy and both officers and members therefore play a part in policy-making and in detailed administration. Bains refers to it as the 'dual nature of management' and likens it (in the words of one witness to the committee) to a scale or spectrum, with the setting of objectives and allocation of major resources at one end, moving through the designing of programmes and plans, to the execution of those plans at the other end. At all points on the scale, both the elected and the official elements are involved, but to varying degrees. This may be illustrated as follows:

Policy/objectives — Members — Officers — Execution/administration

Points of contact

This duality appears in a number of settings. Some of these are *formal*, such as council meetings, committees, joint meetings with other local or regional and central authorities, and ceremonial occasions. There may, for example, be joint meetings of the officers' management team and the P & R committee, and many chief officers attend meetings of the P & R committee as a matter of course. *Semi-official* meetings take place at site visits, disaster areas (such as those damaged by flood) or in departments when a councillor calls in to discuss a constituency matter. And there is an increased tendency for chief officers to attend party group (caucus) meetings.[57] Finally, officers and members may meet *informally* at the club, in the pub or at civic socials. It is usually assumed that the most important of these is the first, particularly committee meetings. At this level there is a close relationship between chief officers and committee chairs (and vice-chairs). This situation may be changing somewhat in so far as councils are setting up panels or 'working groups' of officers and members with the task of examining particular issues or areas in order to discover the facts or possible courses of action rather than make any decisions. In addition, in so far as programme committees have been formed, the committee chairs will each have to relate to a number of chief officers rather than develop a close working relationship with just one.

In the traditional setting, this close relationship between the chair and the chief officer was the result of their working in their particular service area (education, social services, finance, etc.). The chair would be in regular contact with the department; he or she may have had an office there, and would attend pre-committee briefing meetings (and perhaps agenda meetings) so as to be kept informed of latest developments before the formal committee takes place. And in the meantime he or she may be called upon to make decisions or approve the actions of the senior officers.

Where the power lies

Sir John Maud, himself an ex-civil servant, was concerned that members were getting too involved in matters of day-to-day administration at the expense of the officers, whose capacities were thus being under-utilized. Consequently the Maud Report recommended:

It is members who should take and be responsible for the key decisions on objectives, and on the means and plans to attain them. It is they who must periodically review the position as part of their function of directing and controlling. It is the officers who should provide the necessary staff work and advice which will enable the members to identify the problems, set the objectives and select the means and plans to attain them. It is the officer who should direct and co-ordinate the necessary action, and see that material is presented to enable members to review progress and check performance.[58]

In 1989, the Audit Commission suggested that the greater delegation of decision-making to officers would reduce both costs and conflict.[59] And in 1993 the working party report on internal management (see p. 245 above) made recommendations which it was hoped would 'reduce the focus of attention by councillors on detailed administration to enable them to concentrate on strategic issues' [para. 2.7] (though with strengthened scrutiny and monitoring powers).

However, more people see the problem not as one of too much interference in administration by members but rather as one of too much influence on policy by officials: that is, they see the problem as one of 'bureaucracy' or 'managerialism'. After all, members are amateurs (non-experts), they are part-time and they are (largely) unpaid. They can therefore be easily dominated by the full-time professionals, especially when they adopt the corporate approach, with its seemingly conspiratorial groupings, its somewhat alien language and its coordinated advice which is so pre-packaged, plausible and persuasive.

Such dominance by officials may occur because of their superior knowledge, and this may be the product of the way central government relates to local authorities, i.e. dealing with officers rather than councillors, even to the latters' exclusion. For example, in 1982 government inspectors' (HMIs) reports on the effects of expenditure cuts on education provision in certain LEAs were sent to chief officers under conditions of such confidentiality that in some cases elected members were not given the information.[60] Councillors have also complained at being denied access to their local authority's committee proceedings and documents, though this has been substantially overcome by the House of Lords' ruling in the Birmingham case[61] and by the Local Government (Access to Information) Act 1985. (MPs have made similar complaints about their role in Parliament, although, unlike councillors, they have no direct responsibility for administration.)

Sir Horace Cutler, a former Conservative leader of the GLC (1977–81), recently declared that 'it is because we have not enough people with discernment that officials are able to take advantage of elected members and do very much as they please

. . . Paper is useful in baffling councillors when bureaucrats want to get their own way. Documents go on endlessly when it would be perfectly possible to reduce them to the important facts. As a result, policies can be manipulated and distorted so that they slip through in a totally different fashion from what was intended.'[62]

A more striking lack of trust between members and officers was vividly revealed in Walsall Borough Council in 1980. Here the Labour members suspected that when they gained office after the elections officials would undermine or thwart their policies. Consequently, to help secure the achievement of their manifesto objectives, they declared their intention of appointing only officers whose social awareness was 'akin to Labour philosophy' (see too p. 600, note 20). (Such 'politicization' of officials is similar to the 'spoils' system operating in the USA, whereby the top levels of the civil service are replaced when a new party gains the Presidency. The Local Government and Housing Act 1989 now requires appointments to be based on merit alone (though the Widdicombe research showed that such partisan intrusion into the making of appointments was limited in scale).[63] A more moderate approach (which models itself on recent central government practices in Britain and longer experience in France) is being tried in some local authorities: here, special advisers are brought in to provide support services such as research and policy analysis and to advise the council (the majority party) on policy or to help keep policy running in line with party ideology or plans.

The general premise here then is that local government is run by officials; they are 'statesmen in disguise', and the existence of elected members merely provides a democratic veneer.

Such a view is no more tenable than that of the ever-meddling councillor. However, to say that the true situation lies somewhere in between is too simple. There may well be authorities which are substantially run by the officers; and there may be those in which weak or intimidated officers push upwards to councillors trivial administrative decisions. However, it is quite possible to have a combination of these situations so that councillors become heavily involved in routine administrative decisions (see p. 229) while effective control and initiation of major policy decisions rest with the officers. A chief officer has suggested that 'Local government is full of transvestites, members who want to take control of detail and officers who want to make policy.' Furthermore there can be variations among departments within the same authority. In one authority, although the housing manager could himself sanction all repairs and maintenance work below a total of £3·5 million, the children's officer could spend only £10 per case without reference to the committee.[64]

Undoubtedly officers can and do exert substantial influence, since most of the discussion at committee meetings is based on the reports drawn up by senior officers. Most of these reports are well-informed and often based on the guidelines of statute law or central government advice (circulars and official memoranda) which is the familiar province of officers. And although the reports often point out the implications of following certain policy lines or provide a number of options from which the committee may choose, the main themes underlying the reports are influential in the sense of tending to focus discussion and thus limit the range of thinking (especially if there is no alternative paper to consider). In this and other ways, officers, perhaps unconsciously, will filter the information which comes before members. In addition, officers attend committee meetings and they normally speak: indeed some may insist on speaking[65] – they might even have a greater moral claim to local knowledge than the more mobile, less native members. But they need not even speak in order to exercise some influence:

The reality of the formal proceedings of council and committee meetings is that the elected members meet in the presence of officers to consider reports prepared by the officers containing recommendations for action made by the officers. The meetings thus differ from other meetings . . . in that information and advice from experts is rendered in person whilst the process of decision-making is under way. This . . . offers to the officers the opportunity for the well-timed remark, the cautionary aside to the chairman, even the occasional sigh or grimace, which might prevent the councillors taking a decision unwelcome to the officers.[66]

As one chief officer has stated, councillors 'should be led to the right conclusion under the impression that they are arriving at it under their own steam'.[67]

Not all officers, however, are strong-minded or have a 'line' on policy: there may not exist a departmental view on policy, and still less likely is there to be a monolithic official view. Corporate management tends perhaps to encourage such a development, but it is far from being achieved, and it is by no means unknown for differences of opinion among officers to be displayed at committee meetings,[68] which can place the chair in an awkward situation.

The extent of official influence on policy-making is significantly determined by the role played by the committee chairs. They work closely with the senior officers, though how much one will influence the other will depend on personality, on mutual respect and on whether theirs is a close or an arm's-length relationship. In practice there is a range of such relationships, with some committee chairs taking a strong lead and severely limiting the officers' contribution, while others are prepared to play a backseat role, perhaps to the extent of appearing as mouthpiece or ventriloquist's doll to the chief officer. Some chairs surrender, others are captured.[69] Whether the chairs themselves carry influence with their committees will also vary. Some are respected, popular, acknowledged as leaders. Others are seen as party placemen. And in some authorities, they will tend to carry less weight if they have achieved office merely on the basis of 'Buggins' turn next'.

It used to be said that county councils are run by the officers and town councils by the members. The evidence for such a view was related to some extent to the existence or non-existence of political parties or the political zeal of members.[70] However, in so far as it was ever true, recent events will have an impact in that party politics are now more pervasive and reorganization has diluted the town–country distinction.

However, it may be dangerous to try to make any sort of

general statement about the relative importance to decision-making of officers and members. It is 'a fundamental error to believe ... that one set of relationships exist throughout our infinitely variable local government system'.[71] That author goes on to suggest that the relationship depends on a number of characteristics including: (a) the range and size of the authority's service provision, (b) the degree of professionalism among its officers, (c) the existence of political party arrangements, (d) the sensitivity to local public opinion and (e) the extent of central government involvement. On the basis of these factors a range of possible situations is suggested, from those where 'the officer runs the show' to others where 'the party rules and officers do what they are told – or get out'. The emergence of more assertive parties is creating melting pots for many long-standing conventional arrangements and established practices (see p. 465). And the mistrust which can exist between members and officers was illustrated in the local ombudsman's investigation (in December 1988) of the way in which Westminster London Borough council had disposed of cemeteries. He found maladministration arising from a failure to communicate between members and officers, and stated:

Members believed, or gave the impression that they believed, that some officers were intent on 'sabotaging' their policy of running the council on more businesslike lines. Officers felt that their service to the council ... was not valued, and that members did not trust them ... They felt that any suggestion that the ideas of the leading members should not or could not be implemented without amendment would be considered to be undermining the majority party policy. But officers have a duty to give advice to all members even when they suspect it will be unpalatable. Here they failed in their duty.

Within any particular authority the relationship of officers to members will vary with local custom, convention and local political culture: in some authorities, officers will grow up with (or be sharply taught[72]) the notion that policy is councillors' business and officers must keep clear. This was graphically illustrated in

Lambeth LB council in April 1992 when party political differences spilled over into the abuse and baiting of officers (the police were also called in to deal with a brawl between councillors!). A survey in 1992 showed that chief executives find dealing with councillors and political difficulties a stressful aspect of their work;[73] there is clearly a need for greater mutual understanding.[74] The relationship will also depend on personality, since, in practice, power is not shared equally even among members themselves. Chairmanships, council leadership, policy committees, in-groups and out-groups, etc. all have variable effects, and there are individual differences in members' sense of justice or mission, in their tenacity, in their time and devotion to duty. And there are also differences in their 'legitimacy' (their claim to act as decision-makers), especially since some councillors are barely elected and others not elected at all (see pp. 125, 141).

Finally the relative importance of members and officers will vary with the nature of the issue. Matters involving delicate human problems (such as rent arrears by single-parent families) may require the members' common sense rather than the officers' specialized knowledge. Similar considerations apply in controversial matters, likely to arouse strong feelings in the locality, such as the use of the Welsh language in Welsh schools. If, on the other hand, the question is highly technical in character, such as a flood-relief scheme or the purchase of a computer, the tendency is for members to accept the recommendations of the officers.

Rather than deciding whether it is one group or another which dominates, some observers[75] suggest that it is both together, with senior councillors and officers forming a 'dual elite'. Clearly there is much in this interpretation, especially in view of the 'corporate revolution' of the 1970s. Some see the recommendations of the working party on internal management (see p. 245 above) as reinforcing this tendency (though the report does also seek to provide a balance by increasing the 'backbench' councillors' powers to monitor and scrutinize). However, the interpretation may be challenged[76] on various grounds. Firstly, it perhaps too readily assumes a cohesion or unity of view. As we have seen above, this is by no means assured. Secondly, there is the increased readiness of councillors in general, and of party-based councillors in particular, to assert themselves and challenge the official view and the chief officers' 'right to manage'. As the researchers for the Widdicombe Committee found:

... in a situation where quite clearly the political environment of local authorities is changing ... it is almost inevitable that frictions between ... the worlds of members and officers will be created.[77]

And

Whereas in the past chairmen (of committees) saw their role, in many instances, as that of persuading the group to accept lines agreed between themselves and the chief officers, they are now more likely to act as a channel in the opposite direction, from the group to the chief officer, advising that certain recommendations will not be accepted, or that alternative options should be investigated.[78]

Further

It is becoming increasingly common for members to expect free access to whomsoever they wish to talk to in a department, rather than to feel obliged to operate through a chief officer ... There is a growing awareness that policies will be judged by those they affect not in terms of documents agreed in committee or council, but rather in terms of how they are delivered to service recipients.[79]

Thirdly, not only may backbench councillors exercise much influence in private party caucus meetings in devising the party programme, but they can and are likely to press for the full implementation of the manifesto policies[80] (with 63 per cent of councillors seeing this as their primary concern[81]). Fourthly, the experience of the recently hung or balanced councils suggests that much of the decision-making is the result (understandably) of inter-party negotiation and bargaining, with such dealings involving more than simply the party leaderships. The role of the committee chairs is reduced and/or rotated and 'all members ... are politically active and politically important ... a no-majority council enhances the roles of individual council members in decision-making'.[82] Fifthly, there are inevitably inter-departmental conflicts or rivalries, for example, differences over professional territory: does land development 'belong' to the planners, architects or housing managers? Is truancy properly an education or a social service matter? There may be differences too over policy, for example whether to pursue a more or less free market philosophy.

Finally, as suggested above, we must not too readily assume unity within departments. It is becoming more apparent that chief officers experience tensions and pressures from inside their own departments as junior officials bring their own influences to bear (deriving perhaps from their greater specialist expertise, more recent education and training or their experience and contacts developed through area-based administration). This is partly also a consequence of the more consensual or human relations approach to management.

All this is not to deny a place to the 'joint elite' concept of power relationships. But it is clear that power does not lie at any given point in the British system of local government.[83] Instead there are a number of actual or potential centres of power – the policy committee, the officers' team, the individual chief officers or committee chairs (or both together), the party group, the whole council, etc. So, rather than seeing power as consisting of a hierarchy or series of concentric circles spreading from a small apex or central point, it might be more accurate to see local government power-points as consisting of a series or cluster of more or less influential groupings, varying in size in relation to time and issue. If, in general, councillors feel themselves to be somewhat at a disadvantage in their relationship to officers, perhaps they should do something about it by improving their own back-up services and procedures, using such means as properly organized training and secretarial services.[84]

The payment of allowances to members since 1974, the introduction of special responsibility allowances to committee and council chairs in 1980, and the more general payment introduced in 1990 (see pp. 194–6), provide some recognition of the fact that the work can no longer be left on an amateur basis in the hands of relatively few councillors.[85]

11. Finance

The scale of expenditure

Local government is big business. Councils spend nearly £70,000 million a year (over £1,250 per person). This amounts to 25 per cent of all state spending and about one ninth of the National Income (GNP). They manage a total debt of £58,500 million and, as we saw in Chapter 10, local government employs $2\frac{1}{4}$ million staff (about one worker in ten in Britain works for local government). Local authorities are also big landowners, landlords and shareholders.

However, local government has not always been so important in economic terms. In 1951 it was responsible for spending about £1,300 million (about 9 per cent of GNP) and at the beginning of this century the figure was only about £100 million (5 per cent of GNP).[1] Local government has grown as Britain committed itself to the idea of the Welfare State and as legislation has extended the responsibilities of local authorities in the fields of education, housing, social work, transport and the protective services.

Much of local government's expenditure is therefore a result of decisions by the central government and Parliament. For example the Education Act 1944 requires local education authorities to provide schools and teachers, and since the Children's Act 1948 they have been obliged to provide a service for deprived children. In addition the central government may lay down certain standards for those services which may be scrutinized by means of inspection (via Her Majesty's Inspectors, or HMIs). But local authorities also spend money in response to local demands and needs, whether expressed through elections and pressure groups or discerned by professional judgement. Certain services are optional, and local authorities decide whether and at what standard to provide them.

But even then local authorities do not have an entirely free hand to determine their levels of spending. They are faced with pressures which arise from their own local economic and social conditions (they may have a backlog of slums to be cleared or a growing number of old people to be accommodated), or from public expectations and aspirations about the appropriate levels of service (for example, as regards traffic congestion, street cleaning or school crossing patrols). Furthermore, local authorities are committed to certain expenditures under national pay agreements (see Chapter 8) and by joint financing (or 'pooling') schemes, such as for teacher training and advanced further education courses.[2] Finally, there is the legacy of previous spending: if a local authority opens a new school or welfare home, it will be committed to paying for it for many years, for, even if it were closed down in order to save the running costs, loan charges would still have to be paid.

Capital and revenue expenditure

Expenditure on school buildings and residential homes is an example of what is called 'capital' expenditure. Such expenditure implies that the object of expenditure has a long life: it is an asset. Such items are usually very expensive: they involve a heavy outlay, and for that reason they tend to be financed largely from borrowed money (and so repaid over a long period). Short-lived items – fuel, typing paper, the manpower services of teachers etc. – are known as 'revenue' (or current) expenditure. They are consumed as soon as they are purchased or a short time afterwards, and thus are regularly re-purchased. Such items are paid for out of current revenues rather than borrowed money.

The distinction between capital and revenue items is not

always clear-cut: some items could be classified either way (school books for example), but the distinction is important, for in general it is felt that an expensive asset – such as a sports centre or swimming pool, or a fleet of vehicles (refuse wagons or buses) – should in fairness be paid for by the beneficiaries – those who do or could use them. It would be unfair to spend £1 million on a new swimming pool and charge the full cost to the rate-payers in one year: many of those ratepayers will move away from the area or die while the asset continues to give service, and new residents (who will not have paid anything towards the pool) will move in and be able to make use of it. By borrowing money to purchase a capital item, a local authority can spread the cost (of repayment plus interest) over a number of years and so among the actual or potential beneficiaries. Consequently, notwithstanding the high interest charges, a large proportion (normally about 70 per cent) of capital expenditure is financed by borrowing (though the figure has fallen substantially in recent years). Councils thus have a loan debt of £58,500 million (which costs them about £5½ billion a year, which is nearly the same as annual capital spending (see Table 16). Most – nearly 90 per cent – is owed to the government (i.e. to the Public Works Loan Board; see p. 339).

A high proportion of local government expenditure is thus committed in loan charges. As a result any move to cut government expenditure cannot be made 'across the board' (say 10 per cent off all items) because the debt interest expenditure is protected: it *must* be paid or local authorities will be defaulting on their creditors. The cuts must therefore fall more heavily on the other items of expenditure, that is on the services provided by the local authorities.

Local government expenditure

Tables 16 and 17 show that local government is spending some £70,000 million a year. Within this total, the principal item of

Table 16 *Local government expenditure (by service category), 1991*

Current/Revenue items			Capital items	
£m	%		£m	%
		Education, libraries, arts,		
25,413	42	museums, milk and meals	1,443	16
2,713	4	Environmental services	435	5
2,944	5	Roads, lighting, transport	1,311	15
		Housing (incl. subsidies and		
6,232	10	rebates)	4,604	51
5,728	9	Personal social services	193	2
7,621	12	Police, fire services, justice	273	3
		Other (incl. agriculture and		
2,947	5	surplus on trading)	689	8
		Debt interest (current) and		
		repayments (capital) included in		
5,409	9	above figures	0	0
2,140	3	Balance	0	0
61,147	100	TOTAL	8,948	100

Source: UK National Accounts (the 'Blue Book'), 1992 HMSO; *Financial Statistics*, July 1993, HMSO; *Annual Abstract of Statistics*, July 1993, HMSO. NOTE: Figures exclude capital depreciation (of £2,240 million). Expenditure figures are net of service charges/fees (of £4,335 million).

capital expenditure is housing (comprising 50 per cent of that total). Current or revenue expenditure is dominated by education (comprising 42 per cent of that total).

There are considerable differences in the magnitude of expenditure among the different types and tiers of local authority. In England and Wales, county councils spend 85 per cent and the

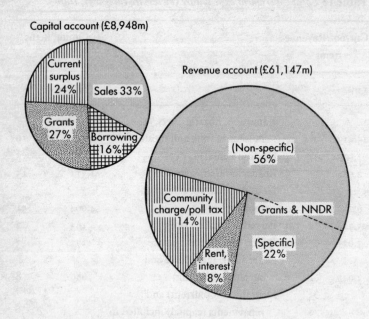

Figure 19 *Local government revenue (1991 figures)*

district councils 15 per cent of their combined total expenditure. In Scotland, too, the regional councils spend 85 per cent and the districts 15 per cent of the total.[3] Among English authorities 49 per cent is spent by shire counties, 25 per cent by metropolitan authorities, 19 per cent by London boroughs and 7 per cent by district councils. Similarly local authorities' income patterns vary considerably, with the shire counties for example depending a great deal more on grants than local tax (precept) revenues.

Local government income

Local authorities derive their income from three main sources: (1) from the rents and fees they charge for services (car parks, bus fares, etc.); (2) from grants or subsidies which they receive

Table 17 *Local government income, 1991*

Current/Revenue				Capital	
£m	%			£m	%
		Grants from central government			
34,500	56	– *general/unallocated*		839	9
		– *specific/allocated to*:			
2,125		education etc.			
3,833		personal social services			
3,173	22	order and safety	152	1,582	18
3,504		housing	972		
.		transport, roads	414		
595		other	44		
47,730	78			2,421	27
.	.	Capital receipts and sales (of council houses etc.)		2,979	33
8,280	14	Community charge/poll tax		.	
5,137	8	Rent, interest, trading surplus		.	
		Surplus/balance from current account (see Table 16)		2,140	24
.		Deficit on capital account/ borrowing from government and/or others		1,408	16
61,147	100	TOTAL (see Table 16)		8,948	100

Source: UK National Accounts (the 'Blue Book') 1992, HMSO; *Financial Statistics*, July 1993, HMSO; *Annual Abstract of Statistics*, 1993, HMSO.

from the central government (housing subsidies, etc.); and (3) from local taxation (the rates or council tax). In addition they

Table 18 *Sources of local authorities' revenue income (selected years)* %

	1975–6	1979–80	1984–5
Fees, etc.			
England and Wales	19·4	21·6	21·2
Scotland	15·0	18·2	19·5
Grants			
England and Wales	53·6	47·3	41
Scotland	58·0	56·1	50
Rates			
England and Wales	27·0	31·1	34·3
Scotland	27·0	25·7	30·5

Source: R. Rhodes, *Beyond Westminster and Whitehall*, Hyman Unwin, 1988.
NOTE: The percentages for each nation do not always total 100 because changes in balances have been omitted.

receive a number of miscellaneous revenues, such as interest and dividends, the proceeds of sales of land and property (such as council houses or county farms) and, for the purpose of capital items, by borrowing. Each of these is dealt with in some detail below, and their relative importance is shown in Tables 16 and 17, and Figure 19. What the tables do not show is how the pattern is changing over the years, notably the rise in the importance of government grants (for example from less than 30 per cent in 1951 to over 50 per cent) and the recent fall in local authority borrowing and the rise in (house) sales income.[4] More recent changes are shown in Table 18.

(1) Charges and miscellaneous incomes

Local authorities have long received small sums of money from a variety of sources – licence fees (dog licences, birth, marriage and death certificates, library fines, etc.), interest on its loans to house purchasers and dividend receipts from its investments (of super-annuation funds for example). Since the Lotteries Act 1976 local authorities have been able to run local lotteries for particular purposes or projects. These have been described as an 'instant success', their turnover increasing from £9·25 million in the first year to £21 million in the following year, and by 1979 about 350 had been registered with the Gaming Board.[5] However, there are significant restrictions involved in their actual operation, such as the permitted amounts to be raised, and a number of local authorities have demurred on moral grounds.

Larger sums are derived, especially recently, from the European Community (see p. 389), from the sale of land and property[6] and from loan repayments from those who borrow from local authorities. They also receive substantial revenues from their charges on a whole range of services. Broadly speaking there are three groups of charges:[7] (a) For *trading* or commercial services, which include industrial waste disposal, passenger transport, harbours and docks, civic aerodromes and markets. Theoretically, as trading undertakings these should raise sufficient revenue from charges to cover costs, but in practice many do not achieve this and have to be subsidized. (b) For *personal* services, such as charges for home helps and for maintaining children or old people in care, or fees for adult/community education classes. Such fees will often take account of the individual's ability to pay[8] and seldom cover the full economic cost of the service. Some critics wish to see such charges abolished altogether on the grounds that they deter those in need, that they often involve high collection costs and that there are considerable inconsistencies and inequities in the various means tests for the different services. (c) For *amenities* such as baths, sports facilities and car parks. The level of charges here will depend on how far the local authorities take account of social criteria: should the ratepayer subsidize a laundry service, in the interests of the needy, or sports facilities, in order to encourage healthy pursuits? Equally, subsidized facilities may, by helping local business, encourage tourism and local prosperity. (Some socialists are critical of this arrangement, as it suggests the

Table 19 *Local authorities' charges and miscellaneous incomes*

Rents and trading (especially transport)	50 per cent
Superannuation investment income and interest	25 per cent
Sales, other fees and charges	25 per cent

deliberate subsidizing of capitalist enterprises, in the same way as the nationalized industries have perhaps provided private enterprise with low-cost supplies.) Alternatively, hefty car-parking fees (for example) may be used as a deterrent to traffic congestion or too rapid a deterioration of the highways. Each council has to make up its own mind about charges.

The single most important charging service is housing. However, for social reasons housing is a service which is (or has been until recently) substantially subsidized both by the central government (via subsidies) and by local authorities (from their rates). In 1976 council rents were meeting only 45 per cent of costs, compared with 75 per cent in 1966.[9] In 1980s, government policy has been to cause rents to rise to a more economic level.

It is sometimes suggested that more income could be derived from charges either by raising their level or by extending their scope.[10] Alternatively, local authorities may 'privatize' or 'hive off' some of their services to private firms. Councils can then collect their local tax to cover the costs of the contracted-out services; or they could allow the firms to collect normal commercial charges from the public.

Such charges would perhaps help to sort out those who really need the services from those who use them because they are free. Furthermore a review of local authority charging policy might help to remove some apparent anomalies, such as charging for day nursery care (under the social services department) but not for nursery schooling (provided by the education departments, the LEAs).

Many would like to extend charges and/or private provision (though others are sceptical).[11] The Government sees charging as another method of increasing accountability, as 'an even more direct way of ensuring that local people can see what they are getting for what they are paying'.[12] But in reality there are great variations in the extent to which local authorities use charges. And with some 40–50 per cent of the population exempt on various grounds (age, income, disability) the potential for raising revenue is clearly limited.[13]

The Local Government, Planning and Land Act 1980 allows councils to charge for planning applications and appeals and for building regulations enforcement as well as allowing LEAs a free hand in deciding their charges for school meals (under the Education Act 1980) – though not for their lessons.[14] (It had also planned to allow LEAs to introduce charges for school transport, but this was defeated in the House of Lords on the grounds that the legislation would discriminate against rural families and religious groups.) The Education Reform Act 1988 and the Local Government and Housing Act 1989 extend the scope for charging in schools (for optional extras) and certain library services, as well as giving the Secretary of State a more general power to allow local authorities to impose charges.

The more general argument against increasing charges is the hardship it might cause to the low-income groups (although this could perhaps be overcome by government grants, such as those paid on a means-tested basis for housing rent allowances or housing benefit). Also there may well be wider social benefits from having, say, a community with general access to low-cost housing and transport.

The issue of *privatizing* local services involves the political question of the proper role of government in society; it is also very much a matter of economics and efficiency. Some councils have adopted the working methods of the commercial world (such as incentive bonus schemes in refuse collection) so that transfer to the private sector may involve no great advantage to the economy as a whole. But there is a widespread feeling, especially in Conservative circles, that much of the work conducted by local authorities could be more effectively undertaken by the private sector (see note 27, p. 601). Consequently, the

Local Government, Planning and Land Act 1980 required councils to scrutinize and justify their use of direct labour (or DLOs – that is, where they employ their own staff rather than outside contractors for building or maintaining roads, parks and housing). DLOs must now submit estimates or 'tenders' in competition with private firms and must achieve given rates of return (or 'profit') or face closure: in effect they are now trading undertakings. In 1985 a survey[15] showed that out of 510 replying, 190 councils had contracted out some of their services. Yet while more councils have since contracted out services, others have brought them back 'in-house', so that the total value of such contracts (in 1987) was only £120 million. But more recent legislation on compulsory competitive tendering (CCT) is altering this situation. Under the Local Government Act 1988, a number of local authority services must now be put out to tender, i.e. the council's direct service provision must bid in competition with private contractors. These include refuse collection, cleaning of buildings and streets, catering, and the maintenance of grounds and vehicles. The Act allows the Minister to designate other services (and management of sports facilities has since been nominated). Although private contractors have won only 17 per cent of the value of current contracts (of £1,753 million), ranging from 25 per cent for refuse collection to 3 per cent for catering,[16] the Government estimates that the result of this injection of competition has been a cost saving of 6·5 per cent,[17] with perhaps £80 million being saved on refuse collection alone[18] (though the Audit Commission believes more savings are possible[19]). Furthermore, while it is estimated that after the implementation of this Act less than 10 per cent of local authority services will be subject to competitive tendering, the Local Government Act 1992 (following the consultation paper *Competing for Quality*, 1991) has identified the 'white collar' (i.e. professional and technical) occupations suitable for competitive tendering and 'market testing'; thus local authority lawyers, accountants, computer and personnel officers will have to submit bids in competition with private firms for the work of the council. There are similar plans for housing management,* police support services, vehicle fleet management, security services, school transport, parking services, theatre management, library services and construction-related services (such as engineering, architecture and estate management).

(2) Government grants

The central government has been helping to finance local authorities since 1835, when grants in aid were introduced to assist local authorities in the cost of transporting prisoners. Subsequently grants were developed for local services such as police and education. Since they helped to finance the cost of particular services, they were known as 'specific' grants. One interesting and notorious form of grant was based on the 'payment by results' system, whereby teachers got paid according to their success in drilling their pupils in the 'three Rs' and getting them through their exams!

Another unusual form of grant was the system of 'assigned revenues'. In 1888 local authorities were empowered to retain and utilize the proceeds of certain taxes (mainly licence duties) collected in their area. Thus tax revenues (sometimes known as 'whisky money') were diverted from the central government to local government. However, this form of financial aid proved to be too erratic in its distribution and insufficiently expansive to keep pace with local authorities' growing expenditures.[20] Consequently, local authorities continued to draw upon government grants.

The character of these grants began to change in the course of the twentieth century. Under the Local Government Act 1929, assigned revenues ceased (apart from a few licence fees, which still exist), and a number of specific grants were replaced by a 'block grant' – a sum of money not tied to any particular service and which the local authorities could use for spending as they saw fit. The aim of this new grant was to place a limit on the

* Under the Leasehold Reform, Housing and Urban Development Act 1993, and beginning in 1996.

government's financial commitment to local government. From 1948 onwards, the block grant was paid only to those local authorities whose means (or rate resources) were below the national average. It was known as the 'exchequer equalization grant'.

In the meantime, specific grants[21] continued to grow in magnitude as services (such as education, housing and roads) expanded. Consequently, in 1958 the Government replaced many of them with a new form of block (or 'general') grant. The equalization grant continued under the name of the 'rate deficiency grant'. Finally, in 1966 these two block grants, together with some of the remaining specific grants (for school meals and milk), were incorporated into a single 'rate support grant' (RSG), which formed the basis of our present system of grant aid up to 1989–90, when it changed to the Revenue Support Grant System (see pp. 314–16). Before we examine the details of current grants, some general aspects must be considered.

(a) The justification for government grants

Government grants to local government may be justified on a number of grounds. In the first place, the central government will wish to encourage the development of certain services which are felt to be in the national interest (education, for example), and it may feel a moral obligation to assist local authorities financially where national legislation compels the latter to provide certain services. Secondly, government grants can help to even out the differences in resources between rich and poor authorities. Thirdly, grants may seek to compensate local authorities for their varying needs to spend, either because of the amount of need in their area (they may have many schoolchildren or old people) or because of the costs involved in meeting those needs (the population may spread thinly, for instance). Fourthly, government grants may seek to reduce the impact of rates (the local tax). The latter is often said to be 'regressive' or unfair to the lower income groups. In so far as central government taxation is 'progressive' (taking proportionately more from the better off), government grants can partially help to balance the tax burden on the local taxpayer; indeed this was precisely one of the Government's lines of defence in introducing the system of community charge (see p. 329). Finally, the central government may pay grants to local authorities to compensate them for any restrictions it may have placed on their other sources of income: thus in 1929, when the Government ceased to allow local authorities to collect rates from agricultural property, their lost income was made up to some extent in the new block grant. Since 1966, government grants have been used for the explicit purpose of keeping the rates or local taxes down, at least in the case of the domestic rate/taxpayer (see p. 312); this was illustrated particularly in 1991 when £4·3 billion was transferred from local taxes to general value-added tax (VAT).

There is, then, a strong case for grants. But some would doubt the wisdom of local government's being so dependent on the central government. Grants to local government have increased substantially in this century: as a proportion of local government income they have increased from 15 per cent in 1913, to 34 per cent in 1950 and to 50 per cent in 1980. Ignoring income from fees, charges and other sources, the ratio of grants to rates changed from 51:49 in 1966 to 65:35 in 1980. In the 1980s this decreased, to 57:43 by 1987. But it has now reached, in effect, 85:15 – see p. 315.

One consequence of such grant aid is that the central government increases its control over local authorities. This appears to be a world-wide phenomenon and is perhaps an inevitable feature of modern society. It is not necessarily or totally undesirable (see p. 362), and for the most part it is not the principle which is in question but the lengths to which it has been taken. In some respects this has been recognized by Government, which has sought to ameliorate the problem by changing the nature of its grants. It is widely felt that grants in the specific form bring closer central controls[22] and they certainly appear to encourage the provision of particular services, which perhaps distorts local authorities' patterns of spending. It was partly for this reason – to give authorities more discretion – that specific grants were largely replaced by the block form. However, over the past fifteen years, there has been a revival in the specific form of grant such that in relative terms they now constitute 28 per cent of current/ revenue grants compared to 17 per cent in 1980. Some of these specific grants include those for which local authorities have to make bids to the government, for example for inner city regeneration (in 'City Challenge') or crime prevention (under the 'Safer City' initiative).

(b) The present grant system

Current grants to local authorities take four forms: (i) the revenue (until 1990, rate) support grant, (ii) specific grants (for police, etc.), (iii) supplementary grants (for transport, for instance), and (iv) housing subsidies (which, like higher education awards and council tax rebates, are a special form of specific grant and are subject to a separate procedure).

(c) The rate support grant (RSG) – 1966–90

Every year, central government departments and local authority associations meet (in the forum of the Consultative Committee on Local Government Finance[23]) to agree a forecast of total 'relevant' expenditure[24] for councils for the coming year. This comprises all local government expenditure except mandatory payments such as student awards, rate rebates and housing subsidies (all subject to separate arrangements). The government would then decide what proportion of this total it was going to finance by grant: from 1977 to 1981 the figure was 61 per cent for England and Wales, and 68·5 per cent for Scotland;[25] for 1985–6, 48·7, 67 and 56·6 respectively, and for 1986–7, 46·4, 66·8 and 56·1. The resulting grant total was the 'aggregate exchequer grant' (or AEG – now known as Aggregate External Finance). From this total were deducted the various small, specific grants (for police, housing improvement, etc.) and supplementary grants (for transport and national parks), both amounting recently to between 28 and 30 per cent of the total (from 17 per cent in 1980). The remainder (70 per cent or more) constituted the rate support

Table 20 *Grants to local government, 1986–7*   £ *million (rounded)*

	England	Wales	Scotland
1. Relevant expenditure	25,329	1,597	3,575
2. Total grant (AEG)	11,764 (46·4%)	1,067 (67%)	2,005 (56·1%)
3. Specific grants	2,606	169	247
4. Supplementary grants	170	21·8	—
5. Rate Support Grant (RSG) [= 2 − (3 + 4)]	8,988	876·2	1,758
Domestic Rate Relief Grant	708 (18·5p)	25·8 (18·5p)	91 (7p)
Block Grant	8,280	850·4 { Resources / Needs	185 / 1,481

Sources: Rate Support Grant Orders; Public Finance & Accountancy, March 1985.

grant (RSG), which was distributed as a general or block grant and was not therefore tied to particular services.

For distribution purposes, the RSG has been divided into three elements: (i) the 'needs' element, which was designed to compensate local authorities for differences in the amounts they need to spend per head of population to provide a given standard of service. It was calculated by reference to a complex formula prescribed annually by the government and based upon an analysis of each local authority's past expenditure, together with some objective indicators of their expenditure needs (factors such as population, number of children, density, etc.); (ii) the 'resources' element, which sought to compensate for the disparities in local authorities' rates/tax resources. The government would prescribe annually a 'national standard rateable value per head' (in 1981 for example it was £178), and those rating authorities whose rateable value (see p. 323) fell below this figure (the majority) would receive payment in proportion to their rate deficiency. Taken together, and assuming local authorities to be providing a given standard of services, the 'needs' and 'resources' elements were to lead to an equalization of rate poundages (the standard rate in the pound which ratepayers have to pay, or Grant Related Poundage (GRP)). In other words these two elements should have enabled local authorities to provide similar levels of service without widely different rate burdens; (iii) the 'domestic' element, which was a form of rate relief for domestic ratepayers: householders thus paid less than industrial and commercial ratepayers, and the difference was made up to the local authorities in the 'domestic' rate relief element of the RSG (a grant amounting (see Table 20) to some 18·5p in the pound for the householder in England and Wales and 7p in Scotland).[26]

The RSG has been the most important financial aid to local authorities, and while the needs and resources elements were largely a continuation of what existed before 1966 when this grant was introduced, the domestic element was new – a response to the then growing concern over the rises in rates. The result was that, while rates appeared to be rocketing, their impact on householders in real terms was barely altered since 1966. This (domestic) element was criticized on the grounds that it was inequitable, being paid on a flat-rate basis regardless of ratepayers' ability to pay. A second criticism was that, by disguising the true cost, it was wastefully drawing resources into the housing sector.

However, in general it was the other elements of the RSG which came in for criticism. In particular, the needs element has been held to be unduly influenced by local authorities' past expenditure patterns, which may not be an accurate guide to local needs.[27] The resources element has been criticized on the ground that rateable values (the basis for this element) were not a fair reflection of property values.

Another more general criticism was that the formulae for RSG distribution could be manipulated by the party in government to suit its own purposes or in response to community pressure groups, with, in general, Labour diverting financial aid to urban areas at the expense of rural, and Conservatives doing the opposite (but see p. 121).

The present Government, however, sought to change the RSG for another reason: to contain local government expenditure. Under the Local Government, Planning and Land Act 1980, a 'block' (or unitary) grants system was introduced (for England and Wales only) whereby local authorities which spent in excess of their 'true needs' (i.e. as perceived by government) would not receive the same proportionate level of grant support as authorities which exercised restraint on their spending. The idea of a 'unitary' grant (combining into one the *needs* and *resources* elements) was commended by the Layfield Committee on Local Government Finance and was accepted by the Government in 1977.[28] It has been seen as a means of penalizing the 'spendthrift' authorities without harming the others, for under the old RSG system, if some councils spent more than the government wished, the latter could take action only by reducing the whole level of its RSG (thus shifting the burden on to the rates of *all* local authorities). Under the 1980 scheme a 'block grant' was calculated for each local authority to cover the deficiency or gap between the cost of providing services comparable with those of similar authorities and the local rate revenue assuming the rate to be set at a particular level (the GRP determined nationally by the government). In effect, the government calculated what the local authority should spend; it then deducted what the standard (or GRP) rate poundage would produce, and the difference paid in grant. A local authority spending above its 'norm' (officially known as Grant Related Expenditure Assessment or GREA) would have to find more from the rates as its grant was reduced or tapered away. Grant fell as the GRP was increased by a 'multiplier' when spending exceeded GREA. Above a certain expenditure threshold, grant was disproportionately withheld.

Local authorities reacted strongly to this legislation. While perhaps having some general sympathy for the general aim of the proposal (to restrain overall local government spending), many authorities felt that extensive powers had been taken to control all local authorities for the sake of a few who acted irresponsibly. And in general it was felt that this was a dangerous attempt to substitute a 'national judgement' about local spending for the 'local accountability' of the authorities themselves (see p. 385). The new grant and rates system (see below and pp. 369, 476) has not substantially changed this.

(d) *The revenue support grant* (*RSG*) – operative from 1990

Under the Local Government Finance Act 1988 (operative from 1990) and the Abolition of Domestic Rates (Scotland) Act 1987 (operative 1989), domestic rates were replaced by the community charge (or poll tax; see p. 326), business rates were 'nationalized' (see p. 327) and the rate support grant was replaced by the 'revenue support grant' (RSG, also known as Standard Spending Grant (SSG)). The aim was to reduce the complexity of the system (for example by simplifying the needs calculation – the former expenditure assessment – from sixty-three indicators or measures to eleven) and to provide greater stability by avoiding the often substantial changes in grant allocation which could affect authorities from year to year. In 1993 the community charge was itself abolished and replaced by the council tax (see p. 333). But the grant system was unchanged.

The essence of the system is that the grant will compensate for differences between areas in their need to provide services (as measured by population and physical/social features, such as numbers in care, incidence of disability, children at risk, etc.), i.e. each authority will have a *needs assessment* or Standard Spending Assessment (SSA); in Scotland it is the Grant Aided Expenditure Assessment. An allowance will then be made for the authority's income from the business rate and its council tax (for which the government will assume a notional or standard level for each property band, and is thus known as 'council tax at standard spending'). Thus:

Revenue Support Grant =

$$\text{Needs Assessment (SSA)} - \left(\begin{array}{c} \text{Business rate} \times \text{local population} \\ + \\ \text{Council tax} \times \text{local householders} \end{array} \right)$$

Authorities whose needs are considered high (in terms of numbers of schoolchildren or elderly residents, for example) will attract higher needs assessments and grant. Thus, since the RSG aims to enable all local authorities to provide a common level of services (based on SSAs) the RSG is alternatively called the Standard Spending Grant (SSG). With the business rate revenue (see p. 327) being distributed nationally on the basis of population (the main criterion of need) and the grant based on needs assessment, then the council tax is the local authority's balancing item. The grant is fixed for the year (in contrast to the previous rate support grant entitlement, which could alter sharply for a local authority during the year or even later since it was based on actual expenditures) and is less likely to change significantly from year to year. Thus the council tax is the variable item which the local authority itself can alter (unless it is 'capped'; see below).

These arrangements will mean that if each local authority spends at the level of its SSA, all local authorities' council taxes will be identical (for each property band; see p. 334 and Appendix 14); where an authority chooses to spend more or is wasteful, the cost will be borne entirely by the (higher) council tax (and equally, underspending will reduce it), since RSG is normally unaltered (unlike the old RSG; see p. 312). Originally, in 1990, the RSG overall provided 50 per cent of local government expenditure (with UBR and community charge at 25 per cent each). But in the 1991 Budget, the Government unexpectedly switched £4·3 billion on to central taxation (VAT) and increased the RSG such that, together with specific grants and revenue from business rates (NNDR or UBR; see below) central support to local authorities now provides some 80 to 85 per cent (according to definition). Thus the community charge (and subsequently the council tax) only had to raise about 15 per cent – thus easing, though not eliminating, its burden on local taxpayers.

It was also intended that the new grants system would not only be less complicated but also provide greater stability and clearer accountability, since changes in the community charge – now council tax – will be due to changes in local spending decisions and not due to grant changes, as often was the case under the rate support grant system. But stability and accountability are undermined by a provision in the legislation (most recently the Local Government Finance Act 1992) that (a) allows the Minister to make one additional grant calculation or adjustment per annum, (b) allows for the payment of an 'additional grant' where exceptional circumstances merit such an award (for example for storm damage), and, above all, (c) gives the Minister the power to limit any local authority's expenditure budget and thus to 'cap' the local tax level.

(3) Rates (substantially abolished 1989–90; see p. 326)

Rates are an important element in local government finance – partly because they have existed for centuries as the only local tax and have provided a substantial proportion of local authorities' revenue, partly because they still exist despite the fact that they have been significantly altered in recent years, and partly because there is a distinct possibility of their being restored in something resembling their original form.

Rates are a form of local property taxation levied on property (real or fixed rather than personal) according to its value. They originated in the Middle Ages, and over the years new and separate rates were established to help to pay for separate services (public health, schools, the poor, highways, water, etc.). These were finally consolidated into a single general rate in 1925 (although in England and Wales water and sewerage rates are still separately assessed and collected). Under the Rating and Valuation Act of that year certain types of local authority were classified as 'rating authorities'. Those which were not so named (counties and parishes in England and Wales; the districts and communities in Scotland) were to raise their finance by 'precepting' the rating authorities (the district councils in England and Wales; the regions and islands in Scotland): in effect this meant that the rating authorities collected the rate for the other authorities (and, since 1981, they also bore the cost of administration).[29] Since the abolition of local rates (see below) we now have 'billing' authorities and 'precepting' authorities. There have been substantial differences in the extent to which authorities depended on rate income.[30]

(a) Liability for rates

Technically, to be liable for rates, property (or 'hereditaments', as they are called) had to be occupied (though not necessarily in a personal sense: a house could be liable for rates if it was empty but contained furniture). However, since 1967 rating authorities had a discretionary power to rate empty properties if they were continuously empty for a given period, usually three or six months. (From 1981 the maximum rate on empty commercial property was 50 per cent; since 1984 empty industrial property has been de-rated.) Whether they decided to rate empty properties and whether they charged full or partial rates would depend on such factors as the administrative costs, the revenue product and whether they thought such an action would encourage owners to utilize the property more quickly or whether it might deter further development.[31] (It should be noted that local authorities themselves pay rates.)

Certain properties have been statutorily exempt from the payment of rates. The main ones include: (i) Crown property, such as government building, military premises, royal parks, etc. (in practice, the Treasury compensates rating authorities with 'contributions in lieu'); (ii) agricultural land and buildings (except the farmhouse), which have been exempt since 1929 (worth £1 billion per annum today), when they were de-rated partly in order to lighten the farmers' burden at that time of economic difficulty; (iii) churches and other buildings used exclusively for religious purposes, charities and related organizations, public parks, police properties, lighthouses, sewers and pumping stations and foreign consulates. Disabled persons were granted rate relief on their properties where these had been specially adapted. In Scotland, industrial property was rated at only 50 per cent, in order to offset the generally higher rate poundages than in England and Wales.

(b) The calculation of the rate

The basic idea of the rating system is quite simple. All property in the area (apart from the exemptions) is given a valuation: this is the 'rateable value'. Every year the rating authority fixed a rate in the pound (per pound of rateable value) and the occupier of that property paid rates at that poundage. Thus, if the rate was 80p and the property's rateable value was £200, the rates due were £0.80 × 200 = £160. The key elements therefore are rateable value and the rate poundage.

The valuation of property is undertaken by the Inland Revenue (England and Wales) and by the Scottish Assessors' Association (although in 1991, valuation of domestic properties was undertaken, on behalf of the Government, by estate agents to provide a set of capital values for the introduction of the council tax). Since the 1939–45 war regular revaluations should have taken place every five years, but in practice they have occurred at very irregular intervals except in Scotland.[32]

The valuation of property for rating purposes is based essentially on the market rent which the property could earn in the course of a year. From this gross or rental value is allowed the deduction of the notional cost of repairs and insurance, etc. For some properties (such as a town hall, school or cinema) it is extremely difficult to assess a rental value and so other bases may be used, such as capital values or profits records. Indeed the rental basis for ordinary purposes may be substantially distorted (for example, because of statutory rent controls) and the use of alternative criteria has been proposed, such as capital values or site values.[33]

Information on the valuation of properties is publicly available in the form of a valuation list (England and Wales) or roll (Scotland), which is usually held at the council offices. Individuals may appeal against the valuation of their property to the valuation court* and beyond that if necessary to the land tribunal. Any structural changes affecting a property's valuation will come to the attention of the local valuation officer normally as a result of the planning permission process.

The rate *poundage* (or simply 'the rate') is the amount per pound of rateable value which is collected from occupiers of property. Up to 1989–90 this rate was determined annually by the local authority (some being issued in the form of 'precepts' on the rating authorities – see pp. 316, 326–7). The basis of the calculation was as follows: each local authority estimates its expenditure for the coming year. (The financial year runs from April to April). It deducts from this figure its known or estimated revenues from charges and grants. This leaves a sum – known as the 'rate-borne expenditure' – which has to be financed from the remaining source of income – the rating of property. The proportion of that rate-borne expenditure figure to the total rateable value in the local authority area (say 80 per cent) shows the poundage (80p) or 'rate' of tax necessary to raise the sum required.[34] Thus for individual ratepayers their property's rateable value multiplied by the rate produces their rate demand.

The rating system has been unpopular because it required lump-sum payments (usually twice a year) rather than regular (and smaller) weekly or monthly payments such as we use to pay income tax ('pay as you earn'). However, after the General Rate Act 1967, the system was modified to allow some rates to be paid in instalments of not more than ten monthly payments. From 1981 this facility applied to all ratepayers except (in England and Wales) for business properties over £2,000 (£5,000 in London) rateable value (in 1985 these rateable value limits ceased to

* Valuation courts, which decide appeals about rateable valuation of property, were reconstituted as Valuation and Community Charge Tribunals, as they dealt with appeals over the community charge. But since the introduction of the council tax in 1992, they are now known as Valuation Tribunals.

apply). The same Act provided an incentive to pay in full by allowing local authorities to give discounts to those who paid promptly.

(c) Criticisms of the rating system

No tax is popular, but rates were particularly unpopular. This is partly because they had to be paid in advance and in a lump sum (even if they are paid in instalments, the demand arrives initially as a lump sum). But rates were also unpopular because the rate (poundage) received a lot of media attention when it was fixed (which usually meant increased) each year. So rates were an overtly painful form of tax. In this respect they differed from income tax and indeed most other taxes that ratepayers have to pay: the total yield from other taxes increases automatically as incomes or prices rise, but that from rates increases only when there is an appreciation in rateable values (following an infrequent, and well-publicized, revaluation survey). Consequently rates lack 'buoyancy' and the rate had to be altered regularly in order to increase the yield.

Rates were also unsatisfactory, as we have mentioned above (p. 315), because their basis (the annual rental value) is inadequate or distorted. Furthermore, it is suggested that they may act as a brake on property improvement, owners being deterred by a threatened rise in their rates through increased revaluation.

However, the biggest criticisms of the rating system relate to its unfairness. In the first place, rate resources are very unevenly distributed among local authorities and are quite unrelated to their varying needs: hence the 'resources' element of the rate support grant (see p. 311). It may be added, however, that no known form of local taxation could easily secure an even or fair distribution of resources. Secondly, rates are said to be 'regressive', that is, relatively they bear most heavily on those with low incomes, since the rate demand is applied to the value of property, not to the occupier's ability to pay. One household may depend on a small income (say a pension), while another identical house, subject to the same rate demand, may enjoy the benefit of several

Table 21 *Rate yields, 1976 (£m) and 1981–2 (£bn)*[35]

	England and Wales	Scotland	Total	1981–2
Domestic	1,565	179	1,744	4·8
Commercial and industrial	1,985	150	2,135	5·0
Other (schools, hospitals, etc.)	450	73	523	1·1
	4,000	402	4,402	10·9

larger incomes.[36] Thus they fail to take account of people's ability to pay.

This last criticism lost much of its force in recent years. This is partly because incomes are taxed nationally (some on a 'progressive' basis) and part of the proceeds help to finance local government in the form of government grants. But mainly it is because since 1967 lower income groups were able to claim rate rebates. Such relief varied with income and family circumstances, but it could amount to as much as £381 per annum (£470 in London in 1980).[37] The average rate rebate was about £100. Rate demands therefore bore a closer relationship to incomes, and recent evidence confirms this.[38] However, there is strong evidence that many groups in society (especially private tenants) did not claim this benefit, although entitled to it. In 1980–81 some 1·45 million eligible householders did not claim, compared to the 3·35 million who did. (The same problems arise with council tax benefit.) And there were others who were outside the rebate scheme although they may be on low income (such as, until 1988, owners of small commercial premises). Also, there is no provision for rebates on water sewerage rates since the separate collections began in 1980–81.

A further criticism is based on the 'beneficiary principle'. Here, rates are criticized because only the householder would pay the rates bill, while other members of the household are not liable, and yet they could benefit from the services provided from the rates and may thus be encouraged to press for greater service provision without feeling any financial 'pinch' (see pp. 331–2).

(d) Merits of the rating system

The rating system has a number of strengths. As a tax, it is simple to administer, difficult to evade and cheap to collect. The total yield of rates up to 1989 was substantial (equivalent to about a 10p income tax) and, being stable from one year to the next, it is reliable and predictable. In addition, since it is truly local in nature, it makes an impact (sometimes very painful) on the ratepayer, and is commonly seen (rightly or wrongly) as the payment for local services. It may thus have the merit of arousing an interest in local government affairs and promote the account-ability of the councillors and officers who spend it. This was enhanced by the requirements under the General Rate Act 1967 that local authorities provide certain specified information with the rate demand, such as description of the property, its rateable value, the amounts in the pound spent on each principal service, etc. Such information has been expanded under current legislation (see pp. 213–14).

A further advantage of the rating system is that, by encouraging a fuller utilization of the household stock and discouraging house-holds from occupying premises which are larger than they need, it helps to mobilize the supplies of housing. A small family or business occupying unnecessarily large premises will be inclined to move to a smaller property because of the relatively heavy rates which large premises attract, and thus make space available for those better able to use it.

Apart from these technical advantages, there is also the perhaps surprising fact that domestic rates in general remained a small and steady proportion of households' disposable incomes – be-tween 2 and 3 per cent, which is roughly what it was in 1935[39] (national taxes are some 47 per cent). This may help to explain why rates were not as unpopular as many people believe.[40]

However, while domestic ratepayers have been protected by the 'domestic' element of the RSG and by rebates, industrial and commercial ratepayers (especially in England and Wales) have been less fortunate: while for the period 1966–74 the overall rate bill rose by 120 per cent, domestic rates payments rose by 80 per cent and non-domestic by 150 per cent. And among the 2 million non-domestic ratepayers businesses as such since 1969 have no local vote (although arguably business is well represented among the membership of most councils and other official bodies). On the other hand, businesses can offset their rates against other taxes (assuming profits are being made) and perhaps pass it on (in whole or part) in higher prices for their product.

(e) Reform of the rating system

Various proposals have been made to reform the rating system. One group of reforms seeks to increase the yield of rates, in particular by shifting the burden of de-rating from local authorities to the central government. Thus if the government sees fit to exempt agriculture or charities from rates, it should reimburse local authorities for the revenue foregone.[41] In effect this did happen indirectly through the resources element of the RSG, and in Scotland there was some direct recognition through the payment of a higher RSG (at 56·1 per cent in 1986–7) to cover the rate relief of charities. However, some critics sought 100 per cent rate liability of all properties; anyone claiming hardship should then be able to approach the central government for financial assistance in the form of grants. A further suggestion is that property revaluation should occur more frequently (the Layfield Committee suggested three-yearly intervals) and that capital values should be used, in view of the narrow base which exists for rental comparisons (see pp. 318–19).

These seem sensible suggestions, but there are technical problems in trying to value agricultural property or undertake more regular revaluations. And the yield may be rather insignificant. But above all are the political problems involved in trying, for instance, to re-rate agriculture or charities. More generally, it is suggested that local authorities which rely heavily on local incomes tend to be parsimonious.[42] The Government's immediate solution, introduced in 1984, was rate-capping, i.e. placing an upper limit on individual local authorities' rate levels when they reach a given point (in 1989 that point was 12·5 per cent above GREA). Then, in 1989–90, domestic rates were abolished – only to be (partially) restored in 1992 in the form of the council tax; see p. 333.

Alternative sources

A second group of reforms have, over the years, been put forward to supplement, or to replace, the rating system.[43] These proposals have comprised a selection of local taxes, including petrol duties, sales tax, employment tax, vehicle duties and, above all, a local income tax. They have been regarded as unacceptable on various specific grounds, including the problems of collection, the scope for avoidance, the small yield, their regressive nature, their intrusion upon the government's revenue sources, their uneven distribution among local authorities and the fact that such new forms of taxation would confuse the public and so jeopardize the delicate thread of accountability which runs between the council and the people.

Governments have rejected such proposals on the grounds that the time was 'not appropriate' for the introduction of new taxes.[44] An example of this was the (Labour) Government's response to the report of the Layfield Committee, which dealt thoroughly and comprehensively with the subject of local income tax (LIT) – widely regarded as the most realistic potential source of local revenue. The Committee was set up in June 1974 in response to widespread public protest over the rises in rates that year: local government was seen to be particularly susceptible to the effects of inflation (some 70 per cent of its expenditure going on wages and salaries), while its rate revenues tend to be rather sluggish (i.e. they lack buoyancy – see p. 320). However, the Layfield

Committee did not consider it feasible to abolish rates. Instead they proposed that a local income tax should be instituted as an additional source of local revenue. The objective was to 'foster the autonomy of local authorities by reducing their dependence on government grants and giving them sources of revenue they can more easily vary under their own control to meet their expenditure requirements'. (In 1993, the former deputy chairman of the Board of the Inland Revenue gave his support for the Layfield proposals, and suggested that, with recent developments in technology, many of the objections made against LIT have been overcome. However, Chancellors of the Exchequer (and/or the Treasury) are reluctant to allow the instruments of economic management, especially direct taxation, to be diverted from their control.)

The Government's response was to deny that a large central grant did undermine local discretion over expenditure: the block grant (RSG) allowed local authorities the freedom to decide their own expenditure priorities. Consequently it saw no need to introduce LIT, and indeed it went further and positively rejected it on the grounds that

the freedom of local authorities to vary the LIT rate would have to be closely constrained so that it did not unduly complicate central government economic and financial management . . . it seems highly questionable whether the majority of electors could be made aware of the LIT element in their normal PAYE deductions as to achieve the [Layfield] Committee's objective of securing an effective local discipline on local authority expenditure decisions.[45]

The present Conservative Government had long pledged itself to abolish domestic rates. It considered a number of alternative revenue sources in a 1981 Green Paper,[46] including a local sales tax, a local income tax and a poll tax. All were rejected and rates were to 'remain for the foreseeable future [as] the main source of local income'.[47] Then in January 1986 the Government published another Green Paper outlining its proposals to abolish domestic rates and introduce a poll tax (residents' or community charge).[48]

Rates reform, the community charge and the council tax

As we have seen above, rates have taken two main forms: (1) domestic; and (ii) non-domestic or business. Under the Abolition of Domestic Rates (Scotland) Act 1987 and the Local Government Finance Act 1988, domestic rates were abolished for Scotland (in 1989) and England and Wales (in 1990) respectively, and business rates have been fundamentally altered. Northern Ireland is un-affected by these changes.

(i) The **domestic rate** was replaced by a 'community charge' or poll tax (or 'service tax'). This was basically a flat-rate levy on all individual adults, determined by each council on an annual basis. Known as the *personal* community charge, a national target or model figure was set (e.g. in 1990 £278 (£300 Scotland, inc. water charge), in 1992 £257), though there were wide variations in the actual charge levels (for example, £438 in Edinburgh (including water charge), to £148 in Wandsworth). Furthermore, individual circumstances affected the amount paid:

(a) Some people (about half a million) were exempt entirely; these included resident hospital patients, those being looked after in residential care or nursing homes and hostels providing a substantial level of care, the severely mentally handicapped, people taken into hospital under the Mental Health Act 1983, members of religious communities, people staying in some night shelters or short-stay hostels, those with no homes, sleeping rough, school students over 18, volunteers working on low pay for charities, prisoners (except those in detention for non-payment of fines or community charge) and foreign diplomats.

(b) Others were entitled to rebates/reductions of up to 80 per cent according to their income and savings. Full-time students and those on Income Support would automatically get 80 per cent rebate; they were thus bound to pay at least 20 per cent of the local charge (though Income Support levels were raised to allow for this). Transitional relief or charge reduction was given to those worst affected by the changeover.

(c) Some paid twice if they had a second home (unless it was used by someone else as their main residence); the charge here was the *standard charge*, and it was determined by the council in whose area the property is located.

(d) Those who moved frequently and used lodgings, hostels or houses of multiple occupation paid the *collective charge*. This would be a proportion of the personal community charge, depending on length of stay (for example, someone who stayed three months paid a quarter of the personal charge). In effect, they paid it (less any rebate) to the landlord (along with the rent) who would pass it on to the council.

In order to collect the community charge, local authorities (in Scotland the regional and island councils and in England and Wales, the boroughs and districts, collectively known as the 'charging authorities' – the others 'precept' on them; see p. 317) drew up community charge registers, based on people's completion and submission of a registration form. People could be fined for non-registration and the community charge registration officer could help compile the register by scrutinizing such local sources as library or education registers, council-house tenancy lists or the electoral register.

(ii) Non-domestic or **business rates** were retained but reformed. Instead of each local authority determining its rate level, the rate (poundage) is set centrally and differently for Scotland, Wales and England and is the same throughout the individual nations (though the business rate will not be uniform in Scotland until 1995); hence it is known as the *uniform business rate* (UBR), or national non-domestic rate (NNDR). The rate will change from year to year, but any increase cannot exceed the rate of inflation (in 1993–4 it was raised by less than inflation). In addition, rateable values are to be regularly up-dated every five years (the first of these in 1989 in England and Wales showed a seven-fold increase since the previous one of 1973).

Certain business properties are exempt. These include agricultural land and buildings; fish farms; lighthouses; sewers; land and structures occupied by drainage authorities; municipal free parks; property used to provide occupations, training, workshops or welfare services for the disabled; property in Enterprise Zones; and churches. Charities automatically receive 80 per cent relief and councils have the discretion to exempt them and other non-profit-making bodies completely or partially.* There is scope for partially exempting empty properties. In general, UBR collects 50 per cent from commerce, 20 per cent from private industry, 10 per cent from public utilities and 20 per cent from schools, hospitals, etc. In 1993–4 (England) the rate was 41·6p (i.e. per £ of rateable value).

The money raised from the UBR and collected locally is transferred to a national pool and then shared out among councils according to the number of adults in their areas. Thus there is an element of redistribution of resources, and in general the North of England benefited most from the reform. But the scheme is criticized because as a tax it does not take account of businesses' differing abilities to pay, nor their differing benefits from council services (though local authorities must still consult local businesses about services (see p. 355)). Furthermore, by centralizing the tax, it reduces (further) local authorities' accountability for meeting business needs. But above all, this system in effect removes from local government one of its own independent sources of income: it is virtually equivalent to an assigned revenue (see p. 307) or government grant.

Objectives of the reforms

The Government's stated purpose of converting domestic rates to the community charge was to spread the cost of local services

---

* Under the 1988 Act there is some provision for 'hardship relief' where a business is facing severe difficulties in paying NNDR. It is at the discretion of the council, and typically applies to such situations as the threatened closure of a key community resource, for example, a village post office.

wider and more equally. Under the financial system operating before 1989–90, about one third of local government expenditure was financed by central grants, a third by sales, rents and charges and a third by ratepayers. Of the latter, business contributed more than domestic ratepayers; yet business as such had no vote to influence council spending decisions, i.e. there was a lack of accountability, and businesses (especially in some local authority areas) felt they were being charged excessive rates to help fund inappropriate local expenditures.

Of domestic ratepayers there were only 19 million compared to 27 million (income) taxpayers and 36 million adults. Among the 19 million ratepayers, 7 million were receiving full or partial rebate, i.e. rate reduction (see p. 370). Thus it was felt that a minority of adults were paying rates, thereby subsidising the services enjoyed by others who would perhaps be inclined to vote for more local service provision because they would not be contributing (directly) towards their cost. It was intended that the community charge would raise people's awareness of local spending and decision-making.* Consequently it was anticipated that excessive council spending in particular, and perhaps their spending in general, would be reduced as more people felt the impact and baulked at the charge they were having to pay.

The impact of payment was to be enhanced in two important ways. Firstly, all charge payers would be issued with a 'ready reckoner' that indicates what the community charge norm (or target figure) was calculated to be: it was a guide or benchmark against which to judge the local council. Since the revenue

---

* A recent opinion poll indicated that nearly one in four voters would be more likely to vote in local elections as a result of the introduction of the community charge, including nearly one in three of those who said they had not previously voted.[49] But the evidence (up to 1992) from Scottish by-elections does not appear to bear this out; thus in some 26 by-elections since March 1989, the average turnout in Scottish districts and regions has been 42 per cent compared to the previous year's by-election average of 40 per cent. The regional elections in 1990 produced a figure of 45·9 per cent, which compares with the previous (1986) figure of 45·6 per cent. The English and Welsh district figures for 1990 and 1991 are ambiguous: see pp. 144–5.

support grant equalizes between local authorities on the basis of assessed need (and the UBR crudely does the same) then a common or national level of charge should help finance a common or standard level of service. Consequently, to reinforce account-ability, local authorities were required, with each community charge bill, to include details of the notional or standard level of community charge for which each local authority could provide a standard level of service. Thus charge payers would be able to compare this to their actual charge and so assess their authority's efficiency and/or spending decisions.

Secondly, as the income from the centre (RSG and UBR) was fixed, any increase in expenditure beyond SSA would (ignoring fee income) fall entirely on to the community charge. Since this was small (25 per cent) relative to grant (50 per cent) and UBR (25 per cent), any increase in expenditure (beyond the notional standard) would trigger a steep rise in the charge. This is known as the 'gearing' effect; in this case it is 1:4, i.e. a £1 rise in expenditure requires a 4-fold rise in community charge (since it is not grant-aided). In Wales the ratio is 1:5.

Each local authority was to be as well off after receiving its share of the UBR and the needs-weighted RSG as any other local authority, so the actual community charge would directly reflect the decisions of the council and (through the ballot box) the wishes of the community. Thus the community charge was designed to place the burden of financing marginal increases in expenditure fully on those who in general benefited from them.

Pros and cons

As a flat-rate charge, it was clearly regressive; since it took the same amount from each individual adult – milkman or millionaire – regardless of income or means, it would be a relatively greater burden on the poor. But the Government rejected this criticism, pointing out that (ignoring fee revenues): (1) half of local authority income came from central government grant, which is substan-tially funded by progressive (heavier-on-the-rich) income tax, capital gains tax and death duties; (ii) a quarter of local income is paid by business; and (iii) about 10 million adults (and some businesses) were totally exempt or received rebates of up to 80 per cent (together with a top-up of Income Support for the remaining 20 per cent where appropriate). Thus it was claimed that the community charge was broadly related to ability to pay for those on low incomes.

A further justification drew on taxation theory. While with the development of progressive income tax it has become widely (though not universally[50]) accepted that taxes should be based on the principle of ability to pay, an alternative principle states that those who benefit from a service should pay for it. On the basis of this 'beneficiary principle' rates were, at least partially, a tax levied on property because property owners benefited from the prevailing services (law and order, highways, sewerage, lighting, gas, etc.). But these days, local services are more personal in nature (education, social services, libraries, etc.) and more widely utilized; hence the community charge or 'benefit tax'.

However, even on the beneficiary principle it could be argued that a fairer or progressive form of local taxation is justified. This arises from the mounting evidence that the higher-income middle-class members of society disproportionately utilize or benefit from community services.[51] In so far as this is true, it would suggest the introduction of some form of property or wealth tax or a local income tax.

A number of other criticisms have been made of the poll tax:

(a) Administration was an enormous problem: registering charge payers, keeping track of those who are mobile, securing payment, processing claims to rebate or exemption. Indeed, it was the 1983 White Paper *Rates* that rejected the poll tax option on the grounds that 'the tax would be hard to enforce ... expensive to run and complicated'. Some estimates suggest that in inner-city areas, some 40 per cent of residents (or 1 million) move in the course of a year, and overall it is estimated that mobility creates a 'leakage' (in potential revenue) of up to 20 per cent. The cost (three times that for the old rates) increased significantly where people pay by instalments (and where there is an 80 per cent rebate, the cost of collection could exceed the revenue).

(b) There was concern at the intrusion into people's privacy, as questions are asked about cohabitation (which could affect liability to pay for another person) or about mental disability or imprisonment (for exemption purposes); and since the register was open to inspection, there were fears over confidentiality (for example among estranged battered wives or refugee students).

(c) There was the risk that people would be deterred from registering to vote in order to evade the tax – indeed there was evidence of considerable electoral non-registration,[52] and by encouraging evasion there was the side-effect of reducing general respect for the law.

(d) Although not legally liable for their payments, it is suggested that families may have discouraged their elderly or disabled relatives or their older children from living with them.

(e) On a wider front, it is believed that the new system may have contributed to the rise in house prices (since the tax – rates – had been removed) and the excessive or wasteful use of housing space.

(f) Finally, although enhanced accountability was one of the main objectives of the new system, this was undermined by widespread rebates (and safety nets[53]), by dubious SSAs, by the continued regime of 'capping' (see p. 324), by allowing one spouse/partner to pay for both (as with rates) and by the fact that many local authorities (such as counties) did not register or collect the charge direct: they precepted (see p. 317). The loss of independent business rate revenue also diminishes accountability.

It also appears that the old rating system was not so flawed, in that non-ratepayers' voting behaviour did not differ from that of ratepayers.[54]

The council tax

The consequences of the introduction of the poll tax/community charge were momentous. There were riots, massive refusals to pay, judicial review, attachment of earnings and benefits, rebellions by poll-tax payers over their surcharge for others' non-payments, threatened or actual imprisonments and warrant sales for non-payment, prosecutions under the Data Protection Act ... followed by a sudden change in government policy on local finance. Mrs Thatcher was forced to resign, at least in part, over the tax issue. In November 1990 John Major became Prime Minister, and Michael Heseltine was brought back into the Government as Secretary of State for the Environment, and thus responsible for local government affairs. He was critical of many of the injustices of the community charge and soon published a review of local finance in the consultation paper *A New Tax for Local Government*, which contained a review of local finance together with plans for further reform. Consequently, the Local Government Finance Act 1992 abolished (in 1993) the community charge/poll tax (on 41 million people) and replaced it with the council tax (on 22 million households).

The council tax is a tax on both the person (like the poll tax) and his or her property (like the rates), and is split equally between the two. It is based on the relative value of people's property and on the assumption that there are two people (adults) in the household. Where there are more than two, the tax bill is unaffected; but where there is only one adult (an estimated 7 million), the 'personal' part of the tax is halved and so there is a 25 per cent discount on the tax bill. In addition, there are categories of people (such as students, residents in welfare homes, those with severe mental impairment) who may be officially disregarded such that a number of multi-occupied houses count as having just one adult and receive the discount. There are also reductions for disabled people who have had their properties

Table 22 *Government projections of average council tax bills in England*
1992

Band	Property value upper limit (£)	Bill (£)	% of homes in band
A	40 000	329	26
B	52 000	384	19
C	58 000	439	22
D	88 000	494	15
E	120 000	604	9
F	160 000	713	5
G	320 000	823	4
H	320 000 +	988	1

NOTE: Houses containing only one adult are
entitled to a 25 per cent discount in each
band. Discounts and exemptions apply in
other special circumstances.

specially adapted. Furthermore, some (for example, empty or
unfit) dwellings are exempt or receive 50 per cent reduction.

The amount of tax will vary according to the value of the
property, for which purpose houses and flats are to be grouped
into eight valuation bands (A to H) (see Table 22 and Appendix
14). Those in the top band will pay about three times as much as
those in the lowest. The property valuation, undertaken in 1991–
2, was intended to be relative rather than absolute or actual, to
provide a base for the tax. The average (for England) is about
£80,000 (which is in Band D), where a household (in 1993)
would pay around £570 if the council spends at government
(standard spending) guidelines (though in practice the range for
band D is £244 for Wellingborough and £295 for Westminster to
£783 in Greenwich, £791 in Newcastle, £987 in Harlow). Those
on low incomes will get rebates of up to 100 per cent (known as
Council Tax Benefit).

Figure 20 *Components of the council tax in a county*

Unlike the community charge, each household receives a single bill. The owner-occupier or resident tenant thus normally pays, though joint owners or joint tenants would be jointly liable (as are husbands and wives or 'as married' partners). (In some cases the owner rather than the tenant is liable.) Unsettled disputes over liability or the level of the bill go to a Valuation Tribunal (see p. 319).

The business rates and grant systems are unchanged, except that grants will be paid separately to each tier. Grants, as we have seen, take account of the differences in the needs and taxable capacity of each area. So if all local authorities spend at the level the government considers appropriate (i.e. the SSA level), the council tax would be the same across the country for all properties in the same value band. Having received its share of grants and NNDR income (which are paid into the local collection fund), each authority will set its own council tax (or precept). The council's tax demand should enable local taxpayers to be able to identify which local authority is responsible for each element of the council tax (see Figure 20).

Capping is retained in the 1992 Act, having, under the Local Government Finance and Valuation Act 1991, been extended to small-spending councils previously exempt.

The proposed new tax has been welcomed by many as fairer, simpler, easier and cheaper to administer than the poll tax (where there is a continuing shortfall in collection, of up to 13·6 per cent in Scotland). It is less easy to evade, and more predictable in its yield, thus fulfilling a number of the principles or canons of a good tax.

Others, however, are fearful of its likely complexity (perhaps requiring another register to reduce evasion). And many, while seeing it as an improvement on the poll tax, regard it as unfair. There is also the problem of changes in regional property values (as with the depreciation in the South East since the 1991 valuation). Like rates, the council tax lacks buoyancy (see p. 320), especially if revaluations are postponed. And there may be problems of collection in so far as the poll-tax resistance has created a more general culture of non-payment or delay.

Others question the validity and fairness of the Standard Spending Assessments – both technically as a way of assessing local need, and on principle in that such assessment should be left to those who are elected to represent localities.[55] And in so far as local decisions are made about the level of the council spending, it is undermined again by the government's power to limit or 'cap' it.*

The continued centralization of the setting of the business rate is similarly denounced. But most fundamental of all is the Government's decision to maintain the present balance in the central–local division of local authority funding. In the 1991 Budget and subsequent legislation (The Community Charge (General Reduction) Act 1991), the Government transferred an additional £4·3 billion to local government (funded by a 2·5 per cent rise in VAT). The result is that local authorities only raise 14 per cent

---

* In 1993–4, the cap applies where councils spend above SSA as follows:

> up to 1% over SSA: 2·5% budget increase allowed
> 1–5% over SSA: 1·75% budget increase allowed
> 5–10% over SSA: 1% budget increase allowed . . .

and so on, until

> 60% over SSA: 10% budget cut.

of their expenditure* from local taxes compared to the 86 per cent coming from central government. This severely undermines local government as a manifestation of local choice and decision-making. Local authorities have become 'mere Whitehall agents'.[56] This is compounded by the severe 'gearing' effect (see p. 330) it creates. Thus a 1 per cent increase in spending needs a 5 to 6 per cent rise in the council tax to pay for it. (In Wales, it is even higher, at 10 to 14 per cent, as the council tax raises only 7 to 10 per cent of revenue.) It is for these reasons that some see the council tax having a short life span.

Alternative strategies

Another area of possible reform is the transfer of some local government services (such as the police or education) to the central government or alternatively the transfer of the cost of certain services (such as teachers' pay). The examples quoted are felt to be particularly appropriate because they are already subject to considerable government intervention. The latter proposal also featured in the 1979 Conservative and Liberal election manifestos. However, there are a number of serious objections to such transfers. In the first place it would lead to a further erosion of local government responsibilities or discretion, and if it were the costs that were transferred it would make councils appear even more as the agents of central government. Furthermore, it might be damaging to the service to have a divided responsibility (and it would inhibit local corporate management). The likelihood of greater public confusion would again endanger accountability. And in the end there might be no net financial gain for local government if the central government simply reduced its grants to compensate. Above all, however, the decision about whether a service should be administered locally or centrally ought to be

* This becomes 21 per cent when allowance is made for council tax benefit, transitional allowances, etc.

Table 23 *Sources of local government capital finance 1991 (and 1987)*

	£m		%	
Capital grants	2,421	(420)	27	(5)
Borrowing – from government – from others	1,408	(3,760)	16	(44)
Other/surplus on current account	2,140	(30)	24	(1)
Sales (e.g. council houses)	2,979	(4,260)	33	(50)
(See Table 17) Total	8,948	(8,470)	100	(100)

Source: UK National Accounts (the 'Blue Book'), 1992, HMSO; *Annual Abstract of Statistics,* 1989 and 1993, HMSO.

NOTE: Total local authority debt = £58,500 m (= ⅓ of National Debt). Annual debt interest = £5,400 m. The above are national figures; as with current expenditure, the actual pattern of capital finance for individual councils will vary from one to another.

decided on its own merits; it should not be seen merely as a device for easing local authority financial problems.[57]

Capital finance

Capital expenditure is spending on items which have a long life, such as houses, vehicles, roads and schools. Such expenditures are traditionally financed by borrowing, but there are other sources (see Table 17, p. 301). These may include the setting up of companies to attract private capital (and have a freer management structure), the *sale* of assets (such as land or houses), money received in the *repayment* of loans by those who have borrowed from local authorities (for house purchase etc.) and revenue from *grants.* The central government provides (capital) grants to local authorities for such purposes as road construction, the purchase of derelict land and the adaptation of properties in smoke-control areas. Local authorities also receive grant-aid from the European Community (EC) for such purposes as industrial redevelopment or school milk. In addition to these, they can, and substantially do, finance their capital expenditures from *current revenues* (council tax, rates, charges, sale of assets, etc.); in recent years there has been a trend in this direction, partly because it is cheaper (as a result of inflation and the high-interest costs of borrowing) and partly for political reasons.[58]

Borrowing

Local authorities are empowered to borrow under the Local Government Acts of 1972 and 1973. There are many ways in which they may raise loans; which precise method they decide to adopt will vary according to current legislation[59] and policy, current financial conditions and the individual judgement (and politics) of the local authority. A large proportion of local government borrowing takes the form of loans from the Public Works Loan Board (PWLB), a government agency comprising twelve Commissioners (originally established in 1815) to lend to public authorities. Under this arrangement each local authority is given a quota which it may borrow from the PWLB (and which it may exceed but at higher rates of interest). Otherwise, local authorities raise mortgage loans from the public, or they issue stock and bonds (these are regularly advertised in the press), or they can raise temporary loans (which do not need loan sanction – see below) such as bank overdrafts. Such borrowing may be expensive when local authorities have to compete with other borrowers and offer attractive interest rates. It can also, on occasion, be rather embarrassing, as when, in 1980, being in dispute with their local authority employers, the National and Local Government Officers' Association (NALGO) threatened to withdraw £2 million of short-term loans from fifteen councils which had borrowed from it! It may be safer and cheaper therefore for local authorities to build up their own reserve funds (for specific capital items) and balances, as indeed most do. Many of them also utilize their superannuation funds; thus, in effect, local authorities 'borrow' from themselves, and indeed some councils are net lenders.

For capital grant and expenditure approval purposes, the government requires local authorities to draw up and submit their proposals; these take the form of 'Transport Policies and Programmes' (TPPs) for roads and transport, 'Housing Investment Programmes' (HIPs) for housing.

Loan sanction

Before 1980, the central government placed strict limits on the amounts which local authorities could borrow. This system of control was known as 'loan sanction'. Under this system local authorities had to obtain explicit permissions from the relevant government department (such as the DES or DSS) before they could borrow money, so that, for example, before raising a loan to finance the building of schools, an LEA had to apply for loan approval. In the early days, such applications were often for individual projects such as a single school, but increasingly approvals were being granted for whole programmes of expenditure, especially in the fields of housing and transport in England and Wales, and more generally in Scotland (where the approvals are given for programmes of expenditure rather than for borrowing as such).

Under the Local Government, Planning and Land Act 1980, local authorities in England and Wales moved closer to the capital control system operating in Scotland (though it was already operating for housing investment and transport policies). Thus under the system now operating central approvals apply to programmes rather than individual projects; relate to expenditure as such rather than borrowing; and relate to one year at a time (though they are accompanied by an indication of the figures likely to be approved in subsequent years). Local authorities thus receive annual capital allocations for capital expenditure, known as prescribed expenditure allocations, under six blocks – housing, education, transport, personal social services, urban aid and all other services (excluding police, probation and magistrates' courts). Authorities are free to aggregate these allocations into a single block and then decide their own levels of expenditure (up to the total) among the different services. The allocations also gave the power to borrow. They can raise the finance for this total in any way they wish, and they can even go some way beyond that figure by using capital receipts such as the proceeds of sales. Specific government approval will still be necessary for capital projects of regional or national importance. The new controls are intended to enable central government to ensure that the total of local authority capital spending each year is consistent with national expenditure plans (in recent years such planning has been too often frustrated[60]), while reducing central government involvement in detailed local capital spending decisions. But many local authorities are suspicious and sceptical about this enhanced freedom from central surveillance (see pp. 384–5), and others say that it can be a wasteful and inefficient system.[61] In 1986 the Government outlined plans for changing these controls.

The capital control system introduced in 1980 (see above) has not worked as the Government anticipated. Together with the rate support grant system, it has created almost a new profession or industry of creative accounting and finance (including such devices as sale and leaseback, advanced purchase, deferred purchase, barters, interest-rate swaps, re-definition/allocation of prescribed expenditure, etc.) that, overall, has been wasteful and distorting. Consequently the Government is now moving back to control capital expenditure levels through control over borrowing.[62] Meanwhile, under the Local Government Finance Act 1988, the Government increased the prescribed list by including assets acquired through barter and property leased for three or more years.

Under the Local Government and Housing Act 1989, local authorities now receive an annual *credit approval* (based on the government's perception of each authority's needs and spending power). Local authorities can also use (i) a proportion of their accumulated capital receipts (from property sales, estimated at £6·2 billion in 1988) for capital expenditure, namely 25 per cent of house sales proceeds and 50 per cent of other sales receipts; the remainder is to be used to redeem debt (over £50 billion and costing some £5 million per annum) and/or for future capital investment, and (ii) current revenues, though it is anticipated that the scope will be limited because of the discipline imposed by capping of the budget and council tax.

Thus in effect, all capital expenditure must be set against a permission to borrow (the credit approvals), plus part of capital receipts (50 or 25 per cent) plus certain other receipts (for example from planning gain and legacies).

While there appears to be some relaxation in direct controls, the indirect control remains and is perhaps more comprehensive in scope or actual coverage. Indeed the aim is to preclude the various creative-accounting devices[63] which have enabled councils to get round spending restrictions.

It may be noted that high interest rates have a strong influence on local authorities' readiness to build up debts. A further consequence has been to alter the pattern of local authority borrowing over the past ten years from a preponderance of borrowing from the private sector (banks etc.) to the present situation where three quarters of local authority debt is owed to the PWLB (with its more favourable interest rates and somewhat easier accessibility).

Financial organization and procedures

Local authorities differ in their internal arrangements for dealing with financial matters. By law they are merely required to 'make arrangements for the proper administration of their financial affairs and ... secure that one of their officers has responsibility for the administration of those affairs'.[64] However, in practice local authorities have adopted a number of common procedures from which it is possible to generalize, and they are all bound by the rules that the financial year begins on 1 April and that it is illegal to budget for a defecit.

As we saw in Chapter 9, local authorities generally have appointed a policy or Policy & Resources (P & R) committee. This committee plays a key role in the coordination and control of the local authorities' financial decisions and actions (for an illustration, see p. 233). However, it is also common practice for the council to create a separate finance committee which works closely with (and is often a sub-committee of) the P & R committee. To facilitate control and coordination, members of the P & R committee (and the finance sub-committee) are drawn from (and are often the chairs of) the service or 'spending' committees.

The chair of the finance committee is a key figure in the local authority, acting in the capacity of a minor Chancellor of the Exchequer and often making a dramatic 'state of the economy' speech at the council's annual budget and rate-fixing meeting. He or she is almost certainly a member of the P & R committee and as chair of the finance committee will have the power to authorize actions (by officers) on behalf of the committee between its meetings. In this respect he or she has a close working relationship with the chief financial officer of the authority (variously entitled the Treasurer or Director of Finance or, more recently, Director of Resources). The latter is the head of the Finance (or Treasurer's) Department, which comprises the senior officials, who are professionally qualified in accountancy, together with the more junior staff, who undertake the more routine processes of collecting money, checking bills and making payments on behalf of the authority.

Preparing the budget

The budget is a statement containing the details of the council's current and capital incomes and expenditures, together with plans for the coming year. While traditionally the budget is drawn up for one year at a time, it has become common practice to develop plans or 'continuation budgets' for several years ahead,[65] based tentatively on the authority's long-term corporate plans (and rolling programmes), together with population forecasts and estimates of need in the local community. This is known as the 'financial plan approach'.

There are broadly two methods of preparing the budget:

(1) The traditional or 'incremental' method, which involves the chief officers and the finance officer calculating the costs of the authority's current activities and making an addition for any expansion or new developments. These estimates are then submitted to the relevant committees (education, social services, etc.) for their approval or amendment. All of the agreed estimates then go to the finance committee, which may make adjustments for inflation and other contingencies. The finance committee will then deduct from the total figure its estimates of incomes from grants and charges (and other incomes such as the use of internal reserves) and make the rate/council tax (or precept) for the coming year (see pp. 318, 326). The P & R committee will also have a part to play here, especially when the finance committee is a sub-committee of P & R.

(2) Rate (now tax) rationing, a process which begins by deciding what is the possible or appropriate level of the council tax. The total product or yield of that charge is then divided among the various services of the authority. It is sometimes held that this approach is more in keeping with the corporate planning system of management (see Chapter 9). In practice, many local authorities these days adopt a combination of the two methods: the finance or P & R committee sets targets or guidelines upon which the service committees base their estimates, but with more or less room for variation.

The budget cycle

Local authority procedures differ in detail, but broadly the budget cycle operates as follows:

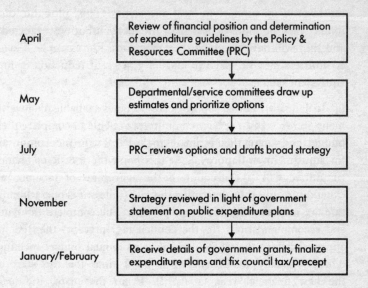

April	Review of financial position and determination of expenditure guidelines by the Policy & Resources Committee (PRC)
May	Departmental/service committees draw up estimates and prioritize options
July	PRC reviews options and drafts broad strategy
November	Strategy reviewed in light of government statement on public expenditure plans
January/February	Receive details of government grants, finalize expenditure plans and fix council tax/precept

Figure 21 *Outline of the budget cycle*

(1) In about mid-March, the P & R or finance committee will start to devise expenditure targets or guidelines for the service committees.

(2) In early autumn the service committees, in drawing up their estimates of expenditure for the next year, will relate the cost of existing services, together with any proposed developments, to these guidelines. This can be a painful process, as committees may have to abandon some of their cherished schemes in order to conform to the target figures. There may be much negotiation, manoeuvring and haggling at this stage between the service committees (and sub-committees) and the P & R and finance committees, and especially within the latter committees, where representatives of the service committees will seek to protect 'their' service. (This may well also have occurred earlier at the target-setting stage.)

(3) In November/December the central government announces

the level of its support to local authorities. This, plus the 'cash limits', may be more or less than the local authorities expected[66] and they will have to adjust their estimates. For example, service committees may be asked to make a 5 per cent reduction or find equivalent savings.

(4) In January/February more detail becomes available on government grants, so that service committees are able to complete their budgets and submit their estimates to the P & R or finance committee for adjustment and approval. At this point the P & R or finance committee will take account of the aggregates of income and expenditure and thus determine the rate (unless it is operating the rate/tax rationing scheme – see p. 344). The complete estimates and recommendations for the council tax (precept) then go for approval before the whole council at its annual budget meeting. This is usually in February, in good time for the start of the new financial year (1 April). From that date, the local authority starts collecting its incomes and spending on the various approved services.

Soon the cycle will start again for the next financial year, though it may be interrupted or influenced by events (such as strikes, inflationary wage settlements or the announcement of new government targets) which have caused councils to levy an additional or 'supplementary' rate or precept midway through the year (but these are now banned; see pp. 474–5).

Control

The most important financial decisions – fixing the council tax and deciding borrowing policy – rest with the council; by law they cannot be delegated. Yet it often appears that the financial control exercised by the council as a whole is little more than a charade, since the estimates always seem to go through 'on the nod', without discussion or alteration. This may in part be due to their complexity and perhaps to the obscurity or esoteric nature of some of the language. Few councillors are financial experts and many feel at a loss.

However, many of the figures merely represent in money terms the nature of most of the local authority's activities: changes tend to be marginal (or 'incremental') and are usually well understood by members of the service committees. And members of the P & R or finance committee build up a familiarity and expertise which allows them to guide the council for purposes of control.

Indeed the whole purpose of the estimates and budgetary procedure is to allow the exercise of control from a central point – the P & R or finance committee. This committee will also monitor progress in the work and expenditure of the local authority. In this respect, at all stages the finance officer and his staff play a leading role – checking that expenditures are in line with targets, that cash flows are running according to plan and reporting on the local authority's finances and any difficulties to the appropriate committee or department.

Control is also exercised through standing orders (see p. 218, and, for illustration, Appendix 12), which are usually supplemented by special rules known as 'financial regulations'. Together these cover such procedures as the composition and role of the P & R and/or finance committee, the drawing-up and submission of estimates, special notification of proposals for large schemes, rules on virement (transfers of funds from one purpose to another) and on tenders (firms' quotations) and the placing of contracts. Another form of control which itself will be set down in standing orders (at least in part) is audit.

The *finance department* inevitably has close contact with all the departments of the authority and the *chief finance officer* (CFO or Treasurer/Director of Finance) has close contacts with other chief officers (especially the chief executive officer) and with the various service committees and their chairs. Under the Local Government Finance Act 1988 (following the Widdicombe Report), councils' chief finance officers are now required to be properly qualified. They also have the statutory duty to restrain what they see as unlawful expenditure or transactions by issuing a 'Section 114 report' to council members and the auditor. This enhanced role has already been exercised (e.g. in Brent London Borough Council in November 1988 and Eastleigh in September 1990), but some people question the competence of treasurers to act in such a quasi-judicial fashion, while others foresee mounting conflict between officers and members.

It is the CFO's job to exercise a general oversight of the local authority's financial practices – methods of payment, timing cash flows, auditing and keeping within guidelines, checking virement, etc. In practice, much of this work will devolve on to senior officers while the CFO will concentrate on the other main role as financial adviser to the council. CFOs will be concerned with the financial implications of the council's overall policy and hence with the specific policies of the service committees and departments. While they may attend these committees or send reports to them, most of their attention will be focused on the finance committee and the P & R committee.

Like the finance officer, these two committees will have two broad roles: firstly, the more routine control function of approving the payment of bills, administration of the authority's superannuation scheme and insurance matters, supervision of the work of the finance department and investment arrangements, etc.; secondly, the more creative function of examining the spending plans and proposals of the service committees, with a view both to their coordination and to assessing their total impact on the resources of the local authority and its broad aims and priorities. This drawing-up of the council's budget is crucial to the operation of the local authority. It requires the close involvement of the P & R and the finance committees with other committees in order to strengthen the corporate approach to the authority's affairs. (A similar and parallel collaboration occurs between the finance department and other departments.) The result of their deliberations is a series of recommendations to the full council.

Audit

This takes two forms:

(1) *Internal*, undertaken by the officials of the local authority's own finance department. They will keep a regular check on incomes from rents, charges and other sources, the receipt of stores, claims for expenses, official receipts, etc. They will be checking the accuracy of stocks and accounts, together with the procedures involved, in order to prevent fraud and the misappropriation of council property. The purpose of internal audit is thus to ensure that the financial dealings of the local authority are undertaken in a proper manner. But additionally, such audit will be concerned to ensure that departmental expenditures are being made in accordance with the approved estimates, and that money is not being unofficially transferred from one purpose to another (otherwise the whole idea of the budgetary procedure is undermined).

(2) *External.* By law, all local authorities are subject to external audit. This itself may take two forms.[67] The first is 'district audit', whereby the country is divided into districts and a district auditor is appointed to each to conduct audits of local authority accounts. Formerly these auditors were appointed by the Minister; since 1982 they are appointed by the Audit Commission (see p. 352). In Scotland, external auditing is the responsibility of an independent Commission for Local Authority Accounts, appointed by the Secretary of State. This Commission recruits its own audit staff, but it also substantially (and traditionally) appoints private practitioners (see below).

The function of district auditors is to inspect local authority accounts in order to detect financial irregularities (fraud), to promote sound financial practices and procedures and to prevent or uncover unlawful payments. In this last capacity they are in effect re-inforcing the *ultra vires* rule (see p. 74), for when they discover expenditure which is outside the legal powers of the local authority, they may refer the matter for a judicial ruling to the courts. (They used to have greater powers: see p. 580, note 68.) The latter can disallow such expenditures and may order repayment by those members and officers who were responsible for the illegal expenditure (or for failure to collect any incomes due).[68] In the twenty-five years 1947–72 the number of cases of reported fraud or unlawful expenditure amounted to about fifty a year.[69]

In 1985–6 councillors in Liverpool and Lambeth were 'surcharged' (heavily fined, at £5,000 each) and disqualified from office (for five years) for 'wilful misconduct in delaying the fixing of their councils' rates' (which is now statutorily timetabled).[70] It led to calls to have the surcharge penalty system (uniquely applicable to local government) abolished. In 1989 the district auditor successfully challenged the legality of some loan deals known as 'swaptions', i.e. where local authorities exchange interest rate charges.[71] And in 1988 ten councillors were surcharged for approving a budget containing an excess rate fund contribution to the housing account.[72] In the same case it was pointed out that councillors could be so penalized even if absent from the meeting; it would depend on the reasons for their absence. Officers too may be surcharged.

Over the years, the district auditors (and internal auditors) have been focusing attention on wasteful expenditures or procedures (mode of borrowing, fuel consumption, cost controls over repairs expenditure, etc.) and increasingly on value for money. In the three years 1970–73, suggestions by the district audit saved an estimated £1·5 million.[73] For the latter purpose, district auditors have started devising 'performance indicators' (output divided by input) for comparing different services and different authorities.[74] And in 1979 the Advisory Committee on Local Government Audit was established, to consider the annual report of the Chief Inspector of Audit[75] and any questions arising from it which were of general interest, and to make recommendations to local authorities in respect of value for money (VFM).

The second form of external audit was 'approved audit'. Here auditors (usually local firms of accountants) had to be approved by the Minister. Where these auditors found cases of illegal expenditure or losses, they had to report the matter to the Minister, who could order an *extraordinary* audit by the district auditor. The Audit Commission is now responsible.

Before each audit, the accounts and relevant documents must be available for public inspection for the previous fifteen working days, and may thus be inspected. And electors may question the auditor about the accounts or make objections/allegations about illegality, losses due to mismanagement, misconduct, etc. It is also possible for the Minister (or Audit Commission, see below) to direct that there should be an extraordinary audit.

External auditors issue a report when they have completed their work, though if a matter is sufficiently important it may be issued beforehand. Audit is announced in advance in the press or public notice boards, and by law the local authority's accounts must be made available to the public (public access in Scotland is no longer more restricted [76]). Members of the public are entitled to raise questions about the accounts with the auditors, and this can be an important aspect of local government accountability (seemingly under-utilized).[77] The auditor may issue a special 'public interest' report, where the accounts appear to be unsatisfactory and things have gone wrong in some way (extravagance, fraud, inefficiency, faulty systems, etc.). There were thirty-six such reports in 1990. Furthermore, if an elector makes objections to the auditor about the accounts, the district auditor may refer the matter to the law court to rule on the lawfulness of expenditure. (In the Camden case, 1982, two members of the council's Conservative opposition party complained to the district auditor that the council had been 'illegally generous' in their pay settlement to striking workers during the 'dirty jobs' dispute in the 1978–9 'winter of discontent'. The auditor took the case to the High Court. The case was dismissed on the grounds that the settlement was within the council's discretion.) Alternatively, the Minister could order the district auditor to hold an extraordinary audit, as in the Clay Cross case (see p. 100). If the district auditor refuses to submit an elector's objection to the court, the latter may go to court for a declaration and if necessary an injunction against the unlawful expenditure.

The Audit Commission

Originating from the Layfield Report (1976), the Local Government Finance Act 1982 made local authorities in England and Wales subject to the 'Scottish' system of audit, with the creation of the Audit Commission. The AC has fifteen members appointed by the government and drawn from industry, local government and trade unions. The aim of this change was to increase the apparent independence of audit, to bring in more private auditors and to increase the efficiency approach to local finances. The AC appoints auditors to inspect local authorities' accounts* (drawing on the District Audit service or, for about 40 per cent of councils, the private sector – local authorities no longer have the choice), but it is specifically charged with promoting more value-for-money (VFM) auditing (for which purpose it absorbed the Advisory Committee). The AC issues auditors with a code of audit practice (approved by Parliament) for use in conducting audits.

In its mission statement (1993) it declares, 'The Audit Commission promotes proper stewardship of public finances and helps those responsible for the management and delivery of public services to achieve economy, efficiency and effectiveness.' It aims to be a 'driving force in the improvement of public services' which it seeks to achieve through 'auditing public service accounts to ensure their probity and regularity and producing national studies of value for money'.

The Commission produces regular and numerous VFM studies (e.g. 1,600 in 1985)[78] and performance indicators and comparisons[79]: see Appendix 15 for an illustration. Its reports cover all aspects of local government – housing, management, vehicle maintenance, parks, policies, education, etc., and its various

---

* Such scrutiny is not free, of course: the commission must cover its costs. Local authorities currently have to pay some £30–40 per hour (in addition to which there are audit fees for certifying/validating grant claims).

VFM studies have identified savings by local authorities amounting to some £2 billion a year.[80] Thus for example in 1988 the AC pointed to the falling school rolls and estimated that empty school places are costing some £250 million a year (though of course local politics and perhaps educational or social reasons may forestall closures of schools). In 1989 it criticized councils for allowing council tenants to fall into arrears of some £500 million. In 1988 the AC criticized local authorities for allowing much of their accumulated land and property (worth £100 billion) to lie idle or under-used, and it suggested that in view of population changes and changing responsibilities (with contracting out etc.) councils should dispose of some 25 per cent of their holdings. (The Government has responded by requiring councils to publish information on their unused land. And under the Local Government, Planning and Land Act 1980, the Minister has the power to require their disposal of land.)

The AC has been instrumental in drawing up (together with the local authority associations) a voluntary code of practice on 'a prudential approach to local authority commitments' to avoid risky financial transactions and the building up of excessive indebtedness (often the result of creative accounting techniques). And under the Local Government Act 1988 (Sec. 30), the AC has been given a pre-emptive or 'stop' power to prevent what it sees as questionable financial deals. This power has been criticized as excessive and undemocratic, and recent cases of surcharge and disqualification of councillors (see p. 350) have led to calls for auditors to shed their quasi-judicial role of initiating such proceedings – indeed the AC has been seen as an instrument in central government control.[81] Others believe that it uses too many business or accounting criteria in its scrutinies and reports; they are afraid that the work of the AC will (together with policies such as the national curriculum in schools) homogenize local authorities and that its tendency to develop a managerial role will impinge on the political aspects of councils' decision-making. Thus, among others, the National Consumer Council has expressed concern that service effectiveness is being neglected in favour of economy and efficiency, and that cost–effectiveness is only cost- and service-cutting.[82] Other critics have suggested that the Audit Commission has perhaps lost some of its traditional auditing cutting edge by focusing too much on VFM and, in view of the apparent recalcitrance of some authorities, that its powers should be increased.[83] However, the AC has rebutted a number of these criticisms (or 'myths'[84]) and now claims to have regard for outcome or quality of service,[85] and it recently declared that '1987–88 was a year in which the Commission's approach to value for money began to bear fruit on a large scale . . . local authorities are now responding positively and enthusiastically to our recommendations'.[86]

In addition to the procedures for the audit of accounts, each local authority must supply annual financial returns to the Minister. These cover income and expenditure and details of rating/tax matters, and they provide an additional safeguard against improper financial activities and are a source of national statistics on local government finance.

Value for money (VFM)

The question of local government's efficiency was raised in Chapter 10. Efficiency may be defined as the maximum outcome or output from a given input of resources. But since the ultimate goal of local government is to enhance the general welfare of society, there can be no easy measure of its 'output'. And even if there were such a measure, allowance has to be made for political factors, both in the narrow (party) sense and in the broader (democratic) sense. Thus local government is subject to regular election, public funds must not be subject to risk, local authorities are subject to public accountability through open committee meetings and the publication of accounts (see above and Chapter 9) and to considerable oversight by the central government (see Chapter 12). On top of all this, local authorities are urged to encourage popular participation, and a number have introduced customer contracts with compensation for late or poor services.

Such features are in many ways very desirable, but they are not without some cost – such as the sudden reversals of policy following elections or the slowing-down of the decision-making process. Perhaps the best example of the latter is the two-tier structure of local government, which could be viewed as a deliberate sacrifice of efficiency for democracy, though others would argue that the large size of our local authorities sacrifices democracy to efficiency of service provision (see Chapter 3). However, as the Layfield Committee pointed out, the public are increasingly concerned at local government's efficiency and effectiveness in view of the steep rises in local taxes, while standards of service fall in spite of the fact that manpower levels appear to be stable. Consequently there have been calls for greater information to be made available to the general public about local government services,[87] a move enhanced by the *Citizen's Charter*, 1991. And under the Local Government, Planning and Land Act 1980 local authorities are required to publish annually their financial and manpower figures, together with information on performances, in order to strengthen local government's accountability to their electors and ratepayers (see too p. 281). (In 1984–5 auditors received 730 questions and objections from members of the public.) Since the Rates Act 1984 they must consult with local business, though nothing of obvious significance has occurred as a result of this requirement.

Constraints

In the pursuit of value for money, local authorities should at least begin with a set of objectives, ranked in some sort of order of priority (based on rational criteria, such as need or expressed demand). Various ways of achieving those objectives should be considered and the most effective projects (those which maximize benefits) chosen and pursued. In Chapter 9 a number of manage-

ment techniques which could help in this respect were outlined.
In addition, local authorities are advised by their own management services units and by outside bodies such as LAMSAC and
LACSAB (see p. 277) or private consultants. And apart from the
work of internal audit and budget monitoring techniques, many
local authorities have established performance review committees.[88]

All of this, however, requires planning and reasonable stability.
In practice, local authorities do not have this stability, partly as a
result of local elections and changing party fortunes, which are
paralleled at national level (with the consequence of significant
changes in economic policy which can vitally affect local government), but also partly as a result of inconsistencies within central
government (or at least a differing view on priorities) with some
departments urging major local government restraint (e.g. the
Department of the Environment) while others urge greater provision (e.g. the Department of Health seeking greater local authority
community care of hospital patients; or the Department of Energy
urging more expenditure on housing insulation grants by local
housing authorities). Perhaps the area of greatest paradox is
within the DoE itself: on the one hand it is urging expenditure
restraint through grant penalties, and on the other it is seeking
inner-city regeneration through 'partnership' schemes and special
grants (or, in some cases, through the creation of special urban
development corporations – UDCs – as in Liverpool, Bristol,
Plymouth and London: see Hackney case, p. 566, note 26).

Furthermore, the central government can also regulate local
authority charges (for instance, for old people's homes, car parks
and even library fines), and they can impose schemes on local
authorities (such as rent and rate rebates, sale of houses, new
charges for old services) that have significant manpower implications for the authorities concerned. In this chapter we have seen
how local government is subject to considerable financial control
and influence, in particular through the RSG settlement and
cash limits (both of which appear rather late for local authority
financial planning purposes), loan sanction and public expenditure

plans. In terms of value for money, therefore, local authorities are not entirely masters of their own fate. As the Layfield Committee commented, 'Our Report finds a lack of clear accountability for local government expenditure, which results from the present confusion of responsibilities between the government and local authorities.' This central–local relationship is considered in the following chapter.

12. Controls and Influences

Local authorities are political institutions: they exercise power. But they themselves are, of course, subject to a substantial degree of control and influence. Such control takes a number of different forms: some of these are widely accepted and cause little offence; others are regarded as exceptionable and give rise to substantial controversy.

Legislative/parliamentary control

In our system of government, Parliament is sovereign: an Act of Parliament becomes the law of the land and cannot be gainsaid. As a consequence, Britain has a 'unitary' constitution, in contrast to those 'federal' systems such as that of the USA, where power is divided and exercised coordinately (or in parallel) by both the central (federal) government and the individual states. In Britain legal authority emanates from Parliament and it may be convenient for Parliament to devolve power on to other bodies (such as local authorities or to regional assemblies like the old Stormont Parliament in Ulster). It may at any time rescind or withdraw that power from them (as indeed it did in the case of Stormont, returning Ulster to 'direct rule' from Westminster in 1972).

Local authorities in Britain therefore exist by virtue of Acts of Parliament: legislation brings local authorities into existence, as the Local Government Act 1888 did (see p. 18), it gives them powers and duties, as the Education Act 1944 did (see p. 78), it will shape their composition and constitution, as the Local Government Act 1972 did, and it may pre-determine their internal arrangements, as the Local Government Social Services Act 1970 did. Local government – with the exception of the City of London, which is technically a common law corporation rather than a statutory one – is thus the creature of Parliament.

Legal/judicial control

As a consequence of their being statutory bodies, local authorities are subject to a high degree of judicial control; that is, there are special remedies against local authorities because they themselves have special rights, powers and duties conferred by statute. We have already seen how they are subject to the principle of *ultra vires* (see p. 74) and how this is reinforced by the scrutiny of external audit (see p. 349). Where the auditor or an individual citizen believes that the local authority is acting *ultra vires* (including unreasonable expenditure) he can seek a declaration and injunction from a court of law, which might subsequently impose the requirement of recompense by repayment (see the London fares case p. 119). In January 1991 Hammersmith and Fulham Council's interest 'swaps' were declared illegal by the House of Lords.

However, the remedy of a High Court declaration or injunction is not confined to cases of *ultra vires*[1] or illegal expenditure: it may be used where an individual's private right suffers particular damage or infringement, for instance against a council which erects a hoarding and blocks the light from a person's windows. An individual will usually conduct his own case. Where the aggrieved persons consist of the general body of ratepayers, as in the Fulham case,[2] court action is normally taken on their behalf by the Attorney-General.

Alternatively, certain kinds of local authority action or decision may be challenged in the courts by means of what are called *prerogative orders.* These are High Court orders usually initiated by an aggrieved individual but pursued by the Crown. They take three forms: (1) the order of *mandamus* (the most frequently used) will require a local authority to carry out a duty imposed on it by law (e.g. to require an authority to issue a precept, invite tenders or to permit the inspection of its records); (2) the order of *prohibition* will restrain a local authority from proceeding further in a situation where it appears to be exceeding its jurisdiction, has disregarded the principles of natural justice or has not followed prescribed procedures (e.g. such an order was made to prevent a police doctor from determining the question of whether a police officer should be retired as disabled, as the doctor had prejudiced the issue in an earlier report[3]); (3) the order of *certiorari* applies, as does prohibition, in those situations where the local authority is acting in a judicial or semi-judicial – as opposed to purely administrative – capacity (as where it is hearing objections to one of its proposals, such as slum clearance). Under this order the action or decision-making procedure does not simply cease, as with the prohibition order. Instead the record or the decision of the authority is sent to the High Court to have its legality inquired into and if necessary to have the decision quashed. The decision of a rent assessment committee, for example, might be quashed on the grounds of bias by its chairman.[4]

The procedure involved in these prerogative orders is cumbersome; as a result there has been a tendency for aggrieved persons to seek judicial redress through actions for a declaration and injunction (see p. 359) or through statutory remedies.[5] The latter may take the form of appeals to the Minister (see p. 366) or statutory appeals.

Since many of the powers conferred on local authorities may affect the interests of individuals, a safeguard is provided in the appeals machinery. In contrast to the procedure for injunctions or prerogative orders, *statutory appeals* are relatively simple and accessible. Under this procedure the individual has the right of appeal, stated in individual Acts of Parliament, against the improper or inequitable use of powers conferred on local authorities by the legislation, such as the granting of licences. Thus, under the Highways Act 1959 owners of properties abutting private streets may appeal to the Magistrates Court against the specification of works served on them by the council for making up the paving and drainage of the street. Similarly, under Housing Acts, property owners may appeal to the county court against a local authority's order requiring the repair, demolition or closure of insanitary property. Finally, appeals may go to the High Court over such issues as clearance orders and compulsory purchase. In some instances, the court's powers will be limited, but in many cases it will be empowered to substitute its own discretion for that of the authority.

Local authorities are, in addition, subject to the control of the courts in much the same way as other organizations or individual people, so that if they are in breach of contract they may be sued (in tort or contract) and if they (through one of their employees) commit a criminal offence proceedings will be taken against them.

Despite their vast powers and responsibilities, however, and notwithstanding the recent spate of notable cases, local authorities are not often taken to court (though there are mounting threats of actions by parents on the grounds that expenditure cuts are causing LEAs to fail in their statutory duties to maintain minimum education standards.[6] It is also suggested that both citizens and lawyers are more ready to make legal challenges these days, partly as a result of excessive or poorly processed legislation by Parliament.) Authorities are normally law-abiding bodies which keep careful track of the legality of their actions by appointing a monitoring officer or other legal staff to advise them. In addition, much control is exercised over them administratively (by Ministers – see below), which reduces the need for judicial control. And finally, judicial intervention occurs only when an aggrieved party (a citizen) institutes the necessary action, and this is not always easy: in spite of the apparently wide-ranging opportunities for redress, the judicial remedies for review and control of local government actions have long been the subject of criticism. The system is held to be confusing and the procedures complex. It is sometimes suggested that they should be consolidated and simplified. It is also felt that the ordinary courts of law are not always well suited to consider the technical issues which may arise in matters such as house repair or demolition. (An alternative system would be a series of courts or tribunals which specialize in administrative justice, such as they have in France.)

Notwithstanding these criticisms, judicial control can be justified on the grounds that it is impartial and not tied to policy matters. Consequently, it helps to secure public confidence that bias and corruption are not present in the administration of local government business. Such suspicions may linger where administrative control alone is involved. However, these suspicions may be assuaged by the introduction (in 1974) of the Local Government Commissioners ('ombudsmen') whose role it is to investigate and remedy maladministration (see p. 422).

Administrative/governmental control

The closest and most continuous form of control over local authorities is that exercised by government departments. Such controls have come into existence piecemeal, as convenience and expediency required. Consequently, they are not uniform in their application and their scale varies from time to time and among the different services.

Government supervision of local authorities has always existed in some form – from the JPs of the Middle Ages, the Poor Law Commissioners of the 1830s and the school inspectors of the 1860s to the powers exercised by the modern Secretary of State. However, although the scale of this control appears to have fluctuated, there has been a more sustained increase since the 1920s and especially since the war.[7]

Justification of government control

Central control of local government may be justified on a number of grounds. Firstly, many of the services for which local authorities are responsible (education, housing, etc.) are national in character and need therefore to be sustained at some minimum standard at least. Secondly, in the interests of social justice the government will try to secure equality of standards and the avoidance of disparities. Besides, many local needs – traffic, fire safety, building controls, food safety, children's services, etc. – are common throughout the country. Thirdly, councils are substantial spenders and taxers (see Chapter 11) and they control too many of the nation's resources to be left alone by the central government, which is generally held responsible for the management of the economy as a whole.

Thus, in general terms, the role of the central government is to secure the national interest over and above the purely local. For example, the Minister may intervene in matters of land use or development. It is sometimes held that central government control is justified because it is more efficient than local government ('auntie knows best'). This may have been true in the last century, when local authorities were far from honest or were often reluctant to spend ratepayers' money, but it is by no means demonstrably true today.

What is true is that the central government can act as a clearing house for useful ideas and good practices which it can disseminate among local authorities. Furthermore it is generally accepted that individuals and local authorities themselves need to have an accessible point of reference in cases of dispute (for example, between two councils regarding an overspill or development project, such as a waste-disposal site, or liability for homeless persons). In such cases the Minister can act as a referee.

These are the justifications for central government intervention in the affairs of local government. Whether they justify the present degree of control is another matter. But before examining the various forms which this intervention may take, it is worth pointing out that central intervention is inevitable, partly because the central government substantially finances local government (see p. 301), which provides a means of intervention; but also because political parties seek to apply their principles throughout the country and, since parties exist at both the national and the local levels, this will provide the necessary motive for intervention.

The forms of control

Acts of Parliament establishing local authority services give Ministers certain general powers to control the way in which councils act, and in some cases these powers may be quite sweeping. Thus the Education Act 1944 makes it the duty of the Secretary of State for Education 'to secure the effective execution by local authorities, under his control and direction, of national policy for providing a varied and comprehensive educational service in every area'. In fact, however, such broad, almost autocratic, powers are rarely found. Furthermore it appears to be a convention that where they do exist they are rarely exercised. (This is not to deny that their mere existence and potential use may be a powerful influence. But see pp. 371.)

It is more usual for the legislation to specify the Minister's powers, and these specific forms of control are much more likely to be used.* In many cases Ministers have conferred on them the power to issue regulations and orders (generally called 'delegated legislation' or 'statutory instruments') to fill in the details of a service outlined in legislation or to bring in new elements and add to that service when circumstances suggest. For example, the Home Secretary issues regulations for the administration and conditions of service of police forces, and the Secretary of State for Social Services does the same for local authorities' arrangements for fostering children or for charges in old people's homes. (A number of Ministers have the power to specify the minimum

---

* For example, it is calculated that in 1988 the Local Government Finance Bill, the Education Bill and the Housing Bill gave 344, 366 and 110 separate statutory controls respectively to the Secretary of State.[8] See too Sec. 53 of the 1990 Planning Act.

and maximum charges which councils may levy.) It is usually by means of such regulations that Ministers try to secure the maintenance of standards in many local government services (as in the regulations concerning school buildings[9] or the qualifications of teachers or house-building). In 1993 the Government unexpectedly scrapped the 1981 Education (Premises) Regulations which local authorities had been preparing for final implementation.

Alternatively, the government may vet and perhaps modify local authority schemes (and their standing orders; see Chapter 9). Many Acts of Parliament require local authorities to submit their schemes for the development of certain services. In the 1960s and 1970s a number of LEAs' schemes for 'going comprehensive' in their secondary schools were rejected as unsuitable by various Secretaries of State for Education. Similarly local authorities' structure plans (see p. 90) have to be approved by the Minister, and they may be altered.[10] So too must housing schemes. More recently (under the Education Reform Act 1988) LEAs are required to submit their schemes for the local financial management of schools (LMS) for approval. Needless to say, schools applying for opted-out/grant-maintained (GM) status require ministerial approval.

Planning is an example (making by-laws is another) of an area where the Minister's consent or approval might be required for individual actions by the local authority. It is regularly needed for compulsory purchase orders and appeals over planning refusals. In the latter cases, an inquiry is usually conducted by a government official (or someone appointed by the government), known as the inspector. Inspectors' reports go to the Minister for his final decision, which in practice normally, but not always, endorses the recommendation of the inspector. As we have seen (in Chapter 4), Ministers take an interest in councils' local structure and development plans, and in recent years London boroughs have complained at the extent to which the Department of the Environment has altered their unitary structure plans.

In this respect, the Minister is often acting as an arbitrator or judge in a dispute between the local authority and its citizens, such as there might be when parents object to the LEA's closure of a school. Or he may act to resolve a dispute between local authorities themselves, for instance over planning or overspill issues or financial liability for students or welfare clients. Similarly he may be called in to deal with disputes between a local authority and its staff over such issues as superannuation rights or conditions of service.

Some legislation gives Ministers important default powers over an authority which is failing to provide a service satisfactorily. If a Minister is dissatisfied with an authority's provision of a particular service he may remove the responsibility from that authority, either taking it over himself (for instance by appointing a school's board of governors, or issuing new street by-laws, where the authority has failed to do so; a recent case involved Norwich council-house sales,[11] and in the 1980s there were plans for commissioners to take over responsibility from Liverpool council.[12]); or, more frequently, transferring responsibility to another local authority or to a special body, as in the Clay Cross case (see note 11). In each case, the financial liability remains with the defaulting authority. (The alternative procedure is for the Minister to issue directions or a default order enforceable through the courts – see p. 359.) In practice, such events are rare, though the tendency of modern legislation to confer default powers on Ministers is increasing.[13]

Influences and informal controls

Besides these formal controls, there exist a number of other points of contact and influence between central and local government. They are less dramatic, but they are equally if not more influential on the operation of local authorities.[14] Thus Ministers may intervene in the appointment (or dismissal) of certain chief officers. For example the appointment of chief constables, fire officers, directors of social services and (in London) senior education officers requires ministerial approval, and normally the local authority is obliged to submit its short list of candidates, many of whom may be vetoed by the Minister as unsuitable in an attempt to safeguard the quality of the service.[15]

Ministers will also seek to maintain the standards of certain services by means of *inspection*, which may be for purposes of securing compliance with statutory requirements (enforcement inspections) or to secure and maintain standards of performance (efficiency inspections). Inspection occurs in the following areas: trading standards/consumer protection, environmental health, ancient monuments and historic buildings, planning, building control, education, police, fire and social services. Thus the police, fire and education services are subject to regular inspection by Her Majesty's Inspectors (HMIs) from the Home Office and the Department for Education (DFE), and social service departments are reviewed by the Social Service Inspectors (SSIs) of the Department of Health. In Scotland the relevant departments are the Scottish Education Department and the Scottish Home and Health Department (in effect they are sub-departments of the Scottish Office). These departmental inspectorates act as the 'eyes and ears' of the central government and can produce some very stern and critical reports (e.g. the Derbyshire police report, 1992). They collect and disseminate information and advice – 'local good practices' – on a large scale. Examples include educational organization and teaching methods, and sheltered housing schemes.

However, much of this information is collected from local government directly by the central government departments, for local authorities are required by law to 'send the Secretary of State such reports and returns, and give him such information . . . as he may require . . .'[16] Innocent as such data collection may seem, it might nevertheless have some influence on the methods and standards of council services, even if it only causes local authorities themselves to analyse and utilize their own findings.

Local authorities have the power (and in some cases the duty) to make by-laws. These must receive ministerial approval before they are valid and enforceable (e.g. in 1980 a number of councils failed to get Home Office approval of by-laws banning dogs in parks), but Ministers will usually short-circuit the process by issuing 'model' by-laws, which tend to be adopted by local authorities if only to save them time and effort. The same arrangement applies to the requirement that LEAs draw up and submit for approval their Instruments and Articles of Government for schools and colleges.[17]

Local authorities are influenced and persuaded by other central government documents. These include memoranda, research reports, White Papers, Green Papers[18] and statements (for instance, the statement on housing investment plans in 1979, which also said that councils would have to raise their rents by 60p per week in the following year, or the Minister's criticism of out-of-town superstores). Some departments regularly publish a news-sheet or bulletin (such as the Treasury's *Economic Progress Report*, the DES's *Reports on Education*, DoEs planning guidance (PPGs) and Design Bulletins (for roads, footpaths, etc.), and the DSS's *Social Work Service*). All of these more or less help to shape local government activity.

Of particular importance in this respect are government circulars, which are sent out very regularly to local authorities explaining new legislation, suggesting new directions in policy or methods of administration, and perhaps explaining government policy. They vary from the relatively trivial circular concerned with minor matters of detail to the highly significant, such as the DES circular 10/65, which requested LEAs to submit their schemes for comprehensive school reorganization, and the DoE circular 21/79, which explained the Government's expectation of a 3 per cent fall in local government expenditure in 1979–80. (Other, less official, 'circulars' include those which are issued to local political parties by the party headquarters, and those which are sent to member authorities by the local authority associations.)

Finally, Ministers can exercise influence personally and directly when they meet local government members and officials at official visits or local government conferences. They can also make their views known through articles in local government journals (such as the *Local Government Chronicle*, the *Municipal Journal*, *Commu-*

nity Care, Public Finance and Accountancy or *Municipal Engineering*) or through well-publicized statements. Two recent examples of the latter include Anthony Crosland's declaration in 1975 that (for local government) 'the party's over' and Michael Heseltine's speech at the local government conference in September 1981 that it was 'closing time' for local authority growth – both of which helped to shape the psychological atmosphere in local government for the years ahead.

Financial controls

The financial relationship between local and central government has been described as the iron fist in the velvet glove. It comprises a mixture of controls and influences. It was observed (on p. 350–51) how the external audit seeks to reinforce the judicial control of local authorities by its concern with the legality of local authority expenditure. Increasingly, however, the Audit Commission is exercising an administrative influence by widening its remit to cover value for money considerations, as a consequence of which it may attempt to guide and advise local authorities (e.g. on staff–pupil ratios, implementing care services, managing arrears).

Stronger and more overt influence is exercised through government grants. This influence may be either particular or general in effect. 'Specific' grants (allocated to a particular service[19]) will tend to encourage the provision of that service, influencing the authority's pattern of service provision (and its corporate plan). It was suggested too (on p. 309) that such grants tend to bring with them rather closer central supervision. The substitution of a 'block' (non-allocated) grant for specific grants, which occurred substantially in 1958, was intended to release local authorities from such close oversight. However, a general grant brings with it the means of a more general control or influence, since all local authorities can be encouraged or discouraged from spending by the central government's increasing or decreasing the proportion of expenditure it is prepared to finance.[20] The adequacy of the government's allowance for cost increases resulting from inflation (the 'cash limits' – see p. 579) is another important factor.

Local resources can be affected by central government in other ways. The government can delay carrying out the revaluation of property. It can determine (through legislation) the de-rating or re-rating of certain categories of property (see p. 317), both of which decisions will impinge on local authorities' tax/rates resources (especially before 1990 when domestic rates were replaced by the community charge). It may issue guidelines and even place upper limits ('capping') on local budgets/taxes. It determines, nationally, the level of the unified business rate (UBR). And it can exercise some influence on local authorities' other main source of income – charges. In a general way it may seek to regulate all charges through a prices policy. More directly, the government can specify or restrict certain local authority fees, such as those for children in care, old people's homes, library fines, or (using heavy persuasion and altered subsidies) council rents. Recent legislation even tells councils what discount they must offer on their council house sales.

In Chapter 11 we saw how local authority capital expenditure has long been subject to loan sanction. Apart from the control element inherent in such a process, additional influences flowed from the various conditions which often accompanied borrowing approval. Until recently, in seeking loan sanction to build houses, local authorities have had to follow certain building standards and conform to certain cost yardsticks.[21] Or in seeking loan sanction to develop nursery education, LEAs found Ministers more favourably disposed to approve certain kinds of project (such as nursery classes attached to primary schools) than others (such as separate nursery school buildings).[22] Finally, central government has an impact on local government's capital finance by changing its policy regarding access to the Public Works Loan Board (see p. 339) and through the interest charged on its loans, and by declaring moratoria on spending (as in 1982 and 1984).

Local authority resources are being regularly committed by the central government when it legislates for new services; for example, the Children and Young Persons Act 1969 introduced the concept of 'intermediate treatment' for young offenders which became the responsibility of the local authority social services departments. Other examples include the national policy of community care for the mentally disabled; and the imposition of the national curriculum in schools; or, through the device of inspection or new regulations, the urging of the expansion or improvement of existing services (police recruitment, fire regulations or schools building standards for instance). Equally, the central government is committing local government resources when it makes public statements on pay norms or sets up pay inquiries and commissions to determine appropriate wage increases, such as the Houghton Committee on teachers' pay in 1974 and the Comparability Commission (Clegg) which was involved in 1979 in the determination of the pay of teachers and other local government employees. It is difficult for councils not to be bound by the recommendations of these bodies.

Consequences of control

The vast array of controls and influences outlined above has given rise to deep concern about central domination and the subordination of local government. Professor Keith-Lucas suggests that local democratic self-government in Britain has become a 'romantic dream'.[23] And the Maud Committee (1967) concluded that British local government has, as a result of central government control, less discretion than local authorities in other countries. It also outlined the dangerous consequences of this excessive control, which it saw causing frustration and discouragement among local government councillors and officers (in 1993, the London Boroughs Association complained of the Government's excessive interference in their unitary development plans, especially their use of new powers under the 1991 Planning and Compensation Act.[24] They also believed that public interest in local government was diminished in so far as people perceived local authorities as little more than puppets dancing at the ends of central government strings with, for example, local authorities simply acting as cyphers or executors of central planning policy.

Another consequence of controls is that local authorities' efficiency and corporate planning may be jeopardized, since different government departments could be pulling local authorities in different, even conflicting, directions. This view was confirmed to a certain extent by the Government's own advisory 'think tank' in 1977.[25] Furthermore, as the Bains and Paterson Reports pointed out (see Chapter 9), central requirements to appoint certain committees, such as social services, reduce local authorities' flexibility for internal organization; similarly, the requirement to appoint (and perhaps have vetted) certain chief officers, such as the director of social services, but not others, creates inconsistencies. The same issues were raised in the consultative paper on internal management of Scottish authorities (1993), and the working party report on English authorities (see p. 245 above) said, 'We believe that the statutory requirement to establish such committees does impose unnecessary constraints on local authorities and inhibits experiments; and that to allow local authorities greater flexibility in the way they carry out functions in no way detracts from their importance. On the contrary, local authorities should be enabled to carry them out in the way they consider most appropriate' (para. 4.26).

As a result a number of remedies have been suggested. These are dealt with below (p. 378). But before examining them, it is important to be aware of the danger of exaggerating the central government's control of local government.

Hidden strengths?

It is easy to overstate and distort the image of the relationship between central and local government. Ministers do not have a free hand to interfere in local government affairs: local authorities are created by Acts of Parliament and these give them a substantially independent existence and range of powers. To intervene,

Ministers must normally be able to point to a statutory power to do so. The wide powers of the Secretary of State for Education (see p. 365) are perhaps exceptional, but even here there are limits, as was shown by the Tameside case of 1976, when the Court of Appeal and the House of Lords decided that the Minister's direction to the LEA (which he believed was acting unreasonably in seeking to reintroduce selective secondary education) was invalid. A number of cases have recently gone against Ministers.[26]

Secondly, the central government is not monolithic. There is no unity or uniformity in the controls exercised by the various government departments: indeed there is considerable variation, even among the different services within the same department, for example between the police services and urban programmes within the Home Office. This may to a large extent be due to the existence of highly integrated vertical 'policy communities'. These are 'networks characterised by stability of relationships, continuity of a highly restrictive membership, vertical interdependence based on shared service delivery responsibilities'.[27] They consist of those people, especially professionals, working in the same field – housing, education, trading standards, environmental health, etc. – whose experience, training, and particular set of values (or ideology) gives them a commitment to their field or service area and allows them to exercise considerable power and influence on policy making across the central–local divide. These networks arise because the central government relies on local authorities to deliver services, for example the DFE itself does not build schools, hire teachers, etc.

Thirdly, while the central government may lay down certain minimum standards, councils have a substantial, though not unlimited, freedom to decide higher standards as they see fit. This derives, in part, from the fact that local authorities themselves raise a significant proportion of their income from local taxes, charges and internal funds, which thus gives them a degree of financial independence (some councils get no grant income).[28]

In addition to their financial and legal independence, local authorities have a considerable degree of political independence: they are, after all, elected bodies, which must carry some weight in the mind of the central government.[29] And where the party in power locally differs from that in power at the centre, there is a greater tendency to resist central dictates (in the 1970s, housing finance reform and council house sales policies were resisted by Labour councils, while comprehensive education plans received filibuster treatment – deliberate delay through talk – from many Conservative councils). The 1980s opened with much united hostility among councils of all political colours to the Government's expenditure cuts, and the AMA mounted a national publicity campaign ('Keep It Local').

Such open hostility and defiance is rare, for central government and local authorities conduct much of their business informally (by means of letters, deputations to Whitehall, telephone calls, etc.) in an attempt to smooth differences and reach compromises. Local authority representatives sit on government advisory bodies (the Housing Services Advisory Group, the Schools Council, the Personal Social Services Council and so on), where they can expound the local government viewpoint. Local authorities (especially through their associations – see p. 401) are in regular consultation with government departments prior to legislation or the publication of circulars (it took six months to negotiate the contents of the circular 10/65[30]). And the local government professional associations, such as the Institute of Housing, the Institute of Rating and Valuation or the Association of Directors of Social Services, are regularly called on to advise the government or participate in a working party which will shape government policy. Indeed, the official Housing Advice Unit in the DoE comprises former local government officers and members of the Institute of Housing.

In addition, local authorities may exercise their own influence on central government through their party machinery. The major parties have regular conferences on local government which provide an opportunity for central and local politicians to get together and exchange views. Both in and out of Parliament, the major parties have local government committees and advisory groups (the latter usually drawing on personnel from local government itself). Ministers are regularly receiving party delegations and deputations from local government (especially in recent years) and they may be similarly confronted when they return to their constituencies at weekends.

Some Ministers may have particular links, past or present, with local government.[31] So too do MPs, who can display their concern about local government through parliamentary questions and adjournment debates. About one third of MPs have had experience in local government, and some of them (24 in 1980, 56 in 1983) have a 'dual mandate' and combine the role of councillor with that of MP. A great deal of MPs' constituency (or 'surgery') matters concern local government, as does a significant proportion of their correspondence.[32] In 1981 Conservative MPs forced their own government to withdraw and substantially revise the Local Government Finance Bill (thereby dropping plans for local rates referenda).

Furthermore, some individual councillors and officers can be quite influential with Ministers and civil servants, on account of their personality, qualifications or expertise.[33]

Local authorities may also exercise influence by forming regional groups and applying collective pressure. In some areas in the 1960s such groups pressed the government to speed up motorway building and reform the Selective Employment Tax (which was adversely affecting the tourist trade). In the 1970s pressure was used in bidding for government economic and industrial aid. And in the 1980s, on a number of occasions, local authorities successfully resisted central government policies.[34]

Finally, what of the claim that local authority services are fragmented and their corporate planning undermined by the central government departments' pursuing different policies and pulling local authority departments in different directions? In 1977 the Government's 'think tank' (CPRS) did find some evidence for this claim – on occasion, the implementation by local authorities of multi-purpose capital projects had been hindered because different elements in the project received different responses – some approved, others refused – from different departments (see note 14). There was also a more general tendency to contradiction between the central spending departments (DSS, DFE, Home Office, etc.) and the control departments (the Treasury and the Department of the Environment) (see note 25).

However, the CPRS report concluded that the claim to lack of co-ordination was exaggerated, and that in many ways the central government was as well forward in the development and application of corporate management as most local authorities were. Nevertheless it did recommend that central government should deal with local authorities more on an inter-departmental programme basis than on a separate service-by-service basis. (In this respect it commended the Scottish system of regional reports.[35] It might be added that the problem is less great in Scotland and Wales because they each have a single department – the Scottish and Welsh Offices – which exercise the responsibilities relating to local government which in England are the functions of the DSS, DoE, DFE, etc.) It also suggested that there should be more contact and mutual understanding between the central and the local authorities (the SIP scheme; see p. 387). And finally it suggested that the central government should reduce its interventions on matters of detail and concentrate instead on key matters, such as the overall size of capital allocations.

Local government expenditure restraint

Despite the Government's efforts, local authorities have maintained their overall level of expenditure. The restraint on their capital expenditure has been offset by a growth in current expenditure, with the result that today local government accounts for almost 25 per cent of total public expenditure, just as it did in 1979, representing 11·5 per cent of total GDP (see Figure 22).[36]

This is not to suggest that councils have not suffered cuts, as such things as the state of school buildings or roads or school meals or discretionary grants bear witness. But some of the 'cuts'

Source: *Financial Statistics*, July 1993, HMSO.

Figure 22 *Local authority current expenditure (percentage of GDP)*
Source: Financial Statistics, July 1993, HMSO.

have been reductions in plans or projections and aspirations. And paradoxically the Government's imposition of spending caps has induced many councils to *increase* their spending up to the official limit (in case that limit is seen as unnecessarily high and subsequently reduced).[37] In addition, councils have acquired new responsibilities (*vide* legislation covering food safety, environmental protection, children, community care, etc.) and have received some transferred central expenditures (such as health and housing benefits). Local authorities have also had to cope with some of the consequences of unemployment and industrial change (e.g. the closure of coal mines, reductions in defence spending) as well as inner-city decay and rising crime. In some cases expenditure has risen as a result of pay awards which have exceeded inflation (e.g. in police and fire services). And service expenditure has increased as a result of overall population growth as well as change in its structure.

Overall, government policy has managed to slow or stabilize the growth of local spending (especially compared to the 1960s and 1970s). There have been efficiency savings and overall staff numbers have begun to fall (see p. 251 and p. 585, note 44). But there are unavoidable pressures for greater expenditure during the 1990s, with the renewed growth in the school population and in the very dependent elderly. Crime figures suggest more spending on police and probation. There is also pressure from users of public services who, encouraged by the 'charters' of both central and local government, seek enhanced standards and quality of provision.

Proposed remedies

Clearly the CPRS report (above) was not content with the state of local–central relations. In this respect the report was echoing the sentiments of the Redcliffe-Maud and Wheatley Royal Commissions of 1966–9 and of the Maud Committee of 1967. It was the latter which most clearly outlined proposals to improve the relationship of local government to central government. It recommended:

(1) abolition of statutory requirements for the appointment of committees and officers;

(2) abolition of ministerial control over the appointment and dismissal of officers;

(3) abolition of the district auditor's power of surcharge (see pp. 349, 580), with its inhibiting effect on initiative by councillors;

(4) abolition of the *ultra vires* principle; instead local authorities should be given general competence to do anything they considered to be for the good of their citizens;

(5) freedom for local authorities to fix their scales for members' expenses;

(6) greater financial freedom for local authorities, with additional sources of revenue to be devised and less detailed government involvement in local capital spending;

(7) simplification of Whitehall's machinery for dealing with local authorities: one department to be responsible for coordinating national policy relating to local government;

(8) the setting up of a Central Office by the local authority associations to conduct negotiations with the central government.

The Layfield Committee,[38] although appointed to 'review the whole system of local government finance ... and to make recommendations', was very concerned about the state of local–central relations. It declared: 'What has been clearly visible over recent years is a growing propensity for the government to determine, in increasing detail, the pace and direction in which local services should be developed, the resources which should be devoted to them and the priorities between them' (Report p. 65). (It also pointed out that the 'drift towards centralization' was even more marked in Scotland than in England and Wales.) In particular, it found 'a lack of clear accountability for local government expenditure, which results from the present confusion of responsibilities between the government and local authorities' (p. xxv).

The Committee then posed a choice: that either an explicitly 'centralist' relationship should be instituted, giving clear and recognized responsibility to the central government for local government expenditure, both generally and among individual authorities; or a more 'localist' solution should be adopted. The latter was favoured by the Committee. It would involve local authorities taking greater responsibility for the conduct of local affairs, including more powers of decision in services such as education, social services, transport and housing (the government was to exercise reserve powers, but these were to be confined to essential issues of national policy and were to be defined by statute). But above all, under this 'localist' solution, local authorities were to have an additional source of revenue in the form of a local income tax (LIT).

In practice, the central government has not accepted the recommendation of the LIT. Indeed, the (Labour) Government did precisely what Layfield feared: it declared for a middle way between the two alternatives posed and argued in favour of a 'partnership' approach to the central–local relationship.[39] (Layfield thought this too vague and that it fudged the issue, and believed that it would only allow the centralist drift to continue.) In the meantime, there have been other developments.

Recent developments

Concern over central intervention in local government affairs is not new: it was expressed strongly in the early nineteenth century,[40] in the late nineteenth century[41] and in the early twentieth century.[42] However, it has been suggested that the situation became worse in the years following the Second World War.[43] In 1956 the Government acknowledged the problem and sought to improve it by tidying the structure (via the Local Government Commissions of 1958–65; see p. 40) and by replacing a number of specific grants by a block grant in 1958 (converted into the RSG in 1966). In 1963 local authorities were empowered to spend up to a 1d. rate on anything which was in the general interests of their area. (Parishes were permitted to spend up to 0.2d. Scotland already had these powers.) In 1968 planning procedures were changed such that local plans (as opposed to the development plans) would no longer need government approval. At the same time there was some relaxation of central control over local authority transport planning, where, with the introduction of Transport Policies and Programmes (TPPs), the Government gave approval for whole programmes of expenditure rather than individual projects (see p. 340). A similar development occurred in 1970 in the field of loan sanction for 'locally determined' schemes of capital development.

Further encouragement was given to local authorities in 1970 with the Conservatives' promise to abolish many of the 1,200 or so controls exercised over local government. Yet, in practice, it seemed that control was *increasing*: local authority social service departments were required to prepare ten-year plans; LEAs were obliged to stop supplying milk in schools to the over-7s (even if the LEA was itself prepared to pay for it); rate monitoring was undertaken by the central government; and the Housing Finance Act 1972 required local authorities to apply a universal system of rent rebates and to raise their rents in line with government policy (see p. 100).

However, the Local Government Acts 1972 and 1973 did remove many controls, including some quite significant ones: indeed one of the purposes of the local government reform was to strengthen and increase the independence of local government by eliminating the smaller and weaker authorities which were often held to be responsible for some of the government's controls (just as the speed of a convoy is dictated by the slowest vehicle).

Thus, apart from the reorganization itself, the legislation reduced the previous mandatory requirements on the appointment of officials and committees, and gave Ministers less power to intervene in appointment and dismissal procedures, including, in 1973, those of chief education officers. Secondly, the power of the district auditor was reduced, so that issues of disallowance and surcharge are now decided by the courts (see pp. 350, 580–81). Thirdly, the 'free 1d.' was increased to 2p, now changed to a per capita maximum (see p. 76), and has a wider application: not only does it apply equally to parishes and communities but it may now be spent in the interests of a part of an area or some of the inhabitants (not all, as had previously been the case). Finally, the Local Government Acts of 1972 (England and Wales) and 1973 (Scotland) empowered local authorities to pay members attendance allowances. (In the meantime, the giant Department of the Environment had been created, and acted, at least to some extent, as the central department for coordinating relationships with local authorities, rather as the Scottish Office and the Welsh Office do.)

All this seemed to reflect a new faith in local government. But there was no real consistency, partly because of the impact of party politics. In 1975 the Labour Government (1974–9) repealed much of the previous government's Housing Finance Act (freeing local authorities to a certain extent) but in 1976 it passed an Education Act which required all LEAs to introduce comprehensive secondary schooling. In addition, economic problems were imposing themselves on the relationship: the Government's incomes policy in 1975 led to local authorities being threatened with a reduction in their RSG if they gave pay rises in excess of £6 per week. In 1978 a new form of control was introduced in the shape of 'cash limits' (see pp. 579, 584). And since the late 1970s, government inspectors have been becoming more directive (rather than merely advisory) in their approach. In broad terms, therefore, it seems that when national resources are scarce or under pressure the central grip tends to tighten.

In response to the economic and financial problems of 1974–5 (when there were numerous rate protests and sporadic rate strikes) the government established two new and important institutions. The first is the Joint Manpower Watch, whereby local authorities (mainly through LACSAB – see p. 252) and the central government together collect and analyse information on local government employment numbers and patterns. This does not give the government any greater control, but it does show its concern and possibly leaves room for influence, perhaps through the effect of a well-timed statement acting on public opinion.[44] The second new body is the Consultative Council on Local Government Finance (or CCLGF, which technically conducts the Joint Manpower Watch through one of its committees). This Council has brought local authorities into the government's budgetary machinery. It meets annually in July and is chaired by the Secretary of State for the Environment and is attended by Ministers and officials from the 'spending' departments (DSS, DFE, HO, etc.) as well as the DoE itself and the Treasury. The local authorities are represented by members and officials from the local authorities' associations. Its purpose is to discuss 'matters of policy affecting local authorities which have major financial implications'.[45] In particular it discusses the local authorities' spending plans, and the government's RSG and its distribution. There is a separate council for Wales for a number of these purposes. In

Scotland, there is no such formal machinery: the Scottish local authorities (since reorganization in 1975) all belong to a single association (the Convention of Scottish Local Authorities – COSLA) and the Secretary of State for Scotland speaks for the central government. Consequently there already exists an ample facility for two-way dialogue between them.

The Consultative Council was a particularly significant step in that it brought together Ministers and the political leaders from local government on a formal and frequent basis for the first time. The essential idea was to let local government make a constructive contribution to government decisions at their formative stages, and especially help to avoid inconsistent and contradictory instructions from government departments. But it is felt that the local authority side is not sufficiently involved in the fundamental public expenditure (PES) decisions, and some local authorities feel sceptical about the consultation, believing that all too often both sides listen to each other but nothing results to deflect the government from a predetermined course. In part this may be due to the local authority associations' having different interests (sometimes reflected in their disagreements over the distribution of the RSG).[46]

The present (Conservative) Government has sought to rationalize controls over local government. In a White Paper (see note 15) published in September 1979, it declared:

Democratically elected local authorities are wholly responsible bodies who must be free to get on with the tasks entrusted to them by Parliament without constant interference in matters of detail by the Government of the day. On the other hand there are certain national policies which it is the Government's duty to pursue even though they may be administered locally; for example, where by statute the responsibilities are shared between central and local government or where the Government of the day may have secured a particular mandate at a general election. It would be inappropriate therefore to abandon all control over local government; to do so would be an abdication of the Government's proper role.

Consequently its intention has been to remove or relax some 300 controls. These include controls over interest rates for various purposes; the hearing of appeals concerning the erection of bus shelters or against bridge restrictions or the provision of street lighting; the prescription of various fees (libraries, testing weights and measures equipment etc. and various licences); the approval of school development plans, of financial assistance to independent schools, of arrangements for the provision of PE clothing, of purchase of equipment for FE colleges; the power to require the submission of housing programmes, control over conditions attached to individual local authority mortgages; the confirmation of noise abatement orders; the consent to disposal of land by non-principal councils; the confirmation of new street by-laws; and the approval of plans for crematoria.

At the same time, the Government has reduced the volume of circulars and other papers issued to local government (they fell from 1,873 in 1978–9 to 592 in 1981–2) and it has been reviewing its need for statistical information from local authorities. In addition, the Government has repealed the Education Act 1976, which means that LEAs are no longer obliged to introduce comprehensive schools and may themselves decide what form secondary schooling will take. In the field of housing (since April 1981) local authorities are no longer bound by minimum (Parker-Morris) standards or maximum (yardstick) costings. And, more generally, the system of control over local authorities' capital expenditure now involves less detailed intervention (see p. 340).

The Local Government, Planning and Land Act 1980

Many people, especially those inside local government, are sceptical about the changes outlined above. Some see them as aimed not so much at reducing the scope of government *interference* in local government affairs but at reducing the scope of *government* generally, in line with current Conservative philosophy. Others see the Government as giving with one hand and taking away with the other. As *The Times* put it, 'Where less government means more.'[47] Thus, under the same legislation which removes or relaxes many controls – the Local Government, Planning and Land Act 1980 – local authorities are required to: (1) publish key information about their finances and their performance generally; (2) to be more publicly accountable for their direct labour organizations, some of which are prevented from undertaking work at the discretion of the Minister; and (3) prepare a register of unused land (following the repeal of the Community Land Act 1975). In addition (4) urban development corporations (UDCs) have been set up, at the Minister's discretion, in eleven inner city areas (such as Bristol, Liverpool and London), with wide powers to by-pass ordinary planning procedures, and twenty-two tax- and planning-free 'enterprise zones' have been established in inner city areas. This is in addition to the Housing Act 1980, which now obliges local authorities to sell (at discount) council houses. And while some local authorities are concerned at (5) the new capital expenditure controls procedure (see p. 340), many have been particularly incensed at (6) the form of the block/support grant system (see p. 309), which (together with the increasing tendency to develop specific grants; see p. 310) has presented a massive threat to local government's already limited freedom.

The legislation of 1980 in particular united the various local authority associations in their opposition to the (Conservative) Government. This unity was unusual; equally unusual was their hostility to the Government, as they were all at the time themselves Conservative-dominated in the composition of their own leadership (see p. 401). The chair of the Association of Metropolitan Authorities appeared to speak for them all when he said that the legislation presented 'the biggest threat to the constitutional independence of local government in this country since the nineteenth century'.[48]

Subsequent legislative developments have increased this anxiety, as they threaten to erode the base of local government. Thus under the Education Reform Act 1988, a national curriculum has been imposed, schools may opt out of LEA control and the Minister's powers have been substantially increased (and enhanced further by the Education Act 1993). Under the Housing Act 1988, council-house tenants can opt to transfer to a non-local-authority landlord, and the Local Government and Housing Act 1989 prevents councils from subsidizing their own rents. The Local Government Acts 1988 and 1992 require a large increase in competitive tendering for council services (see p. 306). The legislation not only identifies the service or function, but stipulates the form of tendering (through detailed regulations), rates of return and the publication of support service costs (which can create the problem of revealing commercially sensitive informa-tion to competitors as well as increasing costs) and gives the Minister powers to intervene, for example through the issue of Secs. 13 and 14 (1988 Act) notices, which may cancel contracts or require re-tendering. And in the field of finance, apart from the enhanced capital control system (p. 340) we have seen the replace-ment of local rates with the unified business rate and the council tax – the latter of which is subject to central limitation or 'capping'.

If this legislation moved many Conservative councils to opposi-tion, anger or anxiety over Government policies, others were more favourably disposed because they saw the legislation (especi-ally the new grant procedures) as a means whereby 'spendthrift' or 'profligate' Labour councils could be penalized and checked. Many of the latter, rightly or wrongly, were seen as actively sabotaging the Government's economic policy by raising their rates/taxes and spending on public services. (In practice many Conservative councils have been hit too – see Chapter 14.)

This argument illustrates the perennial question of 'democracy versus equality' – of how far individual authorities should be allowed to raise service standards above those of their neighbours, and face the consequent judgement of the electors at the next poll.

The relationship between local authorities and the central government has been variously described as that of 'principal and agent', as power-dependency and as a 'partnership'. As *statements* or *prescriptions* of what is desirable or proper, this is clearly a matter of opinion and personal values. There is no formal or constitutional definition of the relationship, and there is no generally accepted theory or philosophy of local government.[49] Too often are local authorities regarded as no more than providers of services. Such a view is widespread, though it is perhaps best exemplified by the central government. For example, a recent government document, while stating that 'local government has a very important role in the democratic life of this country', goes on to state merely that 'local authorities provide or promote a wide range of public services', before it then considers their mode of operation for 'the effective delivery of services'.[50] Such a narrow view clearly forms the Government's perception of its relationship with local government. However, a better understanding and greater cooperation may emerge from a scheme started in 1992 called the Secondment Initiative Programme (SIP). This aims to achieve 140 new secondments between Whitehall and local authorities over three years.[51]

Attempts to assess or *describe* the working relationship are very much a matter of individual judgement. Probably local authorities today are neither mere agents of the government nor equal partners: the relationship is somewhere between. But it is difficult to generalize. Politically, the government controls Parliament and thus can normally push through legislation which will affect the shape and substance of local government. Yet, in practice, local authorities too have a mandate (from their own electors), they have their own source of finance (from council tax and charges) and they have 'know-how' in the sense that they are 'in the field' and responsible for the delivery of a mass of services. As a result, the central government depends upon local authorities' knowledge, field experience and expertise (particularly that of local government officers). This applies more especially to some departments or divisions (education, social services, housing) than to others (the Treasury, energy or trade for example).

While relationships and influences vary among departments and different services, it is generally true to say that what is sought by both sides is agreement and amicable relations rather than hostility and the grudging acceptance of repugnant policies, for ultimately they both share a common concern: the public service. Clashes do occur and some of them become very public (such as the battles Clay Cross in 1972 and Tameside in 1976 (see p. 373), the serious delay in settling the city's rate by Liverpool in 1984 and 1985, or more recently the mass revolt by teachers against school tests). But the use of 'the big stick' can be awkward and embarrassing for central government (as the Clay Cross and the earlier Poplar 1921, Rotherham and Durham 1932 cases well illustrated). And in practice, standards do vary considerably among councils: in spite of central government's apparent dominance, they have not been homogenized.[52] Disagreements are inevitable, since local authorities and central government have different perspectives, different party allegiances and different priorities.[53] This is most obviously illustrated where local authorities are capped. In 1990, twenty-one councils had their community charge compulsorily reduced by the Government. They have since taken the Minister to court to determine the legality of his action – without success. What is needed is a clearer recognition of these differences and a better mutual understanding (promoted perhaps by a greater interchange of staff between central and local government).[54]

Not everyone in local government wants more 'freedom' from central controls: the removal of ministerial control over charges may cause authorities to turn basically free services into money-making ventures; standards of service may be jeopardized if ministerial intervention were to be removed; and certain controls may be welcomed as a means of sustaining local government employment (the need for ministerial approval may delay school closures, for instance). But above all, both inside and out of local government, is the view that real, local self-government is incompatible with social or territorial justice:[55] that social justice requires a high degree of equality in the standards of service from one part of the country to another. Such a view is widely held by Socialists,[56] though not exclusively or universally. It is the Conservatives who have expressed the desire to 'get off the back' of local government (though in practice this does not square with Conservative local government legislation since 1979). It would appear that while the Conservative Party seeks to place an upper limit, a maximum on local authority expenditure and service standards, the Labour Party (through its 1989 proposals for a 'Quality Commission') seeks to impose a minimum or lower limit to local authorities' services provision (which many regard as equally invidious for local government). Paradoxically, the Marxist Left also see a danger in centralization, with local authorities becoming little more than extensions of the capitalist state:[57] hence their advocacy of 'community politics'.

Local government and the European Community (EC)

Increasingly, British local government is having to look beyond the central government to the political institutions of the European Economic Community (EC). Ever since Britain formally joined the European Community in 1973 (under the European Communities Act 1972), local authorities, together with the rest of our society, have become subject to the international laws emanating from the European Commission in Brussels. Local government is experiencing 'Europeanization', as are related professional bodies (such as accountants and auditors), as the Commission harmonizes standards and procedures.

For the most part these laws – generally referred to as 'Community law' – take the form of regulations and directives (or 'secondary legislation'). These regulations seek to standardize throughout the Community such things as weights and measures (packaging, labelling, ingredients); vehicle construction (size, weight, safety); public works contracts (tendering, non-discrimination, advertising); and control of pollution (use of pesticides, herbicides, fertilizers). They will have substantial implications for particular local authority departments, such as those concerned with trading standards, and for particular occupational groups, such as those concerned with environmental health.[58] (The Local Government Information Bureau at 35 Smith Square, London, provides advice on this.) And in recognition of the value it places on its developing relationship with local authorities, in 1989 the European Commission set up an official Consultative Council of Regional and Local Authorities. This was replaced by the Committee of the Regions in 1993. Since local authorities are frequently the bodies reponsible for the implementation or enforcement of EC regulations, this committee provides a mechanism by which the views of local authorities can be taken into account in the early stages of legislation.

However, there are other aspects of Community law which have more general implications for local government. The free movement of labour (one of the 'four freedoms' of the EC) will have an impact on local authority housing policies, especially in relation to the principle of equal access by non-nationals. Other Community laws raise questions about the legality of rate subsidization (e.g. de-rating agriculture). And perhaps hovering in the background is the prospect of scrutiny and control accompanying the financial aid which comes to local authorities from the EC. These funds take the form of loans or grants, e.g. for the purpose of education, training, job creation and rehabilitation, and they derive from the Social Fund, RECHAR, the European Investment Bank and the Regional Development Fund.[59] In 1988 Birmingham Corporation was selected to receive funds of more than £200 million over a five-year period. One problem is that the money passes through the central government, who may make corresponding reductions in its borrowing approvals or grant aid to local authorities. Many local authorities have established EC units, and a number of local authorities have set up offices in Brussels to build up links and sustain communications in order to help negotiate grant aid applications (thus seeking to by-pass central government). In 1993 there were thirteen such offices representing individual councils (such as Birmingham, Kent and Strathclyde). Councils also form consortia to make bids for funds (e.g. East Midlands authorities).

Local authorities, therefore, may obtain substantial material benefit from the EC. And, as in its relations with the British central government, local government is not without influence: apart from briefing Members of the European Parliament (MEPs) (and perhaps influencing them through the party machinery) and sending deputations (lobbying) to the EC,[60] local authorities cooperate jointly with the EC through the International Union of Local Authorities (IULA) and the Council of European Municipalities (CEM – see p. 392). They are also represented on various consultative committees. Evidently 'local government participation in Community affairs is not purely a matter of form. It can and does produce results . . .'[61] But clearly this is not always the case,[62] which may in part be due to inadequate information. Consequently, in 1979 the British section of the IULA and CEM set up the European Information Service.

Information on EC matters also derives from the consultative advisory machinery on EC affairs which exists inside many British government departments. And there is a six-monthly meeting of representatives from British local and central government in the European Joint Group, which meets to consider EC legislation and to act as an information clearing house for local authorities. Together these devices enhance coordination, so that lines do not get crossed when local and central governments are in direct but separate contact with the EC. Thus there is developing another area of common ground between the central government and local authorities.

13. Local Government and the Local Community

We have seen in the last chapter how local government has a close relationship with the central government, and that British local authorities are subject to international (EC) controls as well as the benefits of financial aid (mainly for industrial development). Local authorities have long had other international links, mainly through the International Union of Local Authorities (IULA), an organization, based in the Netherlands, which acts as a spokesman for local government on the international level, provides a forum for the exchange of views on local government policies and supplies services (training, research, information, etc.) for the sixty-three member countries. The latter are particularly useful to the developing countries, but the regular bi-annual conference (which has considered such themes as urbanization, leisure and conservation) is well attended by the membership generally. Similar organizations, though more limited in membership, are the Council of European Municipalities (CEM) and the Conference of Local and Regional Authorities in Europe. More specialized still are the Commonwealth Association of Town Clerks, the Federation of Nature and National Parks of Europe and the International Federation for Housing and Planning. There are similar organizations for recreation administration, for conservation and for public cleaning. Cooperation at a very practical level takes place through the Standing Technological Conference of European Local Authorities (STCELA). This is a new development for the exchange of technical know-how and the benefits of centralized purchasing.[1]

Local government perspectives are thus by no means as narrow as many people imagine. Perhaps the best illustration of this is the involvement of officials from British local authorities in the first elections in Zimbabwe (Rhodesia) in 1980 and in Eastern European countries in 1989–90. British local authorities have also been much involved in the provision of technical help, advice and cooperation for the latter as they emerge from their former communist regimes (though such local authority assistance to developing countries is not always applauded).[2]

However, in this chapter, our primary concern is with the *local* community and local government's varied relationship with its inhabitants.

Local government and other local public bodies

Apart from government departments, the other form of public authority with which local authorities are likely to have contact is the 'quango' or semi-independent government agency. There are many such agencies and, collectively, they present a vast and rather ill-defined area of government. (Indeed, as many of them are regional or local in scale and character, they might even be regarded as another form of local government.) All local authorities have some working relationships with them, especially the public corporations (railways, post office, etc.), in such fields as rating (or payments in lieu), housing and other development, planning controls and amenity arrangements (such as undergrounding power cables). There are also disputes and even legal entanglements (for instance with the post office, for failing to make good a road it has dug up). And there is substantial cross-membership, with, for example, local authority representatives sitting on electricity consumer councils.

Some local authorities have especially close relations (and overlapping membership) with particular government bodies such as the tourist boards, the Countryside Commission and New Town corporations or nuclear power stations (via liaison committees). For example, Somerset County Council has had close links with the South West Road Construction Unit, Norfolk County Council has close links with the Broads Authority, Cumbria County Council with the Lake District Planning Board, and Scottish and Welsh local authorities with their respective Development Agencies. There are also frequent contacts with the Department of Social Security and the Benefits Agency, especially by local social services and housing departments. In recent years a number of councils have signed service-level agreements with local benefits offices to provide for quick and efficient processing of council tax and housing benefits.

Health and water

There are two services which have been particularly important to local government. The first is the National Health Service. By law the 201 English and Welsh District Health Authorities and the fifteen Scottish Health Boards had to set aside a certain number of places for representatives from constituent local authorities. (This has now ceased under the NHS and Community Care Act 1990.[3]) Similarly, local authority members must constitute half of the membership of the Local (Scotland) or Community (England and Wales) Health Councils (the consumer 'watchdogs'). There was also local authority representation on the Family Practitioner Committees (now Family Health Services Authorities) which exist in England and Wales. There continue to be day-to-day working relationships, with local authority social workers employed in hospitals or attached to general practitioners; there are close links between the community physician[4] and local authorities' public analysts and environmental health officers; and there is close collaboration between local authority social services and local health authorities – through what are known as 'joint care planning teams' – to plan and finance local health/welfare projects, such as hostels or sheltered accommodation for patients from psychiatric hospitals. These links are facilitated by the common geographical boundaries of many local authorities and the NHS boards. This could increase as local authorities develop the role of 'consumer advocate'[5] and take the view that local government is responsible for more than just a narrow range of services and specific needs (see p. 490ff). And indeed, a number of councils send observers to the meetings of various local quangos (non-elected public bodies), and their reports form part of the councils' formal business. (In 1993, the Labour Party announced the setting up of a comprehensive 'Quango Watch'.)

The other public body with which local authorities (in England and Wales) had close contact was the water authority. Water supply is a responsibility of regional and island councils in Scotland. Although this is no longer the case in England and Wales, local authorities here have had a continuing interest in water services as providers of fire services and leisure facilities, and, above all, as a consequence of their responsibility for the environment (which includes public health and the wholesomeness of water supplies). From a practical point of view, local authorities have maintained the majority of sewers on behalf of the water authorities under agency agreements.

In England and Wales, under the Water Act 1973, existing water boards were grouped into ten regional water authorities. Local authority representatives constituted a majority of the members of these managing authorities (until the Water Act 1983, after which members were appointed by the Minister) and they also have a strong representation on the regional and local drainage committees. Some local authorities also undertook some of the water authority functions on an agency basis. However, the privatization of the water industry in 1989 and the reform of the NHS in 1990 have obviated much of this.

Close and continuous links between local authorities and these other agencies have been crucial for a truly 'corporate' or community approach to the planning and management of services for the community. But in practice there have been deficiencies. Boundaries do not always coincide, budgets are separate, particular interests are pursued rather than the general interest and there exists a certain amount of resentment on the part of local authorities who, only a few years ago, were themselves responsible for many of these services. Their differing responsibilities sometimes create tensions and indeed legal conflicts (as when Wirral Council sought to prosecute the North West Water Authority in 1989 for its failure to exercise its anti-pollution responsibilities).

Local authority inter-relationships

The 'corporate approach' demands no less of a close working relationship among local authorities than it does between local government and other public bodies. Unfortunately, the history of local cooperation has not been an entirely happy one in this respect, partly because of the differences between the all-purpose authorities ('county boroughs' in England and Wales, 'counties of cities' in Scotland) and the counties in which they were located (see Chapter 3). The reorganization of 1974 eased this problem but did not eliminate it: there has remained considerable hostility among the several parts of the newly formed authorities – resentment at lost functions, allegations of neglect, squabbles and delays over muddled responsibilities. This point is well illustrated by the uneasy relationships which occurred between the GLC and some London boroughs, Greater Manchester and some constituent districts (especially Manchester City), Merseyside County and Liverpool City, and Lothian Region and Edinburgh City Council.[6] There is also the risk of strained relations where 'tier-skipping' occurs, i.e. where a local authority incurs expenditure (from the 'free tuppence'; see p. 75) on an activity which is the primary responsibility of another tier of local government without the consent of the other authority (though the law precludes this from happening in Scotland). A recent survey of local authorities found only 14 per cent of councillors reporting good relations among local councils, and 67 per cent considered the two-tier structure a mistake[7] (but see pp. 105–6). The inter-tier conflict

was one of the reasons given by the Government for the abolition of the GLC and the metropolitan county councils in 1986
(though such action does not eliminate the need for inter-
authority relations: it merely changes their form from county–
district to district–district; see pp. 130–31). And even at the lowest
tier, there are occasions when relations have become so embit-
tered that parishes seek (via the Local Government Boundary
Commission) to opt out of their 'host' district and into
another.[8]

To some extent conflicts are inevitable: old identities and
loyalties underlie the new structures; some of the responsibilities
are split; precepting arrangements can cause ill-will; and frictions
arise from differences in party control. But perhaps above all
each council exists in its own right and will therefore seek
jealously to guard its independence. (Although it is usual to refer
to the 'tiers' of local government, this does not imply a relationship of authority or power. Counties or regions do not have
authority over the district councils, except for emergency planning
situations; nor, except for minor matters like filling vacant seats,
do the districts exercise any legal authority over parishes and
communities.) In such cases of conflict, the Minister may be
called in to arbitrate (see pp. 365–6), or another third party (person)
may be engaged, for instance to decide which authority is responsible for a particular homeless family. Sometimes the issue is
settled in the law courts.[9] Otherwise if it is a dispute of general
interest, it may be carried upwards to the local authority associations (see below).

Fortunately, most local authorities seek cooperative and amicable relations with their neighbours: after all, they have in so many
cases to work together – where powers are shared (as in planning[10]), or where agency arrangements exist (as in much highway
maintenance), or where powers are exercised concurrently (as in
the provision of amenities). Even where functions are apparently
quite separate, there is much need for close consultation. For
example, the county or regional social services departments will
from time to time have to consult with the districts – the housing

authorities – concerning the nature and extent of the special accommodation (sheltered housing) needed for infirm people. Another example is where counties, under their transport role, need to liaise with districts to, say, encourage them to provide car parking and approve their car parking charging policies. Indeed, one recent study[11] of county–district relations has shown that while the amount of contact between counties and districts is surprisingly large, the more extensive contacts are confined to a few services. The same study concluded:

The reality is that inter-tier relationships in a metropolitan area (or elsewhere) are neither intrinsically difficult and conflictual nor intrinsically straightforward and consensual. It all depends on the contextual circumstances impinging upon a particular county–district network and upon individual links therein, particularly the attitudes and interests of key participants ... Several examples were discovered of 'difficult' county–district relationships, in which non-cooperative or indeed obstructive strategies were used; but equally several examples were discovered of relationships which were successful, in that a positive outcome was produced which would not have been possible without inter-tier co-operation ... Conflict in inter-tier relationships is the exception rather than the rule. Most inter-tier relationships work smoothly most of the time ... The defunct metropolitan system was more prone to conflict than the non-metropolitan one ... Handling county–district relations successfully is still a major challenge.

Liaison, coordination and mutual understanding are facilitated by the overlapping of membership among the various tiers of local authorities. This cross-membership at council level, unlike that which occurs at committee level (see below), is not deliberate or consciously planned, yet it does occur on a substantial scale, both between district and county or region and between parish or community and district. Such councillors are said to have a 'dual mandate' (some may belong to three sets of authorities and thus have a 'triple' mandate). The number of councillors with such a dual membership (excluding parishes) is currently 13 per cent[12] (ranging between 2 per cent in London boroughs to 28 per cent

in county councils). In addition, mutual understanding is facilitated by the common background and professional values and
attitudes of the officials involved (and overall most of the inter-
authority relationships are between officials rather than
councillors).

Local authorities form joint committees or establish forums to
discuss common problems and matters of mutual interest –
conservation, structure plans, transport subsidies, libraries, tourism, crime prevention, provision for the arts, etc. Typically, there
are county or regional joint committees comprising representatives
from the county or regional council and from the constituent
district councils. They can be much wider,[13] with the local
authority developing a true community leadership role (see p.
490ff).[14] Where these committees are responsible for allocating
capital expenditure approvals (see Chapter 11), the parish and
community councils will also send representatives.

Such joint committees were strongly advocated by the Bains
Report[15] as a means to 'coordinate the interaction of all county
and district functions and policies for the locality' and for 'coordination and joint planning of the broad overall policies of the
county and the districts within it'. Some of them take the form
of 'area' committees or 'district joint committees'. These may
comprise district and county councillors for the particular area
(together with a team of officers from both tiers) or just the
relevant members of the county council. Their purpose is to
take a community or corporate approach to the problems of the
particular area and the coordination of the local services. However, these committees are non-executive and are not directly
responsible for the provision of services, but are rather a means
of reviewing the services provided and of inviting local public
participation, comment and 'feedback'.[16] But they are not always
so positive and constructive; they may simply vent inter-authority grievances, jealousies or party differences, and thus
languish.[17]

Some of these advisory or consultative committees may specialize in a particular service, e.g. education, where many LEAs have

established district advisory groups to replace the former divisional executives;[18] these often comprise head teachers and officers as well as county and district councillors. They may also contain representatives from the local schools' governing bodies. And these bodies themselves are another example of inter-authority contact, the LEA appointing members to governing bodies from local district and parish or community councils.

Not all of these joint committees are merely consultative or advisory. Some of them are executive; they may specialize in a particular service, such as planning or highways, and they may appoint staff and be given substantial amounts of delegated power. They may thus come to resemble 'quangos' (see pp. 4–6), the best-known example of which was (until its abolition in 1990) the Inner London Education Authority (ILEA), which was a statutory body; but more general examples include those joint authorities established for services such as police, airports or crematoria. The abolition in 1986 of the metropolitan county councils and the GLC led to the creation of a number of joint committees and joint boards (see pp. 105, 120). However, while such bodies bring local authorities together, they do not necessarily achieve the commitment necessary to get results.[19]

More informal groupings may also take place at a local level, particularly among officers, though often on a purely professional rather than a strictly inter-authority basis. Local authorities also frequently share premises and equipment, such as computers, and engage in joint purchasing schemes – in 1970 the Consortium for Purchasing and Distribution (CPD) was formed to provide joint purchasing facilities for a group of local authorities in the south-west of England (the GLC was the main purchaser for London local authorities). There are also a large number of local authority consortia for education system building (such as CLASP), and for housing. Local authorities sometimes join forces to submit joint bids for EC funding (as did Avon, Gloucester and Wiltshire county councils in 1993 to help counter the impact of defence job cuts).

Local authority associations[20]

Local authorities have common interests and common problems. It is therefore not at all surprising that they should join together to consider them. However, their interests and problems are not identical, and as a result they have formed into a number of separate groupings, each representing a different type or tier of local authority though some individual councils do not join.* In England and Wales there is an association for the (non-metropolitan) county councils (the ACC), another for all metropolitan authorities (the AMA) and a third for the district councils (the ADC). Parish and community councils are represented in the National Association of Local Councils and there is a separate association for 'neighbourhood councils' (see p. 453). In addition to these national groupings, there are some area associations, such as the London Boroughs Association, the Association of Greater Manchester Authorities or the Welsh Association of Community and Town Councils, and some specialized bodies, such as the Council of Local Education Authorities (CLEA), the British Fire Service Association and the British Resorts Association.

In Scotland, there is just one association for the various councils: the Convention of Scottish Local Authorities (COSLA), formed at the time of reorganization (1975). It was once hoped that a similar unity might occur in England and Wales, but apart from there being something of a history of disagreements (see below) there were fears over party political domination. (The ACC is usually Conservative-dominated, the AMA Labour-dominated.) It is often said that this fragmentation weakens local government: that a more united voice would be a stronger one. However, some would cast doubt on this assertion[21] and it has

---

* e.g. in 1983 the thirteen Labour-controlled boroughs broke away from the (Conservative-controlled) London Boroughs Association to form the Association of London Authorities. Bromley has left the AMA, and Avon and Derbyshire have left the ACC.

been suggested that Scottish local authorities are less free from central control than their counterparts in England and Wales.[22]

The purpose of these bodies is to protect and advance the interests and powers of member authorities, especially as these may be affected by legislation. Some also have the explicit objective of promoting high standards of administration. For these purposes they nominate members to the various staff negotiating bodies (see Chapter 10) and have formed a number of joint bodies to advise on or provide central services, such as training, management, etc.[23] But above all they discuss issues of common concern to themselves, and negotiate with the central government on matters of local government policy and finance. They may sometimes try to promote legislation to enhance the powers of local government[24] and usually establish a special relationship with certain MPs who will be expected to speak on their behalf in Parliament. The local authority associations often work with the central government, e.g. in drafting codes of conduct and regulations.

Their most important role concerns negotiations with the central government (mainly the Department of the Environment or, for Scotland, the Scottish Office, and to a lesser extent the Welsh Office in Wales). In these negotiations (at the Consultative Council on Local Government Finance, for instance – see p. 382) the associations may present a united front and exercise considerable influence: one Minister has declared that '. . . the Associations have now virtually become a part of the constitution of the country'.[25] But differences (over the distribution of functions or of the RSG, for example) do emerge and they may become quite public. However, it is not easy to assess their impact, since much of their work occurs behind closed doors. Their disputes and disagreements appear to have 'successfully' delayed the reform of local government (see Chapter 3) and they can be said to have lobbied successfully against the 'unitary authority' proposals of the English Royal Commission (see p. 44ff), with a publicity campaign emphasizing the word 'remote'. However, they are powerless to stop a determined government, as the disputes over tax-capping or the metropolitan counties/GLC abolition legislation and the 1980 Local Government, Planning and Land Act have shown. Negotiations gained some concessions in the latter Bill (e.g. capital allocation) but not in the areas of greatest contention (i.e. financial controls).

In similar fashion local authorities may themselves act in a determined way in relation to the interest groups which *they* have to deal with.

Voluntary organizations and pressure politics (or 'lobbies')

The variety of groups

Most of us belong to a pressure group, though we may not normally think of it as such: it may be the tennis club; the AA; the British Legion; the Church; the Red Cross; the RSPCA; the Old Boys' Association; the WRVS; the Parent-Teachers' Association; the WI; the Embroiderers' Guild ... each going about its own business and not interfering in the pursuits of others. We belong because it is convenient: it helps to meet one of our needs or interests.

Some members, however, will want more than this: they will wish to see their interests not merely provided for but also defended against any threats from outside and positively promoted in terms of facilities and resources. This aspect is perhaps most obviously displayed by such groups as trade unions or professional and business associations (such as the Chamber of Commerce or the Licensed Victuallers' Association), but even seemingly innocuous groups like the Old Boys' Association or the PTA can be stung into 'political action' or protest against a local authority proposal to change a school's status, or the squash club can be moved to write to the local paper about the unreasonable increase in the hall letting charges.

For the latter groups, such political action is an occasional event, a by-product of their existence.[26] For the other groups such as trade unions or commercial associations, protecting and furthering the interests of their members is their *raison d'être* and their use of political pressure as a method is commonplace. Consequently we may refer to voluntary organizations as 'interest groups' where they seek to protect and promote the interests of their members by the use, occasional or otherwise, of political methods, i.e. by bringing pressure or influence to bear on governmental authorities to achieve (or resist) changes in public policy. At local level, common examples include teachers' and students' unions, civic societies, residents' or ratepayers' associations, tenant groups, allotment holders, market traders' groups, etc.

A second broad type of pressure group is the 'cause group' – of those who share an attitude and pursue a goal which is not confined to the immediate interests of members of the group but is of more general benefit. Notable examples at national level include Age Concern, CND, the League Against Cruel Sports, Oxfam, the Society for the Protection of the Unborn Child, NCCL, Shelter, the Lord's Day Observance Society and CAMRA. At local level, there may exist branches of these national organizations, and there will be many of purely local origin, for example: a by-pass or motorway action group, a women's aid group, an association for homeless men, an anti-fluoridation group and a host of other amenity and conservation ('green') groups.

Some groups may overlap and be difficult to categorize into one broad type or the other: for example, the trade union UNISON will primarily seek to protect their sectional interests through campaigns against local authority expenditure cuts, but it will also undertake a cause role in so far as it presses (perhaps through the TUC) for better universal retirement pensions or greater priority to be given to the educational provision for the sixteen- to nineteen-year-olds. Other varieties of pressure group may be found locally. Some, such as community groups and Councils of Voluntary Service, are inaugurated by local authorities themselves; others are substantially funded by local authorities or receive material assistance, such as the use of rent-free property, and some are statutory, for example CHCs and the Transport

Users Consultative Committees. Some 'pressure groups' are no more than a local but important employer (Clarks of Street or Fords at Dagenham). Many groups, such as those formed for rent strikes or school-saving campaigns, are short-lived, temporary 'flashes' which wither away once their goal has been gained (or lost). Others are barely organized at all and hardly amount to a pressure group in the normally understood sense, like the 'Grocks [i.e. Outsiders] Go Home' sentiment-cum-movement in Cornwall (local and other public authorities may, of course, act upon one another; but it is uncertain whether such official bodies may be regarded as pressure groups).

The spread of pressure groups

Pressure groups, like political parties, are by no means a new phenomenon in local government, although it does seem that their activities have been increasing in recent years. Nearly 500 civic societies were founded between 1957 and 1970; nearly 200 local consumer groups between 1961 and 1970; and some 16,000 charities in England and Wales alone since 1960. The NCVO has referred to the striking development over the past ten years of 'the growing number and type of self-help organizations particularly in urban areas'.[27] Clearly, many of these are only 'partial' pressure groups, in that their principal focus of activity is not their relations with local authorities and other public bodies. However, in so far as many of them do try to exercise some influence, it is pertinent to ask why their numbers have grown so substantially. Besides, half of the groups listed in the *Guardian Directory of Pressure Groups* have come into existence only since 1960. A number of reasons can be suggested, such as greater leisure, affluence and education, or the emergence of new specialist occupations. It is also perhaps a consequence of the widely reported decline in deference or traditional respect for authority. More likely it is a response to the growth in concentration of power as the state assumes greater responsibilities and business units become bigger and more impersonal. Moran suggests it has to do with the decline of party-class politics[28] while Gyford sees 'the emergence of a more assertive public attitude towards politicians and professional experts, and in the wider society a shift towards greater fragmentation and diversity [has] produced an increasingly sectionalist politics'.[29] Finally, it might be suggested the pressure groups are self-generating in that their presence in society has come to be taken for granted and as their activities and successes are given wide coverage in the media, so are other groups encouraged to form.

Because of their volatility and the problems of definition, it is difficult accurately to determine their number in any particular area, but it is likely to be substantial. In his study of Birmingham, Newton gave a figure of over 4,000 voluntary organizations[30] operating in that city. Of these about one third were politically active, that is 'making demands on public policy and resources', and most (63 per cent) of these were only involved over a single issue. Since they are usually quite specific and limited in their demands, being mostly concerned with individual decisions, they tend to be more sporadic and less institutionalized than those groups which operate at national level.[31]

A comparison with parties

In many ways pressure groups are like political parties, especially newly founded, local or single-issue parties such as the United Country Party, the Wessex Regional Party, the Campaign for a More Prosperous Britain Party, the NHS Supporter Party or the Anti-Poll Tax Party.

However, pressure groups are normally distinguished from parties in that they do not generally seek office but only seek to influence the actions – the authoritative decisions – of those holding office. But with all definitions and classifications there are marginal cases – after all the Labour Party itself is the product of the trade unions' aim to get direct representation for themselves in Parliament, and locally there are close ties between local Labour council groups and trades councils. There may even be factions or pressure groups within the parties, for example CAER – Conservative Action for Electoral Reform. Furthermore there is substantial overlap (some deliberate, some fortuitous) between elected members of local authorities and members of voluntary organizations: in 1967 the Maud Committee showed that 99 per cent of councillors belong to organizations outside the council,[32] and the average councillor belongs to six or seven such organizations. The Birmingham survey showed that one third of politically active organizations had a member serving on at least one statutory, advisory or other public body in the city, and 40 per cent had at least one council member or MP holding an official position in the organization. Such cross-membership will colour the local authorities' attitudes to organizations, and will influence the way the latter operate politically.

How pressure groups operate

Like pressure groups at national level, local groups can engage in public politics in a variety of ways. They may approach the council as a whole (by letter or petition). They may contact and 'lobby' individual councillors, especially committee chairmen and those who show sympathy with their cause (perhaps members of their organization), and ask them to press the matter at council/ committee level. Alternatively, they may negotiate directly with the local authority departments and their officers (again, by letter, petition or delegation). All this implies an initiative by the group itself. In fact, organizations may be approached by the local authority, or they may be automatically consulted in so far as they are represented on advisory bodies: for example teachers' organizations are represented on committees through the process of co-option (see p. 197), and amenity groups and the Country Landowners Association are consulted on development and planning matters.

Some groups will act by seeking the support of other groups ('coalition-building') or the local political parties,[33] especially where the group's cause seems to fit into the party's ideology, or where they can promise or threaten electoral repercussions for the party.[34] Quite often organizations will call on the local MP to intervene, perhaps to prevent the closure of a local hospital or school, and possibly they will appeal to the government (see p. 364), the 'ombudsman' (see p. 422) or even the law courts (see p. 359). At the same time such groups may resort to publicity (via the press, television, leaflets, meetings) and in the last resort take direct action such as demonstrations, sit-ins, squatting, rent strikes or disrupting council meetings. Other influences may result from shared networks of clubs and other bodies.[35]

Which of these different approaches a group will take will depend on a variety of factors:

(a) Is the group attempting to influence policy or just details of administration? Such a distinction is not always easy to make, but the orientation is likely to have some influence on the group's mode of operation. Broadly speaking, if it is a question of administrative detail it might seem reasonable for the group to approach the administrators (the officials), and where policy is involved to approach the policy-makers (the members).[36]

(b) One would expect pressure groups to operate at those points in the local government system where they will be most effective, that is where the power lies. But local authorities will show variations in the locus and diffusion of power (as between committee chairmen, the majority party group, the officers, particular committees and the council as a whole). And pressure groups will vary in their knowledge and understanding of the mechanics of the local government decision-making, both in local government generally and in their own local authority in particular. Some organizations will therefore know who to approach; others will not and may thus simply focus on the most visible or apparently accessible point in the system.

(c) Knowledge of the appropriate 'pressure points' will be aided by having knowledgeable members, especially 'insiders', such as councillors or officers of the council (see p. 407). Newton[37] shows (and the author can confirm from his experience) how these insiders may sometimes find themselves 'wearing two hats'; as members of an outside body they may have to communicate with themselves as members or officers of the local authority!

(d) Effective contact with the local authority need not be confined to cross-membership. The extent to which an outside organization is 'established' or held to be respectable will help to determine the attitude and receptiveness of the authority towards them; that is whether they are regarded as 'in-groups' or 'out-groups'. Their respectability (or 'legitimacy') very much depends on the social standing of their membership, or at least of their officers. Having an MP or other local notable as chairman or committee member is an asset to any group wishing to exercise some influence with the local authority. (Charities received some £350 million from local authorities in 1984 plus £107 million rate relief.)

In this respect a study by Dearlove[38] suggests that the attitude of local authorities to outside organizations will be based not just on the character of the group but also on the nature of its demands and its methods of communicating those demands. Some groups are accepted because their membership contains the 'right' people, or because of the moderateness or usefulness of their cause, or because of the propriety of their methods or 'style'. Other groups become alienated and forfeit their chances to influence the council by appearing too radical, supporting questionable causes (such as 'gay lib' or topless beaches) or resorting to unacceptable methods such as direct action.[39] As a result some groups – out-groups – can find themselves in a very difficult position: if they have the wrong 'image' they will not have the 'ear' of the council and will have to use aggressive publicity-seeking methods which will be less acceptable to the council and will thus further diminish the group's standing and frustrate the achievement of its cause, though Gyford concludes that 'the trend seems to flow clearly in the direction of according greater recognition to sectional interests'.[40] The Widdicombe Committee expressed concern at the way in which some councils discriminated against certain groups on party political grounds.[41]

Apart from their attitude to individual groups, councillors may have a general judgement on pressure groups. This will be coloured no doubt by their experience of particular groups, but it is likely to be generally influenced by the councillor's perception of his own role. We have referred (p. 188) to the 'trustee', 'delegate' and 'politico' types of councillor. One might expect the trustee type to resist sectional interests on principle and conversely the politico to be more accommodating. There is some evidence for this view, but it is not conclusive.[42] What does appear to be more certain is that the older, more experienced councillors are more favourably disposed towards pressure groups than the newer members.

One might also expect Conservative councillors to look quite favourably on pressure groups (especially the welfare, service-providing groups) because they exemplify self-help as well as helping to keep down the council tax. Labour councillors on the other hand might well be expected to cavil at the distortions and inequalities which such groups may introduce. The evidence is, however, conflicting.[43]

(e) While councillors have attitudes towards groups, so do groups have opinions about councillors, and this can affect the way they seek to influence the authority. It is evident for example that many groups operate through the official side of local authorities because of their lack of confidence in councillors.[44]

(f) The timing of the issue (whether it is near an election for example) and the stage at which the outside organization comes to hear of it (whether before or after the relevant committee meeting) will obviously have a bearing on the group's approach. And the nature of the issue itself can be critical: for example, if there is conflict over a local authority's promotion of a Private Bill (see p. 78), pressure groups may have the opportunity for a public hearing before a Parliamentary committee.

(g) The nature of the local party system can be an important factor. If there is a party monopoly or dominance (see p. 149), it would be appropriate for the pressure group to concentrate its efforts on that majority party and perhaps withdraw from any other approaches.

It has been suggested that the more conspicuous their activities are, the less influence pressure groups are likely to exert.[45] This is largely because, as we have seen, local authority members feel there is a 'right' and a 'wrong' way for groups to approach them. The evidence from the Birmingham study suggests that

the local pressure group system seems to operate in such a way that the best-established groups . . . are able to work through their close ties with decision-makers . . . and . . . operate in a relatively quiet and unnoticed way . . . Paradoxically, the noisier and more visible the group the greater the likelihood of its being powerless in the political system.[46]

However, where the group or the issue cannot be accommodated in this behind-the-scenes fashion, the only alternative is for it to go beyond the council and make the matter more public and more obviously political.

The effectiveness of pressure groups

It is clearly difficult to judge the effectiveness of pressure groups at local level since their success will vary with the local authority, the issue or cause and the standing, resources and style of the groups themselves.[47] Slightly more specifically, we can say that a group will succeed or fail according to such variable factors as:

(a) the size of the membership, income and full-time staffing of the group;

(b) the extent of cross-membership and other contacts with the local authority, and its degree of acceptance or establishment;

(c) the 'direction' of its cause, that is whether it runs with, against or across established council policy. This will help to shape the authority's perception of the pressure group as 'helpful' or 'unhelpful';[48]

(d) the methods used by the group and the quality of their arguments;

(e) the extent of public and media sympathy with their cause;

(f) the organization, methods and arguments of counter-groups (such as developers v. conservationists);

(g) the general attitude of the local authority to pressure group politics.

The Birmingham survey suggests that pressure groups are well satisfied with the local authority response. But this may have been due to the fact that their aims were limited to single issues or issues that were congruent to council policy. Nevertheless, Newton suggests that in Britain pressure groups are accepted much more willingly than they are in the USA;[49] 80 per cent of his sample of councillors were described as 'facilitators' rather than 'resistors' of pressure groups. And throughout Britain the extent of support for such groups (especially welfare groups) is indicated by the substantial financial and material assistance which is provided by local authorities.

Pressure groups – threat or promise?

Like political parties, pressure groups are a fact of life. If they did not exist, perhaps they would have to be invented, since they bring with them a number of distinct advantages to the administration of local affairs: they provide expertise;[50] they help to smooth administration by securing cooperation and acceptability of policy; they act as a funnel or filter between the local authority and the various individuals, families, firms etc. who might otherwise separately convey their views and thus deluge the authority; they can scrutinize local government expenditure to detect value for money.

These groups also provide an additional method or source of involvement for the community: anyone can engage in pressure politics; it does not necessarily involve heavy expense, especially since the media seem so ready to provide free publicity for the sake of a story. Armed with the support of others in a group, the individual need no longer feel powerless against the juggernaut local authority. And membership of such a group does not bring with it a continuing commitment which public office or party membership normally requires. Where people feel alienated or estranged from their elected representatives, they can find an alternative voice in the form of a pressure group.

A large proportion of the general public belong to voluntary organizations. A survey published in 1967[51] showed that some 60 per cent of adults belong to one, and a significant proportion of these seem to be active members (though mainly in the non-political aspects of their group). In so far as these organizations do become politically active and establish contacts with the local authority, bridges are being built between the authority and the wider community: the authority has an additional means of gauging public reaction to their proposals and can explain their actions more fully than they could hope to do through the columns of the local press.[52] This mutual exchange of views and information may help to weaken the attitude of 'them and us' which unfortunately bedevils so much of local government's relationship with the public (see p. 430).

Casting a vote is a very generalized expression of opinion about policy: the most conscientious citizen can turn out to vote at every election and yet still have his particular interests overlooked in the manifestos and official policies. Besides, in many areas there are no elections, or the result is a foregone conclusion, and so there is little opportunity for influence. Pressure politics can articulate minority views and injustices which might otherwise go unheard and unacknowledged; in this respect they act as an educative force in society. Professor Richards suggests that pressure groups 'are a particularly valuable element in maintaining a spirit of local democracy as they frequently promote causes that cut across the lines of political party policies'.[53]

Finally, in favour of pressure groups it can be argued that they help to strengthen the democratic process by augmenting the resources of elected members. For those who take a somewhat conspiratorial view of the role of the official in local government, it may be reassuring to see pressure groups helping to restore the balance in favour of the elected member by supplying him or her with information which can augment that provided by the officers of the authority and may, wittingly or not, be biased.

We all have interests and attachments – personal, religious, racial, local, national. We reflect these, or an amalgam of them, when we cast our vote. Voting is thus an individualized registration of our interests. Pressure groups are simply a group or collective form of the same process. As such, they are hardly anti-democratic, and most of them do not deserve the bad name which has derived from the lurid exposures of the influence which some of them have exercised on political decisions during this century (mainly at national level and especially in America).

However, there are certain aspects of pressure groups which do give rise to serious and widespread concern. Principally, they are criticized for distorting or undermining the democratic process of government in its traditional form, in which policy reflects the wishes of the public as expressed through their elected representatives. Through pressure groups, certain interests – especially powerful economic interests – are able to get an unreasonable amount of attention and so distort the balance of local provision, to the detriment of genuine needs. Thus we have a situation 'in which a minority of determined people are able to organize themselves into groups, apply pressure to the right quarter, and so influence decisions which affect us all. Parliamentary democracy has given way to politics by pressure.'[54] Essentially the criticism here is that the interests covered by pressure groups are too limited in scope, and that the already powerful groups accrue extra power through group pressure tactics.[55]

The uneven coverage of interest groups is partly due to the unequal distribution of wealth and other resources in society. It is also due to the fact that overwhelmingly pressure groups are created and run by people from a middle-class background, whose education and ambitions are said to make them 'born organizers'. Thus it could be argued, notwithstanding the prevalence of trade unions, that the working class is under-represented in the pressure group area of politics.[56]

Furthermore, although it has been said that pressure groups provide an opening for greater community involvement in public decision-making, in fact, while many people belong to organizations, most do so for their social, economic or spiritual functions rather than their political activities. A relatively small percentage – 14 per cent[57] – are involved in the organizational or bargaining aspect of their association or society. As Gyford says, '. . . the various groups and individuals which engage in local politics outside the ranks of the national political parties . . . represent a modest widening . . . of the area of debate'.[58]

The other main criticism of pressure groups is their mode of operation: their secrecy. In discussing 'the lobby' at parliamentary level, Professor Finer expressed the concern thus:

When we realize . . . that the debates upstairs [at private meetings of the parties] are conflicts between the claims of the rival lobbies in the parties concerned, surely it is clear that we, the general public, the people who have a right to know, are being denied the opportunity to judge between the true contestants – between the prime movers – between the real issues? Instead we are treated to the premasticated speech, tossed back and forth across the floor of the House, of blocs who have already formed their opinions in secrecy. This secrecy, this twilight of parliamentary debate envelops the lobby in its own obscurity. Through this, above all, the lobbies become – as far as the general public is concerned – faceless, voiceless, unidentifiable; in brief, anonymous.[59]

Room for Reform?

Thus may pressure groups exercise power without responsibility, and many councillors feel that if such people wish to press their 'rights' they should also accept duties and responsibilities, and become more open and accountable, perhaps by helping to shoulder the burden of office as elected members of a public authority. In practice, of course, many pressure groups do shoulder responsibility – for example in providing voluntary services to the community. Nevertheless, one simple reform could help to meet this criticism: the introduction of a register in each local authority area for all pressure groups which are in contact with the local authority. This could be available for inspection by the public and perhaps contain details of the organizations' aims, membership and funding.

Local authorities might also encourage the formation of groups and provide them with information and resources. This would enable a wider cross-section of the community to be represented and act as a counter-weight to the big battalions already well placed. Some authorities already do this, for example by appointing community development officers and associations. And while in their own way, parish and community councils act as community 'watchdogs', some areas are establishing even more local 'neighbourhood' councils (see p. 453). As regards planning, local authorities are required to publicize their plans, to make people who might be affected aware of their rights, and to give them an adequate opportunity of making representations. In 1969, largely in response to the Skeffington Report of the same year,[60] the Government recommended to local authorities that 'the formation of residents' associations should also be encouraged'.[61] In the wake of the Taylor Committee[62] many local education authorities encouraged community participation by appointing parents to school governing bodies (now mandatory under the Education Act 1980 and enhanced in 1986).

However, the opportunities for group formation and participation must be real: they need encouragement as well as resources. Participation 'involves doing as well as talking and there will be full participation only where the public are able to take an active part throughout the plan-making process'.[63] Or, in the words of the Seebohm Committee:

Community development in this country is seen as a process whereby local groups are assisted to clarify and express their needs and objectives and to take collective action to attempt to meet them. It emphasizes the involvement of the people themselves in determining and meeting their own needs. The role of the community worker is that of a source of information and expertise, a stimulator, a catalyst and an encourager ... Community identity may also be developed through organizations such as community centres, clubs, play centres and tenants' associations, where the social service department could provide technical and professional help, information, stimulation and grant-aid.[64]

The Seebohm Committee was aware that 'there is certainly a difficult link to be forged between the concepts of popular participation and traditional representative democracy'.[65] But it also implied that the growth of the Welfare State has altered the relationship between state and people and requires something of a review or revision. The promotion of local groups is one such development. Furthermore, if sufficient such groups are created, then rather than adversely distorting local provision, they may instead provide an invaluable source of information about 'real' needs in the community. In the last resort of course it is the responsibility of the local decision-makers to strike the right balance between the various claims, and there is always the sanction (real or imagined) of the next election if they are seen to be failing in this respect.

The citizen with a grievance

Politics at local or national level is about the resolution of conflicting claims. Inevitably, where interests clash, someone wins and someone else loses, or more likely (in the event of compromise) both win something and lose something.

Local authorities mediate the conflicting claims and interests of the community. Theoretically, they attempt to promote its collective interests as expressed through the ballot box. In practice, owing to a host of imperfections both in the mechanism and in the very concept of representation,[66] the pursuit of the public interest leaves a lot to be desired.

But even with a perfect system of representation (plenty of candidates, perfect communications, high voting turnout, etc.) and with the best will in the world, local authorities are bound to upset some people: the 'general will' takes precedence over the individual in such matters as the compulsory purchase of property, the levying of taxes or the allocation of children to schools. But in a liberal-democratic society, while the majority may rule, they must not ride roughshod over minority interests. The individual must be given a chance to have his or her grievance investigated and redressed.

How should aggrieved individuals seek redress from their local authority? Much will depend on the nature of their grievance: they may have been refused a licence or a council house; they may find that the council has given approval to an objectionable development near their house; they may object to the excessive amount of money being spent on local sports facilities or the inadequate amounts going to the home help service; they may protest generally about the level of the poll tax.

We have already indicated some specific means of remedy – addressing questions to the district auditor (p. 349); presenting objections to the Minister (p. 341); taking legal action (p. 359); or contacting the local MP (p. 375). But the most obvious and sensible starting point is to contact the appropriate councillor, especially through his or her 'surgery'. In practice, it seems that councillors have one such contact per day, on average.[67] However, for various reasons (see p. 443) there may be problems in doing this. The alternative is to approach the local authority itself, though for many people this is a daunting prospect, overlaid with the problem of finding the right department or officer: in the last resort they can simply write to the chief executive officer or the chair of the council. Table 24 shows the differing pattern of contact.

Failing satisfaction here, or if they are uncertain of their case or the correct procedure, complainants may turn to less formal

Figure 23 *Channels of redress*

channels: contacting their local or neighbourhood council (if there is one), approaching a local political party, getting in touch with a relevant pressure group or voluntary organization, informing (or just threatening to inform) the local media.

Although local authorities are not normally deliberately perverse or more self-defensive than other organizations, they do appear to be considerably defective in their machinery for dealing with complaints. The authors of one recent study have said:

From our experience of representing members of the lower socio-economic groups, we have found local authority departments particularly difficult to deal with, not because of any unusual obstinacy on the part of officials or members, but because of a singular lack of adequate and visible procedures, the existing mechanisms frequently being convoluted and Byzantine to a degree.[68]

Table 24 *Extent of contact with councillors and council offices by locational characteristics*

	Contact with councillor %	Contact with council offices %
Housing tenure		
owner occupier	18	50
council tenant	32	47
Length of residence		
up to 5 years	11	44
5 years or more	24	50
Region		
London	14	49
metropolitan England	20	52
rest of England and Wales	22	50
Scotland	21	32
Ratepaying		
pays rates in full	23	53
rates partly rebated	25	50
does not pay rates	18	43
All respondents	20	49

Source: The Conduct of Local Authority Business: Research Vol 3: The Local Government Elector, HMSO, 1986, Table 2.12.

And a former head of the Local Government Information Office states:

Unless something is done to alleviate the public's suspicions that local government is just another part of the bureaucratic machine, resenting criticism and setting itself apart from the community it represents, then it is unlikely that it will survive for very much longer in present form [*sic*].[69]

And it seems that amongst those members of the public (a small minority) who do complain to their councils, over half (54 per cent) proclaim themselves dissatisfied with the way the complaints are handled. (This is a higher proportion than is the case of those complaints going to large firms, the NHS, the central government or the gas and electricity boards.)[70]

However, some of these criticisms may lose their force as local authorities follow the recommendations of their local authority associations and the Commission for Local Administration in England. In 1978 they jointly issued a 'Code of Practice' for local authorities receiving complaints. Among other things, this suggests:

Authorities should ensure that effective and continuing information is available to the public about channels through which queries can be raised or complaints made . . . There should be easy access by the public to those responsible for dealing with queries and complaints whether officers or Members . . . Contact points should be widely publicized, including the names and addresses of Members and appropriate officers. The procedure(s) should ensure that those raising queries are not unnecessarily passed from one place or person to another and that they are dealt with as locally and conveniently as possible . . . Responsibility for dealing with queries and complaints must be firmly established . . . There should be a willingness to see enquirers and complainants particularly when the issues are complicated or the facts need to be clarified . . .[71]

And there is evidence that local authorities are developing a more conscious 'public service orientation' and reminding staff to 'put people first'.[72] This is partly in response to the pressure or threat presented to local government by increased competitive tendering, by greater opportunities for groups (parents of schoolchildren, council house tenants) to opt out of local authority control and by increased numbers of people paying more explicitly for services through the community charge. The central government can also require local authorities to set up appropriate complaints procedures, e.g. on education matters under the Education Reform Act 1988. And local authority associations issue 'model' procedures. In the meantime, local authorities have been improving their general administrative procedures[73] as a result of the reports issued by the Commission for Local Administration (CLA) – the citizen's local 'ombudsman'.

The Ombudsman

Sometimes referred to as the 'citizen's defender', the ombudsman or 'referee' was introduced to deal with local government matters in 1974[74] (1976 in Scotland). The chairman (Dr Yardley) is the senior Commissioner and receives £84,250 per annum. Officially called 'Commissioners for Local Administration' (CLA), there is one for Scotland, one for Wales and three for England. Their function is to investigate and report on any claim by a member of the public that he or she has suffered injustice through maladministration by a local (or police*) authority[75] (except parishes), with a view to securing satisfactory redress for the complainant and better administration for the authorities. (A secondary objective is to encourage authorities to develop and publicize their procedures for the fair settlement of complaints and to settle as many of them as possible.)

'Maladministration' is not defined in the legislation, but refers generally to faulty administration in the *way* in which an authority's decision or action has been taken, rather than the actual merit of the decision. Thus maladministration is taken to cover administrative action (or inaction) based on or influenced by improper considerations (such as bias or unfair discrimination) or improper conduct (such as undue delay, failure to observe established procedures or failure to take account of relevant considerations). Much is therefore left to the interpretation or discretion of the Commissioners themselves.

However, there are a number of areas from which they are explicitly excluded. These include complaints about commercial transactions (apart from the purchase or sale of land and buildings); job grievances and other personnel matters; certain educa-

---

* But not complaints against individual police officers.

tion matters (including the giving of instruction and the internal organization of schools and colleges); and the investigation or prevention of crime (there is a separate machinery for dealing with complaints against the police). Local Commissioners cannot investigate any matter about which the aggrieved person has appealed to a tribunal or to a government Minister or has taken proceedings in a court of law. Nor do they normally pursue the matter if the person has the right of appeal to a Minister, tribunal or court (though this rule may be waived if the Commissioners are satisfied that it is not reasonable to expect the person to use those other rights or remedies). Furthermore, the Commissioners may not look into cases where most or all of the local inhabitants are concerned – a complaint against the general level of rates would not be accepted for investigation. Finally, there is normally a time limit of twelve months within which the complaint must be made (unless there are special circumstances).

In 1988 one of the excluded areas was revised so that the CLA may now (except in relation to police authorities) consider matters concerning the investigation or prevention of crime, such as the way a council deals with matters involving a criminal offence under the trade descriptions and other consumer legislation.

The Commissioners will not normally investigate any complaint until it has been brought to the attention of the local authority or the council's complaints system and that the authority has had a reasonable time in which to reply. If no satisfactory response occurs, the aggrieved person should put his or her complaint in writing and address it to a member (normally a councillor) of the relevant authority with a request that it be sent on to the ombudsman – thus does the local (like the Parliamentary) ombudsman seek to supplement the traditional democratic process rather than supplant it. Under the Local Government Act 1988, complainants may, if they prefer, complain direct to the local ombudsman.

Unless the complaint is withdrawn or settled locally ('out of court', i.e. directly between the local authority and the complainant), and provided that it is within the legitimate scope of the

CLA, an investigation takes place in which a CLA investigator interviews the complainant and will normally visit the local authority concerned, where he or she has, like the High Court, the power (within limits)[76] to examine internal papers and take written and oral evidence from anyone who can provide relevant information. However, all investigations are conducted in private.

When the investigation is completed, a report giving the CLA's findings will be sent to the complainant, the councillor (where appropriate) and the authority (and any person complained against). In addition, a copy is sent to the local media, and it is made available for public inspection. The report is made publicly available, but does not normally give names of individuals. Where the report finds that injustice (anxiety, financial loss, inconvenience, etc.) has been caused to the complainant by maladministration, the authority must consider the report and inform the CLA what action it proposes to take. (Where nothing happens, the CLA may make a further report and the process of publication is repeated.)

Each year the CLA have to prepare a general report on the discharge of their functions. This is received by a body representing the local authority Associations, which normally has the report published together with its own comments.

In reviewing the effectiveness of the ombudsman system, one study has concluded that its impact on local authority procedures has been 'considerable'.[77] Between 1974 and 1978, the English Commissioners received nearly 7,500 complaints – about 2,000 a year (roughly the same, for example, as the South West Regional Gas Consumer Council received). By 1988, the figure had grown to 4,229 (of which half had been received direct and half via a councillor), and in 1992 the figure had reached 12,123. It is difficult to determine whether the increase is evidence of growing maladministration or the result of greater public awareness of their rights and of the Commission's services.

Of the 12,123 cases, 10,610 were considered by the CLA. Of these, the majority – 10,258 or 97·5 per cent – were not investigated beyond the stage of considering the authority's detailed comments on them (e.g. because the council settled the complaint satisfactorily, as in 1,735 of the cases). Or they were discontinued when it became clear that maladministration had not occurred (as in 6,667 cases) or the issue was outside the CLA's remit.

Out of the total of cases considered, only 321 were found to manifest maladministration.

Thus, the findings of the 352 cases fully investigated were:

291 (83 per cent) injustice through maladministration (*58 per cent*);
  30 (8·5 per cent) maladministration but no injustice (*4 per cent*);
  31 (8·5 per cent) no maladministration (*38 per cent*).

(The figures in italics refer to the period 1974–8.[78] The figures for Scotland and Wales show similar amounts of maladministration to those for England.)

Examples of injustice caused through maladministration include the following: delay in processing housing benefit leading to eviction for rent arrears; unfair discrimination in awarding discretionary education grant; a piggery being used without relevant planning permission and the council taking little action in response to complaints about noise and smell; incompetence in granting planning permission for two houses adjoining the complainant's bungalow; failure to act to prevent the demolition of a listed building; and unreasonable delay in carrying out repairs to remedy dampness in a council house. The majority of cases (some 70 per cent) involve housing (especially repairs) or planning matters (especially objections).

The CLA reports tend to be treated with respect by the local authorities. In nearly every case where injustice had been found, the CLA was satisfied with the subsequent action taken by the authority (an apology, provision of accommodation or financial compensation, alteration of procedures, etc.). In only a few cases do local authorities fail to take satisfactory action. There were four such cases in 1987–8, and since 1974, there have been 186 (up to 1992). On at least one occasion the council went to court for a judicial review of the CLA's adverse report and was successful. Normally, the CLA's only sanction here is a second report and reliance on the force of public opinion, though some councils argue that central government constraints on local expenditure and manpower are restricting their ability to provide adequate services or recompense. The CLA was also largely instrumental in the creation of the Code of Practice for receiving and investigating complaints (see p. 421). Since February 1992, it has encouraged the setting up of complaints systems, following the CLA's publication of guidance notes on good administrative practice, 'Devising a Complaints System'. And in 1978 legislation removed a considerable doubt and impediment on local authorities by allowing them to incur expenditure in order to recompense those who suffer injustice as a result of maladministration. And the 1980 Local Government, Planning and Land Act secured the CLA's right of access to relevant information and documents.

The CLA has had a considerable impact on local authority procedures. But reviews of its work[79] have often been critical and have raised a number of questions: should the CLA be empowered to initiate investigations (as has been suggested in such areas as those of child abuse) instead of having to wait for a formal complaint? Should the scope be extended into some of those areas at present beyond the legal competence of the CLA? Is the continued mechanism of funnelling complaints through the councillor an impediment? Should the powers of the CLA be increased (either to insist on adequate – perhaps legally enforceable as in Ulster – redress or greater access to documents, etc.)? Are there too many ombudsmen (they exist separately for the civil service, for the NHS, for local government), thus causing public confusion? Are the CLA themselves guilty of 'maladministration' in taking so long to complete their investigations (the average time being 74·5 weeks (it was 40 weeks in 1981)? Is the system sufficiently well publicized and should other Commissioners appear on television to explain their work as the Scottish ombudsman has done? Is the system (and is it held to be) sufficiently impartial? This last question arises from the fact that, though appointed by the Secretary of State, a number of the Commissioners have a local government background (as member or officer) and the whole system has been financed by the local authority Associations. (The estimated cost of the CLA for England in 1991–2 was £4·9m (i.e. £400 per complaint received, which is the same as in 1987–8, with an expenditure of £1·8m).)

Criticisms like these were levelled at the Parliametary Commissioner for Administration (the ombudsman who investigates the civil service) when he was first established in 1967. Since then his role has been gradually amended so that he is evolving into a more effective and respected institution. The Commissioners for Local Administration appear to be developing in similar fashion. Apart from the developments mentioned above, the Government introduced a number of changes under the Local Government and Housing Act 1989. These were largely in response to the Widdicombe Report,[80] a report by a Parliamentary committee[81] and in response to the pleas of the CLA itself, who refer to the continued 'discouraging feature . . . that a small minority of councils, with blatant disregard for the interests of complainants, were still defying the Local Government Ombudsmen by refusing to implement their recommendations.'[82] The Act now:

(1) requires councils found guilty of maladministration to inform the CLA what steps they are taking to prevent similar injustices occurring; where a council declines to comply with the remedies proposed in the CLA report, that decision must have been taken by the council (not just a committee) and they are required to publish a statement in a local newspaper consisting of the action recommended by the CLA and, if they wish, their reasons for non-compliance;

(2) requires, in most cases, the CLA to name councillors who are involved in such cases and where they have broken the Code of Conduct (see p. 421);

(3) allows the CLA to publish general guidance to local authorities on the principles of good administrative practice;

(4) abolishes the representative bodies (for England and Wales;

see p. 423) so as to remove the possible influence on the work of the CLA of local authorities who compose those bodies;

(5) changes the system of funding such that finance is raised by a deduction from the Revenue Support Grant;

(6) provides additional 'outside' members to the Commissions. Their role would be to help advise on CLA guidance to councils on efficiency and good administrative practice (as in (3) above);

(7) In addition, the Government is reviewing the excluded area of commercial and contractual matters (partly in view of the fact that in some cases, such as market-stall allocations, the commercial aspect is secondary, while in other cases non-commercial considerations have obtruded into tendering/contracting-out procedures).

There is still unease at the refusal of some councils to implement the CLA's recommendations. There have been eighteen cases, involving eight councils, where the ombudsman has required the council to publish a statement (as in (1) above). But one of the Commissioners has stated that 'My experience so far is that the further step of producing a statement has had little effect on those public authorities which set themselves against accepting the referee's verdict.' The Widdicombe Committee and the CLA itself recommended that complainants should have a right to seek judicial enforcement of remedies through the courts. But this has been rejected by the Government on the grounds that it would tend to make the investigations too inflexible, formal and legalistic, such that complainants might find the process more intimidating. This is one of the risks involved in developing the system. There is also the danger that administrators will become over-cautious[83] and that they will lose some of their valuable flexibility and informality (for example, by refusing to give 'off the record' advice to members of the public. However, in its White Paper, *The Citizen's Charter* (1991), the Government states that if difficulties continue over ensuring that local ombudsmen's recommendations are implemented, 'we will take the further step of introducing legislation to make the . . . recommendation legally enforceable'.

The Citizen's Charter also raised the prospect of creating local lay adjudicators to deal with more minor claims of redress. But the CLA fears this may confuse citizens and possibly delay taking up complaints with itself. Meanwhile it is firmly of the view that current restrictions on its jurisdiction should be removed, and that (especially in the light of recent child-abuse cases) it should be able to undertake investigations on its own initiative without receiving a complaint. (In some of the child-abuse cases – such as that of Kimberly Carlile, 1987 – the inquiry lacked the power to compel witnesses to give evidence. The CLA has such a power.) On the other hand, there are those who have pointed to the costs which fall to local authorities as a consequence of CLA inquiries (the cost of officers' time, extra record-keeping, etc., quite apart from any compensation costs or the restructuring of procedures – for which reason even innocent local authorities are known to 'plead guilty' and settle with complainants, just to avoid the time and upheaval of an inquiry). And there is also resistance from councillors: some of them see the CLA as straying illicitly into areas of policy, while others, like MPs, claim that they are themselves 'ombudsmen' and that outside Commissioners are an intrusion.

There is some truth in this claim, as indeed the system originally recognized, by requiring complaints to be channelled initially through the elected representative. However, the evidence points to these representatives being inadequate to the task. This is partly because many have been poor at the constituency role (perhaps preferring to play the 'statesman' – see p. 188); partly because of lack of time (many MPs as well as most councillors are part-time); and partly because of a lack of expertise and power: councillors as individuals have little statutory authority and have until recently had limited access to internal documents.[84] The CLA should therefore be seen as an adjunct or 'back-stop' to the councillor.

A recent study states that 'on almost any index, the LO had

been a force for the good', and it reveals that in England 50 per cent of councils had amended their complaints procedures as a result of the local ombudsman's endeavours. But it went on to suggest that in some local government circles the work of the ombudsman was being taken less seriously than formerly.[85] There is also some concern about the lack of consistency among the different CLAs, while the existence of 'no-go areas' in their remit is felt to add to the public's confusion about the whole institution. Under the Government's current reforms, the CLA is, in its reports, to comment more on the adequacy of local authorities' procedures and will publish general advice on good administrative practice. Judging from the evidence of the Widdicombe Report (see Table 25) there is strong case for trying to raise people's awareness of, and confidence in, the role of the CLA: it appears that the ombudsman would only be people's fifth choice when considering how they would challenge a bad decision by the council, and is considered to be only the fifth most effective in remedying the problem.

Participation

Using conventional measures, British local government does not enjoy a high degree of public participation (i.e. involvement in the State's decision-making process). Appendix 17 indicates the general scale of involvement. As we saw in Chapter 8, less than 1 per cent of the electorate ever serve or stand for election as councillor, a high proportion of seats go uncontested (e.g. 70 per cent in Powys CC, 1985) and the average turnout at local elections is only 40 per cent or less. A survey for the Maud Report[86] found that: between one fifth and one half of the informants were unable to name any service provided by their local authority; over two thirds said they had not heard of anything which their council had done during the previous month; less than one fifth had ever been in touch with a councillor for help or advice; only 7 per cent (1 per cent in counties) had ever been to a

Table 25 *Actions to be taken when faced with a 'really wrong' council decision and 'most effective' action*

	Would take[1] %	Most effective %
Respondent would contact:		
councillor	49	18
council officers	28	4
ombudsman	8	3
MP	47	22
district auditor	2	1
local newspaper/radio	25	15
other people	4	1
Other actions:		
sign petition	53	12
go on protest demonstration	7	1
take council to court	6	4
vote against council	19	4
Other	2	1
None of these	4	6
Don't know	3	9

Source: Widdicombe Report, vol. III, HMSO, 1986, Table 4.7.
[1] Multiple responses.

council meeting; and nearly one quarter felt alienated from the local authority. A different survey[87] found that amongst those who were aware of any participation exercise conducted by their local authority only 12 per cent had in fact participated by returning questionnaires, visiting an exhibition or attending a public meeting, and 42 per cent had declared themselves little or not at all interested in who wins local council elections. A social survey for Matthew Parris MP (April 1981) showed 57 per cent could not name any councillor for their area; 56 per cent could not name their own local authority; two out of three did not know which layer of local government was responsible for different services. Research for the Widdicombe Committee (Vol. 3) found that only 30 per cent could name any of their councillors and only half could correctly name their county or regional council. And a survey for *New Society* (4 March 1982) showed that many people still believed hospitals (59 per cent in the Widdicombe survey) and job-centres were run by local government. British local government is often held to compare unfavourably with other countries in these respects.

These are important findings, but their importance must not be exaggerated. Comparisons with general election results can be misleading, for at national level there is more publicity, the issues are clear, there is perhaps more at stake, electors who are mobile (moving house) have a sustained involvement and the MP will (unlike many local councillors) live in the constituency. Similarly, comparisons with local government elections in other countries must take account of their laws on compulsory voting, polling on Sundays or holidays, or the fact that voters may be electing candidates to national as well as local office. Besides, having a high level of turnout does not necessarily imply a high level of interest, concern or understanding of what the councils are doing. Furthermore, as the Maud Committee itself pointed out,

It is of no particular significance that the public do not throng the public galleries of the councils; at any rate this does not seem to be peculiar to this country ... Local authorities provide a wide range of services to the community and relatively few people need to make contact with their authorities unless things go wrong. The lack of public interest in the work of local authorities may well suggest that the public are satisfied with the services which the local authorities provide. The Social Survey's findings in fact do not show that there is any high degree of dissatisfaction with the services or with the way in which local authorities are run.[88]

Other measures suggest a reasonable level of interest in and commitment to local affairs. Thus an American survey found that in Britain 70 per cent of those interviewed felt that they ought to play an active part in local affairs and 78 per cent felt that they could if necessary alter 'an unjust local regulation'.[89] In another survey, some 65 per cent claimed to be 'quite interested' or 'very interested' in the work of their local council.[90] And in the survey for the Maud Report 52 per cent said that they wanted to know more about their local council.[91] The Widdicombe inquiry found 52 per cent of the public to be well or quite well informed about local government, for example over 50 per cent could correctly name their council's or councillor's political party. And the inquiry revealed a very high (72 per cent) general level of satisfaction with the performance of local authorities.[92]

Furthermore, as we have seen (p. 413), some studies suggest that as many as two thirds of electors claim to belong to at least one voluntary organization, and some 80 per cent of local electors are readers of the local press.[93] Other evidence of a 'rising tide of public involvement' is to be found in the growth of local groups, inquiries at Citizens' Advice Bureaux and in swelling complaints to the CLAs.[94] As a consequence, it may well be that many people are interested in particular aspects of a council's work, rather than have an enduring interest in local government as a whole.[95] Besides which, the governing bodies of schools and colleges, together with the tribunals set up to hear appeals over school admissions or curriculum matters (under the Education Act 1980 and the Education Reform Act 1988 respectively), involve many thousands of such 'lay' members. (There are some 300,000 school governors.)

Notwithstanding what is said above, the apparently low level of active interest in local government is regrettable. But it is not tragic. Nor is it reasonable to cry 'apathy', since some of the explanations lie in the machinery or procedures of local government itself rather than its citizens. The situation is therefore capable of improvement.

Improving participation

The Maud Report made a number of recommendations to raise the level of public interest and participation in local government affairs:

(a) removal of some of the confusing features of local government, such as the aldermanic system and the varying systems of electing councillors;

(b) more education of schoolchildren (and their teachers) in the role and responsibilities of local government in the community;

(c) the development of closer relationships between local authorities and voluntary organizations;

(d) more in the way of advance information to the public on major issues or proposals coming before the council (that is something analogous to government Green and White Papers);

(e) better arrangements at council offices for the public to gain access to responsible officers to raise matters which affect them personally or be put in touch with members if they are dissatisfied with the official response;

(f) easier access for the press to committee meetings; the press should be regarded as partners in the process of informing the public and should be given adequate facilities.

Some of these proposals have been implemented. For example, aldermen have been abolished, and public access to meetings and council documents is increased under the Local Governmment (Access to Information) Act 1985. Others have been rejected. For example, although local government elections are now held on the same day throughout the country, there are still two different systems operating (see p. 131), which leads to confusion. A number of the recommendations have been left to the discretion of local authorities themselves (public access to officers, for instance) and consequently it is difficult to generalize. Certainly a number have attempted to build up their relationships with voluntary organizations by, for example, establishing volunteer liaison officers or funding volunteer bureaux, but it is by no means systematic. In terms of education in schools, there has been no obvious move towards local government or political studies, despite the efforts of the Politics Association and a recommendation in 1978 by Her

Majesty's Inspectors (HMIs), and current official thinking appears to be firmly in the direction of the 'core curriculum' (back to basic subjects) and/or a vocational (work-related) approach. In 1986 Lambeth Council began to pay out baby-sitting fees (under Section 137 of the 1974 Local Government Act) to enable the public to attend its meetings.

The other suggestions and developments are dealt with below. But before turning to them it is appropriate to mention that there was some evidence in the survey for the Maud Report[96] that public understanding of local government was greater in the single-tier authorities than the multi-tier. If this is so then the 1974–5 reorganization to a universally multi-tier system of generally larger local authorities will not have aided public understanding of local government, though the 1986 reform may. And while the 1986 reform may have helped to simplify local government in the metropolitan areas into a single-tier system, it added greatly to its complexity and confusion[97] by the creation of various boards (compounded in these and other areas by the formation of urban development corporations, housing action trusts and grant-maintained schools).

Local authorities have attempted to make themselves more accessible and open to the public, for example, by holding public question sessions and open forums, producing community videos, setting up decentralized information points and by installing complaints systems. They have sometimes run into legal problems, as when the Audit Commission has, on the grounds of illegal expenditure, barred councils from holding public opinion polls or referendums on the question of local reorganization proposals.

In 1993, the Government invited local authorities to follow its lead in being more open, allowing greater access to personal files and providing information about health and safety matters (such as the safety of transport and public places). But they have also been pushed to become more accountable and responsible to their ratepayers and consumers (or users) by the Government: thus the 1980 Local Government, Planning and Land Act requires them to publish information on staffing and finance as well as annual general reports; the Local Government Finance Act 1982 gave ratepayers enhanced powers to inspect and challenge the accounts at audit time; the 1980 Housing Act requires information for tenants; the 1980 Education Act requires information on schools (to allow real choice), which is reinforced by the publication of HMI reports and the involvement of parents in school governing bodies (which now incorporates some 300,000 more people into the political process); the 1986 Disabled Persons (Services, Consultation and Representation) Act requires the greater dissemination of information on services; the 1987 Access to Personal Files Act allows access to housing and social services files (education files became more accessible under the 1980 Education Act); and the 1985 Local Government (Access to Information) Act has made available minutes, agendas and other official documents as well as giving greater public access to committees.

However, local authorities retain discretionary powers to declare certain items as confidential and therefore exempt from disclosure (there are fifteen such categories in the 1985 Act; see pp. 213–4). And there is evidence that some councils seek to avoid disclosure by abusing discretionary powers, by charging unreasonably (e.g. up to £10) when clients want copies of documents, by setting up 'advisory' bodies or working parties (i.e. not proper, and therefore accessible, committees), or by circulating information informally rather than reporting it to committees. In terms of general information, some reports are inappropriate in content or design to be useful to members of the general public. And there is perhaps too often insufficient explanation about complaints procedures.[98]

Communications

Communication is a prerequisite of participation. It has been described as the 'lifeblood of democracy', as it is a vital element in accountability and control. In its broadest sense, communication between the local authority and the community occurs by way of elections, co-option, political parties, pressure groups, area committees and neighbourhood groups, lobbying, open committee meetings, official notices, the media, letters and direct action. In this section, we are concerned with the latter aspects of communications.

Public relations. Communication is a two-way process: from the local authority to the community and vice-versa. It is commonly referred to as 'public relations', which has been defined as 'the deliberate, planned and sustained effort to establish and maintain mutual understanding between an organization and its public' (Institute of Public Relations). The Maud Committee stated that

Public relations are not just a matter of the mechanics of giving information to the public either through the press or over the radio, but also of individual behaviour and attitudes on the part of all who serve the local authority.[99]

This was endorsed by the Bains Report, which said,

. . . the public have a right to information about the affairs of their local council . . . local authorities should themselves adopt an outgoing and positive attitude to the members of the community which they serve and should provide adequate resources, both finance and staff, to finance this.[100]

Legally, local authorities have long been obliged to make available to the public the minutes of their meetings, an abstract of their accounts, information about their expenditures, certain public notices (road alterations, school closures, etc.) and a substantial amount of information about their planning proposals. In practice, local authorities provide more information than this (though there is considerable variation among them). In the 1970s, there was a significant increase in the number of civic or council-sponsored newspapers,[101] progress reports, open days, exhibitions and councillors' open forums (and in 1981 councils were obliged to publish annual reports). Moreover the number of local authorities appointing a specialist officer – the public relations officer (PRO) – increased from 50 to 200 (with subsequent decline to 160, partly through amalgamations with the post of economic development officer), while over 50 per cent of local authorities now have full-time specialist public relations units (though there appear to be relatively fewer public relations staff in district councils).

Briefly stated, the task of PROs is to supply information to the press and public, to instruct those staff responsible for dealing with the public and to organize open days, tours, exhibitions and displays of local services. They might also be involved in the investigation of complaints and the mounting of local campaigns (such as road safety or 'use your vote'). Some, however, are no more than advertising devices for encouraging industrial development or attracting tourists.

Such developments are advocated as a means of bridging the gap and creating a sense of partnership between the citizen, the elected member and the official. Others have seen it as a means of improving the image of local government, of preventing or remedying misunderstandings, of bringing before the public how much they owe to local government (by way of services) and of encouraging greater interest and participation.

However, many of these initiatives in communication have not been sustained. Some have been abandoned as an economy measure – in 1974 the Local Government Information Office, working on behalf of local government generally, was closed down – and others have become piecemeal exercises instead of being systematic and comprehensive. In many authorities there is a long-standing scepticism about public relations: a feeling that it is a waste of officers' time and the council's money; on the other hand there are officers and members (and perhaps journalists) who dislike the centralizing role of the PRO, whom they feel may 'steal their thunder'; some are also fearful of having more 'open' government.[102] Equally, there are members of the public who suspect that it is only a propaganda exercise (or 'whitewash machine') and that PROs (often ex-journalists) have developed a cosy relationship with the local media, with the latter publicizing the councils' conveniently prepared and predigested statements and other releases.

Meanwhile, under the Local Government, Planning and Land Act 1980, local authorities are obliged to publish more information about rate/tax demands and related financial matters and an annual general (or 'stewardship') report; this was developed in the Local Government Finance Act 1988, which incorporated a 'ready reckoner' (in the form of the 'model' or target community charge) into local authorities' community charge bills. The Local Government (Access to Information) Act 1985 takes this further, though we have noted above its limitations, as does the Local Government and Housing Act 1989, which, apart from its require-ments about the ombudsman's reports, obliges councils to publish information about their unused land (this being based on the register of such land made compulsory under the Local Govern-ment, Planning and Land Act 1980). The Education Act 1980 requires more information (to permit parental choice of schools), and the Local Government Acts 1988 and 1992 involve more publicity for purposes of competitive tendering, though it is evident that some authorities are becoming less open as some aspects of their business become more confidential (to consider tenders etc.). Overall, the aim is to help council-tax payers, electors and councillors make comparisons and judgements on their authority's performance, especially since the publication in 1992 by the Audit Commission of performance indicators for local authorities (see p. 282). However, it is fair to say that some authorities and services have been doing something like this for many years.

The media

The development of local broadcasting has increased the impor-tance of radio and television in the reporting and reflecting of local affairs (including phone-in discussion programmes and the broadcasting of live or recorded extracts from council debates).[103] However, the local press remains the most important communication link between the local authority and the community,[104] four out of five electors being regular readers of local newspapers. (During 1975–85 local radio stations increased from 55 to 113, and free local newspapers from 39 to 344.)

Important as they clearly are, local newspapers have been subject to a number of criticisms. In the first place, they tend to present local government affairs in somewhat raw terms: committee meetings are summarized or extracts are culled from official minutes with little or no attempt to interpret them or place them into a wider context of council policy or community development. Consequently, so many of these items tend to become discrete snippets, devoid both of background or sustained interest.[105] Secondly, it has been argued that the local press (especially the weeklies) tends to create an artificial or distorted image of the locality as being essentially united and at harmony with itself, unaffected by social or political division.[106] On the other hand, the press may go to the other extreme and exaggerate the antagonisms which exist in the council and so understate the consensus which may exist on many issues (in the same way as the national press virtually ignores the work of the all-party committees of Parliament). It has been suggested that the media were a significant element in the public disquiet and unrest over the poll tax.[107]

In general, the local press appears to give local government affairs a low priority, devoting few staff or only more junior staff to its reporting. And there is the temptation to seek reader-appeal by sensationalizing news items: after all, they are profit-seeking enterprises (mainly owned by large national companies), not philanthropic bodies working to promote democracy. However, as some editors recognize, the press does and should have a broadly educational and democratizing role, encouraging and leading an interest in civic affairs, rather than simply following or reflecting it.

However, the press is not altogether to blame, since to a large extent it is dependent on the local council for much of its information on local government matters[108] and it may not wish to jeopardize this relationship by being too critical or incisive in its reporting. The press has to walk something of a narrow path between too cosy, bland and passive a relationship with the local authority and a more critical stance which may result in upset, hostility and a closing up of the channels of communication.* Furthermore, in contrast to national politics there are fewer obvious leaders for the media to focus on in local government. Conversely, there are too many local authorities, so that coverage becomes more diffuse and more superficial. And the national media either report local politics for what they infer is its significance for the national scene or they simply do not report local events. There is no television or radio programme that regularly covers local government issues and only one national newspaper has a Local Government Correspondent.

Councils have been accused of being too secretive:[109] as Barbara Castle explained it, 'The tendency is always for the public to be told too little, not too much, because by their very nature, executives tend to be secretive.'[110]

In her maiden speech to Parliament, Margaret Thatcher introduced a Private Member's Bill which subsequently became the Public Bodies (Admission to Meetings) Act 1960. This clarified and secured the right of admittance of the press and the public to meetings of local authorities. This right was apparently extended by the Local Government Act 1972 (for England and Wales) and 1973 (Scotland) to allow access to committees of local authorities. However, much of the work of local government occurs in subcommittees and there has been considerable doubt and variation of practice concerning the public's right of access to these[111] (see p. 214). Furthermore, the public and press can be excluded from

---

* In 1991 the *Sunday Times*' critical reporting of the way Derbyshire CC dealt with its pension fund led to the paper being sued for libel. In February 1992 the Court of Appeal dismissed the claim and emphasized that criticism of the conduct of authorities should be free.

full council and committee meetings if those bodies go into 'camera' or closed session by passing a resolution that 'publicity would be prejudicial to the public interest by reason of the confidential nature of the business to be transacted or for other special reasons'.[112] As a consequence of taking decisions in private session or at sub-committee level, it may be that the press and public become aware of an issue at a stage too late for them to exercise any influence.

In 1975 the central government showed its concern by issuing a circular to local authorities[113] which emphasizes that ready access to full information about a local authority's activities is essential if democracy is to flourish. It pointed out that the legislation of 1960 and 1972–3 sets out minimum requirements only, and it expressed disappointment at the limited moves by authorities to increase their freedom of information in dealing with the press and public. In particular the circular points out that meetings of sub-committees should be open in the same way as full meetings, and that when matters have to be dealt with at private meetings there should be a full explanation of the reasons for the secrecy. Since then the Government has insisted that local authorities provide much more information about specific aspects of their work, including their finances, schools, housing and direct labour organizations (see p. 385). And more recently we have the Local Government (Access to Information) Act 1985 (see p. 213).

Local authorities have raised strong objections to these impositions as yet another example of central interference (and suggesting that central government should put its own house in order[114]). And yet this greater publicity could be to their advantage: it can provide local authorities with an opportunity to blow their own trumpets, to display their achievements, to show they are giving value for money and to rally public support. In addition, by providing more information, they can give the public greater opportunities for comment and for airing views, and thus perhaps avoid frustration and resentment, and forestall outbursts of protest and various forms of direct action. It may also prevent the media providing only one side of a story and the public being given the wrong impression. This often happens in cases where confidentiality is important (as, for example, when children are taken into care), though in such cases the scope for greater explanation will clearly be limited.

Community politics

Communication is, or should be, a two-way process. Local government should be open to the receipt as well as the delivery of information. In the broadest sense this occurs through elections, pressure groups etc.

How, and how successfully, do local authorities receive the community's messages in the narrower, ordinary sense of the term? Ideally, the councillor is the main channel. But in practice there are severe limitations: there is substantial ignorance, lack of esteem, dissociation and even hostility towards councillors[115] due, in part, to the complexity of the local government system and its greater remoteness since reorganization in 1974–5; not all councillors are open to, or adept at, the constituency or 'tribune' role (see p. 188); and difficulties can arise where the councillor lives outside the area or belongs to the 'wrong' party.

Evidently, people prefer to deal with officers.[116] But there are problems here too: crossing the threshold of the town or county hall, locating the appropriate officer, dealing with receptionists, etc. But in general, the main problem is the citizens' (the amateurs) lack of time, knowledge and resources: the local authority (the professionals) has all three. According to the Parris survey (see p. 431), 50 per cent of people feel too ignorant about the system to know who to complain to. And a further survey (Sobol[117]) showed that a majority thought it not worthwhile complaining. The consequence may be a sullen acceptance of or resignation to council policies. But sometimes frustration breaks out into confrontation and direct action – demonstrations, rent strikes, occupation of nurseries or schools or squatting in houses, disturbing council meetings and inquiries or even rioting.[118]

Such events are no doubt partly a reaction to the current economic situation, with cuts in expenditure following years of growth in services and rising aspirations. In part, too, they may be a result of the quickening in the pace of social change, of urban redevelopment and loss of established communities. But it also reflects a reaction to the growth of government and an apparent lack of receptiveness on the part of the authorities. As the Skeffington Report put it:

In the past, local authorities have been more successful in informing the public than involving them. Publicity is comparatively easy, but effective participation is much more difficult . . . We understand participation to be the act of sharing in the formulation of policies and proposals. Clearly the giving of information by the local authority and of an opportunity to comment on that information is a major part in the process of participation but it is not the whole story. Participation involves doing as well as talking and there will be full participation only where the public are able to take an active part throughout the plan-making process.

The report recommended the creation of greater opportunities for public participation in the planning processes of local government (they were largely enacted in the Town and Country Planning Act 1972). But the results have been disappointing in terms of public response. This may be partly due to the language (or jargon) used by the planners; it may be that the public are unprepared for consultation ('Participation does not come naturally, it has to be learned');[119] there is the suspicion too that the consultation is a sham, that the policy is crystallized and more than half decided, or at least the options (or parameters) have been pre-determined.[120] Consequently public meetings which aim to sound out public feeling often leave the public more confused or frustrated.

It is sometimes suggested that information and consultation are not enough: that real participation calls for real partnership, for the delegation of power to neighbourhoods and groups, for citizen control. The argument thus becomes more obviously about the distribution of power and resources in the community. And if the gulf between the governors and the governed becomes too wide, the latter may turn to direct action.

Consequently a number of other participative devices have been developed or suggested, for example in the Seebohm Report. Apart from the establishment of a variety of advice and aid centres (for such services as housing, planning, education, welfare and litigation) there is the encouragement of active involvement of clients in the provision or management of various services. These include mothers helping in nursery classes or playgroups, residents or members helping to run old people's clubs and homes, and volunteers helping in youth clubs or adventure playgrounds. In the field of education, it is intended that there should be more information and choice of schools, and there has been a significant growth in the number of parent–teacher bodies (PTAs) and of parent representation on school governing bodies.[121] As advocated by the Plowden Report[122] there has been some movement towards the development of 'community education' in which schools and colleges are more open to the general public and become a resource for the wider community rather than exclusively for children between the hours of 9 am and 4 pm. In some areas there have been developments in tenant management of estates or tower blocks (and in some cases the establishment of tenant cooperatives). Recent housing legislation – the 'tenants' charter' (1980) – should provide more such opportunities.[123]

Some of these developments have been quite unofficial and due entirely to local initiative, such as the setting up of action groups to monitor redevelopment or rehabilitation programmes, luncheon clubs, 'good neighbour' schemes or community bus services. They may be purely local or indigenous, or they may be an offshoot from a national organization (such as Shelter or Age Concern). The Seebohm Report drew particular attention to the importance of voluntary organizations in community development work (instancing the community projects taking place in North Kensington in London, Sparkbrook in Birmingham and Toxteth in Liverpool).

Similar developments have been started or encouraged (through cash or equipment) by local authorities, especially in response to the creation of educational priority areas (EPAs) and the urban aid programme.[124] Of particular interest has been the appointment of 'community development officers' (sometimes known as social development or social relations officers). Some are appointed by local authorities or other statutory bodies,[125] and others by voluntary organizations including neighbourhood councils. (Many are self-appointed in that youth workers, adult education organizers, librarians or social workers may develop a strong commitment to the community and adapt their role accordingly – in some cases adopting a radical stance and thus placing themselves and the authority in an awkward position.) Apart from giving information and advice to local residents, their function is to identify the needs and problems of the community and to help to deal with these either by calling on official resources or particularly by encouraging local self-help and initiatives. In this latter sense the community worker is acting as a catalyst.

A more radical approach to community work is being developed in areas such as Walsall and Kirklees through multi-purpose and greatly decentralized 'neighbourhood' – virtually walk-in – housing departments.[126] And a number of social service departments are developing the 'patch' system approach to social work services.[127] The aim is to try to 'de-paternalize' services and make them more a real community resource.

An analysis by John Gyford[128] for the Widdicombe Committee has identified two explanations for this increased activism and participation: (i) a more assertive public, which is less prepared to accept the judgements of local politicians and professionals; and (ii) greater social fragmentation and diversity (as a result of changing employment patterns and composition, significant local ethnic concentrations, changing family formations and more individual or customized consumption behaviour). Together, these have 'produced an increasingly sectionalist politics' and a growth in single-issue politics and pressure-group activity. This in turn has been accommodated (at least to some extent) by more open and accessible procedures – in particular by (a) greater consultation with council tenants (especially following the 1980 Housing Act), with business (following the 1984 Local Government Finance Act), with ethnic minorities (through community relations councils and race relations committees), through the establishment of committees dealing with women's issues, and more general schemes involving area/district consultation meetings, advice centres and community newsletters; and (b) various forms of decentralization such as area committees (as in Tower Hamlets LB), community development projects, neighbourhood management and patch systems outlined above.

Thus 'the history of local government over the past two decades has ... been, in part, one of continuing attempts to supplement the institutions of representative democracy and professional service departments'.[129] Such developments challenge what Professor John Stewart sees as the three traditional or common organizing principles of local government in Britain, i.e. hierarchy, uniformity and functionalism (or departmentalism), and consequently they may meet resistance from chief officers, leading councillors, trade unions and political parties. And some see a risk of these developments going too far, that 'an elaboration of consultative mechanisms somehow devalues and even endangers the traditional institutions of representative democracy itself [since] their existence may ... lead to the establishment of a network of consultations and liaison whose existence is rarely visible to the voters at large' and which increases the complexity of the machinery of government and thus its remoteness.[130]

Most of these initiatives in participation have occurred in urban areas. This is partly because urban community problems are more obvious or overt (though not necessarily greater)[131] than rural ones, and also because communication links are easier. But another reason is that urban areas lack local bodies (local councils) to represent them.

Local councils

In this book the emphasis throughout has been on the so-called 'principal' authorities, the regions, counties and districts. In this section attention is drawn to the more local, grassroots councils. These consist of parishes (in England) or community councils (in Wales and Scotland). In urban areas (formerly boroughs and UDCs) they are usually called 'town' councils (entitling them to a 'town mayor'). Collectively, they are all known as 'local councils' and their interests are promoted by the National Association of Local Councils (NALC), which is a federation of county associations (in England and Wales), and the Association of Larger Local Councils (ALLC).

Under the Local Government Act 1972, parish (or town) councils were formed in England from existing parishes. Elsewhere in England (except London) parish councils would be formed (by order of the Minister) (1) where the population contained 200 or more electors; (2) where there were 150–200 electors and a parish meeting passed a resolution to have a council; or (3) in a parish of under 150 electors if the district council agrees. Where there is a parish or (in 6 per cent of cases) town council, there must be an annual meeting open to all electors. Where there is no council, there must be such a meeting at least twice a year (though quite often in practice this does not happen). The parish meeting may appoint a committee. Altogether there are about 10,200 parishes in England, of which 8,159 have a council (containing over 70,000 councillors), about 150 of which comprise group or joint councils, each administering two or more parishes. Local councils cover 14 million people in England (i.e. about 25 per cent of the population). Parishes are to be found predominantly in rural areas and range widely in area (from a few acres to nearly 100 square miles), in population (from 0 to 40,800) and in resources (from a few pounds to £70,000 in the product of a 1p rate).[132] Over the past 20 years, more 'urban' areas (especially in the freestanding towns, have become parished.

However, there are still few in metropolitan areas, and even in rural England their coverage is not universal.

In 1974, Wales was divided up into communities – about 800 in all – based on previous parishes or (where they were requested) urban districts and boroughs. Under conditions similar to those in England they have formed councils in about 750 of them. In certain areas (the larger urban areas)[133] community councils were not permitted; just as in England, it was felt appropriate that no community (parish) should have normally a population in excess of 20,000 (or 20 per cent of the population of the parent district). As a result only about 300 such councils in England and 90 in Wales were created in urban areas. (No parishes were allowed in London.)

The boundaries, status and electoral arrangements of these local councils are likely to change (marginally) as they are subject to review. This is the responsibility of the district councils, who must channel their recommendations through the Local Government Boundary Commission (see p. 51) to the Secretary of State, who makes the final decisions. (In Wales the initial community review is being undertaken by the Commission itself.) In addition, in England it is the district council which determines the number of councillors on a parish council (though the minimum must be five) and (both in England and Wales) the district council has the power to co-opt members on to the parish or community council where they are seriously deficient.

Parish and community council elections take place every four years, the most proximate being in 1995. Councillors are bound by the same conditions (in terms of qualifications, disclosure of interests, etc.) as those in principal authorities, though not subject to the jurisdiction of the local ombudsmen, and they may claim attendance allowances. Interest in becoming a parish councillor has increased over the past twenty-five years, and this is reflected in the higher number of contested elections.[134] The councils themselves feel their role as the voice of their communities is enhanced by the fact that they operate independently of party politics, though some are accused of being somewhat 'cliquish'.[135]

The functions of local councils are broadly four-fold: Firstly, they provide certain services (playing fields, community halls, bus shelters, etc. – see Appendix 10), many of which are run concurrently with the district council. Secondly, they have the power to spend the 'free resource' (or 'free 2p'; see p. 76). Thirdly, they must be consulted about certain matters (such as footpath surveys by the county council and the appointment of governors to local primary schools) and they must be notified by the district council about certain other matters (including local planning applications, particular by-laws, etc.). Fourthly, and perhaps above all, their function is to act as a forum for the discussion of local affairs and to represent the interests of the local community to the district council and other local and national bodies generally. In 1980, this latter function was graphically illustrated in a number of parishes in East Anglia, such as Brandon and Thetford, when under Schedule 12 of the Local Government Act 1972 they conducted local referendums (see footnote p. 457) on the siting of American 'cruise' missiles in their area. A current issue is the opting out of hospitals and schools. For all of these purposes, local councils have the power to precept (see p. 317) upon the district council (the authority responsible for collecting the council tax). For figures see Appendix 11. It may be noted that there are some misgivings at the limited degree of financial accountability of local councils.[136]

The total revenue expenditure of parish councils in England is £108 million (in 1990). An estimated 26,400 people work for these local councils, one third of them on a voluntary basis. Of the remainder who are paid, only 7 per cent are full-time paid staff.[137]

As part of the reorganization process in England, the role and structure (including elections and finance) of local councils is being reviewed, and to this end, a consultation document was issued in 1991. This raised the question of parishes having an enhanced role. This idea has been endorsed by the ACC and ADC as well as by the local councils themselves – especially in relation to their representational role and in the field of planning, highways and environmental powers. But a significant number of local councils stated they neither wished nor were able to take on primary responsibility for such functions. However, in the meantime, district and (especially) county councils have been considering or implementing schemes to devolve more of their responsibilities to local councils, involving such services as libraries, youth services, nursery and community education and the management of schools (the latter being especially significant where closure is threatened). Such a development is partly an aspect of decentralization (or 'subsidiarity') and 'getting closer to the customer' and partly an anticipation of reorganization so that unitary authorities can avoid seeming too large and remote.

The Local Government (Scotland) Act 1973 set up a totally different kind of community council system in Scotland. Although the community councils here have a statutory existence, they do not really form local authorities, since they have no statutory powers or any access, as of right, to public funds.

Initially the Scottish district and island councils were required to consult the public in their areas, then draft schemes for the creation of community councils (which were then submitted to the Secretary of State for Scotland for approval). Fifty-six such schemes have been approved, covering all fifty-three districts and three islands. As in England and Wales, there is considerable variation in the population coverage of the councils: most (75 per cent) have populations of under 5,000 (and 30 per cent have under 1,000), but twenty councils (in the cities) have populations of over 20,000. The schemes also vary in other respects – frequency of meetings and of elections, qualifications of candidates and of electors, methods of balloting, etc.

The schemes also laid down certain conditions for the creation of the councils: at least twenty electors must sign a requisition for elections to be held, and usually a minimum number of candidates must stand. Since the schemes provide for (potentially) 1,343 community councils, some 15,300 councillors are required (in effect, 1 for every 340 people in Scotland). This is in contrast to the 1,600 councillors in the principal councils. It presents a tall order and provides a sure test of community commitment. In practice, the response has been sufficient for 85 to 90 per cent of the proposed councils to have been successfully formed, though in most cases there have not been enough candidates to hold elections and only about one quarter of the council seats have been contested.[138]

According to the legislation, the general purpose of the community councils is:

to ascertain, coordinate and express to the local authorities for its area, and to the public authorities, the views of the community which it represents, in relation to matters for which those authorities are responsible, and to take such action in the interests of that community as appears to it to be expedient and practicable.[139]

For these purposes, the regional, island and district councils are empowered to provide the community councils with finance and other assistance such as may be agreed between them.

The community councils in Scotland, like the local councils in England and Wales, are intended to be broadly based organizations of official standing with which local communities as a whole can identify and through which they can speak and act. Unlike those in England and Wales, they are not a third tier of local government: 'their purpose being to complement local government, not compete with it'.[140] They have the important job of assessing and expressing local opinion, thus bringing to the attention of local authorities and other public bodies any matters of concern to their particular locality. In addition they can collaborate with local authorities in the organization and management of local facilities and services, and initiate community projects. It is a novel scheme in terms of public participation, and one which would, at least in the short term, appeal to many people in (urban) England who feel relatively deprived of a 'voice' at local level.

In 1992 the Government published a consultative document, The Role of Parish and Town Councils in England, which invited views on how they may become more effective as representatives of their communities. In 1993, the Government announced that it felt it inappropriate to enlarge their area of responsibility. But, in view of the reorganization of local government in England, many county and district councils have developed schemes for devolving more functions to local councils (e.g. on an agency basis, for such matters as local planning decisions, village schools, rights of way and minor highways).

Neighbourhood councils

The Royal Commissions in 1969 on local government in England and Scotland each emphasized the necessity of local councils both to provide certain services and to represent the wishes of the inhabitants on matters that affect the local community. These roles were seen as crucial in view of the substantial reduction in the number of councils and councillors which would result from their proposals.

As we have seen, local councils have been established (or re-established) throughout much of Britain. However, in England the local councils predominate in the rural areas and the smaller towns. Very few exist in the large urban areas (e.g. there are two in Manchester and they are not legally permissible in Greater London) with the result that 75 per cent of the population of England live in 'unparished' areas. (In March 1990 Simon Hughes MP introduced a Bill to allow parish councils in London, unsuccessfully.) A further anomaly is that within the same district council some areas are entitled to have a local council while others are not. Consequently, there is strong pressure from many groups in the community for an extension of local councils to the urban, especially metropolitan, areas. This may occur naturally, as districts undertake their parish review (see p. 448). However, such an extension may meet resistance from many existing councillors, partly on the grounds that it would involve a further upheaval in local government so soon after the reorganization of 1974. There may also be opposition (as indeed there has been) arising from the fear of party political rivalry.

In the meantime an alternative is being pursued in the form of 'neighbourhood councils', otherwise known as 'urban parish councils'. These are non-statutory bodies which 'belong to the underworld of local government'.[141] They are based, as the name implies, on a neighbourhood of about 10,000 people (though ranging from under 3,000 to over 20,000). Their existence predates reorganization and they are often the product of local community issues and local action groups which sprang up in response to those issues (see below). They received added impetus from the reorganization of local government, with its creation of larger and what many feel to be remoter forms of local authority.

The Government in the mid 1970s considered giving them statutory status, and has sought mildly to encourage their formation.[142] The Association for Neighbourhood Councils (ANC), a pressure group founded in 1970, has as its principal object the general introduction of neighbourhood councils on a statutory basis[143] in order to give them stability and status (credibility), and also to avoid the possible unrepresentative nature of voluntary groupings. The ANC (in contrast to the Scottish community councils) also wishes to see neighbourhood councils with financial independence (that is, with the right to precept on the rating authorities) and the power to provide certain services and amenities. The ANC publishes a monthly magazine, *Anchor*.

There were 150 neighbourhood councils in 1975 when hopes were high of statutory recognition. But their numbers have dwindled as they lost heart or won recognition as parish/town councils (and host district councils have not always encouraged them). Because they are non-statutory, their size, finance, form and purposes vary considerably.[144] But typically a neighbourhood council has the following objectives: (1) to represent to other organizations (such as government departments, local authorities, public corporations and local industry) the needs and wishes of the local community. In this respect it will act as the 'ears, eyes and mouth' of the community on all aspects of community development. It may campaign for local amenities such as sports facilities, a shopping area, a play space or a community hall; or it may try to protect the local environment by scrutinizing local development plans or raising questions about derelict land or empty properties in the area; (2) to organize or stimulate self-help within the local community in order to improve the quality of life for the residents as a whole. This may include the clearing of dumped material from derelict sites, helping to set up holiday play schemes or 'good neighbour' arrangements; (3) to help those in the community in need of special facilities by providing services and amenities (such as voluntary playgroups, school crossings or youth clubs) and providing advisory services (such as 'problem shops'); (4) to foster or preserve community spirit or identity, and help to create a sense of community responsibility among residents. In other words, the neighbourhood councils may perform roles which are part social and part political. As regards the latter, this does not seem either in practice[145] or in theory[146] to imply party politics.

Neighbourhood councils are potentially an important development in local government. Like the statutory parish and community councils they provide a 'voice for the neighbourhood'. Research has shown that most people identify with, or are conscious of belonging to, a definable area known as the 'home area'.[147] Local councils and neighbourhood councils cover such areas. And, being so local, these councils should be more accessible to the community and their members less anonymous than most councils, boards and commissions. Some people even envisage the development of sub-units based on groups of streets.

The Chairman of the National Consumer Council has spoken[148] of the 'smouldering discontent' among consumers over public services, and how for many people 'life involved banging their heads against the brick wall of bureaucracy'. In this context there is 'a very high level of unhappiness' with the attitudes of council staff. (In August 1991, the NCC found 40–49 per cent of people were fairly or very satisfied with their council. The figure for British Rail was 51 per cent.) Such public feelings are dangerous at a time of mounting unemployment and simmering unease. He advised making public services more accountable to the public they serve by establishing and publicizing adequate complaints and redress systems. A similar warning that 'the monster machine of local government' needs to be geared to the real day-to-day needs of individual people has been expressed by the president of the Association of Directors of Social Services.[149] Neighbourhood councils can play a vital part in this.

We must, however, beware of over-stating their value, actual or potential. There is the danger that yet another council will confuse people or dilute their loyalties to existing local authorities. If they are to be a genuine and effective vehicle for the expression of community or grassroots feeling, they must not become or *appear* to become too formal, bureaucratic or cliquish. Some people may be put off if they see the council becoming too much a part of 'the establishment' and the machinery of consensus politics. Democratic structures do not necessarily pass power over to the people, but too often the power falls into the hands of small groups adroit at committee work (which is essentially a minority skill and interest).

Apart from elections therefore, there must be regular open meetings, newsletters, questionnaires and other means of allowing individuals to express opinions and raise questions – questions which might otherwise go by default because the individual feels overawed, powerless or bemused, or because he or she feels that the matter may be regarded as too petty. Like a speck of dust in the eye, seemingly small matters – litter, dogs, traffic, trees, transport – can loom large in the life of an individual or a small community. Over the past 20 years, local Liberal parties have built up strong support through their policy of taking a deliberate interest in such matters, including broken pavements – hence the term 'pavement (or community) politics'.[150] (During their brief period of political control in Islington in 1982, it was the SDP which initiated an opinion survey of public attitudes to that council and its services.)

Maintaining open channels of communication with the whole community, the neighbourhood and local councils can encourage the 'non-joiners' to participate, and this may be especially important in the inner-city areas. In this way, these councils can put community politics on a more regular basis by enabling ordinary people to band together to exert some influence on the decisions being made every day in town halls, government departments and company offices – decisions which may vitally affect their (our) lives.* This is increasingly important as the scale and penetration of these decisions increase. The neighbourhood and other local councils, in acting both as 'watchdogs' and 'caretakers', can be a means of fusing or combining the old concept of representative democracy with the newer and particularly urban concept of participatory democracy.

---

* A parish poll may be called to put a referendum question (i) by six electors signing a letter to the Parish/Town Clerk to call the necessary initial special meeting, or (ii) at the request of ten electors at the annual meeting.

14. Into the Nineties: Managing (More) Change

Local government is part of the 'body politic' and as such it is in a state of continuous change and development. It has its critics – what social institution has not? In an educated, democratic society criticism is to be expected and welcomed, especially where it is constructive. Consequently, there are many opinions about the shape and direction that local government should take as we approach the twenty-first century.

Firstly, there is the question of structure. The reorganization in 1972 (England and Wales) and 1973 (Scotland) created much dissent and left many elements disgruntled, though a new revision was out of the question in the 1970s. However, there was some (actual or proposed) change by stealth, involving the reallocation or readjustment of functions among local authorities. There was the Labour Government's plan for 'Organic Change' in 1979 (see p. 64) which sought to restore to a number of district borough councils the responsibilities they had previously enjoyed as county boroughs. Under the Local Government, Planning and Land Act 1980, certain planning functions were removed from the counties and consolidated into the districts. There has been a similar rationalization of concurrent functions under the Local Government and Planning (Scotland) Act 1982 (which followed the Stodart Report, though no significant change has resulted from the Montgomery Report – see p. 70 above). There were (1990) plans to change responsibilities for planning and for waste disposal and, in Wales, for libraries. More generally, both the Labour and the Liberal Democratic parties advocate the abolition of the *ultra vires* rules, and propose that councils have 'general competence' powers (see p. 77).[1]

In the 1980s, both the Labour and the Social/Liberal Democrat parties developed policies for a more substantial restructuring of local government. Both opposition parties propose a regional tier of government (with the Labour Party also reviving plans for devolution to Scotland), and a single-tier system of 'unitary' authorities based broadly on enlarged districts. This gained increasingly widespread support (including that of many Conservatives who wished to simplify accountability for the community charge). But if any of these parties win power at Westminster, such changes are unlikely to be pursued in their first term of office: they would have more pressing claims to their attention. Meanwhile, the Conservative Government (in power continuously since 1979) implemented a major reorganization in 1986 through the abolition of the metropolitan counties and the GLC, with their functions transferring to appropriate district/borough councils or to *ad hoc* joint boards. It was argued by the Government that changed circumstances and practical experience had revealed these top-tier authorities to be unnecessary and wasteful[2] (see pp. 57, 105, 119); they had also been Labour-controlled – often stridently so – since 1980–81. Opposition parties have criticized this hastily devised restructuring and have promised at least to restore a London-wide body.

The abolition of the metropolitan county councils threw into greater relief the contrasting (and many would say illogical) status and role of boroughs such as Barnsley, Kirklees, Tameside or Doncaster and such comparable (but relatively functionless) cities such as Bristol, Nottingham, Hull, Plymouth and Southampton. This has been compounded by the abolition of the ILEA (under the 1988 Education Reform Act) and the transfer of its functions to the inner London boroughs, whose populations are often smaller than many non-metropolitan boroughs (such as Bristol etc., above). Meanwhile, in Scotland, there appears to be a growing consensus for the abolition of the regions. Consequently, as we have seen above (p. 60), the Government has inaugurated a full-scale review of the structure of local government in England, Wales and Scotland. For Wales and Scotland the Government has issued clear proposals for restructuring (see pp. 60 and 70) in two White Papers in 1993, subsequently presented to Parliament as the Local Government (Wales) Bill and the Local Government etc. (Scotland) Bill. Both sets of proposals endorse the unitary/single-tier principle and they have found widespread support. However, there has been dissent and criticism locally and nationally, especially in the opposition parties who, regarding Scotland, have accused the Government of gerrymandering, i.e. drawing the boundaries to suit its own electoral advantage. The objections are sufficient for the new structures to be subject to further review and reorganization, though probably on a local and piecemeal scale.

For English local authorities in the shire county areas, uncertainty and anxiety will continue for many months as the Local Government Commission continues its programme of review and reporting (see p. 60). Though there are exceptions (such as Lincolnshire and Gloucester, where the continuation of a two-tier structure has been recommended), the first reports of the LGC have broadly adopted the unitary approach.

In the end, in each case, the outcome will depend on the view taken by the Secretary of State (and Parliament). Clearly, the unitary/single-tier structure is the most likely: for the Government it would appear to save money (though perhaps not immediately) and it would represent a simplification, clearer accountability and a rationalization as a consequence of local authorities' loss of responsibility, with council houses being sold or transferred, schools opting to become grant-maintained, colleges becoming independent corporations, and services being provided under contract by private and voluntary bodies. However, if a unitary system is to be established, it must seek to avoid the situation created in the metropolitan areas, with numerous semi-elected, confusing and unpopular ad hoc bodies.

Secondly, local authorities are still trying to settle their own internal procedures and structures of committees, 'cabinets' and departments,[3] and the appointment and role of their officers. A number of councils are breaking out from the Bains pattern of management by dispensing with the post of chief executive (in some cases by amalgamating it with the treasurer's or by operating at the top with a small corporate team of chief officers); by revising (often reducing) their committees and committee roles (such as separating service-based, decision-making and relatively routine-dominated committees from more open, non-decision-making committees that review and explore policy and strategy, or deal with general (or 'horizontal') issues through area, health, or women's committees etc.); and by amalgamating departments (such as housing and social services or architect's, valuation and estates). Local authorities are being driven (by CCT, LMS, opting out, etc.) or are being encouraged (by the Government, the Audit Commission, the LGMB, etc.) to reconsider the way they go about their business. Consequently, there is considerable movement and diversity among councils in their internal arrangements.[4]

Some of these developments are impacting upon the operation of corporate management (at least in England and Wales),[5] but more significant is the effect of competitive tendering and contracting out, which is leading to many authorities establishing separate boards to oversee their direct service organizations. In so far as councils thus become both client and contractor/provider there is particular concern at the operation of their central departments (finance, legal, personnel, etc.) whose efficiency, speed and costs will affect the ability of the in-house departments to compete and win contracts; in some cases, these functions could be taken over by the service department itself or even bought in from outside.

Furthermore, with the introduction (in 1974–5) of payments to councillors (for attendance at meetings, for special responsibilities and, now, flat-rate payments for all members), the full-time local politician (an estimated hundred or so in 1990, mainly Labour) may become more widespread (as in Sweden). Some would argue that such a development is long overdue, since British local authorities are of a generally higher average size than in most

European and North American countries, and their budgets exceed those of a number of independent sovereign states. Also, elected members are having to become semi-business managers and develop a familiarity with the complexities of the local authority financial system (grants, multipliers, indicators, etc.) and elements of financial management (performance measures, zero-base budgeting, etc.). One further consequence will be the increased need to develop different links between members and officers (and a clearer understanding of their respective roles).

Away from the policy area, there are developments in service delivery, with decentralization and community-based administration. There is more devolution of management responsibility to the point of service provision (residential homes, leisure centres, etc.) – now compulsory in the case of schools and colleges (under the Education Reform Act 1988) in the form of the local management of schools (LMS; otherwise known as budget delegation or local financial management. LEAs must delegate 85 per cent of the education budget to schools). As a result, there is a need for clarification of policy and specification of what managers are expected to achieve and with what resources, as well as appraisal or review of performance (upon which pay and renewal of contract of employment may depend). A further consequence of such accountable-management developments (or 'Volvo-ization') is the reorganization of individual departments, often involving shortened hierarchies. Some have developed market or commercial methods internally, so that service departments 'buy' (through charges) central support services (management, legal, training, computing). There is also a growth in schemes of partnership with private sector business (e.g. for housing, leisure or sports facilities), and for inner-city development. Contracting out ('outsourcing' or 'externalization') is increasing and extending (as contract management) into areas such as the management of welfare homes or the collection of the council tax. And in response to competitive tendering, councils have appointed Directors of Contract Services or created their own companies or semi-autonomous trusts, and there have been employee/management buy-outs (MBOs). In these circumstances the local authority becomes the 'client', which 'buys' services from its own direct service organization (DSO, where the function is kept in-house) or from outside sources. Thus it is suggested that 'compulsory tendering is arguably the most important influence this century on local authorities and the way they operate.'[6] As a consequence, the local authority 'becomes more service-orientated, consumer- and client-led and sharper in its objectives of serving the public'.[7]

The purpose of such developments is to improve economy, efficiency and effectiveness, through more flexible and quicker response and through greater commitment, as managers 'own' the decisions and priorities because they have determined them (within the limits set down); thus they can exercise judgement, initiative and enterprise. But equally important is the political purpose: empowerment. This means greater access, accountability and control by the community (as clients, consumers or users of services), and it is achieved (alongside the neighbourhood or area offices, multi-service centres or 'one-stop shops', 'patch' social work and neighbourhood repair teams, etc.) by means of neighbourhood or area committees, local forums, user-group control or management participation (e.g. tenants, residents or users of leisure facilities). A survey by INLOGOV[8] shows a doubling (from 9 to nearly 20 per cent) in the number of councils using neighbourhood service outlets between 1980 and 1988 (especially in metropolitan authorities). The same survey showed that over 25 per cent had established a system of devolved budgetary control – again double the 1980 figure – and another study concludes, 'Our analysis suggests that decentralisation (broadly defined), far from being a passing fad, can be shown to be a deep-seated trend in the development of the social and economic organization of western democracies which will be of major significance in the 1990s and beyond.'[9] Clearly, in contrast to the recent past, small, not big, is beautiful – although some people are concerned at the cost and others fear for corporate management and coordination of services and unequal treatment/provision (which may be compounded by the quest for local authorities to become 'enablers'; see below).

There are a number of forces ('change drivers') affecting all local authorites – government policies on competition or on 'citizens' charters' and customer care, the impending reorganization of structure, the emergence of corporate issues (such as economic development or environmental policy), the increasing impact of the European Community, new ideas about management and public-service delivery (e.g. performance-related pay, fixed-term contracts of employment, partnerships with other agencies, user-participation and forums) and changing public expectations. Clearly councils have not all responded to these pressures in the same way or to the same extent. A number of authorities take a positive approach to change and are, in the process, helping to 'reinvent' our system of local government. One recent survey by the Local Government Management Board identifies 'leading edge' or pro-active authorities who have recognized the need to develop a capacity to manage change:

Leading-edge authorities embrace the concept of strategic management the better to manage change. Their organizational and management structures recognize the integrated nature of many of the functions they perform. They set up working parties to examine specific issues which are seen to require a corporate approach. Middle-rank officers orchestrate networks across departments. The role of the elected member and the nature of political management assumes a different form ... Formal committee processes are slimmed down in favour of strategy groups and ad hoc working parties, while small groups of prominent members act as custodians of the authority's values and strategic purposes ... They take seriously the dialogue with local residents and service users ... and seek to work ... with other agencies in the public, private and voluntary sectors.[10]

On the other hand, 'many authorites seek to avoid wholesale change. They tackle issues incrementally ... In more than half of all authorities, members were seen as reluctant to respond to change or not fully aware of the pressures.' Thus, for example, only one authority in five has an authority-wide policy on Europe and only a quarter have put their chief officers on a fixed-term contract or performance-related pay.

Overall, however, the impressions from the LGMB survey are 'of sustained rapid change, and of a cumulative impact powerful enough to transform the operations of the local authority ... [amounting to] a transformation of local governance and of local government management', with, for example, almost half of authorities having recast their departments under pressure of the competition requirements and having altered the relationship between their central departments and those providing services to the public. Moreover, four out of five have cut their subcommittees and slimmed down their management team; four out of five now frame 'mission statements' and have put in place arrangements for performance review; a third of authorities have created special posts in strategic management and an authority-wide policy on quality (with a further 40 per cent actively preparing the latter). Two thirds of authorities have revised their structures in the last three years. One of the consequences of these (and other) changes has been to increase staff (and member) turnover, especially among chief officers. In the past four years twenty-three out of thirty-three London chief executives have changed; in the metropolitan boroughs the figure is twenty-one out of thirty-six. Whilst this may be a cause for concern, there is also evidence of gain, in that 'the new ranks of chief executive are certainly more attuned to the new agenda' of putting client needs first and developing new ways of delivering services.[11]

These developments both reflect and propel the new 'managerial revolution' in the public and private sectors. And a recent report on change, drawing on interviews with chief executives, concludes, 'If chief executives have got it right, local government faces more of the same over the next three years.'[12]

Thirdly, whilst party politics are providing a motive force for some of these reassessments, the local party system is itself experiencing important changes. In the last twenty years party politics have obtruded into more council chambers (see Table 9), especially in urban areas.[13] One consequence of this has apparently been the reduction of the number of uncontested seats (e.g., in English county councils, the figures have fallen from 376 in 1977 to sixty-three in 1981 and a mere thirty-three in 1985). Since 1981, we have seen the emergence of the Social Democratic Party which has sought, in alliance with the Liberals, to 'break the mould' of British politics. They have scored some notable election successes (described as 'political earthquakes'), and their achievements at local level have been impressive. In 1981 they had nine council members: in 1986 they had 420 and over 1,000 Alliance (i.e. Social Democrat or Liberal) councillors. Thereafter their fortunes in national politics declined and the two parties subsequently merged (in 1987) to form the Liberal Democrats. Altogether, over the past fifteen years, the tally of Liberal Democrat councillors has increased more than four-fold, so that today there are some 4,500 Liberal Democrat councillors. They now (1993) dominate and run fifty-three councils and either run or share power in more than a quarter of all councils. Their success has led to an increase in the number of balanced or 'hung' councils (where there is no overall control by any one party; see pp. 149, 159). Thus, for example, in 1977 there were five hung counties; in 1989 there were fourteen and in 1993 there were twenty-seven (out of forty-seven).

Meanwhile the Conservatives have had very mixed fortunes. For example, in 1989 they regained control of nine counties, and in 1992 they had (outside London) their best results since 1977. But 1993 was calamitous as they lost control of sixteen county councils (losing 500 seats) and leaving them with control of just one (Berkshire). For its part, after a succession of defeats in general elections, the Labour Party has reviewed its policies and drawn back from its earlier left-wing inclination: the moderates have regained the ascendancy and seek to restore the party's election chances locally and nationally (although 1992 gave the party its worst results for ten years). For a time in the 1980s the Green Party seemed to be making something of a breakthrough into local politics, but their popularity has waned, probably as a result of the economic recession. All such developments have important consequences for the organization and management of local authorities.[14]

Of equal significance, however, are the changing trends *within* the major parties. In the 1970s and 1980s they became more polarized and assertive than they had been for over thirty years.[15] This is partly because, under Mrs Thatcher, the Conservatives espoused the ideology (otherwise known as 'conviction politics' and the 'resolute approach') of monetarism, i.e. deflation through sustained reductions in public sector expenditure (a policy somewhat moderated under John Major). Partly as a reaction to this, Labour moved to the left and proposed to institute a much more planned economy. It has been suggested that Labour changed as a result of having lost the 1979 election on a weak socialist programme and performance in office (1974–9). But it might equally well be contended that the composition of the parties is changing, with the replacement of the traditional upper-class dominance of the Conservatives by the new forces of a radical, thrusting, individualist middle class; whilst in the Labour party, the traditional trade union, working-class dominance is being displaced by the more radical, egalitarian and intellectual middle-class activists.[16] Voters witnessed the results of these latter changes in the 'de-selection' by local Labour parties of some long-standing and moderate councillors. The councils became more involved in national and international issues, with local authorities declaring themselves 'nuclear-free zones' (seeking to ban the deployment of nuclear weapons or the transportation of nuclear waste), calling for boycotts of South African products and investments or holding controversial talks with Provisional Sinn Fein.[17] Whether Labour's recent more moderate stance will de-radicalize such local activities remains to be seen. But more generally, the importance of party politics has become more evident in the past year or two with the increased attention paid by councils (LEAs) to their party representation on school governing bodies.

Officers too are feeling the effects of the more ubiquitous and committed party politics: not only is their professional advice being spurned* or challenged (perhaps on the counter-advice of 'imported' party advisers) but so too (as we saw on p. 287) is their impartial selection and tenure[18] – though some officers themselves have enthusiastically embraced the party commitment, and (in contrast to civil servants) have sought to combine the dual roles of officer and member.[19] As we have seen above (pp. 167, 261) such 'twin-tracking' and other political activity is (under the 1989 Local Government and Housing Act) now prohibited for senior officers. And the combination of tight budgets, assertive party politics, current destabilized conventions,[20] government policies (e.g. on education, housing or CCT) and seemingly perpetual change has caused many senior staff to seek jobs outside local government, or early retirement.[21] While government policies may be causing some officers to leave, others are developing a more openly critical, though not necessarily party political, stance,[22] and some have been encouraged to do so by their professional body.[23]

Fourthly, voters in the 1990s may find a change in the electoral system – to a system of proportional representation (as in Northern Ireland's local government). This is promised not only by the Liberal Democrats should they gain a bargaining position at Westminster, but also by 'Charter 88', a cross-party and non-party movement which seeks to promote social and political rights and freedoms in Britain. There is also considerable public

* Party extremism of the urban Left (the 'loony Left') is mirrored in some councils by the new (or 'raving') Right. One chief officer (in charge of the sale of Westminster's cemeteries in 1988) has declared that, 'I've never had to work in a climate like I worked here – ever, and I've dealt with some pretty difficult Socialist councils before I came here . . . If you put any opposition up, you were either "not one of them", you were opposed to them politically, or you were "negative".' (BBC, *Panorama*, 20 July 1989.) Westminster LB council underwent a special inquiry by the District Auditor and the cemetery sale was subsequently declared unlawful. This council is currently subject to a further inquiry into its alleged manipulation (under the policy known as 'Building Stable Communities') of council house sales to engineer the location of Tory-inclined voters into key marginal wards.

support for such a system, as well as increased interest from the Labour Party.[24] Meanwhile, Labour is in favour of annual elections (the 'thirds' system) for all councils.

It is widely known that the national political scene dominates local election results (see p. 165). Yet there is evidence to show that local factors (issues, personalities, cultures, traditions, etc.) continue to play a significant role in local voting decisions (see p. 167) as revealed by differential trends and patterns (e.g. why there are so few Labour MPs in the south, apart from London, and yet Labour controls so many large towns in that region). This may be increasingly the case insofar as the single-tier structure is adopted to clarify accountability (see p. 62).

The fifth and most crucial area of change or contention in local government is finance. Until recently, local government expenditure increased as a result of new responsibilities (such as community care), improved service standards (e.g. homes for the disabled) and dealing with problems whose scale is growing (such as crime, urban de-industrialization and environmental decay). The problems continue: a growing elderly population, mounting unemployment and increasing obsolescence of capital, buildings, sewerage, etc. In February 1990 the Audit Commission referred to a 'maintenance time bomb' for schools. Local authorities are finding it difficult to cope: they are experiencing 'resource squeeze' and 'fiscal stress'[25] because owing to irregular revaluations rates have lacked buoyancy (see p. 177), and because of reductions in government grant (from 66 per cent in 1976 to 45 per cent in 1989, though grants have since increased; see p. 309).

One strategy which is being developed to save or reallocate resources is 'privatization'. This may take the form of total withdrawal of council provision and the transfer of a service to the private sector (e.g. sports facilities) or to individuals (e.g. selling council houses); or it may involve joint provision of a service with a voluntary or private agency (e.g. homes for the elderly). But most commonly, it consists of competitive tendering by local business and the council's own workforce (or 'direct labour organization') and 'contracting out' council services to private firms or voluntary organizations where it is appropriate (i.e. cheaper). These services may be for the public, e.g. refuse collection (whose privatization was pioneered in 1981 by Southend council) or for the local authority itself (such as legal services, auditing, management consultancy, etc.). Such practices are by no means new: local authorities have long engaged private firms for such things as architecture, building, engineering, industrial waste disposal, school transport, etc. The main advantage of the arrangement is a possible lowering of costs, easier budgeting (with fixed-price contracts) and flexibility for work involving irregular work flows. But critics are fearful of a lowering of standards, of redundancies, of loss of service (through bankruptcies), or being held to ransom over subsequent charges, and above all of the adequacy of control and accountability; there are also doubts about the possible savings to be gained.[26] In 1989 it was estimated that 213 local authorities had contracted out at least one service (40 per cent of refuse and cleaning in London), and the estimated annual savings were £42 million.[27] However, by 1993, only an estimated 17 per cent of the value of contracts had been won by the private sector, and in the area of building cleaning, for example, local authority workforces retain 62 per cent of the contracts.[28]

It has become an issue today because it is being pressed on local authorities by the Conservative central government, who believe it is reducing local authority costs by some 6·5 per cent. Under the Local Government, Planning and Land Act 1980 and the Local Government Act 1988, local authorities must put certain services out to tender and councils must report every six months on the award of contracts. Under the Local Government Act 1992, 'white collar' functions are being put out to tender, with more in prospect.

While councils' own workforces (direct labour or service organizations – DLOs or DSOs) may be awarded contracts (perhaps on condition that they achieve certain rates of return on capital invested and that they publish details of their work and costings),

DLOs may not normally compete for work outside the local authority[29] – even for other councils, so declared the Audit Commission in 1991.

Some councils are allegedly obstructing competitive tendering by demanding excessive performance bonds with unreasonable penalties, time limits or documentation. And others have sought to counter privatization (as well as promote their own social policies such as equal opportunities) by 'contract compliance', i.e. insisting that private firms that have contracts with the council observe certain non-commercial considerations and fulfil stringent conditions regarding health and safety, trade union recognition, fair wages, and the employment of women, immigrants and the handicapped. For example, before abolition, the GLC had contracts worth some £200 million, and nineteen firms were refused business on grounds of alleged discrimination, compared with 130 firms which did comply with the employment practices requirements. Such requirements have now been strictly limited under the Local Government Act 1988, and under the Local Government Act 1992 the Minister has the power to define and forbid anti-competitive behaviour. An alternative strategy in some councils has been to set up 'enterprise boards' (such as Greater London Enterprise, Merseyside Enterprise Board, Lancashire Enterprises Ltd, West Midlands Enterprise Board, West Yorkshire Enterprise Board), to establish or invest in local companies for the purpose of control, to secure local employment and economic growth, as well as providing income. These boards are free of some of the legal constraints which apply to a local authority, though the Local Government and Housing Act 1989 limits the powers of such companies in which local authorities have an interest.

One uncertainty casting a shadow over the policy of competitive tendering and the contracting out of services is that of European law in relation to contracts of employment. Under EC law (Acquired Rights) directive 1977 – the Transfer of Undertakings (Protection of Employment) Regulations 1981 (Acquired Rights) directive, or 'TUPE' – where an undertaking is transferred to another employer, existing employment conditions are also transferred. There have been a number of cases which have gone before industrial tribunals or the employment appeals tribunal (EAT) whereby public sector workers have claimed unfair or illegal loss of employment or pay/pensions as a result of contracts being awarded to private companies. The most celebrated case, in August 1993, was that of the successful Eastbourne dustmen, who had been made redundant when their council's cleansing contract was privatized in 1990. But there have been other cases that have gone against the employees and their unions, and the legal situation remains unclear. Individual cases may turn on the details of the actual procedure involved at the time of the transfer. The general principle hinges on the definition of 'undertaking' (whether it must include premises, goodwill, etc.) and the extent to which it may be deemed to be commercial in nature. The position is likely to remain unsatisfactory until there is a definitive ruling in the European court, and in the meantime TUPE is likely to deter many private contractors from getting involved in council-service provision.

Whatever the outcome, the overall savings from privatization will not be sufficient to free local authorities from dependence on central grants. And such grants provide a means if not a motive for central control.

Central–local government relations should be seen as a major constitutional issue for the 1990s, as it was for the 1980s. It raises fundamental questions about the place of local government in Britain, accountability and the clash of democratic mandates, and the future of Britain as a liberal–democratic state.

The problem has always existed because there is no clear statement of what the relationship is or should be. Britain has no written or codified constitution and, like so much else in our governmental system, the relationship of local government to central government is left to general understandings or conventions, usually characterized as partnership, cooperation or power-sharing. It is often held that in the course of this century, local government has been increasingly subject to central control.

This is difficult to evaluate – like the alleged fall in standards of education or morality, measures are difficult to agree or calibrate. But there is now widespread agreement that the longstanding consensus or concordat between central and local government has been broken in recent years – especially since the advent of Conservative rule in 1979.

It may be suggested that in the period of economic growth (up to the 1970s) local and central government enjoyed an easy-going relationship of incremental growth based on a perception of common interests. (Local government expenditure in real terms increased by 3·5 per cent per annum in the 1960s and 1970s; since 1979 it has been under 1 per cent.) When this growth faltered, the strains began to show as both the Conservative and Labour governments sought to reduce the growth of State (including local government) expenditure, but the underlying consensus remained. This has now been shattered.

The Conservative Government of Margaret Thatcher (elected 1979 and re-elected 1983 and 1987) adopted an unusually forthright and rigid framework for its policies – to the extent that members of the Conservative Party (the so-called 'wets') expressed concern at this uncharacteristic adoption of an ideology. The basis of this doctrinaire approach ('Thatcherism') has been *monetarism*, which implies anti-Statism – or getting the State 'off people's backs'. It is held that the private sector would be more thrusting if there were fewer regulations and controls (over employment, planning, etc.), and it could more effectively and efficiently utilize the resources absorbed (especially through taxation) by the public (state) sector.[30]

In addition, monetarism involves curbing the money supply to control inflation. This involves reducing State expenditure – including that of local government.

The latter policy has been conducted largely through the local government grant system: partly by placing tight cash limits on grants (see p. 346); partly by reducing the proportion of grant support (in England from 61 per cent in 1979–80 to 52 per cent in 1984–5 and 46·2 per cent from 1987 to 1990); and partly by changing the nature of the Rate Support Grant to include (up to 1990) a block grant element (see p. 312). The block grant provided a diminishing proportion of grant aid (the 'taper') for expenditure which exceeded a given 'threshold' level (based on GREAs: see p. 313). Where there was a wholesale crossing of thresholds, then local authorities' grant entitlements were 'clawed back' to allow total grant entitlements to match the total grant available.

Soon after this system was inaugurated (1981) the Secretary of State (Michael Heseltine) announced (volume) 'target' expenditures for local authorities. Where a local authority's expenditure exceeded this guideline figure, it paid the penalty in lost grant (known as 'holdback'), the result of which was to reduce the actual grant proportion (e.g. in 1985–6, 2·8 per cent of the original grant of 48·8 per cent was held back in penalties). These targets were altered so much that councils protested at the difficulty of 'hitting a moving target' (others called it Block Grant Bingo). But the real cause for concern was that rather than monitoring the overall grant figure, the Government was telling each council what it should spend, and further, that it was indicating what councils should spend on particular services. This has been compounded by the resurgence of specific grants (see p. 308) (including one for aspects of education and the new community care, or 'Griffiths', grant for social services) and by the legislation which gives the government power to limit or prohibit councils' subsidies for transport (under the Transport Act 1983) and for council house rents.[31]

Many councils 'overspent' the Government's target figures and lost all or some grant (e.g. nearly £800 million during 1982–4). However, they were often able to make good the loss by raising a supplementary rate (or precept). This avenue was closed by the Local Government Finance Act 1982 which abolished the right of councils in England and Wales to raise supplementary rates/precepts, as was already the case in Scotland. The Act also clarified grant 'holdback' powers[32] and dropped plans for rates referendums.[33]

In Scotland, the Local Government (Miscellaneous Provisions) (Scotland) Act 1981 allowed the Minister to reduce the grant to any Scottish council which was planning levels of expenditure (i.e. in the budget estimates) which he regarded as 'excessive and unreasonable'. Thus facing a loss of grant, councils were expected to cut expenditure and so reduce the rates. In practice a number of (Labour) councils (e.g. Lothian) opted for losing grant. So under the Local Government and Planning (Scotland) Act 1982 the screw was tightened and the Minister could actually limit (or 'cap') the rate of any particular council – thus providing another example of 'fiscal centralism'.[34] These powers were augmented when the scheme was extended to England and Wales (under the Rates Act 1984). The provisions now apply across the country to the council tax, though 'capped' authorities may challenge the approved maximum and negotiate a modification with the Minister.[35] In 1988–9, seventeen councils (plus nineteen joint authorities) were capped (amounting to some 20 per cent of current expenditure).[36] In 1990, twenty-one were charge-capped.

Altogether these are massive central powers – the result of what Professors Jones and Stewart call 'panic ad-hocery'.[37] The balance of the constitution is being changed such that, in relation to local government, central government has come to resemble the Big Brother of George Orwell's *Nineteen Eighty-Four*: indeed rate-capping has been called 'knee-capping'. But before considering the significance of these powers, we should consider why the Government thought them necessary.

The 1983 White Paper *Rates* gives the following reasons. Firstly to protect ratepayers in general against 'excessive levels of expenditure and therefore of rates' (in October 1985, the Government estimated that rate-capping was saving some £300 million per annum). Secondly, the cost of local government is felt to be 'too great a burden on the private sector' and is jeopardizing the economic regeneration of Britain: a reduction in rates would help to reduce the tax burden, increase incentives, increase competitiveness and reduce inflationary pressures. Thirdly, 'the Government necessarily have a major interest in local authority services which

are national in character, such as education, or of national importance, such as the police . . . [and in] the balance between these
and other services'. Fourthly, and above all, the Government is
responsible 'for the broad conduct of the economy' and is 'determined, through firm control, to reduce public expenditure as a
proportion of the Gross Domestic Product' so as to permit a
reduction in public sector borrowing (PSBR, part of which is the
LABR) and thus a lowering of interest rates (to encourage
investment).

Much can, and should, be said about these recent developments
in central–local relations and their bases. On points of detail,
critics have made the following observations: (1) rates form a
small part (2–3 per cent) of business costs, and business taxation
in Britain (including rates) is comparatively light by international
standards; and the effect of selective rate-capping in reducing the
tax burden has been estimated at only about 0·5 per cent; (2)
rates have risen no faster than the retail price index, and have
reflected the inflation rate rather than contributed to it (compared
to the impact of fuel prices, interest rates and subsidies for
housing and transport which the government itself determines),
though the community charge *has* contributed to inflation; (3)
rate increases have largely been a reflection (as indeed intended)
of the Government's own policy of withdrawing grants – both the
penalty withholdings (amounting to £260 million during 1983–4)
for 'overspenders' and the general reduction in the rate support
grant (e.g. in England from 61 per cent in 1979 to 46 per cent in
1986–9),[38] as well as central decisions on such matters as the
development and pay of police, local government implementation
of community care and the statutory sick-pay scheme, keeping
redundant schools open, the 1981 Education Act, the introduction
of the youth training scheme (YTS) and reduced subsidies for
housing benefit; in addition local authorities have been badly hit
by high interest rates, and the heavy bill for housing renovation
(estimated ultimately at some £20 billion); (4) the 'overspend' (at
£900 million in 1984 and £700 million in 1988) was equivalent to
little more than 0·5 per cent of total public sector expenditure,

and local authorities as a whole have not strayed far from the Government's targets (despite the latter's arbitrary nature and frequent inadequate allowance for inflation);[39] indeed as a proportion of the GDP local spending fell from 15.9 per cent in 1974–5 to under 13 per cent in 1982–3 and 11.4 per cent in 1987 (such that the local government spending in Britain was below the average for developed countries);[40] meanwhile central government's spending only changed from 33.3 per cent to 31.6 per cent, largely as a result of significant cuts in capital expenditure, especially housing (its proportion of debt also rose while that of local government fell[41]); (5) some of the biggest overspending (and therefore penalized) councils faced some of the greatest problems of unemployment and deprivation, and capping could further hit many communities in terms of such vital services as schools, libraries, home helps, residential care and housing improvements;[42] (6) the capping mechanisms are unnecessary – indeed they amount to overkill since the worst offenders of overspending (the GLC and the metropolitan counties) have been abolished; and the doubling of the abatement penalties[43] in 1984 had a noticeably cautionary impact on local authorities; (7) there are considerable costs attached to the control process itself, with costs arising from the numerous meetings and mass of communications involved, the production and submission of information, the calculations and assessments, the appeals mechanism, the delays, the altered timetables and the overall uncertainty and demoralization which the whole procedure engenders: capping manifested the twelfth financial system experienced by local government between 1979 and 1984.[44] Indeed, a report[45] by the Audit Commission attacked the block grant system as confusing and perverse. (The Commission has also criticized the capital control system as wasteful.)[46]

The Government has now acknowledged the problems of this grant support system – a large part of what Rhodes calls 'the policy mess' in local–central relations.[47] In 1986, the system of targets and penalties was abandoned (partly, it is alleged, to soothe the shires, which this system hit rather more than the

GREA mechanisms of tapers and clawback). And separate legislation for Scotland (1987) and for England and Wales (1988) has transformed the system of local government finance. Thus apart from specific grants, local authorities now received a fixed Revenue Support Grant (RSG) together with a share of the centrally determined and collected business rates (UBR), which they themselves supplemented with income from fees and from their local poll tax or community charge, which replaced domestic rates in 1989 (Scotland) and 1990 (England and Wales); see p. 326. (Under the Local Government and Housing Act 1989, capital controls have been altered; see p. 328.) In a move to lower the impact of the community charge/poll tax, the Government, in the budget of March 1991, announced the transfer to local authorities of an additional £4.3 billion grant. Thus local government became even more reliant on central funding. When the council tax was introduced to replace the poll tax (in 1993), the balance of local to central funding was unchanged.

In the context of central–local relations, there are a number of points to observe about these financial changes. First it means that some 85 per cent of local finance will come from the government, i.e. RSG + UBR. The remaining 15 per cent (apart from fee income) will rely on the council tax; and any expenditure above the central government's (publicized) norm or standard will fall entirely on the council tax. This is likely to meet strong resistance from tax payers (although one study suggests that council tenants have been relatively unconcerned about increases in rates[48] and other studies suggest a readiness to face higher taxes for more or better services, e.g. in 1992 and 1993 Tower Hamlets LBC staged referendums with just such results). And there will be reluctance from elected members who are concerned about the regressive nature of the tax on lower income groups and from those who are concerned with retaining their seats. It is thus likely to achieve the Government's aim of curbing the overspenders (though capping and tax limitation is retained just in case). But it is also likely to over-constrict the majority of councils, who are having to deal with the costs of implementing such things as the national school curriculum and attainment testing, LMS, training governors, open (school) enrolments, access to personal files, the NHS and Community Care, housing transfers, the Children's Act 1989, the Disabled Persons Act 1990, the transfer of education from the ILEA, new trading standards and pollution legislation, including that of the EC, competitive tendering, lower social security benefits, the loss of the economies of scale through the opting out of school and tenants, etc., let alone spending as a result of their own substantive policies. Apart from this, Britain is unusual in our local authorities having only one local tax source.

One consequence may well be an increase in fee-charging for services (the scope for which has been increased by recent legislation[49]) and/or an off-loading of council services to the central government or into private hands.[50] Others believe that the council tax will be short-lived (just as the demise of the community charge was predicted[51]). In 1992, the former deputy chairman of the Board of the Inland Revenue helped to sustain the possibility of the introduction of a local income tax (LIT) by giving his support to the Layfield Committee's earlier proposals (see p. 324), and he suggested that with the recent developments in technology, many of the technical objections made against LIT have been overcome.[52] Whilst this is the Liberal Democrats' preferred local tax, the Labour Party's intention is to replace the council tax (which they have dubbed 'son of poll tax') with a modified rating system.

There are some who question the need for central government to be concerned with local government expenditure since 'local governments in Britain have been very successful in meeting their spending targets and there is no conclusive evidence that local government spending and taxation decisions have disincentive effects on the economy'.[53] Indeed, David King has suggested[54] that countries with established systems of local government and devolved tax powers appear to show faster rates of economic growth. The present strategy of centralization threatens overload and inefficiency at the centre (e.g. with the DFE having to deal with, potentially, hundreds of opted-out grant maintained schools and City Technology Colleges). Others acknowledge that the government does have a legitimate concern with total expenditure and with local expenditure as a component. But they argue that the government need only control local government expenditure financed by borrowing and central grants; that expenditure financed by rates or the local tax does not impinge on money supply and interest rates,[55] and has a nil or only marginal impact on aggregate demand in the economy.[56] As the *Economist* put it:

One of the few pluralist aspects of the British constitution is the right of elected local councils to decide what level of local services they deem desirable for their areas, and to levy rates accordingly. The proof of this autonomy is that occasionally such services, and such rates, are more lavish than is considered appropriate by central government. Mrs Thatcher regards this autonomy as an offence against her doctrine of public spending restraint and intends to end it.[57]

Furthermore, as Diane Dawson has stated, 'To identify the particular policy objectives of a government with the centre's responsibility for managing the economy is a red herring frequently invoked by governments of both parties.'[58]

It is the view of many that in contrast to recent experience, the central government should avoid getting itself involved in the detailed budgets of individual authorities and that such central interference only confuses accountability. 'Accountability to the Secretary of State is substituted for accountability to the local electorate,'[59] for if the government 'allocates' a particular council an expenditure (i.e. having determined its needs) and a rate or local tax level to cover it, what accountability is there left between the local council and its citizens? Whitehall has displaced Town Hall. Why bother to vote for the council? And how can one vote sensibly when it is impossible, for example, to know whether the tax level is the product of council decisions, outdated property valuation, a government decision to alter the business rate (or delay revaluation), a change in the grant or tax limitation,[60] or inadequate allowance for inflation in the SSA or RSG? (The

SSA system is currently under review by the Department of the Environment. It has been criticized recently on the grounds of its distortion, inefficiency and injustice.[61])

Furthermore, there is considerable doubt about the validity and wisdom of the whole policy of deflation through public sector expenditure reductions. Some (neo-Keynesian) economists argue that it will cripple Britain's industrial base and have intolerable social consequences – in terms of crime, family stress, health and social unrest (such as the urban riots of 1981 and 1985).[62] And standards of basic services are suffering, including housing, roads, transport and education (the last of which has been highlighted by critical HMI reports). Basically they argue for more State expenditure, and conclude that even if the monetarist policy is right in the long run, the price is too high. Some would go further and argue not just that the policy represents the political opportunism of the Conservative central government sequestering Labour councils (which some see further illustrated by the capping in 1990, for example, of twenty-one councils, none Conservative) but also that it manifests blatant class war: that the attack on local spending is an attack on the welfare services of the working class to provide tax cuts for the rich. (The left-wing Liverpool councillors were determined to resist cuts in local services, but they also sought to avoid penalizing the ratepayers as their view was that it was really the Government at fault for 'robbing' the city of £350 million in grants since 1979: hence the deficit budget in 1985–6. For local government as a whole, the estimated loss of grant support for 1979–87 was £17,500 million (see Douglas and Lord, p. 629 below).)

The price of the attack on local government may be too high in another sense. Local government is a system which diffuses power; it provides local opportunities for choice; and it provides alternative solutions (right or wrong) to local problems. It is the existence of local government which provides part of the 'checks and balances' of our unwritten constitution. Its existence helps to render inaccurate Lord Hailsham's description of our political system as an 'elective dictatorship'. Local government is part of the pluralism which characterizes the liberal-democratic state. Indeed Parliament itself provides inadequate checks and balances on the government: there is much official secrecy and there is Crown or 'public interest' privilege. By contrast, local government is more open, it can be taken to court more easily, local people can challenge local decisions, there is more audit and backbench councillors (including the opposition members) have rights of access to officials and information. It is this which is at risk as local decision-making is circumscribed and centralized. As Professors Jones and Stewart have said, with reference to the rate-capping legislation: 'The proposed Bill makes a constitutional change of the greatest significance. It removes from the local authorities that Parliament has set up as elected authorities the right of control over their own tax. It concentrates power to an extent unparalleled in this country since local authorities were created.'[63] The Times, commenting on the continuation of capping, commented that 'An electoral process held sacrosanct when applied to Parliament is rendered meaningless when the same people turn out to vote for their local councils.'[64] Dr J. Cunningham (Labour's Shadow Minister) has declared it 'the biggest step yet ... down the dangerous road to a centralized authoritarian economy'. This was reiterated by the Chairman of the Association of County Councils, who declared: 'The excessive power which central government is proposing will remove from the local voter and ratepayer the right to control their local budgets and determine their local priorities. This is the very essence of local democracy.' And indeed the (Conservative) Minister for Local Government (Tom King) said in 1980: 'If we started to determine [local authorities'] rate levies for them, then I'd accept that that would be a major threat to local democracy.'[65] In Parliament, the centralizing implications of the rate-capping legislation caused ex-Prime Minister Edward Heath to vote against his Conservative Party and defy a three-line whip: he was the first Prime Minister this century to do this. Yet the power to impose a limit has been retained under the new council tax system. In effect, local authorities are taking responsibility or accountability for decisions of the central government.

Local government and the democratic deficit

We referred on p. 473 to monetarism as seeking to reduce the role of the State. This continues in a number of areas: sale of state industries and assets, deregulation of employment and transport, market testing and contracting out services. The Government has introduced a host of measures which many believe will, and are intended to, undermine or marginalize local government. Local authorities have been required to sell much of their housing stock, to contract out services, to limit their subsidies to transport and, above all, to live within severe constraints on resources. A tier of local government (covering 40 per cent of the population) has been abolished, with many functions being transferred to non-elected or indirectly elected boards, thus adding to the 'democratic deficit' in Britain today. More specific (or 'ring-fenced') grants have been introduced (in education and social services), some 35,000 pupils are centrally funded for (assisted) places in private schools, and the determination of teachers' salaries has been taken over by the Government. And under the inner cities regeneration policy, local authorities have been side-lined by Urban Development Corporations (currently twelve), Enterprise Zones, Simplified Planning Zones and Task Forces (and the Minister is increasingly allowing appeals against local planning decisions).

Recent policy has also tended to reduce democratic control over and within the State: thus, the 'democratic deficit'. This arises partly because sections of the State have been privatized (sold or transferred to the private or voluntary sectors), and partly because, where the State continues to provide, control is increasingly indirect and tenuous. The latter is evident in central government, where ministerial responsibility has become diluted or blurred as activities are hived off to departmental (internal or 'Next Step') agencies or to quangos (such as Health Authorities, some of whose functions have subsequently been devolved on to health service trusts). In between lie the contracted out public services (national and local), and it is a moot point as to how far such an arrangement reduces control and accountability. The Government denies (see below) the demo-cratic deficit – indeed it proclaims the opposite.[66] As far as local democracy is concerned, the Government has introduced what has been called a 'torrent of reforms'. These include:

(1) The Education Reform Act 1988. This removes polytechnics and colleges from LEA control; allows schools to opt out of LEA control alongside the separately created City Technology Colleges; requires LEAs to admit pupils to schools up to their maximum capacity; delegates control of finance (85 per cent) and staffing to schools' governing bodies (LMS). The Education (Schools) Act 1992 requires schools to be inspected every four years and to publish annual performance indicators (exam results, truancy rates, etc.). The Further and Higher Education Act 1992 removed sixth form and FE colleges from LEAs and gave them independ-ent corporate status (financed through the Further Education Funding Council).

(2) The Housing Act 1988. This allows council tenants to opt for an alternative landlord and, where appropriate, for estates to be taken into the hands of Housing Action Trusts. Meanwhile, councils have been encouraged to transfer their houses to housing associations (though not encouraged to build). The Housing, Land and Urban Development Act 1993 extends the sale of council houses and sets up the Urban Regeneration Agency.

(3) The Local Government Act 1988. This requires competitive tendering (CCT) for a number of local authority services, includ-ing catering, grounds maintenance, vehicle maintenance, refuse collection, cleaning and (subsequently) sports/leisure facilities; others may be added by the Minister. It also strengthens the ban on political advertising (see p. 175); gives district auditors powers to issue 'stop orders' to prevent unlawful expenditure. The Local Government Act 1992 extends competitive tendering to the 'white collar' activities of local authorities. And under the Trade Union

Reform and Employment Rights Act 1993, LEA careers services are to be put out to tender.

(4) The Local Government Finance Act 1988. This replaced domestic rates with the community charge or poll tax; non-domestic (or business) rates are taken over and redistributed by the government; the Rate Support Grant has become the Revenue Support Grant, which is a fixed amount per annum; the chief finance officer is given the duty to enforce prudence in their council's financial affairs. The Local Government Finance Act 1992 replaced the community charge/poll tax with the council tax, but at the same low level of 15 per cent of contribution to local revenue and under the continued risk of capping.

(5) The Local Government and Housing Act 1989. This is the Government's main reponse to the Widdicombe Report on 'The Conduct of Local Authority Business' (1986). It regulates the appointment and management of staff and restricts their right to engage in political activity; creates a 'monitoring officer' and requires the designation of a head of the paid service; regulates local authorities' interests in companies; controls capital expenditure by limiting borrowing (or credits) and councils' use of their own assets sales receipts; prevents councils from subsidizing their housing rents; permits local authorities to charge for a wider range of services.

It is calculated that since 1979 local authorities have been subjected to some 150 pieces of legislation (though some have been inspired by local government itself). Thus in the words of the Controller of Audit, local government is 'under siege'.[67] Local authorities are being told what do to (impose the national curriculum, raise rents, contract out services, etc.). They are also being by-passed as functions are transferred to other, non-elected, bodies – development corporations, training councils, housing associations and trusts, governing bodies, funding councils – a situation John Stewart describes as 'a New Magistracy'.[68] And there are plans for more services to be removed from council control, such as (starting in 1995) the careers service, police[69] and the national parks. In all there are an estimated 40,000 appointments to such bodies – outnumbering the total number of elected councillors (and MPs).[70] What makes this situation more objectionable is the evidence which suggests that, in making its appointments, the Government is too often favouring Conservative supporters. They often receive higher allowances than councillors, too.[71]

Many of these changes are being made in the name of the citizen and taxpayer, in pursuit of effectiveness, efficiency and economy. They also seek liberation – 'setting the people free' – through the provision of choice, ownership and opportunity. The Minister responsible for overseeing the implementation of the Citizen's Charter, William Waldegrave, has proclaimed that the Government's public service reforms are 'helping to restore a proper balance to the relationship between State and citizen'.[72] He says that accountability is being increased because more information on service procedures and outcomes is being made available, and that there is a greater clarity or transparency of the link between policy formulation and its implementation (i.e. through the purchaser/provider split).

However, he also asserts that 'the key point is not whether those who run the service are elected, but whether they are producer or consumer responsive. Services are not necessarily made to respond to the public simply by giving citizens a diffuse democratic voice in their makeup.'[73] But it may be said that where there is a lack of real choice (as with, say, hospitals or community psychiatric services), the only means of influence is through the political process. In the area of local authority social services, the opportunity for meaningful choice is often extremely limited in practice.

It is true that housing or school opt-outs only occur after a ballot of tenants or parents, but such decisions are binding and cannot be reversed. It is also suggested that many of the changes will only transfer power from one set of professionals to another.[74] And for many of the council tenants, voting takes the form of 'informed acquiescence', i.e. those who do not turn out to vote (where a landlord offers to replace the local housing authority) are deemed to have voted in favour. Apart from all this, it is suggested that while local authorities are now limited in what they can publicize, the Government can use its unlimited powers to convey misleading information which affect people's attitudes and voting decisions.

Some of the 'freedom' is illusory or exaggerated (e.g. all state schools have to conform to the new national curriculum, must regularly test children's attainment according to national guidelines, must appraise teacher performance, etc.), and many of the new bodies lack accountability[75] or accessibility, so that what appear to be more democratic (or populist) decisions actually lead to a greater concentration of power. The Education Act 1993 illustrates this. The Act aims to make it easier for parents/schools to opt out of LEA control and become grant-maintained (with the number of such schools rising from 500 in 1992 to 1500 in 1994). However, the legislation creates another appointed regulatory body (the Funding Agency for the GM schools, or FAS*), and it gives the Minister over fifty new powers. These include the power to take over problem schools, to replace the originating governors of GM schools, to vary school admissions and to require rationalization (to cut surplus places). The Minister will appoint the FAS and guide its activities. The result is that parents may be voting not so much for 'freedom' by opting out but opting for more remote control.

The Act also implies that, coupled with LMS (delegated school budgets), LEAs will degenerate. They do retain responsibility for special needs education, education welfare, psychological testing and securing school attendance, and they may continue to offer services to schools such as curriculum and legal advice, payroll and personnel services, etc.), but it is intended that these

---

* When 10 per cent of schools have opted out, the FAS will begin to share responsibility with the LEA for admissions/allocation of places; when the figure reaches 75 per cent, the FAS assumes the role.

services will be obtained by the grant-maintained schools from the private sector within two years. So local government is at risk of losing perhaps its most crucial function. But as it will occur incrementally, many local authorities face the prospect of years of (more) uncertainty and change (compounded by reorganization).

The enabling council

The present Government increasingly sees local authorities as 'enablers' rather than 'providers'. This concept is most evident in the field of housing, where Government policy has reduced council housing stock through sales of over 1 million dwellings since 1979. It also provides the rationale for the policy of compulsory tendering. It has been given added impetus by the Government's acceptance (in July 1989) of the main recommendation of the Griffiths Report on community care of the elderly and the mentally disabled. Under the NHS and Community Care Act 1990, local authorities have been given the leading role in assessing needs and designing, organizing and purchasing care services and not acting primarily as direct providers.

To many people, especially those who believe in the collective or State provision of goods and services, the concept of the enabling authority represents a threat to local government; it is perceived as a means of lowering or cheapening service standards, of eroding the welfare state (in line with the Government's policy of changing the 'culture of dependency' to a 'culture of enterprise') and of weakening local authorities' political role or 'clout'.[76] Yet the notion is not entirely new; to some extent local authorities have been 'enabling' for many years[77] and it has increasingly wide support (including that of the Labour Party). But it is a matter of scale, emphasis and, above all, meaning. Certainly there are many officers who welcome the managerial freedom which 'the competitive council' should provide, and there are those who support the view that local government has been too 'cocooned by protective legislation'.[78] Nicholas Ridley, when Secretary of State, once declared that his ideal council would be one that met once a year to award contracts for all its services to the private sector (a view which, apart from anything else, overlooks the council's role in drawing up the service/ contract specifications and monitoring its implementation and outcome, together with its role in securing adequate coordination). More recently he has acknowledged that councils should have a providing role,[79] but within a more diverse service provision, with a variety of agencies working alongside councils. Thus:

The role of the local authority will no longer be that of the universal provider. But it will have a key role in ensuring there is adequate provision to meet needs, in encouraging the various providers to develop and maintain the necessary services, and where necessary in providing grant support or other assistance to get projects started, and to ensure that services are provided and affordable for the clients concerned.[80]

Arguably, the essence of government is control or regulation of the community – originally (in the case of local government) in the shape of law and order and, in the 19th century, environmental health, slums, etc. Provision of services came later. In this respect, it is perhaps worth recalling the original reasons for the state provision of services: the family and voluntary sector cannot always provide sufficiently or consistently; the private enterprise or market system can fail to meet the needs (welfare, education, etc.) of those without money and it can exploit its (often) monopoly situation;[81] and there are aspects of society (conservation, public health, etc.) which can only be dealt with on a collective basis.

A broader view of the enabling role sees it as an opportunity to develop more creative local government, with councils more responsive to the needs of their communities and placing themselves at the centre of a network of formal and informal links with local groups, businesses and individuals. Councils here have the role 'to identify and articulate the collective needs and aspirations of its own community' through actions as a lobbyist, promoter, coordinator, managing agent and service provider.[82] This view is expressed by Michael Clarke and John Stewart as one where:

The local authority accepts that its direct provision of services is but one means of providing for the community among many. Its role as an 'enabling' council is to use all the means at its disposal to meet the needs of those who live within its area.[83]

Local authorities are having to learn that they can be local government even where they cannot act directly. The management of influence is required as well as the management of action.[84]

They suggest councils have become so immersed in the business of ensuring services are provided day by day that they have often lost sight of a wider role – acting with and speaking on behalf of their community on issues other than local government services:

In the past local authorities have defined their role by the services provided. Committees, departments and professions have been struc-tured around them. The business of the authority has been to deliver them. Councillors' attention has focused on service production as the main expression of the interface with the community. At times, many seem to have become more absorbed in the problems of production than the needs of the community . . . Freed from the assumption of self-sufficiency and the need to produce all it does directly, the enabling council can define its role not by the services it produces but by a broader agenda of concerns . . . Councillors will focus on whether needs are being met rather than on the detailed problems of production . . . It is a recognition that the role of the local authority can be one of *local government* with concerns for its community which extend beyond service provision . . . It needs to recognise the resources that lie within communities and to develop them.[85]

As a result, local authorities would have the task of constantly searching for gaps and weaknesses in community provision; they would continue to make some direct provision, but they would also work through and with other organizations; aiding, stimulating, pump-priming, advising, guiding, regulating, inspecting.[86] Local authorities should break with their tradition of direct provision or 'self-sufficiency' and analyse 'what local government bureaucracy is good at providing, as well as what it is not so good at accomplishing'.[87] The Audit Commission, as a result of the Education Act 1988, envisages the reorganization of LEAs as they change to become 'leaders, partners, planners, informers, regulators and bankers'.[88]

Local government is understandably cautious and on the defensive; but it shouldn't be, since 'in reality significant opportunities have opened up which will relieve it of the burden of day-to-day management of services to focus on broader policies'.[89] They should 'share the ownership of problem-solving with others'.[90]* In the latter respect councils should consider forming partnerships with, and contracting out services to, other local or public authorities and trusts, the private sector, or voluntary and cooperative organizations, devolving more management to users (e.g. tenants) and helping communities to solve their problems, providing vouchers to enable customers to buy services both within and outside the local authority, surveys to find out what the public thinks, creating forums for discussion of issues, giving publicity to issues of concern, linking groups together. Their overview role is particularly important since, with many and various agencies involved, there will be problems of coordination and steerage as well as the risk of unequal treatment and user access.

Many councillors are concerned about their future not just because of local authorities' reduced role in direct service provi-

* There is a close parallel between this and what has been happening in the field of education, where teachers have become 'facilitators' in the new, student-centred classroom. Teachers are still very much involved in the education process – perhaps more so – but they too are finding it difficult to adjust to a culture in which they are no longer centre-stage with talk and chalk. Under the NHS reforms, health authorities plan and purchase rather than directly provide medical services.

sion but also because of the possible/probable changes in the management of councils: the possibility of the widespread introduction of local authority 'cabinets' and two-tier councillors is unsettling.[91] In the light of this Professor Jones suggests councillors should develop the role of consumer proponent and promote consumer democracy:

In the new era they could take on the role of representing consumers, acting as their champions as they draw up policy and the specification of performance for different services and as they monitor and evaluate the performance of the providers, whoever they are. Councillors would act on behalf of consumers. In this sense 'consumers' means not just those who receive a particular service, but also potential consumers who may be denied access.

Councillors could see themselves as advocates of consumers in their wards, districts and areas, expressing in council and committee meetings (and other settings) the concerns of their constituents. But they need not constrain themselves to services for which the council is or was responsible but may also become involved in other public services . . . and even voice concerns about providers . . . So, instead of championing their 'own' services, councillors could play a lead role in championing their consumers.[92]

But to fulfil this role properly, councils themselves need to be 'enabled'; they need freedom from central controls, less circumvention and unilateral transference of responsibilities by the government, and more financial resources that are truly local. Some councils, in pursuit of the 'consumer watchdog' role, have run into the problem of *ultra vires* (in relation to conducting opinion polls). Thus local authorities also need to be given the power of 'general competence'.[93]

They also need the support, confidence and goodwill of the public. This can be enhanced by the process of enabling, and at the same time it provides one of the motives for this new approach. For it can be seen as a response to the changing environment of local government – the growth of private provision (of welfare, health, housing, transport, etc., much of it encouraged by the Government) and the trend to 'consumerism', where the 'customer is king', increasingly aware of his or her rights, becoming less grateful for services received, seeking variety and quality or value for money (including in taxes, national and local) and exercising choice to express or achieve individual identity through customized design, specialization and 'post-Fordism'.[94] This has thrown into relief the form and content of State provision, and has given rise to the criticism that public services are, variously, too bureaucratic, unresponsive, inflexible, wasteful, impersonal, uniform, paternalistic and professions- or union-dominated.[95] It can be argued that 'it is not merely a matter of building support for local services, but rather that services might not deserve to survive unless they are made more accountable and user-friendly. It may be that the final battle for the future of local government will lie between the decentralisers and the privatisers.'[96] The head of the Audit Commission believes that 'The best of local authority service provision has nothing to fear from competition,'[97] and councils are becoming much more public-service orientated and are 'putting people first' through decentralization, customer contracts, user panels, increased information, consumer (and staff) surveys[98] and other 'marketing' devices.[99]

However, while there are undoubted gains, there are also risks attached to this new competitive environment. In seeking to protect or promote the interests of themselves or their profession, service or council, local authorities and their staff should not lose sight of the public interest nor their sense of public service. The traditions of British public service are something of which we can be proud – integrity, professionalism, fairness and a sense of service. A more commercial culture can soon erode these values and create a more instrumental and selfish attitude and approach.

The challenge of a changing environment

We have seen how local government is responding to changes in its environment or context. Some of these changes (such as the penetration of parties or the greater assertiveness of councillors) are more or less self-induced; others (more limited resources, contracting out, loss of domain) are largely the result of Government policies. But there are others which are effectively beyond control, though they have important implications for local government. These are dealt with briefly below.

Population changes are affecting local authorities in a number of ways. The changing age structure in the 1980s brought a 25 per cent fall in secondary-school rolls and a 50 per cent increase in the vulnerable elderly (over-85s). The former is now being reversed (accompanied by a growth in further and higher education students) but the latter is likely to continue. So too is the fall in the population of working age, and local authorities (an estimated 75 per cent in pre-recession 1989) have experienced shortages of professional staff (such as accountants, lawyers, planners, social workers). This may lead to greater contracting out of services; it may have an impact on personnel policies, such as pay, training and retention, and above all on the recruitment of and greater opportunities for women (with its consequential withdrawal of unpaid, informal care in the community). It is also likely to influence industrial relations and trade union power.

The Henley Centre for Forecasting envisages local authorities continuing to face budgetary constraints throughout the 1990s due to these population changes. With low economic growth and unemployment remaining high, public funds will be stretched.[100]

Population is also on the move, drifting from north to south and moving out of the inner urban areas to the suburbs and beyond – with social, economic and political consequences, and bringing problems of planning, transport, de-industrialization, dereliction and unemployment to local authorities. Over 40 per cent of jobs in manufacturing and mining were lost during the 1980s.[101] Traditional communities are altering with the changing ethnic composition and more generally with the growth of divorce (at 170,000 per annum), reconstituted families and single parents (one in seven families) – all amounting to what has been described as an 'imminent threat to our social ecology'.[102]

Information technology is not new to local government. But it is beginning to affect its operation in new ways. First it is changing the relationship between local authorities' central departments and their service departments as the latter become better informed and less dependent on the former, particularly as service managers are caught up in competitive tendering.[103] It also allows for decentralization without loss of control. Secondly, elected members increasingly have the facility to key in to council mainframe computers and gain access to reports and appropriate data. Some authorities provide their councillors with micro computers for this and related purposes: in a recent survey 16 per cent of councils said they gave members access to information technology to aid their decision-making and casework activities.[104] And thirdly, service users are being informed and empowered by the provision of high street viewdata (in libraries etc.), where they can check such things as their eligibility for benefits, education grants, etc., opening times of council facilities, waiting lists, charges, names of councillors, etc. The survey showed 40 per cent of the councils in the north made such provision compared to only 18 per cent of southern councils.[105]

Finally the European Community has a number of implications for local government. Local authorities are increasingly called upon for information about the EC in general and on particular aspects, e.g. the significance for business of standards, competition and State subsidies. Businesses and local trading standards/consumer protection departments are at the moment affected by some 600 Acts and Regulations, 20 per cent of which emanate from the EC. From 1992 about 80 per cent of the consumer protection legislation is affected by harmonization within the EC. There are literally dozens of EC directives just dealing with additives and materials in contact with food, responsibility for which will fall on local authority trading standards officers. There will be new rules governing waste disposal and other environmental controls (such as transport and highways). There will be new rules governing employment and health and safety; these alone will cost local authorities millions of pounds to implement.[106] And there are special requirements for awarding public works contracts and supplies (e.g., those over £142,000 must be advertised in the *Official Journal* of the EC). There may be problems over recognizing professional qualifications, and there are certain to be movements of businesses, of people changing jobs and a growth in tourism. Education services are affected by all this in terms of curriculum development, languages, etc. and in careers advice and vocational training. But a more worrying conclusion is that 'the development of the European Community . . . seems to be having a centralizing impact upon member-states . . . the institutions of the Community are likely to take greater powers upon themselves. Therefore, unless the position of local government is more firmly entrenched, there could be a real shift of power away from the individual citizen to institutions which seem remote to him or her.'[107] Paradoxically, while the Prime Minister, John Major, argued for greater independence or safeguards for the UK (through opt-out clauses) in the Maastricht Treaty of 1992, he has been less willing to apply the same principle (of 'subsidiarity') to local government within Britain.

Inevitably, complex problems require complex solutions. How well local authorities will provide solutions to the problems outlined above remains to be seen, though many have already displayed initiatives in, for example, supporting their local economy and helping to reduce the impact of unemployment.[108] In the words of the Audit Commission, 'In any period of uncertainty and change, the well-managed organization survives more successfully than the rest. That will be true of local authorities in the next decade.' The AC then provides a checklist of advice for well-managed councils.[109] But their capacity to respond to problems has been hindered by the actions of the Government, with the reorganizations, the creation of special agencies, the reduced resources and the increased steerage of their general and particular expenditure.

Local government has not been alone in this assault by the

'strong State': legislation has significantly curbed the power of trade unions, the church has been attacked for 'interference' in social affairs, the media have been issued 'stop notices' and a standards watchdog for broadcasting, the institutions of higher education have been squeezed financially and are now at risk of losing their autonomy with the loss of academic tenure and the creation of less independent finance bodies, and the legal institutions feel similarly threatened. There is an 'apparent drift towards authoritiarianism',[110] Government policies are moving Britain towards a 'mass society' – where intermediate bodies, between the government and the people, are weak and vulnerable (as they were in Germany prior to Hitler's rise to power).[111] Thus Professor Newton feels that Britain stands within sight of a form of government which is 'more highly centralised than anything this side of [pre-1990] East Germany'.[112]

Local government has been especially hit because it does not operate on the basis of the dominating principle: market forces. Local authorities manifest so much of the 'positive' State for it is not government ministers and their departments which build schools or employ teachers and social workers or plan cities. In so far as the State and its expenditure is to be rolled back, local authorities find themselves in the front line. Lord Jenkins has called it 'civic degradation'.[113]

Thus we return to the opening theme of this book; the proper role of local government in Britain. It is this which is currently under threat.[114] But local authorities have not received much defensive support from the general public – perhaps because the national government gets its own message across more successfully and there is too great a readiness to allow local matters to be subsumed by national.

At one time it was assumed that local government would be 'safe' from excessive central interference because, ultimately, the central government depends upon the goodwill and expertise of local government for the delivery of national environmental, economic and social services. This safeguard is now much less certain as the central government's commitment to such service provision diminishes. Central government does not need the cooperation of local authorities to the same extent as before, since it is no longer so concerned about the delivery of State services, and those programmes which the government does seek to protect or fashion may well be privatized or passed into the hands of the more pliant appointed quangos (such as the urban development corporations, the training and enterprise councils, education funding councils or the new style police authorities).

However, a number of things could happen to change this. The normally non-political public may become more politically active [115] with a new, simpler structure and as 'capping' results in lower service standards. There may be a consumer revolt against so much service delivery by non-accountable quangos. And the Government may find that recent policies (e.g. in the sphere of education) lead to overload at the centre. There is a reservoir of support for local government, in that between 40 and 50 per cent of the population is satisfied with the way their council is running their area, compared to only 30 per cent who were satisfied with the central government's performance (MORI, 1991).

Local authorities can take advantage of a growth in local consciousness and activity: they can harness local and neighbourhood movements both as voluntary providers of community services and as 'power to their elbow' in their relations with the central government. Local government is becoming much more open and accessible, with open committees, access to council documents, decentralized services, community management, consultation schemes, civic newspapers and community radio. [116] Despite what is often said, there is a considerable reserve of faith and goodwill towards local government. [117] Recent polls have shown that 55 per cent of electors disapprove of rate-capping; 36 per cent want less control of councils (against 14 per cent who want more); and they are twice as satisfied with the performance of local government as they are with central government. [118] Two thirds of the public think they get good value for money from local government. [119] Since they are so dependent on central finance, local authorities need not appear as the villains of the piece (as they often did in the depression of the 1930s). Indeed local councils have an opportunity, which some are using, to stem the alleged increasing alienation of the public from established political institutions by listening, by showing understanding, by responding positively and by demonstrating their relevance.

Appendix 1

ENGLAND AND WALES							
1800	SHIRE COUNTIES			BOROUGHS			PARISHES
1830							
1860							
1890	County councils	County borough councils	Non-county borough councils	Urban district councils	Rural district councils	Parish	London County Council
1920							
1950							
1980	Metro-politan counties	Metropolitan district councils	Non-metropolitan county councils	Non-metropolitan district councils	Parish/community		Greater London Council

The Changing Pattern of Local Government

	SCOTLAND			
	COUNTIES	BURGHS	KIRK/ PARISH	1800
Ad hoc bodies associated with local government — considerably absorbed by local authorities during this period though some reappear on a national or regional basis in the period since the Second World War				
				1830
				1860
	County councils			1890
London borough councils		Burgh councils	Parishes	
				1920
	County councils	Burgh councils	District councils	Counties of cities councils	
					1950
Greater London borough councils	Regional councils	District councils	(Community councils)	
				1980

Appendix 2

The Functions of Principal Local Authorities (see p. 506 for notes)

FUNCTION	ENGLAND AND WALES			LONDON	SCOTLAND	
	Metropolitan District	Non-Metropolitan County	Non-Metropolitan District	Borough	Region and/or Island	District
Aerodromes	X	X	X	X	X	
Allotments (a)	X		X	X	X(q)	X
Arts and recreation:						
– Art and crafts support, entertainment, art galleries, museums	X	X	X	X	X	X
– Libraries	X	X	(t)	X	X(s)	X
– Recreation (e.g. parks, playing fields, swimming baths etc.)	X	X	X	X	X	X
– Tourism encouragement	X	X	X	X	X	X
Caravans:						
– Site provision	X	X	X	X	X(s)	X
– Site control, licensing	X	X	X	X	X(s)	X
– Gypsy sites, provision	X		X	X	X	X
– Gypsy sites, management	X		X	X	X	X
Cemeteries and crematoria	X	X	X	X	X(q)	X
Consumer protection	X	X	X	X	X	X

– Food and drugs (composition), trade description, weights and measures	X	X	(t)	X	X	
Diseased animals	X	X		X		X
Education (b) (c) and Careers guidance	X(x)	X		X(d)	X	
Emergency action, natural disaster	X(x)	X	X	X(x)	X	
Environmental health:						
– Building regulations	X	X	X	X	X(q)	X(s)
– Communicable disease control	X	X	X	X	X(q)	X
– Food safety and hygiene	X	X	X	X	X	X
– Litter control	X	X	X	X	X	X
– Public conveniences	X		(w)	X	X(q)	X
– Refuse collection, nuisance control, abatement, clean air	X		X	X	X(q)	X
– Refuse disposal	X(y)	X	(u)	X(y)	X(q)	X
– Rodent control	X	X	X	X	X(q)	X
– Street cleansing	X	X	X	X	X(q)	X
Fire service	X(x)	X		X(x)	X(r)	
Footpaths and bridleways:						
– Creation, diversion and extinguishment, protection	X	X	X	X	X	
– Maintenance, signposting, surveys	X	X		X	X	
Housing(e)	X	X	X	X	X(q)	X
Land drainage (h)	X	X	X	X	X	
Licensing, inspection, registration (f)	X	X	X	X		
Local licence duties collection (g) (e.g. game licences)	X	X	X	X	X(q)	X
Markets and fairs	X	X	X	X		X

FUNCTION	ENGLAND AND WALES			LONDON	SCOTLAND	
	Metropolitan District	Non-Metropolitan County	Non-Metropolitan District	Borough	Region and/or Island	District
Planning:						
– Advertisement control, listed building control	X		X	X(aa)	X(q)	X(s)
– Building preservation notices, derelict land, conservation areas	X	X	X	X(aa)	X(r)	X(s)
– Country parks	X	X	X		X	X
– Development control, local plans, processing of planning applications (i)	X	X	X	X	X(s)	X(s)
– Development plan schemes, structure plans	X(n)	X		X(n)	X	
– National parks (b) (j)	X	X				
Police (b) (k)	X(bb)	X			X(r)	
Rate collection (1)	X		X	X	X	
Registration:						
– of births, marriages, deaths	X	X		X	X	
– of electors	X		X	X	X	
Sewerage (h)	X		X			

					(v)
Smallholdings	X	X		X X	
Social services, social work (b)	X	X		X X	(v)
Traffic, transport and highways:					
– Highways (m)		X	X		X
– Lighting:					
Footway					
Highway	X	X		X X	X X
– Parking: (o)					
Off-street	X	X		X X	X X
On-street	X	X		X X(z)	X X X
– Public transport, road safety, traffic regulation, transportation planning (p)	X	X		X X	X X

Notes on Appendix 2

(a) In England, where they exist, parish councils or meetings are the allotment authorities. In Wales, Allotments Acts powers are exercisable concurrently by district and community councils.

(b) Agency arrangements not permissible.

(c) The councils of non-metropolitan districts and inner London boroughs whose areas serve primary schools are minor authorities for the purpose of appointing managers of these schools except in areas where there is a parish or community council (or, in England, a parish meeting) which can act as a minor authority. Where the area serving the school comprises two or more of the authorities mentioned above they act jointly as a minor authority.

(d) Education is a borough function in outer London; in inner London education was provided, until 1990, by the Inner London Education Authority (ILEA) which consisted of members elected by the public in the inner London boroughs.

(e) County councils have certain reserve powers to provide housing subject to a request by a district council and/or the approval of the Secretary of State. The London boroughs are responsible for the provision of housing. The Greater London Council maintained a stock of housing which it inherited from the former London County Council and also had a strategic role (e.g. aiding the slum clearance programme of the inner London boroughs, provision of housing for Londoners outside London, re-housing GLC and London borough tenants whose accommodation needs change and providing accommodation through a nominations scheme for people on the borough waiting lists for housing). Much of the GLC stock was transferred to the boroughs before the GLC's abolition in 1986.

(f) Not all local authorities are equally responsible for this function; responsibility varies among authorities according to the nature of the activity being licensed/registered (e.g. counties register nursing homes and premises selling poisons; districts licence/register camp sites, race track betting promoters, premises storing explosives etc.). Much is undertaken with special reference to fire safety.

(g) Most local authorities collect local licence duties through the agency of the Post Office.

(h) Under the Water Act 1973 responsibility for water in England and Wales was passed to regional water authorities. They were also given responsibility for sewerage, but they are empowered to enter into agreements with district councils and London boroughs for the carrying out of this function locally. In Scotland, the regional councils are the responsible authorities. In 1986, the GLC's land drainage role was transferred to the Thames Water Authority.

(i) Some matters are reserved to the county and regional councils, i.e. applications straddling the boundaries of national parks and for minerals development.

(j) Two joint planning boards have been set up to administer national park functions in the Lake District National Park and the Peak National Park. For other national parks these functions are administered by a special committee of the county council mainly concerned, which may include representatives of the other county councils and the district councils for the area of the national park.

(k) Many county councils have combined their police forces (e.g. Avon & Somerset). Greater London and certain adjacent areas are policed by the Metropolitan Police Force (administered directly by the Home Office).

(l) Rate demands issued by the district councils include precepts from county and parish councils; those issued by the London borough councils and the City of London before 1986 included precepts from the Greater London Council. In Scotland the regional councils collect rates on behalf of the districts.

(m) The Secretary of State for the Environment is highway authority for trunk roads. District councils may claim the right to maintain unclassified roads in urban areas (this power is distinct from the powers to act under agency agreements). The Greater London Council's responsibility for all principal roads in London other than trunk roads (i.e. the main strategic road network, which are the responsibility of the central government), is now transferred to the London boroughs who were already highway authorities for non-principal roads.

(n)   Metropolitan and London boroughs devise 'unitary development plans' (where local and structure plans are combined). London boroughs must appoint a joint committee to advise them on planning matters of common interest.

(o)   In England and Wales off-street parking is provided as shown, subject to the consent of the county council or the appropriate London borough council. Subject to this consent Welsh district councils are also able to provide on-street parks. The GLC provides on-street parking on the application of the appropriate London borough council.

(p)   London Regional Transport and, following the abolition of the Metropolitan counties in 1986, joint boards ·and members from metropolitan boroughs are the passenger transport authorities and there are passenger transport executives responsible for day-to-day administration. Non-metropolitan county councils are responsible for the co-ordination of public transport in their areas but in some cases district councils run transport undertakings.

(q)   Islands, not regional councils.

(r)   Islands combine with the Highland region.

(s)   Regions only in Dumfries & Galloway, Highlands and Borders.

(t)   Some English districts have been granted limited agency powers for libraries. Welsh district councils may be designated exceptionally to exercise libraries, weights & measures and food & drugs authority functions.

(u)   Welsh district councils (unlike English) have refuse disposal functions (including the disposal of abandoned vehicles) as well as refuse collection. Similarly they are able to provide on-street as well as off-street car parks (subject to the consent of the county council).

(v)   In Scotland smallholdings are administered by the Secretary of State for Scotland and the Crofters' Commission.

(w)   Counties exercise a variety of environmental health functions which complement and impinge upon those of the districts. These include such things as control of toxic waste, the monitoring of noise and atmospheric pollution, the control of diseased animals (rabies, sheep scab etc.) and the analysis of samples (such as suspect food) sent by the district councils.

(x)   The metropolitan and London boroughs provide this service through a joint Fire and Civil Defence Authority in each metropolitan area.

(y)   The Secretary of State can require joint arrangements if necessary.

(z)   The GLC's transport responsibilities transferred to London Regional Transport (an offshoot of the Department of Transport) in June 1984, under the London Regional Transport Act 1984. The Secretary of State has power to ensure that the metropolitan and London boroughs' joint arrangements here are satisfactory.

(aa)   Joint police authorities cover an area of the former metropolitan county councils and comprise members of the constituent (i.e. metropolitan district) councils (as well as JPs). In the case of Tyne and Wear, this extends to include the non-metropolitan county of Northumberland.

(bb)   Some of the former GLC's functions here transferred to the Historic Buildings and Monuments Commission in 1986.

Appendix 3

Election Contests and Turnout 1945–70

Average % polls at local government elections (England and Wales)

Year	County councils	County boroughs	Non-county boroughs and UDCs	RDCs
1945	30·1	45·6	46·4	47·9
1949	42·5	52·2	47·0	51·6
1952	43·2	49·9	50·9	52·0
1955	36·5	43·8	45·0	48·2
1958	33·3	40·3	42·9	46·2
1961	35·7	40·6	42·3	45·0
1964	41·0	40·5	42·0	45·1
1967	38·7	40·3	42·8	42·8
1970	33·8	37·6	40·4	42·3

Uncontested seats (%) at local government elections (England and Wales)

Year	County councils	County boroughs	Non-county boroughs and UDCs	RDCs
1945	43·5	7·8	7·3	59·2
1949	52·1	7·7	19·2	66·5
1952	55·3	12·4	25·4	67·2
1955	60·7	18·5	31·5	72·7
1958	60·9	18·6	32·1	75·2
1961	61·2	12·8	28·5	73·9
1964	55·6	8·8	19·7	69·9
1970	55·0	6·0	23·0	70·0

Source: Registrar General's Statistical Review of England and Wales 1970, Part II; and the Maud Report, Vol. I, p. 93 (amended).

Scottish local authorities 1970

	Uncontested seats (%)	Voting turnout (%)
Scottish local authorities	50	44·1
Counties of cities	0	39·4
Large burghs	14	43·8
Small burghs	40	46·9
Landward areas	67	53·6
Districts	80	53·3

Source: Registrar General of Scotland: *Annual Report 1970*, Part II.

Appendix 4

An Example of a County Council Agenda

Please sign the Attendance Book in the vestibule of
the Shire Hall before entering the Council Chamber

WESSEX COUNTY COUNCIL

LOCAL GOVERNMENT ACT 1972

YOU ARE HEREBY SUMMONED to attend a Meeting of the
Wessex County Council to be held in the Council Chamber,
Shire Hall, Selmer, on Wednesday next, the 6th August, 1986, at
10.30 a.m. The business is specified in the following Agenda.

Anyone requiring further information about the meeting or
wishing to inspect any of the background papers used in the
preparation of the reports referred to in the Agenda is requested
to contact Mr Lionel Hampton, County Secretary and Solicitor's
Dept, County Hall, Selmer.

Dated this 30th day of July, 1986.

Charles Mingus

Chief Executive
County Hall, Selmer.

To: The Meeting of the Wessex County Council

AGENDA

1. The Meeting to be opened with Prayer.

2. To sign the Minutes of the meeting of the Council held on 21 May, 1986.

3. Apologies for absence.

4. Chairman's announcements.

5. Notice of Motion – Hunting.
   Mrs E. Fitzgerald to move, in accordance with notice duly given:
   (i) That the Council welcomes the recent decision of the National Trust to limit the number of occasions that land within their control is hunted over together with the banning of motorized hunt followers, and in indicating its support for these policies, seeks to make provision for similar measures over council-owned land.
   (ii) That this motion be treated as urgent for the purposes of Standing order 26.

6. To consider the reports of the following Committees:—
   A   Policy and Resources Committee
   B   Planning and Transportation Committee
   C   Public Protection Committee
   D   Social Services Committee
   E   Libraries, Museums and Records Committee
   F   Education and Cultural Services Committee

   (Copies of these reports have already been circulated.)

Note: All the reports mentioned above, including any documents circulated previously or with this Summons, are to be considered and taken as part of the Agenda.

Appendix 5

An Example of a Committee Agenda: Wessex County Council Social Services Committee – 12 June 1986

A meeting of the Social Services Committee will be held in the Brubeck Room, County Hall, Selmer, on Tuesday 12 June 1990 at 2.15 pm. This meeting will be open to the public and press, subject to the passing of any resolution under Section 100A(4) of the Local Government Act 1972.

Charles Mingus
County Secretary and Solicitor

1. Minutes of the meeting held on 20 May 1986.
2. Community Services Sub-Committee: to consider the quarterly report of the Sub-Committee.
3. Planning and Resources Sub-Committee: to consider the quarterly report of the Sub-Committee.
4. Grants to outside bodies: to consider a report by the Director of Social Services.
5. Proposed Strategies for the Care of the Mentally Handicapped: to consider the consultation document prepared jointly by the Director of Social Services and the Wessex District Health Authority.
6. Supplementary Benefit Payments to People in Voluntary and Private Residential Care Homes: to consider a report by the Director of Social Services.
7. Report of the Gypsy Sites Panel.
8. Action agreed by the Chairman: to report the action taken in consultation with the Chairman, as set out in the schedule to be laid on the table.

9. To seal and to authorise the County Solicitor to sign any necessary documents arising out of the matters dealt with at the meeting.

10. <u>Any other business.</u>

Appendix 6

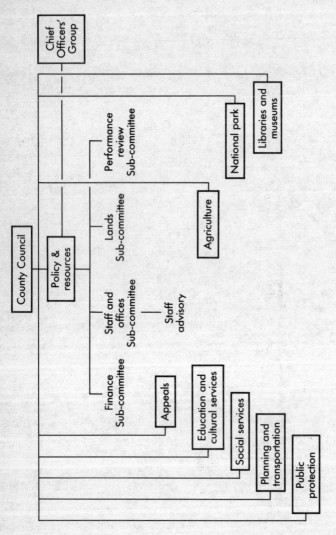

An Example of Committee Structure (Somerset County Council 1980)

Appendix 7

*Chief Executive

Chief Officers' Group

*Chief Executive's Dept	*Education Dept	*Treasurer's Dept	*Surveyor's Dept	Management Services Unit	Fire Brigade	Libraries Dept	County Analyst and Scientific Adviser

Architect's Dept · Social Services Dept · Planning Dept* · Valuer and Estates* · Emergency Planning HQ · County Trading Standards · Museums Dept

* Indicates permanent membership of the Chief Officers' Group (COG)

An Example of Departmental Structure (Somerset County Council 1980)

Appendix 8

Somerset County Council's Education Department (1980)

Appendix 9

Taunton Deane Borough Council Statement of Expenses (1980–81)

The following statement shows how the rate in the pound is made up. It sets out in relation to the Borough Council and the Somerset County Council, in terms of rates in the pound, the expenses, after deducting fees, rents, recoupments etc., of the services and the amount of Government grants and other monies receivable.

| Services | Administering Authority | | Total General Rate |
	Borough council	County council	
	p	p	p
Education		86·5	86·5
Public Health –			
Refuse Collection	2·8		2·8
Waste Disposal		1·6	1·6
Other Health Services	3·3		3·3
Cemeteries and Crematorium Joint Committee	0·5		0·5
Concessionary Bus Fares		13·6	13·6
Social Services		8·4	8·4
Police		3·6	3·6
Fire Service	1·1	14·4	15·5
Highways	19·9		19·9

Services	Administering Authority		Total General Rate
	Borough council	County council	
	p	p	p
Housing – General	6·8		6·8
Housing – Rent Rebates	1·0		1·0
Housing – Rent Allowances	2·7	1·4	4·1
Planning		1·6	1·6
Regional Water Authorities	5·0		5·0
Leisure and Recreation		1·6	1·6
Magistrates' Courts and Probation		2·0	2·0
Libraries	1·8	0·8	2·6
Other Services and Expenses		26·6	26·6
Provision for Inflation			
	45·4	162·1	207·5

| Services | Administering Authority | | Total General Rate |
	Borough council	County council	
Deduct in respect of:			
Addition to Balances:		0·1CR	
Appropriations from Balances	1·4		1·3
Housing Subsidies	18·0		18·0
Government Grants Service Grants		9·7	9·7
Housing Rent Rebates Subsidy	5·0		5·0
Housing Rent Allowance Subsidy	0·9		0·9
	25·3	9·6	34·9
	20·1	152·5	172·6
Rate Support Grant – Needs Element	6·7	43·5	50·2
Rate required for Borough and County Council Services	13·4	109·0	122·4
Estimated product of 1p Rate	£146,651	£731,368	
Estimated Local Deficiency in Rateable Value	£5,007,318		

Appendix 10

Functions of Parish Councils in England and Community
Councils in Wales

A. Powers to provide facilities and/or to contribute towards the provision of facilities by others

1. Allotments

2. *Arts and Recreation*
   Arts and Crafts, support and encouragement
   Community halls, provision
   Recreational facilities (e.g. parks and open spaces, playing fields, swimming baths etc.)
   Tourism, encouragement

3. *Burials* etc.
   Cemeteries and crematoria†
   Closed churchyards, maintenance†
   Mortuaries, provision†

4. *Environmental Health*
   Cleaning and drainage of ponds etc.
   Litter control
   Public conveniences
   Wash houses and launderettes

5. *Footpaths, Roads and Traffic*
   Bus shelters*
   Footpaths – creation and maintenance; signposting*
   Footway lighting, provision*

Parking facilities – cycle and motor cycle parks; off-street car parks*

Rights of way, acquisition and maintenance

Roadside verge, provision, maintenance and protection*

6. Public Clocks

7. War Memorials†

B. Specific powers to receive notifications and represent parish interests to other authorities

1. District councils must notify parish councils in England and community councils in Wales of the following –

a. planning applications received by them where the parish or community council asks to be so notified;

b. intention to make by-laws relating to hackney-carriages, music and dancing, promenades, sea shore, registry of servants and street naming;

c. intention to provide a cemetery in a parish or community;

d. proposals to carry out sewerage works.

2. County councils must consult parish councils in England and community councils in Wales about footpath surveys.†

3. Parish councils in England and community councils in Wales may in certain circumstances withhold consent to proposals for stopping up unclassified highways and footpaths.

4. Parish councils in England and community councils in Wales are 'minor authorities' for the purpose of appointing managers of primary schools serving their area.†

5. Parish councils in England and community councils in Wales may often act as trustees or make appointments to the trustees of local charities.

6. In England, the district councils may confer any power of a parish council on to a parish meeting.

* The exercise of these powers is subject to the consent of the county council.

† These powers or rights, as appropriate, are also available to parish meetings.

Appendix 11

Income and Expenditure Pattern of Parish Councils 1990

Expenditure

Finance charges & insurance – 6·8%	Bank charges	0·3%
	Loans	4·7%
	Other	0·6%
	Insurance	1·2%
Office administration – 26·9%	Clerk's salary	11·0%
	Audit fee	0·7%
	Other	15·2%
Activities – 66·3%	Parks & open spaces	20·4%
	Village/community hall	12·8%
	Burials/crematoria facilities	6·8%
	Indoor recreation	6·6%
	Tourism	4·1%
	Lighting	3·4%
	Footpaths	2·5%
	Public amenities	1·4%
	Car & cycle parks	1·3%
	Allotments	1·1%
	Communications	0·8%
	Litter bins	0·8%
	Competitions	0·2%
	Other	4·1%

Source: The Role of Parish and Town Councils in England, HMSO, 1992.

Revenue

Appendix 12

An Extract from the Standing Orders of Somerset County Council

(reproduced by kind permission)

POLICY AND RESOURCES COMMITTEE

86(1)(a) The Policy and Resources Committee shall consist of 19 councillors, including the Chairman and Vice-Chairman of the Council and the Chairmen of [all the Council's committees]
(2) It shall be the duty of the Committee

(a) to consider and advise the Council regarding:

(i) their strategic policies, and for such purposes to consider the broad social and economic needs of the county (having regard also to any relevant national and regional considerations), to take into account (and to be consulted in the preparation of) any structure plans for the county, and to advise the Council on what their aims and priorities should be, and on methods and programmes for the achievement of those, either in whole or in part;
(ii) their overall level of expenditure both on capital and revenue account, their forward capital programme and the allocation and control of the financial, manpower and land resources of the Council;

(b) (i) to regulate and control the financial affairs of the Council and for such purpose from time to time to embody their directions relating to financial matters in a code of procedure which shall be observed by all committees of the Council;

(ii) to present to the February meeting of the Council each year estimates of income and expenditure of the Council for the next financial year together with a recommendation as to the amount which will be required to be raised by means of precepts in respect of that financial year;

(c)   to keep under review the progress of any of the Council's work and services, the effectiveness of such work and services, and the standards and levels of, and the necessity for, existing services;

(d)   to examine and make recommendations to either the Council or the committee concerned as the Policy and Resources Committee consider appropriate, on any proposal or decision of a service committee for new major policies or services or for any material changes in existing major policies or services, with due regard to any impact upon the Council's strategic policies or resources, for which purpose each service committee is hereby directed to refer any such proposal or decision to the Policy and Resources Committee before it is implemented;

(e)   to keep under review the main policies and aims of the Council and the arrangements for their implementation;

(f)   to ensure that the organization and the management processes of the Council are designed to make the most effective contribution to the achievement of the Council's aims; and to keep them under review, making recommendations as necessary for change in either committee or departmental structures, or the distribution of functions and responsibilities, or Standing Orders;

(g)   to advise the Council on the carrying out of any major building development schemes by the Council in association with any other local or public authority or private developer;

(h)   to ensure that the Council maintain effective liaison with other local authorities and appropriate bodies in respect of matters within the purview of the Committee;

(i)   to ensure the maintenance of an effective public relations service;

(j)   to determine polling districts for County Council elections;

(k)   to recommend to the Council the appointment of the Chief Executive, the Deputy Chief Executive and County Solicitor, the County Treasurer, the County Architect and the County Valuer and Estates Officer;

(l)   to make recommendations to the Council regarding the appointment of:–

(i) councillors to serve on the various committees (including the Staff Advisory Committee and the County Joint Committee);

(ii) persons to serve as additional members of committees;

(iii) councillors and other persons to serve on statutory and other outside bodies or committees thereof under whose constitutions the Council are entitled to representation except in those cases where this power is specifically reserved to another committee;

(m) to act as the controlling committee in relation to the Departments of the Chief Executive, the County Solicitor and the County Architect.

FINANCE SUB-COMMITTEE

87(1)(a) The Policy and Resources Committee shall appoint a Finance Sub-Committee consisting of ten councillors including the Chairman of the Council, the Chairman and four other members of the Policy and Resources Committee;

(b) the Chairman shall be elected from members of the Sub-Committee who are also members of the Policy and Resources Committee.

(2) Subject to the overall control of the Policy and Resources Committee, it shall be the duty of the Sub-Committee

(a)   to advise the Committee as to

– the methods and procedures for controlling the financial affairs of the Council and to supervise their implementation and, where appropriate, give directions;

– the Council's annual capital and revenue budgets and forward capital and revenue estimates for successive years;

– members' allowances.

(b) to make recommendations regarding the granting of supplementary estimates, provided that the Sub-Committee may in their discretion approve any supplementary estimate which the Council are obliged by law to incur or suffer or which is required to meet an unforeseen increase in the level of costs, prices or remuneration; [and in respect of certain other items].

(c) to examine estimates of the cost of proposals by committees and to draw the attention of the Policy and Resources Committee to any points in connection with such estimates or proposals as they may think fit;

(d) to act as the controlling sub-committee in relation to the County Treasurer's department.

Appendix 13

An Example of a Schedule of Delegation of Powers to Officers

The Director of Social Services and in his absence or where appropriate, a Deputy Director (and where specifically mentioned, other officers) have delegated to them the powers set out below, subject to the overall policy of the Council, its Committees and sub-Committees, and the expenditure involved being within the overall estimate provision and to the amounts expended on any individual client (residential placements excepted) not exceeding £250.

(1) To authorize the payment of boarding-out allowances in accordance with the Scale approved by the Committee.

(2) Area Officers to approve or refuse applications from persons wishing to become foster parents to children in care, subject to a report being made to the Care and Community Services Sub-Committee stating the reasons where application is not approved and to the Director of Social Services seeking the observations of any member of the Committee living in that locality.

(3) To authorize, subject to reporting to the Chairman and Vice-Chairman of the Social Services Committee, at the first available opportunity, to grant or refuse permission for a period in secure accommodation in accordance with the law in respect of the children in care of the County Council but admitted to Homes not under the management of this authority, and to authorize the County Solicitor, in consultation with the Director of Social Services, to apply to the Juvenile Court where appropriate for an Order under Section 21(a) of the Child Care Act 1980, enabling a child to

be kept in secure accommodation. (Also exercisable by the Principal Assistant, Children and Families.)

(4) To authorize the County Solicitor or the persons designated in Standing Order 107(a), in consultation with the Director of Social Services or the Deputy Director, Operational Services, to issue a complaint to the juvenile court under Section 43 of the Adoption Act 1958 that a child be removed to a place of safety subject to the action taken being reported to the next meeting of the Care and Community Services Sub-Committee.

(5) To make decisions on or give effect to the recommendations of the Adoption Panel in relation to the acceptance, placement and freeing of children for adoption and to authorize the County Solicitor to make application to Court, on the recommendation of the Adoption Panel and Director of Social Services for a Freeing Order. (Also exercisable by the Principal Assistant, Children and Families and Area Officers as appropriate.)

(6) To give or withhold consent to an application for custodianship, including the payment of allowances. (In disputed cases, the power to hear representations and determine the question will be delegated to the Care of Children Panel).

(7) To deal with the question of charges for children attending day nurseries on the basis of social need. (Also exercisable by the Principal Assistant, Children and Families).

(8) To vary the assessed charge for parental contributions on the basis of social need. (Also exercisable by the Principal Assistant, Children and Families).

(9) To decide the dates of terms and holidays at Day Centres for the handicapped.

(10) To issue permits under the Minibus Act 1977 where appropriate.

(11) To authorize the issue of child employment permits in compliance with County Council Bye-Laws under the Children and Young Persons Act 1933 and to issue licences to perform under the

Children (Performances) Regulations, 1968. (Also exercisable by Senior Administrative Assistant, Support Services under the direction of Principal Assistant, Children and Families.)

(12) The County Solicitor acting in consultation with the Director of Social Services be authorized to institute care proceedings under Section 1, Children and Young Persons Act 1969, other than under Section 1(2)(e) on grounds of education where a recommendation is required to the Special Services Sub-Committee for the Education and Cultural Services Committee by the County Solicitor acting in consultation with the Director of Social Services and the Chief Education Officer.

Appendix 14

Council tax valuation bands

Range of values	Valuation band	Range of values	Valuation band
England		*Scotland*	
not exceeding £40,000	A	not exceeding £27,000	A
£40,001–£52,000	B	£27,001–£35,000	B
£52,001–£68,000	C	£35,001–£45,000	C
£68,001–£88,000	D	£45,001–£58,000	D
£88,001–£120,000	E	£58,001–£80,000	E
£120,001–£160,000	F	£80,001–£106,000	F
£160,001–£320,000	G	£106,001–£212,000	G
exceeding £320,000	H	exceeding £212,000	H

Range of values	Valuation band
Wales	
not exceeding £30,000	A
£30,001–£39,000	B
£39,001–£51,000	C
£51,001–£66,000	D
£66,001–£90,000	E
£90,001–£120,000	F
£120,001–£240,000	G
exceeding £240,000	H

Appendix 15

An Example of an Audit Commission Profile

For purpose of performance review, local authorities receive this information, comparing them with a group (or family) of similar authorities. In this case, for Somerset, the 'family' consists of eighteen county councils.

	Somerset	Family Average	Cost of Difference
PRIMARY SCHOOLS			£000
Pupil/teacher ratio	22·2	21·9	(478)
Salary and oncosts per teacher (£)	12,126	12,711	(859)
Cost per pupil	£	£	
Teaching costs	558	599	(1·336)
Education support staff	32	26	223
Other employees	76	78	(58)
Premises	104	106	(74)
Books and educational equipment	31	25	202
Home to school transport	14	17	(114)
Other costs less income	7	11	(129)
	823	862	(1,286)
Pupils per school	140	142	
Pupils per 1,000 population			
Under 5	11·2	7·1	
5 and over	60·8	65·5	
Number of schools			
Nursery	0	2	
Primary	234	243	
Percentage of primary schools			
50 or less pupils	21%	22%	
51–200 pupils	50%	52%	
201–400 pupils	28%	24%	
401 or more pupils	1%	2%	
Number of FTE Teachers	1,511	1,625	

Appendix 16

The Local Government and Housing Act 1989 – a summary*

Part I: Local Authority Members, Officers, Staff and Committees, etc.

The Act implements the Government's proposals in response to the report of the Widdicombe Committee on the conduct of local authority business. The main effect is to give legal force to many of the conventions under which local authorities have done their business. Local authority staff in politically sensitive posts are required to abstain from public political activity. Councils are required to ensure that they have access to advice on good management and the lawfulness and propriety of their actions. Local authority staff are required to be appointed on merit, and provision is made for uniform rules on staff appointments and discipline. Voting power on local authority committees is, in general, reserved to elected councillors. Local authority committees will have to reflect the political composition of the parent council. New rules are introduced for councillors' remuneration. Public registers of councillors' pecuniary interests will be required. A core of uniform rules on the conduct of local authority meetings will be possible.

● Existing provisions for public inspection of the accounts of local authorities and certain other bodies at the time of audit are amended so that, with effect from the audit of the 1990–91 accounts, no personal information about employees of those bodies can be inspected.

---

* Parts VI, VII and VIII, which relate to housing, are omitted here.

Part II: Local Government Administration

The Act reforms the financial arrangements for the Local Ombuds-men. It will ensure proper publicity for cases where the local authority declines to implement a local ombudsman's recommen-dation. It also gives statutory status to the National Code of Local Government Conduct.

Part III: Economic Development and Discretionary Expenditure by Local Authorities

The Act introduces a new, general power for local authorities to promote the economic development of their areas, subject to certain restrictions on inappropriate activities and procedural requirements. It amends the general residual discretionary spend-ing power ('s. 137') to remove ambiguities, and introduces new limits on that power based on population (i.e. £5 per head in London, £2.50 in counties and districts and £3.50 in parishes/communities). It requires reports from voluntary bodies on the use of grants made by local authorities, and clarifies the power of local authorities to assist advice agencies.

Part IV: Revenue Accounts and Capital Finance of Local Authorities

Part IV introduces a new local authority capital finance system which will replace the present capital controls provided by Part VIII of the Local Government. Planning and Land Act 1980. Whereas the present controls place a limit on the amount of capital expenditure an authority can undertake in any year, the new system will instead focus control on the sources of finance for capital expenditure. The main sources of finance are credit, capital receipts, Government grants and revenue.

• Local authorities will receive credit approvals which will permit them to capitalise expenditure and borrow for it, or to enter into certain forms of credit such as leasing and deferred purchase which are defined as credit arrangements in the Act. Most credit approvals will be given in the form of an annual basic credit approval which can be used for any capital expenditure. But some will be issued in the form of supplementary credit approvals which can only be used for specified purposes such as expenditure on coast protection, estate action projects, or the urban programme. Local authorities will have to set aside 75% of their capital receipts from the sale of council houses, and 50% of most of their other capital receipts, as provision for debt redemption. They will be free to use the remainder of their receipts to finance any capital expenditure whenever they choose.

● The Government supports some local authority capital expenditure, such as transport and urban programme expenditure, through grants. With certain exceptions to be specified in regulations, local authorities will be free to spend their capital grants on top of their credit approvals. They will also be free to finance additional capital expenditure from revenue.

● The Act defines expenditure for capital purposes and local authorities will not be able to borrow or use capital receipts for expenditure which does not come within this definition. Thus ordinary repair and maintenance, such as minor repairs to roofs or windows, would normally have to be financed from the authorities' annual revenue account.

● Local authorities will have to set their community charges or precepts at levels sufficient to meet their revenue expenditure for the year, including a minimum provision to be made from revenue in respect of debt redemption. They will also have to provide for an appropriate level of financial reserves.

● Part IV also provides a comprehensive revision and updating of the controls on the administration of local authority borrowing and introduces a requirement for local authorities to keep their outstanding borrowing and other forms of credit within an aggregate credit limit. These controls replace provisions contained in the Local Government Act 1972 and in some 30 other Acts of Parliament dating back to 1875.

Part V: Companies in Which Local Authorities Have Interests

The Act introduces a new framework to regulate local authority interests in companies. It defines what companies are to be regarded as part of the local authority sector, as being subject to the control, or dominant influence, of local authorities, and provides for rules on their conduct. It also lays down rules for local authority minority interests in companies.

Part IX: Miscellaneous and General

This part includes a wide range of provisions, some of the more important of which are noted below.

● Schedule 5 makes amendments to the Local Government Finance Act 1988 relating to the introduction of the new local government finance system on 1 April 1990. This schedule includes technical amendments, additions and modifications to the existing provisions which are necessary in the light of further detailed consideration of the policy and of the powers which are available for bringing it into effect. The most important provisions concerning the community charge and the new business rate are noted below.

● 1990 sees the end of the domestic rating system and its replacement by the community charge. The Act includes provision for a community charge transitional relief scheme to protect those who would otherwise face a substantial increase in their contribution to local services as a result of the change. The scheme will concentrate help on certain groups of people, principally former ratepayers, and pensioners and disabled persons who did not previously pay rates and are not the partner of a former ratepayer.

● The Act contains a number of other improvements to the community charge system. It clarifies the dates on which someone can become subject to a community charge, and the residence provisions for students; ends the anomaly under which foster children were not exempt and school children lost community charge exemption on reaching their 19th birthday while still in full time education; improves the provisions allowing local authorities to give discounts for prompt payment of the community charge or payment in ways which are cost-effective for the local authority; and increases the discretion available to local authorities in defining classes and multipliers for the standard charge.

• The Act sets out the framework for transitional arrangements for the new business rate, designed to phase in the combined effects of the 1990 revaluation of non-domestic property and the introduction from 1 April of a uniform national poundage, the UBR. It also includes a number of other amendments to the business rate provisions in the 1988 Act, which ensure that the policy operates as intended in respect of matters such as the valuation of composite hereditaments and a number of other types of property and in respect of the rating of empty property.

• The Act also amends a number of other matters concerning the new system of local government finance. In particular there are amendments to clarify and improve the powers contained in the 1988 Act in relation to the grant system and related matters. The main amendments are concerned with flows for information between authorities and other bodies including the Government, and with the calculation of the population figure for each authority for grant and other purposes.

• The Act provides a new power to pay grants to local authorities, which will be used to pay transitional grants to assist with the transfer of responsibility to inner London boroughs and with the introduction of the community charge. There is also a new, statutory basis for payments to local authorities towards the costs of dealing with natural disasters and emergencies.

• There are provisions enabling the Secretary of State to amend existing powers, or to give local authorities new powers, to charge for the services they provide, without resorting to long-winded primary legislation. Section 150 gives the Secretary of State the power to make regulations which allow local authorities in England, Scotland and Wales new powers to charge, on a fixed or variable basis, for their services. Any new charging powers introduced under this section will have to be approved by both Houses of Parliament. The Secretary of State may amend existing charging powers by making regulations under s. 151. Neither of these sections gives the Secretary of State the power to *require* local authorities to charge for any services and s. 152 lists those local authority functions which are excluded from their scope.

Appendix 17

Range of Involvement in Local Politics

Level	Estimated number of people	Estimated % of electorate
Consumer of local government services	40,200,000	98
Votes at local election	17,000,000	42
Knows name of council chairman/mayor	11,500,000	28
Very interested in local affairs	8,000,000	20
Ever contacted local councillor	6,800,000	17
Confident of influencing local council	5,000,000	12
Knows date and place of council meeting	3,200,000	8
Member, principal local authority	21,695	0.05

Source: R. Rose, *Politics in England*, Faber, 1984 (adapted).

Notes and References

1. What Local Government Is

1. See *Sunday Times*, 19 September 1993, p. 15. In 1978 P. Holland MP estimated there were 3,000: see P. Holland and M. Fallon, *The Quango Explosion*, CPA, 1978. See also *What's Wrong with Quangos?*, Outer Circle Policy Unit, 1979, D. N. Chester, 'Fringe Bodies, Quangos and All That', *Public Administration*, Spring 1979, and A. Barker, *Quangos in Britain*, Macmillan, 1982.

2. Estimates vary according to definition. See the *Independent*, 17 March 1994 and *Labour Party News*, January 1994. Cf. *The Times*, 29 January 1994, p. 8. See too P. Holland, *Quelling the Quango*, publisher, 1993.

3. F. A. Hayek, *The Road to Serfdom*, Routledge, 1946, pp. 174–5.

4. See for example J. S. Mill, *Representative Government*, 1861, Chapter XV, and J. Toulmin Smith, *Centralisation or Representation?*, 1848, and *Local Government and Centralisation*, 1851.

5. *The Conduct of Local Authority Business* (Widdicombe Report), HMSO, 1986, p. 47.

6. See also *Local Government Studies*, December 1984, and G. Jones and J. Stewart, *The Case for Local Government*, Allen & Unwin, 1985.

7. See A. Henney, *Inside Local Government*, Sinclair Brown, 1983.

8. See for example 'Abolish Local Authority Funding', *The Times Educational Supplement*, 19 May 1992; 'Honouring Town Hall Humbug', *The Times*, 23 February 1988.

2. An Evolving System

1. This reluctance was a consequence of the prevailing philosophy of *laissez faire*, which implied that the state should not interfere with private interests, especially in business. See D. Fraser, *The Evolution of*

the Welfare State, Macmillan, 1973; A. J. Taylor, *Laissez Faire and State Intervention in Nineteenth-Century Britain*, Macmillan, 1972; and E. J. Evans, *Social Policy 1830–1914*, Routledge, 1978.

2. For example, Liverpool promoted nine such Bills in Parliament in the period 1858–83.

3. The population of Britain, in the years 1801–51, increased from 10·5 million to 20·8 million. Over the same period, individual towns experienced the following population growths: Birmingham 71,000 to 233,000; Liverpool 82,000 to 376,000; Glasgow 77,000 to 345,000; Manchester 75,000 to 303,000; London 865,000 to 2·8 million.

4. Some counties, Yorkshire and Sussex for instance, were divided into separate administrative areas (North Riding, East Riding and West Riding; East Sussex and West Sussex) because of their size or shape. England's fifty-two geographic counties were thus divided into sixty-two administrative counties.

5. This figure included four towns – Canterbury, Worcester, Burton and Chester – which achieved county borough status despite having populations of less than 50,000.

6. A number of individual towns had acquired a variety of powers, for example to establish free libraries, museums, police forces, housing and tramways, largely through private Acts of Parliament.

7. See the *Report of the Committee on the Management of Local Government* (the Maud Report), HMSO, 1967, Vol. 1.

8. It has been suggested that some of the functions of the Countryside Commission, the Housing Corporation and the Scottish Development Agency could be taken over by local authorities. See N. and H. M. Drucker, *The Scottish Government Yearbook 1979*, Paul Harris, 1978.

9. There were eight of these in England; Wales and Scotland had councils with similar functions. They were all abolished in 1980.

10. *Report on Social Insurance and Allied Services*, Cmnd 6404, HMSO, 1942.

11. J. Wiseman, 'Local Government in the Twentieth Century', *Lloyds Bank Review*, January 1966.

12. G. Jones and J. Stewart, 'Against Centralism', *Local Government Studies*, December 1984.

13. The population of Scotland rose from 1·5 million in 1801 to 3 million in 1851. By 1861, nearly one third of Scotland's population was living in one-room dwellings, and Glasgow was described as 'possibly the filthiest and unhealthiest of all British towns in the period'. See M.

W. Flinn, *Chadwick's 'Report on the Sanitary Condition of the Labouring Population of Great Britain'*, pp. 10, 99.

14. Following the Parliamentary Reform Act 1832, a number of non-burghal towns were designated 'parliamentary boroughs', entitling them to elect MPs and set up town councils.

3. The Structure of Local Government

1. See, for example: W. A. Robson, *Local Government in Crisis*, Allen & Unwin, 1968; *Report of the Royal Commission on Local Government in England* (the Redcliffe-Maud Report), Cmd 4040, HMSO, 1969; *Report of the Royal Commission on Local Government in Greater London*, Cmd 1164, HMSO, 1960.

2. *Report of the Royal Commission on Local Government in Scotland* (the Wheatley Report), Cmd 4150, HMSO, 1969, Vol. 1, paras. 1 and 2.

3. Parishes did not exist in Scotland, having been abolished in the Local Government (Scotland) Act 1929.

4. Some shared the provision of services through joint schemes, or they 'borrowed' from their neighbours.

5. *Ad hoc* provision includes such things as gas, electricity and National Assistance. Delegation occurred (usually) when an upper-tier authority arranged for services to be provided by lower-tier authorities (for example education or planning in 'excepted' districts with populations of over 60,000).

6. *Local Government: Areas and Status of Local Authorities in England and Wales*, Cmd 9831, HMSO, 1956, p. 4.

7. ibid., p. 6.

8. See H. V. Wiseman, *Local Government in England 1958–69*, Routledge, 1970, p. 30.

9. The Local Government Commission for England produced separate Reports and Proposals for: West Midlands Special Review Area (1961); West Midlands General Review Area (1961); East Midlands General Review Area (1961); South Western General Review Area (1963); Tyneside Special Review Area (1963); North Eastern General Review Area (1963); West Yorkshire Special Review Area (1964); York and North Midlands General Review Area (1964); Lincolnshire and East Anglia General Review Area (1964); and Lincolnshire and East Anglia General Review Area (1965). (All published by HMSO.)

10. Wiseman, op. cit., p. 1.

11. This did not apply only to seats on local councils: as Richard Crossman recorded in his diary when writing about his decisions on the reports of the Local Government Commissions and their possible impact on his parliamentary colleagues, '... each of them knows that as Minister of Housing [and Local Government] the decision I make may be life or death for them in terms of representation at Westminster'. See R. H. S. Crossman, *Diaries of a Cabinet Minister*, Cape, 1975, Vol. 1, pp. 87, 88. See also F. Mount, 'The History of a Mistake', *Spectator*, 6 October 1979.

12. Crossman (op. cit. above) explains how he took the initiative in setting up the Royal Commission in the fortuitous absence of his strong-willed and sceptical Permanent Secretary. The paradox is that this civil servant became a member of the Royal Commission!

13. Local Government Commission for Wales, *Report and Proposals for Wales*, HMSO, 1963, paras. 14, 16.

14. *Local Government in Wales*, Cmd 3340, HMSO, 1967.

15. Originally this was to be elected and executive – a response to the growing nationalist feelings in Wales at the time.

16. The Redcliffe-Maud Report, Vol. 1, para. 28.

17. *Local Government Reform in England*, Cmd 4276, HMSO, 1970.

18. *Report of the Royal Commission on the Constitution* (the Kilbrandon Report), Cmd 5460, HMSO, 1973. This report produced a number of schemes for devolving power to the regions of Britain, and led ultimately to legislation to set up elected assemblies in Scotland and Wales (subsequently repealed, see note 46 below).

19. The Redcliffe-Maud Report, Vol 11, Memorandum of Dissent, Cmd 4040–41, HMSO, 1969.

20. It is estimated that the reorganized structure transferred twenty seats from Labour to Conservative. See F. Mount, 'The History of a Mistake', *Spectator*, 6 October 1979; B. Keith-Lucas and P. G. Richards, *A History of Local Government in the Twentieth Century*, Allen & Unwin, 1978, pp. 223–4; and P. Hall, 'The Country Fights Back – and Wins', *New Society*, 17 September 1970.

21. *Local Government in England*, Cmd 4585, HMSO, 1971.

22. *The Reform of Local Government in Wales*, HMSO, 1971.

23. Some district councils – former boroughs and UDCs – are entitled to call themselves 'boroughs' and some parishes are known as 'town councils'. In addition, some authorities have retained the title of 'city'.

24. *Local Government in England* (op. cit.), para. 13.

25. The adoption of certain business practices ('corporate management' – see Chapter 9) might be regarded as a further move in this direction. However, for the main thrust of the argument, see J. Dearlove, *The Reorganisation of Local Government: Old Orthodoxies and a Political Perspective*, CUP, 1979. See also the references in note 53, p. 587. While the Maud Report of 1967 (Vol. 2, p. 20) showed that 55 per cent of councillors were managers, farmers, professional workers or employers, and the Redcliffe-Maud Report of 1969 (Vol. 3, p. 132) quotes a similar figure of 51 per cent, the more recent Robinson Report (*Report of the Committee of Inquiry into the System of Remuneration of Members of Local Authorities*, HMSO, 1977, Vol. 2, Tables 10 and 11) shows that at least 65 per cent of councillors are from non-manual occupational backgrounds, and that over 60 per cent of male councillors who are working are from just four groups of occupation (sales, clerical, administration/management and professional/technical). This change may please those who bemoaned the poor calibre of councillors, but it adds credence to those who, like Dearlove, interpret the reorganization of local government in class terms.

26. See G. Jones, 'The Local Government Act 1972 and the Redcliffe-Maud Commission', *Political Quarterly*, April 1973.

27. These services have been transferred into the hands of separate boards and authorities under the NHS Reorganization Act 1973 and the Water Act 1973.

28. Redcliffe-Maud Report, Vol. 1, para. 576 (iv).

29. N. Flynn *et al.*, *Abolition or Reform*, Allen & Unwin, 1985.

30. E.g. boroughs have had difficulties reaching joint decisions because of different party control in Merseyside, W. Yorkshire and Greater London.

31. *Streamlining the Cities*, Coopers & Lybrand Ltd, December 1983 and February 1984.

32. S. Bristow *et al.*, *The Redundant Counties?*, Hesketh, 1983.

33. *Organic Change in Local Government*, Cmd 7457, HMSO, 1979. The philosophy behind organic change is that the structure of local government should not be rigid but should vary between different parts of the country, taking into account local circumstances. However, it may be that the original proposals were a first step towards a general pattern of most-purpose district councils; see J. Stewart *et al.*, *Organic Change*, Institute of Local Government Studies, 1978, p. 4.

34. *Devolution and Regional Government in England*, Labour Party, 1975, p. 8. See also *Regional Authorities and Local Government Reform*, Labour Party, 1977.

35. See J. Stewart, *The Local Government Review Itself Reviewed*, European Policy Forum, 1993.

36. See *Local Government Chronicle*, 16 July 1993, p. 3.

37. See *Local Government Chronicle*, 11 June 1993, p. 12, and 9 July 1993, p. 14; also *Local Government Agenda*, July 1993, p. 1.

38. See *The Times*, 6 May 1993.

39. See *Municipal Journal*, 25 June 1993, p. 4.

40. J. Boynton, 'A Case for Leaving Local Government Alone for the Moment', *The Times*, 26 September 1978. In *Local Government in Britain Since Reorganization*, Alexander suggests that antagonism to the two-tier structure is muted through distaste for further reorganization.

41. There were some reservations by members about the allocation of planning functions and the structure of the island councils.

42. N. and H. M. Drucker, eds., *The Scottish Government Yearbook 1979*, Paul Harris, 1978. A. Dawson, 'The Idea of the Region and the 1975 Reorganization of Scottish Local Government', *Public Administration*, Autumn 1981.

43. 'The imbalance of size has been a natural target for criticism, but the boundaries of the Strathclyde region correspond broadly to a distinctive area with regional characteristics and large-scale problems. Any sub-division would have meant a weakening of administrative cohesion and an impairment of strategic opportunities' (*Brief on Local Government Reform*, Scottish Office, HMSO, 1974).

44. Elections were held in 1974 in readiness for the 1975 start.

45. It has been suggested that this was to give the districts a worthwhile role (see *Municipal Journal*, 16 May 1975).

46. Elected assemblies for Scotland and Wales were to be created under the Scotland Act 1978 and the Wales Act 1978. They were to exercise a number of legislative and/or administrative roles and thus off-load the central government as well as providing a focal point for the expression of local public opinion. However, all this came to a halt when the referendums (March 1979) failed to provide the necessary minimum support, and the Acts were repealed. An outline of the proposed schemes is to be found in the Government's White Paper *Our Changing Democracy*, Cmd 6348, 1975.

4. The Functions of Local Government

1. Attorney-General *v.* Fulham Corporation (1921). Local authorities are 'corporations', i.e. they have corporate status. This means the collection of individuals (councillors) becomes one body, with a name and with 'perpetual succession' (i.e. even though actual members change) and with legal rights and duties. Thus it is a legal *persona*, an artificial person, which is itself (rather than individual, constituent members) capable of holding property, making contracts, suing and being sued.

The powers expressly stated or implied in an Act are in practice extended, in that local authorities may legally also do whatever is 'reasonably incidental' to them (such as employing staff, acquiring property, etc.). But it does not mean 'in connection with', which is too broad or vague.

In the exercise of their powers (particularly their discretionary powers – granting licences etc.), local authorities are expected to act 'reasonably'; otherwise they may be deemed to be acting *ultra vires*. In the Wednesbury Corporation case (1948) it was suggested that reasonableness implies that relevant matters are taken into account and irrelevant ones are excluded, and that decisions are not made in bad faith or for improper purposes; nor should they be just plain arbitrary or perverse.

2. In reality the distinction is not very important since, as the Layfield Committee (1976) pointed out, the bulk of local activity is a mixture of free choice, formal requirements and various pressures and influences: see *Layfield Committee on Local Government Finance*, pp. 403–5.

In practice even some mandatory responsibilities may not be fulfilled by local authorities, or they may be undertaken in purely token fashion, as the provision of county colleges after the 1944 Education Act and provision of health centres after the 1946 Health Service Act were. In other cases there may be uncertainty whether the responsibility is mandatory or not, as in the case of the provision of adult or nursery education. *Note*: legislation may also be required where a local authority wishes to cease a function (e.g. close a dock).

3. Scottish authorities also have the power to spend 'common good' funds: see *Public Finance and Accountancy*, 11 November 1988, p. 14.

4. See 'Aspects of Local Democracy', *The Conduct of Local Authority Business* (Widdicombe), Research Vol. 4, HMSO, 1986. See also C. Crawford and V. Moore, *The Free Two Pence*, CIPFA, 1983. Also

Public Finance & Accountancy, May 1985, which shows that Lancashire spent 99 per cent and Tyne & Wear only 18 per cent of permitted expenditure.

5. 'Local Government Today and Tomorrow', *Municipal Journal*, 1962, p. 27.

6. The Maud Report, Vol. 1, Chapter 4. See also the Redcliffe-Maud Report, Vol. 1, para. 323, and the Wheatley Report, Vol. 1, para. 640.

7. See for example *Local Government Chronicle*, 13 March 1991, p. 26; *Reducing Uncertainty – The Way Forward*, CIPFA, 1992; *The Power to Act*, LGIU, 1991; S. Cirell and J. Bennett, *Municipal Trading*, 1992. See too C. Crawford and C. Grace, *'Conducive or Incidental to'*, INLOGOV, 1993.

8. For example the York Corporation Act 1969 cost £6,000. Today such an Act could be ten times that: some opposed Bills may cost over £1 million. However, under the Local Government Act 1972 (sec. 262) it was intended that certain powers conferred by local Acts should be made generally available to local authorities.

9. There are various types of order, and procedures differ for each. For further details, see C. A. Cross, *Principles of Local Government Law*, Sweet & Maxwell; W. O. Hart and J. F. Garner, *Hart's Local Government and Administration*, Butterworth, 1973; or J. A. G. Griffith and H. Street, *Principles of Administrative Law*, Pitman.

10. The Redcliffe-Maud Report, Vol. 1, paras. 257–8.

11. The Wheatley Report, Vol. 1, paras. 361–9.

12. Joint committees are sometimes formed here too – e.g. Somerset County Council and Taunton Deane Borough Council had a joint planning committee until 1980 when under the Local Government Planning and Land Act 1980 counties lost most of their control responsibilities over 'county aspects' of planning. Note the intention to scrap structure plans, proposed in 1988: see note 19.

13. In some areas, in order to avoid the messy administration which can sometimes occur when responsibilities are claimed, 'excepted districts' have been created whereby the district authorities may, for example, become responsible for the road maintenance of whole areas.

14. A *statutory joint authority* or *board* is a body with its own legal existence, made up of councillors nominated by a number of local authorities, and with the power to precept on those authorities, to employ its own staff and hold its own property.

A *joint committee* is a voluntary, but formal, combination of authorities, having no separate legal existence. It is able to discharge functions but has no power to precept, employ staff or hold property.

A *joint forum* is an informal combination of authorities, such as a regional association or county tourism forum. It has no power to discharge functions, which stays with the individual authorities.

A *lead authority* is one authority acting on behalf of others. It can only be used for service provision and not for deciding another authority's service policy, since the latter is a statutory responsibility of the individual authorities.

An *arm's-length supplier* is a company or other organization under the nominal ownership of one authority but supplying also to others.

15. K. Newton and T. J. Karran, *The Politics of Local Expenditure*, Macmillan, 1985.

16. See, for example, the *Report of the Royal Commission on the Police*, HMSO, 1962. On the question of controls, see G. Marshall, 'Police Accountability Revisited', in D. Butler and A. Halsey, *Policy and Politics*, Macmillan, 1978.

17. In England the Department of Transport, in Wales the Welsh Office and in Scotland the Development Department of the Scottish Office.

18. Under the Transport Act 1968, certain areas of Britain were designated 'passenger transport areas' within which municipal transport was managed by 'passenger transport executives' (PTEs), full-time experts who worked under the control of 'passenger transport authorities' (PTAs), comprising part-time members, mainly representatives of the local authorities in the area. In 1974 the role of the PTAs was taken over by metropolitan county councils and the Strathclyde Regional Council. With the abolition of the Metropolitan counties (1986) the PTAs became joint boards formed from the constituent metropolitan boroughs.

19. The existing procedures have been criticized as too complex, with structure plans often being over-detailed and too often overlapping in content with the local plans. See *The Future of Development Plans*, HMSO, 1986.

20. Largely a result of *People and Planning* (the Skeffington Report), HMSO, 1969.

21. This includes public as well as private developments, so that local authorities themselves have to make applications. However, certain government departments and government properties are excluded. In

addition, certain aspects of 'permitted' development do not require specific applications for permission. These occur under a statutory instrument (the General Development Order) and include, for example, small house extensions.

22. Apart from private health provision, the health service provided under the Employment Medical Advisory Service, and health services in prisons and the armed forces, are technically outside the NHS.

23. See, for example, the Redcliffe-Maud Report, Vol. 1, paras. 259–367.

24. See, for example, the *Report of the Royal Commission on the National Health Service*, Cmd 7615, HMSO, 1979, para. 16.22; *Community Care: Agenda for Action* (Griffiths Report), HMSO, 1988.

25. See C. Game, 'Public Attitudes to the Abolition of the Mets', *Local Government Studies*, September 1987.

5. London's Local Government

1. They were in fact called 'Progressives' and included many Liberals and some Conservatives. They were sometimes also known as 'Municipal Socialists', as they sought to emulate and surpass the achievements of Joseph Chamberlain, mayor of Birmingham in the 1870s.

2. This notion was examined by the Royal Commission on Greater London (Ullswater) in 1921–3. It lacked unanimity, producing three conflicting reports, and consequently no action was taken on its various recommendations.

3. From some 600,000 per day in the 1920s to nearly 1 million in the 1950s. See K. B. Smellie, *A History of Local Government*, Allen & Unwin, 1968.

4. Of these counties perhaps Middlesex was the most notable in this respect, having a number of boroughs which by the criterion of population size merited promotion to county borough status, except that this would have emasculated the administrative county.

5. The London boroughs were given some traffic management responsibilities.

6. See, for example, Professor Griffith's evidence to the Royal Commission (para. 192). See also W. A. Robson, *Local Government in Crisis*, Allen & Unwin, 1967, Chapter XXXI.

7. G. Rhodes (ed.), *The New Government of London: The First Five*

Years, Weidenfeld & Nicolson, 1972; see also the *Local Government Chronicle*, 4 March 1972.

8. *The Times*, 6 July 1978. See also R. Freeman, 'London through the Looking Glass', *New Society*, 27 March 1980.

9. See *Hansard*, 12 April 1982; *The Times*, 24 June 1982, 29 July 1982.

10. White Paper, *Public Transport in London*, Cmnd 9004, 1983.

11. See *The Times*, 20 April 1990 and *Sunday Times*, 25 February 1990. Also D. Walker, 'London cries out for a voice again', *The Times*, 15 January 1988; D. Walker, *Capital Welfare*, RIPA, 1988; P. Kelly, 'London isn't Working', *Midweek*, 27 October 1989; *After Abolition*, NCVO, 1987. Conversely, there is evidence of success; see *Municipal Journal*, 19 February 1989.

6. Local Government Elections

1. Such as voting twice by impersonating someone else, etc. Anyone found guilty of such offences is debarred from voting in the local area in which the offence was committed for five years from the date of conviction.

2. See W. Miller, 'Local electoral behaviour', in 'The Local Government Elector', *The Conduct of Local Authority Business* (Widdicombe), Research Vol. 3, HMSO, 1986; M. and S. Pinto-Duschinsky, *Voter Registration: Problems and Solutions*, Constitutional Reform Centre, 1987.

3. See A. Wigram and E. Lyon, *Local Government Elections – the Case for Proportional Representation*, CAER, 1979; B. Keith-Lucas, *Local Elections –Let's Get Them in Proportion*, Parliamentary Democracy Trust, 1978; V. Bogdanor, 'Why the Local Elections System Makes Us Appear More Divided', *The Times*, 19 May 1980; 'Putting the Local Government Vote in Proportion', *Local Government Chronicle*, 17 December 1982; *Electoral Systems in Local Government*, INLOGOV, 1986.

4. By-elections take place when vacancies occur on the council owing to resignation, death or disqualification of councillors. A councillor may be dismissed as a result of his unauthorized absence from council meetings over a continuous period of six months. However, a by-election would not take place in any of these situations if normal elections were due within six months, unless the council was deficient in membership by a third or more.

5. Up to 1979, members could be disqualified on the grounds of having been surcharged (in effect fined) the sum of £500 or more by the District Auditor. This power ceased as such under the Local Government Act 1972, but see pp. 348, 579.

6. This principle implies that those who make the law should be different from those who operate it and from those who adjudicate when it is broken. For a rather fuller treatment, see C. Padfield, *British Constitution Made Simple*, Heinemann, 1987.

7. See *Municipal Journal*, 2 February 1990. Other estimates put the figure at 130,000; see *Hansard*, 13 June 1989. This Parliamentary debate revealed that twenty-four out of forty Greenwich councillors would be affected by this ban.

8. *Candidates' Expenses at Local Government Elections*, Home Office circular, RPA 263. Also Representation of the People Act 1985.

9. These electoral areas are reviewed from time to time by the Local Government Boundary Commissions (see p. 51), though the local authorities themselves may initiate alterations, counties seeking to change divisions and districts revising wards and parishes/communities. In the case of GLC elections, the boroughs assume the role of electoral areas.

10. 'The Local Government Elector', *The Conduct of Local Authority Business* (Widdicombe), Research Vol. 2, HMSO, 1986.

11. The Conduct of Local Authority Business (Widdicombe Report), HMSO, 1986, p. 170.

12. The Maud Report, Vol. 3, pp. 72–80.

13. See, for example, A. H. Birch, *Small Town Politics*, OUP, 1959; W. Hampton, *Democracy and Politics*, OUP, 1970; F. Bealey *et al.*, *Constituency Politics*, Faber, 1965. Information has also been drawn from L. J. Sharpe, *Voting in Cities*, Macmillan, 1967, and *Power in Britain*, BBC, 1965.

14. See note 10. See also W. Miller, *Irrelevant Elections?*, OUP, 1988.

15. I. McLean and J. Smith, *The UK Poll Tax and the Declining Electoral Roll: Unintended Consequences?*, University of Warwick, 1992.

16. See, for example, Hampton, op. cit., and P. Fletcher, in Sharpe, op. cit.

17. See *Local Government Studies*, Summer 1992, pp. 2–3.

18. J. Stanyer, *Understanding Local Government*, Fontana, 1976, pp. 272, 284.

19. J. Stanyer, 'Why Does Turnout Vary?', *New Society*, 13 May 1971.

20. What these average figures do not show is the wide range of turnout

among local authorities. For example, in the 1973 local elections the districts of Ceredigion and Dwyfor, in Wales, had turnouts of 93·9 per cent and 82·8 per cent respectively, while those in Middlesbrough and Stoke-on-Trent were 18·1 per cent and 22 per cent. On the other hand, high voting turnouts can disguise the fact that a high proportion of seats have gone uncontested, and vice versa.

21. Such a view is at least implicit in the Government's White Papers *Local Government in England*, Cmd 4585, and *Reform of Local Government in Scotland*, Cmd 4583, both HMSO, 1971. See also the Redcliffe-Maud and Wheatley Reports. Some election figures for the old local government system are given in Appendix 3.

22. The Maud Report, Vol. 3, Table 113, p. 82.

23. K. Young, 'Attitudes to Local Government', in 'The Local Government Elector', *The Conduct of Local Authority Business* (Widdicombe), Research Vol. 2, HMSO, 1986.

24. *Attitudes to Local Government – A Survey of Electors*, Joseph Rowntree Foundation, 1991.

25. J. G. Gibson, 'Rate Increases and Local Elections', *Policy and Politics*, Vol. 16, no. 3, 1988; J. Ferry, 'Rates and Elections', *Centre for Environmental Studies Review*, Vol. 5, 1979; C. Game, 'Local Elections', *Local Government Studies*, Vol. 7, 1981.

26. G. W. Jones, 'Varieties of Local Politics', *Local Government Studies*, April 1975.

27. See, for example, W. H. Morris-Jones, 'In Defence of Apathy', *Political Studies*, Vol. 2, no. 1, 1954. See also L. J. Sharpe, 'Instrumental Participation in Urban Government', in J. A. Griffiths, *From Policy to Administration*, Allen & Unwin, 1976.

28. J. M. Bochel, *The Scottish Regional Elections 1986*, Dundee University, 1986. There is a tendency in rural areas towards a lack of contests because the incumbent councillor is often known personally by the electors, who may not wish to give offence by opposing him. Subsequently, many rural councillors become well entrenched and almost irremovable. This has been well illustrated in the study of the Scottish Communities – see R. Masterson and E. Masterman, 'The Scottish Community Elections, the Second Round', *Local Government Studies*, January 1980.

29. *Local Government Studies*, Annual Report 1983.

30. 'The Local Government Councillor', *The Conduct of Local Authority Business* (Widdicombe), Research Vol. 2, HMSO, 1986, Table 4.2.

31. The Maud Report, Vol. 1, p. 134; see also p. 93.

32. The Maud Report, Vol. 5, pp. 48–9.

33. The last time there was an uncontested parliamentary seat in Britain was in 1951, when four constituencies went uncontested. See A. J. Allen, *The English Voter*, English Universities Press, 1964, p. 13.

34. See the Maud Report, Vol. 3.

35. J. G. Bulpitt, in *Participation in Politics*, ed. G. Parry, Manchester University Press, 1971, p. 290. There has been some change in composition since then (see Chapter 8) and some would argue that Bulpitt's warnings were justified: see J. Dearlove, *The Reorganisation of Local Government*, CUP, 1979.

36. Parties are not entirely unwritten elements in local government operations. Many councils' Standing Orders contain references to them; they were recognized in the Representation of the People Act 1969 (which allowed affiliations or labels on ballot papers), and the Local Government Act 1985 requires constituent local authorities to reflect the balance of parties in their appointments to joint authorities (sec. 33).

7. The Political Parties

1. The 'Shetland Movement', an erstwhile party, contains many so-called Independents: see J. M. Bochel and D. T. Denver, *The Scottish Regional Elections 1982*, Dundee University, 1982. In order to cover these various situations, J. Stanyer has suggested a classification as follows: a 'developed' party system exists where parties contest elections and control the council; a 'semi-party' system is where they contest elections but hardly refer to their party labels while in office; a 'concealed' system is one where members are partisan behind the scenes of council work, but do not contest elections using party labels; a council is 'non-partisan' where parties are absent from elections and the council. J. Stanyer, *Understanding Local Government*, Fontana, 1976, p. 136.

2. See H. V. Wiseman, *Local Government at Work*, Routledge, 1967, and the Maud Report, Vol. 5, p. 100.

3. In 1956 a prominent (Labour) city council took it upon itself formally to condemn the British invasion of Suez. In June 1981 the GLC declared a boycott on South African goods as a protest against apartheid.

4. A five-fold classification is suggested by L. Corina, 'Elected Representatives in a Party System', *Policy and Politics*, Vol. 3, no. 1, 1974.

5. Political culture has been defined as 'orientations towards political objects' – A. Almond and S. Verba, *The Civic Culture*, Princeton, 1963. In the local government context, it implies the amalgam of people's judgements and attitudes about political institutions (the council, parties, the town hall, etc.), personalities (the chairman, the officers, social workers) and processes (elections, rate collection, etc.). It also entails an element of how individuals see or feel about their own role in the local political system. e.g. Strathclyde provides an illustration with its tradition of left-wing distrust of voluntary organizations and a preference for working through the Labour party. For a concise account of the general concept, see D. Kavanagh, *Political Culture*, Macmillan, 1972.

6. Some of them could be said to have begun with the Birmingham Liberals under Joseph Chamberlain in the 1860s. See A. Briggs, *Victorian Cities*, Penguin Books, 1968; C. Game and C. Skelcher, 'Manifestos and other Manifestations of Local Party Politics: The Spread of Party Politics since Reorganisation', *Local Government Studies*, 1983.

7. J. Redlich and F. W. Hirst, *A History of Local Government in England*, ed. B. Keith-Lucas, Macmillan, 1958; K. Young, 'Party Politics in Local Government: an Historical Perspective', in 'Aspects of Local Democracy', *The Conduct of Local Authority Business* (Widdicombe), Research Vol. 4, HMSO, 1986.

8. A nice illustration of the resistance to state provision was given by *The Times* in 1854 when it stated, 'We prefer to take our chance of cholera and the rest than be bullied into health.'

9. See W. Thornhill, *The Growth and Reform of English Local Government*, Weidenfeld & Nicolson, 1971, pp. 106–8, 112–13. See also Chapter 5 above.

10. Just as at national level more than half of the seats in Parliament went uncontested prior to the emergence of national parties. See T. Lloyd, 'Uncontested Seats in British General Elections 1852–1910', *Historical Journal*, Vol. viii, no. 2, 1965; J. M. Bochel, *The Scottish Regional Elections 1986*, Dundee University, 1986.

11. It is true that some councillors are deterred by the existence of political parties, but these appear to be few in number. See the Maud Report, Vol. 1, pp. 109, 145; Vol. 3, Table 207.

12. See for example J. G. Bulpitt, *Party Politics in English Local Government*, Longman, 1967; H. V. Wiseman, *Local Government at*

Work, Routledge, 1967; W. Hampton, *Democracy and Community*, OUP, 1970; K. Newton, *Second City Politics*, O U P, 1976; G. W. Jones, *Borough Politics*, Macmillan, 1969. This concentration of study may also be justified on the grounds that, while it may not cover a lot of local authorities, it does cover a lot of Britain's population.

13. See H. V. Wiseman, 'The Party Caucus in Local Government', *New Society*, 31 October 1963.

14. See the Maud Report, Vol. 5, p. 105.

15. See too *New Society*, 4 April 1986, and *Local Government Chronicle*, 3 January 1986.

16. There have been some bitter episodes with party groups disowning or de-selecting councillors; e.g. see 'Manchester Politics', *Economist*, 3 October 1981.

17. In addition they may also determine the choice of co-opted members. See p. 199. Indeed, well-established majority parties could change the number and structure of committees and to a large extent even the internal organization of the authority if they wished. See the *Guardian*, 27 May 1981.

18. See the Maud Report, Vol. 5, p. 98.

19. ibid., p. 104.

20. See J. Gyford, *Local Politics in Britain*, Croom Helm, 1976, pp. 78, 84.

21. The Maud Report, Vol. 5, p. 193.

22. Gyford, op. cit., p. 82.

23. See the Maud Report, Vol. 5, p. 100.

24. See Gyford, op. cit., pp. 86–7, G. W. Jones' article in *Local Government Studies*, April 1975, p. 31, and Table 7.5 in Bennett, *Central Grants* (p. 627 below).

25. See Chapter 8. The October 1974 Parliament comprised only 4 per cent women and 7 per cent working-class members, while the middle-age groups (35–54), with 63 per cent, were well over-represented, and the younger (21–34) and older (55 plus) groups were under-represented with 8 per cent and 29 per cent respectively. See C. Mellors, *The British MP*, Saxon House, 1978; also 'The Times' *Guide to the House of Commons 1974*. On a wider perspective, the role of local politics as a stepping stone to national politics should be noted: Mellors shows that one MP in three has local government experience.

26. See L. J. Sharpe, *Why Local Democracy?*, Fabian Society, 1965; J. M. Bochel, p. 555 above, note 28.

27. See J. D. Stewart, 'The Politics of Local Government Reorganisation', in K. Jones, *The Yearbook of Social Policy 1973*, Routledge, 1974.

28. The Maud Report, Vols. 1 and 2.

29. W. Miller, p. 553 above, note 2, and *Irrelevant Elections*, OUP, 1988.

30. *The Times*, 3 May 1990.

31. Source: K. Newton, *Second City Politics*, OUP, 1976, fig. 2.2. Newton declares that 'local elections are a sort of annual general election'. Another recent study concludes: 'On the whole ... municipal voting in big cities is a product of whatever factors happen at the time to be salient nationally.'

32. See Anthony Steen, 'New Life for Old Cities', *Aims*, 1981. Also G. Cameron, *The Future of British Conurbations*, Longman, 1981. The pattern was not continued in 1983, for while the Conservatives won the Election, they held only five cities after the local elections of that year compared to Labour's thirteen.

33. E.g. the 'Lothian effect', see J. M. Bochel and D. T. Denver, *The Scottish Regional Elections 1982*, Dundee University, 1982.

34. See C. Game, 'Local Elections', *Local Government Studies*, March/April 1981, and references therein; J. Ferry, 'Rates and Elections', *Centre for Environmental Studies Review*, January 1979; G. Jones and J. Stewart, 'The Local Factor in a Local Election', *Local Government Chronicle*, 18 June 1982; see also *Local Government Chronicle*, 17 June 1983, and *Municipal Journal*, 3 June 1983. In May 1979 the local elections happened to coincide with the General Election, and the authors of the second study mentioned in note 28 above show that electors (at least in Liverpool) made use of that unique opportunity to 'split' their vote and separate national issues from local by voting for one party in parliament and a different party in their local council: see W. Harvey Cox and M. Laver, 'Local and National Voting in Britain', *Parliamentary Affairs*, Autumn 1979. C. Rallings and M. Thrasher in *The 1985 County Council Election Results in England* conclude that 'while there might be some national trends evident in local voting behaviour they are by no means the only ... influences ... [a] scan through the results should reveal considerable variation and demonstrates that local elections must be viewed in the light of both national and local circumstances.' See also their article in *Local Government Studies*, January/February 1990. See too G. Green, *Policy and Politics* 1 (1), 1972, and A. Bruce and G. Lee, *Political Studies*, June 1982.

35. W. Miller, p. 553 above, note 2.

36. See J. C. Gibson, p. 555 above, note 25, and W. Miller, op. cit. Also see footnote to p. 329.

37. E.g. see *Economist*, 12 May 1990, pp. 35–6.

38. The adversary or 'yah-boo' system as it occurs nationally is also heavily criticized: see S. E. Finer, *Adversary Politics and Electoral Reform*, Anthony Wigram, 1975.

39. *Municipal Journal*, 4–10 June 1993, p. 15.

40. See *Local Government Chronicle*, 5 March 1982, 18 September 1981.

41. See *The Times*, 24 March 1990, and 7 December 1990.

42. The Maud Report, Vol. 1, p. 110.

43. K. Young, *The Conduct of Local Authority Business since Widdicombe*, Rowntree Trust, 1989

44. ibid., Vol. 5, p. 109, and the Widdicombe Report.

45. Gyford, op. cit., p. 68.

46. Source: *Municipal Year Books.*

47. See, for example, *Local Government Chronicle*, 12–26 April 1991.

48. See *The Conduct of Local Authority Business*, Committee Report and Research Vol. 1, HMSO, 1986.

49 *The Conduct of Local Authority Business: The Government Response*, HMSO, 1988.

8. The Councillors

1. By the Committee on Management of Local Government (Maud), 1967. See also C. Rallings and M. Thrasher, 'Disillusion, Age and Frustration – Why Councillors are Calling it a Day', *Local Government Chronicle*, 9 October 1981.

2. Councils are free to determine the timing of their meetings. Consequently, there are variations, but in very general terms county and regional councils and Scottish districts meet in the daytime (mornings or afternoons); other districts meet in the afternoon or evenings; and the London boroughs meet in the evenings.

3. A local study by Peter Beresford (1983) suggests that the Act is quite effective.

4. *Community Leadership and Representation: Unlocking the Potential*, DoE, 1993, para. 4.24.

5. See *The Times Educational Supplement*, 28 April 1989.

6. See *Local Government Studies*, Sept/Oct 1982.

7. R. V. Clements, *Local Notables and the City Council*, Macmillan, 1969.

8. The Maud Report, Vol. 2.

9. As with MPs, this normally means that the union agrees to make a contribution towards the candidate's election expenses (in effect to the local party funds). However, in local government it is less systematic (e.g., agreements are not signed) and the sums involved are small. Sponsorship normally occurs where the candidate is a member of the union and displays this fact on his election material.

10. The Maud Report, Vol. 1, p. 139.

11. This information is drawn from *The Remuneration of Councillors*, Vol. 2, HMSO, 1977, and the Maud Report, Vol. 2.

12. See J. Gyford, 'Our Changing Local Councillors', *New Society*, 3 May 1984, and 'The Local Government Councillor', *The Conduct of Local Authority Business* (Widdicombe), Research Vol. 2, HMSO, 1986.

13. The Maud Report, p. 143.

14. Thus local authorities' conventions vary in such matters as drawing up agendas, officers attending party meetings, members appointing officers, etc.; See Widdicombe Report. See also K. Young, *The Conduct of Local Authority Business since Widdicombe*, Rowntree Memorial Trust, 1989. For a good illustration see the Statement of Conventions by Cheshire County Council in Widdicombe Report, Annexe H.

15. Thus the chairmen of committees may take decisions on behalf of their committee, for example where the matter is urgent. Furthermore, it would appear that just one person may legitimately constitute a committee – see *Local Government Chronicle*, 30 March 1979, 13 April 1979, 4 May 1979.

16. This dilemma is made no easier when councillors are given such guidance as: 'Your over-riding duty as a councillor is to the whole local community. You have a special duty to your own constituents . . .' (Circular on the National Code of Local Government Conduct, 1975. See note 60 below.)

17. See *Towards a New Governance?*, LGMB, 1993, and *Local Government Chronicle*, March 1993, p. 13.

18. *Community Leadership and Representation*, para. 4.10 (iv).

19. For various studies of this aspect, see K. Newton, *Second City Politics*, OUP, 1976; I. Budge *et al.*, *Political Stratification and Democracy*, Macmillan, 1972; J. Dearlove, *The Politics of Policy in Local Government*, CUP, 1973; J. M. Lee, *Social Leaders and Public Persons*,

Oxford, 1963. In his study 'The Functions and Organisation of Councillors', *Public Administration*, Vol. 51, 1973, G. Jones suggests that, at that time, councillors broadly fell into three groups – 75 per cent mainly concerned with representing the ward and constituents' interests, about 5 per cent acting as general policy-makers and 20 per cent being policy-makers in particular service areas. See also *Local Government Studies*, Sept/Oct 1982.

20. *Community Leadership and Representation*, para. 5.5.

21. *Report of the Committee of Inquiry into the System of Remuneration of Local Authorities*, HMSO, 1977, Vol. 2.

22. The Maud Report, Vol. 1. Also MORI in *Sunday Times*, 19 June 1982. A recent survey of Scottish councillors gives a figure of 120 hours per month: *Local Government Forum*, No. 4.

23. 'The Local Government Councillor', *The Conduct of Local Authority Business* (Widdicombe), Research Vol. 3, HMSO, 1986.

24. The chairman of the council is sometimes known as the 'mayor'; in Scotland he is known as either the 'convenor' or the 'provost'.

25. A. Bloch, *The Turnover of Local Councillors*, Rowntree Trust, 1991.

26. K. Young and N. Rao, *Councillors and the New Local Government*, Rowntree Trust, 1992; see too *The Times*, 29 July 1993, p. 14.

27. See *Local Government Chronicle*, 8 April 1993, p. 6; also *Local Government Studies*, Summer 1992, pp. 5–6.

28. *Community Leadership and Representation*, para. 4.10 (ix).

29. See note 23, above.

30. 'The Political Organisation of Local Authorities', *The Conduct of Local Authority Business* (Widdicombe), Research Vol. 1, HMSO, 1986.

31. See Addenda to the *Report of the Royal Commission on Standards of Conduct in Public Life* (the Salmon Report), Cmd 6524, HMSO, 1976; also see pp. 200–202 above.

32. The Robinson Report, Vol. 1.

33. The Maud Report, Vol. 3.

34. *Community Leadership and Representation: Unlocking the Potential*, HMSO, 1993, para. 4.18.

35. In England and Wales, this system started under the Municipal Corporations Act 1835 and did not apply to many later types of local authority, including UDCs, RDCs and parishes.

36. However, it was not a clean break, as aldermen did not disappear from London until 1977 (GLC) and 1978 (London boroughs); and the City, being exempt from the 1972 Act, still has its aldermen. Further-

more, under that Act, principal local authorities in England and Wales are empowered to confer the title of 'honorary alderman' on anyone who has given eminent service as a past member of the council. He/she may then be invited to attend civic ceremonies, but that is all.

37. By law, police committees must comprise two thirds councillors and one third JPs. This could be regarded as compulsory co-option, but equally it may be seen simply as a joint committee (see p. 221). The distinction is not always clear, especially where the co-option is of a representative nature (see p. 197), for example where a county planning committee provides for the built-in representation of additional members from district councils.

38. Equally co-opted members are disqualified like councillors, the one notable exception being teachers, who since 1902 have been regularly co-opted on to LEA education committees.

39. E. L. Hasluck, *Local Government in England*, CUP, 1948. However, it should be noted that such complaints are not a new phenomenon, having been made at various times in the nineteenth century. See E. P. Hennock, *Fit and Proper Persons: Ideal and Reality in Nineteenth-Century Urban Government*, Arnold, 1973; G. Jones, *Borough Politics*, Macmillan, 1969.

40. Dame E. Sharp in a speech quoted in the *Municipal Review*, November 1960. See also *Public Administration*, Winter 1962.

41. Professor B. Keith-Lucas, *The Mayor, Alderman and Councillors*, Liberal Publications, 1961.

42. The Maud Report, Vol. 5, p. 458; see also pp. 40–46 of the report.

43. ibid., p. 196.

44. The Salmon Report, p. 11.

45. The Maud Report, Vol. 1, p. 143.

46. See, for example, *Municipal Journal*, 28 May 1993, pp. 26–7.

47. *The New Local Authorities*, HMSO, 1972, para. 7.52. Concern at the calibre of members is still being expressed: see R. Garson, 'What Direction Should Local Government's Leaders Take Now?', *Local Government Chronicle*, 2 May 1980, p. 478.

48. *Support Services for Councillors*, Association of Councillors/Charles Knight, 1988.

49. T. Eddison *et al.*, *Strengthening the Role of the Elected Member*, LGTB, 1979; *Support Services for Councillors* (Thomas Report), Association of Councillors, 1982. In recent years, the University of Bristol has run some courses for councillors, as indeed it did in 1979 for newly elected MPs.

50. *The Conduct of Local Authority Business* (Widdicombe Report), HMSO, 1986, p. 163.

51. The various relevant nineteenth-century laws were consolidated in the 1933 Local Government Act and are found in the Local Government Act 1972 (secs. 94–98) and the Local Government (Scotland) Act 1973 (secs. 38–42).

52. *Conduct in Local Government*, Cmd 5636, HMSO, 1974.

53. *Report of the Royal Commission on Standards of Conduct in Public Life 1974–6* (the Salmon Report), Cmd 6524, HMSO, 1976.

54. *Conduct in Local Government*, p. 3.

55. *Report of the Royal Commission on Standards of Conduct in Public Life*, p. 11.

56. *Conduct in Local Government*, p. 11.

57. *Report of the Royal Commission on Standards of Conduct in Public Life*, Addendum by Mrs Ward-Jackson, p. 117.

58. An interesting illustration of this is provided by the former Chief Executive Officer of Wandsworth Borough Council who said that he was sacked for calling in the police to investigate suspected corruption. 'There is an immense amount of corruption going on and it is got away with because people know there is no thank you for reporting it' (*Local Government Chronicle*, 20 April 1979).

59. *Report of the Royal Commission on Standards of Conduct in Public Life*, p. 19.

60. Joint circular, *The National Code of Local Government Conduct*, HMSO, 1975.

61. *The Times*, 20 June 1973.

62. A. Doig, *Corruption and Misconduct in Contemporary British Politics*, Penguin, 1984. This book provides a number of useful case studies of corruption in local government.

63. *Economist*, 30 January 1993.

64. Victims of reported fraud are shown opposite. The Audit Commission report *Protecting the Public Purse* (1994) concluded that 'probity in local government is generally in good order, especially with regard to the honesty of staff.' But it has also revealed many cases of fraud and corruption, totalling £25 million. To counter the greater risks associated with CCT, LMS, etc., some councils are appointing an officer whose sole responsibility ifs fraud investigation.

65. See ACE Bulletin Nov/Dec 1985.

Victims of reported fraud (1987–1992)

	Number	amount £m	% of total amount
Banking and finance	105	490	31
Commercial companies	58	473	29
Public (including investors)	77	230	15
Pension funds	2	147	9
Inland Revenue/Customs & Excise	26	99	6
Local and Central Government	37	17	1
Other	31	129	8
Not known	13	20	1
	349	1605	100

Source: Local Government Agenda, ICSA, September 1993.

9. Internal Organization: The Council and its Committees

1. Standing orders (SOs) are the set of rules by which local authorities conduct themselves. They are rather like a written constitution, explaining the composition, powers and procedures of the local authority's component parts. For example, they would lay down the quorum required for meetings, the procedures for entering into contracts or those matters upon which committees or officers could make (delegated) decisions on behalf of the council. The central government issues 'model' standing orders for the benefit of individual local authorities. An example of a local authority's standing orders is given in Appendix 12. New model SOs are emerging as a result of recent legislation (and under the Local Government and Housing Act 1989, the Minister can require local authorities to make certain types of SOs, known as 'core' standing orders).

2. See P. Cousins, 'Council Leaders: the New Strong Persons in Local Government', *Administrator*, July, 1984.

3. See *Local Government Chronicle*, 19 July 1985.

4. See the Bains Report, *The New Authorities*, HMSO, 1972, para. 4.34.

5. The Maud Report, Vol. 1.

6. The Paterson Report, *The New Scottish Local Authorities: Organisation and Management Structures*, HMSO, 1973, para. 3.10, found some 20 per cent of their sample of local authorities reported having made significant changes in organization since the Maud Report.

7. For details of surveys of local authorities see Occasional Papers by the Institute of Local Government Studies (INLOGOV), 1969, 1970.

8. A. L. Norton and J. D. Stewart, 'The Bains Impact', *Local Government Chronicle*, 9 March 1973.

9. The Bains Report, p. xv and para. 2.3; the Paterson Report, para. 4.3.

10. See for example E. F. L. Brech, *Management: Its Nature and Significance*, Pitman, 1967.

11. For example, whether monitoring should be undertaken by the P & R committee or should form a separate sub-committee function; or whether the chief executive should develop a small inner 'executive office'.

12. See the Bains Report, Appendix J.

13. With the possibility of joint meetings (ibid., para. 5.42).

14. The Paterson Report, para. 4.9.

15. ibid., para. 4.6.

16. J. D. Hender, *Municipal and Public Services Journal*, 15 September 1972.

17. This reflects the view of Sir Andrew Wheatley when he dissented from the Maud Committee Report on the grounds that this would keep council members generally better informed and would avoid the danger of the management board members becoming too remote or detached (see the Maud Report, Vol. 1, pp. 155–6). Bains did, however, follow Maud in pointing out that members have different interests, and implied that some of them could be satisfied in pursuing a purely constituency (rather than policy-making) role. (See the Bains Report, Chapter 3.)

18. See R. Greenwood *et al.*, *The Organisation of Local Authorities in England and Wales 1967–75*, INLOGOV, 1975.

19. See R. Greenwood *et al.*, *In Pursuit of Corporate Rationality: Organisational Developments in the Post-Reorganisation Period*, INLOGOV, 1977.

20. R. S. B. Knowles, *The Law and Practice of Local Authority Meetings*, ICSA, 1987.

21. Greenwood, op. cit., p. 18.

22. Bob Hinings, 'Developments in Organisation and Management', *Local Government Studies: Annual Review*, April 1979. Birmingham City Council provides an illustration. When the Conservatives assumed control

there in 1976, they proceeded to dismantle the corporate machinery and re-establish a more devolved, departmental structure.

23. Professor G. Jones has observed: 'It is still doubtful if the corporate devices will invest the chief executive with the necessary authority to prevail against the tendency to departmentalism that is still inherent in the present system' (G. Jones and A. Norton (eds.), *Political Leadership in Local Authorities*, INLOGOV, 1978).

24. See note 12.

25. Note Avon's battle (May 1990) with the Minister for Education over Beechen Cliff school's opting out of LEA control and thereby upsetting the authority's plans for rationalizing its school usage. Also, see B. Chilton, 'Enabling Local Government to Survive', *Journal of Public Finance*, 1 June 1990.

26. N. Hepworth in *Public Finance and Accountancy*, 9 September 1988.

27. Speech to the Conservative Party Annual Conference, October 1991.

28. See p. 310.

29. 'Invent a Problem', *Local Government Chronicle*, 16 July 1993, p. 13.

30. J. Mc Leod and M. Lee, *Towards a New Governance*, LGMB, 1993.

31. See N. Rao, *Managing Change*, Rowntree Trust, 1993.

10. Internal Organization: The Officers

1. See J. H. Warren, *The Local Government Service*, Allen & Unwin, 1952.

2. This is augmented by general legislation such as the Contracts of Employment Act 1972, the Health and Safety at Work Act 1974, the Employment Protection Act 1975 and the Sex Disqualification Act 1975.

3. See *Local Government Chronicle*, 10 April 1992, p. 7.

4. See the *Report of the Committee on the Staffing of Local Government* (the Mallaby Report), HMSO, 1967.

5. See the *Report of the Royal Commission on Standards of Conduct in Public Life 1974–76* (the Salmon Report), Cmd 6524, HMSO, 1976.

6. See A. Spoor, *White Collar Union*, Heinemann, 1967.

7. *Public Finance and Accountancy*, 2 April 1993.

8. K. P. Poole, *The Local Government Service*, Allen & Unwin, 1978, p. 114; also *Public Finance and Accountancy*, February 1980, p. 26.

9. See the Salmon Report; also 'The Dangerous Ground in Public Life', *Local Government Chronicle*, 20 April 1979, pp. 425–7.

10. See K. Young, *The Conduct of Local Authority Business since Widdicombe*, Rowntree Memorial Trust, 1989.

11. *The Conduct of Local Authority Business* (Widdicombe Report), HMSO, 1986, para. 6.161; 'The Political Organisation of Local Authorities', *The Conduct of Local Authority Business* (Widdicombe), Research Vol. 1, HMSO, 1986. See too p. 561, note 12.

12. See Chapter 6. Teachers are an exception: they can be (and in Scotland must be) co-opted on to education committees.

13. E.g. in 1984 Camden council appointed the left-wing chairman of the social services committee of the neighbouring borough, Hackney, to the post of Director of Social Services. *The Times* declared it to be an 'example of degenerating civic culture'. (See p. 599, note 19.)

14. 'The Political Organisation of Local Authorities', *The Conduct of Local Authority Business* (Widdicombe), Research Vol. 1, HMSO, 1986, Table A49.

15. *Report of the Committee of Enquiry on Industrial Democracy*, Cmd 6706, HMSO, 1977. In October 1979, the Secretary of State for Employment (James Prior) told a Confederation of British Industry conference that the Government believed that greater employee involvement in decisions at work was the right road to good industrial relations and better productivity.

16. See R. Greenwood *et al.*, *In Pursuit of Corporate Rationality*, INLOGOV, 1977.

17. B. Wood, in *Party Politics in Local Government*, RIPA/PSI, 1979.

18. See R. Greenwood *et al.*, *The Organisation of Local Authorities in England and Wales 1967–75*, INLOGOV, 1975, and R. Greenwood and J. Stewart, *Local Government Studies*, October 1972.

19. Greenwood *et al.*, op. cit. (1975). Since then several local authorities have dropped their chief executive posts.

20. In the reports by Maud (1966), Mallaby (1967), Bains (1972) and Paterson (1973).

21. See R. Greenwood, 'The Recruitment of Chief Executive Officers', *Local Government Chronicle*, 19 October 1973. See also Alexander, op. cit.

22. See Greenwood *et al.*, op. cit. (1977) and op. cit. (1975).

23. J. Stewart, *The New Management of Local Government*, Allen & Unwin, 1986.

24. See too LGTB, *Breakout from Bains*, 1987.

25. See for example *Municipal Journal*, 13–19 August 1993, pp. 16–17, and 18 September 1992, pp. 25–6.

26. J. Hunt, CEO of Ealing LB. See *The Times*, 20 May 1993, p. 14.

27. *Municipal Journal*, 11 June 1993, p. 18.

28. See *Local Government Chronicle*, 11 June 1993, p. 15.

29. See *Municipal Journal*, 7–13 December, 1990, p. 7.

30. See *County News*, ACC, October 1992, p. 186, and *The Citizen's Charter. First Report 1992*.

31. BS 5750 is a national standard for quality assurance systems. It is awarded through certification (after assessment by an independent certification body). The aim of the standard is 'to establish, document and maintain an effective and economical quality assurance system that will enable an organization to demonstrate to its customers that it is dedicated to quality and has the ability to meet customers' needs. The principles of BS 5750 ... identify the basic principles and specify the procedures to ensure that its services meet customers' requirements.' In practical terms, this requires the creation (involving staff) and maintenance of a quality manual which concerns procedures. Over 50 per cent of local authorities use the BS 5750 criterion in awarding contracts, which made it a logical step for them to apply the same quality assurance system to their own departments.

Total Quality Management (TQM) is more concerned with attitudes in the organization, and its aim is for everyone to 'get it right first time, every time'. It has four basic principles: (i) the vision and drive for quality has to be led and demonstrated from the top; (ii) TQM is about satisfying customer needs, both internally and externally, at the right cost; (iii) quality is everyone's responsibility; (iv) quality has to be designed and built into a product or service and not just inspected out at delivery stage. It therefore involves finding out what customers want and what the organization can best provide; turning those requirements into written objectives and specifications; and setting up procedures to ensure the specifications are met. See *Municipal Journal*, 21 January 1994, p. 20.

32. See for example *Municipal Journal*, 30 October 1992, pp. 14, 16; 7 May 1993, pp. 18–19; and 13 August 1993, p. 19. See also M. Jacques, 'Britain's Dinosaurs Must Adapt to a Competitive New World', *Sunday Times*, 1 August 1993, and D. Osborne and T. Gaebler, *Reinventing Government*, Plume/Penguin, 1993.

33. H. Davies, *Fighting Leviathan*, Social Market Foundation, 1992.

34. See *Public Finance and Accountancy*, 11 June 1993, pp. 12, 14, 27, 29; *Local Government Chronicle*, 15 June 1990, pp. 17, 26.

35. D. Prior *et al.*, *Is the Citizen's Charter a Charter for Citizens?*, LGMB, 1993. See also *Local Government Chronicle*, 8 April 1993, p. 15.

36. See *Municipal Journal*, 2 October 1992, p. 22; *Local Government Chronicle*, 23 April 1993, p. 16.

37. See for example F. Analoui and A. Kakabadse, *Sabotage: How to Recognise and Manage Employee Defiance*, Mercury, 1991; C. Cockburn, *In the Way of Women*, Macmillan, 1991; C. Hakim in *Work, Employment and Society*, 4 (2), pp. 157–88; J. MacInnes, *Thatcherism at Work*, Open University, 1987; J. Newman and J. Clarke, *Doing the Right Thing?*, Open University, 1993.

38. Greenwood *et al.*, op. cit. (1975).

39. Greenwood *et al.*, op. cit. (1975).

40. Greenwood *et al.*, op. cit. (1975).

41. Further details may be found in the Treasury's *Glossary of Management Techniques*, HMSO, 1967. See too *Public Finance and Accountancy*, April 1983.

42. See, for example, *Output Measurement – Discussion Papers*, published by CIPFA (and previously by the IMTA).

43. See, for example, the Local Government Operational Research Unit report, *Evaluating Alternative Housing Management Strategies*, HMSO, 1973; *Information Techniques in Local Authority Supplies Organisations*, HMSO, 1979; and *Planning Remedial Work on Local Authority Buildings*, HMSO, 1979.

44. ZBB implies abandoning the normal 'continuation' budget and examining the whole basis of funding a service by relating its budget to objectives and levels of service. Thus a service, e.g. fire, is broken into functional components (such as Operations Prevention, Transport, Administration) for which objectives can be set. Alternative levels of service can then be considered, including a minimum or zero-base level. Options can be evaluated and priorities determined.

45. See A. Seldon, 'Local Government Imperialism', *Economic Affairs*, January 1984.

46. See, for example, *Performance Management in Local Government*, published by Epping Forest District Council.

47. See the Layfield Report; also Walker and Henney (p. 623 below).

48. In 1974 the DES established the Assessment of Performance Unit to monitor national levels of pupil achievement. See *Output Budgeting for the Department of Education and Science*, Education Planning Paper 1,

HMSO, 1970, and *Performance Indicators in the Education Service*, CIPFA, 1984.

49. *Which?*, March 1989.

50. MORI 1986.

51. *The Conduct of Local Authority Business* (Widdicombe), Research Vol. 3, HMSO, 1986.

52. W. Miller, *Irrelevant Elections?*, OUP, 1988.

53. For a more general appreciation, see N. Johnson, *In Search of the Constitution*, Pergamon, 1977.

54. Other notable legal cases such as Attorney-General *v.* De Winton (1906) and *Re* Hurle Hobbes ex-parte Riley and another (1944) seem to imply that officers have a duty to the electors and may disobey council instructions. However, this would seem only to apply in cases where the legality of the council's instructions was in serious doubt.

55. The Maud Report, Vol. 5, p. 196. Elsewhere in that report officers are reported to say that 'only a minority of members on their committees make any real contribution' and 30 per cent to 40 per cent of the committee members 'were useless' (p. 42). The Royal Commission on London also noted that a good education officer 'is normally immensely influential in policy as well as in administrative questions' (*Report of the Royal Commission on Local Government in Greater London 1957–60*, Cmnd 1164, HMSO, 1960, para. 469). An example of LAMSAC's work concerned the computerization of refuse collection in 1982.

56. The Maud Report, Vol. 1, para. 109. See also *Local Government Chronicle*, 4 May 1990, p. 19.

57. K. Young and M. Davies, *The Politics of Local Government since Widdicombe*, Rowntree Trust, 1990.

58. ibid., Vol. 1, para. 145.

59. *We Can't Go On Meeting Like This: The Changing Role of Local Authority Members*, Audit Commission, 1990.

60. See *The Times*, 20 May 1982.

61. See *Community Care*, 4 March 1982.

62. See *Municipal Journal*, 21 May 1982. Also article by D. Peschek in *Local Government Chronicle*, 24 April 1981.

63. *The Conduct of Local Authority Business* (Widdicombe), Research Vol. I, p. 133, HMSO, 1986.

64. *Aspects of Administration in a Large Local Authority*, INLOGOV, 1967. At one time during the 1984–5 Militant-dominated Labour

administration of Liverpool City Council, every item of expenditure had to be approved personally by the Chairman of Finance.

65. B. Keith-Lucas, 'Who Are the Policy Makers?', *Public Administration*, Vol. 43, 1965.

66. J. Gyford, *Local Politics in Britain*, Croom Helm, 1976, p. 43.

67. See, for example, M. Kogan and W. Van Der Eyken, *County Hall LEA*, Penguin Books, 1973. It is perhaps not without significance that this study of policy-making was based upon interviews with the *officers*, while the parallel study at national level (*The Politics of Education* by M. Kogan, Penguin Books, 1971) concentrated on elected *politicians.*

68. It is sometimes felt by some chief officers that education gets an unreasonably favourable share of the authority's resources because it has a powerful lobby behind it – parents. However, this can lead to those other officers reacting by 'ganging up' against the chief education officer.

69. See Kogan and Van Der Eyken, op. cit., and K. Wheare, *Government by Committee*, Oxford, 1955, Chapter 7.

70. See G. W. Jones, 'Varieties of Local Politics', *Local Government Studies*, April 1975. Another writer suggests that there may be differences between the political parties when it comes to keeping a rein on officers: see J. Sharpe, 'American Democracy Reconsidered', *British Journal of Political Science*, Vol. 3, no. 1, 1973. See too M. Bichard, 'The Tale of Two Councils', *Municipal Journal*, 21 April 1989, and 'Managing in a Political Environment', *Administrator*, January 1986.

71. *Party Politics in Local Government*, RIPA/PSI, 1979.

72. See, for example, the clerk who wrote, 'In any cases where officials have tried to interfere with policy I have rapped them firmly over the knuckles' (Maud Report, Vol. 5, p. 268).

73. See *Municipal Journal*, 8–14 May 1992, p. 7.

74. See *Local Government Chronicle*, 15 June 1990, p. 17.

75. See P. Saunders, *Urban Politics*, Hutchinson, 1979, A. Blowers, *The Limits of Power*, Pergamon, 1980, and C. Cockburn, *The Local State*, Pluto, 1977.

76. See, for example, the interpretation in S. Barrett and C. Fudge, *Policy and Action*, Methuen, 1981, and C. Ham and M. Hill, *The Policy Process in the Modern Capitalist State*, Wheatsheaf, 1984.

77. *The Conduct of Local Authority Business* (Widdicombe), Research Vol. I, p. 125, HMSO, 1986.

78. Ibid. p. 130.

79. Ibid. pp. 137, 141.

80. C. Game and C. Skelcher, 'Manifestos and other Manifestations of Local Party Politics: The Spread of Party Politics since Reorganisation', *Local Government Studies*, 1983.

81. *The Conduct of Local Authority Business* (Widdicombe Report), HMSO, 1986.

82. See R. Wendt, 'Decision-making in Central and Local Government in the Absence of Political Majority', *Public Administration*, Autumn 1986.

83. On the grounds that there are other strong influences and inputs – see G. Stoker and D. Wilson, 'Intra-organizational Politics in Local Authorities', *Public Administration*, Autumn 1986.

84. The Paterson Report recommended the provision of offices for committee chairmen (and perhaps party leaders), interviewing rooms at headquarters and local offices, libraries and information rooms, assistance with research, dictating, typing, copying and other secretarial services and adequate telephone facilities. See also T. Eddison, *Strengthening the Role of the Elected Member*, LGTB, 1979.

85. Under the reorganization of 1974–5, the number of members (excluding parishes and communities) fell from 42,000 to 26,000; the number of employed staff remained constant at over 2 millions (having risen from a figure of 1·4 million in 1952 and 1·8 million in 1962). A similar problem occurs at central government level with a virtually constant number of ministers having to control a greatly expanded (post-war) civil service.

11. Finance

1. See A. T. Peacock and J. Wiseman, *The Growth of Public Expenditure in the United Kingdom*, OUP, 1961, and the *Report of the Committee on Local Government Finance* (the Layfield Report), Cmd 6453, HMSO, 1976.

2. In Scotland, teacher training and advanced further education (and mandatory grants) are not local authority functions and are financed directly by the central government.

3. The Layfield Report, Annexe 9.

4. See *UK National Accounts*, Central Statistical Office, HMSO; *Annual Abstract of Statistics*, Central Statistical Office, HMSO; *Social Trends*, Central Statistical Office, HMSO; and the *Local Government Trends*, CIPFA.

5. For example, the London Lotteries Club (comprising the GLC and twenty-one boroughs) raised £2½ million up to the beginning of 1980. See the *Local Government Chronicle*, 8 June 1979 and 1 January 1980.

6. The Community Land Act 1975 gave local authorities substantial powers to acquire land for development. This was being implemented slowly by councils, but under the Local Government, Planning and Land Act 1980 the 1975 Act was repealed and the scheme has ceased to operate.

7. A possible fourth group concerns the inter-local authority charges which occur under 'pooled' expenditure arrangements (see p. 94) and where the residents from one local authority benefit from the services provided by another; for example, students travelling to another LEA's college or children being placed in care outside the native local authority.

8. Individual councils may decide to adopt such a policy, but in some services (e.g. for free school meals) it may be laid down by the central government (as indeed might the actual scale of charges; e.g. those for residents of old people's homes).

9. See *Housing Policy Technical Volume 3*, HMSO, 1977. Local authorities are obliged to keep a separate housing account.

10. See *Local Charges as a Source of Local Government Finance*, IMTA, 1968; A. Seldon, *Charge*, IEA, 1979; A. Maynard and King, *Prices and Rates*, IEA, 1972; M. Beasley, 'How Rates Can Be Abolished', *Local Government Chronicle*, 4 January 1980; *Alternatives to Domestic Rates*, HMSO, 1981; *Service Provision and Pricing*, HMSO, 1981; Economic Affairs, July 1984; and S. J. Bailey, 'Paying for Local Government: Charging for Services', *Public Administration*, Winter 1986. Another regular suggestion is that students be paid loans instead of grants. In February 1981, the High Court ruled that Hereford and Worcester LEA was breaking the law in charging for individual music lessons in school time: see *Where*, March 1981.

11. An Audit Commission report (August 1984) was sceptical about the savings achieved by private refuse collection. Yet savings of 3 per cent p.a. are claimed: *LGC Supplement*, 5 July 1985.

12. *Paying for Local Government*, HMSO, 1986, para. 7.3.

13. See Bailey in note 10.

14. See note 10.

15. *Municipal Yearbook 1985*.

16. LGMB CCT Report, May 1993.

17. *Local Government Chronicle*, 13 November 1992, p. 10.

18. S. Szymanski and T. Jones, *The Cost Savings from CCT of Refuse Collection Services*, London Business School, 1993.

19. *Realising the Benefits of Competition*, Audit Commission, 1993.

20. See K. B. Smellie, *A History of Local Government*, Allen & Unwin, 1946, pp. 112–14. Their expansion was mainly hindered by jealous Chancellors.

21. Some of these – police, education, roads – were paid on a percentage basis; others, such as housing, were paid on a unit basis, for instance £5 per house p.a.

22. See the White Paper on Local Government, 1929. In fact this is not easy to determine: it is very much a matter of judgement. For example the police services are closely overseen, but they probably would be even if there were no specific grant. On the other hand there is some evidence that the specific grants which go to housing and transport do bring with them a significant degree of central intervention. (See, for example, P. G. Richards, *The Reformed Local Government System*, Allen & Unwin, 1978, p. 104.)

23. See *Public Finance and Accounting*, 3 August 1990.

24. In England and Wales, they meet under the auspices of the Consultative Council on Local Government Finance. See Chapter 13. 'Relevant' expenditure covers most local authority expenditure but excludes housing subsidies and student mandatory grants, which are paid separately.

25. The percentage figure is higher in Scotland for historical reasons: the amalgam of general and specific grants in 1966 amounted to a higher proportionate figure in Scotland than it did for England and Wales. Also, in Scotland relevant expenditure is differently determined. Scotland's costs are greater too (e.g. harder winters, etc.).

26. In effect, the local authorities transfer some rating responsibilities from domestic ratepayers to the central government to the extent of these figures. Until recently the figure for Scotland was 31p but this was reduced in line with the 1978 revaluation.

27. See, for example, *Local Authority Needs and Resources*, Centre for Environmental Studies Research Paper no. 12, December 1974; also F. Cripps and W. Godley, *Local Government Finance and Its Reform*, CUP, 1976.

28. *Local Government Finance*, Cmd 6813, HMSO, 1977.

29. This implies a common, uniform precept across the county. In fact

(essentially in London) there may be local additions to the basic precept where services are not evenly provided over the whole area.

30. E.g. 97 per cent of spending is funded from rates in Harlow; cf. 8 per cent in Rhondda.

31. A further consideration is whether neighbouring district authorities do so. Any such decision will automatically affect the yield of the county precept from which *all* county inhabitants benefit.

32. In Scotland the regions and islands appoint independent assessors (the Scottish Assessors Association). Their revaluations have been fairly regular (occurring in 1961, 1966, 1971, 1978 and 1985). This is in contrast to England and Wales, which since a partial revaluation in 1956 has only had a revaluation in 1963 and 1973. It was Scotland's 'efficiency' in carrying out a revaluation in 1986–7 that produced some shock increases and led to the introduction of the community charge a year before England and Wales.

33. Site values are said to have the merit of encouraging the development of empty sites. Capital values are said to be more realistic and easier to determine. The Government accepted the advantages of the capital valuation method. See *Local Government Finance*, Cmd 6813, HMSO, 1977.

34. As an illustration, if the local authority's

estimated expenditure is		£40,000,000
and its estimated income is:		
grants	£20,000,000	
charges	5,000,000	25,000,000
then the rate-borne expenditure is		15,000,000
If the total rateable value is		20,000,000
then the rate poundage is	$\dfrac{15,000,000}{20,000,000}$	= 75p per £ R. V.

In actual practice, councils determine the rate on the basis of the 'product of a 1p. rate'. In the example, if 1p rate raises £200,000, then to raise the required £15 million (which is 200,000 × 75) the local authority must charge 75 times the 1p rate.

35. There are some 28 million income earners compared to 20 million ratepayers. Under the Local Government Act 1980 elderly ratepayers in arrears can arrange to have their debts settled from their estate when they die.

36. Source: *Alternatives to Domestic Rates*, Cmnd 8449, 1981; *Economic Progress Report*, January 1982; *Lloyds Bank Review*, July 1982.

37. Note: water and sewerage rates are not eligible for rebate (except for business).

38. In 1963 the *Report of the Committee on the Impact of Rates on Householders* (Allen), Cmd 2582, HMSO, suggested that while rates were regressive, they were broadly proportionate to incomes. It was this report which led to the rate rebate scheme in 1967. The Layfield Report (1976) said that rates were progressive up to £40 per week income, were proportional between £40 and £60 and were less than proportional over £60 per week. See also *Alternatives to Domestic Rates*, HMSO, 1981. In addition 2·45 million of those receiving Supplementary Benefit had their rates paid.

39. See the Allen Report and the Layfield Report, Annexe 19; also *The Times*, 19 April 1980, *Alternatives to Domestic Rates*, HMSO, 1981. K. Newton and T. J. Karran, *The Politics of Local Expenditure*, 1985.

40. S. Weir, 'The Citizen and the Town Hall', *New Society*, 4 March 1982; T. Travers, 'Local Government is More Popular than Politicians Realise', *Local Government Chronicle*, 13 June 1980; C. Game, 'Budget Making by Opinion Poll', *Local Government Studies*, March/April 1982; 'Islington's Rates Survey', *Local Government Review*, 13 March 1982; Coventry's referendum, *The Times*, 26–28 August 1981; Layfield Report (Appendix) 1976.

41. Another case in point is the rate rebate scheme under which the central government reimburses local authorities 90 rather than 100 per cent.

42. See P. Self, in *From Policy to Administration*, by J. A. G. Griffith (ed.), Allen & Unwin, 1978. Thus, it is estimated that while half of the 42 million voters pay rates, only one-third pay full rates.

43. *New Sources of Local Revenue*, RIPA, 1956; S. Hindersley and R. Nottage, *Sources of Local Revenue*, RIPA, 1958; IMTA studies covering, individually, rates, sales tax, local income tax, charges and motor tax (1968–9); *The Future Shape of Local Government Finance*, HMSO, 1971. Britain would appear to be the only country where local authorities rely on only one local tax.

44. *The Future Shape of Local Government Finance*, HMSO, 1971; *Local Government Finance*, HMSO, 1973.

45. *Local Government Finance*, HMSO, 1977, para. 6.12.

46. *Alternatives to Domestic Rates*, HMSO, 1981.

47. *Rates*, HMSO, 1981.

48. *Paying for Local Government*, HMSO, 1986.

49. See *Local Government Chronicle*, 19 February 1988.

50. See W. J. Blum and H. Kalven, *The Uneasy Case for Progressive Taxation*, Macmillan, 1960; Antony Flew, 'Inequality is not Injustice', *Economic Affairs*, IEA, June 1987.

51. See J. LeGrand, *Strategy for Equality*, Unwin, 1982, and *Not only the Poor*, Newtones, 1988; also the study of Cheshire County Council in G. Bramley, 'How Far is the Poll Tax a "Community Charge"?', *Policy and Politics*, July 1989. The suggestion that non-ratepayers vote themselves (free) services paid for by ratepayers is discounted by Miller on the grounds that very few people realized or regarded themselves as non-ratepayers, and 'when it came to voting in actual elections . . . turnout bias toward left or right, rich or poor, council tenant or house-owner was very small or non-existent. In particular, ratepayers and non-ratepayers were almost equally likely to vote.' W. Miller, *Irrelevant Elections?*, OUP, 1988.

52. See *Municipal Journal*, 5 May 1989, p. 9, and *Local Government Chronicle*, 23 June 1989. In the USA this was one of the purposes of the poll tax – hence its abolition (in 1963) as a condition of voting. But it remains as a Residents Tax, e.g. in New Hampshire.

53. The 'safety net' mechanism involves transferring funds such that local authorities, and their local taxpayers, are eased into the new tax system: thus local taxed/rated areas will be 'subsidized' at a decreasing level over four years to avoid the sudden increase in tax. Similarly, the higher-rated areas will find their situation improves over four annual stages. The higher-rated areas are critical of their having to thus support many high-spending authorities. Many critics see the device as a political ploy by the Government to make the scheme's introduction more acceptable as we approach a general election. Clearly, accountability during the four-year period will be compromised. See M. Cowan in *Municipal Journal*, 12 February 1988, and R. Hale in *Public Finance and Accountancy*, 22 February 1988.

54. See W. Miller, *Irrelevant Elections?*, OUP, 1988.

55. See *Local Government Chronicle*, 26 July 1991, pp. 16–17; *Passing the Bucks*, Audit Commission, 1993; *Public Finance and Accountancy*, 14 September 1990, pp. 16–21; *Local Government Policy Making*, July 1993, pp. 67–9.

56. *The Times*, 14 June 1991.

57. In 1934 and 1948 Public Assistance was transferred to the central government partly because of the burden on local authorities, but

mainly for other reasons (uniformity, equity and to de-stigmatize the service).

58. The (Conservative) government is wedded to a monetarist (or deflationary) economic policy: this implies a commitment to reduce the money supply which itself involves substantial reductions in borrowing by public authorities in particular (the 'Public Sector Borrowing Requirement'). However, apart from this there is a broad (party) difference of general philosophy regarding capital expenditure, with Labour largely seeking to spread the benefits and costs of capital projects over a number of years by borrowing, and Conservatives, broadly, believing in living within one's means and seeking to minimize borrowing. Furthermore, the move towards greater revenue financing may be seen as a further move towards the adoption of business methods, since much business finance is raised internally, including sale of assets.

59. Such legislation may for example set limits on local authorities' short-term borrowing as a percentage of its long-term, or it may govern their arrangements for the issue of bonds, mortgages, etc. The Local Authority (Mortgages) Regulations 1974 are an example.

60. Partly because local authorities have been able to spend without approval from their own (revenue) resources and partly by leasing, but also because approved borrowing may run over a long period and become out of phase as capital projects get held up (or suffer what is called 'slippage').

61. See, for example, the critical report of the Audit Commission, *Capital Expenditure Controls*, HMSO, 1985.

62. See *Capital Expenditure and Finance*, HMSO, 1988.

63. See *Local Government Chronicles*, 13 November 1992, p. 3.

64. Local Government Acts 1972 (Sec. 151) (England and Wales) and 1973 (Sec. 95) (Scotland). Under previous legislation some local authorities were required to appoint a finance committee.

65. Especially for capital expenditure. However, in practice this has become extremely difficult because of the uncertainties regarding government grants, economic policy, interest rates and inflation.

66. Local authorities will have some idea of RSG from their Consultative Council (see p. 382) meetings with the central government before the final November meeting. 'Cash limits' started in 1977 and represent the government's allowance for inflation, pay increases, fuel price rises etc. It is the maximum supplement which the government will make to the

RSG. Thus where the actual inflation rate (say 8 per cent) exceeds the government's allowance in cash limit (say 5 per cent), local authorities have to find the extra resources themselves or cut their planned expenditure.

67. They could also choose (as did eight local authorities in England and Wales) to have partial audit by both district and approved auditors. In England and Wales 90 per cent had chosen district audit pre-1982.

68. Before 1972–3, the district auditor himself could actually disallow and 'surcharge' (fine). This was felt by many, for example the Maud Committee (1967), to be excessive, inhibiting local authority activities. Consequently, under the 1972 Act, leniency will be exercised where the persons concerned acted reasonably or in the belief that the expenditure was authorized by law. The Minister retains his discretionary power to approve expenditure of questionable legality. In the Camden wages case (Pickwell *v.* London Borough of Camden, April 1982) the auditor's claim of excessive and illegal expenditure was refused by the court.

69. R. Minns, 'The District Audit', *New Society*, 10 July 1975.

70. The charge was that by delaying the collecting of rate income, they had lost potential interest on the revenue. See *The Times*, 6 March 1986. The Local Government Act 1986 now requires councils to fix a rate by April. On surcharge abolition see *Local Government Chronicle*, 14 February 1986.

71. Some of these are acceptable, as a way of establishing a balance in the debt portfolio; but if it amounts to speculation it is deemed illegal, i.e. *ultra vires*.

72. See *Public Finance and Accountancy*, 22 July 1988.

73. See note 69.

74. See E. C. Thomas, 'The District Audit Since Reorganisation', *Telescope*, November 1976; also L. Tovell, 'The District Auditor and His Place in Local Government', *Local Government Chronicle*, Supplement, 8 June 1979. W. Werry, 'What Does an Auditor Add Up To?', *Local Government Chronicle*, 29 January 1982.

75. See, for example, *The Local Government Audit Service*, the report of the Audit Inspectorate 1979, which makes critical remarks on bonus schemes, building contracts and pooling arrangements for polytechnics. In April 1982 the report criticized overtime payments.

76. Rating and Valuation (Amendment) (Scotland) Act 1984.

77. See note 74.

78. And found improvement opportunities of about £500m. *Annual Report*, HMSO, 1985.

79. *Audit Commission Performance Review in Local Government*, HMSO, 1988.

80. See *How Effective is the Audit Commission?*, 1991.

81. Its independence was cast in doubt because it made a presentation to the Cabinet in 1985. Also over surcharging in 1985 – see *Local Government Chronicle*, 13 September 1985, 25 April 1986, 2 May 1986, 20 April 1990 and 7/14 June 1991.

82. *Measuring Up: Consumer Assessment of Local Authority Services*, NCC, 1986.

83. *Public Finance Accounting*, 16 April 1993, pp. 11–13.

84. See *Local Government Chronicle*, 20 November 1990, p. 16.

85. 'Howard's Way', *Municipal Journal*, 25 March 1988.

86. *Annual Report for 1987–88*, HMSO.

87. For example, *The Consumer and the State – Getting Value for Public Money*, National Consumer Council, 1979. See also 'Value for Money in the Public Sector', CIPFA, 1980; C. Holtham and J. Stewart, *Value for Money*, INLOGOV, 1981.

88. With a view to keeping their committee structure within reasonable proportions, a number of authorities have had second thoughts about these.

12. Controls and Influences

1. *Ultra vires* may be procedural as well as substantive: thus if a council has not followed proper procedure in exercising its rightful powers (such as obtaining magistrates' approval before implementing a nuisance abatement order), the action is unlawful. See too note 1, p. 551.

2. Attorney-General *v.* Fulham Corporation (1921), in which the council went beyond its powers to provide washing facilities by providing a laundering service.

3. R. *v.* Kent Police Authority (1971).

4. Metropolitan Properties Ltd *v.* Lannon (1969).

5. See H. W. Clarke, 'The Prerogative Order', *Local Government Chronicle*, 23 August 1974.

6. Recent cases include the GLC (December 1981) and the West Midlands MCC (January 1982), both of whose supplementary precepts (for subsidized transport) were quashed; similar protests by BL (*v.* Birmingham MCD, February 1982) and GUS (*v.* Merseyside MCC, December 1981) failed.

7. See W. A. Robson, 'The Central Domination of Local Government', *Political Quarterly*, January 1933; B. Keith-Lucas and P. G. Richards, *A History of Local Government in the Twentieth Century*, Allen & Unwin, 1978; the Maud Report, Chapter 4; and the Layfield Report.

8. *What Future for Local Government?*, AMA, 1988. See also *The Times Educational Supplement*, 1 April 1988.

9. For example *Standards for School Premises Regulations 1972*. Strictly speaking such regulations are a legislative form of control as much as administrative.

10. E.g. see *Local Government Chronicle*, 11 April 1980, p. 404. Another instance concerned Manchester's sixth forms: see the *Guardian*, 12 January 1981.

11. In 1972 the Clay Cross Council refused to apply the new (Conservative) Housing Finance Act to its tenants: consequently eleven councillors were surcharged (£63,000) and disqualified from holding office. In 1974 the council went out of existence as a result of local government reorganization, but in the meantime the Minister established a Housing Commission to take responsibility for the housing functions of the local authority. The council refused to cooperate with the Commission and made its work rather difficult.

   An earlier case of a commission being sent in to replace a local authority occurred in 1927, when the Tredegar Board of Guardians was found to be too generous with poor relief. Outside local government, a more recent example concerned the Lambeth, Southwark and Lewisham Area Health Authority, which was replaced by Health Commissioners between 1979 and 1980. Most recently (November 1981–February 1982), the Minister was about to send his own agents in to administer the sale of council houses (and he had won a case in court to prove his right to do so) when the council, Norwich DC, acceded to the Minister's pressure to carry out the responsibility under the Housing Act 1980. In March 1986 the Government appointed a commission ready to assume responsibility for Belfast City Council where members ceased conducting business as a protest against the Anglo-Irish agreement, 1985.

12. See K. Baker, *The Turbulent Years*, Faber Faber, 1993.

13. W. O. Hart and J. F. Garner, *Hart's Local Government and Administration*, Butterworth, 1973, p. 371.

14. See *Relations between Central Government and Local Authorities* by the Central Policy Review Staff, HMSO, 1977.

15. In 1970, for example, half of the lists of candidates for posts of

director of social services were altered following submission to the Minister. See Lord Redcliffe-Maud and B. Wood, *English Local Government Reformed*, OUP, 1974, p. 127. In 1979, the Government issued a White Paper, *Central Government Controls over Local Authorities* (Cmd 7634), which proposed to drop the ministerial vetting of candidates for such posts; this was not legislated for, however. In May 1990 Derbyshire Police Authority proposed to challenge in the High Court the Home Secretary's veto of their choice of John Weselby as Chief Constable.

16. Local Government Act 1972 (Sec. 230) and Local Government (Scotland) Act 1973 (Sec. 199).

17. The 'Instruments' deal with the procedures of governing bodies – their size, membership, meetings, etc. The 'Articles' are concerned with their powers and duties – appointing staff, the conduct of the school, its curriculum, lettings, etc.

18. A White Paper is a government document declaring its policy; a Green Paper is a consultation document indicating the Government's tentative ideas on policy, for discussion purposes.

19. Student grants, for example, within the education service. Such grants may take the form of 'percentage' grants (as in the case of the police, where the central government pays for half of the cost of local police forces – 51 per cent since 1985–6). Alternatively, grants may be paid on a unit basis (such as the traditional form of housing subsidies, where a fixed amount of grant is given to local authorities for each house built).

20. If the government's allowance for inflation (the cash limits) is less than the actual rate of inflation, local authorities will find their resources stretched. Another constraint is the amount of planned expenditure which the government is prepared to recognize as 'relevant' for grant purposes, that is upon which it is prepared to make its proportionate contribution.

21. The building standards have been known as 'Parker Morris' standards after the committee which determined them in 1961. Cost yardsticks are in effect the maximum expenditure per house which the government recognizes as reasonable. In 1980, the Government began to dismantle these controls.

22. See the White Paper, *A Framework for Expansion*, Cmd 5174, HMSO, 1972.

23. B. Keith-Lucas, 'What Price Local Democracy?', *New Society*, 12 August 1976. See also W. A. Robson, *Local Government in Crisis*,

Allen & Unwin, 1968; *Local Government Chronicle*, 9 October 1981, pp. 1041–2; the Maud, Wheatley, Redcliffe-Maud and Layfield Reports.

24. See *Municipal Journal*, 16–22 June 1993, p. 10.

25. See the Central Policy Review Staff's *Relations between Central Government and Local Authorities*, HMSO, 1977; the Layfield Report; and J. A. Taylor, 'The Consultative Council in Local Government Finance', *Local Government Studies*, March/June 1979.

26. Secretary of State for Education and Science *v.* Tameside Metropolitan District Council (1976). See also A. Bradley, 'The Tameside Affair', *Listener*, 5 May 1977. In 1980, a similar event occurred in that the courts declared as unlawful the Minister's appointment of Health Commissioners in place of the Lambeth, Southwark and Lewisham Area Health Authority. In October 1981, the court held that the Minister had acted illegally (on a technicality) in withholding grant from six London Boroughs; in December Hackney successfully challenged his right to withhold part of their inner city 'partnership' grant. In 1990 the High Court initially found against the Minister's approval of Beechen Cliff School to opt out of Avon LEA.

27. R. Rhodes, *Beyond Westminster and Whitehall*, Unwin, 1988. See also J. A. G. Griffith, *Central Departments and Local Authorities*, Allen & Unwin, 1966.

28. See D. E. Ashford, 'The Effects of Central Finance on the British Local Government System', *British Journal of Political Science*, Vol. 4, no. 3, 1974; K. P. Poole, 'England and Wales', *Studies in Comparative Local Government*, Vol. 4, no. 1, 1970. Cf. E. Page, 'Grant Dependence and Changes in Intergovernmental Finance', Strathclyde Studies in Public Policy, 1981; article by D. Wardman in *Local Government Chronicle*, 2 July 1982; A. Robinson, 'The Myth of Central Control', *Listener*, 19 June 1982.

29. It is said that Richard Crossman resisted the proposals to place the NHS in the hands of local authorities (or any other separately elected bodies) because they were too successful in spending money, having the force of 'active' public opinion behind them. A similar point is made in L. J. Sharpe, *Why Local Democracy?*, Fabian Society, 1965.

30. M. Kogan, *The Politics of Education*, Penguin Books, 1971, p. 189.

31. Previous Ministers include Attlee, Morrison and Bevan. The current Conservative Party Chairman, Kenneth Baker, is an ex-councillor as was Patrick Jenkin, a past Environment Secretary. The Minister for Consumer Affairs until 1981, Mrs Oppenheim, was also Vice President of

the Association of District Councils. Lord Bellwin, once the Minister for Local Government, was a prominent councillor and leader of Leeds City Council before the Conservative election victory in 1979, and John Major was a prominent councillor in Lambeth LB.

32. For this information, I am grateful to Edward du Cann, MP, and also the House of Commons Public Information Office. See also F. Willey, *The Honourable Member*, Sheldon Press, 1974; P. Richards, *The Backbenchers*, Faber, 1972; A. Barker and M. Rush, *The Member of Parliament and His Information*, Allen & Unwin, 1971; 'The Times' Guide to Parliament 1979. However, it may be added that MPs are not always the allies of local government: by passing on complaints to the Minister rather than the local authority, the MP (perhaps unwittingly) draws the central government into local affairs. See G. Jones, 'MPs – Eroding the Independence of Local Government?', *Municipal Review*, July 1972.

33. It is claimed that they may carry more influence with Ministers than do MPs: this was suggested by the ex-leader of the Liverpool Council ('Brass Tacks', BBC, 17 July 1979).

34. See H. Drucker *et al.*, *Developments in British Politics 2*, Macmillan, 1986, pp. 142–3.

35. See the Layfield Report, Annex 4.

36. See *The Times Educational Supplement*, 5 May 1989, pp. 14–16, and *Local Government Chronicle*, 4 September 1992, pp. 13–15, and 27 March 1992, pp. 16–17.

37. See *Local Government Chronicle*, 31 July 1992, p. 13.

38. *Local Government Finance* (1976).

39. *Local Government Finance* (1977), para. 2.9.

40. In 1854 *The Times* declared 'we prefer to take our chance of cholera and the rest than be bullied into health'.

41. In 1873, the town of Nottingham published an open letter to the president of the Local Government Board criticizing the degree of ministerial control: see Keith-Lucas, op. cit.

42. See Robson, op. cit.; L. T. Hobhouse, *Liberalism*, H.U.L., 1910, p. 233.

43. See Keith-Lucas, op. cit.; Robson, op. cit.; and see R. Darke and R. Walker (eds.), *Local Government and the Public*, Leonard Hill, 1977, Chapter 1.

44. In 1979 and 1980, the Minister was regularly expressing his concern at local government's failure to reduce its staffing levels, and suggesting that the bureaucrats were protecting themselves from the expenditure cuts. Local authorities replied that their numbers were sustained in part

by government-imposed policies (selling council houses, charging for planning applications, allowing parental appeals against LEA school allocations etc.) which had substantial manpower implications. They also pointed out that 'bureaucrats' constituted only 2 per cent of the labour force. See A. Fowler, 'Who Are the Wicked Bureaucrats?', *Local Government Chronicle*, 11 January 1980.

45. Denis Healey, Chancellor of the Exchequer, House of Commons debates (*Hansard*), cols. 296–7, 15 April 1975.

46. See Taylor, op. cit.

47. *The Times*, 19 February 1980.

48. *The Times*, 20 March 1980.

49. Though there are a number of theories: see W. J. M. Mackenzie, *Theories of Local Government*, LSE, 1961. See also L. J. Sharpe, 'Theories and Values of Local Government', *Political Studies*, no. 80, 1970; O. A. Hartley, 'The Relationship between Central and Local Authorities', *Public Administration*, Winter 1971; *The Times*, 8 July 1972.

50. *The Conduct of Local Authority Business: The Government Response*, HMSO, 1988.

51. See *Municipal Journal*, 2 July 1992, p. 7.

52. Variations in the standards of local authority services are well documented. For example, see: the *Report of the Committee on Local Authority and Allied Social Services*, HMSO, 1968; S. Sainsbury, *Registered as Disabled*, Bell, 1970; B. Davies, *Variations in the Services for the Elderly*, Bell, 1971; B. Davies *et al.*, *Variations in Children's Services Among British Urban Authorities*, Bell, 1972; N. Boaden, *Urban Policy-Making*, CUP, 1971; Newton and Sharpe (p. 618 below). The Chartered Institute of Public Finance and Accountancy (CIPFA) regularly provides useful analyses of local authority expenditures through Statistical Information Service, from which the following examples are taken:

Estimated expenditure per primary pupil (1984–5)

Dudley MD	£623	Powys CC	£926
Newcastle MD	£850	Kent	£639

Estimated expenditure per pupil in special education (1976–7)

Somerset	£930	Gwent	£2,154

Estimated expenditure per head for planning functions (1984–5)

Solihull MD	£2·63	Manchester MD	£12·75

Estimated expenditure per head for social services (1984–5)

Cleveland CC	£46·30	Shropshire CC	£27·81
Manchester MD	£99·62	Dudley MD	£32·44

Expenditure on consumer services (1975–6)
  Powys CC over £1 m   Hertfordshire CC less than £200

Home help contact hours per 1,000 over 65 (1984–5)
  Gwent CC   17,152   Surrey   5,069
  Sunderland MB   26,582   Wirral MB   10,763

Meals delivered to pensioners (1976–7)
  Doncaster MD provided four times those provided by Sheffield

Overall spending per head (1983–4)
  Haringey LB   £697   West Sussex CC   £315
  South Cambs. DC   £24·75   Blackburn BC   £122

It is unwise to draw too hasty conclusions from these figures: such 'league tables' can be misleading unless other factors are taken into account (such as need, costs, alternative provision, etc.). A useful discussion of the reasons for variations is to be found in Boaden, op. cit., note 52. A striking example emerged from a recent report of the Public Accounts Committee. This expressed concern at the substantial variations in expenditure among police forces – hardly the least centrally supervised local service. (See *Fifth Report from the Committee of Public Accounts: Procurement of Police Equipment*, House of Commons Paper 445, HMSO, 1980.)

53. See also P. Saunders, 'Local Government and the State', *New Society*, 13 March 1980; and P. Saunders, *Urban Politics: A Sociological Interpretation*, Penguin Books, 1981.

54. See, for example, J. D. Godfrey and J. S. Stevens, *Training Gamekeepers to be Poachers*, RIPA Report no. 1, Spring 1980.

55. B. Davies, *Social Needs and Resources in Local Services*, Michael Joseph, 1968, and K. Judge, *Rationing Social Services*, Heinemann, 1978. But cf. Darke and Walker (eds.), op. cit., Chapter 14.

56. Darke and Walker (eds.), op. cit.

57. Saunders, op. cit. See also C. Cockburn, *The Local State*, Pluto, 1977; W. K. Tabb and L. Sawers, *Marxism and the Metropolis*, OUP, 1978; and M. Castells, *City, Class and Power*, Macmillan, 1978.

58. E.g. some of the work of British environmental health officers and meat inspectors is carried out in Europe by vets. This may have career implications.

59. A. Norton, 'Local Government and Europe', *Local Government Studies Annual Review*, 1979; J. Redmond and G. Barrett, 'The European Regional Development Fund and Local Government', *Local Government*

Studies, September 1988; A. Davison, *Grants from Europe: How to Get Money and Influence Policy*, Bedford, 1988.

60. E.g. see 'European Pay Off', *Local Government Chronicle*, 14 March 1980.

61. R. A. W. Rhodes, *Local Government and the European Community*, INLOGOV, 1973, p. 7. See too J. Glasson, *Local Authorities Access to EEC Aid*, Oxford Polytechnic, 1984.

62. A. Norton, 'Relations between the European Commission and British Local Government', *Local Government Studies*, January/February 1980.

13. Local Government and the Local Community

1. See D. Peschek, 'Local Authority Technology Co-operation in Europe', *Local Government Chronicle*, 19 October 1979.

2. See *Scottish Government Yearbook*, 1991.

3. See *Working for Patients*, HMSO, 1989.

4. This post replaces that of the old Medical Officer of Health. Doctors are appointed by the health authorities, but since they work in and with the district councils, they have to be formally 'adopted' by those local authorities.

5. See *Local Government Chronicle*, 12 March 1993, p. 13, and *Local Government Agenda* (ICSA), July 1993.

6. E.g. the GLC fares issue was started by Bromley council. On Manchester see: 'Greater Manchester 78', *Guardian*, 27 November 1978; 'Metropolitan Review', *Local Government Chronicle*, 14 March 1980; H. Elcock, 'English Local Government Reformed', *Public Administration*, Summer 1975; and M. Fitzgerald, 'Politics', *Local Government Chronicle*, 28 September 1979. The inquiry into the Toxteth riots in 1981 referred to the strained relations between the two tiers of local government on Merseyside.

7. C. A. Collins, 'Councillors' Attitudes', *Local Government Studies*, April 1980, p. 36.

8. See, for example, the *Somerset Express*, 24 May 1988.

9. For example, Manchester City Council *v.* Greater Manchester Council (1979) and Kensington and Chelsea LB *v.* GLC (1982).

10. One area of potential conflict in the field of planning is being somewhat diminished by the removal of many of the counties' planning

control functions (known as 'county matters') to the district councils, under the Local Government, Planning and Land Act 1980.

11. S. Leach *et al.*, *Two-Tier Relationships in British Local Government*, INLOGOV, 1987. They go on to suggest how these authorities may work together via aligned service boundaries, rearranged departmental responsibilities (including lead departments) and joint provision.

12. 'The Local Government Councillor', *The Conduct of Local Authority Business* (Widdicombe), Research Vol. 2, HMSO, 1986.

13. In 1993 Somerset County Council inaugurated an Environment Forum of some fifty representatives from local councils, government departments and statutory undertakings (rail, waterways, tourism, forestry, etc.), the CBI and Chambers of Commerce (and local industries such as quarrying, farming, construction), voluntary organizations (for sport, leisure, youth, conservation) and interest groups (Country Landowners Association, Archaeological Society, etc.).

14. See *Local Government – The Community Leadership Role*, LGMB, 1993.

15. The Bains Report, Chapter 8.

16. Some are executive in nature: see, for example, T. J. Phillips, 'Area Planning Committees in Walsall', *Local Government Studies*, January 1979. See also Barbara Webster, 'Area Management', *Local Government Studies Annual Review*, April 1979; L. Corina, 'Area Councillors Committees', *Public Administration*, Autumn 1977; and R. Greenwood *et al.*, *The Organisation of Local Authorities in England and Wales 1967–75*, INLOGOV, 1975, section III.

17. A. Alexander, *Local Government in Britain Since Reorganisation*, Allen & Unwin, 1982.

18. Divisional executives were a form of decentralization within counties for the purpose of educational administration. They comprised members of the (county) local education authority and members of the district councils within the divisional area, together with some co-opted members. Their functions varied from county to county, but they normally exercised some powers delegated by the LEA.

19. See *Strategic Government*, Winter 1992, ACC.

20. Apart from the local authority associations, there are some separate associations representing members (the Association of Councillors, for example) and officers (the Society of Education Officers and the Association of Directors of Social Services, for example). These are primarily professional bodies: they do not negotiate pay or conditions of service,

for which they may have separate bodies, such as the Association of Local Authority Chief Executives. There are also party groupings, e.g. Association of Liberal Councillors.

21. See D. Peschek, 'Can the Associations Become One Body?', *Local Government Chronicle*, 14 September 1979. However, one of the objectives of the ACC is the setting-up of a single body to speak for local government in England and Wales.

22. J. Kellas, *The Scottish Political System*, CUP, 1975, p. 143; the Layfield Report, p. 87. Though this contrast has diminished with the Local Government Acts of 1980 and 1982. See D. Heald, 'The Scottish Rate Support Grant', *Public Administration*, Spring 1980.

23. For example, the Local Government Training Board (LGTB); the Local Authorities Management Services and Computer Committee (LAMSAC); the Local Authorities Conditions of Service Advisory Board (LACSAB); the Local Authorities Mutual Investment Trust (LAMIT).

24. Such as the Bill drawn up by the AMA in 1979 seeking extensive powers for local authorities to help small firms in inner cities.

25. Mr Duncan Sandys in a speech reported in the *County Councils Gazette*, September 1956, pp. 195–6. See also A. C. Hetherington, *Local Government Studies*, April 1980, who notes the increasing readiness to hold talks with local authority association representatives at ministerial level.

26. As such they are 'partial' or semi-pressure groups. In practice many people belong indirectly to 'overt' pressure groups in so far as local (or first-order) groups may become members of a regional or a national network (second-order groups). For example, a local sports club may become affiliated to a regional/national body or standing conference which in itself provides no sporting facilities but seeks solely to further sporting interests.

27. D. Hill, *Participation in Local Affairs*, Penguin Books, 1970, p. 200; *Westminster Bank Review*, August 1979; *The Voluntary Sector*, NCVO, 1985. See too S. Lowe, *Urban Social Movements*, Macmillan, 1986; The Wolfenden Report: *The Future of Voluntary Organisations*, 1977; and *Social Trends*, 1989.

28. M. Moran, 'The Changing World of British Pressure Groups', in L. Robins, *Political Institutions in Britain*, Longmans, 1987.

29. J. Gyford in 'Aspects of Local Democracy', *The Conduct of Local Authority Business* (Widdicombe), Research Vol. 4, HMSO, 1986.

30. K. Newton, *Second City Politics*, OUP, 1976. He adds (p. 36) that there might well be another 5,000 which he had not included. There are about 400 such organizations in the area of Taunton, Somerset.

31. See J. Stanyer, *Understanding Local Government*, Fontana, 1976. But see also W. Hampton, *Democracy and Community*, OUP, 1970, p. 244.

32. The Maud Report, Vol. 2, pp. 184–5.

33. For example, the groups resisting the local introduction of nuclear power production may seek the aid of the energy-saving or alternative energy producers.

34. See Hampton, op. cit., Chapter 10.

35. See P. Saunders, *Urban Politics*, Penguin, 1980.

36. Councillors in Britain, however, have been traditionally and notoriously involved in administrative details. See the Maud Report, Vol. 1.

37. Newton, op. cit. He also points to the very large amount of informal contacts, lunchtime chats, etc. It must be quite obvious to councillors or local government officers why they are invited to social occasions or to act as speakers at meetings of local organizations. Nevertheless, even if their goodwill is not thereby engendered, such occasions do provide opportunities for them to be buttonholed or 'lobbied'.

38. J. Dearlove, 'Councillors and Interest Groups in Kensington and Chelsea', *British Journal of Political Science*, Vol. 1, no. 2, 1971, and *The Politics of Policy in Local Government*, CUP, 1973.

39. An example at national level is the RSPCA, which Professor Birch suggests has maintained its parliamentary reputation as a responsible body by successfully restraining the extremists within its ranks who would like to oppose blood sports. A. H. Birch, *The British System of Government*, Allen & Unwin, 1967.

40. Gyford, op. cit.

41. *The Conduct of Local Authority Business* (Widdicombe Report), HMSO, 1986, ch. 8.

42. Newton, op. cit., pp. 132–3.

43. See Dearlove, Hampton and Newton, studies cited above.

44. Newton, op. cit., Chapters 4 and 9. But cf. Hampton, op. cit., pp. 215 and 244.

45. Birch, op. cit., p. 99.

46. Newton, op. cit., p. 88.

47. Some interesting case studies are provided in Hampton, op. cit., Chapters 9 and 10, and in R. Darke and R. Walker (eds.), *Local Government and the Public*, Leonard Hill, 1977.

48. Dearlove's terms.

49. Newton, op. cit., p. 132. Cf. Hill, op. cit., p. 199.

50. In mobilizing the skills and energies of their members in the design and execution of local projects, pressure groups are acting rather like co-opted members at one remove.

51. The Maud Report, Vol. 3, pp. 114–17.

52. The need for this is well illustrated in Hampton, op. cit., pp. 206–13, where he shows significant differences between what councillors perceive to be issues and what the ordinary electorate thinks.

53. P. G. Richards, *The Reformed Local Government System*, Allen & Unwin, 1978, p. 157.

54. P. Rivers, *Politics by Pressure*, Harrap, 1974, p. 7.

55. See Rivers, op. cit., pp. 16–20, and Hampton, op. cit., p. 216.

56. See, for example, Newton, op. cit., pp. 83–4; the Maud Report, Vol. 3, Table 159; Hill, op. cit., pp. 53, 89; G. M. Aves, *The Voluntary Worker in the Social Services*, Allen & Unwin, 1969, para. 38.

57. The Maud Report, Vol. 3, p. 167, Table 167.

58. J. Gyford, *Local Politics in Britain*, Croom Helm, 1976, p. 109.

59. S. E. Finer, *Anonymous Empire*, Pall Mall Press, 1969, p. 145.

60. *People and Planning: Report of the Committee on Public Participation in Planning*, HMSO, 1969.

61. Ministry of Housing and Local Government, Circular 65/69.

62. *A New Partnership for Our Schools*, HMSO, 1977.

63. The Skeffington Report, para. 5.

64. *Report of the Committee on Local Authority and Allied Personal Social Services*, HMSO, 1968, para. 480.

65. Ibid., para. 494.

66. A. H. Birch, *Representation*, Macmillan, 1972.

67. Darke and Walker (eds.), op. cit., p. 73.

68. N. Lewis and P. J. Birkinshaw, 'Local Authorities and the Resolution of Grievances', *Local Government Studies*, January 1979.

69. Laurence Evans, 'Review of Public Relations', *Municipal Year Book*, 1975.

70. *Report of the Royal Commission on the Constitution* 1969–73 (the Kilbrandon Report), Study no. 7, Table 25.

71. *Complaints Procedures: A Code of Practice for Local Government and Water Authorities for Dealing with Queries and Complaints*, Commission for Local Administration in England, 1978.

72. See *The Public Service Orientation*, LGTB, 1985; *Learning from the Public*, LGTB, 1989; *Getting Closer to the Public*, LGTB, 1987.

73. N. Lewis and B. Gateshill, *The Commission for Local Administration, a Preliminary Appraisal*, RIPA, 1978.

74. Local Government Act 1974 and Local Government (Scotland) Act 1975.

75. Except parish and community councils. The addresses of the CLA are: 21 Queen Anne's Gate, London; Portland House, 22 Newport Rd, Cardiff; 125 Princes St, Edinburgh. Contact normally takes place in the first instance through a member of the local authority.

76. Local authorities have some discretion to withhold records or information and can refuse to allow their officers to be interviewed by the ombudsman on grounds of confidentiality.

77. Lewis and Gateshill, op. cit.

78. See note 72.

79. *Your Local Ombudsman. Report for the Commission for Local Administration in England*, 1978. Published annually, the Report for 1981–2 responded to the 'Justice' appraisal (p. 633 below), endorsing its recommendations that CLA should be able to: receive complaints direct; secure legally enforceable remedies; deal with New Towns, school matters and contractual/commercial matters. The CLA also seeks the power to initiate investigations, while 'Justice' wanted independent (central) funding for the CLA. The 1983 Report was highly critical of the negative or inadequate council responses to findings of maladministration. This was reiterated in 1985.

80. *The Conduct of Local Authority Business* (Widdicombe Report), HMSO, 1986.

81. Report of the Select Committee on the Parliamentary Commissioner for Administration, HC (1985–86), 448.

82. CLA, *Annual Report 1991–2*.

83. E.g. see Audit Commission Report, August 1984 (p. 625 below).

84. For example R. *v.* Hampstead BC ex-parte Woodward (1917); R. *v.* Barnes BC ex-parte Conlan (1938); R. *v.* Lancashire CC Police Committee ex-parte Hook (1980). Also C. Webster, 'What Right to Know Has the Member?', *Local Government Chronicle*, 9 November 1979; C. Cross, 'March with the Lawyers', *Local Government Chronicle*, 25 April 1980; H. W. Clarke, 'The Legal Right to Look at Local Authority Documents', *Local Government Chronicle*, 9, 16 July 1982; *Local Government Review*, 1983, pp. 226 and 451.

85. *Complaints Procedures in Local Government*, Centre for Criminological and Socio-Legal Studies, Sheffield University, 1986. See too *Administrative Justice: Some Necessary Reforms*, Report of the Committee of the Justice–All Souls Review of Administrative Justice in the United Kingdom, Oxford, 1988.

86. The Maud Report, Vol. 3. A recent figure is 25 per cent: *New Society*, 4 March 1982.

87. National Opinion Polls, 'Public Participation in Local Government', *Political Economic Social Review*, no. 1, 1975. For 42 per cent figure see *Local Government Chronicle*, 13 June 1980.

88. See the Maud Report, para. 323 and Table 91.

89. G. A. Almond and S. Verba, *The Civic Culture*, Princeton, USA, 1963.

90. The Kilbrandon Report, 1973, Research Paper no. 7, Table 4.

91. See the Maud Report, Vol. 3, Table 38.

92. *The Conduct of Local Authority Business* (Widdicombe Report), Vol. 3, HMSO, 1986.

93. The Maud Report, Vol. 3.

94. See K. Newton and T. J. Karran, *The Politics of Local Expenditure*, 1985.

95. J. Bonner, 'Public Interest in Local Government', *Public Administration*, Winter 1954.

96. The Maud Report, Vol. 3, Chapter 1.

97. See C. Game, 'Public Attitudes to the Abolition of the Mets', *Local Government Studies*, September 1987.

98. See B. Walker, 'Client's Choice', *Social Services Insight*, 20 February 1987. See too P. Birkinshaw, *Open Government, Freedom of Information and Local Government*, Local Government Legal Society Trust, 1986.

99. The Maud Report, Vol. 1, para. 448.

100. The Bains Report, paras. 7.35, 7.39.

101. See S. Jackson (p. 636 below) for an interesting case-study.

102. H. Benham, *Two Cheers for the Town Hall*, Hutchinson, 1964, suggests that local authorities do not aim to maximize their communications with the public because they can administer services more smoothly without publicity. In particular it appears that some Labour councils are suspicious, rightly or wrongly, of press publicity because they feel that newspapers are Conservative in general outlook: see D. Hill, *Participating in Local Affairs*, Penguin Books, 1970; D. Murphy, *The Silent Watchdog: The Press in Local Politics*, Constable, 1976.

103. See A. Wright, *Local Radio and Local Democracy*, IBA, 1982.

104. *Publicity for Work of Local Authorities*, Department of the Environment Circular 47/75. Also see the Maud Report, Chapter 1, and the Royal Commission on Local Government in Scotland (Wheatley) Research Study 2, HMSO, 1969, p. 22, and S. C. Sobol, in *Local Government Studies*, September/October 1981.

105. H. Cox and D. Morgan, *City Politics and the Press*, CUP, 1974; Hill, op. cit., Chapter 6.

106. I. Jackson, *The Provincial Press and the Community*, Manchester University Press, 1971.

107. See *Local Government Studies*, Summer 1993.

108. For example, while the Public Bodies (Admission to Meetings) Act requires local authorities to supply agenda and other papers to the press it does not lay down how far in advance. And the Local Government Act 1972 was silent on the issue of papers for committee meetings, so that local authorities vary in their practices here. See now Local Government (Access to Information) Act 1985.

109. 'Participation', *Studies in Comparative Local Government*, Vol. 5, no. 2, International Union of Local Authorities, The Hague, 1971.

110. R. Burke, *The Murky Cloak: Local Authority–Press Relations*, Charles Knight, 1970, p. vii.

111. A. Harding Boulton, 'Councils, Public and the Press', *Local Government Chronicle*, 31 March 1978.

112. Public Bodies (Admission to Meetings) Act 1960, sec. 1.

113. *Publicity for the Work of Local Authorities*, Department of the Environment Circular 47/75.

114. Referring not just generally to more open government and freedom of information etc. but also specifically to the government's sharing information with local authorities in particular. Local authorities frequently show their frustration at being given too little information too late: they should therefore well understand the public outbursts of those who feel local government is playing the cards too close to its chest. Thus in fairness to the central government, it must be said that some local authorities do lack initiative and do need prodding.

115. See, for example, the Maud Report, Vol. 3, Tables 98, 99; L. Corina, 'Area Councillors Committee', *Public Administration*, Autumn 1977, p. 335; Lewis, op. cit., p. 13.

116. The Redcliffe-Maud Report, Research Study 9; the Wheatley Report, Research Study 2; Hampton, op. cit., pp. 87–8.

117. The Maud Report, Vol. 3, Chapter 1.

118. The riot in the St Pauls district of Bristol in April 1980 and in Brixton in April 1981 led some to suggest that 'no go areas' were beginning to develop in certain (especially immigrant) areas of mainland Britain.

119. Hill, op. cit., p. 150. See also Darke and Walker (eds.), op. cit., Chapter 10.

120. While planning is *not* easy and its results are distant in time, it has nevertheless been suggested that the participation element has been jeopardized by its being left in the hands of the professional planners to arrange: see Darke and Walker (eds.), op. cit., p. 83.

121. Under the Education Act 1980, it is now to be a legal requirement that parents be appointed to school governing/managing bodies. This follows the recommendations of the Taylor Report, *A New Partnership for our Schools*, HMSO, 1977.

122. *Children and Their Primary Schools*, HMSO, 1967. Current legislation is seeking to extend parental choice of schools and also to give greater publicity to their activities – see the Education Act 1980.

123. The Housing Act 1980. In 1975, forty-six local authorities had introduced schemes for tenant participation and a further forty were considering doing so. See Darke and Walker (eds.), op. cit., Chapter 12.

124. Following the recommendations of the Plowden Report certain inner urban areas were given priority (or 'positive discrimination') in obtaining resources to improve their schools and educational opportunities: these were known as 'educational priority areas'. The 'urban programme' started in 1969 when special financial assistance was directed from the central government to certain local authorities containing areas of special social need. While early attention was focused on facilities for children, part of the funds have been used for 'Community Development Projects' which involved more intensive approaches by specially appointed staff who sought to gain the cooperation of all the local central and local social service agencies.

125. For example in rural areas many community development officers are funded by the Development Commission.

126. See *Guardian*, 16 March 1982; *New Statesman*, 19 March 1982.

127. See R. Hadley and S. Hatch, *Social Welfare and the Failure of the State: Centralized Social Services and Participatory Alternatives*, Allen & Unwin, 1981; *Barclay Report*, 'Social Workers: Their Role and Tasks', Bedford, 1982.

128. J. Gyford, 'Diversity, Sectionalism and Local Democracy' in 'Aspects of Local Democracy', *The Conduct of Local Authority Business* (Widdicombe), Research Vol. 4, HMSO, 1986.

129. Ibid.

130. Ibid.

131. See A. Walker, *Rural Poverty*, CPAG, 1978.

132. C. Arnold Baker, *Local Council Administration*, Longcross, 1975.

133. Cardiff, Swansea, Newport, Port Talbot, Merthyr Tydfil and Rhondda. There could be changes here as a result of the current special review.

134. *Parish and Town Councils in England: A Survey*, Aston Business School, 1992.

135. *Role and Activities of Parish and Town Councils in England: Case Studies*, HMSO, 1993.

136. See *Public Finance and Accountancy*, 14 May 1993, pp. 12–14.

137. Ibid.

138. *Community Councils in Scotland*, Central Research Unit Paper, Scottish Office, September 1978. Early analysis of some of the second round of elections suggests an even smaller proportion of contested seats: see M. Masterson and E. Masterman, 'Elections of the Second Generation of Community Councils', *Local Government Studies*, January/February 1980; *Local Government Chronicle*, 22 March 1984.

139. Local Government (Scotland) Act, Sec. 51.

140. *Local Government in Scotland* (Scottish Office Brief), p. 7.

141. M. Minogue, *The Consumer's Guide to Local Government*, Macmillan, 1977, p. 111.

142. *Neighbourhood Councils in England*, Consultation Paper LG4/743/4, Department of the Environment, HMSO, 1974.

143. B. Dixey, *A Guide to Neighbourhood Councils*, The Association for Neighbourhood Councils, 1975.

144. J. Talbot and S. Humble, 'Neighbourhood Councils Defined', *Local Government Studies*, July 1977. Also *An Investigation into Neighbourhood Councils*, INLOGOV, 1977.

145. See note 144.

146. *A Voice for Your Neighbourhood*, Department of the Environment, 1977.

147. The Redcliffe-Maud Report, Vol. 1, p. 99 and Research Study 9; and the Wheatley Report, Research Study 2.

148. At an ICSA–CIPFA conference in November 1981. See also

NCC publications, 'Bureaucracies', 1981, and 'The Neighbourhood', 1982.

149. See *Community Care*, 19 November 1981, p. 3.

150. See A. Godfrey, 'More Pavement Politics', *Local Government Review*, 28 November 1981.

14. Into the Nineties: Managing (More) Change

1. See p. 606, note 90, and *Local Government Chronicle*, 21 June 1991.

2. Reports by management consultants Coopers & Lybrand, *Streamlining the Cities*, suggest that savings will be negligible or nil. A later report by PA Management Consultants (1984) condemns the reorganization for other, non-financial reasons. See too N. Flynn *et al.*, note 29, p. 549 above.

3. E.g. in Bournemouth: see *Local Government Chronicle*, 17 February 1984.

4. See *Getting On With It*, Vols. 1 and 2, LGMB, 1992.

5. See A. Midwinter, *Management Reform in Scottish Local Government*, Strathclyde University, 1982; D. Clapham, 'Corporate Planning and The Cuts', *Local Government Policy Making*, July 1983. See too *Local Government Chronicle*, 27 June 1985, and P. Sabin, in *Local Government Chronicle*, 16 April 1987. The legislation of 1988 and 1989, which gives statutory roles to the finance, monitoring and head of service officers, will also have an impact.

6. *Solicitor's Journal*, 16 February 1990.

7. *Public Finance and Accountancy*, 29 January 1993.

8. *Challenge of Change in Local Government*, INLOGOV, 1988; see too R. Pearson and C. Miller, 'Laying the foundations', *Insight*, 21 February 1989.

9. R. Hambleton, 'The Decentralisation of Public Services', *Local Government Studies*, January 1989.

10. *Survey of Internal Organizational Change in Local Government*, LGMB, 1993.

11. *Local Government Chronicle*, 12 February 1993, p. 16.

12. *Survey of Internal Organizational Change in Local Government*, LGMB, 1993, p. 1.

13. K. Young and M. Davies, *The Politics of Local Government since Widdicombe*, Rowntree Foundation, 1990.

14. See *Local Government Studies*, August/September 1982; *Local Government Studies*, May/June 1983; *Local Government Chronicle*, 3 January 1986; *Managing Hung Authorities*, LGTB, 1985; *Local Government Chronicle*, 12 July 1985.

15. See K. Young, *The Conduct of Local Authority Business after Widdicombe*, Rowntree Memorial Trust, 1989.

16. R. Dahrendorf, *On Britain*, BBC, 1982. See also J. Gyford, *New Society*, 3 May 1984.

17. The GLC did all three, arguing that London's population has a large Irish element, and has suffered the effects of IRA terrorist bombings, or that London is especially susceptible in the event of nuclear attack, i.e. that foreign policy is a quite legitimate pursuit. Others have justified their actions by arguing that national policies may have direct effects on their localities' welfare (e.g. housing or education in immigrant areas) or their economy or community (e.g. in mining or industrial areas) or that (nuclear) civil defence expenditure wastes part of their budgets. A contrary view has been expressed by Prof. Regan. He points to the expenditure of such councils, e.g. on anti-nuclear propaganda and subsidies to unilateralist groups. (Some 'nuclear free zone' councils have blacked firms involved in building or supplying nuclear sites.) He concludes that, 'even if this expenditure is within the law [using the free 2p] it is a distortion of the status and role of local government in our political system. For local authorities to conduct a multi-million pound propaganda campaign on defence is as inappropriate as it would be for a local authority to open an embassy in Albania or purchase anti-aircraft missiles. Some local authorities are now being exploited to serve political ends far removed from their responsibilities' (*The Times*, 5 August 1985).

18. See B. McAndrew, 'Complications of Overtly Political Officers', *Local Government Chronicle*, 22 July 1984, and M. Clarke, 'What Has Happened to the Ground Rules?', *Local Government Chronicle*, 3 August 1984. The resignation or suspension of a number of chief officers recently may have been prompted, in whole or part, by party-political considerations, e.g. James Pailing, Director of Education, Newham LB (1985); Keith Bridge, Humberside MCC Chief Executive (1983); Alf Parrish, Chief Constable, Derbyshire CC (1985–6).

19. In a number of authorities, officers have been encouraged (e.g. by granting/withholding paid leave) to participate in activities of a party political nature. In a number of London Boroughs, an estimated 1 in 8

councillors (known as 'twin-track politicians') works as an officer in another authority; *Sunday Times*, 14 April 1985. See too p. 287 above.

20. Many of the old certainties, traditions and conventions are being challenged and overturned due to the erosion of mutual trust and toleration between members and officers. This is due to the mounting polarization of the parties, the greater assertiveness of the new, younger, more highly educated and less deferential members, and to the strains thrown up by diminished resources (and its incidental politicization of staff). Officers are often having to shed their traditional caution in implementing policies; and if they turn to COG for support or protection, they risk being perceived as conspirators.

The emergence of hung councils is causing similar or other problems – longer meetings, more tortuous consultation, etc. Local authorities are having to devise new procedures and ground rules with regard to drawing up agendas, officer's advice to opposition and minority party groups, the selection and role of chairs, etc. The Widdicombe Committee may well have an impact here, though there is a strong case for leaving local authorities to determine their own arrangements (after all very little of our central cabinet/parliamentary/party government is based on legislative provisions). See C. J. Davies, 'The Changing Roles of Officers and Members', *Local Government Studies*, January/February 1986; K. Walsh, *Ethics and the Local Government Officer*, LGTB, 1984; M. Laffin and K. Young, 'The Changing Roles and Responsibilities of Local Authority Chief Officers', *Public Administration*, Spring 1985; D. Kennedy, 'Officers can support members without being labelled', *Local Government Chronicle*, 14 February 1986. See Cheshire County Council's conventions in the *Widdicombe Report*, HMSO, 1986, Annex H. See also *The Times*, 17 February 1990, p. 3.

21. See *The Times Educational Supplement*, 24 November 1989, p. 22, and *Local Government Chronicle*, 21 August 1992, p. 4.

22. See, for example, *The Times Education Supplement*, 16 June 1993.

23. See SOLACE report in *Municipal Journal*, 1 May 1992, p. 6.

24. A Marplan poll in February 1982 showed 62 per cent in favour of PR.

25. See K. Newton in L. J. Sharpe (ed.), *The Local Fiscal Crisis in Western Europe*, Sage, 1981; also P. Jackson *et al.*, 'Urban Fiscal Decay in UK Cities', *Local Government Studies*, September 1982.

26. See note 11, p. 574 above.

27. See *Public Service Review*, January 1990, and *Public Finance and Accountancy*, 26 January 1990.

28. *Institute of Public Finance*, August 1993.

29. Under the Local Government (Goods and Services) Act 1970. See *Local Government Chronicle*, 30 August 1985 and 6/13 September 1991.

30. See R. Bacon and W. Eltis, *Britain's Economic Problem: Too Few Producers*, Macmillan, 1978.

31. Under the Rating and Valuation (Amendment) Scotland Act 1984, and the Local Government and Housing Act 1989.

32. There had been some uncertainty about the Minister's legal power to withhold grant from overspending councils; this was unsuccessfully contested (January 1983), e.g. by Camden council. It might be added, too, that at one stage the Bill included powers allowing the Minister to penalize councils on conditions drawn up retrospectively, i.e. after the financial year had begun: this was dubbed 'super-holdback'.

33. The original Local Government Finance Bill 1981 would have allowed the Minister to require a local authority to hold a local referendum before it could impose a supplementary rate/precept (as some thirty councils had done that year, including the GLC for its 'Fares Fair' transport subsidies). The Bill was withdrawn in November 1981 after vehement opposition from the local authority associations and a number of MPs: they argued that (i) a referendum was difficult to validate if there was a low poll (it was only 26 per cent in Coventry's experimental rate referendum of August 1981) and if the wording was over-simplified; (ii) that if adopted, referendums should become applicable to central government extra-budgetary tax changes; and, above all, (iii) that referendums would emasculate local responsibility by undermining the value of the ordinary electoral process and reducing councillors to mere delegates and cyphers.

34. See R. Jackman, 'Does Central Government Need to Control the Total of Local Government Spending?', *Local Government Studies*, May 1982; also D. Walker in C. Jones and J. Stevenson (eds.), *Yearbook of Social Policy 1980–81*, Routledge, 1982.

35. Derogation was not taken up by the rate-capped councils in 1985–6, partly in protest at the whole new regime of rate control, and partly because it would involve the central government in detailed scrutiny and approval of individual service levels of the authorities. But a number of councils did negotiate a re-assessment or re-determination the following year.

36. T. Travers, in M. Parkinson (ed.), *Reshaping Local Government*, Policy Journals, 1987.

37. *The Times*, 7 November 1981.

38. This was confirmed and detailed in the report of the Comptroller and Auditor-General, *Operation of the Rate Support Grant System*, HMSO, 1985. And a report by LACSAB, *The Effects of Central Government Initiatives on Local Government* (1984) shows how central policies have themselves added some 16,000 council jobs over five years. In 1985 the Government gave some acknowledgement of the impact of its own policies on local expenditures, e.g. by increasing the police grant from 50 per cent to 51 per cent.

39. P. Smith, 'How Targets Went Wrong', *Public Finance and Accountancy*, December 1983; K. Young, *National Interests and Local Government*, Heinemann, 1983; P. Jackson in *Economic Affairs*, IEA, October 1988.

40. See K. Newton and T. J. Karran, *The Politics of Local Expenditure*, Macmillan, 1985, p. 8.

41. Thus while local government debt fell from 21·7 per cent (of the total public sector) to 18 per cent the Government's rose from 59·7 per cent to 65 per cent over the period 1980 to 1983. It has been suggested that the Government focuses attention on local expenditure and its cuts in order to draw attention away from its inability to control its own spending. The *Financial Times* has said, 'With one or two well publicized exceptions, the local authorities have a record of sound budgetary control which Whitehall should envy' (see Newton and Karran, op. cit., p. 17).

42. It puts things into perspective when we see that as a nation we spend more on alcohol than LEA education, on tobacco than personal social services and on hair and beauty care than refuse collection.

43. For 1984–5 the penalties involved a 2p rate poundage holdback (or abatement) for the first 1 per cent of overspend, 4p for the second 1 per cent, 8p for the third 1 per cent and 9p for each subsequent 1 per cent. In 1983–4, the figures were 1p, 2p, 3p, 5p. For 1985–6 they were 7p, 8p, 9p, etc.

44. G. Jones, J. Stewart and T. Travers, 'Rate Control: the Threat to Local Government', *Local Government Chronicle*, December 1983. A senior civil servant, Sir Antony Part (Permanent Secretary to the Department of Trade and Industry, retired), has commented in relation to the various grant formulae, 'They've got themselves so snarled up

they hardly know what they're doing at the moment' ('Who Rules Britain?', BBC, 19 October 1982).

45. Referring to the uncertainties engendered by fluctuations of the block grant, in targets, in penalty systems and in the GRE assessments, the Report of the Audit Commission, *The Impact on Local Authorities' Economy, Efficiency and Effectiveness of the Block Grant Distribution System* (1984), says that 'The conflicting signals which the grant system contains and the variations in these signals from year to year cause authorities to protect themselves by building up substantial reserves.' This exaggerates apparent overspending, so that in fact 'real overall local government spending last year was probably in line with target'.

The Report also comments critically on (i) the reliability of the information on which GREAs are based, so that some councils receive substantially more or less than their circumstances might warrant; (ii) the divergence of targets from GREAs, so that local authorities lose grant though their spending does not exceed GREA; (iii) the targets which, being related to past expenditure, provide a perverse inducement to spend more (i.e. at least up to target) since spending below target in one year may be 'rewarded' by a lower target (but the same penalties) next year: consequently, (iv) the grant system provides few incentives for local authorities to increase efficiency; (v) the fact that changes in local rates are not a reliable guide to individual councils' changes in expenditure; (vi) the continued central involvement in local affairs which has not been reduced as intended by the new system; (vii) the number of people (over 800) in local government alone who are occupied in grappling with the complex grant system, and (viii) the intricacies of the grant arrangements that (inevitably?) distract too many of the recipients into 'playing the system'. This was reiterated in the report of the Auditor-General: see note 38 above. See also *Public Money*, September 1983.

46. *Capital Expenditure Controls*, HMSO, 1985.

47. R. Rhodes, *Beyond Westminster and Whitehall*, Unwin, 1988, p. 254.

48. *The Future of Local Government in Britain*, ICL, 1988.

49. The Local Government and Housing Act 1989.

50. D. Mason, 'Slimming for Survival', paper to IEA Conference, 27 April 1988, and P. Minford, in *Economic Affairs*, IEA, October 1988.

51. N. Hepworth, 'What Future for Local Government?', *Inquiry*, IEA, 1988.

52. J. Isaac, *Local Income Tax – Options for Change*, Rowntree Trust, 1993.

53. P. Jackson, in *Economic Affairs*, IEA, October 1988.

54. D. King, in *Economic Affairs*, IEA, October 1988.

55. Indeed the main impact of public sector borrowing seems to be on the exchange rate rather than on interest rates, and the latter are largely influenced by external factors anyway, especially US interest rates.

56. G. Jones, 'How to Save Local Government', in *Town Hall Power or Whitehall Pawn?*, IEA, 1980, and J. Barlow, in *Local Government Studies*, May 1981. R. Jackman, in *Local Government Studies*, March 1982.

57. *Economist*, 6 August 1985.

58. D. Dawson in K. Young (ed.), *National Interests and Local Government*, Heinemann, 1983.

59. *Municipal Journal*, 29 July 1983. Such increased direct intervention is evident in the new (1986) joint boards and authorities, e.g. the Transport Minister has imposed a 10 per cent reduction in the expenditure of the new Passenger Transport Authorities 1986–7 (to provide 'a reasonable balance between the interests of public transport users and ratepayers').

60. Indeed, the Auditor-General declared that the grant system was so complex 'that many officers and members had abandoned the attempt to fully understand it' and accountability had diminished because of its ambiguities and confusions: see note 38 above.

61. J. Gibson, *Increasing the Efficiency of the SSAs*, INLOGOV, 1993; see too *Local Government Chronicle*, 8 April 1993, p. 15, and *Public Finance and Accountancy*, 14 May 1993, p. 9.

62. See SOLACE report in the *Observer*, 18 July 1982; T. Blackstone in *The Times Educational Supplement*, 24 September 1982; and a MORI poll (*Sunday Times*, 6 September 1981) which found that nearly half of young unemployed respondents believed that violence to bring about political change is justified. See also B. Stevenson, 'Cleveland's Crazy Cuts', *Local Government Chronicle*, 14 January 1983, and B. Simon, *Marxism Today*, September 1984 (compare with the survey in the *Economist*, 4 July 1982).

63. *Municipal Journal*, 29 July 1983.

64. *The Times*, 8 May 1992.

65. *Public Finance and Accountancy*, January 1984.

66. The whole issue is currently being investigated: see D. Beetham, *Auditing Democracy in Britain*, Charter 1988, 1993.

67. Howard Davies, 'Local Government Under Siege', *Public Administration*, Spring 1988.

68. *Accountability to the Public*, European Policy Forum, 1992. See also *The New Local Governance*, European Policy Forum, 1993.

69. See the White Paper *A Police Service for the 21st Century*, July 1993. This is being reconsidered after severe criticism and substantial amendment of the Bill as it goes through Parliament, March 1994.

70. See *The Times*, 31 May 1993. See too *Municipal Journal*, 20–26 August 1993, p. 10.

71. See the *Observer*, 4 July 1993, p. 11.

72. W. Waldegrave, *Public Service and the Future: Reforming Britain's Bureaucracies*, Conservative Political Centre, 1993.

73. *The Times*, 5 August 1993. See too *Public Finance and Accountancy*, 16 June 1993, pp. 6–7.

74. M. Kogan, in M. Parkinson (ed.), *Reshaping Local Government*, Policy Journals, 1987.

75. This is exemplified in a letter to *The Times*, 20 April 1989, from Harry Greenaway MP, in which he criticized local authorities and welcomed alternative public housing, but was concerned that voluntary housing trusts and associations 'need to be watched carefully . . . management by these associations can be weak and ineffective . . . [and] I cannot tackle the offending association by the democratic processes . . .'

76. Dawn Oliver, 'Law, Convention and Abuse of Power', *The Political Quarterly*, January 1989.

77. Through grants to voluntary bodies (such as CABx, Marriage Guidance, etc.), support to informal carers (such as respite, bathing attendance, laundry, etc.) and contracting out. An estimated 1 million people receive welfare services from the non-statutory sector.

78. Hepworth, op. cit. note 51. The possibilities have been illustrated enthusiastically by one housing manager. 'Just passive enabling will be an inadequate response; the Council must assume the role of strategic housing authority, set the parameters and direct the resources; make things happen in the way and in the timescale it needs. Most of all it must try to ensure that what gets built meets the needs of the locality . . . it is a case of exploiting the volatile and lively environment, forging partnerships and putting up workable ideas. It is a new form of brokerage . . .' D. Hawes, *Municipal Journal*, 10 June 1988.

79. 'The Governing Principle', *Municipal Journal*, 10 June 1988.

80. N. Ridley, *The Local Right: Enabling not Providing*, CPS, 1989.

81. See, for example, S. Mohun, in A. Cochrane and J. Anderson,

Restructuring Britain: Politics in Transition, Sage, 1989.

82. D. Jackson, 'Analysing the Nature of Local Government Today', *Public Finance and Accountancy*, 7 October 1988.

83. M. Clarke and J. Stewart, *The Enabling Council*, LGTB, 1988.

84. M. Clarke and J. Stewart, *Managing Tomorrow*, LGTB, 1988.

85. M. Clarke and J. Stewart, *The Enabling Council*, LGTB, 1988.

86. Some suggestions for the enabling (housing) role were given by the Minister, Michael Howard, in a speech to the IEA, 27 April 1988, such as the assessment of demand and supply, development control, land assembly and site provision, subsidies to the private rented sector, lending to housing associations, repair and improvement grants, allocation of tenancies, monitoring and regulating, and the coordination and provision of housing-related social services and amenities.

87. K. Spencer, *Alternatives to the Direct Delivery of Services by Local Government*, INLOGOV, 1986. It should be noted that indirect provision or administration of services was quite common in the nineteenth century; see, for example, J. Stanyer, p. 636 below.

88. *Losing the Empire, Finding a Role: The LEA of the Future*, Audit Commission, 1989.

89. Hepworth, op. cit. note 51.

90. M. Clarke and J. Stewart, *The Enabling Council*, LGTB, 1988; see too *Partners or Rivals?* [voluntary organizations], LGTB, 1988.

91. N. Rao, *Managing Change*, LGMB, 1993.

92. *Local Government Agenda*, ICSA, March 1993. See too *The Councillor and the Enabling Council*, LGTB, 1990.

93. See the Widdicombe Report, HMSO, 1986; *The Enabling Council*, LGTB, 1988; Maud Report, HMSO 1967; the Local Authorities (General Powers) Bill 1988, a Private Member's Bill introduced by Tony Benn in 1988.

94. P. Hoggett and R. Hambleton, *Decentralisation and Democracy*, SAUS, 1987.

95. R. Harris and A. Seldon, *Over-ruled on Welfare*, IEA, 1979; P. Taylor-Gooby, *Public Opinion, Ideology and State Welfare*, Routledge, 1985; see too *Journal of Social Policy*, October 1983.

96. J. Gyford, in M. Parkinson, *Reshaping Local Government*, Policy Journals, 1987.

97. Howard Davies, 'Local Government Under Siege', *Public Administration*, Spring 1988.

98. E.g. *Tell Us What It's Really Like*, Age Concern, Norfolk, 1989.

99. Marketing is about selling and publicity, and local authorities are having to do their share of these, for example to boost their falling college rolls. But marketing is also about satisfying customer needs, and this applies, as 'social marketing', whether services are free or are charged for. See K. Walsh, *Marketing in Local Government*, Longman, 1989, and *Has Marketing a Role in Local Government?*, LGTB, 1987.

100. *A Glimpse of the Future: Social and Economic Trends for Local Government in the 1990s*, LGMB, 1992.

101. A. Coulson, in *New Directions for INLOGOV*, INLOGOV, 1988.

102. See Professor R. Whitfield in the *Sunday Times*, 4 June 1989.

103. N. Hepworth, 'Changing Relations between Local Government Officers', *Public Finance and Accountancy*, 9 September 1988.

104. *The Challenge of Change in Local Government*, INLOGOV, 1988.

105. Ibid.

106. See, for example, *Municipal Journal*, 5–11 June 1992, p. 20.

107. *Against the Over-mighty State*, Federal Trust for Education and Research, 1988.

108. The Audit Commission is more sceptical here; see its *More Equal Than Others*, in which it points to local authorities' budgetary crises and problems with handling falling school rolls as signs that local government may not be so able to make the necessary decisions to be credible as a centre of genuine discretion.

109. See *The Competitive Council*, 1988, where it advises the well-managed council to: (1) understand its customers; (2) respond to the electorate; (3) set and pursue consistent and achievable objectives; (4) assign clear management responsibilities; (5) train and motivate people; (6) communicate effectively; (7) monitor results; and (8) adapt quickly to change. These principles are also dealt with by M. Clarke and J. Stewart, *Managing Tomorrow*, LGTB, 1988, though they also emphasize the need to work through political processes and to 'rediscover local government'.

110. *Political Quarterly*, January 1989.

111. W. Kornhauser, *The Politics of Mass Society*, Routledge, 1960.

112. K. Newton and T. J. Karran, *The Politics of Local Expenditure*, Macmillan, 1985.

113. 'LGTB Conference', *Insight*, 14 March 1989.

114. It has been suggested that a Bill of Rights for local government

may provide protection: see J. Stewart, 'Now is the time for our Bill of Rights', *Municipal Journal*, 5 June 1981; J. Raine (ed.), *In Defence of Local Government*, INLOGOV, 1981; P. Self, 'Rescuing Local Government', *Political Quarterly*, July 1982; Federal Trust, op. cit. note 107; *Political Quarterly*, January 1989.

115. Though T. Clegg is less sanguine here: see M. Goldsmith (ed.), *Essays on the Future of Local Government*, University of Salford, 1986.

116. See *Local Government and the Public Service Orientation*, LGTB, 1985.

117. See R. Greenwood *et al.*, 'Making Government More Local', *New Society*, 25 February 1982. However, a Gallup poll in 1981 showed only 27 per cent were in favour of more decentralization from London to regional and local authorities.

118. See *British Social Attitudes*, Gower, 1985; Chris Game, 'Opinion Polls can be a Real Asset', *Local Government Chronicle*, 13 September 1985; *Local Government Chronicle*, 20 September 1985. See also Commission on the Constitution Research Paper 7, *Attitudes Survey*, 1973.

119. *Which?*, March 1989.

Further Reading

Serious students cannot rely upon a single book for their knowledge of local government. Yet they face the problem that the literature on local government is constantly growing in volume and diversity: new areas and themes are being explored and older ones are being revisited and researched and perhaps re-interpreted. This is both inevitable and desirable, for our understanding of local government cannot be fixed once and for all, and, in particular, it should not be based simply on an understanding of the statutory and other legal provisions (important though these are).

However, as a bibliography, a long list of books can be off-putting – and academics do get carried away (what enthusiast doesn't?). In what follows, therefore, I have aimed to provide a range of suitable reading from which students can make selections (bearing in mind that a number of the titles listed are alternatives). It is very difficult deciding what to leave out: even authors whose ideas are unacceptable can stimulate lines of thought and provide interesting insights and perspectives.

The list is essentially a list of books, though a few important articles are included. Other articles and books are mentioned in the chapter references. Keen students might also consult the bibliographies contained in *Local Government Studies* for July 1975; J. Gyford, *Local Politics in Britain*, Croom Helm, 1984; and H. V. Wiseman (ed.), *Local Government in England 1958–1969*, Routledge, 1969. There is also a select bibliography on local government published by the Royal Institute of Public Administration (RIPA). And in 1975 there was published an index of articles drawn from eleven journals entitled *The Essex Reference Index: British Journals on Politics and Sociology 1950–73*, edited by K. I. Macdonald, Macmillan, 1975.

Finally, those who wish to keep themselves up to date with developments in local government should regularly consult the journals mentioned in the last section of this list.

1. General reference

Municipal Year Book (annual)

M. Minogue (ed.), *Documents on Contemporary British Government*, Vol. 2: *Local Government in Britain*, CUP, 1977.

Annual Abstracts of Statistics, HMSO (annual).

UK National Accounts, HMSO (annual).

Local Government Financial Statistics (England and Wales), HMSO (annual).

Finance and General Statistics, CIPFA (annual).

L. Golding, *Dictionary of Local Government in England and Wales*, EUP, 1962.

Local Government Trends (annual statistical digest, CIPFA).

Public Domain, CIPFA (annual).

2. General and/or theoretical

The Conduct of Local Authority Business, HMSO, 1986 (the Report of the Widdicombe Committee). (Considers the purpose of local government, the impact of party politics, member–officer relationships and conduct, decision-making, elections, discretionary spending, audit and public challenge.)

'Aspects of Local Democracy', *The Conduct of Local Authority Business* (Widdicombe), Research Vol. 4, HMSO, 1986. (Includes chapters on discretionary spending, rate-setting in Liverpool, history of local party politics, decentralization and local government abroad.)

J. Stanyer, *Understanding Local Government*, Fontana, 1976.

D. Hill, *Democratic Theory and Local Government*, Allen & Unwin, 1974.

W. J. M. Mackenzie, *Theories of Local Government*, LSE, 1961.

L. J. Sharpe, 'Theories and Values of Local Government', *Political Studies*, June 1970.

I. M. Barlow, *Metropolitan Government*, Routledge, 1992.

Introducing Local Government (interactive computer-based programme), LGMB, 1992.

Welcome to Local Government, LGMB, 1992.

S. Leach and M. Stewart, *Local Government: Its Role and Function*, Joseph Rowntree, 1992.

R. Hambledon, *Urban Government Under Thatcher and Reagan*, SAUS, 1988.

Coopers and Lybrand Deloitte, *The Constitutional Role of Local Government*, ACC, 1991.

K. Young, *Essays in Urban Politics*, Macmillan, 1975.

S. Leach, *The Heseltine Review of Local Government*, INLOGOV, 1992.

Redcliffe-Maud and B. Wood, *English Local Government Reformed*, OUP, 1974.

P. G. Richards, *The Reformed Local Government System*, Allen & Unwin, 1978.

A. Alexander, *Local Government in Britain since Reorganization*, Allen & Unwin, 1982.

M. Boddy and C. Fudge, *The Local State: Theory and Practice*, SAUS, 1981.

P. Dunleavy, *Urban Political Analysis*, Macmillan, 1980.

J. Raine *et al.*, *In Defence of Local Government*, INLOGOV, 1981.

E. Butler and M. Pirie (eds.), *Economy and Local Government*, Adam Smith Institute, 1981.

Why Local Government?, LGTB, 1985.

G. Jones and J. Stewart, *The Case for Local Government*, Allen & Unwin, 1985.

J. Stewart, *Local Government: the Conditions for Local Choice*, Allen & Unwin, 1983

B. Houlihan, *Politics of Local Government*, Longmans, 1986.

S. Duncan and M. Goodwin, *The Local State and Uneven Development*, Polity, 1988.

J. A. Chandler, *Public Policy-Making for Local Government*, Croom Helm, 1988.

A. Cochrane and J. Anderson, *Restructuring Britain: Politics in Transition*, Sage, 1989.

C. Mellors and N. Copperthwaite, *Local Government in the Community*, ICSA, 1987.

G. Stoker, *The Politics of Local Government*, Macmillan, 1991.

W. Hampton, *Local Government and Urban Politics*, Longman, 1992.

D. Blunkett and K. Jackson, *Democracy in Crisis: The Town Halls Respond*, Hogarth, 1987.

'Symposium on Local Government', *Contemporary Record*, Summer 1989.

J. Bulpitt, *Territory and Power in the United Kingdom*, Manchester University Press, 1983.

'What is happening to Local Government?', *Local Government Studies*, November 1989.

J. A. Chandler, *Local Government Today*, Manchester University Press, 1991.

3. History

K. B. Smellie, *A History of Local Government*, Allen & Unwin, 1968.

J. Redlich and F. W. Hirst, *The History of Local Government in England*, ed. B. Keith-Lucas, Macmillan, 1970.

B. Keith-Lucas and P. G. Richards, *A History of Local Government in the Twentieth Century*, Allen & Unwin, 1978.

W. Thornhill (ed.), *The Growth and Reform of English Local Government*, Weidenfeld & Nicolson, 1971.

V. D. Lipman, *Local Government Areas 1834–1945*, Blackwell, 1949.

C. J. Pearce, *The Machinery of Change in Local Government*, Unwin, 1982.

D. Fraser, *Municipal Reform and the Industrial City*, St Martin, 1982.

4. The legal context

C. A. Cross, *Principles of Local Government Law*, Sweet & Maxwell, 1986.

W. O. Hart and J. F. Garner, *Local Government and Administration*, Butterworth, 1973.

R. J. Buxton, *Local Government*, Penguin Books, 1973.

S. A. de Smith, *Judicial Review of Administrative Action*, Stevens, 1973.

R. Jeffries, *Tackling the Town Hall*, Routledge & Kegan Paul, 1982.

M. Loughlin, *Local Government, the Law, and the Constitution*, Local Government Society Trust, 1983.

O. Lomas, *et al.*, *Legality and Local Politics*, Dartmouth, 1987.

R. Morris, *Local Government Ground Rules*, Longman, 1990.

M. Loughlin, *Administrative Accountability in Local Government*, Joseph Rowntree, 1992.

M. Supperstone and J. Goudie (eds.), *Judicial Review*, Butterworths, 1992.

Ultra Vires *in the Public Sector: Final Report of the Legal Risk Review Committee*, Bank of England, 1992.

C. Crawford and C. Grace, *Conducive or incidental to: Local Authority Discretionary Powers in the Modern Era*, INLOGOV, 1993.

L. E. Rockley, *Public and Local Authority Acts*, Heinemann, 1978.

L. Bridges *et al.*, *Local Politics and Legality*, Gower, 1987.

M. Loughlin, *Local Government and the Modern State*, Sweet & Maxwell, 1986.

K. Puttick, *Challenging Delegated Legislation*, Waterlow, 1988.

S. A. de Smith, *Constitutional and Administrative Law*, Penguin Books, 1979.

5. Structure

The Structure of Local Government in England, DoE, 1991.

S. Leach and C. Game, 'English Metropolitan Government since Abolition: An Evaluation of the Abolition of the English Metropolitan County Councils', *Public Administration*, Summer, 1991.

S. Leach *et al.*, *After Abolition*, INLOGOV, 1992.

S. Leach *et al.*, *The Heseltine Review of Local Government*, INLOGOV, 1992.

Report of the Royal Commission on Local Government in England 1966–1969 (the Redcliffe-Maud Report), 3 vols., Cmd 4040, HMSO, 1969.

Report of the Royal Commission on Local Government in Scotland 1966–1969 (the Wheatley Report), 2 vols., Cmd 4150, HMSO, 1969.

Local Government in England: Government Proposals for Re-organization, Cmd 4584, HMSO, 1971.

The Reform of Local Government in Scotland, Cmd 4583, HMSO, 1971.

C. Arnold-Baker, *The Local Government Act 1972*, Butterworth, 1973.

P. G. Richards, *The Local Government Act 1972: Problems of Implementation*, Allen & Unwin, 1975.

K. Newton, 'Is Small Really So Beautiful? Is Big Really So Ugly?', *Political Studies*, June 1982.

B. Wood, *The Process of Local Government Reform 1966–74*, Allen & Unwin, 1976.

J. A. Brand, *Local Government Reform in England 1888–1974*, Croom Helm, 1974.

J. Dearlove, *The Reorganisation of British Local Government*, CUP, 1979.

G. Jones, 'The Local Government Act 1972 and the Redcliffe-Maud Commission', *Political Quarterly*, April 1973.

S. L. Bristow, 'Criteria for Local Government Reorganisation and Local Authority Autonomy', *Politics and Problems*, December 1972.

R. A. W. Rhodes, 'Local Government Reorganization: Three Questions', *Social and Economic Administration*, no. 8, 1974.

J. M. De Grove, *The Reorganization of Local Government in England 1972–77: An assessment*, Transaction, 1978.

S. Bristow *et al.*, *Redundant Counties?*, Hesketh, 1983.

N. Flynn *et al.*, *Abolition or Reform?*, Allen & Unwin, 1985.

S. Leach and C. Game, 'English Metropolitan Government since Abolition', *Public Administration*, Summer 1991.

6. Functions

The Functions of Local Authorities in England, HMSO, 1992.

J. Percy Smith and I. Sanderson, *Understanding Local Needs*, Institute for Public Policy Research, 1992.

The Impact of Population Size on Local Authority Costs and Effectiveness, Joseph Rowntree, 1992.

Local Government Community Leadership, LGMB, 1992.

R. Bell and N. Grant, *Patterns of Education in the British Isles*, Allen & Unwin, 1978.

M. Kogan, *Educational Policy Making*, Allen & Unwin, 1975.

M. Kogan, *The Politics of Educational Change*, Fontana, 1978.

N. Rao, *Educational Change and Local Government: The Impact of the Education Reform Act*, Joseph Rowntree, 1990.

N. Rao, *The Changing Role of Local Housing Authorities*, Joseph Rowntree, 1990.

A. Byrne and C. Padfield, *Social Services Made Simple*, Heinemann, 4th ed., 1992.

Report of the Committee on Local Authority and Allied Personal Social Services, Cmd 3703, HMSO, 1968.

J. Pratt *et al.*, *Your Local Education*, Penguin Books, 1973.

T. A. Critchley, *A History of the Police in England and Wales*, Constable, 1978.

S. Elkin, *Politics and Land Use Planning*, CUP, 1974.

J. Gyford, *Town Planning and the Practice of Politics*, University College London, 1978.

J. B. Cullingworth, *Town and Country Planning in Britain*, Allen & Unwin, 1976.

J. B. Cullingworth, *Essays on Housing Policy*, Allen & Unwin, 1979.

D. Regan, *Local Government and Education*, Allen & Unwin, 1977.

O. Hartley, 'The Functions of Local Government', *Local Government Studies*, February 1973.

D. Donnison and C. Ungerson, *Housing Policy*, Penguin Books, 1982.

J. A. Chandler and P. Lawless, *Local Authorities and the Creation of Employment*, Gower, 1985.

P. Lloyd, *Services Administration by Local Authorities*, ICSA, 1985.

M. Campbell, *Local Economic Policy*, Cassell, 1990.

K. Ennals and J. O'Brien, *The Enabling Role of Local Authorities*, Public Finance Foundation, 1990.

S. Ransom, *The Role of Local Government in Education: Assuring Qaulity and Accountability*, Longman, 1992.

M. Kogan and J. Cordingley, *Caring for Education: The Functioning of Local Government*, Jessica Kingsley, 1983

A. Coulson, *Managing Local Economic Development*, LGMB, 1990.

Managing the Local Environment – Local Authorities in Action, LGMB, 1990.

Environmental Practice in Local Government, LGMB, 1990.

The Environmental Role of Local Government, LGMB, 1990.

K. Ennals and J. O'Brien, *The Enabling Role of Local Authorities*, Public Finance Foundation, 1990.

R. Bennett and G. Krebs, *Local Economic Development: Public–Private Partnership Initiatives in Britain and Germany*, Bellhaven, 1991.

M. Campbell (ed.), *Local Economic Policy*, Cassell, 1990.

J. Benington and M. Geddes, *Restructuring the Local Economy*, Longman, 1992.

M. Burton and D. Nicholson, *Local Planning in Practice*, Hutchinson, 1987.

G. Ashworth, *The Role of Local Government in Environmental Protection*, Longman, 1992.

Coopers and Lybrand Deloitte, *Leisure and Recreation*, ACC, 1992.

Coopers and Lybrand Deloitte, *Planning and Transport*, ACC, 1992.

Coopers and Lybrand Deloitte, *Economic Partnerships*, ACC, 1992.

Coopers and Lybrand Deloitte, *Protecting the Community*, ACC, 1992.

Coopers and Lybrand Deloitte, *Caring for the Community*, ACC, 1992.

Coopers and Lybrand Deloitte, *Housing*, ACC, 1992.

P. Hall, *Urban and Regional Planning*, Routledge, 1992.

7. Elections and councillors

Report of the Committee on Management of Local Government (the Maud Report), Vols. 2, 3 and 5, HMSO, 1967.

The Remuneration of Councillors, Vol. 2, HMSO, 1977.

I. Budge *et al.*, *Political Stratification and Democracy*, Macmillan, 1972.

F. Bealey *et al.*, *Constituency Politics*, Faber, 1965.

G. Jones, 'The Functions and Organisation of Councillors', *Public Administration*, Winter 1973.

H. Heclo, 'The Councillor's Job', *Public Administration*, Summer 1969.

R. Gregory, 'Local Elections and the Rule of Anticipated Reactions', *Political Studies*, March 1969.

A. Samuels, 'On Ceasing to be a Councillor', *Local Government Review*, 4 July 1981.

P. Fletcher, 'An Explanation of Variations in Turnout in Local Elections', *Political Studies*, March 1969.

L. J. Sharpe, *Voting in Cities*, Macmillan, 1967.

'The Local Government Elector', *The Conduct of Local Authority Business* (Widdicombe), Research Vol. 3, HMSO, 1986.

C. Martlew, *Local Democracy in Practice*, Avebury, 1988.

A. Young, *Councillor's Handbook*, Harrap, 1987.

Association of Councillors, *Support Services for Councillors*, Knight, 1988.

Councillor's Handbook, Municipal Publications, 1988.

People and Places, HMSO, 1989 (the Boundary Commission).

W. Miller, *Irrelevant Elections?*, OUP, 1988.

M. and S. Pinto-Duschinsky, *Voter Registration: Problems and Solutions*, Constitutional Reform Centre, 1987.

T. Harrison, *Danger Zones: A Guide for Councillors and Officers*, LGC
    Communications, 1993.

'The Local Government Councillor', *The Conduct of Local Authority
    Business* (Widdicombe), Research Vol. 2, HMSO, 1986.

University of Plymouth Local Government Elections unit – produces
    regular and statistical analyses and *The Local Elections Handbook*.

J. Prophet, *The Councillor*, Shaw, 1988.

J. Stewart and C. Game, *Local Democracy – Representation and Election*,
    LGMB, 1991.

J. Barron, *Councillors in Crisis – The Public and Private Worlds of Local
    Councillors*, Macmillan, 1991.

Political Leadership in Local Government, LGMB, 1990.

Why Bother?, LGMB, 1991.

C. Rallings and M. Thrasher, 'Local Elections in Britain', *Parliamentary
    Affairs*, 1988.

C. Rallings and M. Thrasher, 'Turnout in Local Elections', *Electoral
    Studies*, 1990.

C. Rallings and M. Thrasher, 'The Impact of Local Government
    Electoral Systems', *Local Government Studies*, Summer 1992.

C. Rallings and M. Thrasher, *Electoral Reform for Local Government*,
    Electoral Reform Society, 1991.

N. Rao, *Managing Change: Councillors and the New Local Government*,
    Joseph Rowntree, 1993.

8. Parties and politics

J. Gyford, *Local Politics in Britain*, Croom Helm, 1984.

J. G. Bulpitt, *Party Politics in English Local Government*, Longman,
    1967.

Report of the Committee on Management of Local Government (the Maud
    Report), Vol. 5, HMSO, 1967.

J. Dearlove, *The Politics of Policy in Local Government*, CUP, 1973.

A. H. Birch, *Small Town Politics*, OUP, 1959.

P. Saunders, *Urban Politics: A Sociological Interpretation*, Hutchinson,
    1979.

W. Grant, *Independent Local Politics in England and Wales*, Saxon
    House, 1978.

A. Richards and A. Kuper, *Councils in Action*, CUP, 1971.

Local Government Handbook, Labour Party, 1977.

Conservative Political Centre, *Party Politics in Local Government*, 1962.

G. Jones, 'Varieties of Local Politics', *Local Government Studies*, April 1975.

G. Green, 'Politics, Local Government and the Community', *Local Government Studies*, June 1974.

W. Grant, 'Non-Partisanship in British Local Politics', *Policy and Politics*, 1973.

J. Barry, *The Women's Movement and Local Politics*, Avebury, 1991.

J. Alt, 'Some Social and Political Correlates of County Borough Expenditure', *British Journal of Political Science*, 1971.

K. Newton and J. Sharpe, 'Local Outputs Research', *Policy and Politics*, 5, 1977.

S. K. Mitra *et al.*, *Local Government and Urban Poverty*, Sangam, 1991.

J. D. Lees and R. Kimber (eds.), *Political Parties in Modern Britain*, Routledge, 1972.

J. Richardson and G. Jordan, *Governing Under Pressure*, Martin Robertson, 1979.

G. Ben-Tovin *et al.*, *The Local Politics of Race*, Macmillan, 1986.

M. Cowan, *Politics and Management in Local Government*, RIPA, 1983.

J. Sharpe and K. Newton, *Does Politics Matter? The Determinants of Public Policy*, OUP, 1984.

K. Ascher, *The Politics of Privatization*, Macmillan, 1987.

M. Boddy and C. Fudge, *Local Socialism*, Macmillan, 1984.

J. Gyford *et al.*, *The Changing Politics of Local Government*, Unwin Hyman, 1989.

J. Gyford and M. James, *National Parties and Local Politics*, Allen & Unwin, 1983.

'The Political Organisation of Local Authorities', *The Conduct of Local Authority Business* (Widdicombe), Research Vol. 1, HMSO, 1986.

'Aspects of Local Democracy', *The Conduct of Local Authority Business* (Widdicombe), Research Vol. 4, HMSO, 1986.

B. Wood, *The Political Organisation of Local Authorities*, RIPA, 1980.

S. Lansley *et al.*, *Councils in Conflict: The Rise and Fall of the Municipal Left*, Macmillan, 1989.

K. Young, *The Conduct of Local Authority Business since Widdicombe*, Rowntree Memorial Trust, 1989.

N. Carter, *Is There Life After Hanging?* (a study of three counties), University of Bath, 1986.

9. Internal organization and procedures

J. Bourn, *Management in Central and Local Government*, Pitman, 1979.

R. Hambledon, *Policy Planning and Local Government*, Hutchinson, 1978.

T. Eddison, *Local Government Management and Corporate Planning*, Hill, 1975.

R. Greenwood et al., *The Organisation of Local Authorities in England and Wales 1967–75*, INLOGOV, 1975.

R. Greenwood et al., *In Pursuit of Corporate Rationality: Organisational Developments in the Post-Reorganisation Period*, INLOGOV, 1977.

A. Fowler, *Personnel Management in Local Government*, IPM, 1975.

A. Fowler, *Local Authority Manpower*, BKT, 1981.

J. Stewart, *The Responsive Local Authority*, INLOGOV, 1974.

Report of the Committee on Management of Local Government (the Maud Report), Vols. 1 and 5.

J. Skitt, *Practical Corporate Planning in Local Government*, Hill, 1975.

The New Local Authorities: Management and Structure (the Bains Report), HMSO, 1972.

R. S. Knowles, *Modern Management in Local Government*, Butterworth, 1977.

The New Scottish Local Authorities: Organisation and Management Structures (the Paterson Report), HMSO, 1973.

N. Boaden, *Urban Policy Making*, CUP, 1971.

A. Griffiths, *Local Government Administration*, Shaw, 1976; new edition 1989.

R. Ashworth, 'Generalists and Specialists', *Local Government Review*, 27 June 1981.

G. L. Bayley, *Local Government: Is It Manageable?*, Pergamon, 1980.

D. Regan, *A Headless State*, University of Nottingham, 1980.

R. A. W. Rhodes and A. F. Midwinter, *Corporate Management: the New Conventional Wisdom in British Local Government*, University of Strathclyde, 1980.

M. Clarke and J. Stewart, *Developing Effective Public Service Management*, LGMB, 1990.

CCT Survey Reports, LGMB, annual.

Quality and Competition, LGMB, 1990.

Getting on with It, LGMB, 1992.

Internal Management Arrangements, DoE, 1991.

Managing Change, LGMB, 1992.

N. Rao, *Managing Change*, Joseph Rowntree, 1993.

Strategic Role of Local Government in the Community, LGMB, 1992.

New Management Trends, LGMB, 1989.

Fitness for Purpose, LGMB, 1993.

M. Usher and B. Darbourne, 'New approaches to Governance and Service Delivery', *Local Government Policy Making*, October 1993.

K. Shaw and J. Fenwick, 'Client and Contractor Roles in Local Government', *Local Government Policy Making*, October 1993.

G. Stoker, *New Management Trends*, LGTB, 1989.

The Councillor and the Enabling Council: Changing Roles, LGTB, 1989.

I. Sanderson, *Management of Quality in Local Government*, Longman, 1993.

Challenge and Change: Characteristics of Good Management in Local Government, LGMB, 1993.

A. Norton, *The Role of the Chief Executive in British Local Government*, INLOGOV, 1991.

The Role of the Chief Executive, LGMB, 1991.

Community Leadership and Representation: Unlocking the Potential, DoE, HMSO, 1993.

The Internal Management of Local Authorities in England, DoE, HMSO, 1991.

J. K. Friend and W. N. Jessop, *Local Government and Strategic Choice*, Tavistock, 1969.

K. P. Poole, *The Local Government Service*, Allen & Unwin, 1978.

J. Boynton, *Job at the Top*, Longman, 1986.

Information Technology in Local Government, SAUS, 1983.

The Use of Management Services in Local Government, IMS & SOCPO, 1984.

J. England *et al.*, *Information Systems for Policy Making in Local Government*, Longman, 1985.

M. Floyd, *Policy Making and Planning in Local Government*, Gower, 1984.

D. Clapham, *Corporate Planning in Local Authorities*, Glasgow Centre for Urban and Regional Research, 1984.

M. Laffin and K. Young, 'The Changing Roles and Responsibilities of Local Authority Chief Officers', *Public Administration*, Spring 1985.

Report of the Committee on the Staffing of Local Government, HMSO, 1967.

D. Birley, *The Education Officer and His World*, Routledge, 1970.

Brunel Institute of Organisational and Social Studies, *Social Services Departments*, Heinemann, 1974.

B. Wilson, 'Who Would be a Chief Executive?', *Public Administration*, Autumn 1975.

R. J. Haynes, *Organization Theory and Local Government*, Allen & Unwin, 1980.

R. Greenwood et al., *Patterns of Management in Local Government*, Martin Robertson, 1980.

C. Skelcher, 'From Programme Budgeting to Policy Analysis: Corporate Approaches in Local Government', *Public Administration*, Summer 1980.

C. Pinker and A. Dixson, *Solving Local Government Problems*, Allen & Unwin, 1981.

Innovations in Service, LGMB, 1991.

L. Gaster, *Quality at the Front Line*, SAUS, 1992.

A Local Authority's Options for Service Delivery, LGMB, 1990.

Good Management in Local Government, LGTB, 1985.

J. Stewart and M. Clarke, *The Search for Quality*, LGMB, 1990.

G. Stoker and H. Wolman, *A Different Way of Doing Business: The Experience of the US Mayor*, LGMB, 1991.

The Enabling Authority and County Government, ACC, 1991.

M. Green, *Local Government Administration*, Institute of Administrative Management, 1992.

I. Caulfield and J. Schultz, *Planning for Change: Strategic Planning in Local Government*, Longman, 1989.

I. Sanderson, *Management of Quality in Local Government*, Longman, 1992.

C. Skelcher, *Managing of Service Quality*, Longman, 1992.

M. Clarke and J. Stewart, *Getting the Balance Right: Towards the General Management of Local Government*, Longman, 1990.

I. Taylor and G. Popham, *An Introduction to Public Sector Management*, Unwin, 1989.

D. Farham and S. Horton, *Managing the New Public Services*, Macmillan, 1992.

T. Bovaird, 'Recent Developments in Output Measurement in Local Government', *Local Government Studies*, September/October 1981.

The Politics of Decentralization, SAUS, 1984.

K. Walsh, *Ethics and the Local Government Officer*, INLOGOV, 1984.

The Conduct of Local Authority Business (Widdicombe Report), HMSO, 1986.

The Conduct of Local Authority Business: The Government Response, HMSO, 1988.

The Competitive Council, Audit Commission, 1988.

The Enabling Council, LGTB, 1988.

K. Walsh, *Marketing in Local Government*, Longman, 1989.

N. Ridley, *The Local Right: Enabling not Providing*, Centre for Policy Studies, 1988.

The Challenge of Change in Local Government, INLOGOV, 1988.

C. Goodson-Wickes, *The New Corruption*, CPS. 1984.

Managing Tomorrow, LGTB, 1988.

Audit Commission, *More Equal Than Others: the Chief Executive in Local Government*, HMSO, 1989.

The Management of Hung Councils, LGTB, 1985.

B. Hogget and R. Hambleton, *Decentralisation and Democracy*, SAUS, 1989.

J. Stewart, *The New Management of Local Government*, Allen & Unwin, 1986.

J. Barrett, *Organising for Local Government*, Longman, 1988.

R. S. B. Knowles, *The Law and Practice of Local Authority Meetings*, ICSA, 1987.

R. Knowles, *Effective Management in Local Government*, ICSA, 1988.

Qualgos Just Grow, CPS, 1985.

D. Clapham, 'Management of the Local State: The Example of Corporate Planning', *Critical Social Policy*, 14, 1985.

Decentralisation of Social Services Departments, DHSS, 1988.

Audit Commission, *Performance Review in Local Government*, HMSO, 1988.

Audit Commission, *Managing Services Effectively – Performance Review*, HMSO, 1989.

M. Temple, 'Power Distribution in Hung Councils', *Local Government Studies*, July/August 1991.

M. Temple, 'Political Influence in Hung and Non-Hung Councils', *Local Government Policy Making*, July 1993.

S. Leach and J. Stewart, *The Politics of Hung Authorities*, Macmillan, 1992.

Coopers and Lybrand Deloitte, *The Changing Style of Local Government – Enabling in Practice*, ACC, 1991.

J. Stewart, 'The Role of Councillors in the Management of the Authority', *Local Government Studies*, August 1990.

D. Rosenburg, *Accounting for Public Policy: Power, Professionals and Politics in Local Government*, Manchester University Press, 1989.

J. Fairley and S. Marsh, 'The Enabling Committee and How It Works', *Local Government Studies*, Autumn 1992 (economic development and training initiatives).

C. Collins *et al.*, 'The Officer and the Councillor', *Public Administration Bulletin*, December 1978.

A. Alexander, 'Officers and Members', *Local Government Studies*, 1981.

R. Brooke, 'The Enabling Authority', *Public Administration*, Winter 1991.

Working with the Balance LGMB, 1993.

L. Mills and A. Norton, 'The British Local Authority Chief Executive', *Local Government Policy Making*, June 1990.

A Statement on Performance Indicators in the Education Service, CIPFA, 1986.

A. Parker *et al.*, *The Administration of Standards of Conduct in Local Government*, Knight, 1988.

R. Brown, 'Corporate Planning in a Local Authority' [Cambridge CC], in A. Gray and B. Jenkins, *Policy Analysis and Evaluation in British Government*, RIPA, 1986.

A. Doig, *Corruption and Misconduct in Contemporary British Politics*, Penguin Books, 1984.

D. Walker, *Municipal Empire*, Temple Smith, 1983.

A. Henney, *Inside Local Government*, Sinclair Browne, 1983.

T. Mobbs, *Local Government Policy Making Handbook*, INLOGOV, 1983.

Audit Commission, *Economy, Efficiency and Effectiveness*, HMSO, 1983.

R. Jennings, *Going Corporate in Local Education Authorities*, Gower, 1984.

A. Fowler, *Human Resource Management in Local Government*, Longman, 1988.

Local Government and Racial Equality, Commission for Racial Equality, 1983.

H. Elcock and M. Wheaton, *Local Government: Politicians, Professionals and the Public in Local Authorities*, Methuen, 1986.

Politicians and Professionals, LGTB, 1988.

D. Grimshaw and A. Haddad, 'Trends in the Use of Information Technology in Local Government', *Local Government Studies*, July 1988.

S. Baddeley and N. Dawes, 'Information Technology Support for Devolution', *Local Government Studies*, July 1987.

K. L. Kraemer and J. L. King, 'The Role of Information Technology in Managing Cities', *Local Government Studies*, March 1988.

Audit Commission, *More Equal than Others*, January 1989 (the chief executive).

T. Meeson and J. Haward, 'Devolved Management – The Berkshire Experience', *Local Government Studies*, January/February 1990.

Audit Commission, *We Can't Go On Meeting Like This*, HMSO, 1990.

J. Stewart, 'The Role of Councillors in the Management of the Authority', *Local Government Studies*, July 1990.

A. Clarke and A. Cochrane, 'Inside the Machine: the Left and Finance Professionals in Local Government, *Capital and Class*, 37, 1989.

M. Harloe *et al.*, *Place, Policy and Policies: Do Localities Matter?*, Unwin Hyman, 1990.

D. King and T. Pierre (eds.), *Challenges to Local Government*, Sage, 1990.

P. Minford, 'How to De-politicise Local Government', *Economic Affairs*, 9 January 1988.

A. Cochrane, 'The Changing State of Local Government: Restructuring for the 1990s', *Public Administration*, Autumn 1991.

V. Lowndes and G. Stoker, 'An Evaluation of Neighbourhood Decentralisation', *Policy and Politics*, 1992.

G. Stoker, 'Reflections on Neighbourhood Decentralisation in Tower Hamlets', *Public Administration*, Autumn 1991.

R. Brooke, *Managing the Enabling Council*, Longman, 1989.

W. Ball and J. Solomos, *Race and Local Politics*, Macmillan, 1990.

H. Hatry *et al.*, *Efficiency Measurement for Local Government Services*, Urban Institute, Washington, 1979.

M. Laffin, *Managing Under Pressure: Industrial Relations in Local Government*, CUP, 1990.

J. Painter, 'Compulsory Competitive Tendering in Local Government: The First Round', *Public Administration*, Summer 1991.

M. Laffin and K. Young, *Professionalism in Local Government*, Longman, 1990.

M. Clarke and J. Stewart, *General Management in Local Government: Getting the Balance Right*, Longman, 1990.

A. Fowler, *Human Resource Management in Local Government*, Longman, 1988.

S. Rogers, *Performance Management in Local Government*, Longman, 1990.

B. Tanner and D. Rawlinson, *Financial Management in the 1990s*, Longman, 1989.

J. Barratt, *Organising for Local Government*, Longman, 1988.

J. Stewart, *Understanding the Management of Local Government*, Longman, 1988.

The Local Government Administrator's Manual, ICSA.

J. Greenwood, 'Facilitating Officer/Councillor Relationships – Meeting the Post-Widdicombe Challenge', *Local Government Studies*, November 1990.

N. Mallabar, *Local Government Administration*, Business Education, 1991.

10. Finance

Paying for Local Government, Cmnd 9714, HMSO, 1986.

A Handbook of Local Government Finance, CIPFA, 1982.

R. Davy, *Guide to Local Government Finance*, Longman, 1991.

Guide to Local Government Finance, LGUI, 1993.

The A–Z of Council Tax and Council Tax Benefit, ADC, 1992.

C. Harrington and M. Lee, *Council Tax: Your Guide*, IRRV, 1993.

Local Authority Finance: A Glossary, CIPFA, 1985.

A New Tax for Local Government, DoE, HMSO, 1991.

N. P. Hepworth, *The Finance of Local Government*, Allen & Unwin, 1984.

A. H. Marshall, *Financial Administration in Local Government*, Allen & Unwin, 1974.

S. J. Bailey and R. Paddison, *The Reform of Local Government Finance*, Routledge, 1988.

K. Newton and T. J. Karran, *The Politics of Local Expenditure*, Macmillan, 1985.

Audit Commission, *The Impact on Local Economy, Efficiency and Effectiveness of the Block Grant Distribution System*, HMSO, 1984.

Local Government Finance: Report of the Committee of Enquiry, Cmd 6453, HMSO, 1976 (Layfield).

Report of the Committee of Inquiry into the Impact of Rates on Households, Cmd 2582, HMSO, 1965 (Layfield).

The Future Shape of Local Government Finance, Cmd 4741, HMSO, 1971.

Sources of Local Revenue, RIPA, 1968.

A. R. Ilersic, *Rates and Local Government*, Michael Joseph, 1965.

D. S. Lees *et al.*, *Local Expenditure and Exchequer Grants*, IMTA, 1965.

W. L. Abernethy, *Internal Audit in Local Authorities and Hospitals*, Shaw, 1971.

K. Newton, *Balancing the Books: Financial Problems of Local Government in Western Europe*, Sage, 1980.

L. J. Sharpe (ed.), *The Local Fiscal Crisis in Western Europe*, Sage, 1981.

L. Helmore, *The District Auditor*, Macdonald & Evans, 1961.

D. Ashford, 'The Effects of Central Finance on the British Local Government System', *British Journal of Political Science*, 4, 1974.

C. D. Foster *et al.*, *Local Government Finance in a Unitary State*, Allen & Unwin, 1980.

G. Hollis *et al.*, *Alternatives to the Community Charge*, Joseph Rowntree, 1990.

J. LeGrand and G. Bramley, *Who Uses Local Services: Striving for Equity*, LGMB, 1992.

C. Bone, *Achieving Value for Money in Local Government*, Longman, 1992.

A. Midwinter and C. Monaghan, *From Rates to the Poll Tax*, Edinburgh University Press, 1992.

J. Gibson, *The Politics and Economics of the Poll Tax: Mrs Thatcher's Downfall*, EMAS, 1990.

Standard Spending Assessments: A Reappraisal, Society of County Treasurers, 1992.

P. Cook, *Local Authority Financial Management and Accounting*, Longman, 1993.

B. Blake *et al.*, *Local Budgeting in Practice: Learning from Two Case Studies*, SAUS, 1991.

G. Jones *et al.*, *The Way Ahead for Local Government Finance*, INLOGOV, 1982.

T. Burgess and T. Travers, *Ten Billion Pounds*, Grant McIntyre, 1980.

R. J. Bennet, 'The Local Income Tax in Britain: A Critique of Recent Arguments Against Its Use', *Public Administration*, Autumn 1981.

Changing Policies in Local Government, CIPFA, 1984.

R. J. Bennet, *Central Grants to Local Governments*, CUP, 1982.

Alternatives to Domestic Rates, Cmnd 8449, HMSO, 1981.

H. Page, *Local Authority Borrowing*, Allen & Unwin, 1985.

'Why the Rate Burden on Business is a Cause for Concern', *National Westminster Quarterly Bank Review*, February 1984.

H. Elcock and G. Jordan, *Learning from Local Authority Budgeting*, Avebury, 1987.

H. Elcock *et al.*, *Budgeting in Local Government: Managing the Margins*, Longman, 1989.

I. Douglas and S. Lord, *Local Government Finance: A Practical Guide*, Local Government Information Unit, 1986.

A. Midwinter and C. Main, *Rates Reform: Issues, Arguments and Evidence*, Mainstream, 1987.

R. Rose and E. Page, *Fiscal Stress in Cities*, CUP, 1983.

A. Midwinter, *The Politics of Local Spending*, Mainstream, 1984 (esp. Scotland).

T. Travers, *The Politics of Local Government Finance*, Allen & Unwin, 1986.

G. Boyne, 'Rate Reform and the Future of Local Democracy', *Political Quarterly*, October 1986.

A. Midwinter, 'The Poll Tax in Practice: The Distributive and Political Consequences of Rates Reform in the Scottish Highlands', *Local Government Studies*, January 1989.

D. Whitfield, *Making it Public: Evidence and Action Against Privatisation*, Pluto, 1983.

Guide to Local Government Finance in Scotland, CIPFA, 1988.

A Guide to Scottish District Council Finance, Heriot-Watt University, 1988.

A Councillor's Guide to Local Authority Finance, CIPFA, 1990.

S. J. Bailey, *Practical Charging Policies for Local Government*, Public Finance Foundation, 1988.

J. Walker and R. Moore, *Privatisation of Local Government Services*, WEA, 1983.

11. Central controls and other relationships

J. A. G. Griffith, *Central Departments and Local Authorities*, Allen & Unwin, 1966.

Report of the Committee on Management of Local Government (the Maud Report), Vols. 1 and 5, HMSO, 1967.

Local Government Finance: Report of the Committee of Enquiry, Cmd 6453, HMSO, 1976.

E. Sharpe, *The Ministry of Housing and Local Government*, Allen & Unwin, 1969.

D. N. Chester, *Central and Local Government: Financial and Administrative Relations*, Macmillan, 1951.

M. Thrasher, 'The Concept of a Central–Local Government Partnership', *Policy and Politics*, 9 April 1981.

Working Across Organisational Boundaries, LGMB, 1992.

Community Leadership, LGMB, 1992.

N. Lewis, *Inner-City Regeneration – Demise of Local Government*, Open University, 1992.

A. Cochrane, *Whatever Happened to Local Government?*, Open University, 1993.

P. John, *Recent Trends in Central–Local Relations*, Joseph Rowntree, 1990.

C. Carter, *A New Accord: Promoting Constructive Relations between Central and Local Government*, Joseph Rowntree, 1992.

J. Swaffield, 'Local Government in the National Setting', *Public Administration*, Autumn 1970.

N. Boaden, 'Central Departments and Local Authorities: The Relationship Re-examined', *Political Studies*, 28, 1970.

S. Ranson (ed.), *Between Centre and Locality*, Allen & Unwin, 1985.

M. Loughlin (ed.), *Half a Century of Municipal Decline*, Allen & Unwin, 1985.

R. Rhodes, *The National World of Local Government*, Allen & Unwin, 1986.

Improving Relations between Central and Local Government, Joseph Rowntree Memorial Trust, 1986.

Against the Over-mighty State: A Future for Local Government in Britain, Federal Trust for Education and Research, 1988.

A. McPherson and C. Raab, *Governing Education: A Sociology of Policy since 1945*, Edinburgh University Press, 1988.

R. Rhodes, 'Inter-governmental Relations in the post-War Period', *Local Government Studies*, November 1985.

R. Rhodes, *Beyond Westminster and Whitehall*, Unwin, 1988.

M. Parkinson (ed.), *Reshaping Local Government*, Policy Journals, 1987.

K. Young (ed.), *National Interests and Local Government*, Heinemann, 1983.

Auditing Local Government: A Guide to the Work of the Audit Commission, Audit Commission, 1986.

Sir F. Hill, 'The Partnership in Practice', *Political Quarterly*, 2, 1966.

J. Boynton, 'Local Councils in Confrontation: the Current Conflict with the Centre', *Policy Studies*, April 1982.

N. Boaden, *Public Participation in Local Services*, Longman, 1982.

T. Gibson, *People Power: Community and Work Groups in Action*, Penguin Books, 1979.

O. Hartley, 'The Relationship between Central Government and Local Authorities', *Public Administration*, Winter 1971.

C. Hull and R. A. W. Rhodes, *Intergovernmental Relations in the European Community*, Saxon House, 1978.

P. Bongers, *Local Government and 1992*, Longman, 1991.

1992: The Impact on County Councils' Services, CECSNET, 1991

K. Young, 'Inter-tier Political Relations in a Metropolitan System', *Local Government Chronicle*, 9 October 1971.

Local Government Studies, May/June 1982 (issue devoted entirely to central–local relations).

G. Jones, *Introduction to Central–Local Government Relations*, SSRC, 1980.

G. Jones (ed.), *New Approaches to the Study of Central–Local Government Relationships*, Gower, 1980.

Rhetoric and Reality, Society of Education Officers, 1982.

D. Mellor, *The Effects of Central Government Initiatives on Local Government Manpower and Expenditure*, LACSAB, 1984.

M. Goldsmith, *New Research in Central–Local Relations*, Gower, 1985.

R. Rhodes, *Control and Power in Central–Local Government Relations*, Gower, 1981.

C. Crouch and D. Marquand (eds.), *The New Centralism*, Political Quarterly/Blackwell, 1989.

G. Jones, 'The Crisis in Central–Local Government Relations', *Governance*, April 1988.

B. Houlihan, *Housing Policy and Central–Local Government Relations*, Avebury, 1988.

G. Boyne, 'Central Grants and Local Policy Variation', *Public Administration*, Summer 1990.

H. Butcher *et al.*, *Local Government and Thatcherism*, Routledge, 1990.

A Rough Guide to Europe, HMSO, 1993.

Europe: A Guide for Public Authorities, FIS/CIPFA, 1993 (annual subscription).

12. Local councils

Report of the Royal Commission on Local Government in England 1966–1969 (the Redcliffe-Maud Report), Vol. III, Appendix 8, HMSO, 1969.

C. Arnold-Baker, *Local Council Administration*, Longcross, 1989.

W. H. Ousby and B. G. Wright, *A Practical Guide to Local Council Administration*, Knight, 1976.

S. Ellwood *et al.*, *A Survey of Parish and Town Councils in England*, HMSO, 1992.

R. Harrop, *Parish, Town and Community Finance – A Practical Guide*, Knight, 1991.

Coopers and Lybrand Deloitte, *Making the Most of Parish and Town Councils*, ACC, 1992.

Department of the Environment, *Neighbourhood Councils in England*, HMSO, 1974.

Department of the Environment, *A Voice for Your Neighbourhood*, HMSO, 1977.

J. Seabrook, *The Idea of Neighbourhood – what local politics should be about*, Pluto, 1984.

R. Harrop, *Parish, Town and Community Council Finance*, Knight, 1991.

H. Clarke, *Parish, Town and Community Councils: a Guide to Law and Administration*, Knight, 1992.

Role and Activities of Parish and Town Councils in England: Case Studies, HMSO, 1993.

13. Participation

D. Hill, *Participating in Local Affairs*, Penguin Books, 1970.

G. Parry (ed.), *Participation in Politics*, Manchester University Press, 1972.

Royal Commission on Local Government in England, Research Study 9, *Community Attitudes Survey*, HMSO, 1969.

Royal Commission on Local Government in Scotland, Research Study 2, *Community Survey*, HMSO, 1969.

People and Planning: Report of the Committee on Participation, HMSO, 1969.

R. Benewick and T. Smith (eds.), *Direct Action and Democratic Politics*, Allen & Unwin, 1972.

D. Jones and M. Mayo, *Community Work*, Routledge, 1974.

A. Lapping, *Community Action*, Fabian Society, 1970.

W. Hampton and R. Walker, *The Individual Citizen and Public Participation*, Sheffield University Press, 1978.

C. Ward, *Tenants' Takeover*, Architectural Press, 1974.

S. Arnstein, *A Ladder of Citizen Participation*, Royal Town Planning Institute, 1971.

Citizens and Local Democracy: Empowerment – A Theme for the 90s, LGMB, 1992.

J. Stewart, *Accountability to the Public*, European Policy Forum, 1992.

W. Hampton *et al.*, 'Public Participation in Planning Within a Local Representative Democracy', *Policy and Politics*, 7, 1979.

Towards a New Governance? Local Authorities as Democratic Advocates, LGMB, 1993.

D. Prior *et al.*, *Is the Citizen's Charter a Charter for Citizens?*, LGMB, 1993.

J. Gyford, *Citizens, Consumers and Councils: Local Government and the Public*, Macmillan, 1991.

J. Gyford, *Does Place Matter?: Locality and Local Democracy*, LGMB, 1991.

P. McCarthy, *Grievances, Complaints and Local Government*, Avebury, 1992.

Citizens and Local Democracy: A Resources Guide, LGMB, 1993.

V. Lowndes and G. Stoker, 'An Evolution of Neighbourhood Decentralisation', *Policy and Politics*, 1992.

Administrative Responsibility in Local Government, Joseph Rowntree, 1992.

Measuring Up: Consumer Assessment of Local Authority Services, NCC, 1986.

L. J. Sharpe, 'Instrumental Participation and Urban Government', in J. A. G. Griffith (ed.), *From Politics to Administration*, Allen & Unwin, 1976.

S. Baine, *Community Action and Local Government*, Bell, 1975.

W. Harvey Cox, *Cities: The Public Dimension*, Penguin Books, 1976.

A. Brier and T. Hill, 'Participation in Local Politics: 3 Cautionary Case Studies' in L. Robins, *Topics in British Politics*, Politics Association, 1982.

G. Jones, *Local Community*, Harrap 1983.

J. Smith, *Public Involvement in Local Government*, Community Rights Foundation, 1984.

Participation in Public Life at Local Level, EOC, 1985.

R. Bailey, *Access to Local Government Information*, LG & Health Rights Project, 1983.

P. Hoggett and R. Hambleton, *Decentralisation and Democracy*, SAUS, 1987.

P. Wilmott, *Local Government, Decentralisation and Community*, PSI, 1987.

Getting Closer to the Public, LGTB, 1987.

The Public Service Orientation, LGTB, 1985.

Learning from the Public, LGTB, 1989.

Hearing the Voice of the Consumer, PSI, 1988.

K. Spencer, 'Decentralisation and Neighbourhood Management – Is the Mood Changing?', *Local Government Studies*, 1983.

T. Duncan, 'Community Councils in Glasgow', *Local Government Studies*, March 1990.

A. Mabileau *et. al.*, *Local Politics and Participation in Britain and France*, CUP, 1990.

14. Comparative

M. Bowman and W. Hampton (eds.), *Local Democracies: a Study in Comparative Local Government*, Longman Cheshire, 1986.

R. Batley and A. Campbell, *The Political Executive: Politicians and Management in European Local Government*, Cass, 1992.

E. Page, *Localism and Centralism in Europe*, OUP, 1991.

J. Chandler (ed.), *Local Government in Liberal Democracies*, Routledge, 1992.

Coopers and Lybrand Deloitte, *The New Europe*, ACC, 1992.

L. Gain and J. Richardson, *Citizenship and Local Democracy: A European Perspective*, LGMB, 1992.

15. Public relations and the ombudsman

C. O. Bell, 'Local Government Ombudsmen: Progress Through Persuasion', *New Law Journal*, 11 June 1981.

D. Murphy, *The Silent Watchdog: The Press in Local Politics*, Constable, 1972.

A. Sherman, *Councils, Councillors and Public Relations*, Barry Rose, 1973.

A. J. Morris, 'Local Authority Relations with the Local Press', *Public Law*, Autumn 1969.

Justice Report, *The Citizen and His Council*, Stevens, 1969.

Justice Report, *The Local Ombudsmen: A Review of the First Five Years*, Stevens, 1980.

N. Lewis and B. Gateshill, *The Commissioner for Local Administration: A Preliminary Appraisal*, RIPA, 1978.

Complaints Procedures in Local Government, Centre for Criminological and Socio-Legal Studies, Sheffield University, 1986.

Administrative Justice: Some Necessary Reforms, Report of the committee of the Justice–All Souls Review of Administrative Law in the UK, Clarendon, 1988.

M. Simey, *Government by Consent: The Principles and Practice of Accountability in Local Government*, Bedford, 1985.

T. F. Richardson, *Public Relations in Local Government*, Heinemann, 1988.

Public Relations in Local Government, Institute of Public Relations, 1993.

D. Fedorcio *et al.*, *Public Relations for Local Government*, Longman, 1991.

D. Deacon and P. Golding, 'Barriers to Centralism: Local Government, Local Media and the Charge on the Community', *Local Government Studies*, Summer 1993.

B. Franklin, *Public Relations Activities in Local Government, A Research Report*, Centre for Television Research, University of Leeds, 1988.

Effective Communication: A Guide to Public Relations in Local Government, ACC, 1990.

K. Walsh, *Marketing in Local Government*, Longman, 1989.

F. Laws, *Guide to the Local Government Ombudsman Service*, Longman, 1990.

16. The Future

M. Clarke and J. Stewart, 'The Future of Local Government: Issues for Discussion', *Public Administration*, Summer 1990.

M. Clarke and J Stewart, *Choices for Local Government for the 1990s and Beyond*, Longman, 1991.

F. Terry, *The Future Role of Local Government*, Public Finance Foundation, 1990.

J. Stewart and G. Stoker, *The Future of Local Government*, Macmillan, 1989.

H. Davis (ed.), *Reports on the Future of Local Government*, INLOGOV, 1986.

J. Beecham, *Local Government: The Challenge Ahead*, Fabian Tract 521, 1987.

M. Goldsmith (ed.), *Essays on the Future of Local Government*, University of Salford, 1986.

Future Changes in Local Government Structure, Functions and Finance, Association of District Councillors, 1983.

The Future of Local Democracy, SAUS, 1984.

What Future for Local Government?, Association of Municipal Authorities, 1987.

What Future for Local Government?, IEA, October, 1988.

The Future Role and Organisation of Local Government, INLOGOV, 1987.

The Future of Local Government in Britain, ICL, 1988.

Looking Ahead: Local Government in the 1990s, LGIU, 1993.

G. Hollis *et al.*, *The Future Role and Structure of Local Government*, Longman, 1992.

Coopers and Lybrand Deloitte, *The Future of LEAs*, ACC, 1992.

S. Leach (ed.), *Strengthening Local Government in the 1990s*, Longman, 1992.

A Glimpse of the Future: Social and Economic Trends for Local Government in the 1990s, LGMB, 1992.

Choices for Local Government for the 1990s and Beyond, LGMB, 1990.

Change and Challenge, LGMB, 1993.

M. Clarke, 'Changing Prospects for Local Government', *Local Government Policy Making*, October 1993.

S. Young and G. Stoker, *Cities in the 90s*, Longman, 1992.

17. Case studies

(While some of the following works deal with a particular area, others deal with a particular policy or aspect of policy-making. Where this is not self-evident, it is indicated in brackets.)

A. Henney, 'The Cost of Camden', Camden Commercial Ratepayers Group, 1981.

G. Jones, *Borough Politics: A Study of the Wolverhampton Town Council 1888–1964*, Macmillan, 1969.

J. M. Lee, *Social Leaders and Public Persons*, OUP, 1963 (Cheshire).

J. M. Lee *et al.*, *The Scope of Local Initiative*, Martin Robertson, 1974 (Cheshire).

W. Hampton, *Democracy and Community*, OUP, 1970 (Sheffield).

K. Newton, *Second City Politics*, OUP, 1976 (Birmingham).

M. Stacey, *Tradition and Change*, OUP, 1960 (Banbury).

M. Stacey *et al.*, *Power, Persistence and Change: A Second Study of Banbury*, Routledge, 1975.

A. Clipson, *Public Trust – Public Property: Open Government in Bradford*, Bradford Council for Voluntary Service, 1986.

M. Parkinson, 'Decision Making by Liverpool City Council: Setting the Rate, 1985–6', *The Conduct of Local Authority Business* (Widdicombe), Research Vol. 4, HMSO, 1986.

F. Ridley, 'Liverpool is Different', *The Political Quarterly*, 57, 1986.

H. V. Wiseman, *Local Government at Work*, Routledge, 1967 (Leeds).

R. Reiner, *Chief Constables*, OUP, 1991.

Tower Hamlets and Decentralisation, LGMB, 1991.

G. Jones and A. Norton, *Political Leadership in Local Authorities*, INLOGOV, 1978 (a selection of personal portraits).

N. Dennis, *People and Planning*, Faber, 1970.

N. Dennis, *Public Participation and the Planner's Blight*, Faber, 1972 (redevelopment).

J. Beishon, *A Local Government System*, Open University, 1973 (Brighton Marina project).

J. Gower-Davis, *The Evangelistic Bureaucrat*, Tavistock, 1972 (redevelopment).

R. Minns, 'The Significance of Clay Cross', *Policy and Politics*, 4, 1974.

R. Mitchell, 'Clay Cross', *Political Quarterly*, 2, 1974.

S. Ranson, 'Changing Relations between Centre and Locality in Education', *Local Government Studies*, November/December 1980.

R. Farrel, *Local Planning in Four English Cities*, Gower, 1983.

Efficiency in Public Services, CBI, 1984 (privatization).

Local Government and Racial Equality, Commission for Racial Equality, 1982.

D. Rowlands, 'The Impact of the Introduction of Corporate Management on the London Borough of Waltham Forest', Polytechnic of the South Bank, 1981.

D. Skinner and J. Langdon, *The Story of Clay Cross*, Spokesman Books, 1974.

M. Gillard and M. Tomkinson, *Nothing to Declare*, Calder, 1980 (the Poulson affair).

A. P. Brier, 'The Decision Process in Local Government: A Case Study of Fluoridation in Hull', *Public Administration*, Winter 1970.

D. G. Green, *Power and Party in an English City*, Allen & Unwin, 1981 (Newcastle).

A. Blowers, *The Limit of Power: The Politics of Local Planning Policy*, Pergamon, 1980 (Bedfordshire).

R. Glasser, *Town Hall*, Century, 1984 (St Albans).

S. Jackson, *The Anatomy of a Local Government Newspaper*, Welwyn and Hertford District Council, 1984.

A. Alexander, *Borough Government and Politics 1835–1985*, Allen & Unwin, 1985 (Reading).

P. Beresford, *Good Council Guide: Wandsworth 1978–87*, CPS, 1987.

J. Carvel, *Citizen Ken*, Chatto & Windus, 1985.

F. Reeves, *Race and Borough Politics*, Avebury, 1989 (Wolverhampton).

J. Stanyer, *The History of Devon County Council 1889–1989*, Devon Books, 1989.

M. Harloe *et al.*, *Place, Policy and Politics: Do Localities Matter?*, Unwin Hyman, 1990 (seven case studies: Swindon, Teesside, Merseyside, SW Birmingham, Cheltenham, Lancaster, Isle of Thanet).

J. Barry, *The Women's Movement and Local Politics*, Avebury, 1991 (London).

A number of county councils have recently had their histories published, some to celebrate their centenary. See too local authority annual reports and yearbooks.

18. London

The LBA Handbook 1992–3: A Guide to Local Government in London, LBA, 1993.

G. Rhodes (ed.), *The New Government of London: The First Five Years*, Weidenfeld & Nicolson, 1972.

G. Rhodes, *The Government of London: The Struggle for Reform*, Weidenfeld & Nicolson, 1970.

D. Foley, *Governing the London Region*, University of California Press, 1972.

Report of the Royal Commission on Local Government in Greater London, Cmd 1164, HMSO, 1960.

Royal Commission on Local Government in England, Research Study 2, *The Lessons of the London Government Reform*, HMSO, 1968.

D. Donnison and D. Eversley (eds.), *London: Urban Patterns, Problems and Policies*, Heinemann, 1973.

E. Wistrich, *The First Years of Camden*, Borough of Camden, 1972.

W. E. Jackson, *Achievement: A Short History of the LCC*, Longmans, 1965.

A. Saint (ed.), *Politics and the People of London: The London County Council 1889–1965*, Hambledon, 1989.

J. Davis, *Reforming London: The London Government Problem, 1855–1900*, Clarendon, 1988.

P. Hall, *Radical Agenda for London*, Fabian Society, 1980.

H. Cutler, *The Cutler Files*, Weidenfeld & Nicolson, 1981.

D. Owen, *The Government and Victorian London 1855–89*, Harvard UP, 1982.

M. Hebbert and T. Travers, *The London Government Handbook*, Cassell, 1988.

Governing London (weekly).

Audit Commission, *The Management of London's Authorities*, HMSO, 1987.

T. Travers and G. Jones, 'Governing London', *Public Money and Management*, Blackwell, 1991.

S. James, 'A Streamlined City: The Broken Pattern of London Government', *Public Administration*, winter 1990.

T. Travers *et al.*, *The Government of London*, Joseph Rowntree, 1991.

19. Scotland

Shaping the New Councils, HMSO, July 1993 (White Paper on Scotland)

Report of the Royal Commission on Local Government in Scotland 1966–1969 (the Wheatley Report), 2 vols., Cmd 4150, HMSO, 1969.

J. P. Mackintosh, 'The Royal Commission on Local Government in Scotland 1966–1969', *Public Administration*, Spring 1970.

J. G. Kellas, *The Scottish Political System*, CUP, 1985.

G. S. Pryde, *Central and Local Government in Scotland*, Routledge, 1960.

J. B. Miller, *An Outline of Administrative and Local Government Law in Scotland*, Green, 1961.

A. Midwinter *et al.*, *Politics and Public Policy in Scotland*, Macmillan, 1991.

V. D. Lipman, 'Some Contrasts between English and Scottish Local Government', *Public Administration*, 3, 1949.

H. M. Drucker and M. G. Clarke or N. Drucker (eds.), *The Scottish Government Yearbook*, Paul Harris (annually since 1978). D. McCrone (ed.), Edinburgh University Press since 1984. A. Brown since 1990.

J. M. Bochel and D. T. Denver, *The Scottish Local Government Election 1974*, Dundee University, 1974 (and subsequent years).

E. Page and E. Midwinter, 'Remote Bureaucracy or Administrative Efficiency? Scotland's New Local Government System', *Studies in Public Policy* no. 38, Centre for the Study of Public Policy.

R. Young, *The Search for Democracy: A Guide to Scottish Local Government*, Heatherbank Press, Milngavie, 1977.

M. Keating and A. Midwinter, *The Government of Scotland*, Mainstream, 1983.

G. Monies, *Local Government in Scotland*, Green, 1985,

K. Ferguson, *An Introduction to Local Government in Scotland*, Planning Exchange, 1984.

20. Wales

Local Government in Wales: A Charter for the Future, HMSO, 1993 (White Paper on Wales).

G. Boyne *et al.*, *Local Government in Wales*, Joseph Rowntree, 1991.

The Reform of Local Government in Wales: A Consultative Document, HMSO, 1971.

P. Madgwick *et al.*, *The Politics of Rural Wales*, Hutchinson, 1973.

T. Brennan *et al.*, 'Political Parties and Local Government in Western South Wales', *Political Quarterly*, 1, 1954.

I. B. Rees, *Government by Community*, Knight, 1971.

B. Jones, 'Welsh Local Government – a Blueprint for Regionalism?', *Local Government Studies*, September 1986.

21. Journals

Local Government Chronicle (weekly).

Municipal Review (monthly).

Municipal & Public Services Journal (weekly).

Local Government Review (weekly).

Local Government Annotations Service: LOGA (bi-monthly).

Local Government Studies (bi-monthly, with an annual review).

The Local Economy (quarterly, Longmans).

Public Money and Management (quarterly, Blackwell).

Local Government Manpower (monthly, LACSAB).

Local Government Comparative Statistics (annual, CIPFA).

Local Government Policy Making (3 times a year, Longmans).

Local Government Agenda (monthly, ICSA).

Local Government Forum (2 or 3 times a year, LG Unit, Paisley College).

Local Government News (monthly).

Policy and Politics (quarterly, SAUS).

County Councils Gazette (monthly).

District Councils Review (bi-monthly).

Councillors' Bulletins and *Training Newsletters* (LGTB).

Contemporary Record (quarterly).

Strategic Government (quarterly, ACC).

Public Policy and Administration (quarterly).

Teaching Public Administration (bi-annual).

Tramis (leaflet, LGMB).

Index

READ MORE IN PENGUIN

In every corner of the world, on every subject under the sun, Penguin represents quality and variety – the very best in publishing today.

For complete information about books available from Penguin – including Puffins, Penguin Classics and Arkana – and how to order them, write to us at the appropriate address below. Please note that for copyright reasons the selection of books varies from country to country.

In the United Kingdom: Please write to *Dept. JC, Penguin Books Ltd, FREEPOST, West Drayton, Middlesex UB7 0BR*

If you have any difficulty in obtaining a title, please send your order with the correct money, plus ten per cent for postage and packaging, to *PO Box No. 11, West Drayton, Middlesex UB7 0BR*

In the United States: Please write to *Penguin USA Inc., 375 Hudson Street, New York, NY 10014*

In Canada: Please write to *Penguin Books Canada Ltd, 10 Alcorn Avenue, Suite 300, Toronto, Ontario M4V 3B2*

In Australia: Please write to *Penguin Books Australia Ltd, 487 Maroondah Highway, Ringwood, Victoria 3134*

In New Zealand: Please write to *Penguin Books (NZ) Ltd,182–190 Wairau Road, Private Bag, Takapuna, Auckland 9*

In India: Please write to *Penguin Books India Pvt Ltd, 706 Eros Apartments, 56 Nehru Place, New Delhi 110 019*

In the Netherlands: Please write to *Penguin Books Netherlands B.V., Keizersgracht 231 NL–1016 DV Amsterdam*

In Germany: Please write to *Penguin Books Deutschland GmbH, Friedrichstrasse 10–12, W–6000 Frankfurt/Main 1*

In Spain: Please write to *Penguin Books S. A., C. San Bernardo 117–6° E–28015 Madrid*

In Italy: Please write to *Penguin Italia s.r.l., Via Felice Casati 20, I–20124 Milano*

In France: Please write to *Penguin France S. A., 17 rue Lejeune, F–31000 Toulouse*

In Japan: Please write to *Penguin Books Japan, Ishikiribashi Building, 2–5–4, Suido, Bunkyo-ku, Tokyo 112*

In Greece: Please write to *Penguin Hellas Ltd, Dimocritou 3, GR–106 71 Athens*

In South Africa: Please write to *Longman Penguin Southern Africa (Pty) Ltd, Private Bag X08, Bertsham 2013*

READ MORE IN PENGUIN

HISTORY

The World Since 1945   T. E. Vadney
New edition

From the origins of the post-war world to the collapse of the Soviet Bloc in the late 1980s, this masterly book offers an authoritative yet highly readable one-volume account.

Ecstasies   Carlo Ginzburg

This dazzling work of historical detection excavates the essential truth about the witches' Sabbath. 'Ginzburg's learning is prodigious and his journey through two thousand years of Eurasian folklore a *tour de force*' – *Observer*

The Nuremberg Raid   Martin Middlebrook

'The best book, whether documentary or fictional, yet written about Bomber Command' – *Economist*. 'Martin Middlebrook's skill at description and reporting lift this book above the many memories that were written shortly after the war' – *The Times*

A History of Christianity   Paul Johnson

'Masterly ... It is a huge and crowded canvas – a tremendous theme running through twenty centuries of history – a cosmic soap opera involving kings and beggars, philosophers and crackpots, scholars and illiterate exaltés, popes and pilgrims and wild anchorites in the wilderness' – Malcolm Muggeridge

The Penguin History of Greece   A. R. Burn

Readable, erudite, enthusiastic and balanced, this one-volume history of Hellas sweeps the reader along from the days of Mycenae and the splendours of Athens to the conquests of Alexander and the final dark decades.

Modern Ireland 1600–1972   R. F. Foster

'Takes its place with the finest historical writing of the twentieth century, whether about Ireland or anywhere else' – Conor Cruise O'Brien in the *Sunday Times*

READ MORE IN PENGUIN

HISTORY

The Guillotine and the Terror   Daniel Arasse

'A brilliant and imaginative account of the punitive mentality of the revolution that restores to its cultural history its most forbidding and powerful symbol' – Simon Schama.

The Second World War   A J P Taylor

A brilliant and detailed illustrated history, enlivened by all Professor Taylor's customary iconoclasm and wit.

Daily Life in Ancient Rome   Jerome Carcopino

This classic study, which includes a bibliography and notes by Professor Rowell, describes the streets, houses and multi-storeyed apartments of the city of over a million inhabitants, the social classes from senators to slaves, and the Roman family and the position of women, causing *The Times Literary Supplement* to hail it as a 'thorough, lively and readable book'.

The Anglo-Saxons   Edited by James Campbell

'For anyone who wishes to understand the broad sweep of English history, Anglo-Saxon society is an important and fascinating subject. And Campbell's is an important and fascinating book. It is also a finely produced and, at times, a very beautiful book' – *London Review of Books*

The Making of the English Working Class   E. P. Thompson

Probably the most imaginative – and the most famous – post-war work of English social history. 'A magnificent, lucid, angry historian ... E. P. Thompson has performed a revolution of historical perspective' – *The Times*

The Habsburg Monarchy 1809 –1918   A J P Taylor

Dissolved in 1918, the Habsburg Empire 'had a unique character, out of time and out of place'. Scholarly and vividly accessible, this 'very good book indeed' (*Spectator*) elucidates the problems always inherent in the attempt to give peace, stability and a common loyalty to a heterogeneous population.

READ MORE IN PENGUIN

HISTORY

Citizens Simon Schama

The award-winning chronicle of the French Revolution. 'The most marvellous book I have read about the French Revolution in the last fifty years' – Richard Cobb in *The Times*

To the Finland Station Edmund Wilson

In this authoritative work Edmund Wilson, considered by many to be America's greatest twentieth-century critic, turns his attention to Europe's revolutionary traditions, tracing the roots of nationalism, socialism and Marxism as these movements spread across the Continent creating unrest, revolt and widespread social change.

Jasmin's Witch Emmanuel Le Roy Ladurie

An investigation into witchcraft and magic in south-west France during the seventeenth century – a masterpiece of historical detective work by the bestselling author of Montaillou.

Stalin Isaac Deutscher

'The Greatest Genius in History' and the 'Life-Giving Force of socialism'? Or a despot more ruthless than Ivan the Terrrible and a revolutionary whose policies facilitated the rise of Nazism? An outstanding biographical study of a revolutionary despot by a great historian.

Aspects of Antiquity M. I. Finley

Profesor M. I. Finley was one of the century's greatest ancient historians; he was also a master of the brief, provocative essay on classical themes. 'He writes with the unmistakable enthusiasm of a man who genuinely wants to communicate his own excitement' – Philip Toynbee in the *Observer*

British Society 1914–1945 John Stevenson

'A major contribution to the *Penguin Social History of Britain*, which will undoubtedly be the standard work for students of modern Britain for many years to come' – *The Times Educational Supplement*

READ MORE IN PENGUIN

POLITICS AND SOCIAL SCIENCES

National Identity Anthony D. Smith

In this stimulating new book, Anthony D. Smith asks why the first modern nation states developed in the West. He considers how ethnic origins, religion, language and shared symbols can provide a sense of nation and illuminates his argument with a wealth of detailed examples.

The Feminine Mystique Betty Friedan

'A brilliantly researched, passionately argued book – a time-bomb flung into the Mom-and-Apple-Pie image ... Out of the debris of that shattered ideal, the Women's Liberation Movement was born' – Ann Leslie

Peacemaking Among Primates Frans de Waal

'A vitally fresh analysis of the biology of aggression which deserves the serious attention of all those concerned with the nature of conflict, whether in humans or non-human animals ... De Waal delivers forcibly and clearly his interpretation of the significance of his findings ... Lucidly written' – *The Times Higher Educational Supplement*

Political Ideas David Thomson (ed.)

From Machiavelli to Marx – a stimulating and informative introduction to the last 500 years of European political thinkers and political thought.

The Raw and the Cooked Claude Lévi-Strauss

Deliberately, brilliantly and inimitably challenging, Lévi-Strauss's seminal work of structural anthropology cuts wide and deep into the mind of mankind, as he finds in the myths of the South American Indians a comprehensible psychological pattern.

The Social Construction of Reality
Peter Berger and Thomas Luckmann

The Social Construction of Reality is concerned with the sociology of 'everything that passes for knowledge in society', and particularly with that 'common-sense knowledge' that constitutes the reality of everyday life for the ordinary member of society.

READ MORE IN PENGUIN

POLITICS AND SOCIAL SCIENCES

Conservatism   Ted Honderich

'It offers a powerful critique of the major beliefs of modern conservatism, and shows how much a rigorous philosopher can contribute to understanding the fashionable but deeply ruinous absurdities of his times' – *New Statesman & Society*

Karl Marx: Selected Writings in Sociology and Social Philosophy Bottomore and Rubel (eds.)

'It makes available, in coherent form and lucid English, some of Marx's most important ideas. As an introduction to Marx's thought, it has very few rivals indeed' – *British Journal of Sociology*

Post-War Britain   A Political History   Alan Sked and Chris Cook

Major political figures from Attlee to Thatcher, the aims and achievements of governments and the changing fortunes of Britain in the period since 1945 are thoroughly scrutinized in this stimulating history.

Inside the Third World   Paul Harrison

This comprehensive book brings home a wealth of facts and analysis on the often tragic realities of life for the poor people and communities of Asia, Africa and Latin America.

Medicine, Patients and the Law   Margaret Brazier

'An absorbing book which, in addition to being accessible to the general reader, should prove illuminating for practitioners – both medical and legal – and an ideal accompaniment to student courses on law and medicine' – *New Law Journal*

Bread and Circuses   Paul Veyne

'Warming oneself at the fire of M. Veyne's intelligence is such a joy that any irritation at one's prejudice and ignorance being revealed and exposed vanishes with his winning ways ... *Bread and Circuses* is M. Veyne's way of explaining the philosophy of the Roman Empire, which was the most successful form of government known to mankind' – *Literary Review*

READ MORE IN PENGUIN

A CHOICE OF NON-FICTION

Ginsberg: A Biography   Barry Miles

The definitive life of one of this century's most colourful poets. 'A life so dramatic, so dangerous, so committed to hard-volume truth, that his survival is a miracle, his kindness, wisdom and modesty a blessing' – *The Times*. 'Read it to the end' – Michael Horovitz

Coleridge: Early Visions   Richard Holmes

'Dazzling ... Holmes has not merely reinterpreted Coleridge; he has re-created him, and his biography has the aura of fiction, the shimmer of an authentic portrait ... a biography like few I have ever read' –*Guardian*. 'Coleridge lives, and talks and loves ... in these pages as never before' – *Independent*

The Speeches of Winston Churchill   David Cannadine (ed.)

The most eloquent statesman of his time, Winston Churchill used language as his most powerful weapon. These orations, spanning fifty years, show him gradually honing his rhetoric until, with spectacular effect, 'he mobilized the English language, and sent it into battle'.

Higher than Hope   Fatima Meer

A dramatic, personal and intimate biography drawing on letters and reminiscences from Nelson Mandela himself and his close family, *Higher Than Hope* is an important tribute to one of the greatest living figures of our time. It is also a perceptive commentary on the situation in South Africa. No one concerned with politics or humanity can afford to miss it.

Among the Russians   Colin Thubron

'The Thubron approach to travelling has an integrity that belongs to another age. And this author's way with words gives his books a value far transcending their topical interest; it is safe to predict that they will be read a century hence' – Dervla Murphy in the *Irish Times*

READ MORE IN PENGUIN

BUSINESS AND ECONOMICS

From Boom to Bust David Smith

When Margaret Thatcher took office for the third time in 1987 her monetarist experiment had been replaced by more pragmatic policies, inflation and unemployment were both low, and there was even talk of an 'economic miracle'. By 1991 this short-lived boom was just a distant memory.

Atlas of Management Thinking Edward de Bono

This fascinating book provides a vital repertoire of non-verbal images that will help activate the right side of any manager's brain.

Almost Everyone's Guide to Economics
 J. K. Galbraith and Nicole Salinger

This instructive and entertaining dialogue provides a step-by-step explanation of 'the state of economics in general and the reasons for its present failure in particular, in simple, accurate language that everyone could understand and that a perverse few might conceivably enjoy'.

The Economist Economics Rupert Pennant-Rea and Clive Crook

Based on a series of 'briefs' published in *The Economist* , this is a clear and accessible guide to the key issues of today's economics for the general reader.

The Rise and Fall of Monetarism David Smith

Now that even Conservatives have consigned monetarism to the scrap heap of history, David Smith draws out the unhappy lessons of a fundamentally flawed economic experiment, driven by a doctrine that for years had been regarded as outmoded and irrelevant.

Understanding Organizations Charles B. Handy

Of practical as well as theoretical interest, this book shows how general concepts can help solve specific organizational problems.

READ MORE IN PENGUIN

BUSINESS AND ECONOMICS

The Affluent Society   John Kenneth Galbraith

Classical economics was born in a harsh world of mass poverty, and it has left us with a set of preoccupations hard to adapt to the realities of our own richer age. Our unfamiliar problems need a new approach, and the reception given to this famous book has shown the value of its fresh, lively ideas.

Understanding the British Economy
Peter Donaldson and John Farquhar

A comprehensive and well-signposted tour of the British economy today; a sound introduction to elements of economic theory; and a balanced account of recent policies are provided by this bestselling text.

A Question of Economics   Peter Donaldson

Twenty key issues – the City, trade unions, 'free market forces' and many others – are presented clearly and fully in this major book based on a television series.

The Economics of the Common Market   Dennis Swann

From the CAP to the EMS, this is an internationally recognized book on the Common Market – now substantially revised.

The Money Machine: How the City Works   Philip Coggan

How are the big deals made? Which are the institutions that really matter? What causes the pound to rise or interest rates to fall? This book provides clear and concise answers to these and many other money-related questions.

Parkinson's Law   C. Northcote Parkinson

'Work expands so as to fill the time available for its completion': that law underlies this 'extraordinarily funny and witty book' (Stephen Potter in the *Sunday Times*) which also makes some painfully serious points about those in business or the Civil Service.